Security Analysis
and Portfolio Management

Holt, Rinehart and Winston Series in Finance
William Beranek, Consulting Editor

> **Steven E. Bolten:** Security Analysis and Portfolio Management: An Analytical Approach to Investments
>
> **Joseph F. Bradley:** Administrative Financial Management, Second Edition
>
> **Adolph E. Grunewald and Erwin Esser Nemmers:** Basic Managerial Finance
>
> **Paul F. Jessup:** Innovations in Bank Management: Selected Readings
>
> **Glen A. Mumey:** Theory of Financial Structure
>
> **Keith V. Smith:** Portfolio Management: Theoretical and Empirical Studies of Portfolio Decision-Making

SECURITY ANALYSIS AND PORTFOLIO MANAGEMENT
AN ANALYTICAL APPROACH TO INVESTMENTS

Steven E. Bolten
Graduate School of Business, New York University
University of Houston

Holt, Rinehart and Winston, Inc.
NEW YORK   CHICAGO   SAN FRANCISCO   ATLANTA
DALLAS   MONTREAL   TORONTO   LONDON   SYDNEY

Copyright © 1970 as *Investment Analysis* by Steven E. Bolten
Copyright © 1972 by Holt, Rinehart and Winston, Inc.

All rights reserved

Library of Congress Catalog Card Number: 76-157455
ISBN: 0-03-085286-2
Printed in the United States of America
2 3 4 5 038 9 8 7 6 5 4 3 2

To my parents who started me and to
Margie who sustains me

Preface

In recent years the study of investments has shifted dramatically from institutional description to analytical explanation. Starting with the pioneering work of J. Burr Williams, ever deeper exploration has been made into the underlying workings of security price determination, continually incorporating additional pertinent factors such as risk and applying more powerful quantitative techniques. This text provides the reader with an understanding of these recent developments, while merging much of the institutional description into the framework of the analytical explanation.

I believe, and my students, using an earlier version of this text, have demonstrated, that the analytical framework of this text provides an understanding of financial asset evaluation and price determination that allows the reader to explain security prices and to relate specific money and capital market factors as well as corporate events to security price movements. The incorporation of money and capital market factors adds a necessary, but heretofore lacking, dimension to security analysis. In addition, many of the quantitative techniques that have found applications in security analysis and portfolio management are explained with emphasis on their application and their relation to the analytical framework. However, no mathematics beyond high school algebra is required. Much of the recent literature that has been devoted to the investigation of specific types of securities and evaluation problems is synthesized in the text.

Part One introduces the subject, providing the reader with a review of the organization and mechanics of the securities markets, sources of information, and an extensive discussion of the various security evaluation models (Chapter 3). Parts Two and Three elaborate on each of the factors within the models of Chapter 3. Chapters 4 to 7 deal with the various methods of estimating earnings and dividends, while Chapters

8 to 13 deal with the determination of the quality of those earnings and dividends.

Part Four extends the general analysis of Parts One to Three to applications in the evaluation of particular types of securities and variations thereon. Chapter 14 covers bonds; Chapter 15, stocks; and Chapter 16, mutual funds. Part Five discusses the technical analysis, including random walk, charting, and technical indicators.

Part Six describes portfolio analysis, synthesizing the voluminous literature in the area. Chapter 20 develops the theory of modern portfolio management, while Chapter 21 explores its application to the management of the portfolio. Chapter 22 explores some of the more traditional formula planning techniques of portfolio management.

I have successfully used an earlier version of this text and the accompanying questions and problems in the first course in investments on both the undergraduate and the graduate level, covering more of the material more deeply on the graduate level. The students are required to have an introductory macroeconomics or introductory money and banking course and an introductory statistics course as prerequisites and an introductory corporation finance course as a corequisite. However, the text is constructed in modular form, and the money and banking prerequisite may be eliminated without loss of continuity by not assigning Chapters 9 and 10. The elementary statistics prerequisite may be relaxed by not assigning Chapter 7.

The modular construction of the text allows it to be used in several ways. Parts One to Three are a course in the analytical framework of security analysis. To these parts one may add Part Four to broaden the course to include specific securities, Part Five to include technical analysis, and/or Part Six to introduce portfolio analysis. Any combination of the parts may be used to complement the thrust of the course.

I wish to thank the many who have contributed to this book. I owe an enormous debt of gratitude to my colleague and mentor, M. Chapman Findlay III for his brilliant and penetrating comments. Although we do not always agree, I have the deepest respect for his genius and profoundest thanks for his generous cooperation. Professors William Beranek of the University of Pittsburgh and Keith V. Smith of UCLA rendered detailed comments which were most helpful and for which I am most grateful. Professors Fred Renwick, Edward Altman, and John Brosky also commented on certain sections of the manuscript, and I thank them.

I am particularly grateful to my students who struggled through earlier drafts of the manuscript and the questions and problems for their help in smoothing many of the rough spots. Ken McCoin, who created the questions and problems at the end of each chapter, and Joe Landtroop, who worked on many of the examples and the bibliography, saved me countless hours of effort. I thank them for their excellent jobs.

Paula McClain, Iris Mitchell, and Catherine Parker typed the manuscript. Their smiles in the face of seemingly endless revisions saved many a day.

To my wife, Marjorie, goes that special thanks of love for her understanding and encouragement. Her tolerance of my compulsion to complete this book was invaluable; her kind word and warm touch irreplaceable.

Houston, Texas   Steven E. Bolten
October 1971

Contents

PART ONE
Introduction 1

Chapter 1–The Organization and Mechanics of Securities Markets 3
    Origins of the Money and Capital Markets 3
    Characteristics of Securities: Reward and Risk 4
    Characteristics of a Perfect Market: Homogeneity and Numerous Traders 4
    Shifts in Perceived Value 9
    Objective of Security Analysis 9
    Functions of an Organized Securities Market 10
    Examples of Organized Securities Exchanges 10
    Mechanics of Securities Trading 12
    Types of Orders 13
    Other Exchanges and Markets 16
    Summary 17

Chapter 2–Sources of Information 20
    Summary 23

Chapter 3–The Framework of Security Analysis 25
    Stream of Future Benefits 26
    Time Value of the Stream of Future Benefits 26
    Compound Interest 27
    Time Horizons 28
    Components of Security Evaluation 28
    Present Discounted Value 30
    Use of the Present Discounted Value Tables 30
    A Series of Future Benefits 32
    Annuities 33
    PDV of a Common Stock 34
    Forecasting Risk 34

Interest Rate Risk   36
Purchasing Power Risk   38
Business Risk   38
Financial Risk   39
Common Stock Evaluation Framework   39
Summary   48

PART TWO
Introduction   53

Chapter 4–Financial Statement Analysis   55
The Income Statement   55
Income Statement Ratios   62
Common Size Income Statement   63
Statement of Retained Earnings   64
Balance Sheet   64
Balance Sheet Information   66
Common Size Balance Sheet   70
Sources and Uses of Funds Statement   70
Physical Data   70
Stock Market Data   73
Earnings Projections through Ratios   74
Problems with Ratio Analysis   74
Summary   76

Chapter 5–Projecting Earnings under Stable Conditions   80
Historical Growth Rate   80
Aggregate Approach Using Regression Analysis   90
Return on Investment Approach   98
Seasonality   99
Dividend Projections   101
Summary   103

Chapter 6–Projecting Earnings under Dynamic Conditions   107
The Industrial Life Cycle   107
Product Demand Analysis   114
Market Penetration   114
Break-even Analysis   121
New Product Demand Analysis   126
Management Evaluation   127
Summary   127

Chapter 7–Forecasting under Risk   131
Certainty   132
Uncertainty   132
Risk   132

Strategies of Risk   135
Summary   146

PART THREE
Introduction   151

Chapter 8–Interest Rate Risk   154
    Liquidity Preference Framework   155
    Loanable Funds Framework   159
    Portfolio Balance Effect   164
    Investment Implications of Interest Rate Risk   168
    Summary   170

Chapter 9–The Federal Reserve System   174
    Goals of Monetary Policy   174
    Tools of Monetary Policy   177
    Interpreting FRS Activity   179
    Other Indicators of Monetary Climate   181
    Liquidity Thesis of Stock Prices   183
    Summary   186

Appendix 9A Interest Rate Forecasting   189
Appendix 9B Monetary Indicators   193

Chapter 10–The Structure of Interest Rates   205
    Yield Curve   206
    Types of Yield Curves   209
    Bond Maturity, Yield and Prices   210
    Term Structure Theories   212
    Informational Content of the Yield Curve   218
    Yield Spreads   218
    Applications of the Yield Curve   220
    Summary   221

Chapter 11–Purchasing Power Risk   225
    The Concept of Inflation   226
    Measures of Inflation   227
    Pattern of Inflation   228
    Real Rate of Interest   229
    Purchasing Power Risk in the PDV Framework   233
    Summary   238

Chapter 12–Business Risk   241
    Business Risk   242
    Business Risk Measurement   251
    Incorporating Business Risk into the PDV Framework   254
    Summary   256

Chapter 13–Financial Risk 259
    Financial Leverage 260
    Financial Leverage and Securities Prices 263
    Optimal Financial Leverage 267
    Financial Risk in the PDV Framework 269
    Summary 271

Appendix 13A Summary of PDV Framework 274

PART FOUR
Introduction 277

Chapter 14–Special Situations—Bonds 279
    Corporate Bonds 281
    Deferred Call Privilege 291
    Convertible Bonds 293
    Municipal Bonds 303
    Summary 305

Chapter 15–Special Situations—Equities 309
    Mergers and Acquisitions 309
    Warrants 325
    Options 333
    Bankruptcy—Altman's Model 337
    Other Considerations 340
    Summary 342

Chapter 16–Investment Companies 349
    Types of Investment Companies 350
    Management Evaluation 353
    Performance Record 358
    Other Performance Measures 360
    Summary 362

PART FIVE
Introduction 367

Chapter 17–Technical Analysis 369
    Random Walk 369
    Technical Analysis 371
    Empirical Evidence—Random Walk 372
    Empirical Evidence—Technical Analysis 381
    Summary 383

Chapter 18–Charting 385
    Vertical Bar Charts 385
    Chart Patterns 387

Point-and-Figure Chart   394
Summary   398

Chapter 19–Technical Indicators   402

The Breadth of the Market (Advance-Decline Line)   402
Trading Volume   404
Short Positions   405
Odd Lot Theory   406
Insider Transactions   409
Credit and Debit Balances   410
Moving Averages   410
Confidence Index   410
Dow Theory   411
New Highs to New Lows   412
Contrary Opinion   412
Tax Selling and Payment Dates   413
Stock Splits   413
Convertible Bond Premiums Deviations   415
Earnings Patterns   417
Summary   417

PART SIX

Introduction   421

Chapter 20–Portfolio Theory   423

Portfolio Criteria   424
Efficient Set   429
Portfolio Selection   435
Limits of Diversification   437
The Shape of the Risk Function   438
Summary   441

Chapter 21–Portfolio Management   446

Portfolio Objectives   446
Portfolio Size   448
Readjustment   449
Selection Basis   452
Leverage   454
Stock Options and the Portfolio   455
Summary   460

Chapter 22–Formula Plans   463

Dollar Cost Averaging   463
Constant Dollar Plan   465
Constant Ratio Plan   466

Variable Ratio Plans 466
Summary 469

Appendix 471
Glossary 477
Index 503

Security Analysis
and Portfolio Management

Part One

Part I provides the reader with background knowledge of the securities markets as well as an evaluation framework that serves as a foundation for the development of subsequent topics. The history, organization, and mechanics of the securities markets are covered first in order to help the reader understand the practical, working aspects of markets; sources of investment information are surveyed next in order to acquaint the reader with the source of data inputs necessary for financial analysis. In the last chapter of this part, the theoretical framework of security prices is examined.

1
The Organization and Mechanics of Securities Markets

Knowledge of the origin, organization, and mechanics of the securities markets is helpful in achieving success in investment management. This knowledge enables the reader to see the who, what, where, why, and how of the markets. Who participates, what is traded, where it is traded, why it is traded, and how it is traded are the basics of any market. These facts are part of the tool kit of the investor.

ORIGINS OF THE MONEY AND CAPITAL MARKETS

The reader is well aware of the fact that man's first markets used barter as a means of exchange. With the advent of money, however, barter gave way to trade conducted in monetary terms. Money was superior, because it had purchasing power over all goods and services, was more convenient to carry, and was a standard unit that could readily be divided into any desired quantity of purchasing power. The monetary system also fostered the division of labor and specialization, which increased total productivity, allowing production and consumption to be divided in time and giving rise to saving and borrowing.

In addition, money could be used as a store of value. The possessor of money could now spend or save; he no longer had to consume or dispose of his barter. The saver, who accumulates funds in anticipation of future consumption, is a *surplus spending unit*. The dissaver, who spends more now and repays in the future, is a *deficit spending unit*. The deficit spending unit naturally wanted to borrow the surplus spending unit's accumulated funds, so that he could spend more than his income. The deficit spending unit actively sought out the surplus spending unit and attempted to borrow his savings, and when the two units met, the deficit spending unit offered to borrow the money in return for his IOU. The surplus spending unit consented if the borrower's IOU carried a satisfactory guarantee of repayment and interest payment. Thus, the securities market was born.

The securities market, among other things, transfers the surplus spending unit's money to the deficit spending unit in exchange for an IOU, which, in modern terminology, is a security or financial asset, such as a stock, bond, note, bill, or commercial paper.

From this first transfer of funds in exchange for an IOU, the mechanics of joining buyer and seller and transferring securities has developed until today there are several well-organized stock and bond exchanges as well as an efficiently performing over-the-counter market. The *primary markets* facilitate the transfer of the funds to the original issuer from a surplus unit. Transfers of the acquired security by the surplus spending unit that originally bought the security to another unit takes place in the *secondary market*.

CHARACTERISTICS OF SECURITIES: REWARD AND RISK

Securities are financial assets that are used to transfer funds from the surplus spending unit to the deficit spending unit and are the liabilities of the borrower and the assets of the lender. Specific examples of financial assets are government bonds, corporate bonds, and common stocks.

Financial assets have common characteristics that are exhibited to various degrees by the individual asset. All offer some potential reward to the lender, in the form of income or capital gain or both. The income on a financial asset is the interest paid by the borrower for the use of the money, less any expenses incurred by the lender. The capital gain (loss) on a financial asset is the price change of the asset from the time of purchase to the time of sale. The total yield or return is the sum of the income plus (minus) the capital gain (loss). Financial assets may be compared among themselves by their potential return.

Financial assets bear a degree of risk. The best-known risk is the loss of capital, which arises when the financial asset is sold for less than was paid for it. Capital risk itself—fluctuation in the price of the security—is a composite of interest rate risk, purchasing power risk, business risk, financial risk, and forecasting risk. Each of these risks is explored in the text. All financial assets are comparable among themselves according to their degree of risk. In general, the higher the degree of risk associated with a financial asset, the higher the potential reward.

CHARACTERISTICS OF A PERFECT MARKET: HOMOGENEITY AND NUMEROUS TRADERS

A perfectly functioning secondary securities market has certain characteristics and exhibits certain functional processes. First, securities are

Characteristics of a perfect market: homogeneity and numerous traders 5

homogeneous; that is, each security is a perfect substitute for another security. All securities are tailored to the same specifications and are essentially the same product. Second, there are many small traders, none of whom is capable of individually influencing the market. Each of these traders has no-cost freedom of entry into and exit from the market, and each is an informed transactor; that is, the same information is available to all at the same cost, although each investor may interpret it differently.

The price of a security is then determined where the supply offered equals the amount demanded. At a given point in time and under a given market structure, there exists a set of potential suppliers and demanders of a security. Each potential transactor has an idea of the value of the security based on his conception of certain pertinent corporate and market variables, such as expected growth in earnings, dividends, and aggregate economic prospects. The potential transactor is willing to enter the market when his evaluation equals the market price. If he has the financial means with which to buy, his perceived value and willingness may be translated into an actual transaction, a sale recorded on tomorrow's financial page.

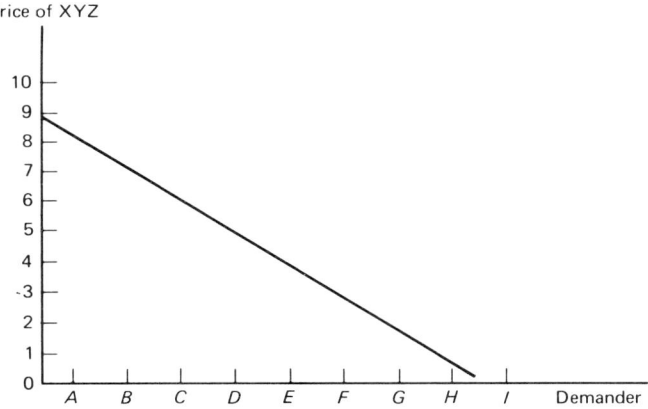

Figure 1.1. Demand for security XYZ.

Figure 1.1 illustrates a set of potential buyers. Each of the nine potential buyers A to I is represented on the horizontal axis; the vertical axis denotes the maximum price per share that each buyer is willing to pay. At most, buyer A is willing to pay $9 per share; buyer I considers XYZ to be worth only $1 per share. The total quantity demanded at each price is the sum of the quantity demanded by each potential buyer willing to pay this price or more. In Figure 1.1, the quantity demanded at $9 is equal to A's demand; at $8 it is equal to A and B's demand, and at $1 it is equal to the total demanded by all nine buyers.

On the other side of any transaction is the set of potential suppliers or sellers of XYZ shares. They, too, have a perceived value at which they are willing to sell XYZ when the market price equals this value. Figure 1.2 illustrates a set of potential sellers. Each of the nine potential sellers J to R has a different value for a share of XYZ. Potential seller J is willing to sell for $1 per share; potential seller R is willing to sell for $9 per share. The total quantity at each price is the sum of the quantity supplied by each potential seller willing to sell at this price. In Figure 1.2, the quantity supplied at $1 is equal to J's supply; at $2 it is equal to J and K's supply, and at $9 it is equal to the total supply of all nine sellers.

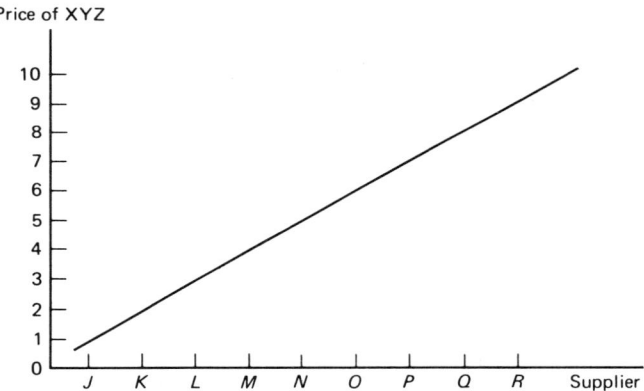

Figure 1.2. Supply of security XYZ.

Table 1.1 is a summary schedule of the potential supply and demand for XYZ shares in which each individual is willing to buy or sell, as the case may be, exactly 1,000 shares at the indicated price. At a price of $9 per share, demand is equal to 1,000 shares, and supply is equal to 9,000 shares. In an auction market this situation cannot prevail for long. All the suppliers are willing to sell, but only one can find a buyer. Because suppliers J to Q are willing to accept less than $9 per share, they lower the asking price in an attempt to bring out the demanders who are willing to buy at a lower price. The price continues to fall as those suppliers who are willing to accept a lower price decrease their asking price to bring out more buyers. Reading down Table 1.1, the amount willingly supplied exceeds the amount willingly demanded, and the process of suppliers reducing their price to bring out willing

Characteristics of a perfect market: homogeneity and numerous traders

demanders continues until the amount demanded equals the amount supplied at 5,000 shares. Here the auctioning process comes to rest at the equilibrium price of $5 per share. In the jargon of the financial analyst, the market is said to be *cleared* at $5 per share.

TABLE 1.1 Schedule of Supply and Demand

Demander	Price	Potential demand, thousands	Potential supply, thousands	Price	Seller
A	$9	1	9	$9	R
B	8	2	8	8	Q
C	7	3	7	7	P
D	6	4	6	6	O
E	5	5	5	5	N
F	4	6	4	4	M
G	3	7	3	3	L
H	2	8	2	2	K
I	1	9	1	1	J

If the price were $4 per share, demand would rise to 6,000 shares, and supply would drop to 4,000. The auction process would now be reversed. Demanders, willing to pay more than $4 per share, would raise the price in an effort to bring out demand at an equilibrium price of $5, the price that clears the market, and an equilibrium quantity of 5,000 shares.

A graphic illustration of equilibrium price is Figure 1.3. Only at $5 and 5,000 shares, where buyer E and supplier N coincide, does the potential demand equal the potential supply. Buyers A to E buy 5,000 shares, and suppliers J to N sell 5,000 shares. If the price rose to $6 per share, the amount supplied would exceed the amount demanded, and the price would be forced back up to $5. In a perfect market the equilibrium price would be reached immediately, for each supplier would be aware of any demander and vice versa, and no one would pay more than necessary. It is clear that in a less than perfect market, however, A might find R and, in A's ignorance of what the potential supply is, agree to a transaction at $9.

Potential transactors will trade among themselves as long as a supplier and a demander can agree on a price. If transactions continuously take place in the market, the market is referred to as *continuous*.

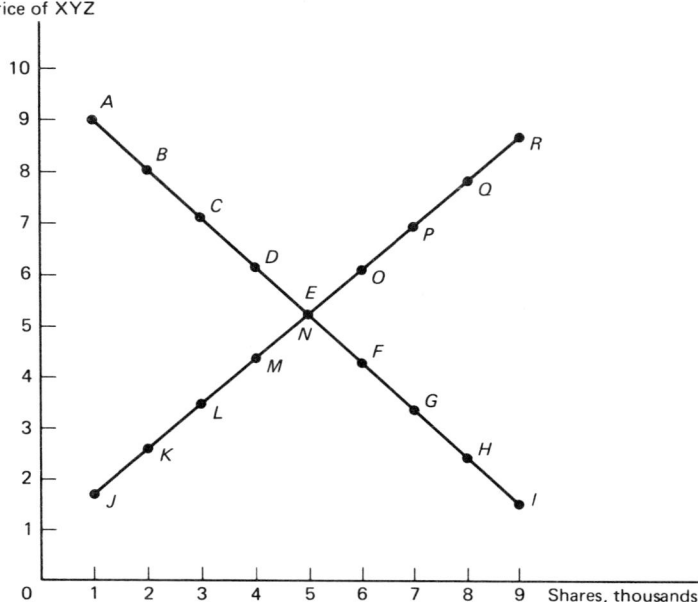

Figure 1.3. Supply and demand for security XYZ.

There are occasions, however, when the transactors cannot agree, and no trade takes place. As illustrated in Figure 1.4, the demanders A to I are willing to pay from $1 to $5 per share for XYZ stock, and the suppliers J to R are willing to sell XYZ stock at $6 to $9 per share. Because the suppliers and the demanders cannot agree on a price, no transactions take place.

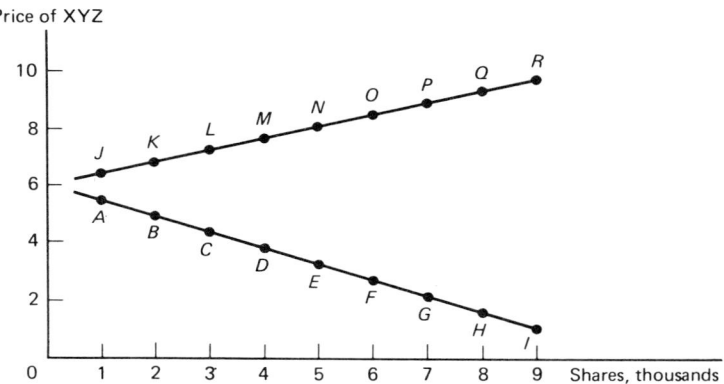

Figure 1.4. Nonfunctioning market.

SHIFTS IN PERCEIVED VALUE

It is unlikely that any securities market continues to clear at the same price. New transactors may enter the market less than completely informed and at different times, causing an oscillation around the equilibrium price as potential transactors attempt to meet one another through their bids and offers.

Large shifts in equilibrium price arise, because the potential transactor's idea of the value of the security changes. For example, his conception of XYZ's growth in earnings or aggregate economic prospects might decline. This could mean that demanders, such as A in Table 1.1, would now think XYZ worth only $8 per share instead of $9, demander B would only pay $7 for XYZ instead of $8, and each demander A to I would pay $1 per share less for XYZ than before Figure 1.5 illustrates this shift in the potential demand schedule. Line AI is the original demand schedule; line A'I' is the new demand schedule. The new equilibrium market clearing price is $4.50 per share and 4,500 shares. A favorable piece of news could make each demander willing to pay more and shift the demand schedule up to the right in Figure 1.5. In a similar manner the supply schedule could shift up to the left in Figure 1.5 if suppliers raised their evaluation of XYZ shares or shift down to the right if suppliers lowered their evaluation of XYZ shares.

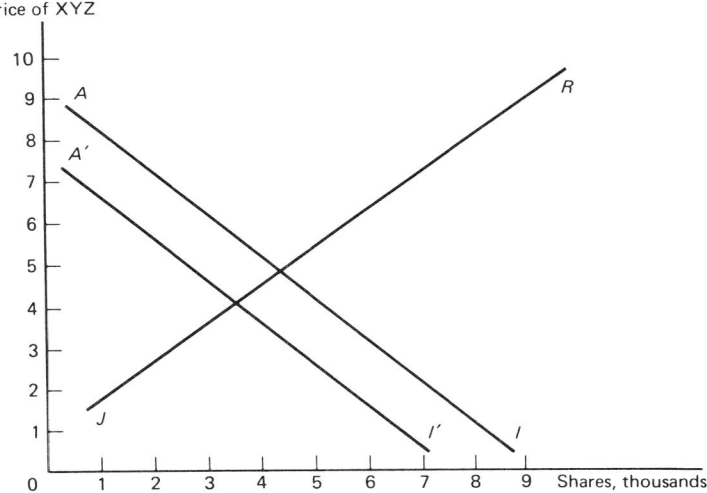

Figure 1.5. Shift in demand for security XYZ.

OBJECTIVE OF SECURITY ANALYSIS

In a perfect securities market, at a given moment in time, there exists a set of potential buyers and a set of potential sellers. Each buyer or seller has evaluated the security according to his knowledge and concept of relevant information. When the price evaluations of the potential buyer and the potential seller coincide, a transaction at a price takes place. The objective of security analysis is to provide a framework for evaluating the individual's desired position on a potential demand and a potential supply schedule or curve.

FUNCTIONS OF AN ORGANIZED SECURITIES MARKET

The primary function of an organized securities market is to encourage and facilitate the coming together of potential buyers and potential sellers. To meet this objective, it is usually necessary for a market to provide an appropriate physical setting, sufficient equipment, and rapid, accurate dissemination of information, such as price, trading volume, and company factors. When a market is properly organized, buyers and sellers are consistently finding one another in a continuous market, because an organized market provides constant contact between buyers and sellers. A continuous market encourages a more rapid and direct determination of the equilibrium price. Most of today's markets attempt to maintain continuous trading but more closely resemble auction markets, in which contact between the buyer and the seller is made at discrete intervals for the purpose of bargaining.

An important benefit of a continuous market is marketability, which allows the securities holder to convert his security into cash. If there is a continuous market, the buyer is more readily found, and the security more readily converted into cash.

Another important function of a market is to expedite additional corporate financing. With the market price as a guide, new corporate issues can be more rationally priced. With a continuous market promoting marketability, the investor is more willing to buy the securities issued in new corporate financing.

EXAMPLES OF ORGANIZED SECURITIES EXCHANGES

New York Stock Exchange—History

The largest organized securities exchange is the New York Stock Exchange (NYSE). Located in downtown Manhattan, it has been a gathering place for potential transactors since the American Revolution. At first, potential buyers and sellers would meet in coffeehouses and offices in the area to trade United States Revolutionary War bonds. In May 1792, a group of these traders formalized the trading procedure

Examples of organized securities exchanges 11

in what has become known as the Buttonwood Tree Agreement and agreed to meet regularly at predetermined hours and places to trade.

Gradually the exchange expanded as the number of securities traded increased. In addition to the Revolutionary War bonds, the exchange handled insurance company stocks, bank stocks, state bonds, and the securities of corporations formed under the then newly enacted limited liability and incorporation laws.

Trading volume was small, however, until the 1830s, when speculation in land and securities grew. Trading swelled until 1836, when a farm crop failure triggered a series of loan defaults, and securities prices plummeted in the ensuing struggle for liquidity. This cycle of boom and bust was to repeat itself again in 1854 and during the Civil War. The end of the Civil War ushered in the era of the great operators. In 1869, Jay Gould tried to corner the entire gold market. The attempt failed and plunged the market into chaos. Manipulators like Commodore Vanderbilt and Jim Fisk would, in terms of today's ethics, defraud each other in the afternoon with questionable stock certificates that had been freshly printed that morning on Fisk's most valuable possession, his printing press. In 1873, Jay Cooke, one of these manipulators, failed, and the ensuing panic temporarily closed the market.

During the second half of the nineteenth century, the great trusts rose to prominence and soon dominated the financial markets. With the advent of these large corporations, the age of the manipulator waned, and the age of the investment banker began. Men like J. P. Morgan put together vast industrial empires. Speculation ran high in the shares of these new corporations, only to falter in 1893 and again in 1903. In 1907, an overextension of credit by the major banks resulted in a panic when a general wave of selling depressed the prices of stocks that had been pledged as collateral for the loans. A liquidity crisis developed in which stock traders were unable to sell their securities in order to repay their loans, and the banks were faced with large losses and insolvency. This disaster was averted through the efforts of J. P. Morgan, who lent his personal fortune and prestige to stem the panic. The events of 1907, however, spurred the United States government to initiate the Federal Reserve System, which today has a commanding position in the securities markets.

The 1920s saw the greatest boom and the greatest bust in the market's history. From 1929 to 1932 the Dow Jones Industrial Average fell 89 percent. This rapid and large decline led to the Senate investigations of 1933 and 1934 and brought about the present NYSE organization[1] and the SEC regulatory apparatus.

---

[1] More detailed histories of the exchange may be obtained in the references at the end of the chapter.

Organization of the NYSE

The NYSE is an association in which membership is restricted to acceptable persons who purchase *seats*. The Board of Governors is the chief policy-making body, and its rulings are executed by a paid, full-time president.

There are basically six types of members: (1) the commission broker, who executes orders received from his firm; (2) the bond broker, who executes bond orders received from his firm; (3) the specialist, who maintains an orderly market; (4) the odd lot specialist, who transacts in less than round lots; (5) the floor broker, who, for a fee, executes orders for the commission broker; and (6) the floor trader, who trades for his own account.

These members, either trading for themselves (traders) or on the orders of others (brokers), deal in the securities that have been admitted—*listed*—for trading on the NYSE. Companies with listed securities have applied for listing and have met certain quality requirements. The members' trading in these securities creates the securities market known as the NYSE.

MECHANICS OF SECURITIES TRADING[2]

Opening an Account

Before opening an account with a broker—a securities firm that executes an investor's transactions for a fee in contrast to a dealer, who trades with the customer for his own account—the beginning investor would be wise to investigate the reputation and financial strength of any prospective brokerage house. In today's market we also want to know if the broker is able to remain financially solvent. A reputable brokerage house endeavors to give the customer honest opinions and adequate information services and is sure that he understands his customer's investment objectives. For example, if the customer's objective is liberal dividend income, a good broker is aware of such preferences and suggests securities compatible with such objectives.

Types of Accounts

Customer accounts are classified by the method by which the purchase is financed, the two most common being the cash account and the margin account.

Cash Account. A cash account is one in which the securities purchased are paid for in full by resources provided by the purchaser. If 1,000 shares

---

[2] More detailed descriptions of security trading mechanics may be obtained in the references at the end of the chapter.

of stock at $10 per share are purchased, the total amount owed and paid by the purchaser is $10,000 (excluding commissions).

Margin Account. A margin account is one in which the securities purchased are paid for in part by funds supplied by the customer and in part by funds borrowed from the brokerage house. The Board of Governors of the Federal Reserve System specifies the particular securities on which a customer may borrow and also fixes the minimum percentage of the purchase amount that the customer must put up in cash, called *margin*. If the margin allowed is 80 percent, then on a $10,000 purchase, the purchaser puts up $8,000 of his own cash, and the brokerage house, if it agrees to, lends the purchaser the other $2,000. The brokerage house, of course, charges interest on the money that it lends.

After the initial purchase, a maintenance margin of something less than 80 percent, usually 25 to 30 percent, is required. Suppose that, in the example above, 10,000 shares are purchased at $1 per share. If the price of the stock drops from the original $10 to $2.60 per share, the total value is $2,600, the amount owed the broker is $2,000, and the customer's equity is $600. Because the equity is less than 25 percent of the present total account value, the customer is required to deposit more equity or sell his securities and repay his loan.

When the customer opens a margin account, he signs a hypothecation agreement that allows the brokerage house to hold the securities in its name and use them for collateral. The securities are then held in what is known as *street name*.

TYPES OF ORDERS

Size of Orders

Customers' orders for stocks can be of two sizes: (1) multiples of 100 shares, a round lot, or (2) less than 100 shares, an odd lot. Round lots account for the vast majority of all shares traded. The odd lot orders are handled through dealers on the floor of the exchange who specialize in odd lot transactions. The odd lot dealer purchases round lots from which he supplies odd lot demand. Usually he maintains an inventory of securities on which he can draw. He may accumulate odd lots until he has a round lot and then sell it. For his services the odd lot dealer receives an odd lot fee of 12.5 cents per share for stocks selling at a price of less than $55 and 25 cents per share for stocks at $55 or more.

Type of Transactions

The *buy* is an order to purchase the securities for the customer's account.

The *sell* is an order to sell securities already owned by the customer that is called a *sell-long transaction*.

The *sell-short transaction* is an order to sell securities borrowed by the customer from his broker. In this transaction, the broker borrows the securities for the customer to sell. The customer must then, at a later date, buy the securities and return them to the lender. The customer attempts to profit by buying back the securities at a lower price than he sold them. In a *short sale* the customer is required to deposit a sum of money to assure that he is able to buy back the securities.

At times, situations known as *short squeezes* develop. Here, short sellers have sold so much borrowed stock that when they attempt to buy it, there is not enough available for purchase to return to the borrower. In this instance the price may rapidly advance as the short sellers attempt to buy the stock.

Limited Orders

Orders may be limited by price. A *market order* commands the broker to execute the order at the most favorable price at that time. In contrast, a limited order to buy or sell requires the broker to execute the order at a particular price or better. For example, if the order is to buy at $40 per share, the broker may not buy the shares at any price above $40.

Orders may be limited by the time allowed for execution. The shortest order is the *fill or kill,* which provides that if it cannot be executed immediately, it expires. The customer may also specify a *day order,* which, unless executed, is canceled at the end of the trading day. Only if the customer specifically renews the order is it reactivated. In a similar manner, orders may be placed which expire in a week, 10 days, or a month or which remain open until executed or explicitly canceled by the customer.

Special Orders

Stop Order. A stop order is one that turns into a market order once the stop price has been reached. For example, if there is a stop order to sell 100 shares at $35 per share, and the stock price falls to $35 per share, the 100 shares are sold at the best immediately available price. The customer may limit the price that he is willing to accept once the stop price is reached, but he runs the danger of not being able to get this price or better and so may never sell his shares. The stop order may be used to buy or sell.

Discretionary Order. A discretionary order allows the broker to exercise his own judgment in buying and selling securities for the customer. This authorization, usually given when the customer feels that the broker is in a better position to handle the account than himself, is revocable at any time.

Floor Procedures and Mechanics of Delivery

After the customer has opened an account and given a buy order to his broker, it is relayed to the broker's representatives on the floor of the exchange. The floor representative proceeds to a trading post where buyers and sellers of the particular security gather. The floor representative asks at what price the stock is trading and receives a reply like "bid 40, asked $40\frac{1}{2}$." The *bid* is the highest price that someone is willing to pay at this time, and the *asked* is the lowest price at which someone is willing to sell. He may then say "bid $40\frac{1}{2}$" and receive the answer "sold" from another representative who is willing to sell the security at $40\frac{1}{2}$. At this point the transaction is complete. If the floor representative is instructed not to pay more than 40, there can be no trade unless the offer is lowered. If there is no trade at this time, he may use the services of a specialist.

Specialist

The specialist is a member of the New York Stock Exchange whose function it is to maintain a continuous, *orderly* market. In doing so, the specialist at times acts as a broker and at other times as a dealer. If the traders cannot agree on a price with the floor representative, the floor representative may deliver the order to the specialist, who collects such orders to buy and sell a given stock and executes a transaction when buy and sell orders can be matched at a given price. In this transaction the specialist is acting as the broker's agent and receives a commission. The specialist's book contains limit and stop orders, and he is obligated to execute these orders at the current price before trading for his own account.

When he acts as a dealer, the specialist is obligated to buy and sell a stock at all times, although, of course, he is not obligated to buy or sell at the customer's price. When the floor representative in the example above inquires as to price, it is usually the specialist who responds with the bid and asked prices. When the specialist does respond, he obligates himself to purchase or sell at least one round lot at these prices for his own account. The spread between the bid and asked is the specialist's potential profit (or loss).

Delivery and Clearance

After the floor representative has completed the transaction, it is reported to the exchange, which flashes notification to its members over the stock exchange ticker. The customer is notified of his transaction and either billed for the purchase or, if selling, requested to supply the duly endorsed stock certificate to the selling broker within 5 business days.

The seller's stock certificate is then forwarded by the broker to the transfer agent, usually a commercial bank, who removes the seller's name from the stockholder list and adds the purchaser's name. The new certificate issued by the transfer agent with the purchaser's name is forwarded to the registrar, who countersigns the certificate to ensure its validity and checks to see that the number of new shares issued equals the number of old shares canceled. The certificate is then forwarded to the purchaser's broker.

OTHER EXCHANGES AND MARKETS

American Stock Exchange

The American Stock Exchange (ASE) is the second largest exchange. It functions with the same objectives as the NYSE and operates in a similar manner. The American Stock Exchange, however, generally trades in smaller and less well-known securities.

Over-the-Counter (OTC)

The OTC is not really an exchange or a physical place to trade but is a telephone-connected network of dealers who, for a profit, buy and sell securities. These securities are taken from the dealer's own portfolio, and the difference between the price he paid for the security and the price he sold it for is his profit. This is in contrast to the broker, who does not own the securities but for a fee brings the buyer and the seller together. Any public transaction that does not take place on an exchange is considered to be an OTC transaction.

Among the securities usually traded OTC are bank and insurance company stocks, government and corporate bonds, foreign stocks, and the less widely held and less well-known common stocks. The securities of these smaller companies generally exhibit more price volatility and lower marketability. In terms of the number of different issues traded, the OTC market is larger by far than any exchange.

Regional Exchanges

Various regional exchanges, patterned after the New York and American Stock Exchanges, have been established around the country. These exchanges serve as trading arenas for the securities of local companies as well as many of the securities listed on the New York exchanges.

Among the larger of these are the Pacific Coast and Midwest Stock Exchanges. Among the reasons for trading on these regional exchanges are the time differences from New York, which allow for trading after the New York exchanges close, the avoidance of the New York State tax on the transfer of securities, and the acceptance of institutional members, such as mutual funds.

Other Markets

A so-called *third market* exists in which stocks listed on the exchanges are traded over-the-counter. This third market is used by large institutional traders, because the transaction costs are lower than those of the organized exchanges. A so-called *fourth market* exists in which institutions trade directly among themselves rather than through a dealer or an exchange. This procedure usually decreases the transaction costs, although a fee is customarily paid to the individual or service that introduces the buyer and seller.

Regulation

In the aftermath of the 1929–1934 stock market slide, the federal government chartered the Securities and Exchange Commission (SEC) to supervise and enforce the newly enacted securities laws. These laws require that corporations and brokers who sell securities to the public provide investors with all relevant and reliable financial information. The law requires that a prospectus detailing pertinent business and financial information be provided to prospective purchasers when the firm sells securities in the primary market. Annual reports of financial condition must be filed by corporations. Investment companies and the mutual funds—companies whose primary purpose is to invest in the securities of other firms—are supervised by the SEC.

The New York and the American Stock Exchanges and the National Association of Securities Dealers—the OTC dealers' association—police their members in an attempt to forestall misconduct or unethical trading procedures.

SUMMARY

Securities and securities markets have developed substantially from the first crudely exchanged IOU's between the borrower and the lender. The securities themselves have taken on many forms, such as stocks, bonds, and variations thereon, but all financial assets still retain the common characteristics of reward and risk. The potential reward comprises the income, which is in the form of dividends or interest, and the capital gain (loss), which reflects the difference in the price paid for the asset and the price received for it. The total reward is commonly referred to as the asset's yield or return. Similarly, all financial assets have a degree of risk. Capital risk, which reflects the sale of a financial asset for less than was paid for it, is a composite of interest rate risk, purchasing power risk, business risk, financial risk, and forecasting risk.

The securities markets also exhibit certain common characteristics that theoretically resemble a perfectly competitive market. The potential supply and the potential demand for a security are reflected in a schedule of perceived values. Where the potential supply equals the potential demand, the market is cleared, and the equilibrium market price determined. The price may fluctuate as the suppliers and demanders seek to arrive at the equilibrium price or as the supply and demand schedules shift in response to an adjustment in perceived values. The objective of security analysis is to discover where one fits on the supply or demand schedule for a particular security.

The major function of a securities market is to facilitate the exchange of securities among transactors. To this purpose several exchanges have been organized. Among the best known are the New York Stock Exchange, the American Stock Exchange, various regional exchanges, and an informal network of dealers known as the over-the-counter market. These exchanges have developed various mechanics for trading securities, such as different types of orders, the procedures for trading and delivery of the securities, and the functions of the various members of the exchange.

QUESTIONS

1.1   Enumerate the risk-reward characteristics common to all financial assets.

1.2   What are the characteristics of a perfectly functioning securities market?

1.3   Why might the characteristics of the actual securities market differ from those of a perfectly functioning securities market?

1.4   What is the objective of security analysis?

1.5   What are the functions of an organized securities market? How does an investor benefit from an organized securities market?

1.6   Explain the following: (*a*) cash account, (*b*) margin account, (*c*) maintenance margin, (*d*) street name.

1.7   Explain the sell-short transaction.

1.8   Explain the following: (*a*) market order, (*b*) limit order, (*c*) stop order, (*d*) discretionary order.

1.9   What are the functions of the specialists?

1.10   In what way is the investor protected by the securities laws?

REFERENCES

Baumol, William J. *The Stock Market and Economic Efficiency,* New York: Fordham University Press, 1965.

Bellemore, Douglas H., and John C. Ritchie, Jr. *Investments: Principles, Practices and Analysis,* Cincinnati: South-Western Publishing Company, Incorporated, 1969.

Clendenin, John C., and George A. Christy. *Introduction to Investments,* 5th ed., New York: McGraw-Hill Book Company, 1969.

Eiteman, Wilford J., and Sylvia C. Eiteman. *Nine Leading Stock Exchanges,* Ann Arbor: The University of Michigan Press, 1968.

Engel, Louis. *How to Buy Stocks: A Guide to Making More Money in the Market,* 5th ed., New York: Bantam Books, Inc., 1962.

Graham, Benjamin, David L. Dodd, and Sidney Cottle. *Security Analysis,* 4th ed., New York: McGraw-Hill Book Company, 1962.

Leffler, George L. *The Stock Market,* 3d ed., revised by Loring C. Farwell, New York: The Ronald Press Company, 1963.

Prime, John J. *Investment Analysis,* 4th ed., Englewood Cliffs, N.J.: Prentice-Hall, Inc., 1967.

2
Sources of Information

If the conceptual framework that the investor uses to judge his position in the market is to be valuable, it must have inputs. The grist for the mill of security analysis is information. Once it is decided what factors are important in determining a stock's value, actual figures must be gathered and used in the evaluation. Because it is important that the investor know where to get appropriate input data, this chapter is devoted to a summary of information sources.

Individual Investor Investigation

The aware individual knows that the various goods and services that he uses daily are possible rich sources of information. A new restaurant chain, a new and improved product at the grocery store, or good customer relations with a firm might just be the clue to a well-run, potentially profitable organization.

The infamous "tip," although a source of individually gathered data, has produced so notoriously bad a track record for "tip" followers that such information should be independently verified before being used as data inputs.

Brokerage Houses

Almost all brokerage houses publish and have reports and comments on various companies readily available. Many times these reports are taken as suggestions when they are intended only as information sources, and rarely do brokerage houses make a direct sell suggestion. Therefore, the investor must be careful to gather the information and to judge his potential position within the context of his evaluation framework. The *Wall Street Transcript* compiles weekly issues of many of these reports.

The Press

General news offers information that may be of consequence in the evaluation of a firm. Dow Jones and Company operates a news ticker that disseminates items in a matter of moments. Several magazines, such as *Newsweek, Business Week,* and *U.S. News and World Report,* carry substantial business and financial news in addition to political and social news.

The daily newspapers are a major source of general information. The more financially oriented papers, such as the *Wall Street Journal,* provide a wealth of financial news with an emphasis on news of significance to individual industries, companies, or markets.

Several journals are also specifically devoted to finance. *Barron's* and the *Commercial and Financial Chronicle* are both financial publications that discuss specific corporate, industry, and economic events in addition to providing stock price and market statistics. Other journals provide specific investment suggestions. Among these are *Forbes, Financial World, Magazine of Wall Street,* and *O-T-C Chronicle.*

The *Financial Analysts Journal* is the professional journal devoted to the field of security analysis. It generally carries the writings of practicing analysts and less theoretically oriented academic articles.

Trade Journals

Every major industry grouping has at least one trade journal that covers the events of the industry and the companies in it. *Electronic News* and *Chemical Week* are two such journals. Because of their narrower interest these journals are among the first to gather news on product development, management change, pertinent general economic considerations, and other corporate developments. These journals are probably closer to the heart of an industry than any other published source of information.

Investment Services

Many companies engage in the business of providing information to investors. Among the better known are Moody's Investor Services and Standard and Poor's. Moody's manuals contain statistical data on companies in the industrial, public utility, municipal government, transportation, and financial fields. Most pertinent events in a company's recent history may be found in Moody's manuals, which are published yearly and updated daily. Moody's also publishes the *Bond Survey,* the *Stock Survey,* and bond quality ratings.

The Standard and Poor's Corporation (S&P) publishes the *Corporate Record,* which is similar to the Moody's manuals. S&P also publishes the monthly *Stock Digest,* an abridged compilation of selected statistics on more than 4,000 companies, and the *Industry Surveys,* studies of industry operating characteristics and financial data on individual companies in each industry. Other S&P publications include the *Earnings Forecaster,* which provides a compilation of earnings estimates; the *Register of Corporations Directors and Executives;* the *Outlook;* the *Stock Market Encyclopedia;* and the *ISL Daily Stock Price Record,* a compilation of stock prices and bond ratings. The S&P *Compustat* tapes are computerized data banks of corporate financial statistics.

Value Line Investment Service surveys some 1,100 companies, reports on them, and through its own evaluation system, ranks them as to investment attractiveness. Arthur Wiesenberger and Company publishes an annual study with quarterly updates of closed-end and open-end investment companies. Vickers Associates also publishes several services on mutual funds.

Other available publications include the following: General: Babson Reports, Inc., United Business Service Reports, Dun & Bradstreet: *Key Business Ratios in 125 Lines and Credit Reports;* Technical analysis: Indicator Digest, Inc., Dow Theory Forecasts, Drew Investment Associates, Inc. Convertibles: R. H. M. Associates, Kalb, Voorhis & Company; Chart services: M. C. Horsey & Company: *The Stock Picture,* Trendline Corporation: *Trendlines' Current Market and Daily Basis Stock Charts,* Chartcraft, Inc., Morgan, Rogers & Roberts, Inc.: Point and figure charts.

Government Publications

The *Federal Reserve Bulletin,* published by the Federal Reserve System, is the most comprehensive body of monetary statistics. Included are data on banks, credit, interest rates, employment, prices, and so on. The Federal Reserve Bank of St. Louis publishes for free weekly distribution national figures on credit, bank reserves, money supply, interest rates, and so on. The St. Louis Federal Reserve also publishes information on the balance of payments and an economic and financial series. The Federal Reserve Bank of New York publishes a monthly bulletin that describes the current money and capital market situation.

The Department of Commerce publishes the monthly *Survey of Current Business* and the biannual *Business Statistics.* The former gives current business statistics, including many financial statistics; the latter is a historical compilation of the monthly issues. The Department of Commerce also issues the monthly *Business Conditions Digest,* a publication for economy forecasting, using indicators that have historically led, lagged, or coincided with the general economy. The Department of Labor publishes the *Monthly Labor Review,* with statistics on employment and prices.

The SEC publishes the *Statistical Bulletin* and its *Annual Report.* The *Statistical Bulletin* has data on the volume of trading on organized exchanges, security prices, and new issues. The *Annual Report* contains information on the legislative acts administered by the SEC, new securities offerings and listings, and SEC actions. The 10-K form is a detailed, annual financial report compiled by the company and filed at the SEC. The SEC also publishes the record of insider[1] trading.

The *Statistical Abstract of the United States* is an annual compilation of most of the statistical series gathered in the United States. It is a prime starting point in searching for data series. The Federal Trade Commission (FTC) and SEC jointly issue the *Quarterly Financial Report for Manufacturing Corporations,* which produces a corporate balance sheet and income statement for each industry and for various sizes of corporations.

The Company

The company's annual and quarterly reports are a source of information. The balance sheet, income statement, and, with increasing importance, accompanying footnotes give clues to the profitability of the enterprise. The auditor's statement may give an indication of any irregularities. The accompanying information may give some indication of management objectives, product development, future plans, and so on. The company's sales literature may give some indication of its product potential and its marketing ability. Any recent, new offering prospectus may give information on products, patents, employees, and so on, that is not otherwise readily available.

Others

The NYSE and the American Stock Exchange both publish information on their operations and on companies listed on their exchanges. Many large banks publish letters that contain information on the economy and banking. Several newsletters, such as the *Kiplinger Letter* from Washington, D.C., are available and offer pertinent information.

SUMMARY

Once the investor has decided what factors he will consider in evaluating a security, he must know where to get the specific information. Areas of information about which the potential transactor must know are current economic conditions and business, political, and market events. Various sources, ranging from private investment advisory sources to government departments, publish such information. The investor must locate the appropriate source and keep abreast of the ever-flowing new information.

---

[1] An insider is a director or officer of the company or any individual or corporation that owns more than 10 percent of the company's stock.

QUESTIONS

2.1 Why are trade journals excellent sources of investment information?

2.2 Why should an investor read such government publications as the *Federal Reserve Bulletin?*

2.3 If you were considering investing in a mutual fund, what sources of information would you use to make your decision?

2.4 What would be a likely source of information for someone considering bonds as an investment?

2.5 If you were seeking information as to which company in a particular industry had the greatest percentage of increase in assets or had the highest earning per share last year, what sources of information would you use?

2.6 As an exercise, go to your library and list, according to the categories found in Chapter 2, the available sources of information.

REFERENCES

Comen, Edwin Truman, *Sources of Business Information,* Berkeley: University of California Press, 1964.

Standard & Poor's Services:
    Trendline Publications. Stock market charts.
    The Outlook. Market advice on individual stocks.
    Dividend Record. Detailed information on dividends.
    Industry Surveys. Economic and investment analysis of leading industries.
    Corporation Records. Financial information for leading corporations.
    Listed Stock Reports. Profiles on individual companies.
    American Exchange Stock Reports. Individual reports on active stocks.
    Unlisted Stock Reports. Individual reports on many OTC stocks.
    The Review of Securities Regulation. Regulations affecting securities.
    Register of Corporations Directors and Executives. Directory of individuals.
    Convertible Bond Reports. Information required for evaluation purposes.
    Called Bond Record. Reports bond and preferred stock calls.
    ISL Daily Stock Price Index. Daily price record of stocks and warrants.

Walter, H. C. (ed.), *Investment Information and Advice: A Handbook and Directory,* Whittier, Calif.: FIR Publishing Co., 1964.

3
The Framework of Security Analysis

This chapter explores the major theoretical underpinnings of security evaluation. Every security's (financial asset) value is a function of the promised reward to its owner. The larger and more secure the reward, the higher the value of the asset. The theoretical framework of security analysis must include some factor that accounts for the size and the security of the reward.

The promised reward accrues to the financial asset owner during a period of time. For example, the owner may receive $1 per year in interest. Given a positive rate of interest, money grows in time, and money received earlier can earn more interest than money received later. Thus, the reward received earlier is more valuable than the later reward, and the theoretical framework must include some factor that accounts for the time value of money.

Each financial asset has its own degree of risk that reflects the following major risks that may be attached to any financial asset: (1) forecasting risk, (2) interest rate risk, (3) purchasing power risk, (4) business risk, and (5) financial risk. The first risk is that the expected reward may not be what actually occurs. This is called the *forecasting risk*. Because all financial assets are to some degree in competition with one another, there is the chance that other assets may offer larger rewards and lower the worth of the presently owned financial asset. This is commonly called the *interest rate risk*. There is also the chance that the value of the accruing reward will be worth less because of inflation. Inflation erodes purchasing power and reduces the amount of goods and services that the dollars of accrued reward are worth. This is called the *purchasing power risk*. There is the risk that business competition and conditions may impair the promise to pay the reward. This is called the *business risk*. There is also the risk that the methods used to finance the corporation may impair the promise to pay the reward. This is called the *financial risk*. It is necessary, therefore, to include in the theoretical framework some factors that account for these risks.

STREAM OF FUTURE BENEFITS

The promised reward to the financial asset owner may be thought of as a stream of future benefits. In the case of a savings and loan deposit, the stream is the dividend paid by the savings and loan association to the deposit owner. For example, a promised return of 5 percent per year rewards the owner with $5 for every $100 he has on deposit. The stream of benefits is announced in advance by the savings and loan association and is almost certainly paid as promised. As long as the owner holds this savings and loan account, he may reasonably expect a steady reward of $5 per year per $100. Likewise, a United States government bond (the debt of the United States government) may promise to pay $6 per year per $100. The United States government's promise to pay dollars is almost completely guaranteed, because the government can issue new money at any time. Because both the savings and loan associations and the United States government may be expected to meet their promise to pay, there is little forecasting error attached to these securities.

A share of common stock is also associated with an expected future stream of benefits. On purchasing the shares, the owner is entitled to all residual profit after prior claims, such as bond interest, are met. The stockholder may be indifferent, ignoring tax effects, to receiving the expected residual directly in the form of dividends or having it wisely invested for him by the corporation in business expansion.[1] The former gives the owner immediate benefits; the latter gives him benefits in growing stock values. On purchasing the stock, the owner expects to receive a specific reward per share. The owner's chance of not getting these expected per share benefits is naturally much greater than in the instance of the United States government bond, and thus the forecasting risk is greater.

It must be emphasized that all financial assets have part of their value in the promised or expected reward that accompanies owning them. The greater the chance of the expected reward's not being paid, the greater the forecasting risk.

TIME VALUE OF THE STREAM OF FUTURE BENEFITS

Money has a time value. A savings and loan account that promises a 5 percent return grows from $100 to $105 in a year. This $5 growth

---

[1] Eugene M. Lerner, and Willard T. Carleton, *A Theory of Financial Analysis*, Harcourt, Brace & World, Inc., New York, 1966, pp. 121–123.

is accomplished through the passage of time with no other effort by the account owner because of the presence of a positive rate of interest.

If the account owner withdraws the $5 reward and allows the original $100 to remain on deposit at the savings and loan for another year, he receives another $5. For every year that the original $100 remains on deposit, the owner receives $5. This is known as *simple interest*. Table 3.1 illustrates the effect of time on the owner's reward when the simple interest process is applied to the original $100 investment. For every additional year that the money is left on deposit, an additional $5 reward is earned.

TABLE 3.1 An Illustration of Simple Interest

Original deposit	Time, years	Annual interest, 5 percent
$100	1	$5
100	2	5
100	3	5
100	4	5
100	5	5
100	6	5
100	7	5

COMPOUND INTEREST

If the $5 per year reward is allowed to accumulate, the original $100 deposit becomes $105 after the first year. In the second year the account grows to $110.25, because the promised 5 percent is paid on the $105 on deposit at the end of the first year. Every year thereafter the expected 5 percent is paid on the original deposit plus the accumulated rewards of the prior years, as illustrated in Table 3.2. This is known as *compound interest*. With compound interest the expected future stream of

TABLE 3.2 Effect of Compound Interest

Original deposit	Time, years	Annual interest 5 percent	Deposit at year's end
$100	1	$5.00	$105.00
100	2	5.25	110.250
100	3	5.512	115.762
100	4	5.788	121.550
100	5	6.078	127.628
100	6	6.381	134.009
100	7	6.600	140.709

benefits grows from year to year. When the concept is applied to common stock, it is called *growth*.

TIME HORIZONS

Different financial assets have different life expectancies or holding periods. Each financial asset entitles its owner to reap the future stream of expected benefits for the life of the asset. The 6 percent United States government bond can have a life ranging from a period of days to more than 20 years. If it has a 20-year life, the owner is entitled to $6 reward per $100 of bond every year for 20 years. At the end of 20 years, the government returns the owner's original investment, the bond ceases to exist, and the reward payments cease. The savings and loan account has an infinite life expectancy. The savings and loan shareowner and his heirs can leave the deposit untouched, allowing it to accumulate the reward until the savings and loan association ceases paying it.

A share of common stock also has an infinite time horizon. As long as the shareholder or his heirs maintain ownership, they are entitled to receive the expected future stream of benefits until the company ceases to exist. Since the life expectancy of most companies is infinitely long, the stockholder's time horizon is also infinite. Few, if any, publicly owned companies go into business with the expressed purpose of going out of business. Almost all companies are operated as "going concerns," which implies perpetual operation. One can hardly imagine a spokesman for General Motors saying that they will produce transportation equipment for only a few more years and then go out of business. It is more reasonable to imagine General Motors' announcing that they will produce transportation equipment forever.

COMPONENTS OF SECURITY EVALUATION

Up to this point, there have been three components of security evaluation: (1) a stream of expected future benefits, (2) a time value of money, and (3) a time horizon over which the benefits are to be received. The fourth component, risk, is discussed later in this chapter.

The next step is to combine all three components into a single security evaluation model. Let us start by asking what the value of a $100 savings and loan account over a 3-year time horizon will be if the time value of money is 5 percent. We can sum the original amount and the benefits earned during the first year to find the accumulated amount in the second year, then sum the accumulated amount in the second year and the benefits earned on this amount during the second year to find the accumulated amount in the third year, and so on. Table

Components of security evaluation 29

3.3 illustrates this process. The original amount at the beginning of year 1 is $100. Five dollars of interest is earned during year 1, making an accumulated total of $105 at the beginning of year 2. Interest of $5.25 is earned during year 2, making the accumulated amount at the beginning of year 3, $110.25. Interest of $5.51 is earned during year 3, making the value of the savings and loan account $115.76.

TABLE 3.3 Value of $100 in 3 Years at 5 Percent Interest

1 Year	2 Account beginning of year	3 Interest	4 (2 + 3) Account end of year
1	$100.00	$5.00	$105.00
2	105.00	5.25	110.25
3	110.25	5.51	115.76

In general terms, where M equals the original deposit, r the time value of money, F the future value at the end of each year, and n the number of years in the time horizon:

Year 1 $\begin{cases} \text{Accumulated amount at beginning of year 1} = M \\ \text{Interest earned during year 1} = rM \end{cases}$

Year 2 $\begin{cases} \text{Accumulated amount at beginning of year 2} = M + rM \\ \text{Factor } M \text{ gives } M(1 + r) = F_1 \\ \text{Interest earned during year 2} = [M(1 + r)]r \end{cases}$

Year 3 $\begin{cases} \text{Accumulated amount at beginning of year 3} = M(1 + r) \\ \qquad\qquad + [M(1 + r)]r \\ \text{Factor } (1 + r) \text{ gives } [M + rM](1 + r) = M(1 + r)(1 + r) \\ \text{Combining } (1 + r) \text{ gives } M(1 + r)^2 = F_2 \\ \text{Interest earned during year 3} = [M(1 + r^2)]r \\ \text{Accumulated amount at end of year 3} = M(1 + r)^2 \\ \qquad\qquad + [M(1 + r)^2]r \\ \text{Factor } (1 + r)^2 \text{ gives } (1 + r)^2(M + rM) = M(1 + r)^2(1 + r) \\ \text{Combining } (1 + r)^2 \text{ gives } M(1 + r)^3 = F_3 \end{cases}$

If $M = 100$, $r = 5$ percent, and $n = 3$, the value of the $100 deposit at the end of 3 years is $100(1 + 0.05)^3 = \$115.76$, or the same as summing the interest earned and adding it to the original amount, as in Table 3.3. In general terms the future value of any amount at a compound interest is

$$F = M(1 + r)^n$$

where n is the years in the time horizon. By combining these three components of security evaluation into a systematic framework, we can determine the future value of a present sum of money.

PRESENT DISCOUNTED VALUE

Once we have a method of determining the future value of a present sum of money, we can ask the reverse question: What is the present sum of money that is worth a promised future reward? In other words, what would one be willing to pay now for the right to receive a future sum of money?

In terms of the formula framework, the promised future reward F of the present sum M is

(3.1) $\quad F = M(1 + r)^n$

and the reverse or present sum M of the promised future reward M is

(3.2) $\quad M = \dfrac{F}{(1 + r)^n}$

Equation (3.2) says that the offer of a promised future reward F, in n years, is worth the present sum M if one's time value of money is r.

For example, if $F = \$115.76$, $r = 5$ percent, and $n = 3$, one would be willing to pay $M = \$100$. It is as if the owner of the savings and loan account in the previous examples offered to sell you his account today, provided that you cashed it in 3 years for \$115.76. Note that the promised future value F of \$115.76 is worth only M or \$100 today because of the time value of money r.

USE OF THE PRESENT DISCOUNTED VALUE TABLES

The specific figures used in the present discounted value (PDV) framework may be read from prepared PDV tables, such as Table 3.4. After finding the appropriate r on the top row, one reads down the corresponding column until reaching the appropriate time horizon n line. The figure in the r row and n column is the present discounted value for \$1 received n years hence at an r rate of discount. This figure multiplied by the total dollar amount of the promised future payment is the PDV.

Example 3.1.

$F = 100 \qquad n = 3 \qquad r = 5$ percent.

Looking in Table 3.4, we find $r = 5$ percent and then search the 5 percent column until $n = 3$ years. Then, where $r = 5$ percent and $n = 3$ years, the discount factor equals 0.864. Multiply 0.864 times \$100 to get a PDV of \$86.40.

If r or n changes, the discount factor also changes.

TABLE 3.4 Present Value of $1 Due at the End of *n* Years

Year	1%	2%	3%	4%	5%	6%	7%	8%	9%	10%	12%	14%	15%
1	.990	.980	.971	.962	.952	.943	.935	.926	.917	.909	.893	.877	.870
2	.980	.961	.943	.925	.907	.890	.873	.857	.842	.826	.797	.769	.756
3	.971	.942	.915	.889	.864	.840	.816	.794	.772	.751	.712	.675	.658
4	.961	.924	.889	.855	.823	.792	.763	.735	.708	.683	.636	.592	.572
5	.951	.906	.863	.822	.784	.747	.713	.681	.650	.621	.567	.519	.497
6	.942	.888	.838	.790	.746	.705	.666	.630	.596	.564	.507	.456	.432
7	.933	.871	.813	.760	.711	.665	.623	.583	.547	.513	.452	.400	.376
8	.923	.853	.789	.731	.677	.627	.582	.540	.502	.467	.404	.351	.327
9	.914	.837	.766	.703	.645	.592	.544	.500	.460	.424	.361	.308	.284
10	.905	.820	.744	.676	.614	.558	.508	.463	.422	.386	.322	.270	.247
11	.896	.804	.722	.650	.585	.527	.475	.429	.388	.350	.287	.237	.215
12	.887	.788	.701	.625	.557	.497	.444	.397	.356	.319	.257	.208	.187
13	.879	.773	.681	.601	.530	.469	.415	.368	.326	.290	.229	.182	.163
14	.870	.758	.661	.577	.505	.442	.388	.340	.299	.263	.205	.160	.141
15	.861	.743	.642	.555	.481	.417	.362	.315	.275	.239	.183	.140	.123
16	.853	.728	.623	.534	.458	.394	.339	.292	.252	.218	.163	.123	.107
17	.844	.714	.605	.513	.436	.371	.317	.270	.231	.198	.146	.108	.093
18	.836	.700	.587	.494	.416	.350	.296	.250	.212	.180	.130	.095	.081
19	.828	.686	.570	.475	.396	.331	.276	.232	.194	.164	.116	.083	.070
20	.820	.673	.554	.456	.377	.312	.258	.215	.178	.149	.104	.073	.061
25	.780	.610	.478	.375	.295	.233	.184	.146	.116	.092	.059	.038	.030
30	.742	.552	.412	.308	.231	.174	.131	.099	.075	.057	.033	.020	.015

Year	16%	18%	20%	24%	28%	32%	36%	40%	50%	60%	70%	80%	90%
1	.862	.847	.833	.806	.781	.758	.735	.714	.667	.625	.588	.556	.526
2	.743	.718	.694	.650	.610	.574	.541	.510	.444	.391	.346	.309	.277
3	.641	.609	.579	.524	.477	.435	.398	.364	.296	.244	.204	.171	.146
4	.552	.516	.482	.423	.373	.329	.292	.260	.198	.153	.120	.095	.077
5	.476	.437	.402	.341	.291	.250	.215	.186	.132	.095	.070	.053	.040
6	.410	.370	.335	.275	.227	.189	.158	.133	.088	.060	.041	.029	.021
7	.354	.314	.279	.222	.178	.143	.116	.095	.059	.037	.024	.016	.011
8	.305	.266	.233	.179	.139	.108	.085	.068	.039	.023	.014	.009	.006
9	.263	.226	.194	.144	.108	.082	.063	.048	.026	.015	.008	.005	.003
10	.227	.191	.162	.116	.085	.062	.046	.035	.017	.009	.005	.003	.002
11	.195	.162	.135	.094	.066	.047	.034	.025	.012	.006	.003	.002	.001
12	.168	.137	.112	.076	.052	.036	.025	.018	.008	.004	.002	.001	.001
13	.145	.116	.093	.061	.040	.027	.018	.013	.005	.002	.001	.001	.000
14	.125	.099	.078	.049	.032	.021	.014	.009	.003	.001	.001	.000	.000
15	.108	.084	.065	.040	.025	.016	.010	.006	.002	.001	.000	.000	.000
16	.093	.071	.054	.032	.019	.012	.007	.005	.002	.001	.000	.000	
17	.080	.060	.045	.026	.015	.009	.005	.003	.001	.000	.000		
18	.069	.051	.038	.021	.012	.007	.004	.002	.001	.000	.000		
19	.060	.043	.031	.017	.009	.005	.003	.002	.000	.000			
20	.051	.037	.026	.014	.007	.004	.002	.001	.000	.000			
25	.024	.016	.010	.005	.002	.001	.000	.000					
30	.012	.007	.004	.002	.001	.000	.000						

Example 3.2.

$$F = 100 \quad r = 5 \text{ percent} \quad n = 5$$
Discount factor = 0.784
PDV = $100 \times 0.784 = $78.40

Note that the farther in the future the promised reward, the lower the PDV.

A SERIES OF FUTURE BENEFITS

Some promises of future rewards come as a series of future rewards. Instead of the promise of one reward 3 years hence, the promised reward is delivered in annual or quarterly installments for a particular length of time. For example, a United States government bond might promise a $100 per year reward for 10 years plus the return of the original $1,000 investment at the end of the tenth year. This series of annual benefits is illustrated in Table 3.5.

TABLE 3.5 A Series of Future Benefits

Year	Benefit
1	$ 100
2	100
3	100
4	100
5	100
6	100
7	100
8	100
9	100
10	1,100

The promised future reward is $100 per year, but the more distant the reward, the less valuable it is today because of the time value of money. The first year's $100 reward is worth more than the second year's, because one has to be compensated for the interest that could be earned on the $100 for the additional year.

If the time value of money is 10 percent, $100 received at the end of year 1 is worth only $90.90, that is, $100 multiplied by a discount factor of 0.909, obtained from the intersection of the 10 percent column and the 1-year row in Table 3.4. The $100 received at the end of year 2 is worth only $82.60. Table 3.6 computes the present value of each year's promised benefit. The sum of each year's present value is $1,000.40, the PDV of the entire series of benefits.

TABLE 3.6 Computation of the PDV

Year	Benefit	PDV at 10 percent discount factor	
1	$100	90.90	
2	100	82.60	
3	100	75.10	
4	100	68.30	
5	100	62.10	Total
6	100	56.40	interest
7	100	51.30	
8	100	46.70	
9	100	42.40	
10	100	38.60	
10	1,000 (return of principal)	386.00	
		1,000.40*	

* Rounding errors account for the $0.40 error.

In terms of the formula, the PDV of a series of future rewards is the sum of each year's future value. The PDV of the first year's benefit is $F_1/(1+r)^1$ and for the nth year $F_n/(1+r)^n$.

Therefore, the PDV of any series is

$$\text{PDV} = \frac{F_1}{(1+r)^1} + \frac{F_2}{(1+r)^2} + \frac{F_3}{(1+r)^3} + \cdots + \frac{F_n}{(1+r)^n}$$

or, where Σ means the sum of,

$$\text{PDV} = \sum_{j=1}^{n} \frac{F_j}{(1+r)^j}$$

ANNUITIES

A series of equal promised future rewards received annually for a stated number of years is an annuity. Table 3.7 is an example of an annuity for $100 received for 10 years.

The PDV of an annuity may be computed by summing the PDV of each reward (as in Table 3.7) or by discounting the annual stream by the factor found in Table 3.8. The discount factor at 10 percent for $1 received annually for 10 years is 6.145; that is, $1 received annually for 10 years is presently worth $6.145 when discounted at 10 percent. This factor of $6.145 multiplied by the $100 value produces a net worth of $614.50. The sum of the PDV of each year's reward is also equal to $614.50. The annuity tables are a method of discounting equal future rewards.

TABLE 3.7 An Example of an Annuity

Year	Reward	10 percent discount factor	PDV
1	$100	0.909	$ 90.90
2	100	0.826	82.60
3	100	0.751	75.10
4	100	0.683	68.30
5	100	0.621	62.10
6	100	0.564	56.40
7	100	0.513	51.30
8	100	0.467	46.70
9	100	0.424	42.40
10	100	0.386	38.60
		6.144*	$614.40

* The sum of the individual year's discount factors is equal to the annuity factor in Table 3.8.

PDV OF A COMMON STOCK

Like any other financial asset, common stock has a present discounted value and fits into the PDV framework. The promised future rewards are the dividends that the shareowner expects to receive. The time value of money is as applicable here as in the case of a bond, for the promised future rewards are to be received during some future time period. The time horizon, however, is indefinite, for the company expects to be a going concern during an infinite period of time. In terms of the PDV formula, the stock price is

$$\text{PDV} = \frac{D_1}{(1+r)^1} + \frac{D_2}{(1+r)^2} + \frac{D_3}{(1+r)^3} + \cdots + \frac{D_n}{(1+r)^n}$$

or

$$\text{PDV} = \sum_{j=1}^{\infty} \frac{D_j}{(1+r)^j}$$

where D = expected dividends in years 1 to n; $j = 1, \infty$

FORECASTING RISK

The particular values of the promised future rewards are much harder to predict for common stocks than for bonds and most other financial assets. Dividends are not usually so stable as interest on bonds. Divi-

TABLE 3.8 Present Value of $1 per Year for *n* Years

Year	1%	2%	3%	4%	5%	6%	7%	8%	9%	20%
1	0.990	0.980	0.971	0.962	0.952	0.943	0.935	0.926	0.917	0.909
2	1.970	1.942	1.913	1.886	1.859	1.833	1.808	1.783	1.759	1.736
3	2.941	2.884	2.829	2.775	2.723	2.673	2.624	2.577	2.531	2.487
4	3.902	3.808	3.717	3.630	3.546	3.465	3.387	3.312	3.240	3.170
5	4.853	4.713	4.580	4.452	4.329	4.212	4.100	3.993	3.890	3.791
6	5.795	5.601	5.417	5.242	5.076	4.917	4.766	4.623	4.486	4.355
7	6.728	6.472	6.230	6.002	5.786	5.582	5.389	5.206	5.033	4.868
8	7.652	7.325	7.020	6.733	6.463	6.210	5.971	5.747	5.535	5.335
9	8.566	8.162	7.786	7.435	7.108	6.802	6.515	6.247	5.985	5.759
10	9.471	8.983	8.530	8.111	7.722	7.360	7.024	6.710	6.418	6.145
11	10.368	9.787	9.253	8.760	8.306	7.887	7.499	7.139	6.805	6.495
12	11.255	10.575	9.954	9.385	8.863	8.384	7.943	7.536	7.161	6.814
13	12.134	11.348	10.635	9.986	9.394	8.853	8.358	7.904	7.487	7.103
14	13.004	12.106	11.296	10.563	9.899	9.295	8.745	8.244	7.786	7.367
15	13.865	12.849	11.938	11.118	10.380	9.712	9.108	8.559	8.060	7.606
16	14.718	13.578	12.561	11.652	10.838	10.106	9.447	8.851	8.312	7.824
17	15.562	14.292	13.166	12.166	11.274	10.477	9.763	9.122	8.544	8.022
18	16.398	14.992	13.754	12.659	11.690	10.828	10.059	9.372	8.756	8.201
19	17.226	15.678	14.324	13.134	12.085	11.158	10.336	9.604	8.950	8.365
20	18.046	16.351	14.877	13.590	12.462	11.470	10.594	9.818	9.128	8.514
25	22.023	19.523	17.413	15.622	14.094	12.783	11.654	10.675	9.823	9.077
30	25.808	22.397	19.600	17.292	15.373	13.765	12.409	11.258	10.274	9.427

Year	12%	14%	16%	18%	20%	24%	28%	32%	36%
1	0.893	0.877	0.862	0.847	0.833	0.806	0.781	0.758	0.735
2	1.690	1.647	1.605	1.566	1.528	1.457	1.392	1.332	1.276
3	2.402	2.322	2.246	2.174	2.106	1.981	1.868	1.766	1.674
4	3.037	2.914	2.798	2.690	2.589	2.404	2.241	2.096	1.966
5	3.605	3.433	3.274	3.127	2.991	2.745	2.532	2.345	2.181
6	4.111	3.889	3.685	3.498	3.326	3.020	2.759	2.534	2.339
7	4.564	4.288	4.039	3.812	3.605	3.242	2.937	2.678	2.455
8	4.968	4.639	4.344	4.078	3.837	3.421	3.076	2.786	2.540
9	5.328	4.946	4.607	4.303	4.031	3.566	3.184	2.868	2.603
10	5.650	5.216	4.833	4.494	4.193	3.682	3.269	2.930	2.650
11	5.988	5.453	5.029	4.656	4.327	3.776	3.335	2.978	2.683
12	6.194	5.660	5.197	4.793	4.439	3.851	3.387	3.013	2.708
13	6.424	5.842	5.342	4.910	4.533	3.912	3.427	3.040	2.727
14	6.628	6.002	5.468	5.008	4.611	3.962	3.459	3.061	2.740
15	6.811	6.142	5.575	5.092	4.675	4.001	3.482	3.076	2.750
16	6.974	6.265	5.669	5.162	4.730	4.033	3.503	3.088	2.758
17	7.120	5.373	5.749	4.222	4.775	4.059	3.518	3.097	2.763
18	7.250	6.467	5.818	5.273	4.812	4.080	3.529	3.104	2.767
19	7.366	6.550	5.877	5.316	4.844	4.097	3.539	3.109	2.770
20	7.469	6.623	5.929	5.353	4.870	4.110	3.546	3.113	2.772
25	7.843	6.873	6.097	5.467	4.948	4.147	3.564	3.122	2.776
30	8.055	7.003	6.177	5.517	4.979	4.160	3.569	3.124	2.778

dends may grow at a constant rate, grow at various rates in time, decline, change with competition, or change irregularly. If dividends take the pattern illustrated in Table 3.9, the PDV of the common stock at a discount factor of 6 percent is $317.78.

TABLE 3.9 PDV of Common Stock

Year	Dividend	PDV at 6 percent discount factor
1	$ 1	0.94
2	1	0.89
3	2	1.68
4	2	1.60
5	3	2.25
6	10	7.00
7	10	6.65
8	10	6.27
9	10	5.92
10	10	5.58
10*	500	279.00
		317.78

*Share sold at end of year 10 for $500.

This difficulty in predicting the size and the timing of the dividends as well as determining if the company has the ability to pay the expected dividend is known as the forecasting risk, and later chapters deal with methods of coping with it. Forecasting risk is peculiar to the financial analyst, because it is his risk of an incorrect forecast. Any possible error lies with him, not with the corporation. The possibility of the corporation's inability to pay the expected dividends is captured in the concepts of business and financial risk.

INTEREST RATE RISK

The time value of money may change from one period to the next. Today the United States government may be willing to pay 8 percent per year to borrow money. The 8 percent rate is the market rate of interest determined by the supply and demand for credit. At some future date the market rate may be more or less than 8 percent. If one can receive a pure interest return of 8 percent,[2] the time value of money

[2] As we shall see in Chapter 11, the pure interest rate refers to that rate of interest paid by borrowers who have no business or financial risk, for example, the United States government. The pure interest rate comprises the real interest rate plus the purchasing power risk premium and in the context of investments is sometimes called the *default-free interest rate*.

Interest rate risk

is 8 percent. This pure rate of interest is that rate demanded of the riskless borrower by the suppliers of funds (the surplus spending units).

As the pure interest rate changes, the PDV of a financial asset also changes. Potential changes in the pure interest rate, which may lead to a decline in the market price of the security, are the interest rate risk. For example, the PDV of a United States government bond promising $100 for each of the next 10 years and the return of $1,000 in principal at the end of the tenth year at a time value of money of 10 percent is

$$PDV = \sum_{j=1}^{10} \frac{F_j}{(1+0.10)^j}$$
$$PDV = \$1,000.00$$

The same bond at a time value of money of 6 percent is

$$PDV = \sum_{j=1}^{10} \frac{F_j}{(1+0.06)^j}$$
$$PDV = \$1,394.00$$

When the time value of money decreases, the PDV of a given stream of future benefits is higher. Conversely, if the bond in the example is sold when the time value of money is 6 percent and the time value of money rises to 10 percent, the value (PDV) of the bond drops.

Volatility

The infinite time horizon makes stocks more volatile than most financial assets, because their longer time horizon makes their PDV more sensitive to a change in the time value of money. For example, the PDV of a $1,000 bond promising a future reward of $30 per year for one year will vary from a PDV of $1,004.79 when the time value of money is 2½ percent to $990.40 when the time value of money is 4 percent. A 10-year $1,000 bond promising $30 per year will vary from a PDV of $1,043.70 when the time value of money is 2½ percent to $918.86 when the time value of money is 4 percent. Table 3.10 illustrates the effect of the time horizon on PDV volatility. The longer the time horizon, the more volatile the PDV of the financial asset. Because stocks have an infinite time horizon, they are the most volatile.[3]

---

[3] B. Malkiel, "Expectations, Bond Prices, and the Term Structure of Interest Rates," *Quarterly Journal of Economics,* May, 1962, pp. 199–206. Noncallable preferred stocks and perpetual bonds also have infinite time horizons.

TABLE 3.10 PDV of a $1,000 Bond Paying $30 per Year Interest for Various Time Horizons and Time Values of Money

Time value of money, %	PDV
Time Horizon for 1 Year	
2½	$1,004.79
3	1,000.00
3½	995.16
4	990.40
Time Horizon for 10 Years	
2½	$1,043.76
3	1,000.00
3½	958.43
4	918.86
Time Horizon for 50 Years	
2½	$1,141.80
3	1,000.00
3½	802.73
4	785.87

PURCHASING POWER RISK

Money is worth only what it will purchase. If the price of goods and services rises faster than your income, you are earning less in terms of real goods and services. The owners of a financial asset must be sure that their return is greater than the rise in prices if they are to keep their ability to purchase goods and services from declining. Thus, part of the pure interest rate demanded by lenders reflects a premium for purchasing power risk. Generally, the higher the anticipated rise in prices, the larger the purchasing power risk premium and the higher the pure interest rate. The other part of the pure interest rate is the real interest rate, that is, that part which remains after the purchasing power risk premium is removed. The real interest rate is the return to lenders before consideration of the other risks.

BUSINESS RISK

Each company is subject to risks that are peculiar to its industry or operating environment. Some companies, for example, deal in very speculative projects, operate in countries with unstable governments, or are sensitive to the business cycle. Operating factors which increase the probability that the expected future stream of benefits may not be realized or which interfere with the company's ability to meet its obligations are collectively called the business risk. Where the business risk is present, investors demand a premium above the pure interest rate. The more business risk present, the higher the premium demanded.

FINANCIAL RISK

Financial risk is peculiar to the financing of the corporation. Corporations that rely on debt to finance their asset acquisitions inject a prior claim on earnings before dividends can be paid. This prior claim increases the probability that the expected dividends may not be paid. Where financial risk is present, the investors demand a premium over and above the pure interest rate. The more financial risk present, the higher is the premium demanded.

COMMON STOCK EVALUATION FRAMEWORK

Dividend Model

The common stock evaluation framework is the PDV model. The individual investor examines the facts about a company and decides on its future stream of benefits, the pure interest rate, the purchasing power risk, business risk and financial risk premiums demanded. Once he has decided on specific figures for each of these factors, he combines them into the PDV framework and computes the price he is willing to pay.

$$\text{PDV} = \frac{D_1}{(1+r)^1} + \frac{D_2}{(1+r)^2} + \cdots + \frac{D_n}{(1+r)^n}$$

where $r = i + p + b + f$
i = real interest rate
p = purchasing power risk premium
b = business risk premium
f = financial risk premium
D_j = forecasted dividend per share in year j; $j = 1, n$

The PDV of a common stock is today's price that the individual potential transactor is willing to pay. The prevailing market price on the exchange is that at which the potential seller and potential buyer (see Chapter 1) have identical PDV evaluations of the same common stock. The other potential buyers and sellers have different PDV values that are not observed in the marketplace.

Capital Gains Model

Despite the fact that the value of the share is dependent on the infinite stream of future dividends, many investors concentrate their attention on the expected future price of the stock. These investors hope to gain by selling their shares at a higher price some time in the future. The anticipated benefits are then the dividends received in each of the n years during which the stock is held plus the price received when the stock is sold in year n. In formula terms this is

$$(3.3) \quad \text{PDV} = \frac{D_1}{(1+r)^1} + \frac{D_2}{(1+r)^2} + \cdots + \frac{D_n}{(1+r)^n} + \frac{P_n}{(1+r)^n}$$

where D_j = dividend in year j; $j = 1, n$
P_n = share price when sold

Note, however, that the price for which the share is sold in year n (P_n) must itself represent the present discounted value of the future stream of dividends from year n to infinity. The person to whom the share is sold in year n is basing his evaluation on the then prevailing expected stream of dividends. The price at this future date P_n reflects the anticipated stream of dividends from year n to infinity and the discount factor r prevailing in year n. For P_n to be higher than the purchase price P_1, the expected stream of dividends has to have been growing[4] as anticipated in year 1, or to have been revised upward since year 1, or the discount factor r has to have remained constant or decreased from year 1. The investor who purchases a share now in the anticipation of selling it later at a higher price is only deluding himself unless the expected future price is supported by the dividend expectations of this future date.

Capitalization Models—No Growth Case

The purchase of a share of common stock entitles the owner to all future dividends. The price of the share should then reflect the present discounted value of all these anticipated future dividends. Each dividend in this future stream from now until infinity has an effect on the present discounted value of the share, although the more distant dividends have much less, if any, significance because of the time value of money.

Investors have telescoped the PDV evaluation of the infinite stream of dividends into the shorthand dividend capitalization model because of the difficulty of dealing with the infinite stream. This model expresses the share price P as the dividend D_1 in year 1 divided by the discount factor r:

$$(3.4) \quad P = \frac{D_1}{r}$$

[4] As one progresses into an infinite future stream of growing dividends, the larger dividends become more valuable (are subject to a smaller discount for time) and the present discounted value of the stream increases, if everything else remains unchanged.

Common stock evaluation framework

From Equation (3.4), we can derive what is commonly called, in the language of the investor, the price-dividend ratio P/D. The P/D is derived by solving Equation (3.4) for $1/r$:

(3.5) $\quad \dfrac{1}{r} = \dfrac{P}{D_1}$

The P/D ratio indicates, in the language of the investor, the number-of-times dividend at which the stock is selling.

The P/D ratio is merely a shorthand representation of the PDV evaluation framework. Assuming that the dividend is constant in time, the derivation of the P/D from the PDV is as follows:

(3.6) $\quad \text{PDV} = \dfrac{D_1}{(1+r)^1} + \dfrac{D_2}{(1+r)^2} + \cdots + \dfrac{D_n}{(1+r)^n}$

Multiplying Equation (3.6) by $(1+r)$ gives

(3.7) $\quad \text{PDV}(1+r) = D_1 + \dfrac{D_2}{(1+r)^1} + \dfrac{D_3}{(1+r)^2} + \cdots + \dfrac{D_n}{(1+r)^{n-1}}$

Subtracting Equation (3.6) from Equation (3.7) gives

(3.8) $\quad \text{PDV}(1+r) - \text{PDV} = D_1 - \dfrac{D_n}{(1+r)^n}$

Combining terms in Equation (3.8) gives

(3.9) $\quad \text{PDV}(r) = D_1 \left(1 - \dfrac{1}{(1+r)^n}\right)$

As n, the time horizon, approaches infinity, Equation (3.9) becomes

(3.10) $\quad \text{PDV}(r) = D_1$

(3.11) $\quad \text{PDV} = \dfrac{D_1}{r}$

Now, since PDV is the observable price in the market place $(\text{PDV} = P)$,

(3.12) $\quad P = \dfrac{D_1}{r}$

Equation (3.12) is the dividend capitalization model of Equation (3.1). Solving Equation (3.12) for $1/r$, we get the P/D ratio. Therefore, the P/D ratio approximates the present discounted value framework of an infinite stream of future dividends.[5] To explain the price of a stock with

---

[5] The P/D ratio remains a reasonable approximation even if we drop the assumption of constant dividends, as long as there are no sharp changes in dividends between consecutive years. In subtracting Equation (3.6) from Equation (3.7), the intervening dividends between year 1 and year n approximately cancel out.

this model, we must be able to forecast dividends and explain the discount factor.

The other capitalization model is the earnings capitalization model. Instead of capitalizing dividends, the model capitalizes earnings:

$$(3.13) \quad P = \frac{E_1}{r}$$

From Equation (3.13), we can derive what is commonly called, in the language of investors, the price-earnings ratio P/E. The P/E is derived by solving Equation (3.13) for $1/r$:

$$(3.14) \quad \frac{1}{r} = \frac{P}{E_1}$$

The P/E_1 indicates, in the language of the investor, the number-of-times earnings at which the stock is selling.

As in the case of the P/D, the P/E is a shorthand representation of the PDV evaluation framework. Assuming $E = D$ and substituting a constant earnings E for the D in Equations (3.6) to (3.12) gives

$$(3.15) \quad \text{PDV} = \frac{E_1}{(1+r)} + \frac{E_2}{(1+r)^2} + \cdots + \frac{E_n}{(1+r)^n}$$

$$(3.16) \quad \text{PDV}(1+r) = E_1 + \frac{E_2}{(1+r)^1} + \frac{E_3}{(1+r)^2} + \cdots + \frac{E_n}{(1+r)^{n-1}}$$

$$(3.17) \quad \text{PDV}(1+r) - \text{PDV} = E_1 - \frac{E_n}{(1+r)^n}$$

$$(3.18) \quad \text{PDV}(r) = E_1\left(1 - \frac{1}{(1+r)^n}\right)$$

$$(3.19) \quad \text{PDV}(r) = E_1$$

$$(3.20) \quad \text{PDV} = \frac{E_1}{r}$$

$$(3.21) \quad P = \frac{E_1}{r}$$

Equation (3.21) is the earnings capitalization model of Equation (3.13). Solving Equation (3.21) for $1/r$, we get the P/E ratio. Therefore, the P/E ratio approximates the present discounted value framework of an infinite stream of earnings when $E = D$. To explain the price of a stock with this model, we must be able to forecast the earnings and explain the discount factor.

The earnings capitalization model and the dividend capitalization

Common stock evaluation framework

model produce identical results only in the no growth case where dividends are constant and equal to earnings. If expected dividends remain constant, the quantity of earnings assets from which they are generated must also remain constant. The latter does not remain constant, however, if some of the earnings are reinvested instead of being paid as dividends.[6] The only way in which the quantity of assets may remain constant is for all the earnings to be paid out as dividends. Therefore, dividends must equal earnings.[7] When dividends equal earnings, the two capitalization models give identical results.[8] When a portion of earnings is retained, however, as in the growth models, the earnings capitalization model is incorrect, as discussed in the next section.

It is most important to note that the P/E and P/D ratios are simplified representations of the entire infinite time horizon of the PDV evaluation framework. The P/D shorthand does not avoid any of the necessary considerations of forecasting the future stream of benefits, estimating the pure interest rate, or determining appropriate purchasing power, business, and financial risk premiums. The potential investor should not allow the P/E or P/D shorthand to mask the consideration of all the factors in the PDV framework. If he does, he cannot explain share price movements that result from changes in the components of the discount factor r. For example, the P/E or P/D, by themselves without resorting to the PDV evaluation framework, cannot explain the change in stock price from Example 3.3 to Example 3.4.

Example 3.3.

Interest rate risk i = 2 percent
Purchasing power risk p = 0 percent
Business risk b = 2 percent
Financial risk f = 2 percent
Total risk r = 2 percent + 0 percent + 2 percent
    + 2 percent = 6 percent
$D_1 = \$10$ $D_2 = \$10$
$D_3 = \$10$ $D_4 = \$10$

---

[6] The firm may, of course, reinvest some of its earnings just to replace the depreciated assets.

[7] For example, if we assume that a firm with a given quantity of assets earns $1 a share and profitable projects return 10 percent on investment, the firm could reinvest the $1 instead of paying dividends and have earnings grow in succeeding years to $1.10, $1.21, $1.33. With the growing earnings stream, we anticipate higher dividends. If the firm paid its entire $1 earnings in dividends, it could not expand its earning assets and would earn $1 in succeeding years, and we expect constant dividends.

[8] M. Gordon, *The Investment, Financing and Valuation of the Corporation,* Richard D. Irwin, Inc., Homewood, Ill., 1962, chap. 5.

The stock is sold at the end of year 4 for $90.

$$PDV = \frac{10}{(1+.06)^1} + \frac{10}{(1+.06)^2} + \frac{10}{(1+.06)^3} + \frac{(90+10)}{(1+.06)^4}$$

$PDV = 9.43 + 8.90 + 8.40 + 79.20 = 105.93$

$PDV = 105.93$

$$\frac{P}{D} = \frac{105.93}{10} = 10.6$$

Example 3.4. If all else remains the same but $i = 4$ percent and $f = 4$ percent, $b = 2$ percent, $p = 0$ percent.

$$PDV = \frac{10}{(1+.10)^1} + \frac{10}{(1+.10)^2} + \frac{10}{(1+.10)^3} + \frac{100}{(1+.10)^4}$$

$PDV = 9.09 + 8.26 + 7.51 + 68.43 = 93.29$

$$\frac{P}{D} = \frac{93.29}{10} = 9.3$$

A reliance solely on the P/E or P/D ratio cannot explain the change in the price. The use of the P/E or P/D ratio masks the fact that the business and financial risks are higher in Example 3.4 than in Example 3.3. The failure to consider each component of the PDV framework separately does not reveal the higher business and financial risks, and the price change cannot be accurately explained by using only the P/D ratio.

The examples also demonstrate that stock prices can change if any of the factors in the PDV framework change. In the examples the increase in the business and financial risks cause a stock price decline. In analyzing a company, the investor must look into every one of the components and not rely on the P/E or P/D shorthand if he intends to understand stock price movements.

The Growth Model

We may incorporate a growing stream of expected benefits into the PDV framework. When dividends are anticipated to grow at a constant rate g, the future stream is

Year	Dividend
1	D_1
2	$D_1(1+g)^1$
3	$D_1(1+g)^2$
4	$D_1(1+g)^3$
n	$D_1(1+g)^n$

Substituting this future stream into the PDV framework yields[9]

$$(3.22) \quad \text{PDV} = \frac{D_1}{(1+r)} + \frac{D_1(1+g)}{(1+r)^2} + \frac{D_1(1+g)^2}{(1+r)^3} + \frac{D_1(1+g)^3}{(1+r)^4} + \cdots$$
$$+ \frac{D_1(1+g)^{n-1}}{(1+r)^n}$$

By the same arithmetical steps used in Equations (3.6) to (3.12), we can multiply both sides of Equation (3.22) by $(1+r)/(1+g)$ and, subtracting Equation (3.22) from the results, derive

$$(3.23) \quad \text{PDV}\frac{(1+r)}{(1+g)} - \text{PDV} = \frac{D_1}{(1+g)} - \frac{D_1(1+g)^{n-1}}{(1+r)^n}$$

As n approaches infinity, Equation (3.23) becomes

$$(3.24) \quad \text{PDV}\frac{(1+r)}{(1+g)} - \text{PDV} = \frac{D_1}{(1+g)}$$

If $P = \text{PDV}$, Equation (3.24) becomes

$$(3.25) \quad P\frac{(1+r)}{(1+g)} - P = \frac{D_1}{(1+g)}$$

Solving for D_1 gives

$$(3.26) \quad P(1 + r - 1 - g) = D_1$$

$$(3.27) \quad \text{and } P = \frac{D_1}{r-g}$$

Thus, the PDV framework and the accompanying shorthand are applicable to a growing stream of dividends.[10]

If we drop the assumption that $E = D$, the substitution of E for D in the growth model seriously violates the theoretical evaluation frame-

---

[9] E. Lerner and W. Carelton, *op. cit.*, pp. 105–106.

[10] In the continuous case, where the growing stream is continuously compounded instead of at discrete time intervals, the PDV framework is

$$P = \int_0^\infty D_0 e^{gt} e^{-rt} \, dt$$

which, when integrated, is

$$P = \frac{D_0}{r-g}$$

The model must be constrained so that r is always greater than g; otherwise, the PDV of the stock would be infinite. See D. Durant, "Growth Stocks and the Petersburg Paradox," *Journal of Finance*, September, 1957, pp. 348–363.

work. The growth in the expected future dividend stream is a function of the retained earnings that are reinvested in profitable projects instead of being paid in dividends. It is double counting to include both the earnings and the future growth in dividends derived from their reinvestment. In terms of Equation (3.27), if we substituted E for D, we should be counting the same factor twice: once in the form of earnings and once in the growth factor g derived from their reinvestment.

Looked at in another way, higher future dividends as the result of reinvested earnings are an alternative to present dividends and are not an addition to the dividend stream. We can only count as a benefit that which we actually receive, and we receive only dividends, not retained earnings.[11] For example, assume that a firm with a given quantity of assets earns $1 a share and its investments return 10 percent. The firm can reinvest the $1 instead of paying dividends and have earnings grow in succeeding years to $1.10, $1.21, $1.33, and so on, or it can pay the entire $1 in dividends, not expand its assets, and earn $1 in the succeeding years. If the firm pays its entire earnings in dividends, it cannot grow; but if it reinvests its earnings in order to grow, it cannot pay out its earnings in dividends. Because receiving dividends now and reinvesting earnings in the anticipation of larger, future dividends are mutually exclusive alternatives, it is double counting to include, in one model, present earnings and the future growth in dividends caused by their reinvestment.

The effect of retained earnings and the anticipated growth that they cause are, of course, incorporated into the model through the growth factor g. If the initial dividend is low because of the high retention of earnings, we expect the future dividend stream to grow. The resulting higher g makes $r - g$ smaller and the price of the stock higher for any given dividend D_1.

As in the case of the constant stream, the growth model shorthand formulation offers serious pitfalls for the analyst who uses the model without careful attention to all the relevant evaluation factors. It may be unwarranted to assume that a constant growth in dividends is infinitely sustainable. If the analyst wishes to incorporate varying growth rates into the future stream of benefits, he must return to the original present discounted value formulation (dividend model) and estimate each future year's dividends. It is possible, however, that a constant growth rate may be sustained for a relatively long period. In this case, the growth model shorthand formulation can be a reasonable representation of the PDV framework, because the value of the more distant benefits, in which the growth rate is likely to change, approaches zero.

[11] John Burr Williams, *The Theory of Investment Value*, chap. 5, as reprinted in Hsiu-Kwang Wu and Alan J. Zakon, *Elements of Investments,* Holt, Rinehart and Winston, Inc., New York, 1965, pp. 147–161.

Of course, if the analyst is using the shorthand and a change in the growth rate does occur, his evaluation of the stock may be incorrect.

The necessity of examining each of the factors that influence the discount factor is not avoided in the growth model. The discount factor r remains a major consideration in the stock price and, if altered, changes the stock price. The analyst must investigate the interest rate risk, the purchasing power risk, the business risk, and the financial risk attached to any stream of dividends.

The Price-Earnings Ratio

Despite the theoretical inconsistencies in discounting earnings (see the section on capitalization models), practitioners tend to rely heavily on *ad hoc* models that use earnings instead of dividends. The most common is the price-earnings ratio, which, as we have seen, is a shorthand PDV evaluation formulation using earnings instead of dividends.

Practitioners apparently use earnings as indicators of future dividends; fluctuations in near-term earnings expectations alter investor expectations of the future stream of dividends and cause the stock price to fluctuate. It is obvious that, in most cases, earnings must precede the payment of dividends and that dividends are directly related to the firm's earnings and stage of development.[12]

Firms with growing streams of earnings tend to postpone dividends in favor of reinvesting earnings in profitable expansion. As explored in Chapter 6, firms have a life cycle in which various sales, earnings, and dividend patterns generally emerge. After the initial, unprofitable organizational and developmental years, the firm should experience a rapid upsurge in sales and earnings if it is to survive. This rapid upsurge in earnings usually requires an accompanying rapid expansion of the firm's assets, which is financed, in part, by the reinvestment of most, if not all, profits. Consequently, dividends are either nonexistent or miniscule, and earnings grow much more rapidly than dividends during this period. In the second stage of the firm's life, the pressing need for asset expansion slackens. Dividend patterns are established at some percentage of earnings and then grow proportionately with them. In the third stage of growth, the profitable opportunities wane, and dividends grow more rapidly than earnings.

By using earnings as a proxy, investors can get an indication of future dividends, which may not be contained in the very low dividends in the first stage of the life cycle. Earnings in this stage may be an expedient proxy, although not a substitute, for the expected future stream of dividends.

---

[12] The subsequent chapters that deal with forecasting seek to forecast earnings for the purpose of forecasting dividends.

Investors who use the P/E tend to overvalue the future stream of benefits because of the double counting problem. These investors can still judge stock price changes, however, if their earnings predictions are accurate, because changes in earnings lead to changes in the size of the expected future stream of dividends, which, in turn, lead to adjustments in the stock price.

Again, it must be emphasized that the use of the price-earnings ratio does not avoid the necessity of examining each of the factors in the discount rate r as well as forecasting future dividends.

SUMMARY

The analysis of any financial asset involves a careful scrutiny of each of the components that are factors in the asset's value. Every financial asset has a promised future stream of benefits that must be discounted back to the present at some time value of money. Financial assets also involve, to varying degrees, risks that must be taken into account. These risks are interest rate, purchasing power, forecasting, business, and financial risks. On one extreme, United States government bonds involve only interest rate and purchasing power risk, and, on the other extreme, common stocks involve all risks.

The PDV framework is a concept that allows a systematic consideration of all the components of financial asset evaluation. Within this framework, the investor must consider the future stream of benefits, the time value of money, and purchasing power, business, and financial risks. By putting actual values on each of the components, the individual investor can place himself on the appropriate potential supply and potential demand curves in Chapter 1.

There are several variations to the PDV framework. The dividend model discounts the expected stream of future dividends. The capital gains model discounts the expected future dividends during the period the stock is held and the future price at which the stock is expected to be sold. The capitalization models contract the infinite stream of future dividends to the price-dividend ratio. Under the assumption of constant dividends, earnings equal dividends, and the PDV framework reduces to the price-earnings ratio. The price-earnings ratio is a shorthand for the PDV framework and does not eliminate the need for the careful analysis of all the components in the framework. The growth model incorporates a growing stream of dividends into the PDV framework. This model is usually based on a constant growth rate, which is assumed to continue from now until infinity. This assumption may mislead the analyst into overlooking cyclical or irregular earnings patterns. Although the discounting of earnings is incorrect, because it double counts the future stream of benefits and leads to higher than warranted stock price evaluations, many investors still use the shorthand price-earnings ratio. By using earnings as indicators of future dividends, they may be able to anticipate stock price changes, because earnings changes cause changes in the expected future stream of dividends, which, in turn, change the stock price. In none of the models is the necessity of examining each of the factors in the discount rate r, in addition to forecasting the future stream of dividends, avoided.

QUESTIONS

3.1 Explain each of the major risks attached to any financial asset.

3.2 The interest paid on a United States government bond is usually less than the interest paid by a corporate bond issued in the same time period. How can this be explained in terms of the risks attached to a United States government bond?

3.3 What are the components of security evaluation?

3.4 What is an annuity? Give several examples.

3.5 Why are common stocks with their infinite time horizon more sensitive to changes in the time value of money and therefore more volatile?

3.6 Why should an investor not rely on the simplified P/E and P/D ratios as representative of the entire infinite time horizon of the PDV evaluation framework.

PROBLEMS

3.1 Locate the following from the PDV tables:
(a) The factor for the present value of a sum to be received in eleven years at 12 percent.
(b) The factor for the present value of an annuity to be received for twenty-one years at 9 percent.
(c) The future value of $1 at the end of four years at 15 percent.
(d) The interest rate necessary for $1 received twenty-four years from now to have a PDV of $0.31.
(e) The number of years necessary for the PDV of a $1 yearly annuity at 6 percent to be worth $9.30.
(f) The present value of $1 to be received at the beginning of the nineteenth year at 10 percent.

3.2 Compute the future value of a $1,000 savings and loan account for a three-year period at an interest rate of 4 percent per year.

3.3 Compute the future value of $1,000 placed in the same account but with the interest compounded semiannually.

3.4 What is the present discounted value of a $90 interest payment received annually from a corporate bond for the next ten years if the time value of money is 10 percent?

3.5 If the redemption value of a 6 percent United States government bond is $1,000 and the bond is redeemable in eight years, what is the present price of the bond if the time value of money is 8 percent?

3.6 A particular common stock pays a constant $2 dividend as a matter of policy. If the discount factor is 5 percent, what is the PDV of the stock with the capital gains model? What is the PDV of the stock with the dividend capitalization model? What conclusion can be drawn concerning the two models?

3.7 If a common stock is selling at $50 a share and it has a P/E ratio of 20, approximately what is the discount factor r?

3.8 What is the PDV of a $1 dividend stream growing at 5 percent for three years if the discount factor is 4 percent? Find the stock's price over an infinite time horizon if the growth and discount rates remain constant. Explain your results.

3.9 What is the PDV of a dividend stream from 100 shares of a common stock for the next ten years if the stock pays a $1 annual dividend, regardless of splits, and regularly splits 2 shares for 1 every 3 years and the time value of money is 7 percent.

3.10 Compute the PDV of one share of a common stock for the next 4 years given:
  (a) The dividend is currently $1 per share and is increasing at the rate of $0.25 per year at the end of each year for the next 5 years.
  (b) Inflation is increasing at an additional 1 percent a year for the next 3 years.
  (c) $i = 2$ percent, $f = 0$ percent, $b = 2$ percent, $p = 1$ percent at the beginning of year 1.
  (d) The stock is expected to be selling at $25 a share.

REFERENCES

Bauman, W. Scott. "Investment Returns and Present Values," *Financial Analysts Journal,* vol. 25, pp. 107–120, November–December, 1969.

Foster, Earl M. "The Price-Earnings Ratio and Growth," *Financial Analysts Journal,* vol. 26, pp. 96–103, January–February, 1970.

Gordon, Myron J. *The Investment, Financing and Valuation of the Corporation,* Homewood, Ill.: Richard D. Irwin, Inc., 1962.

Hubbard, Charles L., and Clark A. Hawkins. *Theory of Valuation,* Scranton, Pa.: International Textbook Company, 1969.

King, Benjamin F. "Market and Industry Factors in Stock Price Behavior," *The Journal of Business,* vol. 39, pp. 139–190, January, 1966.

Lerner, Eugene M., and Willard T. Carleton. *A Theory of Financial Analysis,* New York: Harcourt, Brace & World, Inc., 1966.

Lindsay, John R., and Arnold W. Sametz. *Financial Management: An Analytical Approach,* Homewood, Ill.: Richard D. Irwin, Inc., 1967.

Peterson, D. E. *A Quantitative Framework for Financial Management,* Homewood, Ill.: Richard D. Irwin, Inc., 1969.

Van Horne, James C. *Financial Management and Policy,* Englewood Cliffs, N.J.: Prentice-Hall, Inc., 1968.

Weston, J. Fred, and Eugene F. Brigham. *Managerial Finance,* 2d ed., New York: Holt, Rinehart and Winston, Inc., 1966.

Williams, John Burr. *The Theory of Investment Value.* New York: Augustus M. Kelley, Publishers, 1965.

Part Two

In Part I we introduced the basic PDV evaluation framework and its major components. Part II concentrates on the future stream of benefits component, that is, the numerator in the PDV framework. This entails a careful examination of the projection of earnings from which the expected stream of future dividends is derived and the forecasting risk.

As a point of departure, we explore the techniques of financial statement analysis. This involves us with balance sheet, income statement, and ratio analysis. Financial analysts commonly use each of these to gather information used in forecasting earnings. We attempt to see what particular bits of information might be gathered and how they might be pertinent to earnings forecasting.

From financial statement analysis, we investigate earnings forecasting under stable conditions. The statistical techniques that are applicable and the restrictive nature of the assumptions underlying them are also discussed.

Once we move from stable conditions to dynamic conditions, new considerations have important bearing on earnings forecasting. Dynamic shifts in the firm's product markets and factor (raw materials) markets must be analyzed for their potential impact on the firm's earnings.

We introduce break-even analysis as a possible forecasting aid.

Forecasting risk is the risk that the investor's earnings forecast is inaccurate and causes him financial loss. Several methods for improving earnings forecasting are suggested and explored.

Although dividends, not earnings, are the stockholders' future reward and the stream on which the PDV is computed, Part II concentrates on earnings estimation techniques as the method of deriving divided expectations, because within the earnings estimates lies the dividend estimate. Dividends are a function of earnings. Without earnings, dividends cannot be paid. But dividends tend to lag earnings, in many cases, by relatively long and unpredictable lengths of time, and the direct forecasting of dividends over the infinite time horizon of a stock is often very difficult and inaccurate. Nearer-term earnings estimates, however, imply an expected dividend stream; that is, earnings have an informational content about future dividends. An increased (decreased) earnings forecast implies an increased (decreased) dividend stream. It is frequently assumed[1] that dividends are directly proportional to earnings by the retention rate λ, so that in the PDV framework

$$D = (1 - \lambda)E$$

or

$$P = \frac{(1 - \lambda)E}{r - g}$$

We can also assume that the timing of future dividends is related to that of the earnings stream, so that the lag between higher earnings and higher dividends is a specific number of years. Each earnings estimate then has an implied dividend stream, although each analyst may interpret the implication differently and derive a different expected dividend stream from a given earnings estimate.

For our purposes, then, we estimate the reasonable foreseeable earnings and assume an implied dividend stream from them. This procedure allows us to capture changes in the expected future stream of dividends in our PDV evaluation as well as providing techniques for refining our estimates.

---

[1] E. Lerner and W. Carelton, *op. cit.*, and Ezra Solomm, *Theory of Financial Management*, Columbia University Press, New York, 1963.

4
Financial Statement Analysis

The first component of the PDV framework to be examined is the forecasting of the future stream of benefits. This is perhaps the most refined and widely used component of the framework. For years, financial analysts have been using financial statement analysis in an attempt to glean indications of the company's future earnings and dividend performance.

This chapter explores financial statement and ratio analysis. The more commonly used analytical techniques and ratios and their weaknesses are discussed. The following chapters explore methods of processing financial statement analysis into earnings projections and their implied dividend streams and of handling forecasting risk, that is, the possibility of incorrect projections.

THE INCOME STATEMENT

The annual income statement issued by a company is an accounting picture of the past year's income, expenses, and profits. A typical income statement is illustrated in Table 4.1.

Income Statement Terms

Sales. Sales or revenues are the money collected or accrued for the products sold or the services rendered.

Cost of Goods Sold. Cost of goods sold represents all the costs incurred in turning raw material and labor into the finished products. It is computed by adding the cost of raw materials to the inventory at the beginning

TABLE 4.1 Basic Incorporated Income Statement, 19

Net sales		$19,500,000
Cost of sales and operating expenses		
Cost of goods sold	$13,200,000	
Depreciation	2,700,000	
Selling and administrative expenses	1,500,000	17,400,000
Operating profit		$ 2,100,000
Other income		
Dividends and interest		305,000
Total income		$ 2,405,000
Less: interest on bonds		405,000
Profit before provision for federal income tax		$ 2,000,000
Provision for federal income tax (calculated at 50% rate)		1,000,000
Net profit for year		$ 1,000,000

of the period and subtracting the inventory at the end of the period. For example,

Inventory, January 1, 1970 (1 million units @ $1)		$1,000,000
Purchases		
Raw materials	$300,000	
Labor	500,000	800,000
Cost of goods available for sale		$1,800,000
Inventory, January 1, 1971 (250,000 units @ $2)		500,000
Cost of goods sold		$1,300,000

Inventory evaluation presents some problems. For example, if the 1/1/70 inventory cost was $1 per unit but the cost of the goods produced in 1970 was $2 per unit, was the cost of the 1/1/71 inventory $1 or $2 per unit? Under the first-in first-out (fifo) method, the inventory sold first is that which was produced at $1 per unit, and the value of the inventory remaining at 1/1/71 is $2 per unit, the cost of the last goods to be finished. In the example above, the cost of the goods sold is computed on a fifo basis. Under the last-in first-out (lifo) method, the inventory sold first is that which was produced at $2 per unit, and the value of the 1/1/71 inventory is $1 per unit, the cost of the first goods to be finished. For example, the cost of goods sold in this case under lifo is as follows:

Inventory 1/1/70 (1 million units @ $1)		$1,000,000
Purchases		
Raw materials	300,000	
Labor	500,000	800,000
Cost of goods available for sale		$1,800,000
Inventory 1/1/71 (250,000 units @ $1)		250,000
Cost of goods sold		$1,550,000

During periods of falling prices, lifo usually produces higher earnings than fifo, because the less costly inventory is sold first. During periods of rising prices, the earnings effect is reversed.

In projecting earnings, it is important to be aware of any earnings increase or decrease that may have arisen because of a shift from lifo to fifo or vice versa; and if inventory is a relatively large asset, to be aware of the evaluation method. For example, if the lifo basis is used, the inventory value may be understated in an inflationary period. It is also important to be aware of the lifo versus fifo effects on earnings when comparing earnings projects for different companies.

Depreciation, Amortization, and Depletion. Depreciation is an expense that represents a year's portion of the capital asset's (any asset with a life expectancy of more than 1 year) cost due to wear, use, or obsolescence. Amortization is the depreciation of an asset other than a capital asset, and depletion is depreciation of a natural resource, such as oil. For example, a machine that costs $10,000 and has a useful life of 10 years wears out one-tenth of its cost every year, so that after 1 year the machine is worth only $9,000, and after 2 years only $8,000, and so on. The machiney is depreciating at a rate of $1,000 per year.

The rate of depreciation is arbitrarily determined under the Internal Revenue Code and computed by artificial accounting procedures. There are several depreciation choices; the most common are (1) straight-line, (2) double declining balance, and (3) sum of the year digits.

The straight-line method, as illustrated in Table 4.2, depreciates the asset in equal yearly installments during the life of the asset.

The double declining balance (DDB) method accelerates the depreciation to twice the straight-line percentage that would be charged on the

TABLE 4.2 Straight-Line Depreciation

Year	Asset value (Beginning of Year)	Depreciation	Asset value (Year End)
1	$10,000	$1,000	$9,000
2	9,000	1,000	8,000
3	8,000	1,000	7,000
4	7,000	1,000	6,000
5	6,000	1,000	5,000
6	5,000	1,000	4,000
7	4,000	1,000	3,000
8	3,000	1,000	2,000
9	2,000	1,000	1,000
10	1,000	1,000	0*

* Asset has zero salvage value.

value of the asset at the end of the year. For example, if the straight-line depreciation is 10 percent, the DDB method each year depreciates twice this, or 20 percent of the asset's undepreciated worth, as illustrated in Table 4.3. This has the effect of making the depreciation greater than

TABLE 4.3 Double Declining Balance Depreciation

Year	Asset value (Beginning of Year)	Depreciation	Asset value (Year End)	Straight-line depreciation
1	$10,000	$2,000	$8,000	$1,000
2	8,000	1,600	6,400	1,000
3	6,400	1,280	5,120	1,000
4	5,120	1,024	4,096	1,000
5	4,096	820	3,276	1,000
6	3,276	655	2,621	1,000
7	2,621	655*	1,966	1,000
8	1,966	655	1,311	1,000
9	1,311	655	656	1,000
10	656	655	0	1,000

* Switch to straight-line depreciation on remaining value.

straight-line in the earlier years and less than straight-line in the later years of the asset's life. The usual practice, however, is to switch to straight-line depreciation of the remaining value once it is greater than the DDB depreciation, as given in Table 4.3. The effect of the DDB is to increase current expenses and reduce reported income and income taxes in the earlier years of the asset's life. Table 4.4 illustrates the effect of DDB on taxes and reported income. As long as the firm continues to grow rapidly enough so that the largest portion of its assets are in the earlier years of their lives, the effect of DDB is to reduce taxes and reported earnings and hence increase the firm's cash flows in the early years of the asset's life.

TABLE 4.4 Effect of Double Declining Balance on Taxes and Reported Income for First Year of Asset's Life

	Straight-line	Double declining balance
Sales	$100,000	$100,000
Cost of goods sold	50,000	50,000
Depreciation	10,000	20,000
Net operating income	40,000	30,000
Taxes (50%)	20,000	15,000
Net income	$ 20,000	$ 15,000

The sum of the year digits (SOY) method also accelerates the depreciation charges and puts the greater portion of depreciation in the earlier years of the asset's life. In the SOY method, the years of the asset's life are summed. The total years remaining in the asset's life are divided by the summed figure. This fraction is multiplied by the asset's original cost less any salvage value. The product of the multiplication is the depreciation for the year. For example, as illustrated in Table 4.5, the summed years of the asset's life are 15 ($5 + 4 + 3 + 2 + 1$), and in the first year $5/15$ of the asset's original cost is depreciated. In the second year $4/15$ of the asset's original cost is depreciated. The effect of SOY on income is similar to that of the DDB. In the earlier years reported income and income taxes are less than under the straight-line method. In the later years the reported income and income taxes are higher than under the straight-line method.

TABLE 4.5 Sum of the Year Digits Depreciation

Year	Asset value (Beginning of Year)	Depreciation	Depreciation factor	Straight-line depreciation
1	$15,000	$5,000	$5/15$	$3,000
2	10,000	4,000	$4/15$	3,000
3	6,000	3,000	$3/15$	3,000
4	3,000	2,000	$2/15$	3,000
5	1,000	1,000*	$1/15$	3,000

* Asset has zero salvage value.

Economic Depreciation

The income statement depreciation expense is an artificial accounting procedure. The investor is really interested in the economic, not the accounting, life of an asset. The economic life of a machine is measured in the years during which the machine has the ability to produce revenue-generating goods competitively. A brand-new machine to produce buggy whips is probably worth less than a 10-year-old machine to produce chewing gum. In forecasting earnings, the investor wants to know the machine's revenue-generating ability and operating cost rather than its age.

Noncash Expense (Depreciation). A noncash expense is an expenditure in which no money changes hands in the current period; it is merely a bookkeeping entry. Depreciation is an example of a noncash expense. Depreciation arises because wear occurs during a period of years, although the actual cost outlay for the asset occurred at the beginning of its life. The original cash outlay is capitalized (added to the company's assets) and only charged against income as it is depreciated. Thus, when a new machine is purchased, the asset cash is decreased, and the asset machinery is increased. But there is no effect on income. Only when the machine is depreciated is there an expense charged against income; but, at this time, no cash changes hands. It is important in forecasting earnings to distinguish between those expenses which are capitalized and do not affect income until depreciated and those expenses which are not capitalized and immediately affect income. For example, the earnings of two companies within an industry may not be directly comparable if one company chooses, within the tax law, to capitalize and then depreciate a certain expense and the other immediately charges this expense against income. Other noncash expenditures are depletion and the amortization of patents, intangible assets, research and development, and good will.

Net Cash Flow. Net cash flow is the actual cash that is available to the company from its operations and other income statement sources during the accounting period. To compute net cash flow, we compare all the sources from which actual cash comes into the possession of the company with all the uses of cash that actually require cash payment by the firm. Basic Incorporated (Table 4.1) generated cash inflow from net sales and other income, while disbursing cash for raw materials and labor (cost of goods sold), selling and administrative expenses, interest, and taxes. The cash inflows and outflows for Basic are as follows:

Inflows		Outflows	
Net sales	$19,500,000	Cost of goods sold	$13,200,000
Other income	305,000	Selling and administrative expense	1,500,000
	$19,805,000	Interest	405,000
		Taxes	1,000,000
			$16,105,000

Net cash flow for Basic would be the difference between the inflows and the outflows, or $3,700,000.

The astute reader will note that depreciation is not included in the calculation of the cash outflow, although it is an expense, because no actual cash is disbursed, as explained above. In the typical case it is therefore possible to calculate net cash flow by summing the net profit and the depreciation for the year, which in the case of Basic Incorporated is $3,700,000, the same figure calculated above.

Selling and Administrative Expenses. Selling expenses include salesmen's salaries, commissions, advertising, and all other expenses connected with selling the product. Administrative expenses include office payroll, executive salaries, and other expenses concerned with administrative affairs.

Operating Income. Operating income is equal to operative revenues or sales minus operating expenses. Operating revenues and expenses are those directly incurred in the production of the goods or service.

Nonoperating Income and Expenses. Nonoperating income is income from sources other than those directly related to the usual operating routine of the company. Among the most common nonoperating expenses and income are (1) nonrecurring gains and losses, (2) contingency reserves, (3) income from subsidiaries and affiliates, and (4) tax loss carry-forward benefits and tax credits.

Nonrecurring items are usually not expected to repeat themselves and cannot be expected in the future stream of benefits. Nonrecurring items usually arise as one-time occurrences, such as the sale of an asset. For example, if the company sells an old plant that has a book value of $1,025,000 for $1,000,000, it has a nonrecurring loss of $25,000 that lowers net income before taxes by $25,000. Since the unusual $25,000 loss will not occur next year, earnings for this year are not a true indication of the future stream of benefits. Only if the nonrecurrent loss is so great as to endanger the company's future or promises to recur with regularity may it have bearing on the future stream of benefits.

Contingency reserves are provisions for possible future expenses, such as uncollectable accounts receivable. In forecasting future earnings, the adequacy of these reserves must be judged.

Income from subsidiaries and affiliates that is not included (consolidated) with the parent company's statement is nonoperating income. A company may own another company's stock and receive dividends that may be recurring but are not considered operating income. Losses and income of subsidiaries that are not included in the parent's income statements must be considered in forecasting earnings.

Tax loss carry-forwards are allowed tax deductions against current profits. If the company experienced a loss last year, it may reduce this year's taxable income by the amount of the loss. Tax credits are reductions in tax payments, allowed by the government in an effort to encourage a particular type of investment spending.

Other Features of the Income Statement. As a check on the usefulness of reported income in forecasting earnings, the investor may check to see if the reported tax rate (taxes/net income before taxes) agrees with the tax rate that would be paid by a company with only regular income. For example, assume that a firm with only regular income will pay 50 percent of its earnings in taxes. If the firm had earnings before taxes of $1,000,000 and paid only $250,000 in taxes, it paid only 25 percent of its earnings in taxes. This difference between the usual 50 percent rate and the actual 25 percent may imply a need for significant adjustment of the reported income statement before it is indicative of future earnings. For example, substantial nonrecurring capital gains might cause a lower than expected tax rate and be of important bearing on future earnings forecasts.

The footnotes and the auditor's certification accompanying the financial statement are also important clues to the income statement's applicability to future earnings.

Probably one of the most important indications of the income statement's applicability to future earnings is its consistency in time. If the accounting approach is consistent, present statements may very likely give insight into future statements.

INCOME STATEMENT RATIOS

A ratio is a comparison of one income statement figure with another that may be used for common comparison among various companies and among years for the same company. It is important to remember that ratios are generally only symptoms of the underlying condition of the firm. If one of the symptoms seems to be out of line when compared with the usual case, the analyst is alerted to give further examination to the firm's condition. Therefore, ratio analysis is generally used only in comparison with certain accepted ratio standards and not in the absolute evaluation of share prices (see later section of this chapter under "Problems with Ratio Analysis"). Particular ratios and trends in certain ratios may give clues to future earnings. For example, profit margins may indicate the efficiency with which sales are converted to profits.

Among the more useful ratios (as computed from Table 4.1) are the following:

1. Pretax ratio profit margin:

$$\text{Income before taxes/sales}$$
$$\$2,000,000/19,500,000 = \$0.1025$$

2. Posttax profit margins:

$$\text{Net profit/sales}$$
$$\$1,000,000/19,500,000 = 0.0513$$

3. Operating margins:

$$\text{Operating income/sales}$$
$$\$2,100,000/19,500,000 = 0.1077$$

4. Earnings per share:

$$\text{Net profit/outstanding shares}$$
$$\$1,000,000/1,000,000 = \$1.00$$

5. Tax ratio:

$$\text{Taxes paid/earnings before taxes}$$
$$\$1,000,000/2,000,000 = 0.50$$

6. Interest coverage (an indication of the firm's ability to meet interest payments):

$$\text{Earnings before interest and taxes/interest}$$
$$\$2,405,000/405,000 = 5.94$$

Trends in sales, pretax earnings, net profits, and earnings per share may also help in forecasting future earnings. It is imperative to note, however, whether the stated growth rate is a compound or simple rate of growth as well as the size of the base from which the company has grown. It may be easier to double sales of $1 million than to double sales of $500 million.

COMMON SIZE INCOME STATEMENT

The common size income statement is an income statement in which all figures are expressed as a percentage of sales. Table 4.6 is an example of a common size income statement. The major advantage of a common size income statement is the standardized presentation that eliminates the bias of size and makes all companies directly comparable.

TABLE 4.6 Common Size Income Statement, 19

				Percentage		Percentage
Net sales				$19,500,000		100.00
Cost of sales and operating expenses						
Cost of goods sold	$13,200,000		67.69			
Depreciation	2,700,000		13.84			
Selling and administrative expenses	1,500,000		7.70	17,400,000		89.23
Operating profit				$ 2,100,000		10.77
Other income						
Dividends and interest				305,000		1.56
Total income				$ 2,405,000		12.33
Less: interest on bonds				405,000		2.07
Profit before provision for federal income tax				$ 2,000,000		10.26
Provision for federal income tax				1,000,000		5.13
Net profit for year				$ 1,000,000		5.13

STATEMENT OF RETAINED EARNINGS

The statement of retained earnings is an accounting of the accumulated net income not paid out in dividends but retained in the business for reinvestment. Table 4.7 illustrates a statement of retained earnings. The common dividend is a distribution representing part of the stream of benefits to shareholders. The preferred stock dividends take prior claim on the earnings but are usually limited in amount.

TABLE 4.7 Statement of Retained Earnings

Accumulated Retained Earnings Statement (Earned Surplus), 19

Balance January 1, 19		$4,485,000
Add: net profit for year		1,000,000
Total		$5,485,000
Less: dividends paid		
On preferred stock	$ 90,000	
On common stock	400,000	490,000
Balance December 31, 19		$4,995,000

The payout ratio is the common dividend/earnings available to common stock and reveals the percentage of net profits paid to stockholders. In this example, the payout ratio is $400,000/\$1,000,000 = 40$ percent. The amount and percentage of retained earnings (one minus the payout ratio) may give some indication of the funds available for those investments which will generate future earnings. A higher retention rate may indicate increased future earnings.

BALANCE SHEET

The balance sheet represents the company's financial position at a point in time and reflects the accumulation of assets and liabilities. Table 4.8 illustrates a balance sheet.

Terms of Balance Sheet

Assets. Assets are what is owned by the company.

Current assets include all assets that will, in the normal course of business, become cash, be consumed, or be sold within 1 year. These generally include (1) cash in the form of currency and bank demand deposits; (2) marketable securities, such as United States Treasury bills; (3) accounts receivable, which are the debts of customers, less any provision for estimated uncollectable accounts receivable; and (4) the inventory of goods for sale.

Long-term assets are assets that will generally not become cash within

TABLE 4.8 Basic Incorporated

Balance Sheet, December 31, 19

Assets			Liabilities and stockholders' equity		
Current assets			Current liabilities		
Cash		$ 2,250,000	Accounts payable	$ 3,000,000	
Marketable securities at cost (market value: $4,710,000)		4,650,000	Notes payable	2,550,000	
			Accrued expenses payable	990,000	
Accounts receivable	$ 6,300,000		Federal income tax payable	460,000	
Less: provision for bad debts	200,000	6,100,000	Total current liabilities		$ 7,000,000
Inventories		4,500,000	Long-term liabilities		
Total current assets		$17,500,000	First mortgage bonds, 5% interest due 1975		8,100,000
Investment in unconsolidated subsidiaries		1,200,000	Total liabilities		$15,100,000
Property, plant, and equipment					
Land	$ 450,000		Stockholders' equity		
Buildings	10,400,000		Capital stock		
Machinery	3,850,000		Preferred stock, 5% cumulative, $100 par value each; authorized, issued, and outstanding, 18,000 shares	1,800,000	
Office equipment	300,000				
	$15,000,000				
Less: accumulated depreciation	5,400,000				
Net property, plant and equipment		9,600,000	Common stock, $5 par value each; authorized, issued, and outstanding, 1,000,000 shares	5,000,000	
Prepayments and deferred charges		400,000	Capital paid in excess of par	2,205,000	
Goodwill, patents, trademarks		400,000	Accumulated retained earnings	4,995,000	
Total assets		$29,100,000	Total stockholders' equity		$14,000,000
			Total liabilities and stockholders' equity		$29,100,000

the course of 1 year. These include (1) gross plant, property, and equipment or fixed assets with a life expectancy greater than 1 year; (2) net plant, property, and equipment—the gross figure less any depreciation that has accumulated during the life of the assets; and (3) goodwill or intangible assets, such as a patent, franchise, or the amount paid in excess of the accounting asset value for a purchased asset.

Liabilities. Liabilities are the company's debt to its suppliers, creditors, and stockholders.

Current liabilities are those debts which will, in the normal course of business, be paid within 1 year. These generally include (1) accounts payable—the company's debt to its suppliers; (2) notes payable—the company's short-term debt to its creditors; (3) federal taxes payable, the company's tax debt to the government due within 1 year; and (4) long-term debt due within 1 year—the company's debt to its long-term creditors that is due within 1 year.

Long-term liabilities are the company's long-term debt owned to its creditors, usually its bondholders.

Stockholders' equity is the amount owned by the stockholders after everyone else's claim has been satisfied. The preferred stockholders have preference on a specified amount of the residual, and the remainder belongs to the common stockholders. The remainder is divided into common stock, capital paid in excess of the par value of the stock, and accumulated retained earnings.

BALANCE SHEET INFORMATION

The balance sheet reveals information on the company's liquidity, utilization of assets, and financing, all of which may aid in forecasting future earnings.

Liquidity

A company's liquidity position is an indication of its ability to meet the more immediate cash needs of normal, as well as unusual, operating conditions. Current assets are the most quickly converted to cash, and current liabilities present the most pressing need for cash. Therefore, the analysis of liquidity concentrates on these areas. A shortage or inability to raise cash to meet immediate needs may impair the company's ability to generate future earnings. The working capital position, which is current assets minus current liabilities, is a frequently used indication of liquidity. In the balance sheet in Table 4.8 working capital is $10,500,000 ($17,500,000 — $7,000,000).

Certain working capital ratios are indicative of the quality and adequacy of the working capital position. Among the ratios that indicate the quality of the working capital position are (1) the current ratio (current assets/current liabilities), $17,500,000/$7,000,000 = 2.5$; (2) the quick ratio (cash, marketable securities, and accounts receivable/current liabilities), $13,000,000/$7,000,000 = 1.86$. Among those working capital ratios which indicate working capital quality are (1) Accounts receivable turnover, indicating the quality of the accounts receivable (sales/accounts receivable), $19,500,000/$6,300,000 = 3.09$. The average collection period is also an indication of accounts receivable quality: $360 \div$ sales/accounts receivable $= 116.5$ days. When these accounts receivable ratios are compared with normal collection time and turnover for the industry or the company, an indication of the speed with which customers are paying their debt to the company is obtained. A fast payment record indicates a high quality of accounts receivable. (2) Inventory turnover, indicating the quality of the inventory; that is, a comparatively low turnover may indicate that the inventory is not selling or is out of date, and a comparatively high turnover may indicate costly inventory procedures (cost of goods sold/inventory), $13,200,000/$4,500,000 = 2.93$.

Utilization of Assets

An important indication of future earnings performance may be found in how efficiently management is utilizing its assets to produce sales and profits. When compared with industry standards, indications of efficient asset management are:
1. return on investment
    net profit/total assets
    $1,000,000/29,100,000 = .0344$
2. net profit + interest on long-term debt/total capital
    $1,405,000/22,100,000 = .064$
3. net profit/common equity
    $1,000,000/12,200,000 = .082$
4. profit before taxes/total capital
    $2,000,000/22,100,000 = .090$
5. profit before depreciation and taxes/total assets
    $4,700,000/29,100,000 = .1615$
6. fixed asset turnover
    sales/net plant, property and equipment
    $19,500,000/9,600,000 = 2.031$
7. Book value of assets is the accounting worth of the assets owned by stockholders after all prior claims are satisfied. Book value tends to be misleading because it is so arbitrarily determined under the depreciation rules and usually bears little resemblance to the economic worth of the assets. Even in liquidation where asset value

is of prominent importance, book value is usually far from the actual liquidation proceeds.

assets — liabilities = stockholders equity = $12,200,000
book value per share $12,200,000/1,000,000 = $12.20

Financing

The balance sheet also reveals how a company has financed itself among the various sources of funds available. The capital structure is the proportion of long-term debt, preferred stock and stockholder's equity (common stock and capital surplus plus retained earnings) in a firm's financing. For example, the capital structure of the company in Table 4.8 is:

Long-term debt	$ 8,100,000	36.65%
Preferred stock	1,800,000	8.14
Stockholders' equity	12,200,000	55.21
	$22,100,000	100.00%

The debt/equity ratio, along with the times interest earned ratio, is one of the most important indications of the company's financial risk. The debt/equity ratio represents the proportion of debt to equity. In the example, the debt/equity ratio is $8,100,000/14,000,000, or 0.57 to 1. The more debt in a capital structure (the higher the debt/equity ratio), the more cash expense obligations the company has. If these cash expense obligations, such as bond interest, are not met, the company may be forced out of business. A large cash obligation in relation to the company's cash generation is indicative of great financial risk.

In addition to affecting the risk associated with future earnings, the use of debt also affects earnings. Leverage is the use of debt in an attempt to increase return on equity. The difference between the return on an investment and the cost of financing the investment is the residual to the common stockholders. If the difference is positive, the stockholders benefit. If the difference is negative, the stockholders must make up the difference. This causes a decrease in the return on equity and magnifies the decrease in earnings per share (see Chapter 13). In Table 4.9 the use of one-half debt to finance the company instead of all common stock has increased stockholders' returns from 5 to 7.5 percent.

Convertible Securities

Conversion is the privilege of a senior security holder, such as a bond or preferred holder, to convert his senior security into common stock. For example, a company might have $100,000 5 percent bonds convertible into stock at $10 per share. If these bonds were converted into common stock, the number of outstanding shares would increase by

Balance sheet information

TABLE 4.9 Illustration of Positive Leverage

	Company X		Company Y	
Financing	$50,000	5% debt	0	debt
	$50,000	Common stock	$100,000	Common stock
		(5,000 shares)		(10,000 shares)
Sales	15,000		15,000	
Cost of goods sold	5,000		5,000	
Operating profit	10,000		10,000	
Bond interest	2,500		0	
Profits before taxes	7,500		10,000	
Taxes (50%)	3,750		5,000	
Net profit	3,750		5,000	
Earnings per share	$0.75		$0.50	
Return on equity	7.5%		5%	

10,000. If this figure were large in relation to the present number of shares outstanding, it could greatly affect future earnings per share. For example, in Table 4.10 the earnings per share fell from $2.25 to $1.25 when the $100,000 5 percent bonds were converted into 10,000 shares. The effect of conversion on earnings per share was rather large for the company in Table 4.10, because the conversion represented a large increase in the number of shares.[1]

TABLE 4.10 Effect of Conversion on Earnings per Share

	Before conversion	After conversion
Capital structure	$100,000 5%	0
	Bonds convertible into	
	10,000 shares	
	10,000 shares common stock	20,000 shares common stock
Sales	100,000	100,000
Cost of goods sold	50,000	50,000
Operating profit	50,000	50,000
Bond interest	5,000	0
Pretax profit	45,000	50,000
Taxes (50%)	22,500	25,000
Net profit	22,500	25,000
Earnings per share	$2.25	$1.25

[1] Opinion 15 of the Accounting Principles Board now requires the firm to report earnings per share on an adjusted basis, giving effect to potential dilution.

COMMON SIZE BALANCE SHEET

The common size balance sheet is a balance sheet in which all the figures are expressed as a percentage of total assets or total liabilities. Table 4.11 is an example of a common size balance sheet. As in the case of the common size income statement, it offers a standardized presentation that eliminates the bias of size and makes all companies directly comparable.

SOURCES AND USES OF FUND STATEMENTS

The sources and uses of funds statement for a corporation represents where the cash came from and where it went. It gives an indication of what assets were acquired and how they were financed. From this, the investor can judge if the company has invested wisely in an effort to generate future revenues.

Uses of funds are increases in assets and decreases in liabilities. For example, increases in cash, accounts receivable, inventory, and plant, property, and equipment; and decreases in accounts payable, notes payable, long-term debt, and stockholders' equity are uses of funds. Sources of funds are the reverse; that is, decreases in assets and increases in liabilities.

The sources and uses of funds statement may be constructed by comparing the company's balance sheets from one period with another and recording the increases and decreases in assets and liabilities. For example, the decrease in cash for the company in Table 4.12 from $100,000 to $50,000 is a source of funds of $50,000. Table 4.12 illustrates two balances for one company and the construction of a sources and uses of funds statement from them.

PHYSICAL DATA

Indications of future earnings may come from data on the firm's physical size. For example, certain physical data on capacity may be an important indication of the company's ability to generate future earnings. A company that is presently operating at capacity and must wait several years for additional capacity to come on stream may have a limited earnings growth in the near future.

Other physical indications of efficiency are sales per employee or profit per employee, particularly in the service-oriented industries, in which plant and equipment outlays are small. The share of market may be an important indicator of future earnings in marketing-oriented com-

TABLE 4.11 Common Size Balance Sheet

Assets		Percentage		Percentage
Current assets				
Cash			$ 2,250,000	7.73
Marketable securities at cost (market value: $4,710,000)			4,650,000	15.98
Accounts receivable	$ 6,300,000	21.65		
Less: provision for bad debts	200,000	0.69	6,100,000	20.96
Inventories			4,500,000	15.46
Total current assets			$17,500,000	
Investment in unconsolidated subsidiaries			1,200,000	4.12
Property, plant, and equipment				
Land	$ 450,000	1.54		
Buildings	10,400,000	35.73		
Machinery	3,850,000	13.23		
Office equipment	300,000	1.03		
	$15,000,000	51.53		
Less: accumulated depreciation	5,400,000	18.54		
Net property, plant, and equipment			9,600,000	32.99
Prepayments and deferred charges			400,000	1.38
Goodwill, patents, trademarks			400,000	1.38
Total assets			$29,100,000	100.00
Liabilities				
Current liabilities				
Accounts payable	$ 3,000,000	10.31		
Notes payable	2,550,000	8.77		
Accrued expenses payable	990,000	3.41		
Federal income tax payable	460,000	1.56		
Total current liabilities			$ 7,000,000	24.05
Long-term liabilities				
5% first mortgage bonds due 1975			8,100,000	27.84
Total liabilities			$15,100,000	51.89
Stockholders' equity				
Capital stock				
Preferred stock, 5% cumulative, $100 par value each; authorized, issued, and outstanding 18,000 shares	$ 1,800,000	6.19		
Common stock, $5 par value each; authorized, issued, and outstanding 1,000,000 shares	5,000,000	17.18		
Capital surplus	2,100,000	7.21		
Accumulated retained earnings	5,100,000	17.53		
Total stockholders' equity			14,000,000	48.11
Total liabilities and stockholders' equity			$29,100,000	100.00

TABLE 4.12 Sources and Uses of Funds Construction ABC Company

Balance sheet, December 31, 1970 Assets		Balance sheet December 31, 1971 Assets		Net change
Cash	100,000	Cash	50,000	−50,000
Securities	50,000	Securities	0	−50,000
Accounts receivable	75,000	Accounts receivable	150,000	
Inventory	50,000	Inventory	100,000	
Plant and equipment	1,000,000	Plant and equipment	1,000,000	
Accumulated depreciation	200,000	Accumulated depreciation	300,000	
	800,000		700,000	
Goodwill	100,000	Goodwill	100,000	
Total assets	1,175,000	Total assets	1,100,000	−75,000
Liabilities and equity		**Liabilities and equity**		
Accounts payable	25,000	Accounts payable	50,000	+25,000
Notes payable	50,000	Notes payable	0	−50,000
Long-term debt	300,000	Long-term debt	250,000	
Preferred stock	200,000	Preferred stock	0	
Common stock	100,000	Common stock	150,000	
Capital surplus	400,000	Capital surplus	450,000	
Retained earnings	100,000	Retained earnings	200,000	
Total liabilities and equity	1,175,000	Total liabilities and equity	1,100,000	−75,000

Sources and Uses of Funds Statement, 19

Sources		Uses	
Cash	50,000	Accounts receivable	75,000
Securities	50,000	Inventory	50,000
Plant and equipment depreciation	100,000	Notes payable	50,000
		Long-term debt	50,000
Accounts payable	25,000	Preferred stock	200,000
Common stock	50,000		425,000
Capital surplus	50,000		
Earnings	100,000		
	425,000		

panies. Sales per share may be an indication of possible growth in future earnings if profit margins are to be increased. A large sales per share base means a relatively small increase in the profit margin ratio may cause a relatively large increase in earnings per share. Physical reserves per share may be important for mineral companies. Geographical or customer concentration may be important for companies that operate in particular areas or among few customers. Such concentration exposes these firms to the risks inherent in these customers. Various firms or industries may have physical data that is peculiar to themselves. The analyst should be aware of any such data.

STOCK MARKET DATA

Various characteristics of the stock in the marketplace may have some bearing on the analysis. Among these are the prevailing price/earnings ratio, the prevailing dividend yield, the historical price volatility of the stock, the number of shares readily available for trading (floating supply), and the ratio of net asset per share to market price per share, in potential liquidation situations.

The price/earnings ratio relates the price of the stock to the earnings and, as we have seen in Chapter 3, is a shorthand evaluation of the future stream of earnings. For example, if Basic Incorporated is earning $1 per share and selling at $10 per share, the price/earnings ratio would be 10. In practice, this ratio has often been used to capitalize the present or near-term earnings per share to arrive at the going concern worth of the enterprise. Analysts have frequently assumed that the present price/earnings ratio appropriately reflected the risks attached to the particular earnings and have concentrated on projecting future earnings per share, multiplying the historical price/earnings ratio and the projected earnings per share to determine a value. As we have seen in Chapter 3, however, this may cause the analyst to overlook important money and capital market factors as well as changes in business and financial risk, all of which bear on the security's value.

The dividend yield is the relation of the per share dividend to the market price of the share. For example, if Basic Incorporated paid $0.40 per share dividend and sold at $10 per share, the dividend yield would be 4 percent. To many investors, particularly those interested in current income and averse to the uncertainty of expected future growth being achieved and translated into higher share prices, the dividend yield measures the attractiveness of the security to other current income-producing financial assets and the general price level of the market. For example, in choosing between the shares of American Telephone and Telegraph and a savings and loan account, the income-oriented investor would favor the one with the higher current yield.

The historical price volatility of the shares may be the result of a limited supply of shares available for trading (floating supply). In certain instances many of the shares issued and outstanding are closely held by stockholders who have no intention of selling the stock almost regardless of the price, as, for example, in the case of a partially owned subsidiary. Because of a small floating supply it may be very difficult to acquire or sell a relatively large number of shares within a reasonable period of time without distorting the price. In such a case, many large investors, such as mutual funds and financial institutions, may abstain from purchasing the stock, despite a favorable opinion of the company, because of the uncertainty imparted to the future price by the limited market for the stock. On the other hand, some investors may be attracted to the stock for the very reason that it is in short supply and has large price volatility, because they envision a chance to profit from the exaggerated price movements of such a situation.

The ratio of net assets per share to the market price per share may be used by the investor in a potential liquidation situation. The investor stands to profit if the realized distribution from the proceeds of the sale of the assets is greater than the price that he paid for the stock. The investor may use this ratio in attempting to determine whether or not the realized distribution will be larger than the share price.

EARNINGS PROJECTIONS THROUGH RATIOS

Analysts have frequently used the ratios developed in this chapter to project future earnings for the firm. For example, if Basic Incorporated announced plans to add $10,000,000 of new productive capacity in the next year, the analyst might derive an estimate of future earnings, including the effect of the additional capacity, as follows: (1) derive the new net plant, property, and equipment figure by adding the new capacity's cost to the old figure for a total in this case of $19,600,000, (2) derive the expected net sales by multiplying the asset turnover ratio by the new net plant figure to get $39,810,000, (3) apply the debt/equity ratio to the financing needed to build the new capacity to get $5,700,000 of new debt and $4,300,000 of new equity, (4) compare the new equity funds needed to the cash available to determine whether or not any additional shares must be sold, (5) apply the net profit margins to the expected sales to get $2,042,000 in expected profits, (5) divide the expected net profits by the number of shares expected to be outstanding after any new financing and get the earnings per share. The analyst would, as a check, probably apply the rate of return on total capital, including the new financing, to get $2,054,000 (0.064 × 32,100,000) as expected earnings and reconcile any difference with the previous estimate.

PROBLEMS WITH RATIO ANALYSIS

The incorrect use of the ratios presented in this chapter may be misleading. Ratios must be used with caution. The use of isolated ratios without

Problems with ratio analysis

the examination of the broad profile of all the ratios may incorrectly convince the investor that the company's future is bright, when the overall picture may look otherwise.

At various times in the year, the ratios may seem better than at other times. The seasonality inherent in ratios requires a careful examination of several time periods. Trends in ratios may be more important indications of future earnings than isolated observations.

The comparability of ratios among companies and industries is also treacherous. For example, the profit margin of a company operating solely in a politically unstable country may not be so indicative of future profits as the profit margin of a company operating in a more politically stable country.

The components of the ratio may move in different directions and may lead to misinterpretation. For example, the return on equity for a company might be 10 percent in each of 2 years, which would imply no change in the underlying operating efficiency of the company. This return on equity pattern could arise, however, as follows:

	Year 1	Year 2
Equity	100,000	100,000
Sales	100,000	50,000
Net income	10,000	10,000
Profit margins	10%	20%
Return on equity	10%	10%

In this example, the decline in sales could indicate a deteriorating market position or market for the product. The management's efficiency in operation is perhaps being applied to a disappearing market and will prove fruitless in the future. Looking only at the return on equity would not indicate this possibility; because it is unchanged, it gives the appearance of a constant situation.

The most misleading part of ratio analysis is that it misses the entire concept of economic value as introduced in the PDV evaluation framework. It concentrates mostly on providing clues to future earnings and gives no indication as to the effects of the time value of money or purchasing power risk. What few clues that it gives on financial and business risk are handled in isolation from the PDV framework of analysis.

There is no conceptual interaction among the variables in ratio analysis, as there is in the PDV framework. If one ratio changes, it does so in isolation without any conceptual influence on the evaluation of the security, but the PDV framework provides a conceptual analysis for incorporating all the pertinent considerations. Financial statement and ratio analysis may best be used for the inputs that it provides to the PDV framework.

SUMMARY

The financial statements of a company consist of an income statement, a balance sheet, a statement of retained earnings, and a sources and uses of funds statement. From the analysis of these statements it may be possible to gather certain information and indications about future earnings. Certain pertinent ratios, trends, and figures may provide clues to the company's future. Financial statements and ratio analysis itself, however, provide only a limited contribution to the PDV framework of security evaluation. It may provide some inputs to the framework on future earnings and business and financial risk. It fails to provide information on the other needed inputs of interest rate and purchasing power risk and to provide a framework for analyzing the interaction of all the inputs in security evaluation.

QUESTIONS

4.1 Could the application of the fifo inventory pricing method result in a higher or lower cost of goods sold than the lifo method? Explain.

4.2 Explain why a rapidly growing firm would gain by using the double declining balance method of depreciation.

4.3 Define cash flow, and explain its significance in the framework of investment analysis.

4.4 Why should an investment analyst compare the reported tax rate with the normal tax rate?

4.5 Define the following: (*a*) liquidity; (*b*) book value; (*c*) capital structure.

4.6 How is the debt/equity ratio, along with the times interest earned ratio, used to analyze the degree of financial risk of a company?

4.7 Define financial leverage, and explain its effect on earnings per share.

4.8 Explain the effects of convertible securities on earnings per share and the debt/equity ratio.

4.9 What information is provided by a corporation's sources and uses of funds statement?

4.10 Discuss the pitfalls inherent in ratio analysis.

PROBLEMS

4.1 Illustrate the effects of the fifo inventory pricing method versus the lifo method on earnings per share, using the following data:

R. J. Lowrie Co., Inc.
Statement of Purchases and Materials Use
for the Quarter Ending December 31, 1971

1971			Units	Unit cost	Materials issued	Units
Oct.	1	Inventory	500	$10.00	Oct. 10	300
	23	Purchase	300	10.50	25	400
Nov.	12	Purchase	800	10.90	Nov. 15	600
Dec.	2	Purchase	900	11.00	Dec. 4	700
	15	Purchase	1000	11.20	20	900
					28	300

Quarterly data
Sales 60,000
Operating and administrative expenses 15,000
Taxes 50%
Common stock shares outstanding 1,000

4.2

Net sales		$2,000,000
Cost of sales and operating expenses		
Cost of goods sold	1,000,000	
Depreciation	100,000	
Depletion	50,000	
Selling and administrative expenses	500,000	1,650,000
Operating profit		350,000
Other income		
Dividend and interest		50,000
Gain on sale of old plant		200,000
Total income		600,000
Less: interest on bonds		50,000
Profit before taxes		550,000
Total taxes include 50% federal income taxes		225,000
Net profit		325,000

From the income statement above solve the following problems:
(a) Compute the firm's cash flow.
(b) What is the total of the firm's nonoperating income?
(c) Compute the reported tax rate.
(d) What was the amount of nonrecurring capital gains?
(e) What was the tax rate paid on nonrecurring capital gains?
(f) Compute the following ratios: (1) pretax ratio margin; (2) after tax profit margin.

4.3

E. M. Wolf Construction Co. Inc.
Balance Sheet, December 31, 19

Assets			Liabilities and stockholders' equity		
Current assets			**Current liabilities**		
Cash		$ 60,000	Accounts payable	$150,000	
Marketable securities, at cost		100,000	Notes payable	200,000	
Accounts receivable		350,000	Accrued expenses payable	50,000	
Inventories		500,000	Federal income tax payable	75,000	
Total current assets		$1,010,000	Total current liabilities		$ 475,000
Property, plant, and equipment			**Long-term liabilities**		
Land	$400,000		First mortgage bonds, 5% interest due 1975		525,000
Buildings	200,000		Total liabilities		$1,000,000
Machinery	200,000				
Office equipment	115,000			*Stockholders' equity*	
	915,000		**Capital Stock**		
Less: accumulated depreciation	250,000		Common stock, $1 par value each; authorized, issued, and outstanding 100,000 shares	100,000	
Net property, plant, and equipment		665,000	Capital paid in excess of par	350,000	
Prepayments and deferred charges		10,000	Income for year	50,000	
Goodwill, patents, trademarks		15,000	Accumulated retained earnings	200,000	
Total assets		$1,700,000	Total stockholders' equity		700,000
			Total liabilities and stockholders' equity		$1,700,000

From the balance sheet above solve the following problems if sales were $2,000,000 and no dividends were paid:

(a) Compute the firm's working capital position.
(b) Compute the following ratios: (1) current ratio; (2) quick ratio; (3) accounts receivable turnover; (4) return on capital; (5) return on investment.
(c) What percentage of the capital structure is composed of long-term debt? What percent is stockholders' equity?
(d) Compute the debt/equity ratio.

REFERENCES

Bellemore, Douglas H., and John C. Ritchie, Jr. *Investments: Principles, Practices and Analysis,* 3d ed., Cincinnati: South-Western Publishing Company, Incorporated, 1969.

Graham, Benjamin, David L. Dodd, and Sidney Cottle. *Security Analysis,* 4th ed., New York: McGraw-Hill Book Company, 1962.

How to Read a Financial Report, New York: Merrill Lynch, Pierce, Fenner, and Smith, no date.

Hubbard, Charles L., and Clark A. Hawkins. *Theory of Valuation,* Scranton, Pa.: International Textbook Company, 1969.

Myer, John Nicholas. *Financial Statement Analysis,* 4th ed., Englewood Cliffs, N.J.: Prentice-Hall, Inc., 1969.

5
Projecting Earnings under Stable Conditions

This chapter explores several methods by which the information gathered from financial and ratio analyses may be refined into earnings projections for the PDV framework. Various estimating procedures for use under stable economic and business conditions are explored. With a stable rate of growth and environment, the company's past performance may be a good indication of the future. This stability allows forecasting future earnings and dividends with statistical methods, such as historical growth rate extrapolation; aggregate economic forecasting, using regression analysis; and the rate of return approach. Methods of adjusting for seasonality, the use of quarterly data in forecasting earnings, and a procedure for forecasting dividend policy, all under stable conditions, are also included in this chapter.

HISTORICAL GROWTH RATE

Assuming that the circumstances under which the firm operated in the past will continue unchanged in the future, the investor may use the historical growth rate in the firm's sales or earnings in forecasting future earnings. For example, if the past years had produced a constant 10 percent annual increase in earnings per share, the earnings per share projections from a base of $1 per share would be as follows:

Year	Earnings per share
0	$1.00
1	1.10
2	1.21
3	1.33
4	1.46
5	1.61

Computation of the Growth Rate

Various methods of computing the historical growth rate are used. Among the more commonly used are (1) graphic presentations, (2) the simple growth rate, (3) the compound growth rate, (4) the moving average, and (5) a fitted trend line.

Graphic Presentations. The arithmetic chart, as illustrated in Figure 5.1, and the semilogarithmic chart, as illustrated in Figure 5.2, are graphical representations of part changes in earnings.

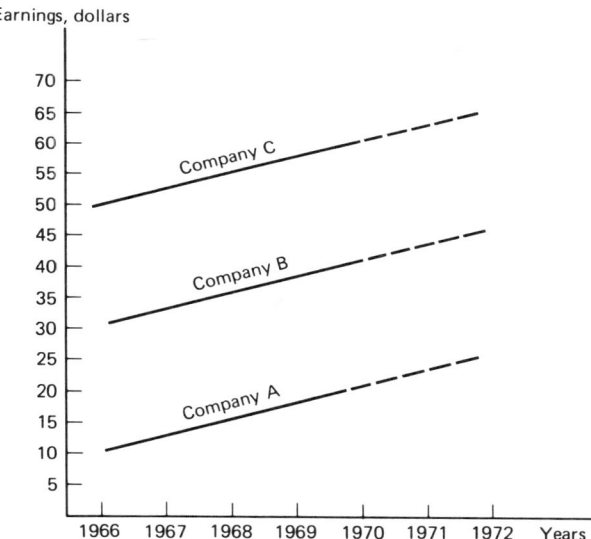

Figure 5.1. Arithmetic graph.

The arithmetic chart in Figure 5.1 represents the absolute change in earnings over time, with points closer to the origin on the horizontal axis farther in the past. In Figure 5.1, the year 1966 is closer to the origin and the year 1970 is farther from the origin. The vertical axis represents the absolute earnings recorded for each year. Each ruled demarcation on the vertical axis is equidistant from the next, and each equal distance represents an equal absolute earnings quantity. To construct the line of absolute growth, the recorded earnings in 1966 and 1970 are plotted on the chart and connected by a straight line. By extending this line (the broken line in Figure 5.1) into future years, the investor may get an idea of future earnings levels if the pattern of 1966 to 1970 continued. In Figure 5.1, company A's increase in earnings from $10 million in 1966 to $20 million in 1970 covers the same

Projecting earnings under stable conditions 82

distance on the graph as company B's increase from $30 to $40 million and company C's $50 to $60 million increase. From Figure 5.1, it seems that all three companies grew at the same rate, because all had the same absolute increase in earnings despite the fact that A's earnings grew at a rate of 100 percent, B's earnings at a rate of 33⅓ percent, and C's earnings at a rate of only 20 percent from 1966 to 1970.

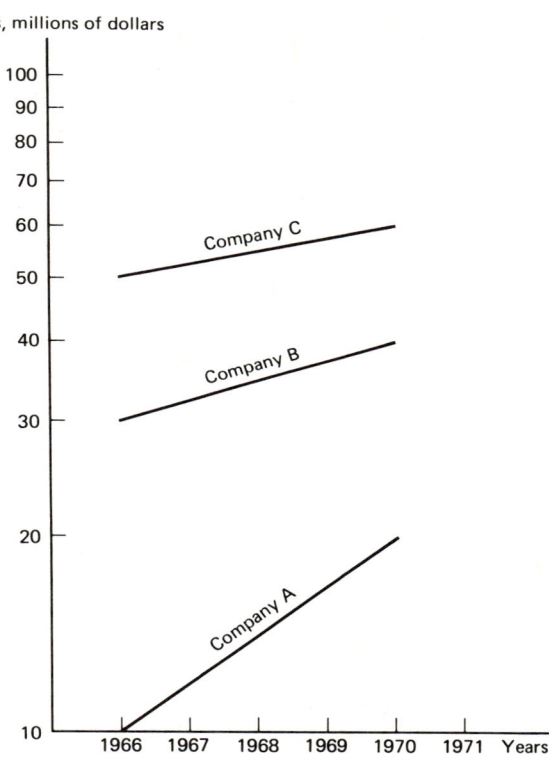

Figure 5.2. Semilogarithmic graph.

Semilogarithmic charts graphically represent the historical growth rate in percentage terms. Again the horizontal axis measures time in the same manner as the arithmetic chart, but the vertical axis is now scaled so that equal distances between lines represent equal percentage changes rather than equal amounts. To construct the line of the rate of change in earnings, the recorded earnings in 1966 and 1970 are plotted on the chart and connected by a straight line. By extending this straight line into future years, the investor may determine future earnings if the 1966 to 1970 rate of change remained the same. In Figure 5.2, company A's $10 million earnings increase from $10 to $20 million appears as a doubling of earnings, company B's $10 million earnings increase from $30 to $40 million appears as a one-third increase, and company C's $10 million earnings increase appears as a one-fifth increase. The semilogarithmic chart more clearly reveals different growth rates among the companies.

Simple Growth Rate. The simple annual growth rate is the rate at which the base period figure will have grown to reach the terminal figure. The simple interest concept discussed in Chapter 3 is the identical concept. For example, if earnings per share were $1 in 1966 and $1.40 in 1970, the simple rate of growth would be 10 percent. In formula terms,

$$E_t - E_b = E_b \cdot g \cdot t$$

where E_t = terminal year earnings
E_b = base year earnings
g = simple rate of growth
t = number of years between base and terminal year

In the example

$$\$1.40 - \$1 = \$1 \cdot g \cdot 4$$
$$10\% = g$$

If the simple growth rate had been constant in the period 1966 to 1970, the earnings per share pattern would have appeared as follows:

1966	1967	1968	1969	1970
$1.00	$1.10	$1.20	$1.30	$1.40

Compound Growth Rate. The compound annual growth rate is the rate at which the base period figure will have grown to reach the terminal figure if each previous year's growth in earnings had been added to each year's earnings before the growth rate had been applied. The compound interest rate, discussed in Chapter 3, is the identical concept. Instead of computing interest solely on the principal, as in simple interest, compound interest is computed on the principal and the interest that has been earned already.

The compound interest formula is

$$F = M(1 + r)^n$$

where F = future sum or terminal year earnings
M = present sum or base year earnings
n = number of years
r = compound rate of interest

Projecting earnings under stable conditions 84

To find r if earnings per share went from $1 in 1966 to $1.46 in 1970, the investor would solve

$$\$1.46 = (1 + r)^4 \, \$1$$

From Table 5.1, $1 will grow to be $1.45 in 4 years at a compound growth rate of 10 percent. The pattern of earnings per share in this example, if the compound growth rate were constant between 1966 and 1970, would be as follows:

1966	1967	1968	1969	1970
$1.00	$1.10	$1.21	$1.33	$1.46

TABLE 5.1 Compound Sum of $1

n	1%	2%	3%	4%	5%	6%	7%	8%	9%	10%	n
01	1.0100	1.0200	1.0300	1.0400	1.0500	1.0600	1.0700	1.0800	1.0900	1.1000	01
02	1.0201	1.0404	1.0609	1.0816	1.1025	1.1236	1.1449	1.1664	1.1881	1.2100	02
03	1.0303	1.0612	1.0927	1.1249	1.1576	1.1910	1.2250	1.2597	1.2950	1.3310	03
04	1.0406	1.0824	1.1255	1.1699	1.2155	1.2625	1.3108	1.3605	1.4116	1.4641	04
05	1.0510	1.1041	1.1593	1.2167	1.2763	1.3382	1.4026	1.4693	1.5386	1.6105	05
06	1.0615	1.1261	1.1941	1.2653	1.3401	1.4185	1.5007	1.5869	1.6771	1.7716	06
07	1.0721	1.1487	1.2299	1.3159	1.4071	1.5036	1.6058	1.7138	1.8280	1.9487	07
08	1.0829	1.1717	1.2668	1.3686	1.4775	1.5939	1.7182	1.8509	1.9926	2.1436	08
09	1.0937	1.1951	1.3048	1.4233	1.5513	1.6895	1.8385	1.9990	2.1719	2.3580	09
10	1.1046	1.2190	1.3439	1.4802	1.6289	1.7909	1.9672	2.1589	2.3674	2.5937	10
11	1.1157	1.2434	1.3842	1.5395	1.7103	1.8983	2.1049	2.3316	2.5804	2.8531	11
12	1.1268	1.2682	1.4258	1.6010	1.7959	2.0122	2.2522	2.5182	2.8127	3.1384	12
13	1.1381	1.2936	1.4685	1.6651	1.8857	2.1329	2.4098	2.7196	3.0658	3.4523	13
14	1.1495	1.3195	1.5126	1.7317	1.9799	2.2609	2.5785	2.9372	3.3417	3.7975	14
15	1.1610	1.3459	1.5560	1.8009	2.0789	2.3966	2.7590	3.1722	3.6425	4.1773	15
16	1.1726	1.3728	1.6047	1.8730	2.1829	2.5404	2.9522	3.4259	3.9703	4.5950	16
17	1.1843	1.4002	1.6529	1.9479	2.2920	2.6928	3.1588	3.7000	4.3276	5.0545	17
18	1.1962	1.4283	1.7024	2.0258	2.4066	2.8543	3.3799	3.9960	4.7171	5.5599	18
19	1.2081	1.4568	1.7535	2.1069	2.5270	3.0256	3.6165	4.3157	5.1417	6.1159	19
20	1.2202	1.4860	1.8061	2.1911	2.6533	3.2071	3.8697	4.6610	5.6044	6.7275	20
21	1.2324	1.5157	1.8603	2.2788	2.7860	3.3996	4.1406	5.0338	6.1088	7.4003	21
22	1.2447	1.5460	1.9161	2.3699	2.9253	3.6035	4.4304	5.4365	6.6586	8.1403	22
23	1.2572	1.5769	1.9736	2.4647	3.0715	3.8198	4.7405	5.8714	7.2579	8.9543	23
24	1.2697	1.6084	2.0328	2.5633	3.2251	4.0489	5.0724	6.3412	7.9111	9.8497	24
25	1.2824	1.6406	2.0938	2.6658	3.3864	4.2919	5.4274	6.8485	8.6231	10.835	25

Problems With Simple and Compound Growth Rates and Graphs

The investor must be careful in interpreting simple and compound growth rates, especially as indicators of future earnings patterns. Among the most important considerations are the selection of the base and terminal years and hidden pattern of intervening years. By selecting different base and terminal years, the investor may change the growth rate. In specific terms, the following earnings pattern may be considered:

1965	1966	1967	1968	1969	1970
$0.10	$1.00	$1.10	$1.20	$1.30	$1.40

The simple growth rate from 1966 to 1970 was 10 percent; the simple growth rate from 1965 to 1970 was 260 percent. Any of the visual, simple, or compound methods of determining growth rates may lead to distorted conclusions under these circumstances. The investor must be careful to select reasonable, representative base and terminal years.

The simple, compound, and visual methods of determining growth rates also suffer from a failure to expose potentially meaningful figures that may occur between the base and terminal years. For example, the following earnings per share pattern may be considered:

1966	1967	1968	1969	1970
$1.00	$1.10	$3.00	$2.50	$1.40

The simple growth rate from 1966 to 1970 is 10 percent, and no notice is made of the sharply higher earnings in 1968 and 1969 or the sharp drop in 1970. The earnings of these 3 years may have significant bearing in future earnings that would escape the investor who relied solely on the mechanically computed 1966 to 1970 growth rate.

Moving Average Growth Rate

The moving average growth rate is the average growth rate for a selected number of past years. As a new year's growth rate is added to the computation, the earliest year's growth rate is removed. For example, if the following earnings pattern were considered:

1965	1966	1967	1968	1969	1970
$1.00	$1.05	$1.16	$1.28	$1.54	$1.84

A 3-year moving average of growth in earnings per share would take the first three growth rates, those between 1965 and 1966, 1966 and 1967, and 1967 and 1968, add them, and divide the sum by 3 to find the moving average growth rate from 1965 to 1968, which in the example is

$$\frac{0.05 + 0.10 + 0.10}{3} = 8.3\%$$

In 1969, the 1965 to 1966 growth rate would be dropped, and the 1968 to 1969 growth rate of 20 percent added:

$$\frac{0.10 + 0.10 + 0.20}{3} = 13.3\%$$

And in 1970, the 1966 to 1967 growth rate would be dropped, and the 1969 to 1970 growth rate of 20 percent added:

$$\frac{0.10 + 0.20 + 0.20}{3} = 16.7\%$$

The moving average growth rate detects accelerating and decelerating rates of growth that the simple, compound, and visual methods do not. An accelerating of decelerating pattern may be a significant indication of future earnings.

The moving average approach also lessens the problem of base and terminal year distortion and gives weight to the intervening years. The effects of an abnormal base or terminal year are tempered by the inclusion of other years. The significance of intervening years is not overlooked, for all years are included in the moving average. The major disadvantage to the moving average is its sluggish response to a significant change. It may take several years before the full effect of a shift in earnings growth is fully reflected in the moving average, because it will take several years to eliminate all the earlier, preshift annual growth rates included in the moving average. Under stable conditions, the moving average growth rate may be applied to the most recent earnings to gain an indication of future earnings.

Trend Line

The statistically fitted time series trend line may be the most precise procedure for determining historical growth rates. This procedure determines the path that most closely summarizes the direction of all the earnings taken in a selected time span. Consider the following earnings per share pattern of a firm from year 1 to year 10:

Year	1	2	3	4	5	6	7	8	9	10
Earnings per share	2	4	7	9	10	14	16	17	16	19

The objective of the time series trend line is to plot a line through these earnings observations, as graphed in Figure 5.3, that minimizes the sum of the squared distances between it and the observations.[1]

---

[1] For a discussion of regression analysis see Taro Yamane, *Statistics: An Introductory Analysis,* Harper & Row, Publishers, Incorporated, New York, 1967, pp. 368–430; Ya-un Chou, *Applied Business and Economic Statistics,* Holt, Rinehart and Winston, Inc., New York, 1963, pp. 404–438; and Lincoln Chao, *Statistics: Method and Analysis,* McGraw-Hill Book Company, New York, 1969, pp. 324–355.

Historical growth rate

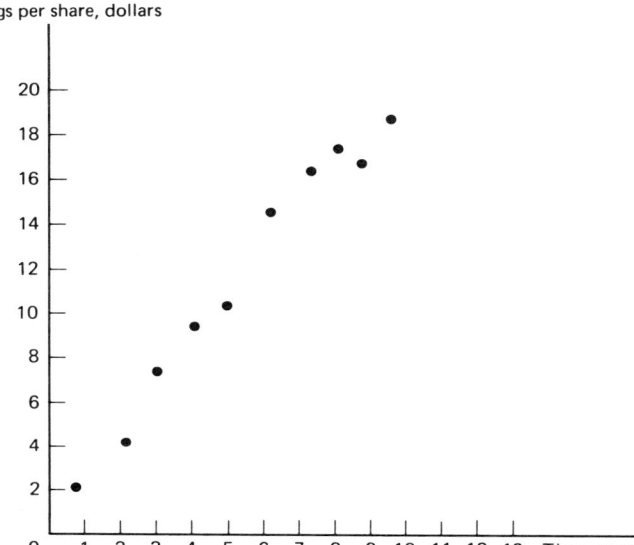

Figure 5.3. Earnings per share in time.

The computational mechanics of the time series trend line are used to determine the slope of the trend line (how rapidly it is raising or declining in the time span) and the intercept (the estimated value in the base year). The formula description of the trend line is

$\hat{Y}_x = a + bx$
$\hat{Y}_x$ = estimated position of trend line in year x
a = intercept of trend line
b = slope of trend line
x = number of years away from base year

To find the value of Y_x at any point in time x, the slope and the intercept must first be determined. The slope b is

$$b = \frac{\Sigma XY - \Sigma X \Sigma Y/n}{\Sigma X^2 - (\Sigma X)^2/n}$$

The intercept a is

$$a = \frac{1}{n}[\Sigma Y - b\Sigma X]$$

ΣXY = sum of cross product of $x \cdot y$

To compute the necessary sums of squares ΣX^2 and cross products ΣXY, Table 5.2 is constructed.

TABLE 5.2 Worksheet for Trend Line Computations

Year	X Year No.	Y Earnings	XY	X^2
1	0	$2.00	0	0
2	1	4.00	4.00	1
3	2	7.00	14.00	4
4	3	9.00	27.00	9
5	4	10.00	40.00	16
6	5	14.00	70.00	25
7	6	16.00	96.00	36
8	7	17.00	119.00	49
9	8	16.00	128.00	64
10	9	19.00	171.00	81
Total	45	114.00	669.00	285

$\Sigma(XY) = 669.00$
$\Sigma(X^2) = 285$

Then

$$b = \frac{669.00 - 45(114.00)/10}{285 - (45)^2/10}$$

$$= \$1.891$$

$$a = \frac{1}{10}[114.00 - (1.891)(45)]$$

$$= \$2.89$$

Figure 5.4 is a graphic presentation of trend line fitted to Figure 5.3. To find any point on the line, we can substitute for X in the formula

$\hat{Y}_x = a \quad + B \quad \cdot \quad X$
$\hat{Y}_x = \$2.89 + \$1.89 \cdot (X) =$
$\hat{Y}_0 = 2.89 + 1.89 \cdot (0) = 2.89$
$\hat{Y}_1 = 2.89 + 1.89 \cdot (1) = 4.78$
$\hat{Y}_2 = 2.89 + 1.89 \cdot (2) = 6.67$
$\hat{Y}_3 = 2.89 + 1.89 \cdot (3) = 8.56$
$\hat{Y}_4 = 2.89 + 1.89 \cdot (4) = 10.45$
$\hat{Y}_5 = 2.89 + 1.89 \cdot (5) = 12.34$
$\hat{Y}_6 = 2.89 + 1.89 \cdot (6) = 14.23$
$\hat{Y}_7 = 2.89 + 1.89 \cdot (7) = 16.12$
$\hat{Y}_8 = 2.89 + 1.89 \cdot (8) = 18.01$
$\hat{Y}_9 = 2.89 + 1.89 \cdot (9) = 19.90$
$Y_{10} = 2.89 + 1.89 \cdot (10) = 21.79$

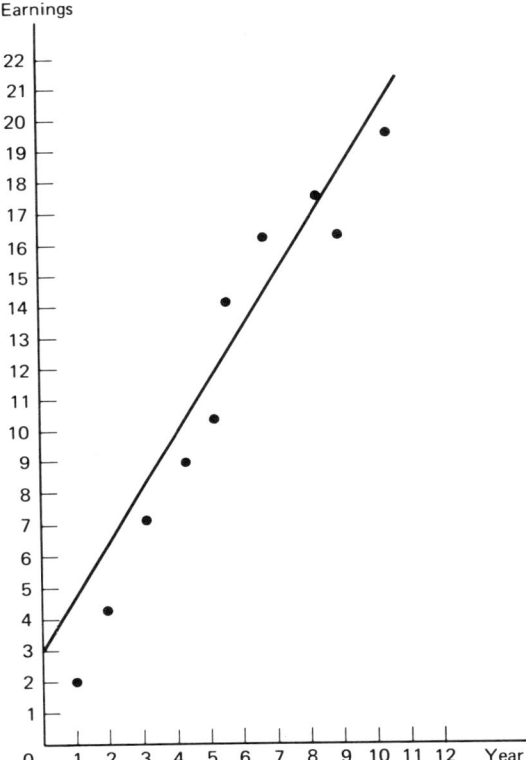

Figure 5.4. Fitted trend line.

To project future earnings using a fitted trend line, the value of X is increased beyond the selected time span. For example, the estimated earnings in $X = 11$ would be

$$Y_{11} = \$2.89 + \$1.89 \cdot (11) = \$23.68$$

Problems with Trend Line Forecasting

The selection of the base and terminal years remains a shortcoming of trend line forecasting. An abnormal base or terminal year could easily distort the fit of the trend line and forecasts.

When using the trend line for forecasting, it must be assumed that the conditions that prevailed during the selected time span will continue in the future. Stable conditions imply that such important considerations as industry technology, competition, and political environment are constant; if the conditions are unstable, accurate forecasts are difficult.

In terms of Figure 5.3, the observations (earnings) may abruptly shift upward after year 10, as illustrated in Figure 5.5. The trend line in

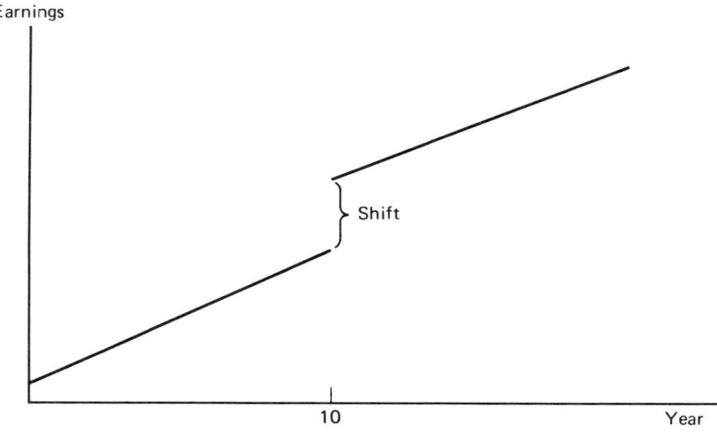
Figure 5.5.

Figure 5.4 would not detect this shift for some time, and any projection based on the computed trend line would be incorrect.

AGGREGATE APPROACH USING REGRESSION ANALYSIS

The application of historical growth rates in forecasting earnings relies solely on earnings information and assumes a continuation of the previous earnings pattern. The aggregate approach broadens the investigation for clues to future earnings beyond the earnings themselves into the general economic, industry, and company operating environments.

The procedure is first to isolate and estimate the major economic influences on the firm's profits. Among the commonly employed economic indicators are gross national product (GNP) and personal income. Second, the relevant industry's sales are related to the selected economic indicator. Third, the company's market share of its industry is determined. Fourth, estimated profit margins are applied to projected company sales to derive earnings forecasts. Schematically, this approach resembles the following:

Economic
indicator
 ↓   {Regression estimation
Industry
 sales
 ↓   {Market share
Company
 sales
 ↓   {Profit margins
Earnings

Despite the broadened area of investigation, the aggregate method still depends on stable relationships between each of the steps in the investigation. For example, the investor must be able to conclude that a particular level of GNP implies a particular level of industry sales.

Estimation of the Aggregate Variable

The pertinent macroeconomic indicator varies among industries. For example, in the farm machinery industry, farmers' personal disposable income is probably the most significant macroeconomic indicator. In the automobile industry, the pertinent variable might be nonfarm personal disposable income. In the industrial machinery industry, it might be corporate profits. The most encompassing of all macroeconomic variables, however, is GNP, the total value of all goods and services produced during the year.

The analyst must relate the appropriate economic indicator to the industry sales, through regression analysis. After the regression analysis has established this relationship, the analyst must obtain an estimate of the future value of this indicator. Applying this relationship to the projected economic indicator value, the analyst arrives at an estimate of projected industry sales.

Projections of these economic indicators may come from any of several sources. Official government publications, such as the *Annual Economic Report of the President* and the Department of Commerce's *U.S. Industrial Outlook,* give indications of official thinking on macroeconomic trends. Many trade and business publications carry estimates of economic indicators based on surveys, econometric models, and other sources.

The range of estimated economic indicators may make them less useful for forecasting. It may be necessary to reconcile the differences among the various estimates. If the investor has one forecaster in whom he has the most confidence, the investor may use his estimate. Alternatively, the investor may average the various estimates to arrive at one figure for use in his forecasting. Another procedure is to take the most frequently mentioned forecast as the estimated economic indicator value. The investor must be prepared to readjust his analysis, however, to meet revised economic forecasts.

Relating Industry Sales to Macroeconomic Variables

The historical relationship between the industry's sales and the selected economic indicator is determined by regression analysis. As GNP increases, it could be reasonably expected that the industry's sales also increase. Under stable conditions there may be a cause-and-effect relationship, so that as GNP advances by $10 billion, industry sales may advance by $1 billion. Regression analysis determines the correlation

Projecting earnings under stable conditions 92

between GNP and industry sales that best describes the historical relationship. When the historical relationship has been established, it is related to the forecasted macroeconomic variable to arrive at projected industry sales.

Table 5.3 and Figure 5.6 describe the relationship of automobile sales to GNP. As GNP rises, automobile sales rise. The most precise description of this relationship is the regression line that minimizes the squared difference between the observations (dots) in Figure 5.6 and the regression line.

TABLE 5.3

Year	X GNP*	Y Auto Sales†
1955	$ 397 (bil)	$ 36.3 (bil)
1956	419	34.1
1957	443	36.3
1958	445	31.6
1959	483	36.9
1960	503	37.0
1961	519	34.4
1962	556	40.1
1963	591	43.4
1964	632	45.8
1965	684	53.2
1966	750	53.9
1967	794	53.7
1968	866	60.7
Total	8082	597.4

* Data reflect revisions: 1955–1962 in July 1964 *Survey of Current Business;* 1963–1964 in July 1966 *Survey of Current Business;* 1965 in July 1967 *Survey of Current Business;* and 1966–1968 in July 1969 *Survey of Current Business.*

† Retail sales: passenger cars, other automotive dealers. Data from *Statistical Abstract of the United States.*

The fitting of a regression line is similar to the trend line fit used with historical earnings growth rates. The sum of the squares (ΣX^2) and the sum of the cross products (ΣXY) must be computed as in Table 5.4. The intercept a and the slope b are

$$b = \frac{\Sigma XY - \Sigma X \Sigma Y / n}{\Sigma X^2 - (\Sigma X)^2 / n}$$

$$a = \frac{1}{n}[\Sigma Y - b \Sigma X]$$

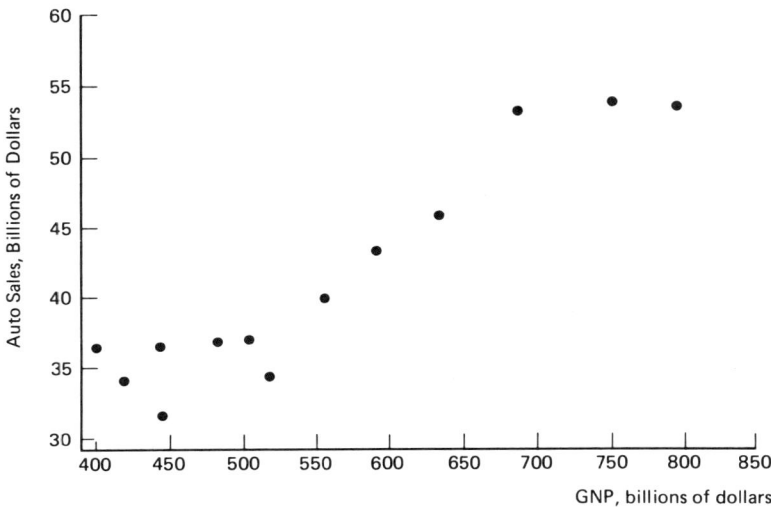

Figure 5.6. Automobile sales versus GNP, 1955 to 1968.

TABLE 5.4 Work Sheet 1 for Simple Regression Analysis

Year	XY	X^2
1955	14,411.1	157,609
1956	14,287.9	175,561
1957	16,080.9	196,249
1958	14,062.0	198,025
1959	17,822.7	233,389
1960	18,611.0	253,009
1961	17,853.6	269,361
1962	22,295.6	309,136
1963	25,649.4	349,281
1964	28,945.6	399,424
1965	36,388.8	467,856
1966	40,425.0	562,500
1967	42,637.8	630,436
1968	52,566.2	749,956
Total	362,037.6	4,951,692

(1) Sum $Y = (N)a + (\text{Sum } X)b$
(2) Sum $XY = (\text{Sum } X)a + (\text{Sum } X^2)b$
(1) $597.4 = (14)a + (8,082)b$
(2) $362,037.6 = (8,082)a + (4,951,692)b$
$a = 8.0285 = 8.0$
$b = .06001 = 0.06$

Solving for *a* and *b*, one gets

$a = 8.0$

$b = 0.06$

The regression equation

$$\hat{Y} = 8.0 + 0.06(X)$$

describes the best-fitted regression line and says that for each $1 billion increase in GNP, automobile sales may be expected to increase $60 million. For example, if GNP rose to $1,000 billion in 1969, auto sales could be expected to be $68 billion.

The regression line or equation may be a better fit in some industries than in others. Various statistical measures indicate the accuracy of the

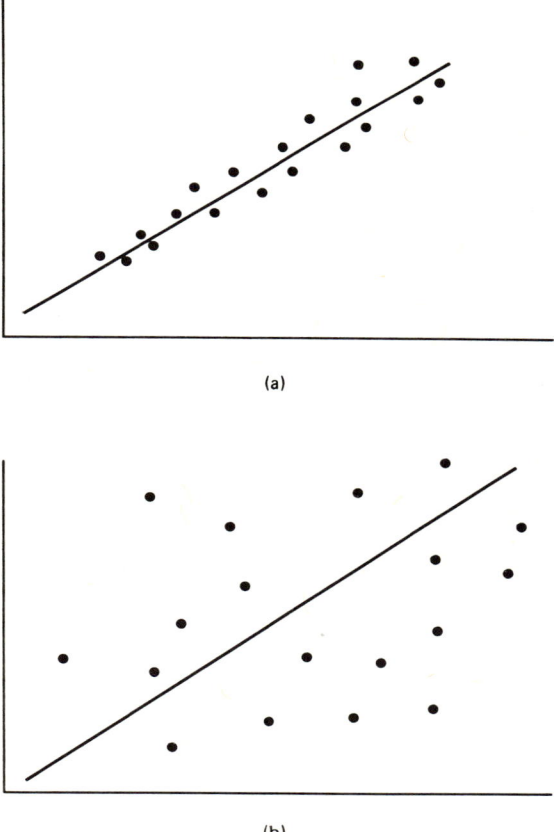

Figure 5.7.

fit. Among the most common are the standard error of the estimate and the coefficient of determination.

The standard error of the estimate measures the difference between the actual observation and the estimated value that lies on the regression line. In Figure 5.7(a), there is a smaller standard error of the estimate than in Figure 5.7(b), because the estimated regression line is closer to the actual observations. The closer the estimated automobile sales to the actual automobile sales for each GNP observed, the smaller the standard error of the estimate. Table 5.5 shows what the estimated automobile sales $\hat{Y}$ would be if the actual observed GNP X were substituted into the computed regression equation. Table 5.5 also shows the difference between the estimated automobile sales and the actual automobile sales Y observed at each level of GNP.

TABLE 5.5 Work Sheet 2 for Simple Regression Analysis

Year	GNP X	Estimated auto sales $\hat{Y}$	Auto Sales Y	Difference $\hat{Y} - Y$	(Difference)^2
1955	397	31.8	36.3	−4.5	20.25
1956	419	33.1	34.1	−1.0	1.00
1957	443	34.6	36.3	−1.7	2.89
1958	445	34.7	31.6	+3.1	9.61
1959	483	37.0	36.9	+0.1	0.01
1960	503	38.2	37.0	+1.2	1.44
1961	519	39.1	34.4	+4.7	22.09
1962	556	41.4	40.1	+1.3	1.69
1963	591	43.5	43.4	+0.1	0.01
1964	632	45.9	45.8	+0.1	0.01
1965	684	49.0	53.2	−4.2	17.64
1966	750	53.0	53.9	−0.9	0.81
1967	794	55.6	53.7	+1.9	3.61
1968	866	60.0	60.7	−0.7	0.49
				Total	81.55

$$\hat{Y} = a + bX = 8.0 + 0.06X$$

$$S_{y \cdot x} = \sqrt{\frac{\Sigma(Y - \hat{Y})^2}{n}} = \sqrt{\frac{81.55}{14}} = \sqrt{5.825} = 2.41$$

The standard error of the estimate is computed, as illustrated in Table 5.5, in the following steps: (1) take the difference between the estimated $\hat{Y}$ and the actual automobile sales Y at each level of GNP, (2) square the differences, (3) sum the squared differences, (4) divide the sum of the squared differences by the number of observations, and (5) take the square root of the figure in step 4. In the example in Table 5.5, the sum of the squared differences is 81.55. The sum of the squared difference divided by the number of observations (step 4) is 5.825. The square root of 5.825 (step 5) is 2.41.

The coefficient of determination R^2 is also a measure of closeness of fit. The higher the R^2, the closer the fit. A perfect fit would have R^2 equal to 1. The R^2 measures the improvement of the regression line fit over the average line fit or, in other words, how much of the total deviation from the average is explained by the regression line.

The computation of the R^2 is as follows:

1. Compute the total squared deviations of the actual automobile sales at each level of GNP from the average automobile sales:

$$\Sigma(Y_x - \bar{Y})^2$$

2. Compute the total squared deviation of the estimated automobile sales at each level of GNP from the average automobile sales:

$$\Sigma(\hat{Y}_x - \bar{Y})^2$$

3. Divide the total squared deviations from the average figure into the total squared deviation from the estimated figure to get R^2:

$$R^2 = \frac{\Sigma(\hat{Y}_x - \bar{Y})^2}{\Sigma(Y_x - \bar{Y})^2}$$

Table 5.6 illustrates the computation of the R^2. The total squared deviations from the average figure is 1,111.66, and the total squared deviations from the estimated figure is 1,030.33. The R^2 is 0.9268, which indicates a relatively close fit. As the R^2 diminishes, the accuracy of the relationship between the economic indicator and the industry's sales decreases. At a very low R^2, the results of the aggregate approach may be unreliable.

The Firm's Market Share

The firm's share of the market is the next step in estimating future earnings under an aggregate approach. It is easier to determine the firm's historical market share if the industry is well defined and there are only a few major companies, as in the automobile industry. If there are a large number of small companies, however, it may be difficult to determine the firm's market share. If the conditions are stable, the firm's historical market share should be maintained in the future. Thus, when GNP has been estimated, industry sales may be forecasted by the regression relationship and a company's sales projected. In the example, if Ford Motor Company had historically received 25 percent of the automobile market and the projected industry sales were $68 billion, its projected sales would be $17 billion.

TABLE 5.6 Computation of R^2: $\bar{Y} = \dfrac{\Sigma Y}{n} = \dfrac{597.4}{14} = 42.7$

Year	$Y - \bar{Y}$	$\Sigma(Y - \bar{Y})^2$	$\hat{Y} - \bar{Y}$	$\Sigma(\hat{Y} - \bar{Y})^2$
1955	−6.4	40.96	−10.9	118.81
1956	−8.6	73.96	−9.6	92.16
1957	−6.4	40.96	−8.1	65.61
1958	−11.1	123.21	−8.0	64.00
1959	−5.8	33.64	−5.7	32.49
1960	−5.7	32.49	−4.5	20.25
1961	−8.3	68.89	−3.6	12.96
1962	−2.6	6.76	−1.3	1.69
1963	+0.7	0.49	+0.8	0.64
1964	+3.1	9.61	+3.2	10.24
1965	+10.5	110.25	+6.3	39.69
1966	+11.2	125.44	+10.3	106.09
1967	+11.0	121.00	+12.9	166.41
1968	+18.0	324.00	+17.3	299.29
Total		1,111.66		1,030.33

$$R^2 = \dfrac{\Sigma(\hat{Y} - \bar{Y})^2}{\Sigma(Y - \bar{Y})^2} = \dfrac{1,030.33}{1,111.66} = 0.9268$$

Predicting Future Earnings

When the firm's sales projection has been made, the investor may apply the historical profit margin ratio to sales to derive the total profits of the company. In the example, if after tax profit margins were 10 percent, predicted earnings would be $1.7 billion. To determine the earnings per share, this figure is divided by the total number of shares outstanding.

Advantages of the Aggregate Approach

The major advantage of the aggregate approach is its consideration of more than just earnings. This approach recognizes the influence of the economy on a firm's earnings. This approach also allows for more flexibility than the mechanical projections of the historical earnings growth rate approach. For example, the individual analyst can decide among aggregate economic forecasts on which to base his projections, and if he is optimistic, he may use a higher estimate in order to raise his earnings projection.

The aggregate approach assumes that conditions identical with those in the past will prevail in the future. If the relationship between GNP and industry sales, the firm's market share, or the firm's profit margins changed, the stable conditions assumption would be violated. The problem of the base and terminal years selection also remains in the aggregate approach. The choice of an abnormal base or terminal year may distort the regression results.

There is also a tendency when using the aggregate approach to forecast only 1 year in advance and to depend on the forecasting to the exclusion of all the other considerations in the PDV framework. The 1-year forecast fits into the P/E shorthand of the PDV framework, so that an investor may be misled into assuming that an increase in next year's earnings will necessarily increase the observed PDV of the stock (the market price). The analyst should never fall into the trap of concentrating on only one factor in the PDV framework to the exclusion of the others.

RETURN ON INVESTMENT APPROACH

Another method for forecasting earnings is the return on investment approach. In this approach the historical rate of return on investment is applied to a projected total investment base. If the company has demonstrated a rate of return of 10 percent a year, the next year's total investment base is projected at $10 million, the forecasted earnings would be $1 million.

The rationale for using this approach is that the necessary information is readily obtainable and that firms have target rate of return objectives that they attempt to maintain. It is argued that investment plans are made in advance and can be readily estimated by a scrutiny of the company's reports and its capital sources, principally retained earnings and borrowings. The target rate of return is the return on investment that the firm attempts to earn from each investment. The firm feels it must earn at least this stated return on its investment if it is to cover the cost of capital used to buy the investment and to maintain its earnings pattern. Under stable conditions, it may be reasonable to assume that future investments will return the historical rate of return.

The advantage of the return on investment approach is the relative ease with which it can be computed. The information is relatively easy to obtain, and the computational procedures are quick. This approach continues to assume, however, that stable conditions will prevail and that investment plans are unlikely to change rapidly. The accuracy of this method may be reduced in industries of low capital investment. If earnings increases arise with no additional investment expenditures, it is difficult to correlate future earnings with investment. The accuracy may also be impaired if unforeseen start-up costs or delays are encountered in the development of the investment's profit potential.

As in the aggregate approach, the analyst may overemphasize a 1-year earnings forecast, to the exclusion of the other factors in the framework. This approach also ignores the influence of the aggregate economy on the forecast.

SEASONALITY

Sales and earnings are usually reported on a quarterly basis. These reports may contain indications of the entire year's earnings. The analyst must be very careful, however, to consider seasonal factors before using quarterly earnings to forecast the entire year's earnings. The quarterly results are not necessarily equal to one-fourth of the entire year's operations. For example, a Christmas tree ornament manufacturer is very likely to earn most, if not all, of his profits in the fourth quarter of the year. In this case, an unprofitable first quarter may not be indicative of the entire year's results. Other examples of seasonal profit patterns are the fruit packer and the ice manufacturer.

Seasonal Adjustment

Adjusting quarterly earnings to account for the seasonal variation is one mechanical method by which some indication of the full-year earnings under stable conditions may be obtained. One simple seasonal adjustment method, as illustrated in Table 5.7, is to:

1. Compute the average quarterly earnings for the last several years, as in columns 1 to 3 in Table 5.7.

TABLE 5.7 Seasonal Adjustment of Quarterly Earnings

Quarter	Year	(1)	(2)	(3)	(4)	(5)	(6)	(7)
		Quarterly Earnings			Actual Quarterly Earnings/Average Quarterly Earnings			Seasonal Index Columns (4+5+6)/3
		1	2	3	1	2	3	
1		$1.50	$1.75	$2.00	1.50	1.40	1.33	1.41
2		0.90	1.15	1.40	0.90	0.92	0.93	0.92
3		1.00	1.25	1.50	1.00	1.00	1.00	1.00
4		0.60	0.85	1.10	0.60	0.68	0.73	0.67
Total		4.00	5.00	6.00				
Average quarterly earnings		1.00	1.25	1.50				

2. Compute the actual quarterly earnings as a percentage of the average quarterly earnings for the last several years by dividing each actual quarterly earnings by its average quarterly earnings, as in columns 4 to 6 in Table 5.7.

Projecting earnings under stable conditions 100

3. Compute the averages of the step 2 percentages for each quarter to arrive at a seasonal index (column 7).

4. Divide the latest quarterly earnings by the seasonal index to arrive at the estimated average quarterly earnings and then multiply the estimated average quarterly earnings by 4 to arrive at a full-year earning estimate.

For example, it can be seen in Table 5.7 that the first-quarter earnings have averaged 141 percent of average quarterly earnings in the last 3 years. If the first-quarter earnings of the fourth year were $3, we should expect average quarterly earnings to be

$$\left(\frac{3.00}{1.41}\right) = \$2.13$$

and full year earnings to be

$$4 \times \$2.13 = \$8.52$$

Predictive Quality of Quarterly Reports

How accurate or reliable are quarterly reports in indicating full-year earnings? Brown and Niederhoffer[2] attempted to construct measures of full-year earnings per share based on reported quarterly earnings and on the previous year's earnings. Each constructed measure was compared with the actual full-year earnings of 519 companies to determine how accurate it was in predicting the full-year earnings.

The four measures based on annual data were:

1. Last year's earnings per share
2. Last year's earnings per share plus the change in earnings in the more recent year
3. Last year's earnings plus the same percentage of change as occurred in earnings per share in the most recent year
4. Last year's earnings per share plus the average change in earnings per share from 1962 to 1965

The measures based on quarterly data were:

1. Four times the most recent quarter's earnings per share
2. Last year's earnings per share plus the same percentage of change as occurred between earnings up to this quarter of this year and this quarter of last year
3. The sum of the earnings in the most recent four quarters
4. Last year's earnings plus four times the difference between the

---

[2] See Philip Brown and Victor Niederhoffer, "The Predictive Content of Quarterly Earnings," *Journal of Business*, October, 1968.

average quarterly earnings up to the end of this quarter of this year and this quarter of last year

5. Average quarterly earnings up to the end of this quarter multiplied by the ratio of the average annual earnings in the last 2 years to the average quarterly earnings up to the end of this quarter for the last 2 years

6. Average quarterly earnings up to the end of this quarter multiplied by the ratios of the annual earnings up to this quarter's earnings for the last 2 years

7. The same as 5, except that the ratio is computed for earnings in the last 3 years

8. The same as 6, except that the ratio is computed for earnings in the last 3 years

Brown and Niederhoffer tested the difference between these constructed measures of full-year earnings and the actual full-year earnings. The measures based on annual data had an absolute average percentage error of from 20.8 to 32.3 percent in the years tested; that is, if you had estimated full-year earnings by any of the four annually based measures, you would have erred by over 20 percent, on the average. The quarterly measures based on the first quarter reports fared better, with an absolute average percentage error of 17.4 to 28.2 percent. This error was reduced to 13.9 to 20.0 percent for measures based on second-quarter reports, and to 9.3 to 15.0 percent for measures based on third-quarter reports. Although the absolute average percentage error seems high, Brown and Niederhoffer concluded that the interim reports could be used in predicting annual earnings,[3] and that their error in prediction decreased as the quarters progressed further into the year.

The error involved in applying these mechanical rules for using quarterly data to predict annual earnings highlights the questionable nature of the stable conditions assumptions. These mechanical rules should have produced more accurate estimates if conditions repeated themselves. If stable conditions do not exist, these mechanical rules lead to inaccurate forecasts. If too much emphasis is placed on these earnings forecasts, to the exclusion of other PDV framework factors, the price of the stock is not explained.

DIVIDEND PROJECTIONS[4]

A projection of future dividends may now be made from the earnings estimates. Although dividends and earnings tend to move together, spe-

---

[3] *Ibid.,* p. 498.

[4] See John Lintner, "Distribution of Incomes of Corporations among Dividends, Retained Earnings, and Taxes," *American Economic Review,* May, 1956, pp. 97–113.

cific methods for forecasting dividends are used. The most commonly used is the target pay-out approach.

In the target pay-out approach the firm is assumed to have set a pay-out ratio that it historically adheres to under stable conditions. For example, a firm may have a 50 percent pay-out ratio, implying that $0.50 out of every $1 earned is paid out in dividends. When the target pay-out ratio has been established, the firm adjusts dividends in relation to earnings, so that the pay-out ratio moves toward the target pay-out ratio. The firm usually adjusts gradually and partially toward the target pay-out, so that if earnings decline, it is not necessary to cut the dividend.

In formula terms, the next year's dividend D_{t+1} is equal to the last year's dividend D_t plus some adjustment C to bring the pay-out ratio P of this year's dividend to next year's earnings E_{t+1} in line with the target pay-out ratio P^*, so that

$$D_{t+1} = D_t + C(P^* - P)E_{t+1}$$

If $\quad P^* = 0.5$
$\quad E_{t+1} = \$1$
$\quad D_t = 0.30$

$$P = \frac{D_t}{E_{t+1}} = \frac{0.30}{1} = 0.3$$

$\quad C = 0.5$
$\quad D_{t+1} = \$0.30 + 0.5(0.5 - 0.3)\$1$
$\quad\quad\quad = \$0.40$

In the example, the firm has selected a target pay-out ratio of 0.5 and it adjusts halfway to this target pay-out ratio ($C = 0.5$) as earnings increase. If the target pay-out ratio has been achieved in period $t + 1$, D_{t+1} would have equaled $0.50. Since the adjustment was made only halfway, the D_{t+1} equaled $0.40. The use of the target pay-out ratio without a knowledge of how rapidly the firm wishes to adjust to it may be misleading. Note, however, that when a certain dividend D_t has been established, there is little tendency for a reduction in D_t. Only if P exceeds P^* is there a reduction in D_t.

The choice of the target pay-out ratio may depend on such conditions as the firm's needs for liquidity and expansion. High expansion needs may cause a slow adjustment toward the target pay-out ratio. Low expansion needs may cause a rapid adjustment. Other considerations in the target pay-out selection are bond indenture restrictions and stockholders desires. The firm's bondholders may deliberately restrict dividend payments in an effort to ensure reinvestment and the maintenance of the firm's ability to meet future interest payments. The firm's stockholders may desire dividend payments now rather than wait for increased payments later or for future capital gains. For example, some stockholders depend on dividends for daily living needs and would prefer a stock that paid regular and generous dividends.

SUMMARY

Under stable conditions, which assume the continuation of present trends in earnings, various approaches for forecasting the earnings factor in the PDV framework are applicable. The historical growth rate approach extrapolates the present trend in earnings by considering only the earnings pattern itself. The statistical procedure used in this approach ranges from trend line fitting to simple growth calculations. The aggregate approach, by regression analysis, relates the industry and the company's earnings to macroeconomic factors, such as GNP. This approach attempts to allow for the changing economic environment and includes consideration of more factors than earnings. The return on investment approach projects the firm's investment and forecasts the expected profit to be made from the investments. This approach assumes that a firm's investment plans are well known in advance and that its rate of return is constant.

Quarterly earnings reports may also indicate future earnings if adjustment is made for seasonality. Various quarterly measures of full-year earnings produce reasonably accurate estimates. Future dividends may also be forecast after the firm's target pay-out ratio and speed of adjustment to it are estimated.

All the approaches in this chapter are concerned with forecasting future earnings or dividends. All exclude consideration of the other factors in the PDV framework. The analyst who relies strictly on his ability to forecast earnings may be correct in this forecast but wrong in his forecast of market price performance.

QUESTIONS

5.1   What are the advantages of using a moving average growth rate as an indicator of growth rather than the simple, compound, or visual methods? What are the disadvantages?

5.2   What problems may be encountered when using trend line forecasting?

5.3   Describe the procedure used in the aggregate approach for projecting earnings.

5.4   What do the standard error of the estimate and the coefficient of determination measure?

5.5   What are the advantages of the aggregate approach to earnings projection? What are the disadvantages?

PROBLEMS

5.1 Plot earnings per share for the following firms and compute the approximate simple and compound growth rates.
Firm A: 0.90, 1.03, 1.08, 1.12, 1.15, 1.20
Firm B: 1.00, 1.10, 1.25, 1.36, 1.50

5.2 Compute the 3-year moving average growth rate of the following annual dividend stream; graph the actual dividend stream and the moving average stream.
Firm A: 0.25, 0.29, 0.34, 0.39, 0.43, 0.50, 0.54, 0.60, 0.68, 0.75
Firm B: 0.50, 0.58, 0.67, 0.75, 0.80, 0.87, 0.85, 0.94, 1.00, 1.07

5.3 Using the time series trend line, compute next year's estimated earnings per share (the stock split two for one in 1967):

Year	1963	1964	1965	1966	1967	1968	1969	1970	1971
Earnings per share	1.00	3.00	4.00	6.00	4.00	4.50	5.50	7.00	?

What is the estimate for 1975? Graph the actual earnings per share against the trend line's predicted earnings per share for the years given.

5.4 Find the regression line that best describes the historical relationship between a firm's earnings per share and the price of its stock on the security exchange.

Average price of stock	20.00	21.25	27.00	30.00	28.00	35.50
Earnings per share	1.00	1.15	1.50	2.00	1.80	2.20
Year	1966	1967	1968	1969	1970	1971

What is the predicted price of the stock in 1972 if its earnings are expected to be $2.40 per share?

5.5 An analyst is using regression analysis to estimate a construction company's annual revenue. He is using the number of housing starts per year as an economic indicator. Another analyst has suggested lagging the company's revenue 1 year behind the housing starts for this year in order to obtain a better fitting regression line. Would the analysis be correct to do so?

Housing starts, mil	8.0	6.3	7.4	8.4	8.9	8.4	8.0
Revenue, mil	2.2	5.1	4.0	4.6	5.2	5.6	5.1

5.6 Estimate next year's earnings per share for a farm equipment manufacturing company given the following data:

Year	0	1	2	3	4	5	6	7
Farmers' disposable income, bil	19.4	20.1	21.8	21.0	22.8	23.0	21.7	24.4
Industry sales, mil	769	800	820	810	840	845	819	870

The firm's share of the market is 10 percent, and its profit margin is 4 percent of sales. There are 1,000,000 shares of common stock outstanding. Farmers' disposable income is estimated to be 28 billion for the year. The firm's tax rate is 50 percent.

5.7 Given below is a record of the quarterly per share earnings of a manufacturing company. Year 6 first-quarter earnings per share were $1.85. Estimate this year's earnings per share.

Quarter	1	2	3	4
Year				
1	1.50	1.00	1.75	2.00
2	1.00	1.00	1.75	1.85
3	0.75	1.00	1.25	1.50
4	1.75	2.00	2.10	2.35
5	1.25	1.75	2.00	2.50
6	1.85			

5.8 Historically, a firm has paid the following dividends in relation to yearly earnings per share:

Year	1	2	3	4	5	6	7
Earnings per share	0.75	0.87	1.05	1.15	1.26	1.30	1.38
Dividend	0.30	0.35	0.42	0.46	0.51	0.52	0.56

The firm has a target pay-out ratio of 45 percent. Compute the actual average pay-out ratio and next year's dividend if earnings are projected at $1.50 per share. The adjustment factor is 0.52.

REFERENCES

Brown, Philip, and Victor Niederhoffer. "The Predictive Content of Quarterly Earnings," *The Journal of Business*, 41:488–497, October, 1968.

Clelland, Richard C., et al. *Basic Statistics with Business Applications*, New York: John Wiley & Sons, Inc., 1966.

Kane, Edward J. *Economic Statistics and Econometrics*, New York: Harper & Row, Publishers, Incorporated, 1968.

Lintner, John. "Distribution of Incomes of Corporations among Dividends, Retained Earnings, and Taxes," *The American Economic Review*, 46:97–118, May, 1956.

Mascia, Joseph S. "Corporate Earnings Predictions," *Financial Analysts Journal*, 25:107–110, July-August, 1969.

Neter, John, and William Wasserman. *Fundamental Statistics for Business and Economics,* 3d ed., Boston: Allyn and Bacon, Inc., 1966.

Newell, Gale E. "Is Quarterly Financial Data Adequate for Investment Decision Making?" *Financial Analysts Journal,* 25:37–43, November-December, 1969.

Yamane, Taro. *Statistics: An Introductory Analysis,* 2d ed., New York: Harper & Row, Publishers, Incorporated, 1967.

6
Projecting Earnings under Dynamic Conditions

Unlike the stable conditions in the last chapter, dynamic conditions are associated with changing earnings potentials. Extrapolation of the past and present trends is no longer meaningful, because the future earnings potential is based on factors that did not previously exist. The parameters of the situation change under dynamic conditions. The changes may emanate from shifts in the demand for the company's product, alteration in the competitive strategy, product innovation, management reorganizations, or any other event that alters the firm's foundation for earnings.

Dynamic conditions are associated with large shifts in earnings and dividend expectations and with large market price movements.[1] The analyst must spot dynamic conditions, pinpoint their origins, and relate the event to future earnings. This chapter explores the dynamic conditions in the life cycle or growth pattern of the industry and in the product demand pattern of the firm. This chapter then investigates the break-even approach, which allows the analyst to relate these dynamic conditions to future earnings, and discusses new product innovation and management evaluation.

INDUSTRIAL LIFE CYCLE

The industrial life cycle, as illustrated in Figure 6.1, goes through three distinct stages of growth.[2] The initial pioneering stage, the investment maturity stage, and the stability stage are characterized by various growth patterns in sales and earnings as the industry is born, matures, and stabilizes in time in the competitive economic environment.

[1] J. Murphy, Jr., "Earnings Growth and Price Change," *Financial Analysts Journal,* January–February, 1968, pp. 97–99.
[2] Julius Grodinsky, *Investments*, The Ronald Press Company, New York, 1953, pp. 64–77.

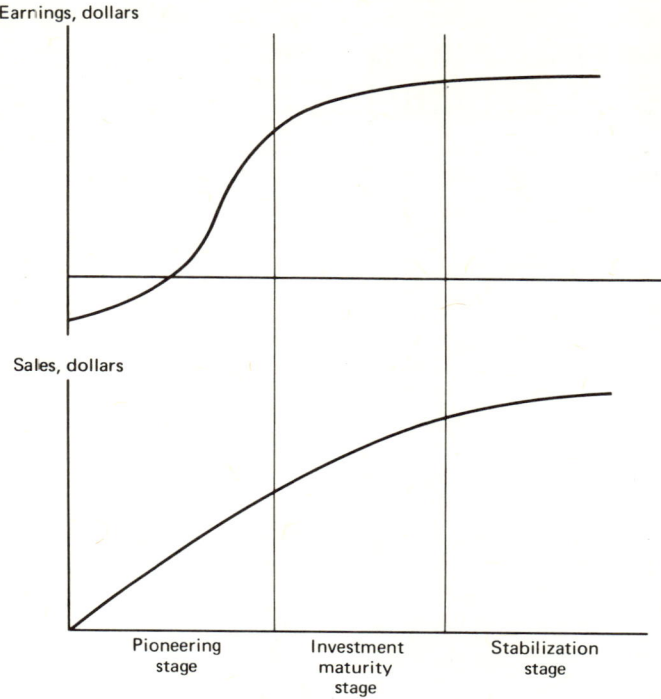

Figure 6.1. Industrial life cycle.

Pioneering Stage

From the birth of the industry until its maturity stage, an industry passes through the pioneering stage. In this stage the industry, if it is to survive,[3] experiences rapidly expanding sales demand, usually growing at an increasing rate. The initial idea or product manifests usefulness in the economy by providing an essential service or good. As sales grow rapidly, large profit opportunities become apparent. High profit margins and high returns to capital are anticipated after the initial losses associated with the first years of organization and development. These anticipated abnormally high returns usually arise because the first companies in the market capture unique competitive positions. Being the first, they usually develop production technology, marketing channels, brand identification, production capacity, personnel adequacy, and general experience before later-entering competitors. As sales expand rapidly in this stage, the individual firms may not have to face stiff price competition, because the demand for the product may be greater than the production capacity and new firms may be hindered in entering the

[3] The highest mortality rate among firms occurs early in the pioneering stage.

industry by licensing or similar barriers. Thus, prices and profit margins may be kept high.

The analyst must recognize the birth of an industry of economic consequence. This may occur as an entirely new industry with new companies or in a previously existing industry that has been reborn with new products, process technology, or any other dynamic change. In the pioneering stage the stable conditions and methods of forecasting earnings are not meaningful, because there are few, if any, past or present trends with which to forecast. The analyst must depend to a great extent on his entrepreneurial instincts in forecasting earnings. He must attempt to envision the product's sales potential within the economy's needs. He must also determine if sufficient financial backing is available. Without financial backing the best product may never develop a sufficient competitive position to survive. The analyst must also evaluate the management's ability to guide the company through the pioneering stage, that is, the ability to coordinate the product's production and sales with financial backing to ensure survival. Because information is generally scarce during the pioneering stage, the analyst must depend to a large degree on subjective evaluations, which adds to the speculative nature of investing in pioneering stage companies.

Pioneering Stage in the PDV Framework. During the first years of life, the companies in the industry may experience low profits or losses although anticipating large profits within the near future and accelerating growth throughout the latter part of the pioneering stage. An earnings pattern, such as illustrated in Table 6.1, might be typical of a pioneering stage company. Assuming that the firm pays half of its earnings in dividends, the PDV would appear as

$$\text{PDV} = \frac{\$0}{(1+r)^1} + \frac{0}{(1+r)^2} + \frac{0}{(1+r)^3} + \frac{0.25}{(1+r)^4} + \frac{1}{(1+r)^5}$$
$$+ \frac{2}{(1+r)^6} + \frac{4}{(1+r)^7} + \sum_{j=8}^{\infty} \frac{D_j}{(1+r)^j}$$

The analyst's price evaluation of the share at the beginning of year 1 is based on the expected dividends implied in the firm's expected earning power. Although pioneering stage firms usually do not pay dividends, the analyst must evaluate the dividend stream for what he believes it would be worth if he sold the share at any future point. The earnings stream may be looked on as an indicator of the future dividend potential. In this hypothetical case, the analyst could sell the shares at the end of year 7 and receive at that time the PDV of the sum of the expected dividends for year 8 to infinity. If he sold the share at the end of year 2, he would expect to receive at this time a price equal to the

PDV of the sum of the expected dividends from year 3 to infinity. The price at any future year would reflect the PDV of the remaining stream of dividends. The analyst then compares his PDV of the future stream of dividends from year 1 to infinity with the actual market price to determine if he wants to buy or sell his shares. Table 6.2 shows the PDV of this dividend stream at the beginning of years 1, 3, and 7 at a discount factor of 10 percent. If all the other factors in the PDV framework were held constant, the analyst could evaluate the share at $22.65 at the beginning of year 1, $30.13 at the beginning of year 3, and $40 at the beginning of year 8.

TABLE 6.1 Hypothetical Pioneering Stage Company Earnings

Year	1	2	3	4	5	6	7	8+
Eps	-$1	-$0.50	0	$0.50	$2	$4	$8	$8

TABLE 6.2 Year PDV of Table 6.1 Dividend Stream at 10 Percent if Bought at Beginning of:

Year	Dividend stream	Year 1	Year 3	Year 8+
1	0.00			
2	0.00			
3	0.00	0	0	
4	0.25	0.17	0.23	
5	1.00	0.62	0.83	
6	2.00	1.13	1.50	
7	4.00	2.05	2.73	
8+	4.00 each year	18.68	24.84	40.00
		22.65	30.13	40.00

With the PDV framework it can be seen why the stock prices of pioneering stage companies are more volatile, more susceptible to market fluctuations, and sell at high P/E's. The high P/E is the result of the shortening of the PDV framework to the P/E shorthand. The market price P is a reflection of the future dividends implied in the expected stream of earnings while the present year's earnings E are low. Therefore, the price that reflects earnings and dividends several years away is compared with the present low earnings, and a high P/E is the result. In the hypothetical case in Table 6.1, the P/E of $21.33/-$1 is a meaningless concept. At the beginning of the year 3 the P/E of $30.13/0.17$ is 177, also a meaningless figure.

The stock price volatility is the result of the uncertainty surrounding the projected earnings and dividends and the earnings and dividends growth pattern. If, in this hypothetical case, the projected earnings pattern depended on the development progress of a particular product, delays in this progress could force the analyst to assume a new pattern of anticipated dividends based on losses to year 3 instead of year 2 and no profits until year 5. If the earnings pattern changes, the PDV of the dividend stream has to change, and because pioneering stage companies are more prone to encounter unforeseen delays or favorable events that change the anticipated earnings and dividend pattern, the stock price tends to be more prone to fluctuation.

The PDV of the pioneering stage company is primarily dependent on forecasting of future earnings and dividends. The projected earnings and dividend pattern may vary quite sharply during the organization and development period. The stock price will react to these changes in the forecasted pattern. Because these changes usually occur more frequently and in larger magnitude than changes in the other PDV factors, forecasting risk dominates the evaluation of pioneering stage companies.

The end of the pioneering stage is usually accompanied by the first industry shake-out, in which the weaker competitors fall and a slow-down occurs in the industry's growth rate. Frequently, the shake-out is accompanied by downward adjustments in expected earnings and dividends and lower stock prices. There is no set number of years during which an industry remains in the pioneering stage, but the recent trend has been for shorter periods between the industry's birth and its first shake-out. This shorter time in the pioneering stage seems to be the result of the more rapid technological progress and more swiftly changing markets of today's commerce.

Investment Maturity Stage

After the industry has gone through the pioneering stage, it enters the maturity stage. The high profits on capital have, by the end of the pioneering stage, attracted sufficient competition to supply the rapidly growing product demand. The stronger, more efficient companies start to encroach on their competitor's market share, usually by reducing profit margins. The companies consolidate into a limited number of financially strong, well-managed firms. The market is supplied, and the initial sales surge of the pioneering stage gives way to a more gradual growth and stronger price competition for larger market shares. The product usually becomes more standardized, and unless there is a dynamic shift, the earnings of companies in the industry grow at a steadier, more moderate rate.

Maturity Stage in the PDV Framework. As the industry matures, the more stable conditions lend themselves to the forecasting methods of the pre-

Projecting earnings under dynamic conditions 112

vious chapter. Unless some dynamic event shifts the anticipated earnings and dividend pattern, the companies in the maturity stage generally exhibit consistent growth patterns. It may be expected that earnings and dividends for these companies will grow at a reasonably consistent rate, in line with the growth in the economy. In this stage, firms typically adopt a dividend pattern that they follow throughout the maturity stage. The constant growth models[4] may become more applicable. These models, such as

$$P = \frac{D_1}{r - g}$$

take advantage of the relatively stable growth rate to telescope the growing PDV framework to the shorthand model above. The advantage of this shorthand model, however, seems to offer little gain at a potentially large disadvantage. Because of the relative ease of predicting earnings and their implied dividend stream during the maturity stage, there is little to gain by assuming a constant growth rate g, but, by doing so, we eliminate the model's sensitivity to cyclical earnings fluctuations. It is probably better, therefore, to remain with the more explicit **PDV** framework.

Stabilization Stage

At some point in the maturity stage, the industry's sales start to stagnate. New products and technologies successfully challenge the older ones, and the mature companies fail to respond to the challenge. The industry's products become standardized, and profit margins and return on capital slump to the minimum level necessary to maintain the firms in business. Although these firms remain profitable, their earnings growth lags, and their investment opportunities diminish. Emphasis is generally placed on dividend maintenance rather than earnings growth.

Stabilization Stage in the PDV Framework. Because of the emphasis on dividend maintenance and the lack of growth, the future earnings and dividends of these stabilization stage companies are relatively easy to forecast. Because of the established markets, standardized products, and lack of investment opportunities, these companies generally tend to have less business and financial risk than those companies in the pioneering and maturity stages. The major PDV factors in the evaluation of these companies are the pure interest rate and purchasing power risk premium. Thus, even in unstable price and interest rate periods, the price of these securities tends to fluctuate less, because of the presence of less business, financial, and forecasting risk.

The P/E of stabilization stage securities is also less than for the se-

[4] See Chap. 3.

curities of the other two stages despite the lower degree of the business, financial, and forecasting risks. The discount factor r comprises mainly real interest rate and purchasing power risk and leads to a lower r. But, because of a lower growth rate, the capitalization rate for the future stream of dividends in the shorthand formula $P = D_1/r - g$ is higher. If the real interest rate and purchasing power risk premium compose most of the discount factor r, a low g leads to a larger capitalization rate and lower P/E. For example, as illustrated in Table 6.3, a maturity stage company with a business risk of 2 percent and a financial risk of 2 percent would have a discount factor r of 10 percent if the pure interest rate (the real interest rate plus the purchasing power risk premium) were 6 percent. If this company's growth rate were 5 percent, its capitalization rate would be $r - g$ or $10\% - 5\% = 5\%$. The stabilization stage company with a business risk of 1 percent and no financial risk would have a discount factor r of 7 percent. If this company had a growth rate of 1 percent, the capitalization factor would be $r - g$, or $7\% - 1\% = 6\%$. For given earnings and dividend of $1 per share, the P/E would be 20 for the maturity stage company and $16\frac{2}{3}$ for the stabilization stage stock.

TABLE 6.3

Maturity stage company	Stabilization stage company
$P = \dfrac{D}{r-g}$	$P = \dfrac{D}{r-g}$
$E = \$1.00$	$E = \$1.00$
$D = E$	$D = E$
$r = i + b + f$	$r = i + b + f$
$i = 6\%$	$i = 6\%$
$b = 2\%$	$b = 1\%$
$f = 2\%$	$f = 0\%$
$r = 10\%$	$r = 7\%$
$g = 5\%$	$g = 1\%$
$P = \dfrac{\$1.00}{0.10 - 0.05}$	$P = \dfrac{\$1.00}{0.07 - 0.01}$
$P = \$20.00$	$P = \$16.67$
if $i = 8\%$	if $i = 8\%$
$r = 12\%$	$r = 9\%$
$P = \dfrac{1.00}{0.12 - 0.05}$	$P = \dfrac{1.00}{0.09 - 0.01}$
$P = \$14.28$	$P = 12.50$

Summary

The industrial life cycle is a representation of an industry's life. The pioneering stage takes the industry from its birth through rapid growth to the maturity stage. In the maturity stage the industry settles into a reasonably consistent and upward growth pattern until the stabilization stage, in which growth rates decline to relatively minor levels, usually less than that of the general economy. The PDV evaluation framework applies in all three stages, although each stage emphasizes different PDV factors. In the pioneering stage forecasting risk is emphasized in the question of whether the product will sell and produce earnings and dividends as projected. In the maturity stage all the factors must receive careful attention, for, in general, all are of major importance. In the stabilization stage, the real interest rate and purchasing power risk receive the emphasis, for the other risks are usually minimized.

PRODUCT DEMAND ANALYSIS

Product demand analysis is an attempt to identify the factors underlying an industry's sales potential. It pinpoints the various influences on the demand for a product. By evaluating these influences, the analyst attempts to detect dynamic shifts in the firm's sales and earnings potential.

The analyst may work with industry classifications to become familiar with the demand factors that are peculiar to an industry. He may need a concept of an industry. Among the criteria for an industry is that the companies within the grouping engage in direct price competition with one another. For example, the companies within the steel industry may bid on the same project. The companies within the industry engage, as a group, in direct price competition with another group, such as the steel industry versus the aluminum industry. The companies within the group should be generally affected by the same general economic, political, and social considerations, such as Arabian crude oil producers. If the companies become multi-industry firms, it may be necessary to evaluate the demand factors in each division when forecasting earnings.

MARKET PENETRATION

Among maturity stage companies, increased market penetration is one possible dynamic shift. The percentage of the industry's market supplied by any one firm is usually increased at the expense of another company within the industry. For example, the automobile market has been divided among the big three manufacturers. A relatively small increase in one of the three's market share could mean substantial earnings improvement for this firm and usually lower earnings for the other two.

The basic approaches to increasing market penetration are price and nonprice competition. With price competition the competitors attempt to undersell one another with the same product. This may result in lower future earnings for all competitors if they meet one another's price reduction without more than proportionately increasing sales. If the firms feel this may be the case, the competitors may turn to nonprice competition to increase market penetration.

Major nonprice competitive devices are (1) advertising, (2) brand identification, (3) patents, (4) technology, and (5) marketing channels. Through advertising, the firm attempts to inform potential buyers about its product and perhaps sway them to the firm's product. Through brand identification, the firm attempts to establish an image for its product that is distinguished from the competitor's and likely to lessen price comparison. Through patents and technology, the firm attempts to sell the product on its technological advantages rather than through direct price competition. Through marketing devices, such as franchises and distributorships, the firm attempts to compete by controlling the channels of distribution rather than direct price competition. The analyst should be aware of the price and nonprice strategies of competitors and attempt to estimate how shifts in these strategies may affect future earnings.

Enlarged Demand

Another possible dynamic shift in sales and earnings potential may arise through increased demand. Increased demand may arise because of decreased prices, increased prices of competing products, or changes in taste, income, and demography.

Price Elasticity of Demand. The price elasticity of demand measures the change in the quantity of a product demanded in relation to the change in the product's price. Usually when price is decreased, the demand for the product increases; and when the price is increased, the demand for the product decreases. For example, Table 6.4 and Figure 6.2 illustrate the relationship between price and demand. At 10 cents, the highest price, the quantity demanded is 1,000 units, the least demanded. As price decreases by 1 cent a unit, the quantity demanded increases by 1,000 units.

TABLE 6.4 Relationship between Price and Demand

Price, cents	Quantity demanded, units
10	1,000
9	2,000
8	3,000
7	4,000

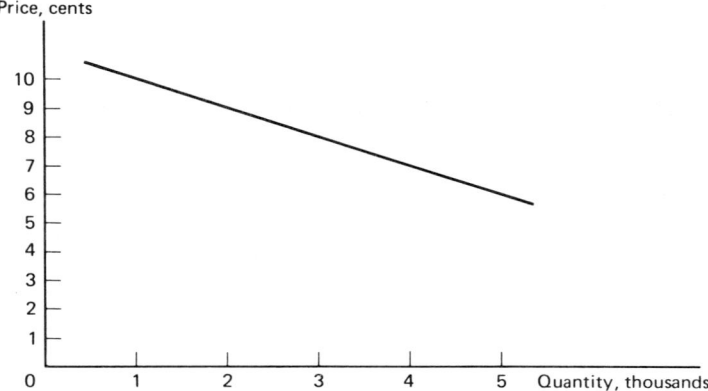

Figure 6.2. Demand curve.

The specific measure, price elasticity, compares the relative change in the quantity demanded to the relative change in the price:

$$\text{Price elasticity} = \frac{\text{relative change in quantity demanded}}{\text{relative change in price}}$$

The relative change in the quantity demanded is

$$\frac{\Delta Q}{Q}$$

where Q = quantity demanded before price change
ΔQ = difference between quantity demanded before and after price change

The relative change in price is

$$\frac{\Delta P}{P}$$

where P = price before price change
ΔP = difference between price before and after change

Therefore, the elasticity is

$$e = \frac{\Delta Q/Q}{\Delta P/P}$$

where e = price elasticity

In Table 6.4, the pure elasticity of demand is

$P = 10¢$
$\Delta P = 10¢ - 9¢ = 1¢$

$Q = 1{,}000$ units
$\Delta Q = 1{,}000 - 2{,}000 = 1{,}000$ units
$$e = \frac{1{,}000/1{,}000}{1/10}$$
$e = 10$

An elasticity of 10[5] implies that the demand for the product is very responsive to price changes and that a 1 percent change in price causes a 10 percent change in the quantity demanded in the opposite direction.

It should also be noted that the degree of elasticity varies at different prices. For example, when the price drops from 8¢ to 7¢, elasticity equals

$$e = \frac{1{,}000/3{,}000}{1/8}$$
$e = 2.67$

It is reasonable to suspect that at different points on the demand curve, the elasticity of demand changes if for no other reason than at some point the market becomes saturated with the product.

There are various degrees of elasticity. A product is said to be elastic, inelastic, or unit elastic, depending on the degree to which the quantity demanded responds to price changes. Table 6.5 illustrates the degrees of elasticity. The elastic product exhibits a proportionately larger change in demand than the change in price and has an elasticity of greater than 1. This implies that if the price were increased, the total revenue generated by the product would decrease, because the increased price would not offset the decreased demand. For example, if the Houston Astros raised the price of a ticket from $5 to $7, the number of tickets that they would sell would drop from 1 million to 0.5 million. The price elasticity of demand would be

$$e = \frac{500{,}000/1{,}000{,}000}{2/5} = 1.25$$

Total revenue from ticket sales would drop from

$1{,}000{,}000 \times \$5 = \$5{,}000{,}000$

before the price increase to

$500{,}000 \times \$7 = \$3{,}500{,}000$

after the price increase.

---

[5] Price elasticity is customarily expressed in absolute terms, and so the minus sign in this example is deleted.

TABLE 6.5 Degrees of Elasticity

Elastic	Unit elastic	Inelastic
$e > 1$	$e = 1$	$1 > e > 0$
$\dfrac{\Delta Q}{Q} > \dfrac{\Delta P}{P}$	$\dfrac{\Delta Q}{Q} = \dfrac{\Delta P}{P}$	$\dfrac{\Delta Q}{Q} < \dfrac{\Delta P}{P}$
If price falls:		
Larger total revenue	Constant total revenue	Smaller total revenue
If price rises:		
Smaller total revenue	Constant total revenue	Larger total revenue

The inelastic product exhibits a proportionately smaller change in the quantity demanded for a change in the price and has a price elasticity of less than 1. This implies that if the price were increased, the total revenue generated by the product would increase. For example, if a razor blade manufacturer sold 50 million blades at $0.10 each and then raised the price to $0.15 each, he would sell only 45 million blades. The price elasticity of demand would be

$$e = \frac{5/50}{0.05/0.10}$$

$$e = 0.2$$

The razor blade manufacturer's total revenue, however, would rise from $5 million to $6.75 million.

The analyst should be aware of the product's price elasticity, so that he may relate price changes to earnings forecasts. In the specific case of the razor blade manufacturer, the increased revenues generated by the price rise should, if profit margins remain unchanged, lead to a rise in earnings. In this example, if net profit margins were 10 percent, earnings should rise from $500,000 to $675,000. In contrast, the analyst would probably lower his estimate of future earnings for the Houston Astros if they raised ticket prices.

Certain product characteristics are generally associated with the various elasticities. Among the factors usually considered are (1) durability, (2) urgency of need, (3) availability of substitutes, (4) range of uses, and (5) price. The more durable the product, the more postponable the purchase and the more elastic the demand, because the old product itself is a competing factor in the demand. The more urgent the need, the less elastic the demand, because the demander is less prone to worry about price. The less available the substitutes, the less elastic the demand, because there is no satisfactory replacement. The larger the number of uses for a product, the higher its price elasticity, because there are more uses for the product when the price declines. At the lower price, the market is still not saturated, because it has expanded into new uses. A minimal price for a product tends to make the product inelastic, for the difference in price is relatively inconsequential in the purchasing decision.

Cross Price Elasticity. A dynamic shift in demand may arise when price changes occur in a competing industry. The cross elasticity of demand measures the relative change in the quantity demanded for the product in response to the relative price change in a competing product. For example, the quantity of chicken demanded increases as the price of beef increases. The cross elasticity between the two would be

$$ec_b = \frac{\Delta Q_c/Q_c}{\Delta P_B/P_B}$$

where ec_b = cross elasticity
Q_c = quantity of chicken demanded before beef price increase
ΔQ_c = difference in quantity of chicken demanded before and after beef price increase
P_B = price of beef before beef price increase
ΔP_B = difference in price of beef before and after price increase

If the price of beef rose from $1 to $1.20 per lb and the quantity of chicken demanded rose from 1,000 to 1,300 lb, the cross elasticity of chicken and beef would be

$$ec_b = \frac{300/1{,}000}{0.20/1}$$
$$ec_b = 1.5$$

If the price of chicken were $0.30 per lb, total chicken revenue would rise from

$0.30 × 1,000 lb = $300
to $0.30 × 1300 lb = $390

after the price of beef rose.

Income Elasticity. The income elasticity of demand is measured by the relative change in the quantity demanded divided by the relative change in income:

$$ey = \frac{\Delta Q/Q}{\Delta Y/Y}$$

where ey = income elasticity of demand
ΔQ = difference between quantity demanded before and after change in income
Q = quantity demanded before change in income
ΔY = change in income
Y = income before change in income

For example, if you purchased 10 bunches of flowers per year for your girl friend when you earned $10,000 per year and 12 bunches per year after you started earning $11,000 per year, your income elasticity of demand for flowers would be

$$ey = \frac{2/10}{\$1,000/10,000}$$

$$ey = 2$$

With an income elasticity of demand of 2, the sale of flowers should respond strongly to a change in income. An income elasticity greater than 1 implies a proportionately larger increase in the quantity demanded than the increase in income. An income elasticity of less than 1 implies a sluggish response in demand to a change in income.

The analyst must be aware of a product's income elasticity, so that he may relate the effects of income changes[6] to earnings forecasts. Luxury items, such as ocean cruises, jewelry, and imported gifts, are typically sensitive to changes in income. The sales and earnings of companies with these products are likely to fluctuate with changes in personal income. Impending slowdowns or drops in personal income should lead the analyst to infer a dip in earnings for these companies. On the other hand, rises in personal income should not encourage the analyst to predict proportional increases in sales and earnings for those companies whose products are not income-inelastic, such as bread bakers. It is improbable that the consumer's purchase of bread will increase because his income has increased; rather, a sufficiency of bread is all that he requires at all levels of income.

Other Shifts. Other dynamic shifts in demand may come from changes in taste, government policy, or demographic factors. A shift in taste to a sportier car or an acceptance of men's colognes may dramatically shift a firm's sales and earnings potential. A government policy shift from foreign to domestic programs or a special government tax incentive for medical care or urban redevelopment may also shift a firm's sales and earnings potential. An increased birth rate may increase the earnings potential of a baby food manufacturer. The analyst must remain alert

[6] Income changes are associated with changes in economic activity which, among other reasons, may be caused by government fiscal and monetary policies and which affect the purchase of capital goods as well as consumer goods.

to these changes and be able to incorporate them into his earnings forecasts.

The future earnings potential may shift dynamically with changes in the cost of raw materials to a firm. The inputs necessary to the firm's production may vary in cost as demand is varied for the inputs or as the supplier's cost changes. For example, a copper wire fabricator who uses raw copper as an input to his wire production would have his earnings potential affected if the price of raw copper rose. If, at the same time, the copper wire fabricator also faced an elastic demand curve, so that he could not raise prices without causing a decline in total revenue, his profit margins would shrink and his earnings potential would decline. The analyst must, therefore, be able to relate price changes in both the firm's products and supplies to future earnings patterns.

Summary

The firm's future earnings and dividend potential, one part of the PDV framework, is affected by shifts in the quantity sold, in the product price, and in the price of its supplies. A shift in price may cause future total revenue to rise or decline, depending on the price elasticity of demand. Independent of price, the quantity of the firm's product demanded may shift because of changes in taste, income, demography, government policy, the price of competing products, and the market penetration of competitors. When such shifts occur, the analyst must spot them and relate their effect to potential earnings. A change in the cost of raw materials also affects a firm's ability to earn. If the firm is unable to pass rising costs on to the customer, its potential profit margins and earnings are less. The analyst must be aware of these shifts and incorporate them into his earnings forecasts.

BREAK-EVEN ANALYSIS

Break-even analysis[7] is one method of quantitatively incorporating dynamic shifts in prices and demand into earnings forecasts. The break-even analysis shows the relationship among the selling price, fixed costs, variable costs, and product demand. When all these factors are combined in the analysis, earnings forecasts can be made by various assumptions about the factors.

The break-even point is that level of sales at which total revenues equal total costs. Total cost is equal to fixed costs plus variable costs. Fixed costs are those which are incurred by the firm regardless of the level of output. In contrast, variable costs vary directly with output.

[7] For simplicity of exposition we use linear relationships, implying perfectly competitive markets, although the nonlinear case allows us to more accurately associate the elasticities of this chapter to the analysis.

As illustrated in Figure 6.3 and Table 6.6, the sales revenue must cover the fixed costs of the operation and the variable costs associated with the output until the point at which profit begins. No profit is obtained until the break-even point is passed. After the break-even point is reached, each additional dollar of sales revenue contributes to profits after the variable costs have been subtracted. If the fixed cost FC is $100,000, the variable cost VC is $0.20 per unit, and the selling price P is $1 per unit, the total cost TC of X units is

$$FC + VC(X) = \text{total cost}$$
$$\$100{,}000 + 0.20(X) = TC$$

Total revenue TR is

$$P(X) = TR$$
$$\$1(X) = TR$$

The break-even sales quantity X is where total revenue equals total cost:

$$FC + VC(X) = P(X)$$
$$100{,}000 + 0.20(X) = \$1(X)$$
$$X = 125{,}000 \text{ units}$$

In this example, variable cost is 20 percent of every sales dollar. Therefore, up to $125,000, 80 percent of every sales dollar contributes to fixed cost after the 20 percent is subtracted from the sales price to cover variable costs. After the break-even sales quantity of $125,000, 80 percent of every dollar is profit, and 20 percent covers variable costs. If there are no dynamic shifts in prices or costs, the analyst may use this analysis to forecast earnings at expected sales levels.

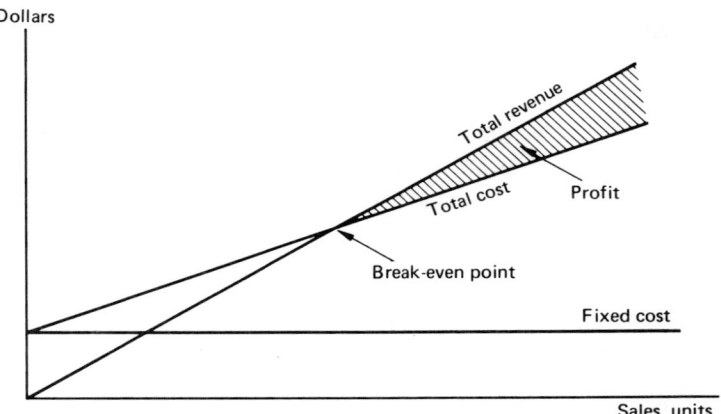

Figure 6.3. Break-even chart.

TABLE 6.6 Break-even Analysis

1 Sales volume, units	2 FC	3 VC	4 (2 + 3) TC	5 TR	6 (5 − 4) Operating profit
0	$100,000	$ 0	$100,000	$ 0	$−100,000
25,000	100,000	5,000	105,000	25,000	− 80,000
50,000	100,000	10,000	110,000	50,000	− 60,000
75,000	100,000	15,000	115,000	75,000	− 40,000
100,000	100,000	20,000	120,000	100,000	− 20,000
125,000	100,000	25,000	125,000	125,000	0
150,000	100,000	30,000	130,000	150,000	+ 20,000
175,000	100,000	35,000	135,000	175,000	+ 40,000

If the selling price shifts upward, however, to $1.20 per unit, the break-even point, as illustrated in Table 6.7, is

$$P(X) = FC + VC(X)$$
$$\$1.20(X) = \$100,000 + \$0.20(X)$$
$$X = 100,000 \text{ units}$$

With the increased price, the break-even point is lower, at any given fixed and variable costs, than before because of increased profit margins. Further, with a price increase, total revenue is higher at each level of unit sales. For example, at a sales level of 125,000 units at $1.20 per unit, projected operating earnings are $25,000, instead of $0 when the price was $1 per unit.

TABLE 6.7 Break-even Analysis

1 Sales volume, units	2 FC	3 VC	4 (2 + 3) TC	5 TR	6 (5 − 4) Operating profit
0	$100,000	$ 0	$100,000	$ 0	$−100,000
25,000	100,000	5,000	105,000	30,000	− 75,000
50,000	100,000	10,000	110,000	60,000	− 50,000
75,000	100,000	15,000	115,000	90,000	− 15,000
100,000	100,000	20,000	120,000	120,000	0
125,000	100,000	25,000	125,000	150,000	25,000
150,000	100,000	30,000	130,000	180,000	50,000
175,000	100,000	35,000	135,000	210,000	75,000

The quantity demanded may very likely change with the increase in price because of the price elasticity of demand associated with the product. The analyst must determine the effect of the price increase on the expected level of sales. If the product has an inelastic demand, the price increase may not affect or greatly reduce the expected sales level. If, in this example, the expected sales level before the price increase was 175,000 units, for a total revenue of $175,000 and an operating profit of $40,000, the increased price might drop expected sales volume to 150,000 units, for a total revenue of $180,000 and an operating profit of $50,000. If the demand were elastic, the price increase would lead to a decline in total revenue and operating profits.

A cost shift would also affect earnings forecasts. If, for example, the price of raw materials fell, causing variable cost to decline from $0.20 to $0.10 per unit, the break-even point, as illustrated in Table 6.8, would be

$$P(X) = FC + VC(X)$$
$$\$1(X) = \$100,000 + \$0.10(X)$$
$$X = 111,111 \text{ units}$$

With a selling price of $1 per unit and a variable cost of $0.10 per unit, each dollar of sales contributes $0.90 to fixed costs up to the break-even point and $0.90 to profit after the break-even point. The break-even point is lower than the 125,000 units in Table 6.7, and earnings at each sales level are higher. When the shift is in cost reduction, the analyst is not concerned with any price elasticity of demand effects unless the cost reduction is likely to lead to a price decrease.

TABLE 6.8 Break-even Analysis

1 Sales volume, units	2 FC	3 VC	4 (2 + 3) TC	5 TR	6 (5 − 4) Operating profit
0	$100,000	$ 0	$100,000	$ 0	$−100,000
25,000	100,000	2,500	102,500	25,000	− 77,500
50,000	100,000	5,000	105,000	50,000	− 55,000
75,000	100,000	7,500	107,500	75,000	− 32,500
100,000	100,000	10,000	110,000	100,000	− 10,000
111,111	100,000	11,111	111,111	111,111	0
125,000	100,000	12,500	112,500	125,000	+ 12,500
150,000	100,000	15,000	115,000	150,000	+ 35,000
175,000	100,000	17,500	117,500	175,000	+ 57,500

By using break-even analysis, the analyst should be better able to forecast earnings when dynamic shifts occur in either price, cost, or quantity demanded. Break-even analysis may be used to determine the effect of output on expected earnings.

High Fixed Cost versus Low Fixed Cost Companies

Figure 6.4(a) illustrates the break-even chart of a high fixed cost company, and Figure 6.4(b) that of a low fixed cost company.

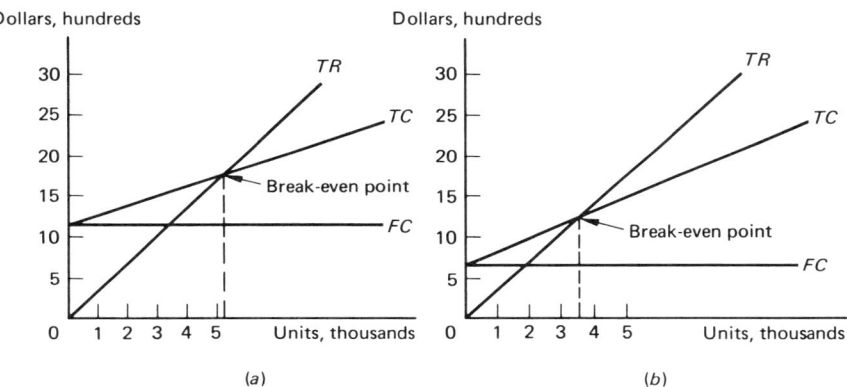

Figure 6.4. A comparison of high fixed cost and low fixed cost break-even points.

The high fixed cost company typically has a large investment in machinery and low variable costs. The low variable costs mean that a high proportion of each sales dollar contributes to fixed costs and then to profits, after the break-even point has been reached. Generally, because of the high fixed costs, the break-even point is higher than that of a low fixed cost company.

In contrast, the low fixed cost company has a lower break-even point and usually higher variable costs. Therefore, after the break-even point has been reached, each additional dollar of revenue minus variable costs contributes less to profit than in the high fixed cost company.

When the analyst foresees a total revenue increase in a high fixed cost–low variable cost company, he expects a relatively larger increase in expected earnings than in a low fixed cost–high variable cost company, because of the larger contribution to profit from each revenue dollar. Coupling his knowledge of the company's cost structure with the product's price elasticity of demand, the analyst should gain insight into the company's future earnings. For example, a sales increase in a high fixed cost–low variable cost company could add substantially to its profits, because the largest portion of each additional sales dollar, after the break-even point, becomes profit. But, in the low fixed cost–high variable cost company, the same increase in sales has a smaller percentage effect on profits.

Earnings Projections

Given a knowledge of the elasticities and break-even factors affecting a firm, the analyst is in a reasonable position from which to evaluate various changes in the operating environment of the firm. If total profit equals the difference between total revenue and total costs, any firm's earnings may be viewed as

$$\text{Profit} = P(X) - (FC + VC(X))$$

The total demand X is a function of the product's price elasticity, the income elasticity, market size, and the firm's penetration of the market, and cross-price elasticity. The total costs are a function of the fixed costs and the variable costs, which themselves are determined by the cost of the input factors. With this in mind, an analyst should be able to relate, for example, a price increase to the firm's overall profitability, so that if the firm increases its price, X may be expected to decrease. If the price elasticity of demand is greater than 1, the analyst should anticipate a decline in revenue. If the price of raw materials increases, the analyst should expect VC to rise and the total profit to fall unless an offsetting rise in P is anticipated. If the demand X for the product is curtailed because of changes in consumers' taste, income, government restriction, or some other limitation, the analyst should expect profits to fall accordingly. In the specific case of oil producers operating in countries that arbitrarily set restrictive quotas on the quantity of crude oil that they may pump, the analyst should expect an adverse effect on profits. Although the list is too extensive to cover every specific company and product, we should be aware that in forecasting earnings and dividends for the PDV framework, we may translate any change in the firm's operating conditions into its effect on profit through the elasticities and break-even characteristics of the firm.

NEW PRODUCT DEMAND ANALYSIS

Companies in the pioneering stage do not readily lend themselves to the break-even analysis. Their dynamic shifts generally come as innovations. These companies develop around new products, markets, patents, or services. Generally there is little, if any, defined market structure or industry history. The analyst may have to resort to his entrepreneurial insight to forecast earnings. Regardless of the difficulty, some earnings pattern projection must be made because of the effect on the stock price, as mentioned in the earlier part of this chapter.

MANAGEMENT EVALUATION

It is important that the corporation be given proper guidance. It must know what to invest in and how to finance its investments, develop its technical skills, and sell its products. The responsibility for this guidance lies with the management. A shift in management may be the dynamic change needed to push the company forward. Yet, management's effect on future earnings is intangible and hard to quantify. The analyst must search for clues to determine if management will deliver the earnings that he forecasts. Among the major areas that the analyst searches are management's motivation, depth, past performance, and plans and objectives.

Clues to management's motivation may come from several areas. A substantial stock ownership by all the management should indicate a personal involvement with the success of the company. Personal interviews, reported interviews, and a willingness to communicate with potential stockholders may also be clues to management's motivation.

The depth of management may also be an important consideration. The company should be more than a one-man operation, so that if he departs, there are several others to carry on. There should be sufficient representation in the company to provide careful supervision of all functions from financing to marketing and stockholders' representation.

The management's record may also provide clues. The management's record of past successes or failures may be indicative of their ability to meet the analyst's projected earnings. A record of firsts in ideas and accomplishments may indicate a capable management.

Management's ideas about the future may also provide clues to their capabilities. Imaginative ideas that are well conceived, carefully financed, and based on what the analyst believes are sound entrepreneurial concepts may convince the analyst that the management is capable of meeting earnings forecasts. Ill-conceived ideas, for which careful implementation has not been planned, should be a warning sign to the analyst.

The analyst must be prepared to form his own earnings forecasts independent of management's forecasts and determine if he believes management will meet his estimates. Management evaluation should be incorporated into the earnings forecasts as a part of the forecasting risk that the analyst's earnings estimate will not be realized. The analyst may adjust his earnings estimate to account for this risk.

SUMMARY

Projecting earnings under dynamic conditions requires the analyst to know the stage of the industrial life cycle that the industry is in. By applying the appropriate forecasting concepts, he is able to forecast a firm's earnings and dividends.

The industrial life cycle comprises three categories: the pioneering stage, the investment maturity stage, and the stabilization stage. In the pioneering stage, forecasting risk is emphasized in the PDV framework. In the investment maturity stage, all the PDV framework factors receive careful attention. In the stabilization stage, the real interest rate and purchasing power risk factors receive the emphasis.

Through product demand analysis concepts, the analyst may be able to forecast earnings when dynamic shifts occur in market penetration, prices, costs, or the quantity demanded. The price elasticity of demand allows the analyst to judge the effect of a price shift on the quantity demanded. Similar elasticity concepts for income, competitive prices, and other factors allow the analyst to judge their effect on the quantity demanded. Cost reductions may also influence the analyst's earnings forecasts.

One method of incorporating all these demand and cost concepts into one forecasting tool is break-even analysis. The break-even analysis allows the analyst to forecast earnings for any expected level of sales under the product demand and cost concepts that he assumes.

The analyst must evaluate management and determine if he believes that they are capable of realizing the earnings and expected dividends that he forecasts.

QUESTIONS

6.1 Describe the characteristics of a company in the pioneering stage.
6.2 With respect to the PDV framework, what are some of the typical characteristics of a pioneering stage company?
6.3 Describe the characteristics of a company in the investment maturity stage.
6.4 How is a firm in the stabilization stage characterized in the PDV framework?
6.5 Explain product demand analysis and its significance as an investment tool.
6.6 What are the major devices for nonprice competition?
6.7 What factors might cause an increase in demand?
6.8 Explain the price elasticity of demand concept.
6.9 What are the factors that affect the price elasticity of demand?
6.10 Explain the concept of cross-price elasticity.
6.11 What is income elasticity of demand?
6.12 What is break-even analysis, and what relationships does it illustrate?
6.13 What information can be taken from a break-even chart?

6.14 Explain why an analyst could expect a relatively larger increase in expected earnings from a high fixed cost–low variable cost firm, when total revenue is increased, than from a low fixed cost–high variable cost firm.

6.15 What are some of the methods by which an analyst can evaluate the quality of a company's management?

PROBLEMS

6.1 The steel industry has announced a price increase of $0.05 per ton for next year. Three years ago, steel was also increased $0.05 per ton, and car makers had to increase the average price of a car by $100, or 2.5 percent. Demand was 100,000 units less than that projected for the period, or a 3.1 percent decrease. Next year's projected volume is 3,500,000 units before a price increase of 2.4 percent. From the historical data, compute the expected new volume of sales.

6.2 Air freight between two cities is $20 per hundred weight, and the motor freight volume is 500,000 lb. If a $2 decrease in air freight rates is expected to cause a 150,000-lb decrease in motor freight volume, what is the cross-price elasticity of demand for motor freight?

6.3 Compute the income elasticity of demand for good A and good B:

		1969	1970
	Income (bil)	$525.00	$551.25
Good A	(mil)	795.00	858.60
Good B	(bil)	30.00	31.00

Which good could be classified as a luxury?

6.4 A company sells its product for $5 per unit. Its variable costs are $1 per unit, and its fixed costs are $60,000. Compute the firm's break-even point and its operating profit on sales of 50,000 units. What is its break-even point if the selling price per unit is $6.

6.5 Compute the break-even point and the operating profit on sales of $100,000 for firm A and firm B, given the following information:

	Firm A	Firm B
Selling price per unit	$ 5.00	$ 5.00
Fixed cost	50,000	10,000
Variable cost per unit	1.00	4.00

Compute the profits at $200,000 of sales for each firm. Compare the operating profits before and after the sales increase. What significance do you draw from the results?

6.6 Careful analysis of a manufacturing company has revealed that total operating costs for the firm is given by the equation $s = Q^2 + 10$, in millions of dollars, where Q is the quantity in thousands of units. The company sells its product for \$7,000 per unit. Construct a break-even chart, and compute the firm's fixed cost and its break-even point(s). At what level of sales will it be maximizing profit?

REFERENCES

Findlay, M. Chapman, III, and Edward E. Williams. *An Integrated Analysis for Managerial Finance,* Englewood Cliffs, N.J.: Prentice-Hall, Inc., 1970.

Grodinsky, Julius. *Investments,* New York: The Ronald Press Company, 1953.

Lerner, Eugene M., and Willard T. Carleton. *A Theory of Financial Analysis,* New York: Harcourt, Brace and World, Inc., 1966.

Liebhafsky, Herbert H. *The Nature of Price Theory,* Homewood, Ill.: The Dorsey Press, 1965.

Richmond, Samuel B. *Operations Research for Management Decisions,* New York: The Ronald Press Company, 1968.

Samuelson, Paul A. *Economics: An Introductory Analysis,* 6th ed., New York: McGraw-Hill Book Company, 1964.

Van Horne, James C. *Financial Management and Policy,* Englewood Cliffs, N.J.: Prentice-Hall, Inc., 1968.

Watson, Donald S. *Price Theory and Its Uses,* 2d ed., Boston: Houghton Mifflin Company, 1965.

Weston, J. Fred, and Eugene F. Brigham. *Managerial Finance,* 3d ed., New York: Holt, Rinehart and Winston, Inc., 1969.

7
Forecasting under Risk

When the analyst forecasts earnings, he encounters forecast risk or the error of incorrectly estimating future earnings. Strategies have been developed to bring the forecasting risk of any projection into clear focus. The most appropriate strategy would be complete accuracy, but this is impossible. The approach has, therefore, been to convert the uncertain future earnings performance into a situation of risk and then to apply the various risk strategies.

The objective of these strategies is to convert a situation in which nothing is known about future earnings to one in which the analyst has at least subjectively clearly focused on possible outcomes and their chances of occurring. This transformation from uncertainty to an array of possible outcomes is accomplished when the analyst constructs this array, either through an educated guess or with the aid of various forecasting models.

When the array has been established, the analyst may apply statistical techniques to satisfy himself as to which possible outcome is the most appropriate and the risk of not realizing this particular estimate. This application of statistical techniques should serve as a guide in selecting the best estimate and in presenting the associated risks; but it never, of course, eliminates the possibility of the analyst's being incorrect, although it may serve to improve his thinking about the forecast and thus reduce error. If the analyst had based his evaluation, at a given discount factor r derived from the historical quality of the earnings stream, on an implied future dividend stream derived from a specific earnings estimate in the array and the actual earnings and the associated implied dividend stream were higher than his forecast, the stock price should be correspondingly higher than his valuation. Conversely, actual earnings and implied dividends below his forecast from the array should lead to a correspondingly lower stock price than his valuation.

The various strategies explored in this chapter are (1) those based on the educated guess and (2) those based on forecasting models. The former include the expected value approach and the certainty equivalent approach. The latter include the sensitivity analysis of a profit and loss model and simulation. The statistical techniques employed are usually measures of expected value and dispersion, including the use of the probability of joint occurrences.

These strategies are attempts at organizing the analyst's logic in forecasting earnings. The effort is to ensure that no important variable is overlooked and to quantify the analyst's own opinion as to the risk of this estimate not being realized.

CERTAINTY

Certainty is encountered when only one outcome is possible, and it is known. This occurs in the world of earnings forecasts only when the future earnings are accurately and invariably known in advance. It is rarely, if ever, the case that future earnings are known in advance. Perhaps, only in the case of United States government bonds is the dollar amount of interest, the future stream in the PDV framework, known with certainty. For the world of certainty there is no forecasting risk. When the analyst moves into the world of other securities, particularly common stocks, he encounters and must handle forecasting risk.

UNCERTAINITY

In the uncertain situation, the analyst faces an unknown set of earnings, with an unknown probability of occurrence. The analyst is totally in the dark as to which earnings figure is most likely to occur or how the earnings possibilities are clustered around the mean. Under uncertainty, it is impossible to compute the mean or the standard deviation and to talk of probabilities. Rather, the analyst is concerned with general principles to maximize his utility or to minimize his losses.

RISK

In contrast with certainty, the circumstances of risk have the analyst facing a spectrum or range of possible earnings forecasts. In a risk situation the analyst is facing a set of possible earnings, each with a known or estimated probability of occurrence. In this particular risk situation, the probabilities are subjectively derived by the analyst, who, by doing so, converts the situation from uncertainty to risk. To each forecast is attached some subjectively derived probability of its occurring. For example, a set of possible earnings forecasts might appear as follows:

Possible earnings	Probability
$0.80	0.05
0.90	0.10
1.00	0.20
1.10	0.30
1.20	0.20
1.30	0.10
1.40	0.05
	1.00

The possible earnings of $0.80 and $1.40 each have a 5 percent chance of being realized. The earnings of $0.90 and $1.30 each have a 10 percent chance of occurring. The earnings of $1 and $1.20 each have a 20 percent chance of occurring, and the earnings of $1.10 have a 30 percent chance. The extreme earnings of $0.80 and $1.40 have the least chance of occurring, and the middle value of $1.10 has the most chance of occurring. There is a 100 percent chance that the earnings will occur between $0.80 and $1.40, because all the chances of occurrence fall in this range. If this set of possible earnings were plotted, it would resemble Figure 7.1.[1]

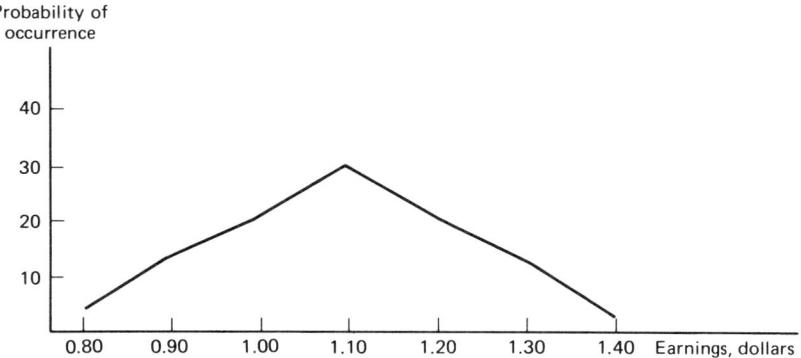

Figure 7.1. Distribution of possible earnings.

This set of possible earnings is a known or assumed probability distribution and is described by its mean and its standard deviation. The mean or expected value of this distribution is the earnings that are most

---

[1] Figure 7.1 is drawn as a continuous distribution by connecting all the plotted points. Throughout the text we follow this procedure for illustrative purposes. This practice is reasonable, because analysts cannot deal with an infinite number of outcomes and tend to visualize each security in terms of certain good and bad outcomes. See G. L. S. Shackle, *Uncertainty in Economics,* Cambridge University Press, New York, 1955.

likely to occur. To determine what is most likely to occur, each possible earnings must be included in the expected value according to its probability of occurrence. In effect, we are taking a weighted average of the form

$$u = \sum_{i=1}^{n} X_i(p_i)$$

where u = mean
X_i = possible earnings
p_i = probability of possible earnings

In this example, the mean is

$u = \$1.10$

The standard deviation measures the dispersion of the probability distribution. It indicates how closely grouped the possible outcomes are around the mean. To determine how far away from the mean the individual observations are, we find the differences squared between the mean and these observations. Then, to find the most likely distance between the mean and the individual earnings, each of the differences is weighted by its probability of occurrence, summed, and the square root taken in the form of

$$\sigma = \sqrt{\sum_{i=1}^{n} (X_i - u)^2 p(X_i)}$$

where σ = standard deviation
u = mean
X_i = possible earnings
$p(X_i)$ = probability of possible earnings

In this example, the standard deviation is

$\sigma = 0.14$

The probability distribution in this example has a mean of $1.10 and a standard deviation of $0.14. If the distribution is normal, as in the example, statistical inference tells us that there is a 95 percent chance that the realized earnings will be within $1.10 ± $0.28, or a range of $0.82 to $1.28.[2]

---

[2] For a discussion of statistical inference see J. Neter and W. Wasserman, *Fundamental Statistics for Business and Economics*, Allyn and Bacon Inc., Boston, 1966. From statistical inference, the analyst can infer that 95 percent of the possible earnings per share in the normal curve will occur within two standard deviations on either side of the mean. This may not be the case in each individual earnings estimate, but in many estimates for many companies, the probability is that the estimate will, 95 percent of the time, occur within two standard deviations of the mean.

Every probability distribution has its own mean and standard deviation, the value of which may vary among distributions. A distribution may have the same mean as another distribution but a smaller standard deviation. This would signify that, although the most likely earnings were the same, the other possible earnings were more closely bunched around the mean than in the distribution with the larger standard deviation. The analyst may, therefore, be more certain that realized earnings will be closer to the expected value. For example, in the following sets of possible earnings the mean is $1.10, and the standard deviation is $0.11:

Possible earnings	Probability
$0.90	0.10
1.00	0.20
1.10	0.40
1.20	0.20
1.30	0.10

The plot of this probability distribution would look like Figure 7.2. The entire spectrum of possible outcomes is covered in a narrower range, and the analyst may be 95 percent certain that the realized earnings will be $1.10 ± $0.22, or between $0.88 and $1.32.

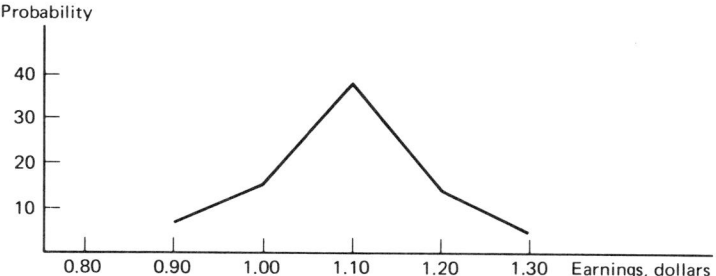

Figure 7.2. Distribution of possible earnings.

In comparing two companies, one with the earnings distribution in Figure 7.1 and the other with that in Figure 7.2, the analyst encounters less forecasting risk in the latter. As a general rule, the smaller the standard deviation, the less the possible forecasting error.

STRATEGIES OF RISK

Various strategies have developed for handling forecasting risk. These methods are designed to allow the analyst to focus on all possible outcomes and to derive the probability of their occurrence. These methods attempt to transform uncertainty to risk and, thus, allow the analyst to improve his estimating procedure. These methods generally do not eliminate the possibility of an incorrect estimate, but they do serve as guides in selecting a more probable estimate and establishing an indication of the chances of an incorrect estimate. Most involve adjusting the future stream of benefits in some manner so as to limit the possibility of overestimate. The most commonly used technique is the expected value approach. A second technique, the certainty equivalent approach, adjusts the expected value to account for forecasting risk. A third approach, sensitivity analysis, forces the analyst to concentrate on the most important factors in the firm's earnings potential in the hope of improving the forecast. A fourth approach, simulation, attempts a reconstruction of the earnings potential by sampling the factors of the break-even analysis. Finally, the analyst's evaluation approach attempts to evaluate the accuracy of the analyst's forecast as a technique in picking out the best earnings estimates.

Expected Value Approach

First, the analyst must construct a probability distribution of earnings potential. The analyst must ask himself what he believes the chances are for any particular earnings estimate to be realized. For example, he must draw on past experience and declare that he expects the chances of the firm's realizing $1 per share to be 20 percent and that he expects the chances of $1.10 to be 30 percent. In the risk example earlier in this chapter (see Figure 7.1) the analyst had decided to construct the following probability distribution:

Possible earnings	Probability
$0.80	0.05
0.90	0.10
1.00	0.20
1.10	0.30
1.20	0.20
1.30	0.10
1.40	0.05

The expected value or most likely to occur estimate is $1.10, so that the analyst would use this figure.

The use of the expected value forces the analyst to search deeper behind his first estimate to place some sort of confidence index on his forecast and explore the possibilities on either side of the estimate. An explicit probability distribution, such as above, would convey to the analyst's clients his own feelings on an earnings forecast that had only a 30 percent chance of occurring. The client may not be willing to make an investment on only a 30 percent chance.

The use of the expected value may be criticized because of its highly subjective derivation of the probabilities. Because each of the probabilities attached to the estimate is only an indication by the analyst, much of the analyst's personal biases and suspicions are involved. This subjectivity may unduly distort the picture, although it is possible that the probabilities may reflect the true variability imparted to the company's earnings potential from its actual operating conditions.

Another criticism of using just the expected value is that it ignores the standard deviation concept embodied in the probability distribution. Without any indication of the dispersion, the analyst is forfeiting a look at the possible forecasting error attached to this particular value. If the analyst forecasts earnings as the expected value $\pm$ three standard deviations ($u \pm 3\sigma$), the potential forecasting error would be seen. Depending on the investor's aversion to forecasting risk, the low, high, or any estimate in between could be used. As we shall shortly see, the certainty equivalent approach attempts to take the expected value and the standard error into consideration.

A last criticism of the expected value approach is its failure to force the analyst to focus on the probabilities attached to each of the factors assumed in each earnings estimate, such as economic conditions and profit margins. For example, the analyst might consider that there is a 40 percent chance of a recession and lower sales and a 60 percent chance of prosperity and higher sales. The analyst might believe that there is a 40 percent chance of low raw material costs and good management's causing high earnings potential and a 60 percent chance of low earnings potential, regardless of the economic climate. The analyst's feelings may be summarized in the following grid:

	Recession (0.4)	Prosperity (0.6)
High earnings potential (0.4)	$1.10	$1.40
Low earnings potential (0.6)	$0.80	$1.00

If the earnings potential is high, the analyst predicts a $1.10 earnings per share in recession and $1.40 earnings per share in prosperity. If the earnings potential is low, the analyst predicts $0.80 per share in recession and $1 in prosperity.

With this grid the analyst may now see what he can expected under various combinations of conditions. The possibility of a combination of a recession and high earnings potential is 16 percent, or the probability of a recession times the probability of high earnings potential. The probability of each combination is summarized in the following grid:

	Recession (0.4)	Prosperity (0.6)
High earnings potential (0.4)	16%	24%
Low earnings potential (0.6)	24%	36%

The combination of prosperity with low earnings potential has the greatest chance (36 percent) of occurring. When the analyst is forced to examine the probabilities attached to all the factors in the earnings forecast, he receives a clearer picture of the forecasting risk.

Certainty Equivalent Approach

The analyst may attempt to adjust for the risk in his forecast by reducing the earnings and the accompanying dividend estimates. This approach requires that the analyst adjust his dividend estimate to a level that he feels certain will occur. In the PDV framework the analyst would adjust each year's forecasted dividends by some factor B_i, where i can equal 1 to n, as in the following illustration:

$$\text{PDV} = \frac{B_1 D_1}{(1+r)^1} + \frac{B_2 D_2}{(1+r)^2} + \cdots + \frac{B_n D_n}{(1+r)^n}$$

To determine the appropriate B coefficient, the analyst must ask himself how averse he is to taking one more forecasting risk. He may start by asking himself for what certain earnings estimate he is willing to trade an uncertain estimate of $1 one year hence. If he answered $0.90, the B_1 coefficient would be 0.9 for this estimate. He could then ask himself for what would he trade an uncertain estimate of $1 two years hence, and he might respond with $0.70. This gives a B_2 coefficient of 0.7. He could repeat this procedure of trading certain estimates for uncertain estimates for each year in his time horizon. By applying these B coefficients, the analyst could reduce the forecast to a level that he felt certain would occur.

Further, when using the certainty equivalent approach, the analyst has, theoretically, eliminated all business and financial risk considerations that may have affected the earnings, and he should use the riskless interest rate as his discount factor. Although theoretically correct, it is unrealistic to assume that the analyst has eliminated all these considerations, and this detracts from the practical application of this method.

The certainty equivalent approach may be criticized for the same reasons as the expected value approach. The associated probabilities are subjectively derived, and the analyst is not forced to focus on all the factors involved. It does, however, increase the focus on the analyst's feeling for the risk involved in each forecast.

Sensitivity Analysis

The analyst may attempt to estimate earnings through a profit and loss analysis model. This would require that he identify all the factors that are pertinent to a firm's total cost and total revenue. For example, several products catering to various markets may produce revenue. This would require the analyst to estimate selling prices and sales for each product and market. Total cost will probably arise from several different areas. Raw materials are one variable cost. If different types of raw materials are used, the analyst must be prepared to investigate each raw material source and its cost factors. Labor is another cost. The analyst must decide which labor costs are fixed and which are variable, as well as estimating the cost associated with the various types of labor, such as skilled and unskilled or union and nonunion. Cost consideration must also be given to the interest or financing costs of any anticipated expansion.

In order to incorporate all these factors into the earnings forecast, the analyst might construct the following model. This model is an attempt to pinpoint clearly all the pertinent variables and isolate each, so that the analyst may clearly see the effect of any one variable on the total picture.

The variables:

P = total profits
TC = total costs
TR = total revenues
S_i = selling price of product i
X_i = sales volume of product i
FC = fixed costs
VC = variable costs
RM_i = raw material cost of product i
Int = financing costs of expansion
Lab_i = labor cost of product i
Q_{i_j} = quantity of raw material j used in product i
F_j = price of raw material j
L_{i_j} = quantity of labor j used in product i
J_j = price of labor used in product j

The model:

(7.1) $\quad P = TR - TC$
(7.2) $\quad TC = FC + VC + Int$
(7.3) $\quad VC = \sum_{i=1}^{n} (X_i \cdot RM_i) + \sum_{i=1}^{n} (Lab_i \cdot X_i)$
(7.4) $\quad TR = \sum_{i=1}^{n} (S_i X_i)$
(7.5) $\quad RM_i = F_j Q_{i_j}$
(7.6) $\quad Lab_i = J_j L_{i_j}$

Starting from the input equations (7.5) and (7.6), the analyst estimates what quantities of labor and raw materials are necessary to produce a unit of product i. Thus, he is forced to look at each type of labor involved and each raw material involved in product i. It may happen that the labor required in a particular project is to come under minimum wage laws or a new union contract that, otherwise, might have gone unnoticed. The variable cost can then be estimated by multiplying the estimated sales of each product i by the raw material costs and labor costs of each product i as in Equation (7.3). Total cost may be projected by adding the variable costs to the fixed costs and any financing costs of expansion Equation (7.2). Total revenue may then be estimated by Equation (7.4), in which the estimated unit sales of product i are multiplied by the estimated selling price of product i. Total profit is the difference between the total revenue and total costs, as in Equation (7.1).

When the analyst has constructed these representative equations, he can change his estimate of any of the variables, such as sales X_i or raw material cost RM_i, for any product. Then, he can recalculate the equations with the changed values and determine how sensitive the profits are to them. If a large change in any one variable causes a little change in profits, he probably turns his attention to other, more influential variables, thus allowing him to become more accurate in estimating the more important variables. Repeating this process of changing variable values, the analyst is able to construct a set of profit estimates depending on the variable values. This set of forecasts reflects what he considers to be the range of the earning forecasts, given possible variable values.

The following example illustrates sensitivity analysis. The XYZ Corporation produces two products X_1 and X_2:

Strategies of risk 141

	X_1		X_2	
	Q	F	Q	F
Raw materials:				
Lead	10 lb	$0.10	0	$0.10
Steel	5 lb	0.05	5 lb	0.05
Nuts and bolts	1 lb	0.25	1 lb	0.25
Plastic	0	0.50	4 lb	0.50
	L	J	L	J
Labor:				
Skilled	3 hr	$2.00	1 hr	2.00
Unskilled	7 hr	$1.00	4 hr	1.00

Q = quantity of raw material
L = quantity of labor
F = price of raw material
J = price of labor

Raw materials for product X_1 include 10 lb of lead, 5 lb of steel, 1 lb of nuts and bolts. Raw materials for product X_2 include 5 lb of steel, 1 lb of nuts and bolts, and 4 lb of plastic. Labor for product X_1 includes 3 hr of skilled and 7 hr of unskilled labor per unit. Labor for product X_2 includes 1 hr of skilled and 4 hr of unskilled labor. Sales of product X_1 are estimated at 1,000,000 units at $20 per unit, and sales of product X_2 at 500,000 units at $15 per unit. XYZ plans no expansion during the coming year and has a fixed cost of $2,000,000.

XYZ's labor costs per unit are

$$L_1 = J_1L_{11} + J_2L_{12}$$
$$= (2)3 + (1)7$$
$$= \$13$$
$$L_2 = J_1L_{21} + J_2L_{22}$$
$$= (2)1 + (1)4$$
$$= \$6$$

XYZ's raw materials costs per unit are

$$RM_1 = F_1Q_{11} + F_2Q_{12} + F_3Q_{13} + F_4Q_{14}$$
$$= (0.10)10 + (0.05)5 + (0.25)1 + (0.50)0$$
$$= \$1.50$$

$$RM_2 = F_1Q_{21} + F_2Q_{22} + F_3Q_{23} + F_4Q_{24}$$
$$= (0.10)0 + (0.05)5 + (0.25)1 + (0.50)4$$
$$= \$2.50$$

XYZ's variables costs are

$$VC = X_1(RM_1 + Lab_1) + X_2(RM_2 + Lab_2)$$
$$= 1,000,000(14.50) + 500,000(8.50)$$
$$= 14,500,000 + 4,250,000$$
$$= \$18,750,000$$

XYZ's total costs are

$$TC = FC + VC + Int$$
$$= \$2,000,000 + 18,750,000 + 0$$
$$= \$20,750,000$$

XYZ's total revenue is estimated at

$$TR = X_1(S_1) + X_2(S_2)$$
$$= 1,000,000(\$20) + 500,000(\$15)$$
$$= \$27,500,000$$

XYZ's profits are estimated at

$$P = TR - TC$$
$$= \$27,500,000 - 20,750,000$$
$$= \$6,750,000$$

If the analyst believes that the price of steel might rise to $0.07 per lb and sales might rise to 1,100,000 for product X_1, he could substitute these figures in the analysis and arrive at a new earnings estimate, based on these possibilities. Under these assumptions, variable cost would rise from $1,610,000 to $20,360,000, and total revenue would rise to $29,500,000. Profits would be $7,140,000. The analyst could repeat his profit calculation, assuming as many different values for factor as he desired.

The advantages of the sensitivity analysis are that it forces the analyst to concentrate on all the factors involved and allows him to try out various possibilities that may occur. The difficulty may be in getting the information to construct a reasonably accurate profit and loss analysis.

Simulation

Using the same model of the firm's operations as in the sensitivity analysis, the analyst may use a simulation approach to generate an earnings estimate and potential forecast error.[3] The method of simulation is to select random values for the variables in the analysis, work through the model to determine the profit potential under each set of variable values, and then array the results to determine which profit is the most likely to occur and with what dispersion.

[3] D. Hertz, "Risk Analysis in Capital Investment," *Harvard Business Review*, January-February, 1965, pp. 95–106.

The analyst is required to assign values and their probability of occurring to each of the factors in the break-even analysis. This means that he must either consult historical data to determine the probability distribution of the price of each raw material, labor, and any other factor or construct a subjective probability distribution based on what he believes will be the possible prices of raw materials, labor, and so on. In the example, the analyst would be required to construct probability distributions for such factors as the following:

Lead prices
Steel prices
Nuts and bolts prices
Plastic prices
Selling prices of each product
Quantity of each product sold

Graphically, the estimated probability distributions might resemble those in Figure 7.3.

After these probability distributions have been constructed, the analyst randomly selects values from each of the distributions and substitutes them into the profit and loss analysis. For each set of randomly selected values, the analyst computes a profit. After this has been repeated several times, a pattern begins to emerge; one computed profit appears more often than the others. The simulated profits also begin to fall within a range, beyond the boundaries of which no simulated profit occurs. After many computed profits based on different sets of randomly selected variable values, a simulated profit pattern in the form of a probability distribution emerges.

For example, after the first 100 simulated profit computations have been made, using the computer, the following pattern may have emerged:

Earnings, millions	Number of Appearances
$10	3
11	7
12	5
13	10
14	15
15	20
16	15
17	10
18	5
19	7
20	3

This probability distribution is represented in Figure 7.4.

Forecasting under risk 144

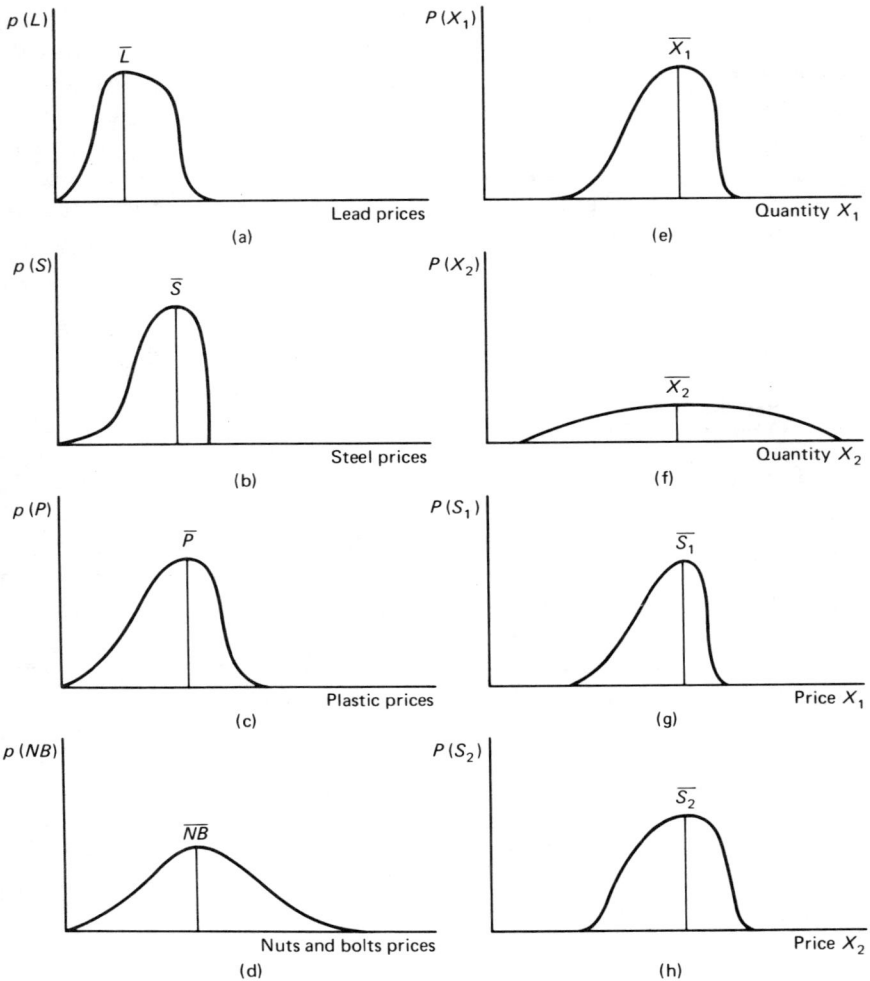

Figure 7.3. Probability distributions of profit and loss analysis variables.

This probability distribution of the simulated profits gives the analyst a representation of the firm's earnings potential. From this probability distribution, the analyst can compute the expected earnings and the standard deviation. With these statistics in front of him, the analyst can decide for himself how great the forecasting risk is and how much risk adjustment he wishes to make. It may, for example, be that the range of the probability distribution discourages the analyst from making a forecast.

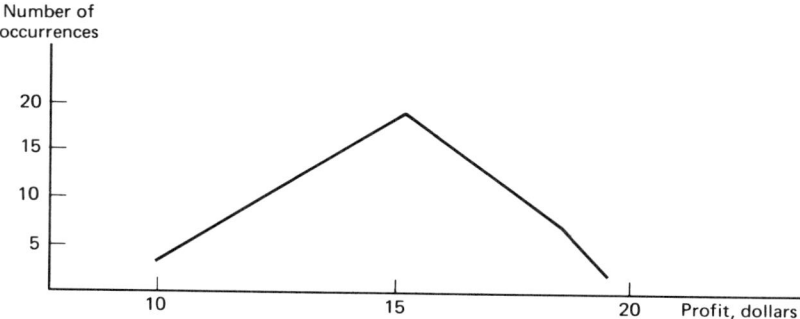

Figure 7.4. Probability distribution of simulated profit.

Analyst's Record

There may be reasons to believe that some analysts are either more accurate than others in their earnings forecasts or more prone to be optimistic or pessimistic. When one is depending on the analyst's forecasts, it is important to be aware of the probability of an incorrect earnings or price movement forecast from any analyst. One method of determining the probability that an analyst's forecast will be correct is to answer the question: given the analyst's forecast of an upward movement in stock price, what is the probability of the stock price rising?

There are two possible events connected with the analyst's forecast of a stock price rise. One, the price can rise, or, two, it can fall. The probability of a price rise is reflected in the frequency with which it occurs in the sample. We can represent this as $P(B_1)$, where B_1 is a price rise. But we want to know how many of these price increases were associated with a forecast of rising prices. We can represent this as $P(X_1/B_1)$, where X_1 is the forecast of a price rise. The observed frequency of a price rise forecast in a price rise situation is the probability of the price's increasing times the probability of a price rise forecast's having been made, or $P(B_1) \cdot P(X_1/B_1)$.

The only other possible event connected with the analyst's forecast of an increase in price is that the price falls. The probability of a price's falling regardless of the analyst's forecasts is $P(B_2)$, or the observed number of price declines among all the stocks the analyst forecasts. The probability that, given that prices did fall, the analyst had made a forecast of rising prices is $P(X_1/B_2)$.

The total probability of the analyst's predicting a price increase is the probability of a price increase forecast when prices both fell and rose, $P(B_1)P(X_1/B_1) + P(B_2)P(X_1/B_2)$.

Therefore, the probability that prices will rise, given a rising price forecast $P(B_1/X_1)$, is the probability $P(B_1) \cdot P(X_1/B_1)$ of price rise forecast in a price rise situation, divided by the total probability of a rising price forecast's having been made in the first place, $P(B_1)P(X_1/B_1) + P(B_2)P(X_1/B_2)$. This would be

$$P(B_1/X_1) = \frac{P(B_1)P(X_1/B_1)}{P(B_1)P(X_1/B_1) + P(B_2)P(X_1/B_2)}$$

where B_1 = stock price increase
B_2 = stock price fall
X_1 = forecast of stock price increase
X_2 = forecast of stock price decrease

In this instance, if $P(B_1/X_1)$ were 87 percent, we could say that this analyst should be accurate on 87 percent of his forecasts of rising prices. If we wanted to know how accurate the analyst would probably be on his forecasts of falling prices, we could compute

$$P(B_2/X_2) = \frac{P(B_2)P(X_2/B_2)}{P(B_2)P(X_2/B_2) + P(B_1)P(X_2/B_1)}$$

By this approach, it may also be possible to gain a feeling for the analyst's bias in his assumptions on earnings potential. If X_1 were the analyst's optimistic forecast assumptions and X_2 his pessimistic earnings forecast assumptions, we could ask the question: given his forecast assumption, were his earnings forecast high B_1 or low B_2 in relation to the actual results? The probability of a high earnings estimate, given high assumptions, is

$$P(B_1/X_1) = \frac{P(B_1)P(X_1/B_1)}{P(B_1)P(X_1/B_1) + P(B_2)P(X_1/B_2)}$$

If it turns out that this probability is rather large, we may assume that the analyst is overoptimistic, and his earnings forecast must be reduced. If the probability of realizing a low estimate, given low assumptions $P(B_2/X_2)$, is large, we may assume that the analyst is biased to lower estimates and adjust accordingly.

SUMMARY

Forecasting risk is the potential error that the earnings forecast by the analyst will not be realized. Within the PDV framework this means that the expected future stream of benefits may not be realized. The change in this stream affects the PDV of the financial asset.

Forecasting risk, in the context of security analysis, has the analyst facing a probability distribution of possible earnings that is constructed by the analyst. In contrast with risk, the situation of certainty has an inevitable, foreseen outcome; and the situation of uncertainty gives no indication of the probability distribution connected with the various earnings possibilities.

Among the methods of handling forecasting risk are the expected value, certainty equivalent, sensitivity analysis, simulation, and analyst evaluation approaches. The expected value approach uses the earnings estimate that is most likely to occur. The expected value approach may be adjusted to allow probabilities to be attached to each assumed factor that goes into the earnings estimate, so that various combinations of probabilities and factors may be included. The certainty equivalent approach attempts to adjust the estimate for forecasting risk according to the analyst's desire to avoid this risk. Sensitivity analysis forces the analyst to focus on each factor of the total profit picture and allows him to experiment with possible changes in the various factors and observe the effects on potential profit. Simulation constructs a probability distribution of the potential earnings from randomly selected values for each factor. This portrays the potential earnings pattern for the analyst and allows him to grasp the entire situation more clearly. Finally, the analyst himself may be evaluated in terms of how accurate his forecasts are likely to be. By these evaluations some insight may be gained into the analyst's personal biases.

QUESTIONS

7.1 Distinguish between uncertainty and risk.

7.2 What is the mean of a distribution, and how is it computed? What is the standard deviation of a distribution, and how is it computed?

7.3 What are some of the criticisms of the expected value approach?

7.4 Explain the sensitivity analysis approach to risk forecasting.

7.5 What advantages does the simulation approach have over the sensitivity analysis approach?

7.6 Explain why the analyst's record approach may be considered an indirect approach to forecasting risk.

PROBLEMS

7.1 Compute the mean and standard deviation of the following earnings distribution:

Possible earnings	1.50	1.60	1.70	1.75	1.80	1.85	1.95
Probability	0.05	0.07	0.13	0.20	0.25	0.18	0.12

7.2 An analyst estimates that there is a 75 percent chance that a firm will receive a large contract if next year is a prosperous year for a certain industry. He feels that there is a 60 percent chance of prosperity next year. He estimates that the firm will have the following probability of earnings if it receives the contract, and less than $1 per share if it does not:

Earnings	1.00	1.10	1.15	1.20	1.25	1.30	1.40
Probability	0.05	0.10	0.20	0.30	0.20	0.10	0.05

What is the probability that the firm will earn $1.20 per share if next year is a recessionary year?

7.3 From the following model and cost information, list those variables which when increased 10 percent effect a greater than 10 percent change (either increase or decrease) in profits:

P = total profits
TC = total cost
TR = total revenue
S = selling price of product
X = units of product
FC = fixed cost
VC = variable cost
M = material cost per unit
L = labor cost per unit
A = advertising cost per unit

$P = TR - TC$
$TC = FC + VC$
$TR = X \cdot S$
$VC = X(M + L + A)$
$FC = \$10,000$
$X = f(A) = 10,000A + 1,000$
$M = 0.75$
$L = 1.00$
$A = 0.50$
$S = 5.00$

7.4 Simulate Problem 7.3 using random values for the variables in the analysis. Array the results for each set of variable values to determine which profit is most likely to occur and with what dispersion.

7.5 During the last year, an analyst predicted that out of the 20 companies in a particular industry, 16 would have significant increases in their price. At the end of the year, only 12 did. What is the probability of the analyst's successfully predicting an increase in a stock's price?

REFERENCES

Dyckman, T. R., S. Smidt, and A. K. McAdams. *Management Decision Making under Uncertainty,* London: Macmillan & Co., Ltd., 1969.

Hamburg, Morris. *Statistical Analysis for Decision Making,* New York: Harcourt, Brace & World, Inc., 1970.

Hertz, David B. "Risk Analysis in Capital Investment," *Harvard Business Review,* 42:95–106, January-February, 1964.

Hillier, Frederick S. "The Derivation of Probabilistic Information for the Evaluation of Risky Investments," *Journal of the Institute of Management Sciences,* 9:443–457, April, 1963.

Luce, R. Duncan, and Howard Raiffa. *Games and Decisions,* New York: John Wiley & Sons, Inc., 1957.

Raiffa, Howard. *Decision Analysis: Introductory Lectures on Choices under Uncertainty,* Reading, Mass.: Addison-Wesley Publishing Company, Inc., 1968.

Richmond, Samuel B. *Operations Research for Management Decisions,* New York: The Ronald Press Company, 1968.

Schlaifer, Robert. *Probability and Statistics for Business Decisions: An Introduction to Managerial Economics under Uncertainty,* New York: McGraw-Hill Book Company, 1959.

Yamane, Taro. *Statistics: An Introductory Analysis,* 2d ed., New York: Harper & Row, Publishers, Incorporated, 1967.

Part Three

The preceding part concentrated its efforts on forecasting the future stream of benefits that were to be discounted back to the present. This part turns its attention to exploring the discount factor r.

The discount factor r is revealed by the end of the part to be the summation of all four components: real interest rate i, purchasing power risk p, business risk b, and financial risk f, so that $r = i + p + b + f$.

The discount factor is the denominator of the PDV evaluation framework. The numerator is the future stream of benefits. When the two are combined in the PDV framework, the student of investments should have a working concept of what determines the security prices, how to evaluate a security to his own satisfaction, and how to incorporate the changing events of the financial markets and of the individual corporation into his price evaluation.

The discount factor comprises several factors, each of which represents an adjustment for time or risk. The first factor that this part considers is the time value of money. The time factor in the discount factor is the same as the real rate of interest.[1] In order to evaluate financial assets, it is necessary to know what determines the real rate of

---

[1] That part of the pure interest rate which remains after the purchasing power risk premium is subtracted (see Chaps. 3 and 11).

interest and what causes it to fluctuate. This part is partly devoted to the theories of interest rate determination, the major components and parties involved in interest determination, and the forecasting of interest rates.

The investment implications of the real interest rate on the PDV evaluation framework are discussed. The prevailing PDV of a future stream of benefits has a time factor equivalent to the existing real interest rate. A future PDV of the same stream has a time factor equal to the real interest rate that prevails at this future date. A decline in the real interest rate causes the PDV of a given stream to increase, and a rise in the real interest rate causes the PDV of a given stream to decrease. The potential change in the PDV caused by a shift in the real interest rate is interest rate risk. When the real interest rate is more likely to rise from its prevailing level, the chance of a decline in the PDV is increased. When the real interest rate is more likely to decrease from the prevailing level, the chance of a rise in the PDV is increased. The existing real interest rate reflects this anticipation of a change with a tendency to retard further increases in the real interest rate at "high interest rates" and further decreases at "low interest rates."

The second factor considered in this part is purchasing power risk. Its determination and effect on the pure interest rate are discussed. The real interest rate is demonstrated to be the pure interest rate minus the purchasing power risk premium. Exploration of the theoretical effects of inflation on fixed and variable income securities is undertaken.

The third risk factor explored is business risk. This is the risk connected with the operating environment of the enterprise. This part attempts to explore suggested methods of classifying operating environments to arrive at homogenous business risk classifications and to measure business risk.

The fourth risk factor of the discount factor is financial risk. This is the risk connected with the financing of the firm. Part of this part is devoted to the exploration of leverage, its possible effects on earnings performance, and how it is measured.

Part III explores the components of the discount factor. The first chapters discuss the pure interest rate

$(i + p)$, the factors in the determination of the interest rate, the importance of the Federal Reserve System in the determination of the real interest rate, and the term structure of interest rates. The later chapters examine purchasing power risk and its part in the determination of the pure interest rate, business risk, and financial risk.

8
Interest Rate Risk

Interest rate risk refers to the effect that a change in the pure interest rate[1] has on the PDV of a security. As defined in Chapters 3 and 11, the pure interest rate comprises the real interest rate i plus the purchasing power risk premium p, so that the pure interest rate equals $i + p$. Changes in the pure interest rate can arise from changes in i or p. We postpone the discussion of the purchasing power risk premium and its effect on the pure interest rate until Chapter 11. Meanwhile, the discussions of interest rate risk and determination use the pure interest rate. If all the other factors in the PDV framework remained unchanged, an increase in the pure interest rate, whether it came from an increase in the real interest rate component i or the purchasing power risk premium p, would decrease the PDV. Similarly, a decrease in the pure interest rate would increase the PDV. This may be seen from the PDV evaluation framework in Chapter 3, in which

$$\text{PDV} = \sum_{i=1}^{n} \frac{F_i}{(1+r)^i}$$

where F_i = future benefits in year i

$r = i + p + b + f$

where i = real interest rate factor
p = purchasing risk factor
b = business risk factor
f = financial risk factor

Therefore, if i increases, the denominator increases and the PDV or price of the security decreases. If i decreases, the denominator decreases

---

[1] The pure rate of interest has no associated business or financial risk and is best approximated by a United States government security.

Liquidity preference framework

and the price of the security increases. For example, the PDV of a 19-year, 5 percent United States government bond would be $1,000 if the pure rate of interest were 5 percent. The PDV would rise to $1,132.20 if the interest rate declined to 4 percent and, conversely, decline to $887.50 if the interest rate rose to 6 percent.

Every financial asset is directly affected by changes in the pure rate of interest. It is the common thread that connects all security markets and all security price movements. When the analysts speak of a broad, market price movement, they have to consider the fluctuation in the interest rate risk component of the PDV framework, for it is the major factor that has to move simultaneously in the same direction for all securities. One estimate maintains that approximately 50 percent of the price movement in common stocks is related to these broad, market movements.[2]

Since the pure interest rate risk component is potentially so influential in the PDV framework of all securities, the analyst must know what determines the pure interest rate and what causes it to fluctuate. This chapter explores the liquidity preference and loanable funds theories of interest rate determination. The chapter then demonstrates how the portfolio balance of the securities markets may be disturbed and the effect these disturbances may have on interest rate determination. The effect of interest rate change in the PDV framework is explored.

LIQUIDITY PREFERENCE FRAMEWORK

In the liquidity preference framework, the interest rate is determined at the point at which the supply of money equals the demand to hold money. The interest rate is viewed as the rate necessary to entice potential money holders to demand the money stock supplied.

The money stock is, for the most part, controlled by the Federal Reserve System, the government's monetary authority. At any point in time, the Federal Reserve determines what stock of money it feels will best serve the desired monetary policy and attempts to influence the banking system so as to reach this goal. The Federal Reserve does not respond to the profit opportunities of higher interest rates, as would the profit-maximizing investor, but instead, adjusts the money stock to policy goals. If policy goals change and dictate the desirability of a different interest rate or money supply, the Federal Reserve alters the money supply to foster the new desired interest rate or money supply. In the sense that Federal Reserve–induced money supply variations are dictated by policy decisions rather than the interest rate per se, the

---
[2] B. King, "Market and Industry Factors in Stock Price Behavior," *Journal of Business,* January, 1966.

money supply is relatively interest-inelastic.[3] In Figure 8.1, the money stock M^1 appears as a vertical straight line.

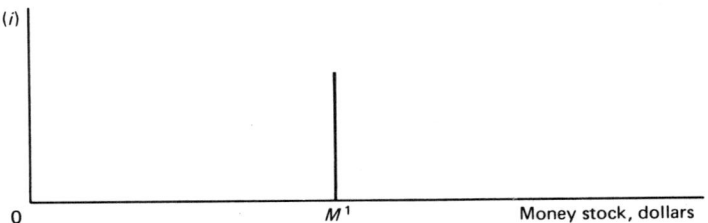

Figure 8.1. Stock of money.

The demand for money has two basic components: the transactions demand and the speculative demand. The transactions demand for money arises out of its capacity as a medium of exchange. As more goods and services are bought and sold, more money is needed to support this trade. As income increases, it may generally be expected that the transactions demand for money will advance in a similar manner, because more goods and services will be bought. Assuming that customary payments habits are maintained as income rises, there should be a definite relationship between income Y and the transactions demand for money M_T, as illustrated in Figure 8.2.

A certain proportion of the money stock will be demanded for transactions at each level of income. In Figure 8.2, the transaction demand for money is assumed to be ⅓ the level of Y, or in algebraic terms:[4]

$$M_T = \tfrac{1}{3} Y$$

The second component of the demand for money, that which must take up the remaining money stock, is the desire to hold speculative balances. Speculative balances are money balances specifically held idle in the anticipation of a capital gain on securities or a higher interest rate. These balances are not used for transactions purposes but are retained for the purchase of securities when the prospects of capital gains are high. When the interest rate is low and securities prices are high,

---

[3] This is a simplistic representation, because the interest rate may deviate from the Federal Reserve's desired target because of factors beyond its control, for example, the public's demand for currency. This deviation will cause the Federal Reserve to alter the money supply in an effort to return the interest rate to the desired level.

[4] The transactions demand may also be curvilinear. For example, see William Baumol, "The Transactions Demand for Cash: An Inventory Theoretic Approach," *Quarterly Journal of Economics,* November, 1952, pp. 545–546, and J. Tobin, "The Interest Elasticity of Transactions Demand for Cash," *Review of Economics and Statistics,* August, 1956, pp. 241–247.

the desire to hold speculative balances is high, because the opportunity cost of forfeiting the low interest rate is small and the probability of a decline in securities prices is considered to be large. The lower the interest rate i, the more speculative balances M_S are demanded. The higher the interest rate, the less speculative balances are demanded, as illustrated in Figure 8.3, because of the higher opportunity cost of hold-

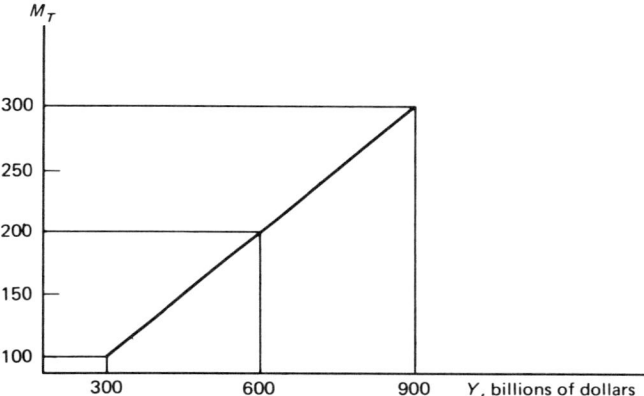

Figure 8.2. Transactions demand for money.

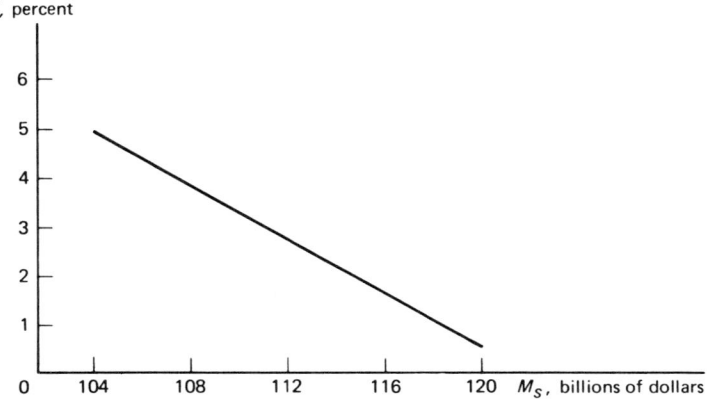

Figure 8.3. Demand for speculative balances.

ing idle balances and the possibility of a capital gain if the interest rate declines. At some very low interest rate, in this case 1 percent, the demand for idle balances becomes very large, perhaps infinite, and the largest possible among speculative balances is held under the current levels of income and money supply, in this case, $120 million. In Figure 8.3, the speculative demand for money is $120 billion at a 0 percent interest rate and declines $4 billion for every 1 percent increase in the interest rate. In algebraic terms this is

$$M_S = 120b - 4b(i)$$

The total demand for money, taken from the example, is the sum of the transactions demand plus the speculative demand:

$$M_T + M_S = \tfrac{1}{3}Y + 120b - 4b(i)$$

This total demand has to equal the fixed money stock M^1; that is, all the money outstanding has to be demanded for either transactions or speculative purposes:

$$M^1 = M_T + M_S$$

With income Y at a certain level, the remainder of the money stock has to be absorbed into speculative balances. This can occur only when the interest rate i is such that people demand the exact amount of the money stock remaining. For example, if income were $300 billion and the money supply were $200 billion, the interest rate would be

$$M^1 = M_T + M_S = \tfrac{1}{3}(Y) + 120b - 4b(i)$$
$$200 = \tfrac{1}{3}(300b) + 120b - 4b(i)$$
$$5\% = i$$

This is the interest rate at which the money supply equals the money demanded, and it is illustrated in Figure 8.4, in which the demand for money $M_T + M_S$ crosses the supply of money M^1.

A Change in the Interest Rate

The interest rate may change if either the supply of money or the demand for money $M_T + M_S$ shifts.[5] In this framework, the demand for money can shift only when the level of income Y shifts, causing increased demand for transaction balances. The supply of money, however, may shift at the discretion of the Federal Reserve System. Shifts here are more frequent and more pronounced than shifts in income and are, therefore, dominant in the short run. A decrease in the money stock in Figure 8.4 to M^2, or $192 billion, would, for example, cause interest rates to rise to 7 percent. At the new $192 billion supply of money the previously prevailing interest rate of 5 percent would not equate the demand with the supply, as demonstrated below:

$$M_T + M_S = \tfrac{1}{3}(Y) + \$120b - 4b(i)$$
$$= \tfrac{1}{3}(300) + 120b - 4b(5)$$
Money demand $= \$200$ billion

[5] This assumes that everything else, such as payment habits, technology, tastes, and financial innovation, is held constant, which may not be an unreasonable assumption in the short run.

There is now $8 billion more demand than supply. In an effort to raise their money balances to the desired level, individuals sell securities. This causes interest rates to rise until the desire for speculative balances is sufficiently curtailed and the demand and supply for money are equated, as illustrated below:

$$M^2 = M_T + M_S = \tfrac{1}{3}(Y) + 120b - 4b(i)$$
$$192 = \tfrac{1}{3}(300) + 120b - 4b(i)$$
$$7\% = i$$

An increase in the money stock would cause interest rates to decrease in the short run.

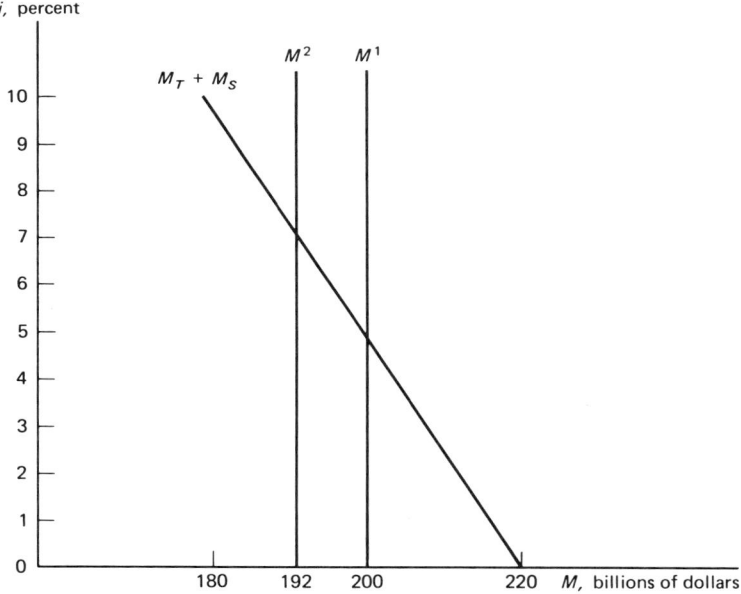

Figure 8.4. Supply and demand for money.

LOANABLE FUNDS FRAMEWORK

The other major monetary theory of interest rate determination is the loanable funds theory. The loanable funds theory attempts to determine the interest rate at which the supply of funds entering the financial markets equals the demand for funds in the financial markets. The usual procedure of the loanable funds analysis is to identify the total supply of funds and the total demand for funds entering the financial market. In general, the higher the demand in relation to the supply, the higher the interest rate necessary to equate the supply and demand.

Supply of Loanable Funds

The three major sources of loanable funds are the net savings of households, the dishoarding of money, and the change in the amount of money supplied by the banking system.

Net Savings. The net savings of households are defined in the national income accounts as the difference between disposable personal income and personal consumption expenditures after borrowings are subtracted. In short, all the income that is not spent or paid out in taxes is savings, and net savings are that figure less personal borrowings. It is what the surplus spending unit has left to lend. Some part of those savings finds its way directly into the financial markets in the form of security purchases; the majority of these savings enters the capital markets through financial intermediaries, such as banks and savings and loan associations. In general, personal savings are not a function of the interest rate but instead depend on the level of personal income. At any particular level of income Y, savings are likely to be a fixed percentage of this income. In terms of Figure 8.5, savings S are independent of the interest rate i and are a vertical, straight line.

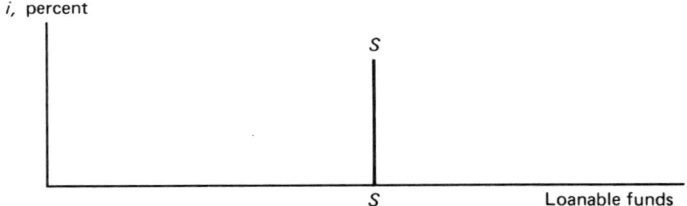

Figure 8.5. Loanable funds provided by savings.

Dishoarding. The dishoarding that may add to the supply of loanable funds is the activation of idle balances. In dishoarding, idle balances are activated. This decision to activate idle balances is directly related to the interest rate, as we saw in the liquidity preference theory. At the higher interest rate, there is less desire to maintain idle balances, because it is more costly to do so at the higher interest rate and potentially profitable speculations begin to appear. Figure 8.6 illustrates the relationship between the desire to maintain idle balances M_S and the interest rate i. Given any particular money stock M, the amount of dishoarding that occurs is the amount by which the actual money stock held exceeds the desired level of idle balances. When the actual amount of money held is more than the demand, the holders attempt to correct this imbalance by lending or investing. As they continue to dishoard, they supply funds to the market in their efforts to reach their desired money holdings. When the actual level of funds is less than the desired holdings, the reverse of dishoarding (hoarding) occurs and funds are withdrawn from the markets.

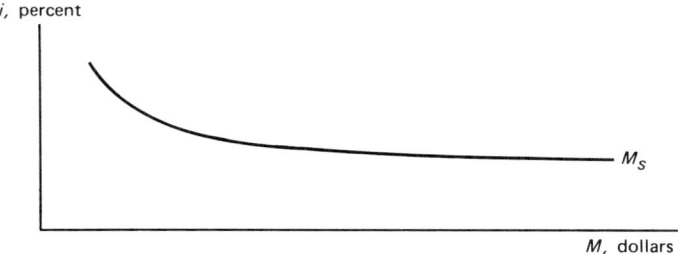

Figure 8.6. Idle balance as a function of the interest base.

Change in Money Supply. The change in the money stock ΔM is associated with Federal Reserve policy. Federal Reserve's moves to increase the money stock tend to provide funds to the financial markets, and its moves to decrease the money stock tend to restrict funds to the financial markets. As in the liquidity preference framework, the money stock is determined independently of interest rate considerations, as illustrated in Figure 8.7.

The total supply of loanable funds S_{LF} is then the sum of the savings S, dishoarding ΔH, and change in the money stock ΔM:

$$S_{LF} = S + \Delta H + \Delta M$$

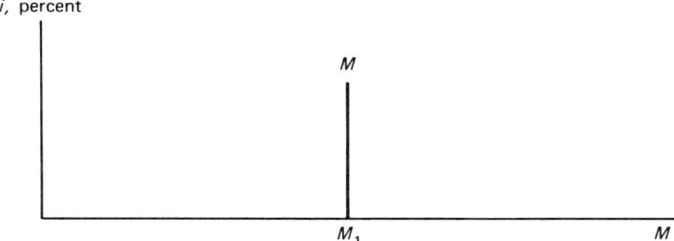

Figure 8.7. Change in money supply in relation to interest rates.

In Figure 8.8, the supply of loanable funds provided by savings is represented by the vertical straight line SS and is determined by the level of income. When we add to this the loanable funds provided by dishoarding, we get the line $S + H$ (see Figure 8.8). Above interest rate i^1 the supply of loanable funds is increased by the effect of dishoarding, because at interest rates larger than i^1 the desire to hold idle bank balances is less than the actual amount held. At interest rates less than i^1 the desire to hold inactive bank balances is greater than the actual money balances, and, in an effort to build up idle balances, people withdraw funds from the markets. To the sum of savings and dishoarding we can add the change in the money stock ΔM, as illustrated in Figure 8.9 to get the total supply of loanable funds. As can be seen in Figure 8.9, the addition of ΔM adds a fixed amount ΔM to all points on the SH line, so that the $S + H + \Delta M$ line is exactly parallel to SH and represents more loanable funds at each interest rate.

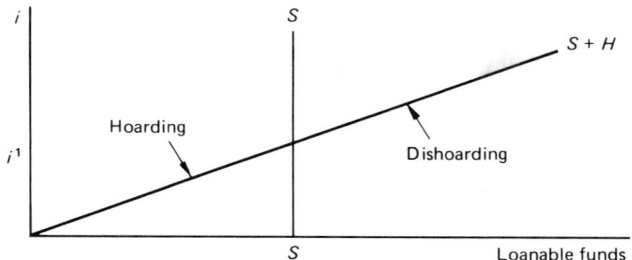

Figure 8.8. Supply of loanable funds from savings and dishoarding.

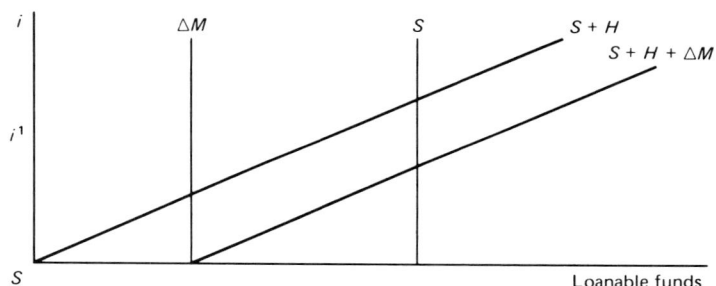

Figure 8.9. Supply of loanable funds from all sources.

Demand for Loanable Funds

The demand for loanable funds comes from the deficit spending units of business and government.

Government Demand. The government's demand for funds is basically independent of the interest rate. It is determined by the difference between tax revenues and expenditures. When the government is running a deficit, its demand for loanable funds increases, and when the government is running a surplus, its demand for loanable funds decreases. As illustrated in Figure 8.10, the government's demand G is interest-inelastic.

Figure 8.10. Government demand for funds.

Business Demand. The business sector's demand for loanable funds is sensitive to interest rates. The higher the interest rate, the less funds businesses demand because of the fewer profitable projects available at these higher rates. Therefore, business's demand for loanable funds (B) may be drawn as in Figure 8.11, with a downward sloping curve.

The total demand for loanable funds D_{LF} is then the sum of the government and the business sector's demand:

$$D_{LF} = B + G$$

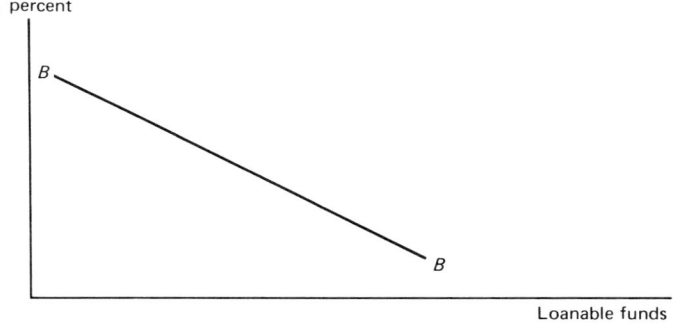

Figure 8.11. Business demand for funds.

Graphically the total demand would appear as in Figure 8.12, as a downward sloping function of the interest rate.

Interest Rate Determination

Where the supply of loanable funds and the demand for loanable funds equate, as in Figure 8.13, the interest rate i^* is determined. Figure 8.13 is Figure 8.12 superimposed on Figure 8.9. In Figure 8.13, the market for loanable funds is in equilibrium at i^*. The interest rate under the loanable funds framework, at this point in time, is i^*.[6] Shifts in either the demand for funds or the supply of funds would cause a new interest rate: For example, an increase in the money supply ΔM would cause $S + H + \Delta M$ in Figure 8.13 to shift downward to the right and force interest rates down. Here, as in the liquidity preference framework, the Federal Reserve has the power to influence the determination of interest rates. It may be the most powerful, because it has specific interest rate targets and the power to adjust the interest rate to its desires, whereas other participants in the loanable funds market are interest-sensitive and must adjust themselves to the interest rate.

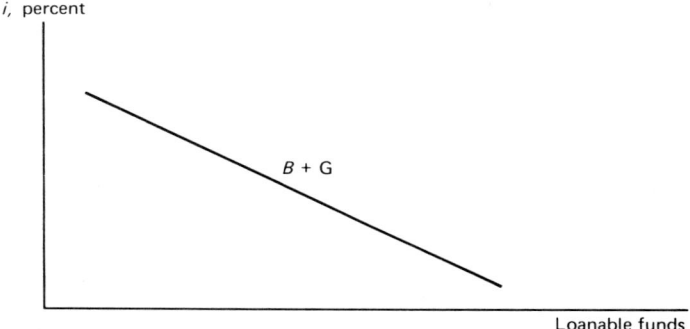

Figure 8.12. Total demand for loanable funds.

PORTFOLIO BALANCE EFFECT[7]

As in the liquidity preference theory, the amount of securities and money held by individuals must be the amount that they desire to hold. If the proportion of money in the portfolio is above the desired percentage, the portfolio holders trade money for securities at higher than previously prevailing prices, forcing up the price of securities and increasing the percentage of the total portfolio that is composed of securities. In the opposite situation, in which the proportion of money held in the portfolio is below the desired percentage, the portfolio holder sells securities at lower than previously prevailing prices to acquire money, forcing down securities prices and increasing the percentage of the total portfolio devoted to money.

[6] This is not necessarily an equilibrium interest rate. If investment plus government spending at i^* does not equal savings, income shifts, causing savings to shift, thus shifting the supply of loanable funds and the demand for loanable funds. See M. Polakoff, et al., *Financial Institutions and Markets,* Houghton Mifflin Company, Boston, 1970, part I, Art. 2.

[7] Much of the following discussion is based on Basil Moore, *An Introduction to the Theory of Finance,* The Free Press, New York, 1968.

Portfolio balance effect 165

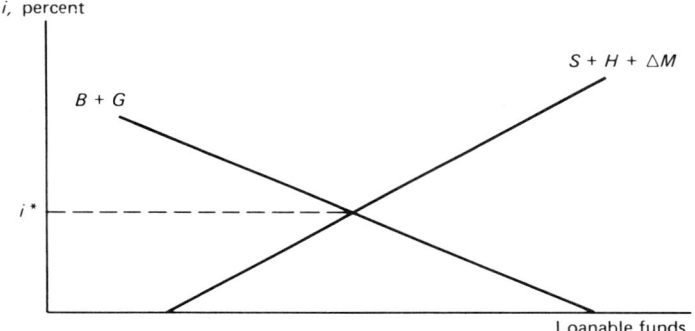

Figure 8.13. Supply and demand for loanable funds.

When portfolio holders are purchasing securities, the interest rate falls. When portfolio holders are selling securities, the interest rate rises. The interest rate settles into a temporarily stable position when the percentage of money desired in the portfolio is equal to the desired percentage. This can be illustrated in Figure 8.14. The desired portfolio balance between money M and securities FA is represented as the PP line. Each point on the PP line represents the desired portfolio balance between M and FA at every interest rate. The lower the interest rate, the higher the desired percentage of money in the portfolio, because the opportunity cost of idle balances is lower and the capital gains potential of securities is lower. Thus, as one moves down the PP line to the right, the desired percentage of money in the portfolio increases.

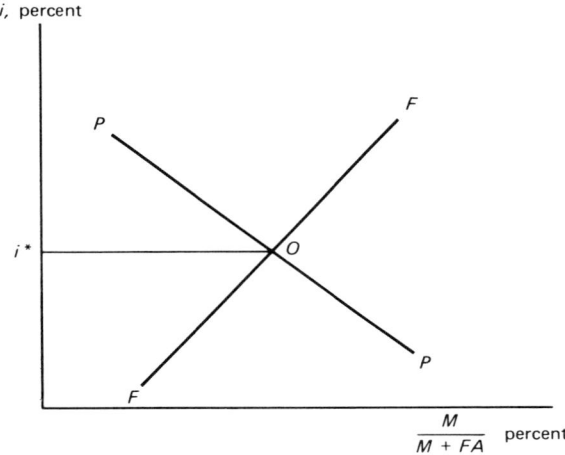

Figure 8.14.

The actual portfolio balance possible within the existing money and securities stocks is represented by the *FF* line. If the actual portfolio balance is not the desired balance at the prevailing rate of interest, portfolio holders adjust their holdings until the actual equals the desired balance at a new interest rate. For example, if the actual percentage of securities is higher than desired, portfolio holders sell securities. This causes securities prices to fall and interest rates to rise, while the value of the money in the portfolio remains constant. This has the effect of increasing the proportion of money in the portfolio. This adjustment process continues until the desired percentage on the *PP* line and the actual percentage on the *FF* line coincide at a point *O* and interest rate i^*. At this point, the existing stocks of money and securities are represented in the portfolio to the satisfaction of the portfolio holders. This position point *O* is maintainable only as long as the actual portfolio maintains these proportions.

At the interest rate i^*, the demanders of loanable funds (businesses and the government), are issuing debt (financial instruments) that may upset the portfolio balance achieved at point *O*. This new flow of securities into the loanable funds market is probably not in the exact proportions as already exist within the existing stocks. This flow of securities at a different proportion shifts the *FF* line and upsets the portfolio balance achieved at point *O*; that is, the *PP* and *FF* lines no longer intersect at i^*. In an effort to absorb these new securities into the existing stocks the portfolio holders adjust their holdings to reach a new point of balance. This adjustment causes price disturbances in the markets. Because the flow of these new securities is continually present in the marketplace, portfolio balance effects are also likely to be experienced on a continual basis. The more disproportionate the new flow, the larger the necessary portfolio adjustment and the greater the price volatility in the markets.

Another portfolio balance disturbance may arise when action is taken to alter the percentage of money in the existing stock of money and securities. This is accomplished when some of the existing securities (money) in the portfolio are exchanged for money (securities) issued by the government for monetary policy purposes. When the Federal Reserve System (FRS) decreases the money supply, it generally does so by exchanging government securities for money held in portfolios. This withdraws the money from the portfolio and increases the stock of securities in the portfolio. After this exchange operation the percentage of money in the portfolio is decreased (a shift to the left in the *FF* curve in Figure 8.14). This exchange process causes the portfolios to be unbalanced at the interest rate i^* in Figure 8.14. In order for portfolio holders to be satisfied with this increased proportion of securities and decreased proportion of money, the interest rate must rise. To increase the money supply, the FRS reverses the process and exchanges its money for the securities in the portfolios. This increases the percentage of money in the portfolio and forces a downward interest rate adjustment.

In the short run, the effect of the flow of new securities on the interest rate adjustment is generally less pronounced than the effect of the monetary authority's altering of the existing portfolio proportions. The immense size of the existing stock of money and securities compared with the relatively small size of the flow of new securities means that adjustments in the existing stocks of money and securities require rather substantial adjustment in the interest rate in comparison with the interest rate adjustment needed to absorb the flow of new securities. The process may somewhat resemble the movement of an iceberg. The flow of new securities is the more obvious top of the berg but the larger part is below the water.

A second reason that a shift in the existing portfolio rather than the new flow seems to dominate in the short run is the adjustment time needed to redress the initial unbalancing. Portfolio holders do not instantaneously adjust their portfolio to a new desired balance whenever it is disturbed. Generally the process requires that the new portfolio balance be determined and adjustment toward it be undertaken in a period of time. The shorter the time necessary to complete this lagged adjustment process, the larger the adjustment burden on the stocks rather than on the flow of new securities. Because the flow occurs in time, it takes a fairly lengthy period for it, building up like sediment, to influence the total adjustment. The influence of a change in the existing portfolio stocks of money and securities, however, on the interest rate adjustment is not so constrained by its size as the flows are. A change in the existing stocks may allow rapid adjustment in the interest rate to return the portfolios to balance. Because the money and securities markets are liquid and capable of rapid, large adjustments, changes in existing stocks are likely to have a greater effect than the flow of new securities in the larger adjustment.

The portfolio balance effect demonstrates the importance of the Federal Reserve System in the more rapid, larger shifts in the interest rate and, consequently, securities prices. As in the liquidity preference and loanable funds framework, the FRS is generally a dominant factor and demands our further study in the next chapter.

The portfolio balance effect also demonstrates how the loanable funds flows and the liquidity preference stocks work in tandem to produce continual market fluctuations in the interest rate and that, in the short run, the larger, more rapid interest rate adjustments occur because of changes in the existing stocks of money and securities in the portfolio. The interest rate may fluctuate as portfolio holders attempt to regain a desired portfolio balance after the flow of new securities has created an imbalance or after the Federal Reserve has created an imbalance among the existing stocks of money and securities. The latter imbalance generally causes the more severe adjustment.

The lags in adjusting to the desired portfolio when the imbalance has occurred make it difficult to predict the interest rate movements. When the portfolio holders adjust rapidly, the effect on the interest rate occurs rapidly. When the portfolio holders adjust slowly, the effect on the interest rate occurs slowly. Because there is so much flexibility in the portfolio holders' timing decision, the adjustment process may very well require different lengths of time to affect the interest rate fully. In addition, lags make it difficult to discern the effect of any particular initial imbalance. As the lagged effect of one initial imbalance begins to blend with that of a more recent imbalance, the two effects become indistinguishable. The time for the interest rate adjustment to be completed and the eventual magnitude of the cumulative influence of these various imbalances become difficult to discern.

INVESTMENT IMPLICATIONS OF INTEREST RATE RISK

In explaining the PDV of a stream of future benefits at a given point in time, the investor must discount each future benefit back to the present by the pure interest rate (the real interest rate, which reflects the time value of money, including consideration for anticipated changes in the rate, plus the purchasing power risk premium). At this given point in time, the appropriate pure interest rate is that which exists on a financial asset with no business or financial risk, such as a United States government security. For example, if the existing pure interest rate were 6 percent, the PDV of $10 received at the end of each year for the next 10 years would be

$$\text{PDV} = \sum_{i=1}^{10} \frac{\$10}{(1+0.06)^i}$$
$$= \$73.59$$

This PDV enables the investor to compare the current market price with his evaluation and determine if, in his opinion, the stock is *overvalued* or *undervalued*. In the evaluation procedure, the existing pure rate of interest is appropriate.

Interest rate risk arises when we attempt to estimate or forecast what the PDV of the same stream will be at a future date. The value of the stream on this future date is dependent on the pure interest rate that exists then. For example, suppose that 1 year later we have the identical stream to that used above; that is, we shall receive $10 at the end of

Investment implications of interest rate risk

each year for the next 10 years. If the pure interest rate had, in the interim, increased to 8 percent, the PDV would be

$$PDV = \sum_{i=1}^{10} \frac{\$10}{(1 + 0.08)^i}$$
$$= \$67.10$$

The identical stream has decreased in PDV solely because the pure interest rate has increased. This decrease in the PDV, which resulted directly from the increase in the pure interest rate, is interest rate risk. General price decreases in financial assets can be explained by increases in the pure interest rate.

If the investor anticipates an upward shift in the interest rate, he should not be willing to purchase the security based on the pure interest rate that presently exists. Although the PDV of the stream may seem undervalued when the interest rate is 6 percent, the PDV will not be so high when the interest rate rises to 8 percent, and the investor suffers a potential capital loss. For example, continuing to use the same $10 stream, at a 6 percent interest rate, the investor should be willing to pay $73.59 for the stream, which 1 year later, because of the rise in the interest rate to 8 percent, would be worth only $67.10. The investor is exposed to a potential $6.49 loss. Many analysts and investors make the error of confining their evaluation to the existing pure interest rate. They decide if the security is overvalued or undervalued in the context of the general market, based on the existing interest rate, only to find that the PDV has changed in the future, because of a change in the pure interest rate.

Just as an increase in the pure interest rate decreases the PDV of a given stream of future benefits, a decrease in the interest rate increases the PDV of a given stream. For example, if the pure interest rate had decreased to 5 from the 6 percent in the first example of the $10 stream, the PDV would be

$$PDV = \sum_{i=1}^{10} \frac{\$10}{(1 + 0.05)^i}$$
$$= \$77.22$$

The PDV would have increased $3.63 solely because the pure interest rate had decreased from 6 to 5 percent.

Note, when the interest rate is "high" and more likely to decline than rise, the PDV is more likely to rise in the future than decline. Interest rate risk, as reflected in the potential decrease in the PDV, is then less than it would be if an increase in the pure interest rate were more likely. Therefore, at a "high" interest rate, where the anticipation of a decrease is greater, interest rate risk is lower than at a "low" interest rate, where the anticipation of an increase is greater. To account for some of the difference in interest rate risk at "high" and "low" interest rates, investors incorporate the risk consideration into the pure interest rate. Thus, at a "low" interest rate, investors are less willing to supply funds (buy bonds) to the financial markets, exerting upward pressure on the pure interest rate; further reductions in the rate are resisted, and part of any potential decline is partially offset by the investors' unwillingness to supply all the funds demanded at the decreased rate. At a "high" interest rate, investors are more willing to supply funds to the financial markets, exerting downward pressure on the interest rate; further increases in the rate are resisted, and part of any potential rise is probably partially offset by the investors' willingness to supply funds at the increased rate. This implies that an increased anticipation of a shift in the interest rate might actually cause the pure interest rate to move in the direction of the expected shift, and security prices to move in the opposite direction, even before some administratively controlled indication of the rate, for example, the prime rate,[8] changes. But the important lesson to learn is that security prices will change from their present levels when interest rates change.

SUMMARY

Interest rate risk is associated with all financial assets. It is the exposure to a decline in the PDV of the asset that results from an increase in the pure interest rate. The pure interest rate comprises the real interest rate, which reflects the time value of money, plus the purchasing power risk premium.

Several conceptual frameworks for the monetary determination of the interest rate have been developed. One, the liquidity preference theory, determines the interest rate where the supply and the demand for money are equal. The supply is determined by the Federal Reserve System. The demand for money comprises the need to use money in transactions and the desire to hold money idle for speculative purposes. The supply and the demand for money are equal at the interest that makes the money demanders content with holding whatever money balances that they have left after satisfying their transactions demand.

The loanable funds theory envisions the interest rate as determined by the intersection of the supply and the demand for loanable funds.

---

[8] The prime rate is the interest rate that the banks charge their best customers and is administratively fixed by the banks.

The price of credit that clears the loanable funds market is the interest rate.

The portfolio effect demonstrates how the balance in the public's portfolio of securities and money can be upset by the issuance of new securities in a proportion that is not equal to the desired proportion that prevails in the present portfolio or by an attempt on the part of the Federal Reserve System to alter the present balance. When the balance is upset, there will be price disturbances in the financial markets as the public readjusts its portfolio to regain the desired balance. The action by the Federal Reserve is the dominant one of the two and causes the more pronounced portfolio imbalances and market disturbances.

Interest rate risk has important implications for investment policy. If the interest rate increases, the PDV of a given stream of future benefits decreases. If the interest rate decreases, the PDV of a given stream increases. Securities that seem to be undervalued in the present market, using the existing pure interest rate to compute the PDV, may seem to have been overpriced at a future date if the pure interest rate rises and, as a consequence, the PDV declines. Of course, if the pure interest rate decreases, the PDV increases, and the security may seem to have been undervalued.

At a "high" interest rate, the anticipation of a decrease in the rate should be greater than at a "low" interest rate, and the interest rate risk is mitigated. This lessening of the risk should retard any further increases in the rate. Conversely, at a "low" interest rate, the anticipation of an increase in the rate should be greater, and further decreases in the rate should be retarded.

QUESTIONS

8.1 What are the determinants of the pure interest rate? Why is a United States government bond a best approximation of the pure interest rate?

8.2 What determines the stock of money?

8.3 What are the chief components of the demand for money, and how are these components expressed functionally?

8.4 How is the interest rate determined in the liquidity preference framework?

8.5 The interest rate changes if either the supply of money or the demand for money shifts. In the liquidity preference framework, what causes shifts in the demand and supply curves?

8.6 Describe the three major sources of loanable funds.

8.7 What determines the government's demand for loanable funds? What determines the business sector's demand for loanable funds?

8.8 Explain how the interest rate is determined under the loanable funds theory.

8.9 Explain the short-run portfolio balance effect on interest rates of a flow of new securities.

8.10 Explain why interest rate risk is lower when interest rates are "high" and higher when interest rates are "low."

PROBLEMS

8.1 If income in billions of dollars is 400, graph the total demand for money, for various rates of interest, if the transactions demand is equal to one-fourth the level of income and the speculative demand equals $150b - 400b(i)$.

8.2 What are the respective interest rates in Problem 8.1 if the money supply equals 226, 230, 242? In the short run, what effect does an increasing supply of money have on interest rates?

8.3 If the speculative demand for money in Problem 8.1 is shifted so that it equals $170b - 400b(i)$, what are the respective interest rates if the money supply again equals 226, 230, 242? What can be concluded about the effects of short-run shifts in the demand for money on interest rates?

8.4 Compute the interest rate from the following system of equations in the loanable funds framework:

$$S = \frac{1}{10} Y$$
$$H = 180b - 300b(i)$$
$$G = T - E = \frac{1}{20} Y - 20h$$
$$B = 300b - 500b(i)$$
$$Y = 400$$

8.5 What is the interest rate in Problem 8.4 if the money stock is increased by $20b$ dollars?

8.6 Assume that most analysts expect a sharp increase in business activity during the next 2 years. They cite the present, relatively low interest rates as a prime stimulant. They expect the interest rates to increase 2½ percent during the period, as a result of an increased demand for funds. A particular government bond with an infinite life and an annual $5 interest payment is selling for $100. How much should an investor be willing to pay for the bond if it is his intention to sell it 2 years hence?

REFERENCES

Dunkman, William E. *Money, Credit, and Banking,* New York: Random House, Inc., 1970.

Homer, Sidney. *A History of Interest Rates,* New Brunswick, N.J.: Rutgers University Press, 1963.

Jackendoff, Nathaniel. *Money, Flow of Funds, and Economic Policy,* New York: The Ronald Press Company, 1968.

Lapkin, David T. *Money, Banking, and the Nation's Income,* Austin, Texas: Business Publications, Inc., 1969.

Lutz, Friedrich A. *The Theory of Interest,* Dordrecht: D. Reidel, 1968.

Moore, Basil J. *An Introduction to the Theory of Finance: Assetholder Behavior under Uncertainty,* New York: The Free Press, 1968.

Polakoff, Murray E., et al. *Financial Institutions and Markets,* Boston: Houghton Mifflin Company, 1970.

Weintraub, Robert E. *Introduction to Monetary Economics,* New York: The Ronald Press Company, 1970.

Woodworth, George Walter. *The Money Market and Monetary Management,* New York: Harper & Row, Publishers, Incorporated, 1965.

9
The Federal Reserve System

The need to study the Federal Reserve System (FRS) in security analysis should be fairly obvious. Because the interest rate is a major factor in determining the price of securities and the FRS is a major factor in determining interest rates, the analyst must understand FRS operations. It is necessary to understand what motivates the FRS to influence the interest rate, so that the analyst is aware of the potential action that the FRS is likely to undertake in a particular situation. The analyst must also know the various tools that the FRS may use in its efforts to reach its policy goals and the possible effects of these tools. It may be very difficult to determine the thrust of FRS policy without a knowledge of the FRS method of operation. It is also necessary that the analyst be attuned to the various indicators of FRS policy, so that he may keep track of the FRS operations. These indicators may give the analyst a clue to the direction and strength of monetary policy and the changing financial environment.

This chapter discusses the goals, the tools, and the indicators of monetary policy. In addition, it explores the relationships between monetary policy and stock prices.

GOALS OF MONETARY POLICY

The FRS has four major policy goals: full employment, price stability, economic growth, and balance of payments equilibrium.

Full Employment

Full employment is attained when all who are seeking work are employed. The Employment Act of 1946 specifically empowered the government to use its resources to facilitate full employment within the constraints of a competitive enterprise system and stable purchasing power.

The reality of 100 percent employment is another matter. At all times there is frictional unemployment. People in these categories of unemployment are temporarily between jobs. These workers have been temporarily displaced by plant relocation, new technology, and similar occurrences but within a relatively short period of time will find new jobs. A more realistic approach to full employment may then be an employment level at which the only unemployment is frictional. This may entail as much as 3 to 4 percent of the labor force's being unemployed. Under these circumstances the FRS may adopt a 4 percent unemployment rate as its guideline in this area. If unemployment rises above this guideline level, the FRS may then direct its policy to encourage employment. Of course, the guideline level of unemployment may vary in time, depending on the policies and economic objectives of the government, and the analyst must be aware of this change.

Price Stability

The goal of price stability implies that the FRS tolerates only an acceptable level of inflation. It is accepted that a certain small amount of inflation may be necessary in a growing economy to facilitate the smooth adjustment of a rapidly changing technology. The question remains, however, as to what is an acceptable rate of inflation. In the past, inflation up to 2 percent per year has been tolerated as a necessary amount. When the FRS becomes concerned with the pace of inflation, the analyst may expect monetary policies to become restrictive and to encourage higher interest rates.

The measurement of inflation presents difficulties. The three most common indices of inflation are the wholesale price index, the consumer price index, and the gross national product (GNP) price deflator. Although these are the most frequently used indices, they all have their shortcomings. For example, the introduction of a new fabric into men's shirts may have caused the price to double but the life of the shirt to triple. In this case, whether price has risen or not is open to serious question. The indices may also reveal different findings. At times, the consumer price index rises while the wholesale price index remains constant. Generally, the analyst must look to statements by members of the Board of Governors, the chief policy-making group of the FRS, to determine the FRS's concern with inflation when the situation is not obvious.

Economic Growth

The goal of economic growth is to encourage a sustainable increase in real output. This is measured by the increases in GNP per capita. What is a sustainable rise in GNP per capita and what is nonsustainable and will degenerate into inflation, however, are vague. The FRS's concern with economic growth seems to arise only during periods of unemployment and elicits an expansionary monetary policy by the FRS. The analyst might, therefore, first watch the employment index in attempting to detect changes in monetary policy. When the government vocally stresses the need for economic growth, it seems that this goal dominates FRS action.

Balance of Payments Equilibrium

The goal of balance of payments equilibrium requires that the United States international accounts in trade and capital movements be in balance. Again, measurement problems make interpretation of the figures difficult. The United States has been running a deficit in its balance of payments that at first received official sanction as a method of supplying the rest of the world with a sound currency system. Periodically, however, these deficits cause concern among the foreign holders of the dollar and instigate crises of confidence. At these points, the FRS usually resorts to monetary policy measures, that is, actions by the FRS that tend to reassure the foreign holders of the dollar's soundness. These measures may include a hike in the discount rate or other moves designed to support the value of the dollar in relation to foreign currencies. Efforts to support the dollar's value tend to increase interest rates. Monetary policy aimed at the balance of payments is usually accompanied by flamboyant speeches that the analyst may clearly recognize as a clue to the FRS's concern with the balance of payments. Frequently, the balance of payments has drawn second place when in conflict with domestic goals.

Priority of Goals

There are no clear priorities among these four goals: As the need for attention in any one of the four general areas becomes apparent, the FRS's thoughts and actions are dominated by their concern with this area. This implies that the analyst must be prepared to follow the indicators within all four areas plus the statements of the FRS to determine which policy goal will next dominate.

It cannot be overemphasized that the analyst must be ever alert to the changing policy direction of the FRS. The largest market adjustments generally occur in conjunction with the turning points in FRS policy. It is these changes in policy which shape future interest rate movements.

Conflicts among the Goals

It may be even more difficult for the analyst to detect FRS policy when two or more areas of concern simultaneously seem to be pressing. When this occurs, the appropriate policy for dealing with the situation may not be obvious. For example, in a period of rising prices and declining employment, the appropriate policy is not obvious. Rising prices call for restrictive money policy and higher interest rates; declining employment calls for expansionary monetary policy and lower interest rates.

The goals of full employment and growth usually call for expansionary monetary policy and lower interest rates. The goals of price stability and balance of payments equilibrium usually call for restrictive monetary policy and higher interest rates. Whenever there is a combination of goals in which one calls for expansionary monetary policy and the other for restrictive monetary policy, the analyst must search for clues as to which policy will prevail. Several times the FRS has tried to combine policies and has, in the opinion of some economists, opted for price stability over full employment and for balance of payments equilibrium over economic growth, although both the evidence and the FRS policy seem to be vague in these situations. At one time, the FRS instituted "operation twist," an attempt to keep short-term interest rates high because of the balance of payments considerations and long-term interest rates low because of full employment considerations. Under this policy, the analyst must be aware of the effect of the different interest rates in his particular area of the financial markets (see Chapter 10 on the term structure of interest rates).

TOOLS OF MONETARY POLICY

The FRS has four major tools for implementing its policy goals: open-market operations, the discount mechanism, reserve requirement changes, and the regulation of interest on commercial bank time deposits.

Open-Market Operations

The FRS alters the securities portfolios of commercial banks and individuals with open-market operations. The operations are conducted daily in the government bond market and are reported weekly in the FRS report. In comparison the other tools are rarely used. When the FRS sells government securities, it exchanges government securities for the money in the public's portfolios. The initial effect of a securities sale is pressure on the securities market, a decline in securities prices, and a higher interest rate. Because the FRS restricts its securities purchases and sales to the United States government bond market and usually to United States Treasury bills, the initial increase in interest rates occurs there first. There may be a lag before the repercussions are felt in the other financial markets, particularly the stock market, as portfolio holders adjust the composition of their portfolios to align with the new interest rates. This adjustment entails selling other types of securities to invest in the now higher-yielding government securities.

The FRS sale of bonds has the effect of reducing the reserves at commercial banks, lessening their liquidity position. This means that the banking system has less money to supply to the loanable funds market. This curtailment of supply tends, in the short run, to increase the interest rate necessary to equate the supply with the demand.

The purchase of securities has the opposite effects. The initial impact is to lower interest rates and to start an expansion in commercial bank reserves. This causes portfolio imbalance as the proportion of money in the portfolio expands, forcing readjustments in other financial markets. This expanded commercial bank reserve position enables the banks to supply more funds to the market, putting downward pressure on the interest rate.

Discount Mechanism

The discount mechanism allows a commercial bank to borrow reserves from the FRS. When the bank is short of funds, it may temporarily borrow additional reserves from the FRS at an interest rate known as the discount rate. The FRS may tighten its willingness to lend reserves by either refusing to lend or increasing the discount rate. A reduction in the availability of funds at the discount window or a higher cost prods the commercial bank to reduce the availability of funds to its borrowers and charge higher interest rates. The FRS may use the announcement of a change in the discount rate as a signal of its monetary policy intentions. This announcement itself may be a clue to the analyst.

Reserve Requirements

The reserve requirement compels the commercial banks to maintain a certain percentage of their assets in cash reserves or on deposit at the FRS. The higher this required percentage, the less per dollar of deposits the banks are able to loan. An increase in the required reserve percentage applies pressure on the banks' ability to supply the loanable funds market and puts upward pressure on the interest rate. This increase may also force a readjustment in the portfolio of some commercial banks as they sell securities to raise the necessary cash reserves. This puts further pressure on the interest rate and upsets the portfolio balance, causing readjustment in all the financial markets.

Interest Rate Regulation

The FRS has curtailed the banks' ability to raise funds during periods of high interest rates by regulating the rates that banks could pay on time deposits. The banks have come to rely on their *certificates of deposit* to attract additional reserves. When the interest rate on these deposits becomes noncompetitive with other interest rates and cannot be raised because of FRS regulation, the banks lose this source of funds.

Without these reserves the banks may be forced to curtail supplying funds to the markets, thereby forcing up interest rates.

INTERPRETING FRS ACTIVITY

Every Friday, the FRS publishes a statement on the principal factors affecting member bank reserves (see Figure 9.1) and indicators of monetary conditions. From these monetary statistics, the analyst should be able to gain information on the direction of FRS policy, the climate for interest rates, and potential changes in general monetary conditions.

Sources

Reserve bank credit
    United States government securities
    Acceptances
    Loans and advances to member banks
    Float
Gold stock
Treasury currency outstanding

Uses

Money in circulation
Treasury cash holdings
Treasury deposits at FRS
Foreign deposits at FRS
Other deposits at FRS
Other FRS accounts

Member bank reserves = total sources − total uses

Figure 9.1. Selected items affecting member bank reserves.

Important indications of FRS policy come from an examination of Federal Reserve credit. Federal Reserve credit consists mainly of the securities owned by the FRS, loans and advances to member banks, and float.[1] An increase in Federal Reserve credit is usually associated with an expansionary monetary policy, and a decrease with a restrictive monetary policy. When open-market operations are expansionary, the amount of government securities owned by the FRS rises as the FRS buys securities. This causes downward pressure on the interest rate. The advances to member banks are the loans made by the FRS through the discount mechanism. An expansion in these loans means that more

---

[1] Float arises in the Federal Reserve's check-clearing process. The FRS gives credit to the bank in which a check is deposited (the collector). If the FRS is unable to notify the bank on which the check is drawn (the payer) within the prescribed time, both the payee and the collector believe that they have the funds, and in effect the FRS has extended credit to the payee until he is notified.

reserves have been made available by the FRS to the commercial banks. This figure has a tendency to rise, however, during restrictive monetary policy periods, because it is here that banks turn for additional funds when the availability of funds declines in other areas. Therefore, this figure must be looked at only in terms of the other factors in Federal Reserve credit. Float is the credit extended by the FRS to the commercial banks to facilitate check clearing. If the mechanics of the check-clearing process are delayed, the amount of float increases. Such delays commonly occur at peak seasonal periods, such as Christmas and Easter holidays, when the slower mail delivery disrupts the clearing process. To get an accurate feeling for monetary policy, the analyst must be aware of unusual movements in float and member bank borrowings. The analyst generally concentrates on the changes in the FRS's government securities account. The analyst must also endeavor to distinguish between defensive and dynamic FRS policy actions.

The FRS is unable to control all the factors involved in member bank reserves, such as currency held by the public. To compensate for this and keep monetary conditions in line with monetary policy, the FRS may undertake open-market operations and discount policies that are not intended to change monetary policy but only to compensate for movements in the uncontrollable factors. Such uses of Federal Reserve credit are *defensive* in that they defend the current policy. Those which are intended to alter monetary policy are *dynamic* actions.

Among the other uses affecting member bank reserves (see Figure 9.1) are gold and Treasury currency outstanding. Among the other uses affecting member bank reserves are money in circulation, Treasury cost holdings, and deposits of the FRS, foreign deposits, and other deposits at the FRS. All these factors are beyond the control of the FRS, and the FRS must compensate for changes in them. For example, if the public decided to hold more money in circulation, member bank reserves would decline. This would alter the commercial banks' ability to supply funds to the financial markets, in opposition to the FRS policy intentions. To bring the member bank reserves position back to the desired level, the FRS might purchase United States government securities. This would be a purely defensive action not intended to shift monetary policy.

When these uncontrollable factors change early in the weekly reporting period, the FRS usually has sufficient time to realize it and is very likely to take a defensive, compensatory action. When these uncontrollable factors occur late in the week, the FRS may not be able to compensate for them before the weekly report is issued. The suggestion has been made[2] that a 6-day average for the factors be taken as the Monday

---

[2] Hobart Carr, "Why and How to Read the Federal Reserve Statement," *Journal of Finance,* December, 1959.

figure and the difference between this figure and that of the previous Wednesday be considered the change that took place early enough in the week for the Federal Reserve to compensate. The difference between the 6-day average and the reported figure of the most recent Wednesday would be considered the changes for which the FRS did not compensate. With this approach the analyst may be better able to judge the degree to which any FRS action was defensive or dynamic.

OTHER INDICATORS OF MONETARY CLIMATE[3]

The various indicators described below reflect the prevailing monetary climate and have in them the seeds of future interest rates and FRS policy. As we have seen, the interest rate is one of the major factors in evaluating a security (the denominator of the PDV framework is partially composed of the interest rate). In addition, the interest rate itself is a major symptom of the money and capital market conditions in which the evaluation of the financial asset is to occur. If the analyst is attempting to forecast future values, he must forecast interest rates, as well as the other factors in the PDV framework, to reflect the future market conditions under which he expects to realize his forecast. The indicators discussed here and especially trends in these indicators offer the astute analyst clues to the future market climate, interest rates, and FRS monetary policy, as well as reflecting present market conditions. Changes in each of the indicators may be taken as a loosening (higher financial asset prices) or tightening (lower financial asset prices) of the financial markets, principally by the FRS. Trends and particularly reversals in trends of these indicators may be insights into changing market conditions.

The money supply, defined as currency in circulation plus demand deposits, is one important indicator of the monetary climate. Increases in the money supply, in the short run, apply downward pressure on the interest rate and increase the liquidity of the economy. Changes in the money supply are the primary motivating force behind portfolio balance adjustments. When the money supply increases to a larger than desired proportion of the public's portfolio, the effort to return the desired balance to the portfolio leads to financial market price adjustments. The FRS may also watch the money supply as a guide in implementing policy.

Member bank reserves are the difference between total sources and uses of reserves (see Figure 9.1). The larger the member bank reserves, the greater the banks' ability to make loans and the potential supply of funds to the markets. When the member bank reserves are in excess

---

[3] See Appendix 9B for the charts of various indicators.

of the required amount, the system is in a position to expand its loan activities. Excess reserves are defined as the difference between actual member bank reserves and required reserves. The relationship among these monetary indicators is illustrated in Figure 9.2.

```
     Monetary Base
  -  Currency in circulation
     Member bank reserves
  -  Required reserves
     Excess reserves
  -  Bank borrowings at the FRS
     Free reserves
```

Figure 9.2. Relationship among monetary indicators.

Free reserves are the difference between the excess reserves and the reserve borrowings of commercial banks through the FRS discount mechanism. When reserves are borrowed, the commercial banks have expanded their ability to lend; but, at the same time, they have restricted their liquidity by increasing their indebtedness to the FRS. As commercial bank borrowings at the FRS increase, the unfettered base from which they can expand shrinks. The FRS generally takes this increase in borrowing as an indication of tightening monetary conditions and uses the free reserves figure as an indication of the banks' ability to supply the demand for loans. The lower the free reserves figure, the tighter the monetary situation and the more the upward pressure on interest rates.

The monetary base is the sum of member bank reserves plus currency in circulation. The FRS considers this figure the primary monetary support for economic activity and may use it as a guide to policy actions. The higher the monetary base, the less the pressure on interest rates to rise, because the banks' potential to supply loan demand is higher.

Because of the increasing importance of certificates of deposit and time deposits as sources of bank funds, the analyst must be cognizant of these figures. Rapid withdrawals of time deposits without replacement from other sources impairs the banks' ability to supply funds to borrowers and causes upward pressure on the interest rate.

The various interest rates themselves and the expectations of interest rate movements are also significant indicators of the monetary climate. We shall see in the term structure of interest rates (Chapter 10) that the interest rate on various maturities may yield insight into future interest rate movements. The commonly used interest rates are connected with the markets in which banks raise funds. These include the rates on Eurodollars,[4] Federal Funds,[5] and competing liquid instruments, such as commercial paper, all of which indicate the degree of liquidity within the banking system. A high interest rate on these funds usually accompanies tight conditions in the banking system. The discount rate and the prime interest rate, which banks charge their most credit-worthy customers, are other indicative interest rates, although they are administratively determined and tend to lag behind movements in other rates.

The FRS is also guided by the amount of loans outstanding at commercial banks. If the level of commercial bank loans is relatively high in relation to reserves and deposits, it is taken as an indication that the banking system is tight and will be unable to continue supplying funds at the present rate. Interest rates might be expected to rise in such a situation.

LIQUIDITY THESIS OF STOCK PRICES

Beryl Wayne Sprinkel contends that monetary changes lead stock price movements because of the changing liquidity that accompanies monetary changes.[6] Sprinkel examined business cycle data from before the First World War and found that stock prices tended to lead economic activity. While the economic activity was still rising, stock prices had already turned down and continued down after the peak in economic activity had passed. Before the trough in economic activity had been reached, stock prices started rising and were usually well above their lows when the business cycle bottomed out. Sprinkel concluded that "stock prices and economic activity typically move in the same direction a little over two-thirds of the time but go in opposite directions nearly one-third of the time, and this is the third that is the most interesting, most difficult to predict, and yet potentially most profitable."[7]

Sprinkel also observed that the monetary changes, as measured by the rate of growth in the money supply, had a longer lead over economic activity than stock prices did. He concluded that monetary changes lead stock prices (see Figure 9.3). Sprinkel observed that the average lead

---

[4] Eurodollars are dollars owned by foreign accounts and borrowed by United States banks to support their lending activity.

[5] Federal Funds are 1-day, interbank loans from a bank with excess reserves to a bank with insufficient reserves. This rate is particularly sensitive to short-run liquidity conditions and is usually among the first to indicate changing market conditions.

[6] Beryl W. Sprinkel, *Money and Stock Prices,* Dow Jones-Irwin, Inc., Homewood, Ill., 1966.

[7] *Ibid.,* p. 118.

of monetary growth change to the business cycle peak was 19 months, compared with 4 months for stock prices. Before the upturn in the business cycle, the average monetary lead was 7 months, and the average stock price lead 5 months.

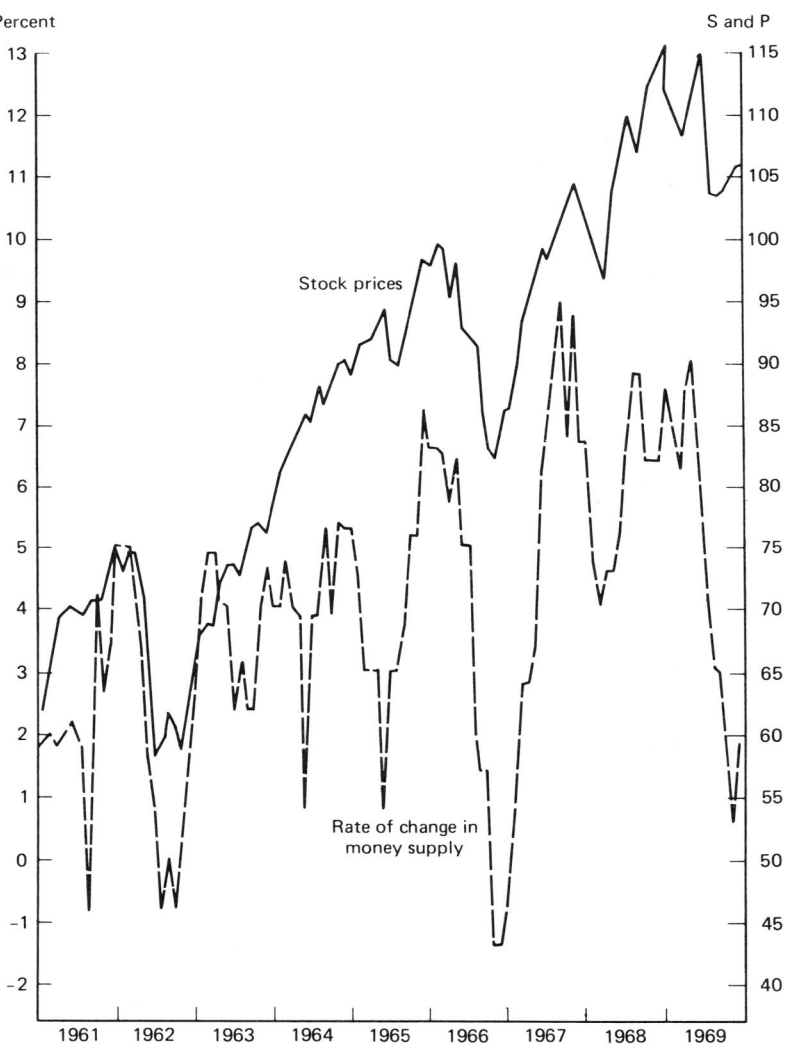

Figure 9.3. Stock prices and change in money supply.

Source: Standard and Poor's 425 Industrial Average, Survey of Current Business, Annual Rate of Monthly Change, Six-month Moving Average, (based on Federal Reserve Bulletin).

Without testing, but observing that this lead was highly variable, Sprinkel applied this observed lead relationship to the Standard & Poor

425 Stock Industrial Index. Taking a 6-month moving average of the annual rate of monthly change in the money supply, he assumed that declining stock prices would occur 15 months after the peak in monetary change and that rising stock prices would occur 2 months after the bottom in monetary change. The results showed that, on the average, the monetary signals were given within 8.1 percent of stock market peaks and 8.6 percent of stock market troughs. Where the monetary signal was incorrect, Sprinkel explained that those stock price movements were unrelated to basic economic conditions but instead were related to some other forces, such as Second World War political considerations.

One consideration that Sprinkel failed to elaborate on is the difficulty of detecting the peaks and troughs in an indicator as variable as changes in monetary growth. As may be seen in Figure 9.3, even in retrospect, the exact determination of the peaks and troughs is difficult. It is even more difficult to distinguish the turning point when working with the most recent data.

Causal Relationship

The causal relationship between monetary changes and stock prices is in the desired degree of liquidity in the portfolios of the public. At first, as business activity grows, the public demands more liquidity for transaction purchases. This is first accomplished by conserving cash balances and using previously inactive balances. Second, as interest rates rise and the economy approaches full employment, the Federal Reserve System starts to tighten the money supply to combat potential inflation. This causes a tightening of the liquidity, and the public starts to adjust its portfolio out of less liquid assets into more liquid ones. Third, the attempt to adjust portfolios to more liquid positions spreads throughout the financial markets, and the full effect of the change in liquidity is felt in the markets; and security prices reach their lowest levels. Fourth, after the liquidity effect has worked through the markets, it reaches into the demand for real goods, such as cars and machinery. The demand for real goods shrinks as the public continues to seek liquidity, and economic activity declines. Because the change in the money supply must first work its way through the financial markets before affecting real economic activity, stock prices decline before economic activity.

The reverse process occurs during the upswing in stock prices. As economic activity declines, the desire for liquidity diminishes. Usually, the Federal Reserve System is now expanding the money supply to combat the economic decline and is adding liquidity. With less need for liquid assets and more liquidity than desired, the public shifts out of very liquid assets, like savings deposits, into less liquid assets, like bonds. As this shift continues, the range of assets affected increases and eventually the still less liquid assets, such as stocks, are purchased, and stock prices rise. After the adjustment has worked through the financial markets, the effects begin to be felt in the demand for real goods. And again, the financial markets, including stocks, have turned up before economic activity.

It is worth noting the difference between the liquidity thesis and the PDV framework. In the liquidity thesis the changes in liquidity work directly on the demand for assets and cause, at the peak, a shift from the less liquid stocks to the more liquid bonds. This implies that first stock prices fall and then bond prices, as people move from the less liquid stocks to the more liquid bonds. The PDV framework allows liquidity to work through the interest rate, and therefore, at the peak, the sale of the more liquid bonds has to occur before stock prices are affected. This implies that bond prices fall and then stock prices. This seems a little more logical, because the Federal Reserve System alters the money supply with operations in the bond markets and because the economy's primary store of liquidity and most sensitive area to changes in liquidity needs is in the bond market.

SUMMARY

The importance of the Federal Reserve System in the determination of interest rates makes it necessary to examine its operations and understand its motives. The analyst who is able to analyze the Federal Reserve System's actions correctly has added insight into interest rate risk.

The Federal Reserve System is motivated to action in an effort to achieve its goals of full employment, price stability, economic growth, and balance of payments equilibrium. When the economic indicators reveal that one or more of these goals is not being met, the FRS attempts, through monetary policy, to push the economy toward a satisfactory performance in this area. The different goals evoke different policy operations and may sometimes be in conflict with one another. At this time, it is the analyst's responsibility to determine which goal has priority.

To accomplish its goals, the FRS has the tools of open-market operations, the discount mechanism, reserve requirements, and the regulation of interest rates. By careful observation of these tools and other monetary indicators, the analyst may be able to detect the direction and degree of monetary policy and relate it to interest rate prospects.

The liquidity thesis of stock price movements maintains that changes in the money supply growth rate are a cause of stock price movements. The proposed thesis is that the changing liquidity needs of the public and the changing liquidity supplied by the FRS cause portfolio imbalances that must be worked out through financial asset price adjustments and then finally through the portfolio of real assets.

QUESTIONS

9.1 Explain the major policy goals of the Federal Reserve System.

9.2 What indexes are commonly used to measure inflation? What are their shortcomings?

9.3 Describe the four major tools used by the FRS to implement its monetary policy.

9.4 What effect does the sale of bonds by the FRS have on commercial banks?

9.5 Explain how changes in the discount rate may signal changes in the FRS's monetary policy.

9.6 What are the components of Federal Reserve credit? What do changes in the amount of credit signal?

9.7 Distinguish between defensive and dynamic FRS policy actions.

9.8 Define the following terms and explain their significance as monetary indicators:
(a) Money supply
(b) Member bank reserves
(c) Excess reserves
(d) Free reserves
(e) Monetary base

9.9 According to Sprinkel, what are the relationships among economic activity, stock prices, and monetary changes?

9.10 Distinguish between the liquidity thesis and the PDV framework.

REFERENCES

Carr, Hobart C. "Why and How to Read the Federal Reserve Statement," *The Journal of Finance,* 14:504–519, December, 1959.

Dunkman, William E. *Money, Credit, and Banking,* New York: Random House, Inc., 1970.

The Federal Reserve System Purposes and Functions, Washington, D.C.: Board of Governors of the Federal Reserve System, 1963.

Freund, William C., and Edward D. Zinbarg. "Application of Flow of Funds to Interest Rate Forecasting," *The Journal of Finance,* 18:231–248, May, 1963.

The Investment Outlook, New York: Bankers Trust Company, 1970.

Klein, John J. *Money and the Economy,* New York: Harcourt, Brace & World, Inc., 1965.

Lapkin, David T. *Money, Banking, and the Nation's Income,* Austin, Texas: Business Publications, Inc., 1969.

Mayer, Thomas. *Elementary Monetary Policy,* New York: Random House, Inc., 1968.

Roosa, Robert V. *Federal Reserve Operations in the Money and Government Securities Markets,* Federal Reserve Bank of New York, 1956.

Samuelson, Paul A., et al. *Controlling Monetary Aggregates,* Federal Reserve Bank of Boston, 1969.

Sprinkel, Beryl Wayne. *Money and Stock Prices,* Homewood, Ill.: Richard D. Irwin, Inc., 1964.

Woodworth, George Walter. *The Money Market and Monetary Management,* New York: Harper & Row, Publishers, Incorporated, 1965.

Appendix 9A
Interest Rate Forecasting

Several attempts to build interest rate forecasting models within the loanable funds framework have been undertaken. The central approach is to identify the various users or demanders of funds and the various suppliers of funds and then to estimate the amount of funds demanded or supplied by each at a particular interest rate. Because the demand and the supply are estimated independently, the two are not equal in the initial estimating procedure; instead there is a gap between the projected supply and the projected demand. To close this gap and bring equality to the supply and demand, as must exist for the loanable funds market to clear, the interest rate must adjust. For example, if projected demand exceeded projected supply, the interest rate would have to rise, as in any supply-demand situation. The rise in the rate would curtail some of the demand and bring forth additional supply until the two were equal.

Table 9A.1 illustrates an estimated supply and demand framework. The demanders are the deficit spending units—those units in the economy who spend beyond their individual savings in order to supplement their investment programs. The suppliers are the surplus spending units and the financial intermediaries who gather the funds from the surplus spending units and channel them to the deficit spending units. The securities offered by corporations and governmental units, in the form of bonds and stocks, comprise one of the major demands in the loanable funds market. The securities purchased by individuals and financial intermediaries provide the funds supplied. The forecaster must attempt to estimate the amount of funds demanded by each of these units during the coming period. This requires that the forecaster be familiar with the factors that influence each category of demand. The demand for investment funds mainly comes from corporations, home buyers, and governmental units.

TABLE 9A.1 Estimated Supply and Demand for Loanable Funds (in $ billions)

Funds demanded (securities offered)		1969 (projected)
Investment funds		
Real estate mortgages	28.5	
Corporate bonds	15.0	
Corporate stocks	1.6	
State and local governments	9.5	
Foreign securities	1.7	
Term loans	1.0	57.3
Short-term funds (including consumer credit)		29.1
Federal government		3.4
Total funds demanded		89.8
Funds supplied		
Savings institutions		
Life insurance companies	8.9	
Pension funds	13.0	
Fire and casualty insurers	3.0	24.9
Deposit type savings institutions		15.5
Investment companies		1.8
Commercial banks		21.0
Business corporations		10.9
Other investors		11.0
Residual: individuals and others		4.7
Total funds supplied		89.8

SOURCE: Banker's Trust Investment Outlook for 1969.

Corporate demand is influenced by the interest rate, the prospects for profit, the need for liquidity, the internal funds available for financing, the expected rate of inflation, tax policies, and other factors. The forecaster must analyze all the factors that have implications for the corporate demand for funds and decide the level of demand that he expects from this demander at a specified interest rate.

The federal government's demand for funds is influenced by its expected revenue and spending actions. The state and local governmental units are more sensitive to local bond referendums and elections than to any particular interest rate. When interest rates on state and local government securities exceed legal ceilings, however, this category of demand declines, because these governmental units cannot legally sell bonds at higher rates.

Real estate mortgages are another major category of demand for funds. The analyst seeks to estimate this demand in light of statistics on household formations, new housing starts, housing permits, the existing stock of housing, apartment vacancy rates, and other factors at the assumed rate of interest.

Another major category of demand is the short-term loans and credits demanded by the business sector and the consumer. Here again, at the specified rate of interest, the forecaster estimates the demand from this category based on such things as personal income, buyers expressed intentions, business inventories, and any other information that he considers pertinent to the demand for short-term funds. Once the individual categories have been estimated—and the categories may be as finely drawn as the forecaster chooses—the estimates are summed and the total demand figure derived.

Next, the forecaster repeats the process for the suppliers of funds. The major suppliers to the market are the savings institutions and the banking system. Among the savings institutions, the forecaster must decide on the amount of funds that the life insurance companies, the savings and loan associations, the mutual savings banks, and the corporate pension funds are each going to supply. To a great extent, the amount that they supply depends on the rate of interest that they pay their depositors, the need for life insurance, and the enlargement of pension fund requirements. The banking system, including the Federal Reserve System, supplies the market with funds, depending to a great extent on Federal Reserve policy and commercial bank lending activity. The state and local governments, through the pension funds that they administer for their employees, supply funds to the market. The United States government, through its trust funds, such as social security, and the lending activities of its agencies, also supplies funds to the market.

The *residual* suppliers are the foreign investor, the individual investor, and the corporation seeking investments in securities. These suppliers are the most sensitive to the interest rate. The forecaster must estimate their supply to the market at the specified interest rate, fully aware that it is in these *residual categories* of suppliers that most of the adjustment to close the gap centers. After estimating all the suppliers, the forecaster sums them to find the total supply of funds to the market.

When the total supply is compared with the total demand, the gap appears. The direction in which the interest rate must move is readily apparent from the relationship of the two totals. If the supply exceeds the demand, the interest rate must fall if sufficient demand is to be generated and sufficient supply curtailed to bring equilibrium to the market. If the demand exceeds the supply, the interest rate must rise. The degree of the rise or fall in the interest rate is indicated by the magnitude of the gap. The larger the gap, the larger the change in the interest rate from the initially specified level to bring equilibrium to the market.

To determine the interest level necessary to bring equilibrium to the markets, a new interest rate is specified, and the process of estimating the supply and demand at this new level of interest is repeated. The process is repeated until the forecaster feels that he has the interest rate that equates the supply and demand for funds. Of course, the computer simplifies the task of repeating the calculations.

Although this process of interest rate forecasting has not been extremely accurate in the past, the potential for at least detecting the direction of interest rate change is good. As economists are uncovering more of the factors involved in the investment processes of each supplier and demander, more and more accuracy may be introduced into the forecast.

Appendix 9B
Monetary Indicators

Prepared by Federal Reserve Bank of St. Louis

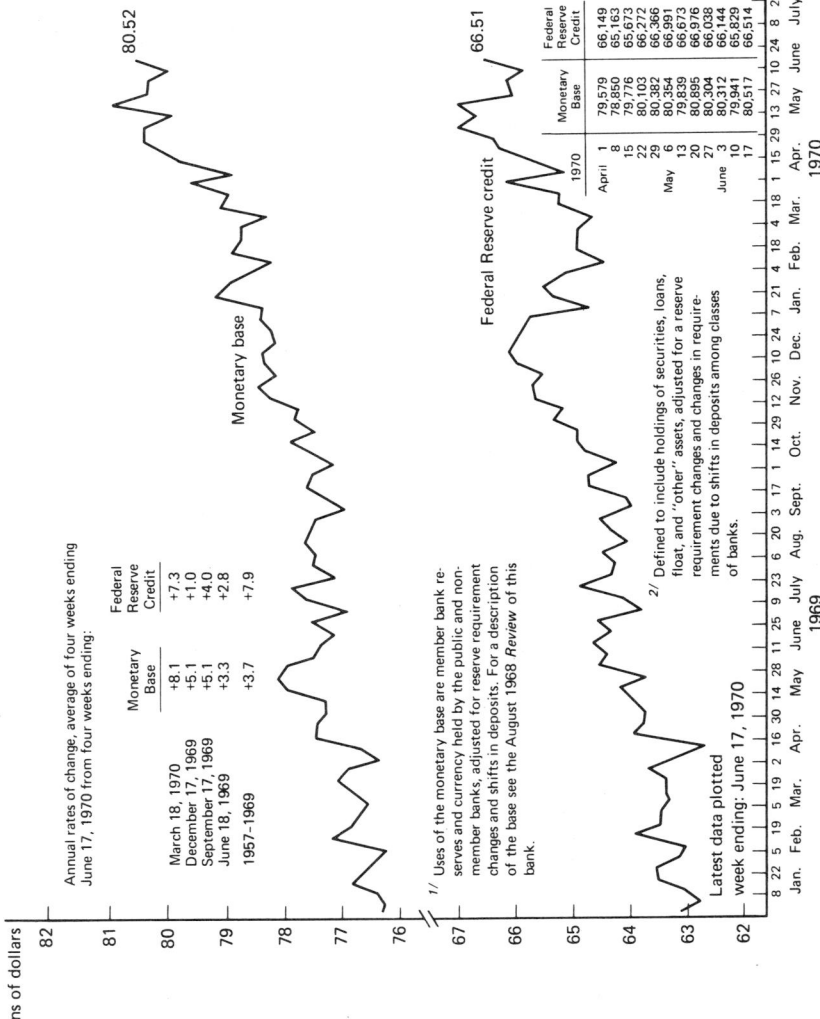

Figure 9B.1. Monetary Base,[1] Federal Reserve Credit,[2] Averages of Daily Figures, Seasonally Adjusted by This Bank.

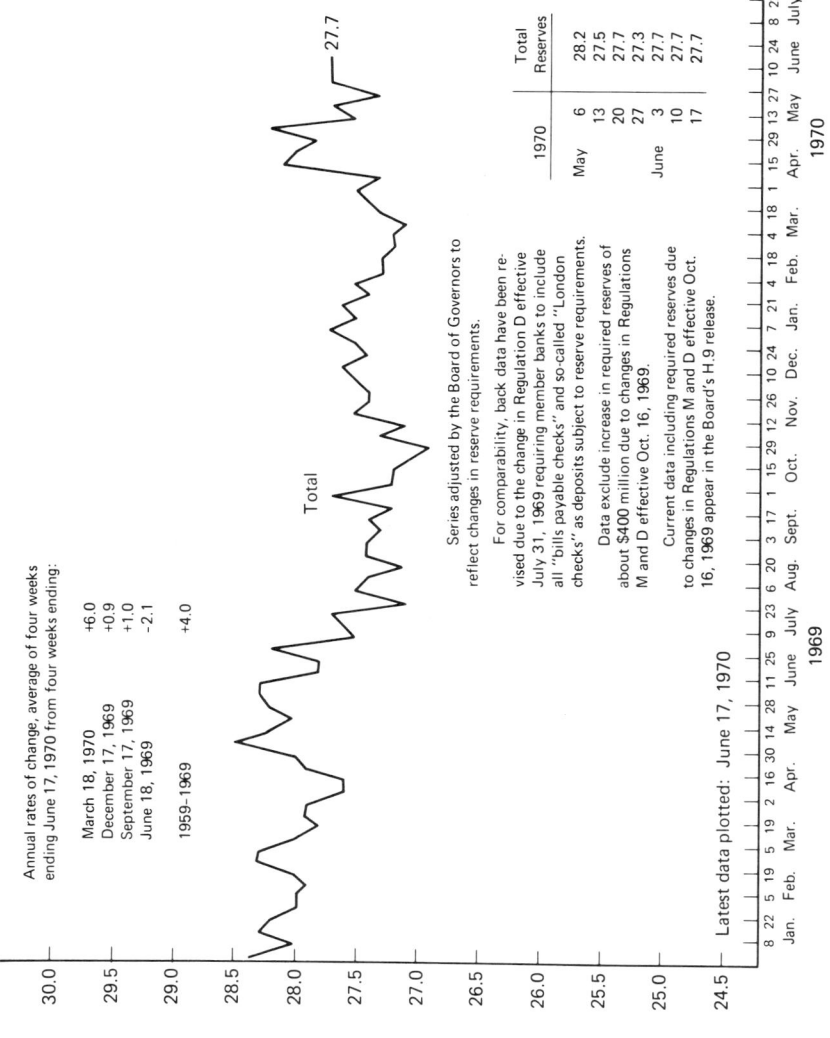

Figure 9B.2. Reserves, All Member Banks in the Nation, Averages of Daily Figures Seasonally Adjusted.

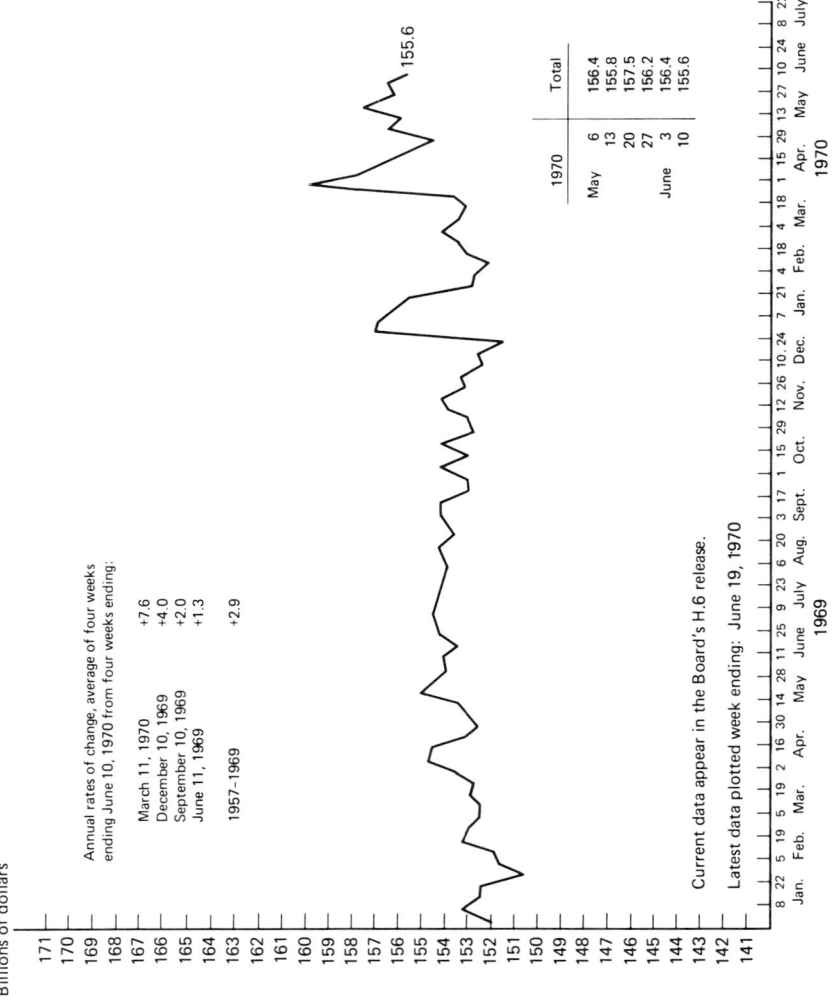

Figure 9B.3. Demand Deposit Component of Money Stock, Averages of Daily Figures Seasonally Adjusted.

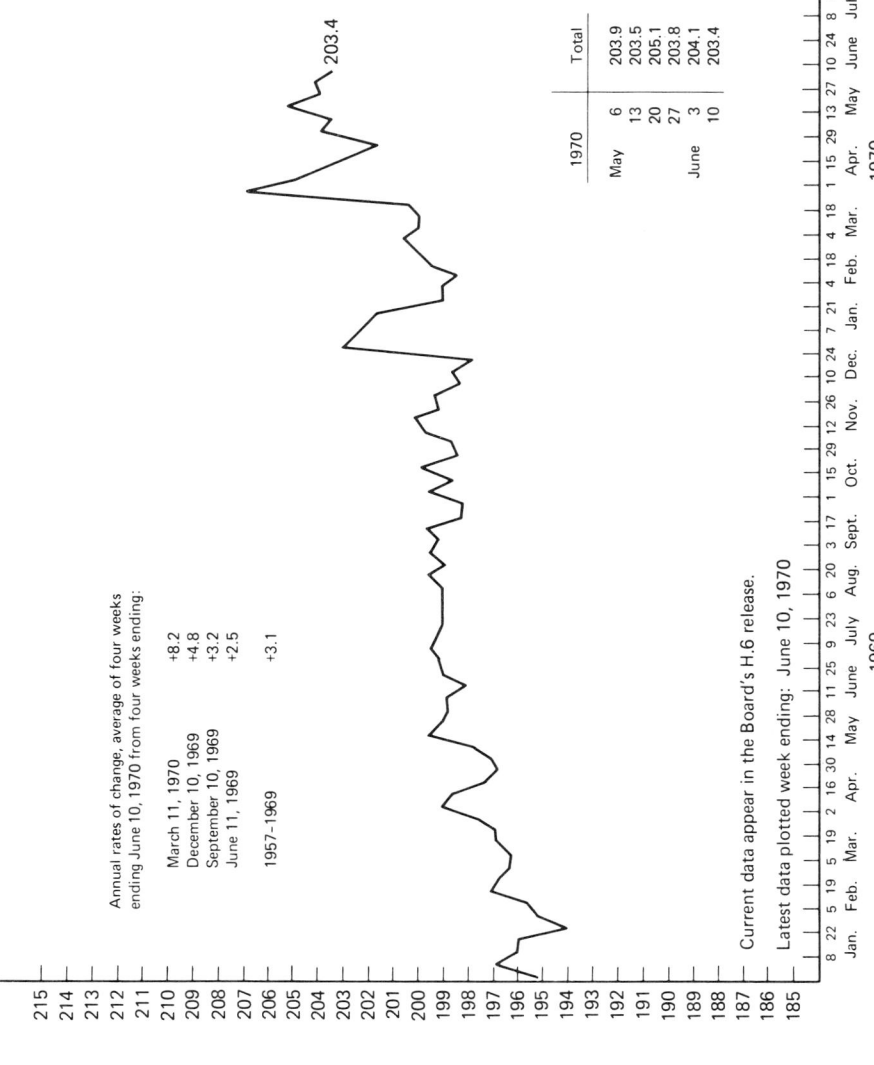

Figure 9B.4. Money Stock, Averages of Daily Figures Seasonally Adjusted.

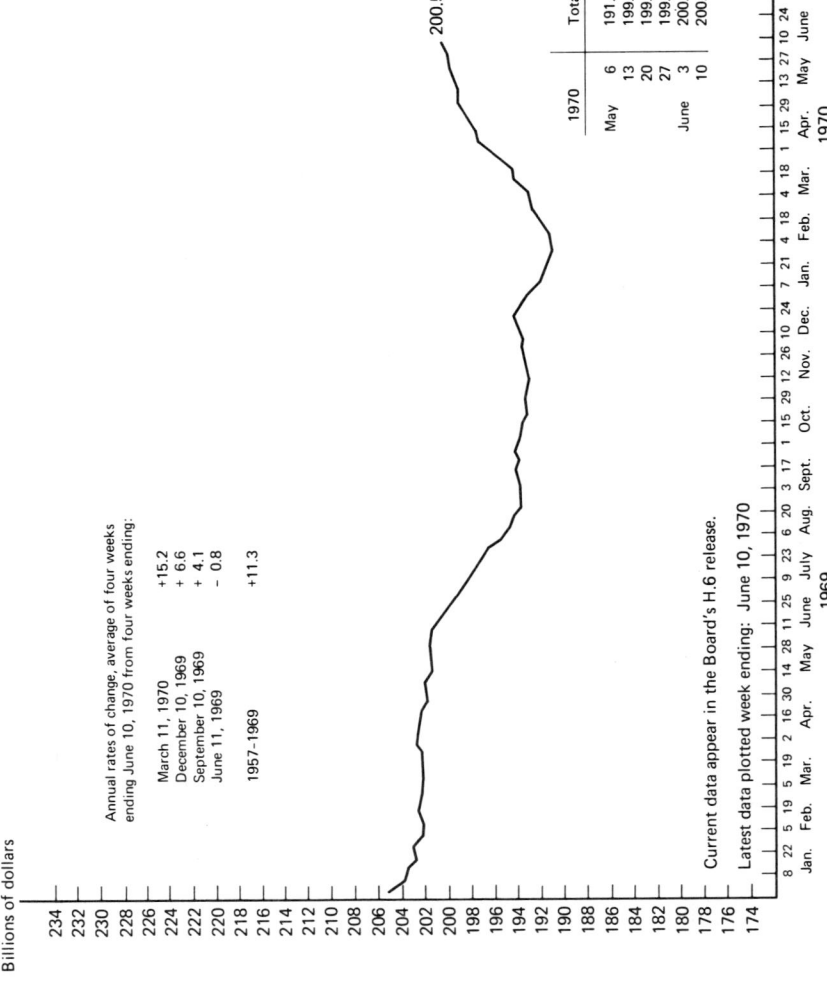

Figure 9B.5. Time Deposits, All Commercial Banks, Averages of Daily Figures Seasonally Adjusted.

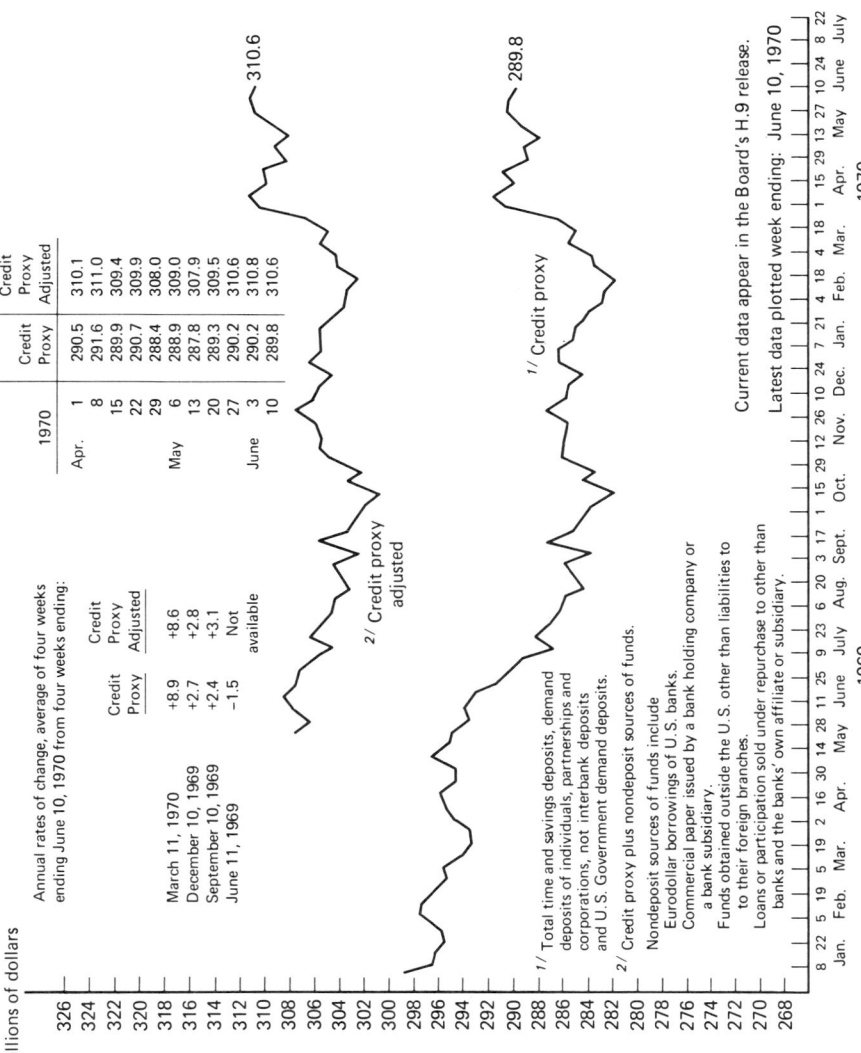

Figure 9B.6. Member Bank Deposits Subject to Reserve Requirements[1] (Credit Proxy), Averages of Daily Figures Seasonally Adjusted.

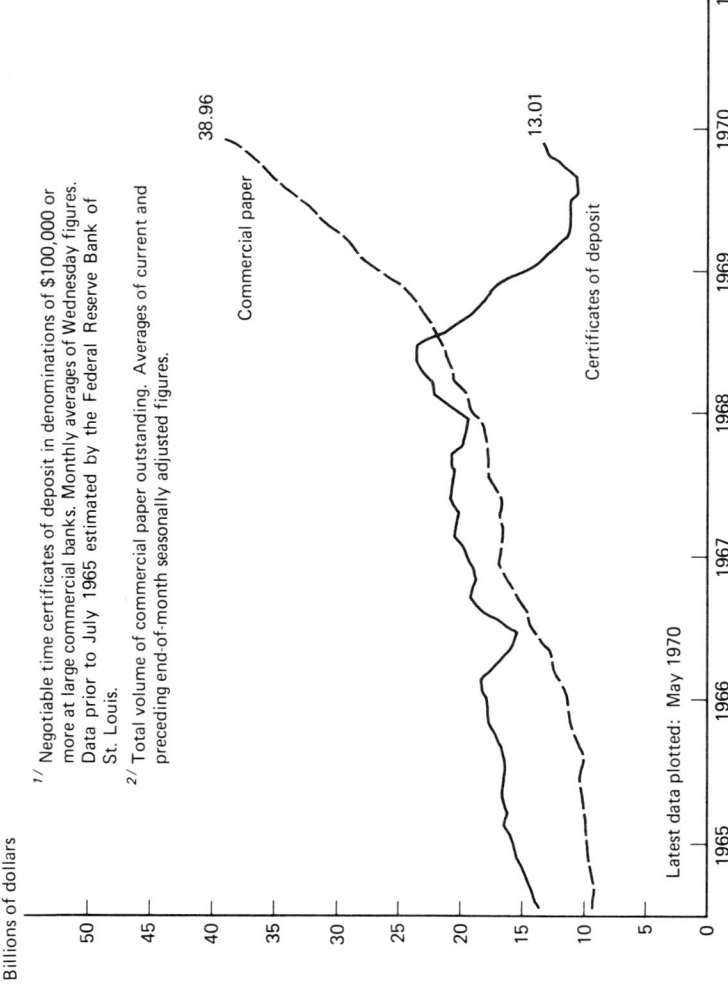

Figure 9B.7. Certificates of Deposit[1] and Commercial Paper[2] Outstanding Volume.

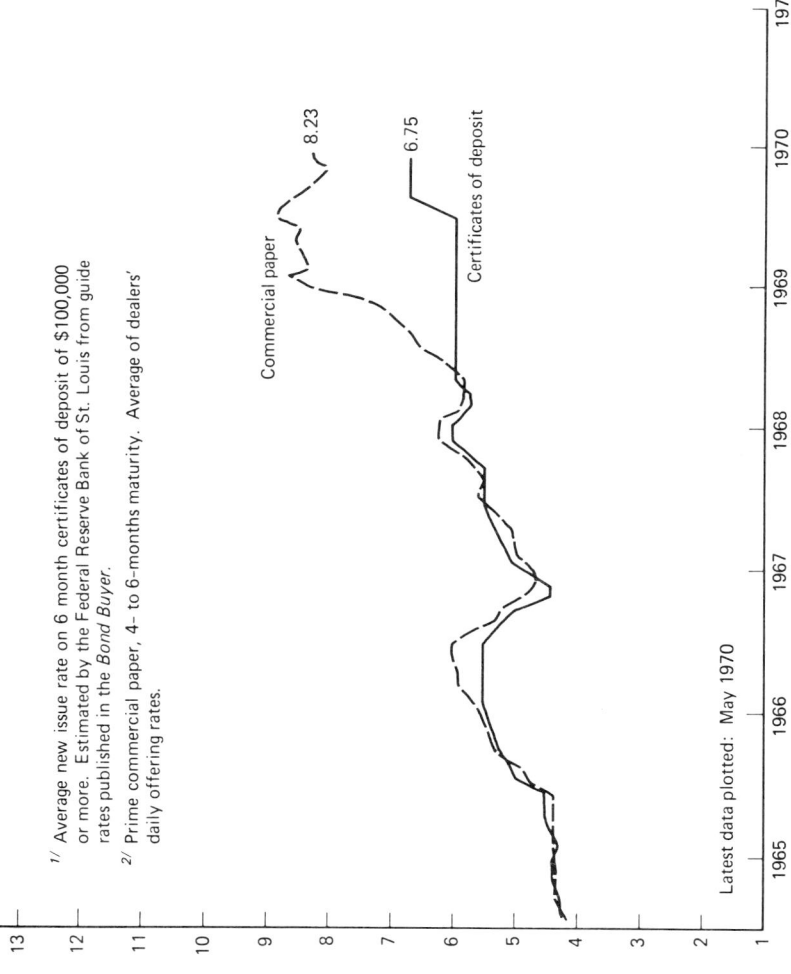

Figure 9B.8. New Issue Rate on Certificates of Deposit,[1] Dealers' Offering Rate on Commercial Paper.[2]

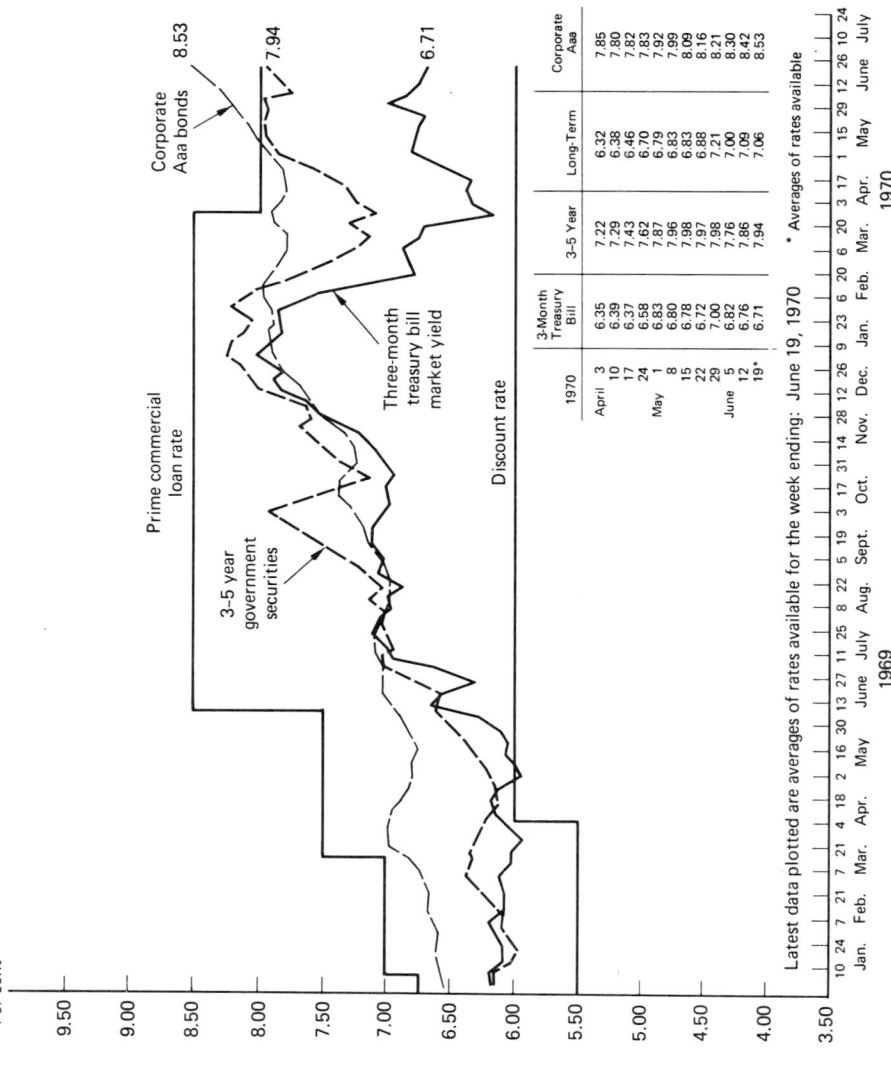

Figure 9B.9. Yields on Selected Securities, Averages of Daily Rates Ended Friday.

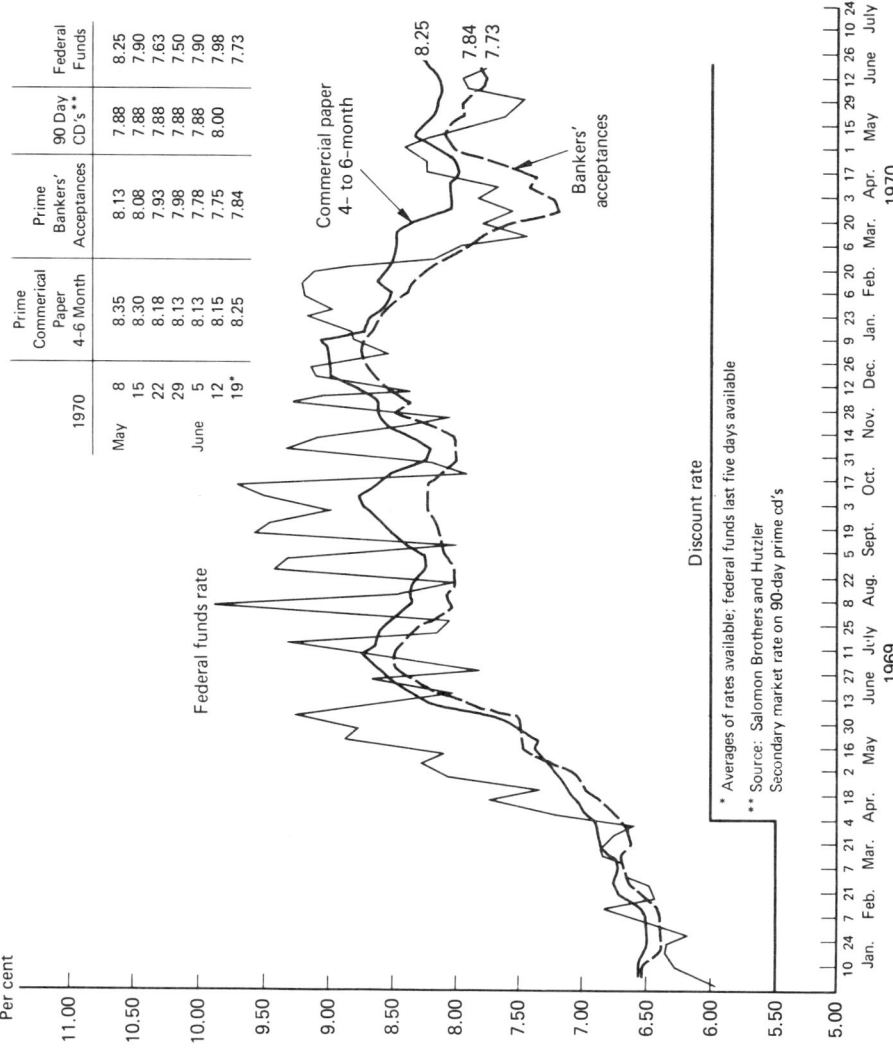

Figure 9B.10. Selected Short-term Interest Rates, Averages of Daily Rates Ended Friday.

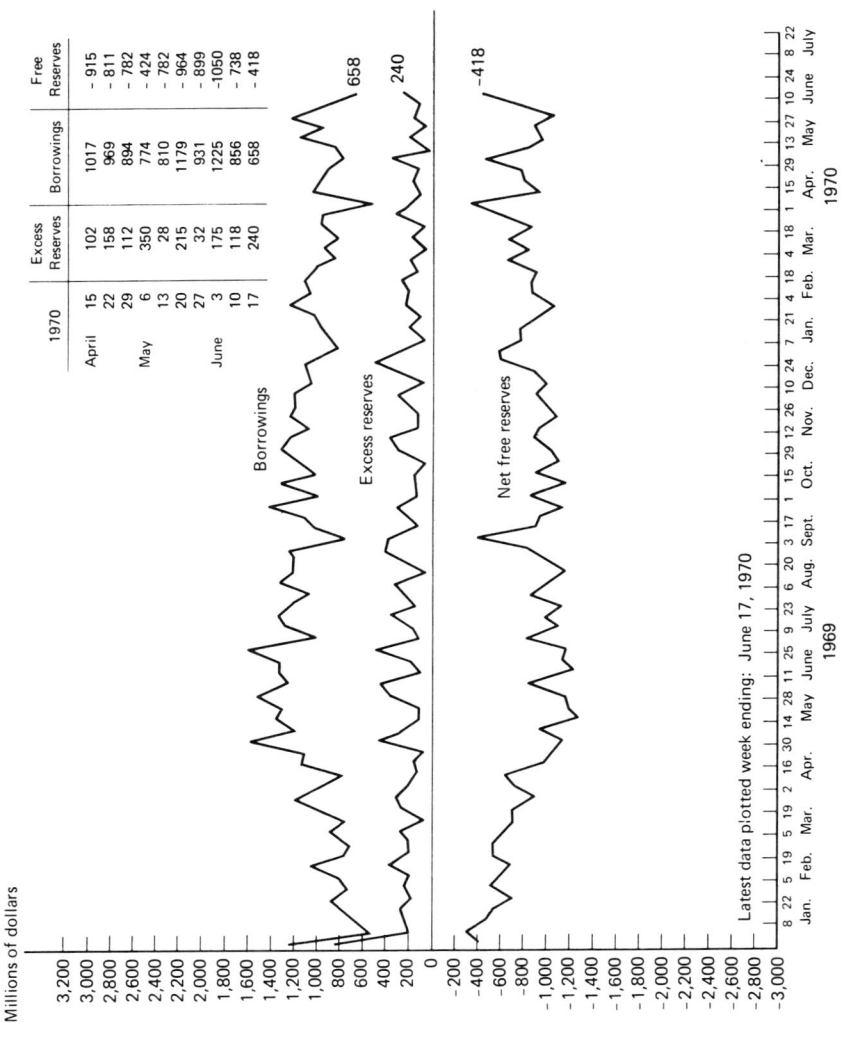

Figure 9B.11. Borrowings and Excess Reserves, All Member Banks in the Nation, Averages of Daily Figures.

10
The Structure of Interest Rates

Up to this point we have been discussing the interest rate as if it were one figure. In reality, however, there is a spectrum of interest rates prevailing in the financial markets at any point in time. There is the spectrum of rates known as the term structure of interest rates. This spectrum describes the rates among securities of the same risk but different maturities. For example, all United States government bonds, regardless of maturity, are of the same quality.[1] But all United States government bonds do not have the same yield. The interest rate varies among the maturities, so that a government bond of 1-year maturity may yield 3 percent and a government bond of 5-year maturity may yield 5 percent.

There is also the spectrum of rates among securities of the same maturity but different risks. This is known as the yield spread. For example, the yield on a United States government bond might be less than the yield on a corporate bond of the same maturity. The former's yield is less, because it has only the interest rate factor i and the purchasing power risk premium p; the later is exposed to business and financial risk as well.

The implications of a term structure of interest rates are quite direct for the analyst who is concerned with the analysis of bonds. Does he commit himself to the long-term bonds or the short-term bonds strictly on the basis of yield, or are the interest rate risks and purchasing power risks involved with the various maturities sufficient to alter his decision? Is there any method by which the analyst might increase his return by purchasing different maturities? In order to answer these questions, the

[1] United States government bonds have no business or financial risk, and all respond to the same changes in interest rate and purchasing power risk. However, the degree of the response in the price may vary with the maturity. See B. Malkiel, "Expectations, Bond Prices and the Term Structure of Interest Rates," *Quarterly Journal of Economics,* May, 1962, pp. 199–206.

analyst must be familiar with the yield curve, the form it may take, the effect of maturity on yield and price, and the theoretical framework within which these yield curves are constructed. Equipped with this knowledge, the analyst may be in a position to behave more rationally in the bond market.

The effect of the term structure of interest rates on stock prices is not so apparent. Because interest rates do play a large part in stock price determination, it is important to study all the aspects of the interest rate. But it is vague as to which of the maturities within the term structure is the most influential on stock prices. The temptation is to assume that the long-term maturities, perhaps the longest of the entire spectrum, are the most influential because of the infinite time horizon associated with the PDV stock evaluation framework. This fails to recognize the counter argument that the most influential interest rate is that which most directly competes for the investor's dollar purchase. If the investor is interested in the short term, it may very well be the short-term rate that is the most influential in his evaluation of common stocks. At the present state of knowledge there is little evidence to support either the short-term or the long-term interest rate as the most appropriate in stock evaluation. It is fortunate for the investor that the entire spectrum of interest rates tends to move in the same direction. All that is required of the analyst is that he himself be aware of which rate he is most concerned with, according to his own time horizon and utility. If he does this, he places himself on the schedule of potential transactors and in the appropriate market position.

There may also be informational content about interest rate risk (Chapter 8) in the yield curve. If investors' expectations are incorporated into the term structure of rates, the direction and magnitude of expected changes in the pure interest rate are revealed in the curve. The investor who examines the yield curve for its informational content about expected future interest rates may not be so readily unaware of prospective interest rate changes.

The yield spread is also of concern to the analyst. The behavior of the yield spread in the business cycle and the market cycle has been used by some to predict future market trends and to judge the present stage of the market cycle. Other analysts have used the yield spread behavior to attempt to increase their return on their investments.

This chapter examines the yield curve and its variations, the relationship of the yield and price movements of bonds to their maturity dates, the theories of the term structure, and the cyclical behavior of the yield spread.

YIELD CURVE

The yield to any bond is the discount rate that equates the future stream of benefits to the present price. We can see that the yield is the discount factor r, where

$$\text{PDV} = \frac{I}{(1+r)^1} + \frac{I_2}{(1+r)^2} + \frac{I_3}{(1+r)^3} + \frac{I_n}{(1+r)^n} + \frac{P_n}{(1+r)^n}$$

where I = annual interest, dollars
r = discount factor
PDV = prevailing market price of bond
P = return of principal
n = year

For example, a 4 percent 20-year, $100 par bond paying $4 per year in interest and selling for $87.45 in the marketplace would yield 5 percent to maturity:[2]

$$\$87.45 = \frac{4}{(1+0.05)} + \frac{4}{(1+0.05)^2} + \frac{4}{(1+0.05)^3} + \cdots + \frac{4}{(1+0.05)^{20}} + \frac{100}{(1+0.05)^{20}}$$

The yield is based on the annual interest paid to the bondholder and the return of capital expected at maturity. To remain competitive with the current market yield, the price of the bond must move inversely with the interest rate. If the current market yields rose to 6 percent, the price of the 4 percent 20-year bond would have to decline to $76.89:

$$\$76.89 = \frac{4}{(1+0.06)} + \frac{4}{(1+0.06)^2} + \frac{4}{(1+0.06)^3} + \cdots + \frac{4}{(1+0.06)^{20}} + \frac{100}{(1+0.06)^{20}}$$

Conversely, if the current market yield fell to 3 percent, the price of the bond in this example would rise to $114.96:

$$\$114.96 = \frac{4}{(1+0.03)} + \frac{4}{(1+0.03)^2} + \frac{4}{(1+0.03)^3} + \cdots + \frac{4}{(1+0.03)^{20}} + \frac{100}{(1+0.03)^{20}}$$

Table 10.1 illustrates a yield table from which it is possible to determine a yield to maturity, given the selling price of the bond, the original yield

---

[2] This yield may be approximated with the following formula:

$$\text{Yield} = \frac{\text{annual coupon payment} + \dfrac{\text{capital gain (loss)}}{\text{no. years to maturity}}}{\dfrac{\text{current price} + \text{redemption value}}{2}}$$

at issue (coupon rate), and the years remaining to maturity. For example, the $87.45 price of the 4 percent 20-year bond has a 5 percent yield, according to the table.

TABLE 10.1 Prices of a 4 Percent $100 Bond for Various Maturities and Current Market Yields

	Current market yield				
Years to maturity	3%	4%	5%	6%	7%
½	100.49	100.00	99.51	99.03	98.55
1	100.98	100.00	99.04	98.09	97.15
2	101.93	100.00	98.12	96.28	94.49
3	102.85	100.00	97.25	94.58	92.01
5	104.61	100.00	95.62	91.47	87.53
7	106.27	100.00	94.15	88.70	83.62
10	108.58	100.00	92.21	85.12	78.68
15	112.01	100.00	89.53	80.40	72.41
20	114.96	100.00	87.45	76.89	67.97
25	117.50	100.00	85.82	74.27	64.82
30	119.69	100.00	84.55	72.32	62.58
50	125.81	100.00	81.69	68.40	58.52
100	131.64	100.00	80.14	66.76	57.19

SOURCE: *Comprehensive Bond Values Tables*, 4th pocket edition, Financial Publishing Company, Boston, 1958.

To derive the yield curve, the analyst must take all the bonds of the same risk and determine the yield for each maturity. The series of bonds with the most uniform risk is probably United States government bonds. Their risk exposure is limited to interest rate risk and purchasing power risk, and maturities are, theoretically, exposed to the same changes in interest rates and inflation. Therefore, we concentrate the discussion on the term structure in the government bond market.

Once the analyst has the various bond maturities with equal risk, he must compute the yield for each maturity. In this case of the United States government bonds, this requires the yield on maturities ranging from days to almost 30 years. Between the two extremes is an array of time periods. For example, Table 10.2 would be a listing of the maturities and their corresponding yields. A graphic representation of Table 10.2 is Figure 10.1. Here the analyst would plot the years to maturity on the horizontal axis and the yield that corresponded to this maturity on the vertical axis. Each yield on the curve is comparable with the other, because the differences in annual interest payments have been eliminated in the computation of the yield to maturity.

TABLE 10.2 Hypothetical Maturities and Associated Yields

Years to maturity	Yield
1	2½%
2	2¾%
3	3
4	3¼%
5	3½%
10	4
15	4½%
20	5
25	5
30	5

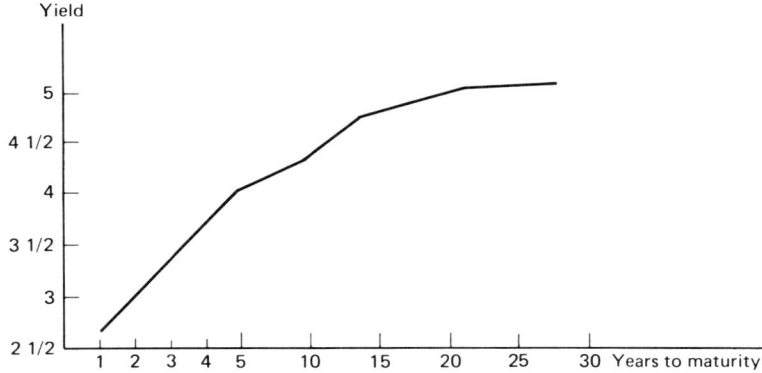

Figure 10.1. Yield curve.

TYPES OF YIELD CURVES

The yield curve generally assumes four different shapes, as illustrated in Figure 10.2. The upward-sloping yield curve is characterized by lower yields in the shorter-term bonds and higher yields as the length of time to maturity increases. The downward-sloping yield curve is characterized by higher yields in the shorter-term maturities and lower yields as the length of time to maturity increases. The flat yield curve is characterized by the same yield throughout the spectrum of maturities, so that the short-term and the long-term maturities have the same yield. The fourth yield curve is the humped yield curve, so called because the curve first rises and, after reaching an apex, falls as maturities lengthen. The appearance of the curve is such that there is a hump either shortly after the most immediate maturities or toward the middle or intermediate-term maturities.

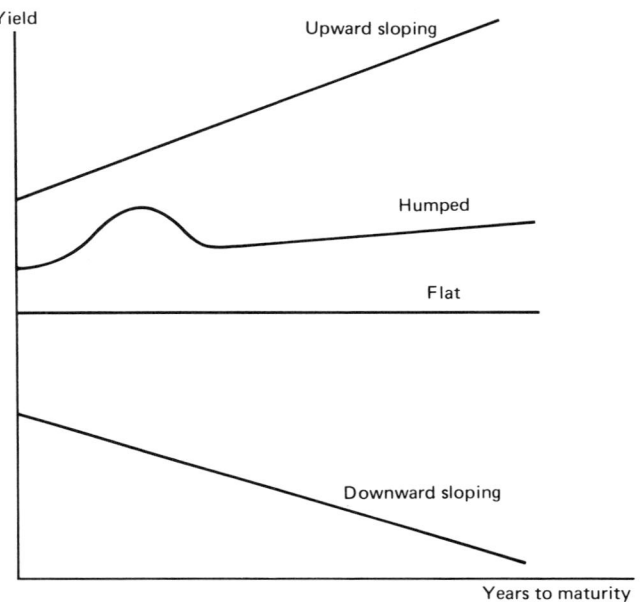

Figure 10.2. Types of yield curves.

Generally, a particular shape of the yield curve is associated with a particular stage in the business cycle. Each of the explanations of the term structure, to which this chapter shortly turns, offers an explanation of the various shapes within the context of the theory and the business cycle. Each shape may also have different implications for interest rates and financial market behavior. First, however, we must explore the relationship of the relative maturities to the price and yield of the bond.

BOND MATURITY, YIELD, AND PRICES

We have already touched on the inverse relationship between bond yield and price. As may be seen in Table 10.1, the price of the bond falls as the current market yield rises. In Table 10.1 the price of the 4 percent 20-year bond drops from $114.96 when the current interest rate is 3 percent to $67.97 when the current interest rate is 7 percent. The mathematics of this inverse relationship are fixed. It must occur whenever interest rates change, but the impetus and the process of change are not connected with this fixed relationship. The impetus and process of change find their origins in the loanable funds market and the portfolio balance effect. Recalling the theory discussed in previous chapters, the interest rate necessary to equate the supply and demand for new funds may not be the same as that which prevailed in the previous markets. The interest rate on the new funds would upset the previous balance in the bondholders' portfolios, and in an effort to regain a desired balance, these bondholders would adjust their portfolio of bonds by either buying or selling in the markets. If the adjustment process calls for the sale of bonds, the price of bonds declines, and the interest rate must rise. The interest rate falls if the adjustment calls for the purchase of bonds.

As may be seen in Table 10.1, a change in the current market rate of interest causes the price of longer-term maturities to fluctuate more than that of shorter-term securities. Note in Table 10.1 that a change in the current market interest rate from 4 to 5 percent causes the bond price of the 1-year maturity to decline from $100 to $99.04 or 0.96 percent; the 10-year maturity bond price declines from $100 to $92.21 or 7.79 percent, and the 20-year bond price declines from $100 to $87.45 or 12.55 percent. Again this is a fixed, mathematical relationship that must be so under the PDV formula. The longer the term to maturity, the larger the absolute price adjustment to bring the yield on the future benefits in line with the current yields, because the adjustment occurs in the difference between the return of the principal of the bond and the price paid in the market. Because the return of the principal is more distant for the longer maturities, it is worth less because of the time value of money. Therefore, a bigger adjustment is needed in the present to bring the yields, including the return of principal of the bond, in line with the market.

Another fixed relationship is that for any given change in the current market price, the yield on the shorter-term bonds fluctuates more than that on the longer-term bonds. This is the reverse relationship of the price movements associated with yield changes.

There are historically observed, but not necessarily fixed, relationships among the price, yield, and maturity of bonds. The entire term structure of rates tends to rise and fall together, although not necessarily to the same degree along the entire maturity spectrum. In a period of rising interest rates the analyst could reasonably expect both the long- and short-term rates to rise. Disturbances in one sector of the spectrum may be expected to transmit themselves to the other sectors, although the full effect of the disturbance may be dampened, because the yields on the shorter-term securities fluctuate more than those on the longer-term securities. Thus, in the market cycle, the analyst may expect all interest rates to fluctuate, with the most fluctuation in yield occurring in the shorter-term securities and the most fluctuation in price occurring in the longer-term securities.

TERM STRUCTURE THEORIES

Segmented Markets Framework

The rigid segmented markets framework suggests that the market for bonds is segmented into separate submarkets according to maturity of the bonds and that the participants in each submarket are locked into and unwilling to move into another submarket. The participants who buy bonds in each maturity range do not move to another maturity range, because of possible legal restrictions and portfolio requirements, regardless of expected interest rate fluctuations. For example, the commercial banks have traditionally confined their activity to the more liquid, shorter-term securities, because they must be in a position to meet the demands of their depositors almost immediately. Unlike the banks, life insurance companies, do not experience sudden, perhaps unexpected, demands. They, therefore, confine their investment to those bonds with the longer, less liquid maturities.

Similarly, the supply of bonds in each maturity depends on the time period for which the funds are needed or the type of asset to be purchased with the borrowed funds. If the funds are borrowed to finance capital investment, such as a new plant, long-term bonds are sold so as not to impair the liquidity position of the borrower. Therefore, the supply of bonds to the market is also restricted to various submarkets.

With both the supply and demand for bonds restricted to submarkets, the interest rate in each submarket is determined by the supply and demand in this particular submarket, independently of the other submarkets. This also implies that the bonds in one maturity range are not substitutes for those in another. In this case, an oversupply in the long-term maturities would depress prices and raise yields in the longer-term submarket without affecting the yields and prices of the short-term bonds.

The empirical evidence does not support the rigid inflexibility of the market segmentation framework. Although it is found that certain institutions concentrate their portfolios in either the long- or short-term maturities, none of the institutions is so inflexible that it does not substitute among securities in a relatively wide range of maturities.[3] In the aggregate, the maturity composition of institutional portfolios is found to be variable. The supply of bonds is also found to be relatively variable in relation to interest rates. At the higher levels of interest rates the sale of bonds tends to be deferred, and many corporations sell short-term obligations to meet their immediate needs.[4] Deferral of state and local municipal bonds is also common at the higher levels of interest rates. An examination of individual commercial bank portfolio procedures also suggests that there is more flexibility in purchasing among the various maturities than is maintained in the rigid segmentations framework.[5] These results suggest a less rigid segmentation in which long- and short-term participants move to the intermediate-term segment if it is attractive.

The less rigid segmented market framework retains sufficient validity and empirical support so that it aids in explaining the various shapes of the yield curve. The upward-sloping yield curve, which is characteristic of the declining phase of the business cycle, is associated with (1) an increased demand for short-term securities, (2) a decreased supply of short-term securities, and (3) an increased supply of longer-term securities. During the economic downturn, businesses reduce their inventory and liquid receivables. This allows them to repay their short-term borrowings and curtails the demand for short-term funds. At the same time, commercial banks are experiencing an accelerated inflow of demand deposits and have excess funds that must be invested. This creates an increased demand from the banks for the shorter-term securities that commercial banks generally hold for liquidity reasons. With the increased demand and the decreased supply in the shorter-term segment of the market, the prices of the securities are bid up and the yields fall. In addition, during the declining phase of the cycle, the Federal Reserve System, which deals mainly in the short-term instruments, is actively demanding securities in an effort to supply funds through its open-market operations.

In the long-term segment of the market, meanwhile, the demand for securities remains relatively constant, but the supply increases. The supply of mortgages tends to run countercyclically and increases in the downturn. The United States Treasury exchanges its short-term debt for longer-term debt, increasing the supply of long-term securities during the downturn, in an attempt to minimize debt costs and to lengthen the maturity structure of the debt. This increases the supply of long-term

---

[3] B. Malkiel, *The Term Structure of Interest Rates,* Princeton University Press, Princeton, N.J., 1966.

[4] *Ibid.,* p. 154.

[5] *Ibid.,* p. 163.

securities and, with the constant demand, forces prices to fall and yields to rise.

The downward-sloping yield curve may also be explained by the segmented markets framework. In the expansion phase of the business cycle, the supply and demand conditions in each segment of the market reverse themselves from the declining phase. The supply of securities in the short-term segment increases as business firms finance their expanded inventories and receivables. The commercial banks lose demand deposits and sell off their excess holdings of short-term liquid assets. The Federal Reserve System sells short-term securities in an effort to soak up funds. These actions lead to an increased supply of securities and a decreased demand for securities in the shorter-term segment, which forces down prices and forces up yields. In the long-term segment, the supply of mortgages is decreased and the Treasury stops selling long-term bonds in an effort to minimize costs. This forces the long-term yields to decline, and hence the yield curve slopes downward.

The humped yield curve is also explained by the segmented markets framework. Within this framework the long-term borrowers and lenders and the short-term borrowers and lenders concentrate strictly within their own segment; they do not bother to shorten or lengthen their relevant maturity ranges. The intermediate maturities' supply and demand determines their yield independently of the other two segments. If the supply of intermediate maturities is greater than the demand, the yield must rise and may very well rise to a level above the other two market segments. Although this seems to be a reasonable explanation within the very rigid, inflexible segmented framework, the empirical evidence of substantial flexibility, particularly between the intermediate and the other two maturity ranges, detracts from this explanation. We must turn elsewhere for a more satisfying explanation of the humped yield curve.

Expectation Framework

In direct opposition to the segmented markets framework, the expectation framework maintains that the maturity composition of the securities has no effect on the yield curve. According to this framework, the long-term rate is equal to the sum of the expected short-term rates, so that the investor is indifferent between buying one long-term bond or a series of short-term bonds in the same maturity range. For example, the yield on a 3-year bond should be equal to the yield on three 1-year bonds, one of which was purchased at the beginning of each of the 3 years.

This can best be demonstrated by an example.[6] Assume that the market consisted of a 2-year bond yielding 3 percent and a 1-year bond

---

[6] We assume no transactions costs, uniform expectations, certainty of interest and principal, and profit maximization in using this simple example.

Term structure theories 215

yielding 2 percent. The potential investor who wishes to invest for a 2-year period has two alternatives:

Alternative A: Buy the 2-year bond and receive a 3 percent yield
Alternative B: Buy the 1-year bond, receive a 2 percent yield for 1 year and at the end of this year take the proceeds from the matured 1-year bond and reinvest them in another 1-year bond

Naturally, the investor is going to take the alternative with the higher yield. If alternative A yields him more than alternative B, he buys alternative A instead of alternative B, and vice versa. Because the two alternatives are substitutes for one another, investors keep switching from one to the other until they have made the two exactly equal in yield. The only way that alternative B can be equal to alternative A is if it, too, yields 3 percent in the same 2 years. The only way that this can happen is if the second 1-year bond purchased in alternative B brings the yield up sufficiently from the 2 percent of the first 1-year bond to equal a 3 percent average yield for the 2-year period. This implies that the second 1-year bond in alternative B must yield 4 percent for the second year, for this is the only way that the yield on alternative B can equal 3 percent in the 2-year period.

This implies that the average of the expected short-term yields

$$\frac{2\% + 4\%}{2} = \frac{6\%}{2} = 3\%\text{[7]}$$

is equal to the long-term yield (3 percent) of the same maturity. If the expected yield on the second 1-year bond in alternative B were greater than 4 percent, investors would switch from alternative A to alternative B, for it would yield more. This would drive up the price of alternative B (lower its yield) and drive down the price of alternative A (raise its yield) until the two yields were again equal.

The essence of the expectations framework is that the shape of the yield curve is determined by investors' expectations of short-term yields within the maturity of the competing long-term bond. When investors expect interest rates to be higher in time, we have an upward-sloping yield curve (see Figure 10.2). If they expect interest rates to be lower, the yield curve slopes downward. The flat yield curve indicates that they expect them to remain the same. This could also explain the humped

---

[7] For simplicity of exposition, the arithmetic average was used, although it is only an approximation of the more accurate geometric average. If the geometric average were used, the equilibrium between the two alternatives would be

$$(1 + 0.03) = \sqrt{(1 + 0.02)(1 + r)}$$

where r is the equilibrating expected future 1-year rate 1 year from now.

yield curve, but it is more realistic to use the segmented or eclectic framework in this case.

The liquidity premium version of the expectations framework maintains that there is a natural tendency for yields to rise as the maturity lengthens because of risk aversion. Because there is greater potential price fluctuation in the longer maturities, the long-term yields have to be higher to induce the investors, regardless of their expectations, to purchase the long-term bonds. Therefore, the natural tendency is for the long-term yields to be higher than the short-term yields. This *liquidity premium* causes an upward push on all the yield curves. The upward-sloping yield curve tends to be steeper, the downward-sloping yield curve tends to be less steep, and the flat curve tends to have a slight upward slope.

The empirical evidence on the expectations thesis has been divided. Several researchers have found that the expected yields implied in the term structure prevailing at a particular time did not occur at the future date. They concluded that expectations were not the determining factor in the term structure. Mieselman found that when forecasting error (incorrect expectations) was taken into consideration, the expectations framework had empirical validity.[8] In other words, the expectations hypothesis was an appropriate explanation of the term structure under a given set of expectations, but the future change in the set of expectations made it seem as if the forward rate implied in the term structure was incorrect. The forecasting error was the reason that it seemed that expectations were not the determining factor. Others have concluded that the short-term yields have been lower than the long-term yields, and the liquidity premium is an important factor in determining the term structure.[9]

The shapes of the yield curve may be partially explained by the expectations theory. From the example it is obvious that if investors demand liquidity premiums or expect yields to rise in the future, the longer-term maturities must yield more than the shorter-term maturities if the two are to be equal alternatives. In a period of low yields and sluggish economic activity we expect that yields would have to rise from their depressed level. With expectations of rising yields the longer-term yields have to be higher than the shorter rates, and the yield curve slopes upward. In a period of high yields, we expect that yields would decline. Investors would then be willing to accept lower yields on the longer-term securities because of the expectation that the high shorter-term

[8] D. Mieselman, *The Term Structure of the Interest Rate,* Prentice-Hall, Inc., Englewood Cliffs, N.J., 1962.

[9] R. Kessel, *The Cyclical Behavior of the Term Structure of the Interest Rates— Occasional Paper No. 91,* National Bureau of Economic Research, New York, 1965.

yields are only temporary and that any investment in them now would lead only to a lower yielding reinvestment when the short-term securities matured. The flat yield curve suggests that investors expect interest rates to remain unchanged.

The explanation of the humped yield curve is not so obvious. Investors must hold a series of varying expectations. First, investors must assume that yields will rise quite sharply from their present levels for a few years. Then rates must be expected to decline rapidly and sharply to lower levels and then rise again to a new plateau on which they are expected to remain.[10] The awkwardness of the explanation for the humped yield curve forces us again to look elsewhere.

Eclectic Framework

The eclectic framework draws on both the expectations and the segmented markets frameworks. As in the expectations framework, it assumes that if investors start expecting higher short-term interest rates, they shift out of the long-term bonds into the short-term bonds, forcing up the long-term yields. With diverse expectations among investors some expect rates to rise, and others expect rates to fall. As in the segmented markets framework, it assumes that various bond buyers have preferred maturity ranges and require a yield premium to switch from their preferred positions to another maturity range.

We are now able to explain the humped yield curve. Starting with the expectations theory, we may assume that the term structure is settled into a posture in which all the short-term and long-term alternative yields are equal. All investors who believe that yields are going to rise invest in short-term securities, and all investors who believe that yields are going to fall invest in long-term securities. An increase in the supply of intermediate-term bonds necessitates a higher yield than previously existed in order to sell these bonds. This makes the yields on the intermediate bonds higher than before, when the expectations on yields were formed. The alternative of switching to these intermediate-term bonds instead of staying with the short-term bonds and reinvesting is more attractive, and short-term holders switch to the intermediate-term bonds. By the same token, those investors who are expecting declining yields and invest in long-term bonds also have their expectations altered, and the intermediate-term bonds are more attractive than remaining with the long-term securities. They sell their long-term bonds and buy the intermediate-term bonds. If, at the same time, the short-term holders demand a premium to switch from their preferred short-term position to the intermediate-term position and the long-term holders demand a premium to switch from their preferred position to an intermediate-term

---

[10] B. Malkiel, *op. cit.*, pp. 202–203.

position, the yields on the intermediate-term bonds must be higher than either the long- or the short-term yields.

INFORMATIONAL CONTENT OF THE YIELD CURVE

There may be informational content about interest rate risk (Chapter 8) in the yield curve. If investors' expectations are incorporated into the term structure of rates, the direction and magnitude of expected changes in the pure interest rate are revealed in the curve. As we have seen in this chapter, long-term government bonds experience a greater price fluctuation in response to a given change in interest rates than shorter-term bonds do. Therefore, the longer-term bonds have a greater interest rate risk. Because investors tend to incorporate some interest rate risk considerations into the yields on bonds, the relationship between longer-term bond yields and shorter-term yields may reflect investors' appraisal of interest rate risk. Substantially lower yields on the longer-term bonds would, for example, be indicative of investor expectations of declining future interest rate, that is, lower interest rate risk. Substantially higher longer-term rates than short-term rates may be indicative of investor expectations of rising future interest rates. A greater magnitude in the differential between the short-term and the long-term yields may indicate that investors are expecting a large shift in interest rates. A steeply ascending or declining yield curve may indicate that investors expect the shift in the pure interest rate to be close at hand. A less steeply sloped yield curve may indicate expectations of a less imminent change in the pure interest rate.

YIELD SPREADS

The relationship between yields on securities of the same maturity but different risk is known as the yield spread. For example, the spread between United States government bonds and corporate bonds of the same maturity is one yield spread. Usually the higher-grade bonds yield less than the lower grade bonds. The yield spread is expressed as the positive difference between the two.

The cyclical behavior of the yield spread has been for the spread to narrow throughout the major part of the expansion but to widen at the peak in the business cycle (see Figure 10.3a). Apparently, as the expansion gains momentum, investor confidence in the ability of the riskier borrowers to meet their bond interest obligations is enhanced; that is, investors feel that there is less business and financial risk attached to the interest payments stream than before. Therefore, the investors switch from the less risky bonds (little or no business and financial risk) that they now own to the higher-yielding lower-grade bonds to which they have now attributed less business and financial risk. This creates a greater demand for the lower-grade bonds than for the higher-grade bonds and narrows the yield spread. At the peak in the business cycle, there is usually an increased outpouring of new corporate bond issues, while Treasury financing declines because of increased revenues. This forces yields to rise in the corporate bond market as supply expands and to decline in the government bond market as supply decreases, and the yield spread widens.

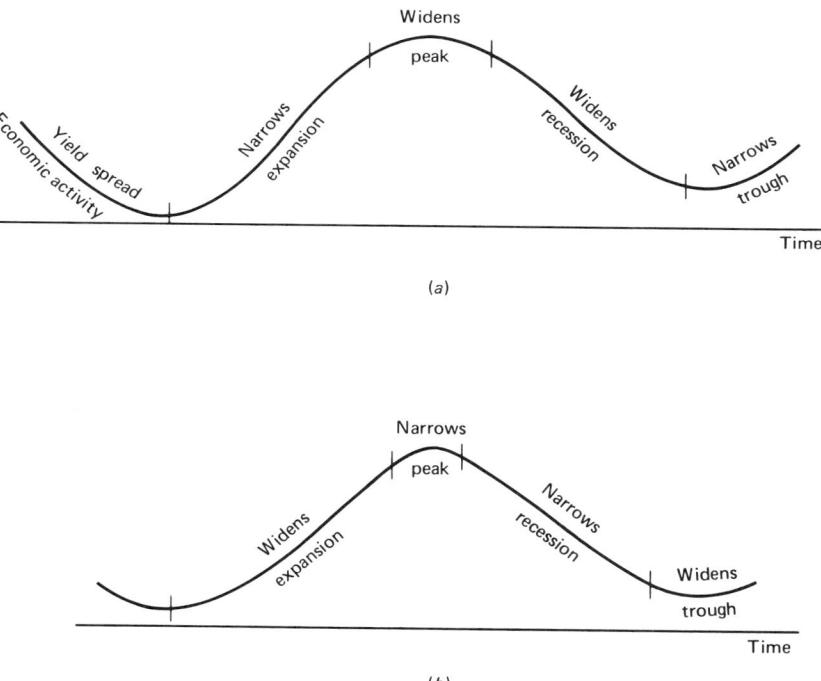

Figure 10.3. Schematic representation of yield spreads. (a) Bond yield spread; (b) Stock-bond yield spread.

In the declining phase of the cycle, the reverse occurs. The yield spread widens throughout the major part of the decline, only to narrow at the bottom of the cycle. Investors begin to lose confidence in the ability of the lesser-quality bonds to meet their bond interest obligations, and they are no longer so willing to purchase the lower-quality bonds. They shift their demand to the higher-quality instruments, thus lowering the yields on the high-quality bonds and raising the yields on the lower-quality bonds. This widens the yield spread. At the bottom of the business cycle, the yield spread narrows as Treasury financing increases to support deficit spending fiscal policy and corporate borrowing declines. This increases the supply of higher-quality government issues, raising their yields, and decreases the supply of lower-quality corporate issues, decreasing their yield.

There is also a yield spread between common stocks and bond prices (see Figure 10-3b). During most of the expansion phase of the business cycle, the price of common stocks usually rises faster than the dividend payment, causing the dividend yield on common stocks to fall. At the same time, the yield on bonds is usually rising in response to corporate demand for investment funds. Because the yield on bonds tends to be above the dividend yield on common stocks, this implies that the yield spread is widening. Toward the peak of the market cycle, the yields on bonds become so much more relatively attractive to the income-oriented investor than the yield on common stocks that he may sell his stocks for a position in bonds. This sale of stocks weakens stock prices and raises stock yields. The purchase of bonds raises bond prices and lowers bond yields. The combination of the two narrows the yield spread.

In the declining phase of the business cycle, the yield spread between stocks and bonds narrows. Typically, stock prices decline and bonds increase in the declining phase of the business cycle. This raises dividend yields and lowers bond yields, narrowing the stock-bond yield spread. Toward the bottom of the cycle, however, some bondholders switch from bonds to stocks because of the latter's more attractive yields. Bond prices fall, raising bond yields. Stock prices rise, lowering stock yields. The combination of the two widens the stock-bond yield spread.[11]

APPLICATIONS OF THE YIELD CURVE

If the yield curve is shaped as in Figure 10.4, the investor may be able to increase his profit if he undertakes a strategy known as *riding the yield curve*. If, for example, the investor feels that the yield curve is to remain in a similar configuration for 2 years, he can purchase the bonds that lie less than 2 years to the right of the break in the yield curve, that is, the point at which the yield curve slopes downward. The investor sacrifices little yield by buying these bonds, because the yield is about the same as bonds of longer maturity. If he holds these bonds

---

[11] The stock-bond yield spread uses the simple dividend yield. This dividend yield is not necessarily indicative of the expected yield to stocks, some of which comes in the form of price appreciation. Therefore, the stock-bond yield spread is a historically based indicator, not a valid theoretical interpretation of market prices.

past the breaking point, however, they start to appreciate in price because of the lower yield on the shorter-term bonds. Simply by waiting for the bonds to pass from the higher yields of the longer term to the lower yields of the shorter term (after the breaking point), the investor has earned substantial capital gains. For example, if the investor bought a bond paying $40 per year interest with 7 years left to maturity and sold it after holding it for 2 years, he would have received the 4 percent annual interest payment and the capital gain of 4.61 percent, because he would have paid $1,000 for the bond and would have sold it 2 years later for $1,046.10, the price appreciation associated with the decline in the interest rate from 4 to 3 percent. By this investment strategy the investor can get a greater return than buying either the long-term or the short-term bonds and holding them to maturity. Caution must be taken, however, that the entire yield curve does not shift upward during the period the investor holds the bonds. If the curve does shift upward, the bond price may not have declined at the end of the holding period, as illustrated by the dotted line in Figure 10.4.

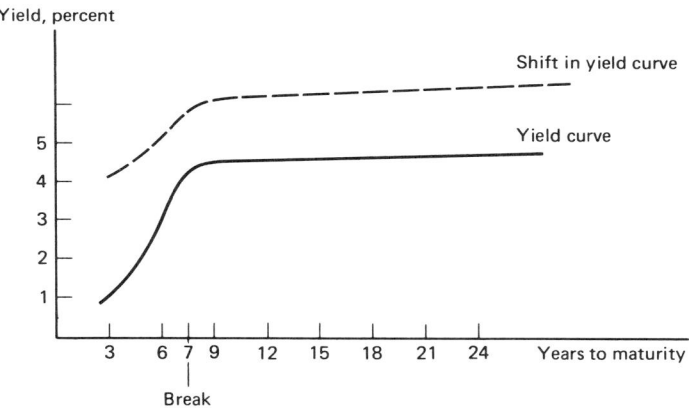

Figure 10.4. Riding the yield curve.

SUMMARY

This chapter is devoted to the term structure of interest rates—the relationship among the yields on the various maturities of securities with the same risk. This relationship is represented by the yield curve. The four general forms of the yield curve are the upward-sloping, the downward-sloping, the flat, and the humped.

The theoretical framework in which each type of curve may be explained are the segmented markets, expectations, and eclectic. The segmented markets framework maintains that each submarket yield within the market is independently determined from the others, because the suppliers and demanders of bonds are themselves segmented into various maturity ranges by the constraints of law and portfolio considerations. Although this framework seems to have some validity, the empirical work does not support a very rigid segmentation of the market. The expectations framework maintains that the term structure is strictly a function of investors' expectations as to what the yields on intervening short-term securities between the present and the maturity date of a long-term security will be. The behavior of these investors is such that the expected average yield on the intervening short-term securities must be equal to the yield on the long-term security. If the expected yield is higher on one or the other, investors switch to the higher-yielding alternative and return equality to yield expectations. The empirical support for the expectations thesis is also ambiguous. The eclectic framework draws on both of the other frameworks and tends to offer a more reasonable, if not totally satisfactory, explanation for the humped yield curve.

The yield spread is the relationship of bonds with the same maturity but differing degrees of risk. The behavior of the yield spread tends to narrow during the major part of the business expansion but widen at the peaks in business activity. In the declining phase of the business cycle, the yield spread has a tendency to widen but to narrow at the troughs in business. The stock-bond yield spread tends to widen at the trough and during the expansion phases of the business cycle and narrow at the peak and during recessionary phases of the business cycle.

QUESTIONS

10.1 Define the following terms: (*a*) yield spread, (*b*) yield, (*c*) yield curve.

10.2 Explain the inverse relationship between bond prices and bond yields.

10.3 What are the four types of yield curves, and what does each type characterize?

10.4 Why does the price of longer-term maturities fluctuate more than that of shorter-term securities when the current market rate of interest changes?

10.5 Explain the segmented markets theory of the term structure of interest rates.

10.6 How does the segmented market framework explain the various shapes of the yield curve?

10.7 Explain the expectation theory of the term structure of interest rates.

10.8 What is the liquidity premium?

10.9 How are the shapes of the yield curves explained by the expectations theory?

10.10 Explain the humped yield curve by the eclectic framework.

10.11 What information may be gleaned from a yield curve?

10.12 What explanation can you give for the cyclical nature of the yield spread?

10.13 What do rising bond yields and falling stock yields usually signal? Explain.

10.14 Explain the meaning of the phrase "riding the yield curve."

PROBLEMS

10.1 Compute the price of a $1,000 per value, 6 percent coupon rate bond that matures in 10 years if (a) the current market yield is 4 percent and (b) the current market yield is 7 percent.

10.2 Compute the yield to maturity for each of the following $1,000 bonds:

United States Government Bond

Years to maturity	Current price	Coupon rate
½	1,019.80	6%
1	1,022.50	5%
2	980.70	2%
3	1,007.00	4%
4	936.90	3%
5	1,000.00	6%
6	806.70	3%
7	865.80	5%

10.3 Graph the yield curve described in Problem 10.2. What is the shape of the yield curve?

10.4 An investor purchased a $1,000 corporate bond for $1,000 when the current market yield was 6 percent. The bond is in the first year of its 30-year life. The investor expects to sell the bond at the end of 3 years, during which time he expects the current market yield to fall 2 percent. Compute the investor's expected capital gain.

10.5 At what point in time should the investor described in Problem 10.4 sell his bond to maximize his capital gain if the yield structure for the bond during the next 8 years is expected to be as follows:

Year (from present)	1	2	3	4	5	6	7	8
Yield	7%	6%	5%	3%	5%	6%	6.5%	7%

Compute his maximum capital gain.

REFERENCES

Conard, Joseph W. *An Introduction to the Theory of Interest,* Berkeley: University of California Press, 1959.

Culbertson, J. M. "The Use of Monetary Policy," *The Southern Economic Journal,* 28:130–137, October, 1961.

Kessel, Reuben A. *The Cyclical Behavior of the Term Structure of Interest Rates,* Occasional Paper 91, National Bureau of Economic Research, New York: Columbia University Press, 1965.

Keynes, John Maynard. *The General Theory of Employment, Interest and Money,* London: Macmillan & Co., Ltd., 1935.

Malkiel, Burton G. *The Term Structure of Interest Rates: Expectations and Behavior Patterns,* Princeton, N.J.: Princeton University Press, 1966.

Meiselman, David. *The Term Structure of Interest Rates,* Englewood Cliffs, N.J.: Prentice-Hall, Inc., 1962.

Struble, Frederick M. "Current Debate on the Term Structure of Interest Rates," *Federal Reserve Bank of Kansas City Review,* pp. 10–16, January–February, 1966.

Van Horne, James. "Interest-Rate Risk and the Term Structure of Interest Rates," *The Journal of Political Economy,* 73:344–351, August, 1965.

11
Purchasing Power Risk

The value of money is represented by the goods and services that it buys. When the investor commits his funds to the purchase of a financial asset, such as a share of stock or a bond, he has forfeited the possibility of enjoying the ownership of some product or service for as long as he holds the security. If, during this holding period, the price of the desired product or service rises, the investor actually loses purchasing power. This loss of purchasing power is tantamount to an actual loss in dollars. For example, the price of a new car may have risen from $2,000 to $3,000 during the holding period. The additional $1,000 that it now costs the buyer to acquire the services of the new car is a cost to him, for the services from the car are the same as they would have been at the lower price. In percentage terms, the investor who delayed in the purchase of the car lost 50 percent in the value of his money. Using the example above, the investor needs a return of at least 50 percent from the securities that he purchased just to break even in terms of purchasing power.

Every rise in prices penalizes the return to the investor, and every potential rise in prices is a risk to the investor. The investor must incorporate some purchasing power risk factor into the PDV evaluation framework. To do this, the investor must understand what rising prices mean and how to quantify the risk. Toward this end, this chapter explores the definition of inflation and the quantitative measures of inflation. The chapter examines the concept of the real rate of interest and the effects of inflation on the creditor and the debtor. After we have these concepts in mind, we investigate the implications of inflation on stock prices. Finally, some of the empirical work in this area is discussed.

CONCEPT OF INFLATION

Inflation is a rise in the prices of commodities and services that are included in the usual standard of living.

The two major types of inflation are *demand-pull* and *cost-push*. The analyst must be in a position to recognize the symptoms and economic causes of both in order to incorporate an estimate of purchasing power risk into the PDV framework. Demand-pull inflation is characterized by a demand for goods and services in excess of their supply. At a full employment level of operations, the economy is able to supply no more than it is presently producing until the work force or the machinery of production expands. If the demand by the consumer, the businessman, and the government is greater than the full employment supply, the available goods must be allocated among the demanders. This is accomplished, as we previously saw in the discussion of market operations, by an increase in the price of the commodity, which discourages some of the demanders and brings supply and demand into equality.

The symptoms of demand-pull are low unemployment, high consumer buying intentions, high corporate investment intentions, and high government expenditures. With low unemployment there is little slack in the economy's ability to meet a spurt in demand. At low levels of unemployment, the economy is particularly vulnerable to inflation. If consumer buying intentions spurt because of changes in attitude, pent-up liquidity, unusually rapid growth in incomes, or some other reason, the additional demand pressure may just tip the economy into inflation. The same could be said for a sudden increase in corporate capital investment. The additional demand could tax the economy's ability to supply the goods and services and raise prices. Government spendings could also generate demand beyond the supply, as in the case of unanticipated war expenditures. Increased demand from these sectors of the economy could cause inflation if it exceeded the economy's ability to supply the goods and services.

Cost-push inflation is associated with the price increases that tend to accompany increases in the costs of production. After wage and raw materials prices increase, producers attempt to pass on some or all of these increased costs to the consumer through higher prices. This causes inflation in the general price level. Usually the environment in which this type of inflation flourishes is during the period of many large labor contract negotiations, when wage earners are dissatisfied with their present salaries and expect further price increases to erode their purchasing power. This environment encourages large wage demands and price increases. The spiral of wage increases, price increases, further wage increases, and further price increases threatens to continue unless the monetary and fiscal authorities intervene. Cost-push inflation may continue after demand-pull conditions cease to exist.

The usual inflationary pattern is for a sudden increase in demand during a period of full employment. This starts prices rising and ellicits corrective monetary and fiscal policy, which eventually dampens the excess demand. Meanwhile, the cost-push inflationary conditions have developed, and prices continue to rise, despite the slackened demand. Eventually, the cost-push conditions subside, and the inflation is checked. The analyst must be cognizant of where the economy is in the pattern, so that he may judge when purchasing power risk will subside. Regardless of the type of inflation, it erodes the purchasing power of the dollar and costs the investor who postponed consumption.

MEASURES OF INFLATION

The three most commonly cited measures of inflation are the consumer price index, the wholesale price index, and the gross national product price deflator. The consumer price index (CPI) attempts to measure the general level of the goods and services that compose the standard of living of the typical American family. The CPI approach is to construct a representative basket of goods and services that are commonly used by the consumer and to price these items in the marketplace continually. Among the items included are food, shelter in the form of rent or mortgage payments, medical services, cleaning, and laundry. When the components of the CPI rise in price, the consumer has experienced inflation. Because this index includes services, it has an upward bias. This bias arises because services that are offered by individuals are less likely to experience increases in productivity. Therefore, as the economy advances and demands more services, prices rise. It has become almost accepted in today's economy that the CPI experiences a mild increase even if aggregate demand is not excessive.

The wholesale price index (WPI) attempts to measure the general price level of the raw materials commonly used in the production of finished goods. Examples of the commodities in this index are hides, copper and other metals, textile products and foodstuffs. Because this index reflects the prices of the intermediate raw materials, it tends to lead price changes in the finished goods. The WPI does not include services and is not so prone to rise unless aggregate demand is excessive. For these reasons, the monetary authorities tend to watch this index more closely than the others in judging the price stability of the economy. Consequently, the analyst should consider movements in the WPI one of the primary indicators of potential inflation. The non-food commodities are often segregated into a separate index to eliminate the more erratic and less indicative food price changes.

The gross national product price deflator is the adjustment factor used to express the final value of all the goods and services produced in real dollar terms, that is, as if there were no price increases. The GNP price deflator is a more sluggish indicator of inflation because of its broad base. Again, as in the case of the CPI, the index includes services and has an upward bias.

PATTERN OF INFLATION

The pattern of inflation, as described in the previous sections, may be traced in Table 11.1. In 1963 and 1964 there was a relatively high unem-

TABLE 11.1 Price Indexes and Economic Activity

Period	WPI 1957–1959 = 100	CPI 1957–1959 = 100	Unemployment rate, percent	Government budget surplus (or deficit)
1963	100.3	106.7	5.7	(4.6)
1964	100.5	108.1	5.2	(5.2)
1965	102.5	109.9	4.5	(4.5)
1966	105.9	113.1	3.8	(5.7)
1967	106.9	116.3	3.8	(7.2)
1968	108.7	121.2	3.6	(16.9)
1969:				
First quarter	111.7	125.6	3.5	(1.9)
Second quarter	113.2	127.6	3.4	15.4
Third quarter	113.6	129.3	3.8	(2.5)
Fourth quarter	115.1	131.3	3.5	(5.6)
1970:				
First quarter	116.6	133.2	4.4	(3.5)

SOURCE: *Federal Reserve Bulletin.*

ployment rate, signifying sufficient slack in the economy to meet a sudden spurt in demand. During these years, the WPI remained essentially unchanged; because of its upward bias, the CPI rose slightly from 106.7 to 108.1, despite the high unemployment rate. After 1965, as the unemployment rate rapidly declined, the pace of inflation accelerated. Also, during this period there was a sudden and rapid increase in the government expenditures to finance the Vietnamese War. The combination of the heightened government demand on top of a fully employed economy sent prices spiraling upward in a demand-pull inflation. In the second half of 1969, the demands on the strained economy relaxed, as shown by the increasing unemployment rate. But, despite the return of some slack to the economy, prices continued to rise at a rapid rate. Obviously, the economy had entered into a cost-push inflationary period. No longer was it necessary to raise prices to allocate the supply among the excessive demand, but price continued to rise in response to the cost-push considerations of higher wages and costs of production. After several years of conditioning, the labor force expected inflation and had suffered because of long-term contracts that locked their salaries into a fixed dollar amount. Now, at the termination of these contracts, labor unions were asking for large salary increases to compensate for the past and expected future inflation. This raised the manufacturer's cost and, in turn, his selling price. So despite the cooling of the economy, prices continue to rise. Only after some period of readjustment when expectations of future inflation subside does the economy pass from a cost-push inflation to relatively stable prices.

REAL RATE OF INTEREST

Up to this point, we have been referring to the pure interest rate. The pure interest rate comprises the real interest rate (the time value of money) plus the purchasing power risk premium. The pure interest rate is observed in the market as the yield on bonds that have no business or financial risk, such as a United States government bond. With the introduction of purchasing power risk, there is another consideration besides the time value of money in the determination of the pure interest rate. Part of the pure interest rate must reimburse the lender for the expected amount of lost purchasing power that he incurs for the duration of the loan. That part of the pure interest rate which remains after the percentage of decline in purchasing power has been removed from the pure interest rate is the real rate of interest, that is, what the loan has cost the borrower in terms of real goods. To compute the real rate of interest, we subtract the percentage of purchasing power lost to inflation from the pure rate of interest. For example, if the pure interest rate were 9 percent and the GNP price deflator were 5 percent, the real rate of interest would be 4 percent.

The pure interest rate is determined not only by the factors discussed in Chapter 8, for example, Federal Reserve policy and the supply and demand for funds, but also by the purchasing power risk present, that is, inflation. Changes in any of the determining factors could change the pure interest rate.

Creditor-Debtor Relationship

During periods of unexpected inflation, the debtor benefits. In terms of real dollars and what they buy, the debtor repays the loan in less valuable dollars than those which he originally borrowed. The borrower has already purchased some real asset, such as machinery, with the funds, and the creditor had to postpone the purchase of real goods or services. By the time the debtor repays the creditor, the same dollar purchases less. The debtor has gained at the expense of the creditor.

The creditor, meanwhile, has suffered a loss in purchasing power. If he had fully anticipated the inflation, he would not have lent his funds at the original interest rate. Instead he would have demanded a sufficient interest rate to cover the loss in purchasing power as well as to provide a reasonable yield.[1] The implication is that the creditor must anticipate the inflation to be experienced during the life of the loan. It is possible that even during periods of mild inflation, the creditor is not correctly anticipating inflation. In this instance, he may not be demanding a sufficient reward for purchasing power risk, and interest rates do not respond to price increases. When the anticipation of inflation becomes widespread among lenders and borrowers, however, interest rates begin to respond to price increases. The creditor demands higher interest rates to protect his purchasing power, and the debtor is willing to pay these higher rates in anticipation of repaying the creditor in cheaper dollars.

Price Anticipation Effect[2]

The price anticipation effect thesis states that changes in the interest rates observed in today's financial markets are influenced by expected changes in the price level. For example, if the real rate of interest were 3 percent and the expected change in the price level were 5 percent, the pure interest rate observed in the market would be 8 percent. If the real rate remained the same but the expected price change rose to 6 percent, the pure interest rate would be 9 percent.

Figure 11.1 illustrates the relationship between pure interest rates and the GNP price deflator index of inflation for the period from 1961 to 1969 in the United States. It is apparent from Figure 11.1 that the pure rate of interest has risen with increased price levels but that the real rate of interest has remained relatively unchanged. The increase in the pure rate, however, did not respond immediately to the increase in prices. Only after a considerable lag did the pure rate of interest start

---

[1] As an alternative to providing funds to the markets at a rate that is insufficient to protect against inflation, the investor might purchase real assets, such as a car, or maintain his short-term Treasury bills, which are not a perfect hedge against inflation but allow the investor to transfer his funds to longer-term securities once the purchasing power risk premium is sufficient. In either case, funds are kept off the market, forcing up interest rates until the purchasing power risk premium is sufficiently high to afford protection against the anticipated inflation.

[2] See for example, William Gibson, "Price Expectations Effects on Interest Rates," *Journal of Finance,* March, 1970, pp. 19–34.

to rise along with prices. During the time lag, prices rose at "moderate rates," and the rate of interest remained relatively steady. Only after the rate of increase in the price level accelerated sharply, approximately in the second half of 1964, did the pure interest rate accelerate. It is also apparent from Figure 11.1 that the real interest rate may move independently from the observed pure rate in response to money and capital market conditions other than inflation. At times, the real interest rate has moved down while the pure rate has moved up.

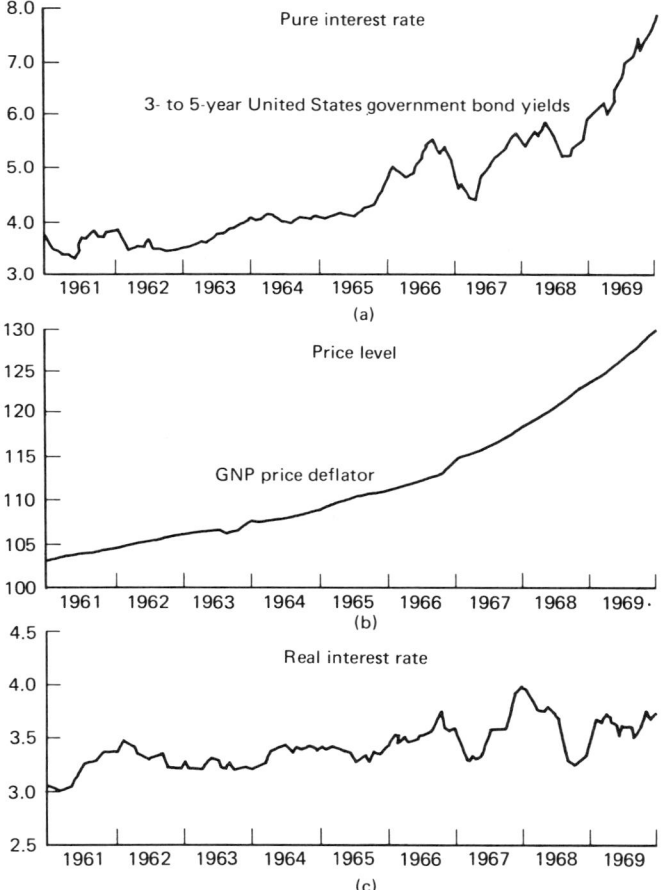

Figure 11.1 (a) Pure interest rate, (b) price level, and (c) real interest rate.

The lesson to be learned from Figure 11.1 is that the pure interest rate comprises two components, the price expectations component and the real interest rate component. To explain the former, we must relate the changes in prices to the pure rate of interest. Lenders increase the interest rate that they demand during inflation, and borrowers increase the interest rate that they are willing to pay during inflation. It takes both parties a length of time, however, to adjust their expectations about inflation. Only after some period of rising prices do they anticipate further inflation and start adjusting their interest rate demands accordingly. In the instance of an expected acceleration in the pace of inflation, the pure interest rate rises until it is high enough to compensate for the expected decrease in purchasing power that accompanies the inflation. When the expected rate of inflation stabilizes, the purchasing power risk component of the pure interest rate also stabilizes at the level that offsets the depreciation of the dollar. As long as the rate of inflation remains constant at the expected pace, the pure interest rate, given the real rate, also remains constant at the level sufficient to compensate for the expected decline in purchasing power. In the case of an expected reduction in the rate of inflation, the purchasing power component of the pure interest rate declines, because the anticipated decline in purchasing power has lessened, and the pure interest, given a particular real rate, declines. In general, after an initial delay, the purchasing power component of the pure interest rate rises as the expected rate of inflation accelerates and declines as the expected rate decelerates.

The real rate of interest component is separately determined by the underlying conditions in the supply and demand for funds. Given stable prices, it is still possible for the rate of interest to increase because of the restrictive Federal Reserve policy, high loan demand, or a reduced supply of funds. It has been quite common for the Federal Reserve to initiate restrictive monetary policy during periods of inflation. Because price stability is one Federal Reserve objective, unacceptable levels of inflation trigger a tight money response. Tight money is generally followed by higher real interest rates. The effect is to increase real interest rates during inflation, putting further upward pressure on the pure rate of interest.

Besides the evidence presented in Figure 11.1, economists have observed this relationship between prices and pure rates of interest in other countries and at other times. For example, it has been noted that the Great Depression of the 1930s saw the lowest interest rates in the history of the United States, and it was a period of falling prices. Countries such as Brazil and Argentina, which have experienced rapid and large inflation, have had unusually high pure rates of interest. In these countries interest rates rose with price increases and fell with price declines. On the other hand, Switzerland, with one of the most stable price level records, has historically experienced one of the lowest pure rates of interest.

PURCHASING POWER RISK IN THE PDV FRAMEWORK

We are now in a position to ask ourselves, how can we incorporate purchasing power risk into the PDV evaluation framework? We can incorporate it as part of the discount factor r, so that $r = i + p$, where i represents the real part of the pure interest rate and p represents the purchasing power risk premium part of the pure interest rate. If i equaled 3 percent and p equaled 3 percent, the discount factor would be 6 percent. If the expectations of price increases continued to rise to, say, 4 percent and were incorporated into the pure interest rate, the discount factor $i + p$ would have to rise to 7 percent. The higher the discount factor, the lower the PDV of a given future stream of benefits. For example, the PDV of a bond that pays an interest of $50 per year for each of 10 years and then returns $1,000 in principal would be $927 at 6 percent and $859 at 7 percent. The inflation has impaired the value of the fixed income stream. During periods of inflation, fixed income stream securities, such as already issued bonds, lose value.

The possible effect of inflation on common stocks, however, is not so clear-cut. An increase in the discount factor, as in the case of the fixed income stream bond, tends to lower the PDV of the common stock, but the inflation may also stimulate higher expected future earnings and dividends. If the increase in the expected future dividends is higher than the increase in the discount factor, the PDV of the common stock actually rises. For example, if, before inflation, ABC Corporation were expected to earn $1 per share in each of the next 5 years and sell for $10 per share at the end of 5 years,[3] the PDV of the stock at 6 percent would be

$$\text{PDV} = \frac{1.00}{(1 + 0.06)} + \frac{1.00}{(1 + 0.06)^2} + \frac{1.00}{(1 + 0.06)^3} + \frac{1.00}{(1 + 0.06)^4} + \frac{1.00}{(1 + 0.06)^5} + \frac{10.00}{(1 + 0.06)^5}$$

PDV = $11.66

If inflation forced interest rates up to 7 percent but allowed the ABC Corporation to earn $1.25 per year for the next 5 years and sell at $10 a share at the end of the fifth year, the PDV would be

$$\text{PDV} = \frac{1.25}{(1 + 0.07)} + \frac{1.25}{(1 + 0.07)^2} + \frac{1.25}{(1 + 0.07)^3} + \frac{1.25}{(1 + 0.07)^4} + \frac{1.25}{(1 + 0.07)^5} + \frac{10.00}{(1 + 0.07)^5}$$

PDV = $12.22

---

[3] Assuming that ABC Corporation paid out its entire earnings in dividends, although we could assume any payout ratio and use the resulting implied dividends in the PDV evaluation.

The overall effect of the inflation would be to raise the ABC stock price.

The increase in earnings during the inflation may be the result of price increases in the company's products, gains from inventory profits, or increased profit margins as wage and raw material costs fail to keep pace with the increase in prices. An earnings increase may also result if the company attempts to maintain its profit margin ratio, for at an increased selling price a given profit margin leads to a large dollar profit per unit sold.

Not all corporations, however, are in a position to benefit from inflation. Many corporations are unable to increase their selling prices. Some are restricted by competition that prevents them from effectively raising prices. Others face price-elastic demand curves and would actually generate less revenue if they raised their prices. Still others are faced with regulatory agencies that control their pricing structure. Even if these last companies could raise prices to increase earnings, the time lag involved in securing the price increase from the agency would postpone the investors' expectation of receiving the future benefits and penalize the PDV of the firm. If the firm is unable to increase expected earnings as rapidly as the discount factor increases, the PDV of the stock must fall. For example, if the ABC Corporation in the previous illustration could raise earnings and dividends by only $0.10 per share in each of the next 5 years instead of $0.25 per share, the PDV would be

$$\text{PDV} = \frac{1.10}{(1+0.07)} + \frac{1.10}{(1+0.07)^2} + \frac{1.10}{(1+0.07)^3} + \frac{1.10}{(1+0.07)^4} + \frac{1.10}{(1+0.07)^5} + \frac{10.00}{(1+0.07)^5}$$

PDV = $11.63

Despite the increase in expected dividends, the PDV of the stock declined. In terms of the P/E shorthand, the price-earnings multiple has shrunk from $11.66 \times$ ($11.66/$1) in the preinflation period to $10.57 \times$ ($11.63/$1.10) after the inflation has had its effect. Therefore, in judging the effect of inflation on stock prices, the analyst must be very careful to consider both the effect on earnings and expected dividends as well as on the discount factor.

Inflation may also affect stock prices by altering the relative value of the equity and the fixed claims on the company. It has generally been assumed that inflation would lessen the value of the fixed claims on the company and increase the value of the equity. The reasoning behind this assumption is that business firms are net debtors, and in periods of inflation net debtors gain at the expense of creditors. Therefore, the firm and the equity claims on the firm would be worth more.

The presence of depreciation may decrease the equity claim value during inflation.[4] Because depreciation is the recovery of investment, it is part of the *gross return to equity*. The present discounted value of the expected depreciation represents an asset of worth to the equity holders. This asset may be looked on as debt owed the company by the United States Treasury. Because the expected depreciation is fixed, it decreases in real value with inflation. The effect of inflation on the real value of the debt owed by the company is to reduce its real value, that is, decrease the present discounted value of the future stream of interest payments. Inflation decreases the firm's assets represented by the present discounted value of the expected depreciation and decreases the firm's liabilities. The effect of inflation on the total real value of the firm depends on the magnitude of the decrease in assets versus the decrease in liabilities. If the depreciation decrease is larger (smaller) than the liability decrease, the real value of the firm declines (increases) during inflation. Therefore, it is implied that corporations must not only be net debtors but have low annual depreciation charges to qualify as good inflation hedges.

It is important to note the differences between the incorporation of the inflation effect into (1) the PDV framework and (2) the creditor-debtor framework. In the former, the effect of inflation is considered in both the earnings and the discount factor. In the latter, the concern is only with the asset-liability relationship. If the asset-liability relationship does not determine stock price, empirical evidence should reveal little or no relationship between it and stock price movements.

Empirical Evidence

Several studies have attempted to discern if corporations are net debtors and if they gain during inflation because of the composition of their assets and liabilities. The procedure was to calculate the monetary assets (fixed dollar claims, for example, cash on hand and accounts receivable) and monetary liabilities (fixed dollar obligations, for example, accounts payable, long-term debt) of the corporation and to subtract one figure from the other. If the monetary assets exceeded the monetary liabilities, the firm was considered a net creditor. If the monetary liabilities exceeded the monetary assets, the firm was considered a net debtor. One study found that the percentage of firms that were net debtors varied from 40 to 60 percent in a 32-year period and that, most of

---

[4] Donald A. Nicholds, "A Note on Inflation and Common Stock Values," *Journal of Finance,* September, 1968, pp. 655–657.

the time, the percentage was 50 percent. This implied that, although half the firms gained from inflation, the other half lost and that to assume that firms in general gained from inflation was misleading.[5] Looking at the stock price performance of net creditor and net debtor firms during inflationary periods, another study found a mixed pattern of performance. Stocks of some of the net creditor corporations, which we should expect to decline in inflation, actually rose in price. In contrast, stocks of several net debtor firms, which would be expected to benefit from inflation, declined. The conclusion of this study was that investors' penchant for stocks during inflationary periods was unwarranted.[6]

Observed in the light of the PDV framework, the results of these studies involving the asset-liability composition of the firm and the effect of inflation do not seem reasonable explanations of stock price behavior during inflation. Unless the change in the real dollar asset-liability composition during inflation influences the expected earnings of the firm, it has no bearing on the future stream of earnings and the rate at which it is discounted. Therefore, we should expect stock price performance to be independent of this consideration, as demonstrated by the inability of these studies to explain the effect of inflation on stock prices satisfactorily.

Many studies have concluded that, in the long run, stock prices rise sufficiently to protect the investor from the loss of purchasing power.[7] The Clendenin study found that the growth in earnings and dividends in a portfolio of good-grade stocks had, on average, outpaced the rise in the general price level in the last 50 years. The increase in earnings and dividends has been approximately $1\frac{1}{2}$ to 2 percent higher than that in the general price level. This was taken to justify the purchase of relatively large amounts of common stock in inflationary periods.

Two serious exceptions to this conclusion, however, were noted. The growth rate of dividends for income-oriented stocks did not, on average, outpace the rate of inflation. In fact, this group of stocks had an indicated real growth rate of zero, implying that they barely preserved the

---

[5] L. DeAlessi, "Do Business Firms Gain From Inflation?" *The Journal of Business*, April, 1964, pp. 162–166.

[6] G. L. Bach and A. Ando, "The Redistributional Effects of Inflation," *Review of Economics and Statistics*, February, 1957, pp. 1–13.

[7] See, for example, J. C. Clendenin, "Price-Trend Variations and the Tenets of High-Grade Investments," *Journal of Finance*, May, 1959; W. J. Eiteman and D. S. Eiteman, *Common Stock Values and Yields, 1950–1961*, The University of Michigan Press, Ann Arbor, 1962; E. L. Smith, *Common Stocks as Long-Term Investments*, The Macmillan Company, New York, 1924; R. A. Bing, "Stocks: A Hedge against Inflation . . . but Not All Stocks at Any Time," *The Commercial and Financial Chronicle*, vol. 205, no. 1.; J. Lorie and L. Fisher, "Rates of Return on Common Stocks," *Journal of Business*, January, 1964.

investors' purchasing power. The entire protection against the loss of purchasing power came from the growth stocks in the sample, which experienced a 3.2 percent real growth rate. This observation is explained in the PDV framework. The increase in the expected dividends of the income-oriented stocks did not rise sufficiently to counteract the depressing effect of the increased discount factor during periods of inflation. The second major exception came in periods of inflation when the increase in earnings and dividends lagged behind the increase in the general price level. During periods of rapid inflation, stocks seemed to offer insufficient protection against inflation. This, too, may be explained in the PDV framework. The rapid rise in the general price level may have caused a rapid rise in the discount factor beyond any reasonable increase in the expected dividends in the near future. With the discount factor rising faster than the expected dividends, the price of the stock would have to decline.

The 1924 study by E. L. Smith also concluded that, in periods of inflation and in the long run, stocks were more profitable investments than fixed income securities. The more recent study by Lorie and Fisher showed that the average stock on the New York Stock Exchange gained 9.03 percent per year before taxes from 1926 to 1960. This was far in excess of the yield on fixed income securities during the same period and in excess of the rate of inflation during the same period. Bing found that from the early 1920s to the early 1960s the price of stocks held for periods of 5, 10, and 20 years rose faster than the CPI, and in the entire 40 years, the Dow Jones Industrial Average had risen six times but the CPI had risen only 3.6 times. He concluded that stocks were a good long-term inflationary hedge. He credited this to the fact that earnings in the long run experience a compounding effect from the reinvestment of retained profits and that the rate of inflation during the same long-run period was relatively mild. Bing found, however, that as the length of the holding period for stocks declined, there were frequent instances, usually in the 5-year periods, in which stocks offered insufficient protection of the investor's purchasing power. Again, the explanation could be that in the shorter run, inflation causes a more rapid and larger increase in the discount factor than in the expected earnings. It takes a period of time for the anticipation of future price increases to subside and the earnings to grow through the compounding effect of reinvestment and profit margin adjustments. Only after these have occurred do the stock prices rise in response to the initial inflationary pressures.

The Eitemans' study also concluded that a portfolio of stocks is an effective long-run hedge against inflation and provides a better yield than bonds. There were short periods within the longer span, however, that did not provide purchasing power protection.

A study by Sidney Homer[8] provides the most convincing evidence that rapid inflation may, in the short run, actually depress stock prices. Homer found that, although in the long-term period from 1900 to 1966 the WPI rose 3 percent and stock prices 5 percent, the short-term holding periods of 1 to 2 years that were associated with inflation produced fewer years of rising stock prices and a smaller percentage of increase in stock prices than those years not associated with inflation. The unusual depression years saw both stock and general price levels fall drastically. The 9 years with mild deflation of between 2 and 5 percent produced 6 years of rising stock prices and only 3 years of declining stock prices, with an average annual increase in stock prices of 9 percent. The 21 years in which the WPI fluctuated between ± 1 percent produced 16 years of rising stock prices and only 5 years of declining stock prices, with an average annual return of 15 percent. When the WPI rose between 2 and 5 percent, stock prices rose in 10 out of 14 years but gained only 9 percent. In the 16 years of rapid inflation, when the WPI rose more than 5 percent, stock prices rose in 9 and fell in 7 years, with an average price increase of only 6 percent. Using only the data since 1945, Homer found that stock prices rose only about half of the periods in which the general price level rose 5 percent or more. The conclusion is that severe inflation depresses stock prices in the short run. The explanation, again, lies in the more rapid and larger advance in the discount factor than in the expected dividends.

SUMMARY

When the investor postpones his purchase of goods or services and instead buys a security, he runs the risk that inflation will lessen the purchasing power of his money during the time that he holds the security. In order to protect himself from this loss of purchasing power, the investor must cover the anticipated inflation and still receive a reasonable reward. Therefore, we can expect that as the anticipation of inflation rises, the yield on investments does also.

The effect of this anticipation of price increases on fixed income securities is to lower the price, because the PDV of the future, fixed stream of interest is discounted at a higher rate. The discount factor has risen with the increase in the yield required by lenders. The price anticipation effect is not so obvious when it comes to common stocks. As in the case of the fixed income securities, the discount factor rises,

---

[8] Sidney Homer, "Price Inflation Has Not Been Good for Stock Prices," *The Commercial and Financial Chronicle,* January, 1967. Recent evidence supporting Homer's observation was found by F. Reilly, et al., "Inflation, Inflation Hedges and Common Stock," *Financial Analysts Journal,* January–February, 1970, pp. 104–110.

but it is possible that the inflation sufficiently increases expected dividends to offset the price-depressing effects of the increased discount factor. Every company is an individual case, because some will and some will not be able to raise earnings and dividends expectations either sufficiently or rapidly enough to compensate for the increased discount factor.

The empirical evidence seems to support the PDV framework. In the long run, when earnings have had an opportunity to grow sufficiently and the inflation rate has slackened, investors' return from common stocks has tended to outpace the rate of inflation and to provide protection against the loss of purchasing power. In the short run, however, when the rate of inflation is relatively high and rapid, the expected per share earnings and dividends do not increase so rapidly or so much as the discount factor, and hence stock prices are depressed.

QUESTIONS

11.1 Describe the two major types of inflation and the symptoms of each.

11.2 Describe the usual inflationary pattern.

11.3 Explain the common measures of inflation. What are the biases and shortcomings of each?

11.4 Why is purchasing power risk included as a component of the pure interest rate?

11.5 Why must creditors anticipate the amount of inflation to be experienced in the life of a loan?

11.6 What is the price anticipation effect?

11.7 Explain the price expectations component of the pure interest rate. What determines the real rate of interest component?

11.8 What are some of the ways in which a company can experience an increase in earnings during periods of inflation?

11.9 What general assumptions have been made about the effects of inflation on debt-equity structure of a company?

11.10 Explain the following statement: The presence of depreciation may decrease the equity claim value during inflation.

11.11 Differentiate between the inflation effect in the PDV framework and the creditor-debtor framework.

11.12 What was the conclusion of the Clendenin study? What exceptions were noted?

11.13 What conclusion can be drawn from the Homer study? Explain the results using the PDV framework.

REFERENCES

Ball, Robert James. *Inflation and the Theory of Money,* Chicago: Aldine Publishing Company, 1965.

Bing, Ralph A. "Stocks a Hedge against Inflation—but Not All Stocks at Any Time," *The Commercial and Financial Chronicle,* May 25, 1967, pp. 1, 24.

Clendenin, John C. "Price-Level Variations and the Tenets of High-Grade Investment," *The Journal of Finance,* 14:245–270, May, 1959.

Coleman, Sylvan C. "Inflation and the Stock Market in the Past Fifty Years Here and Abroad," *The Commercial and Financial Chronicle,* 204:1, 24, Nov. 3, 1966.

Conard, Joseph W. *An Introduction to the Theory of Interest,* Berkeley: University of California Press, 1959.

Friedman, Milton. "Factors Affecting the Level of Interest Rates," *Savings and Residential Financing 1968 Conference Proceedings,* pp. 10–27, September, 1968.

Gibson, William E. "Price Expectations Effects on Interest Rates," *The Journal of Finance,* 25:19–34, March, 1970.

Homer, Sidney. "Price Inflation Has Not Been Good for Stock Prices," *The Commercial and Financial Chronicle,* Jan. 26, 1967, pp. 3, 111–113.

———. "Inflation and the Capital Markets," *Financial Analysts Journal,* 25:143–145, July–August, 1969.

——— **and R. Johannsen.** *The Price of Money,* New Brunswick, N.J.: Rutgers University Press, 1969.

"Inflation and Interest Rates: A Long Observed Link," *Morgan Guaranty Survey,* pp. 6–11, January, 1970.

Reilly, F. K., G. L. Johnson, and R. E. Smith. "Inflation Hedges and Common Stocks," *Financial Analysts Journal,* 26:104–110, January–February, 1970.

Sauvain, Harry C. *Investment Management,* 3rd ed., Englewood Cliffs, N.J.: Prentice-Hall, Inc., 1967.

Youhe, William P., and Denis S. Karnosky. "Interest Rates and Price Level Changes, 1952–69," *Federal Reserve Banks of St. Louis Review,* 51:18–38, December, 1969.

12
Business Risk

Up to this point, we have attempted to deal with the forecasting risk inherent in the financial analyst's projection of expected earnings and with the interest and purchasing power risks connected with the evaluation of every projected earnings stream. Now we turn our attention to the business risk attached to the evaluation of a particular projected earnings stream and the expected dividend stream derived therefrom.

Business risk is independent of the other risks involved in the evaluation of financial assets. If interest rates rise or fall, all stock prices may fluctuate, but the business risk associated with any particular income stream is not affected.[1] The business risk is associated with each individual company and not with general financial market conditions, as are the real interest rate and purchasing power risks. Analyzing business risk requires a study of the operating conditions of each company and the variability that these conditions impart to the expected stream of earnings. The more variability imparted, the greater the business risk that shareholders incur. The presence of business risk adds to the total risk that must be considered in evaluating the expected stream of earnings and dividends. The greater the business risk, the less valuable the present discounted value of the expected stream of dividends.

In exploring business risk, this chapter pinpoints the external and internal considerations that affect operating conditions and contribute to business risk. Then, it proceeds to examine various attempts to classify firms according to their business risk and to quantify business

---

[1] The earnings forecast may be affected by the change in interest, for example, a construction firm. The firm's business risk is not affected, however, because the firm's response to the change in the interest rate should have already been established; that is, the variability in the firm's operating income caused by a change in the interest rate has already been established. Only if the response to a change in the interest rate is altered is business risk affected.

risk. Finally, an attempt to incorporate business risk into the PDV evaluation framework is undertaken.

BUSINESS RISK

Business risk is strictly a function of the operating conditions of the firm and is not affected by the general fluctuations of the financial markets caused by interest rate changes or by the manner in which a firm finances itself. If the operating conditions are such that they increase the probability of the firm's not achieving its expected earnings growth in operating earnings (deviating from its expected operating trend or performance), the quality of the earnings stream is impaired, and the investor faces the risk that he will not receive the benefits that he has anticipated. For example, the operating conditions of an oil company drilling in a hostile political environment, in which it is exposed to expropriation, entail more business risk than an identical oil company drilling in a hospitable political environment. A less extreme example is a textile company whose one product is woolens and which is exposed to the vagaries of fashion, imported woolens, and synthetic fabrics. As opposed to a diversified textile manufacturer which produces various styles of fabric and synthetics and which is engaged in foreign operations, the one-product textile manufacturer's operation obviously entails more business risk.

Business risk may then be defined as the variability or deviation from the trend in expected operating earnings due to operating conditions. Figure 12.1 illustrates this concept. The deviation of the actual operating earnings from the expected trend in operating earnings in Figure 12.1a reflects the business risk inherent in this operating earnings stream. Because the deviations from the expected operating earnings are larger in Figure 12.1b than in Figure 12.1a, the business risk inherent in the operating earnings stream in 12.1b is greater. If we think of business risk as deviations from the trend in expected operating earnings, a United States government bond would have no exposure to business risk. Because the United States government is not expected to have revenues that greatly differ from its expenses, in the long run, it should have no expected operating earnings from which to deviate. And, as long as it remains a sovereign state and can issue dollars to meet its debt obligations, there is no possible way that operating conditions can impart variability to the investor's expected stream of benefits. On the other hand, the bond of a state or local government may have business risk exposure. Because the local government's ability to raise funds (its taxing power) is limited by such operating conditions as land values, population changes, and local income, it is possible that deviations can occur from what the investor expects the local government to earn. The most

Business risk 243

obvious exposure to business risk occurs in the securities of corporations. Operating conditions vary substantially from industry to industry and from company to company. Each industry and firm has its own operating conditions that cause its operating earnings to be more or less variable in response to such things as the business cycle, government policy, competition, and labor negotiation.

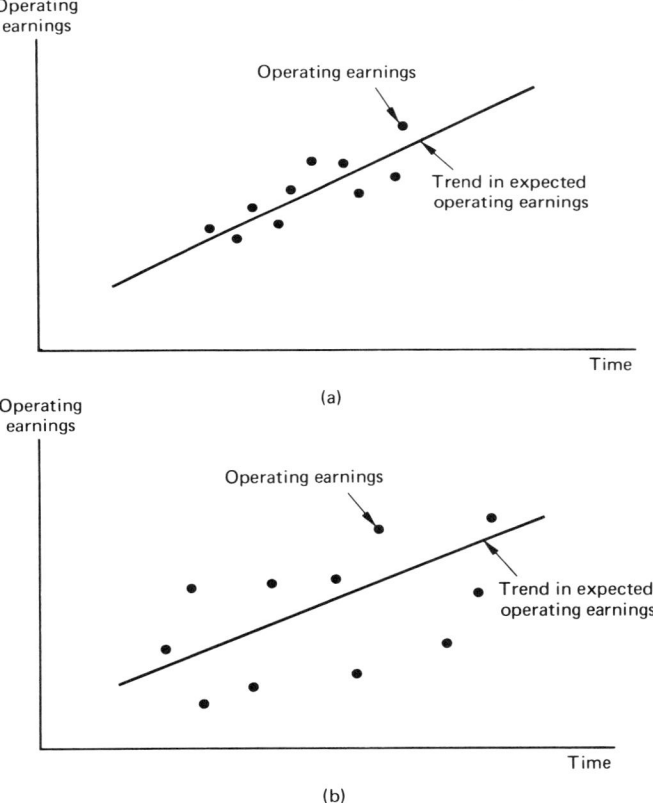

Figure 12.1. Business risk. (a) Little business risk; (b) Substantial business risk.

External Business Risk

External business risk is usually beyond the control of the firm, but it may still account for a large part of any deviation in the operating earnings from the expected trend. In the majority of cases, it is associated with the economic operating environment in which the firm exists. Each firm faces its own external risks, depending on the specific operating environmental factors that it must deal with. For example, a domestically based firm faces different external risk factors from a foreign-based firm, and a retail food chain faces different operating environmental risks than an oil exploration company. Even firms within the same industry differ in the degree to which they are exposed to the various risk factors present in the industry's operating environment. For example, the oil refiner with substantial crude oil reserves may be exposed to less external business risk due to changes in the price of crude oil than the oil refiner without any crude oil reserves.

Although the list of external factors that may affect business risk in every individual firm is too long to enumerate here, we may explore certain general operating characteristics of any firm that are affected by the economic operating environment. In general, the external operating environment affects (1) the quantity of the firm's sales, (2) the quality of the firm's sales, and (3) the price and quality of the firm's supply of production inputs, for example, labor and raw materials.

Quantity of Sales. Fluctuations or unexpected curtailment of growth in the firm's sales may occur because of factors beyond its control (although, as we shall see in the next section, to reduce internal risk proper anticipatory action may offset these external factors.) The size of the sales base, regardless of management's efficiency, limits the maximum profit potential of the firm, for no firm can have an operating income that is greater than its operating revenues.

The business cycle is probably the major external factor in causing sales to fluctuate. Many firms find that beyond their control sales fluctuate with the business cycle. The automobile manufacturers have typically experienced sales declines in recessions and sales increases in booms. Conversely, the residential home building industry has typically experienced a countercyclical fluctuation in sales. Demographic considerations beyond the control of the firm may also influence the quantity of sales. For example, the birth rate affects the sales of a baby food manufacturer, and regional immigrations affect the sales of regional retail chains, banking institutions, and electrical utilities. Government fiscal and antitrust policy decisions also affect a firm's sales. For example, a shift in United States government spending from the space program to other areas of the economy limits the sales of aerospace manufacturers who produce for the space program. A government decision to limit the availability of credit may curtail the ability of local governments to raise funds and, indirectly, curtail the sales of a firm that sells sewage disposal equipment to these local governments. The decision of a competitor to enter the market may also affect the sales potential of the firm.

Quality of Sales. External risk factors also affect the quality of the sales. By quality we generally mean the degree to which the operating environment makes the sales level prone to fluctuations and deviations from expectations. For example, a company whose sales are to only one customer is exposed to an abrupt, sharp decline in sales if this customer curtails its orders. A specific example of this external risk is the firm whose sole customer was the United States government's space program. Congressional failure to appropriate funds for the program could eliminate this firm's one customer. Similarly, in other industries, the quality of the sales is reflected in the customers served. In the electrical utility industry, the analyst might look for the breakdown of the company's customers according to industrial, residential, and agricultural categories. A large proportion of industrial customers indicates cyclically prone sales. A firm engaged in catering to a fad generally has a poorer quality of sales. For example, the sales of the dress manufacturer who caters to one style, of the record company that handles only one type of music, and of the hula-hoop manufacturer are all very prone to rapid changes in consumer tastes.

Price and Quality of Inputs. There are also various external considerations that affect the operating efficiency of the firm. The firm has, for example, little control over the tariff and import quota policy of the government, the demands of labor unions, and the actions of foreign governments who may control needed raw materials. Any of these factors could seriously impair the firm's ability to make operating revenues into operating profits. Although management cannot specifically control these external risks, it can take internal actions, which are within its control, to counter the effects of these external risks. The appropriateness of these internal actions is a reflection of internal business risk.

Internal Business Risk

The internal part of business risk is associated with the efficiency with which the firm conducts itself within the operating environment imposed by external business conditions. Given the firm's profit potential, which is established by the external risk factors, internal business risk is a reflection of how well the firm and its management achieves this profit potential.

As in the case of external business risk, internal risk considerations are individual to the firm and impossible to enumerate in complete detail. There are several general categories, however, within which internal business risk may be considered. These are (1) asset utilization, (2) countercyclical response, (3) diversification, and (4) operating skills.

Asset Utilization. How effectively does management utilize its assets? The analyst would like to know if the firm generates more sales per dollar of assets than its competitors. This might be measured differently among industries. For example, the analyst might look for the system load factor (the utility's average sales to its capacity) in the electrical utility industry. In the airline industry, the analyst would look to the airline's load factor (the number of passengers flown in relation to the airline's capacity), the loan to deposit ratio for banks, and the sales to total assets in other industries.

Countercyclical Response. How efficient is the firm in responding to the business cycle? If the firm is in a position to adjust quickly to changes in demand, rapidly curtailing expenses and production during declines and rapidly expanding during upswings, there is less deviation from the expected operating earnings. As a generalization, it may be expected that firms with large fixed plant, high fixed operating costs, and inflexible production methods are exposed to more internal business risk in the business cycle. For example, the automobile manufacturer with its large fixed plant and long planning time is less able to respond to the business cycle than the retailer who is able to curb quickly new orders for merchandise and shift marketing tactics.

Diversification. The appropriately diversified firm is probably exposed to less business risk, because disappointing results in one division of the firm may be offset by good results in another. The diversified firm may find that different operating conditions among the divisions impart variability to the operating income at different times in the business cycle. This could mean that for the entire company the net effect in the cycle is to minimize the deviations from the trend in expected operating earnings. For example, if a firm had the following two divisions, one of which had operating income that behaved cyclically and the other of which had operating income that behaved countercyclically in the following fashion:

	Division	Normal	Recession	Boom
Operating income	1	$1 mil	$0.8 mil	$1.5 mil
	2	1 mil	1.2 mil	0.5 mil
Total operating income		2 mil	2 mil	2 mil

the variability in the total operating income would be eliminated because of the opposing cyclical pattern in the operating income of the divisions.

Diversification can also enable a firm to counter the external risks associated with the price and the quantity of inputs. For example, the firm may acquire the supply of its raw materials, thus assuring itself of a steady supply and a reasonably constant price. The copper refiner who acquires a copper mining operation has assured himself of a supply of copper ore. The commercial banks that seek funds in new sources when previous sources are no longer available to meet the needs are another example. For example, the commercial bank can acquire reserves in Europe and in the commercial paper markets when government policy restricts the availability of funds.

Operating Skills. Any operating skills that enable management to achieve the firm's sales potential and to convert sales revenues into operating income reflect on internal business risk. Internal business risk is diminished if the management is able to maintain effective internal controls, retain key executives, keep pace with or lead in technological, marketing, and production innovations. This is reflected in such management actions as the profitable implementation of automation, proper patent protection, the correct forecasting of the profitability of projects, and the garnering of monopoly power.

An Illustration

Table 12.1 illustrates the deviation from the trend in expected operating earnings caused by business risk. The chewing gum manufacturer faces less business risk than the farm equipment manufacturer as measured by the deviation of the actual from expected earnings. For the chewing gum manufacturer actual operating earnings deviated from expected operating earnings by $25,000 in the recession year and $2,500 in the boom year, compared with $115,000 and $92,500 for the farm equipment manufacturer. There was no deviation for either company in the normal year of the business cycle when actual operating earnings and expected earnings were equal. After the first year, the irregularities of demand that accompany the business cycle forced the actual operating earnings to deviate from the expected earnings, which had been projected to grow at 10 percent per year for each firm. As can be seen from Table 12.1, the variability in operating earnings in this case arose from the more pronounced effect that the business cycle had on the sales of the farm equipment manufacturer and its higher fixed costs of operating. The fixed costs of the chewing gum manufacturer were $400,000 less than those of the farm·equipment manufacturer for the same level of sales. The chewing gum producer's variable costs were 50 percent of sales against 10 percent of sales for the farm equipment producer. This cost structure allowed the chewing gum producer to adjust more rapidly to the irregularities of demand and mitigate the effect

TABLE 12.1*

	Chewing Gum Manufacturer, Inc.					
	Year					
	1		2		3	
	Normal		Recession		Boom	
Sales		$1,000,000		$1,000,000		$1,100,000
Fixed costs	250,000		250,000		250,000	
Variable costs	500,000		500,000		550,000	
Total costs		750,000		750,000		800,000
Operating earnings		250,000		250,000		300,000
Expected operating earnings		250,000		275,000		302,500
Deviation		0		(25,000)		(2,500)

	Farm Equipment Manufacturer, Inc.					
	Year					
	1		2		3	
Sales		$1,000,000		900,000		1,161,111
Fixed costs	650,000		650,000		650,000	
Variable costs	100,000		90,000		116,111	
Total costs		750,000		740,000		766,111
Operating earnings		250,000		160,000		395,000
Expected operating earnings		250,000		275,000		302,500
Deviation		0		(115,000)		92,500

* The sequence of economic conditions was chosen to illustrate the three general types, although in reality any particular sequence may occur.

on his earnings. The farm equipment manufacturer, on the other hand, was unable to adjust so rapidly and experienced wider fluctuations in earnings.

This variability in actual operating earnings from the trend in expected operating earnings has a significant impact on the PDV of the stock and the risk that the investor experiences when he purchases the stock. The difference between the PDV of the expected stream of operating income (ex ante) and the PDV of the actual stream (ex post) represents the potential risk to the investor and is a historical indication of expected business risk. The greater the difference, the larger the business risk, and the larger the business risk factor b. To illustrate the effect of earnings variability on stock prices, assume the following:

1. The chewing gum manufacturer's operating earnings per share are expected to grow at 10 percent in each of the next 3 years and then stabilize at the third year's operating earnings per share level for the following 22 years.

2. The actual earnings per share are dependent on the economic environment and are as follows:

Year	Economic environment	Actual EPS	Expected EPS
1	Normal	$2.50	$2.50
2	Recession	2.50	2.75
3	Boom	3.00	3.02
4	Recession	2.50	3.00
5	Normal	3.00	3.00
6	Normal	3.00	3.00
7–25	Normal	3.00	3.00

3. The chewing gum manufacturer's operating earnings are discounted at 10 percent.

4. The farm equipment manufacturer's operating earnings per share are expected to grow at 10 percent in each of the next 6 years and then stabilize at the sixth year's level for the following 19 years.

5. The actual operating earnings per share are dependent on the economic environment and are as follows:

Year	Economic environment	Actual EPS	Expected EPS
1	Normal	$2.50	$2.50
2	Recession	1.60	2.75
3	Boom	3.95	3.02
4	Recession	1.60	3.32
5	Normal	2.50	3.65
6	Normal	2.75	4.02
7–25	Normal	3.00	4.00

6. The farm equipment manufacturer's operating earnings are discounted at 15 percent.

7. Each firm has 100,000 shares outstanding, no income taxes, pays no interest, and pays all its operating earnings out as dividends, although we could assume any proportional relationship between operating income and dividends and use the implied dividends in the PDV evaluation. Given these assumptions, let us compare the PDV of each firm's expected future dividends based on its operating earnings with its own actual stream of dividends. The present discounted value of the expected dividends for the chewing gum manufacturer is

$$PDV = \frac{2.50}{(1+0.10)} + \frac{2.75}{(1+0.10)^2} + \frac{3.02}{(1+0.10)^3} + \frac{3.00}{(1+0.10)^4}$$
$$+ \frac{3.00}{(1+0.10)^5} + \frac{3.00}{(1+0.10)^6} + \sum_{j=7}^{25} \frac{3.00}{(1+0.10)^j} = \$26.55$$

The present discounted value of the actual dividend for the chewing gum manufacturer is

$$PDV = \frac{2.50}{(1+0.10)} + \frac{2.50}{(1+0.10)^2} + \frac{3.00}{(1+0.10)^3} + \frac{2.50}{(1+0.10)^4}$$
$$+ \frac{3.00}{(1+0.10)^5} + \frac{3.00}{(1+0.10)^6} + \sum_{j=7}^{25} \frac{3.00}{(1+0.10)^j}$$

$PDV = \$26.01$

The PDV of the expected dividends from the operating earnings for the farm equipment manufacturer would be

$$PDV = \frac{2.50}{(1+0.15)} + \frac{2.75}{(1+0.15)^2} + \frac{3.02}{(1+0.15)^3} + \frac{3.32}{(1+0.15)^4}$$
$$+ \frac{3.65}{(1+0.15)^5} + \frac{4.02}{(1+0.15)^6} + \sum_{j=7}^{25} \frac{4.00}{(1+0.15)^j}$$

$PDV = \$22.38$

The PDV of the actual dividends from the operating earnings for the farm equipment manufacturer would be

$$PDV = \frac{2.50}{(1+0.15)} + \frac{1.60}{(1+0.15)^2} + \frac{3.95}{(1+0.15)^3} + \frac{1.60}{(1+0.15)^4}$$
$$+ \frac{2.50}{(1+0.15)^5} + \frac{2.75}{(1+0.15)^6} + \sum_{j=7}^{25} \frac{3.00}{(1+0.15)^j}$$

$PDV = \$17.34$

The PDV of the expected stream of dividends for the chewing gum manufacturer is $26.55. The PDV of the actual stream of dividends for the chewing gum manufacturer is $26.01, or a decrease in value of $0.54 from what was expected. The PDV of the farm equipment manufacturer's expected stream is $22.38. The PDV of the actual stream for the farm equipment manufacturer is $17.34, or $5.04 less than was expected. The variability in the operating earnings has introduced risk into the stocks of both companies, for each company has suffered a decline in value for its shares because of the deviation of the actual operating earnings and the implied dividends from the expected operating earnings and implied dividends. The farm equipment concern, however, has had a greater risk exposure than the chewing gum manufacturer, as demonstrated by the greater potential decline in its PDV. These examples demonstrate that the various operating conditions of different firms impart different degrees of potential deviation in the actual operating earnings from the expected operating earnings. This potential deviation, in turn, imparts risk to the security holder who must adjust his evaluation for the increased risk by a larger business risk factor b.

BUSINESS RISK MEASUREMENT

Financial analysts have long recognized the existence of business risk and have attempted to incorporate the concept into their analysis. The most frequently used procedure among practicing analysts is to classify the companies according to product or method of marketing. This procedure led to the standard industry classifications by which most analysis is presently done. For example, there is the drug industry, the automobile industry, the integrated oil companies, the nonintegrated oil companies, the paper industry, and so on. This classification system arose out of the recognition that the various industry categories had different operating conditions and that the business risk in each industry was reflected in different operating characteristics. Once these industry classifications had been established, the next step was to decide subjectively that certain industries were exposed to greater business risk than others and should therefore sell at lower earnings multiples. The logic ran that if industry 1 sold at a multiple of 10 times earnings and had less business risk than industry 2, the latter industry would have to sell at a multiple lower than 10. This system gives only a comparative consideration among various business risks and gives no indication of what to expect if the entire structure of multiples for all industries changes. Also, no indication is given as to the appropriate absolute multiple value applied to each industry to reflect its particular business risk. Concurrent with the recognition of the varying degrees of business risk among industries, the financial analyst assumed that the companies within an industry classification were rather closely grouped around the same multiple, with any deviation from this multiple due to the internal business risk of each firm.

To incorporate business risk in this analysis, the analyst had to be sure that his industry classifications were standard among all analysts, constant in time, and that each industry and each company within each industry maintained the same comparative business risk position. To compensate for business risk, the price earnings multiple was lessened by some subjective amount that seemed to maintain the relationship among the companies and the industries.

The first academicians also used this industry classifications system and established an *equivalent risk* class of firms in their empirical tests. They defined this as a homogeneous set of firms, all of which were perfect substitutes for one another, and postulated that all firms within a risk class faced the same degree of business risk. In practice, this meant that the academicians used industry classifications analogous to those used by the financial analysts. The academicians carried it even one step farther than the analysts did and assumed that every company within each industry faced identical business risk (homogeneity) and that every industry faced a different degree of business risk (heterogeneity).

When these assumptions were tested, the results did not support the homogeneity of intraindustry business risk and were divided on the heterogeneity of interindustry business risk. One test[2] examined sixty-one firms from eight different industries by a relative measure of the deviation in operating income[3] and the statistical technique of analysis of variance. The assumption of intraindustry homogeneity was not supported; that is, firms within the same industry did not necessarily face the same degree of business risk. Another test[4] used the relative deviation of a firm's rate of growth in net operating income from the firm's

---

[2] R. Wippern, "A Note on the Equivalent Risk Class Assumption," *Engineering Economist,* Spring, 1966.

[3] The measure used was the variability in net operating earnings expressed as the standard error of the estimate for a logarithmic regression of observed annual net operating income on time.

[4] N. Gonedes, "Test of the Equivalent-Risk Class Hypothesis," *Journal of Financial and Quantitative Analysis,* June, 1969. The measure of relative deviation used was

$$BR_{it} = \frac{R_{it} - K_i}{K_i}$$

where BR_{it} = deviation measure for ith firm at time t
R_{it} = growth rate of ith firm's net operating income during t
K_i = compound growth rate of ith firm's net operating income in last 10 years

compound rate of growth in net operating income. This study concluded that six out of the eight industries tested violated the assumption of intra-industry homogeneity. Therefore, it is inappropriate to assume that internal business risk was the same for all firms within an industry. This study found, however, in contrast to the first study, that there was sufficient evidence to support interindustry heterogeneity. This conclusion implies that industry operating conditions, especially those brought about by external considerations, expose each industry group to different degrees of business risk.

TABLE 12.2 A Measure of Business Risk

(1) Year	(2) Expected	(3) Actual	(4) Deviation	(5) Deviation^2
1	4.30 (mil)	4.60 (mil)	−0.30	0.09
2	4.30 (mil)	4.60 (mil)	−0.30	0.09
3	4.30 (mil)	3.35 (mil)	+0.95	0.90
4	4.30 (mil)	4.70 (mil)	−0.40	0.16
5	4.30 (mil)	4.50 (mil)	−0.20	0.04
				1.28

Average of expected operating income = 4.30 (mil)
Residual variance = deviation^2/n = 0.256

$$\text{Business risk} = \frac{\text{residual variance}}{\text{average expected earnings}} = \frac{0.256}{4.30} = 0.06$$

$n = 5$

What apparently is needed is a standard of business risk that ignores the traditional industry classification system but includes both internal and external business risk considerations. One possible method is to compute a standardized residual variance of operating income.[5] For example, Table 12.2 illustrates a hypothetical case in which the expected stream of operating earnings is $4.30 million for each of the next 5 years. The actual operating income for each of the 5 years is recorded in column 3. The deviations of the actual from the expected are recorded in column 4, and the squared value of the deviations are recorded in column 5. The residual variance is the sum of the squared

---
[5] T. Yamane, *Statistics: An Introductory Analysis,* Harper & Row, Publishers, Incorporated, New York, 1967, pp. 390–391.

deviations divided by the number of years observed *n*. And, to keep the scale factor constant, the average deviation is divided by the average expected operating income.

The business risk measure in this example ignores the industry classification system and simultaneously considers both internal and external business risk. The measure may be computed for any company in any industry. By using the operating income, it catches the effect of both types of business risk. Of course, it is a historical measure and is subject to change. But it does allow the analyst to compute an absolute measure of business risk and make a quantitative comparison of business risk among companies. If one company has a residual variance of 0.06 and another company 0.03, the former is exposed to twice the business risk of the latter.[6]

This particular measure of business risk is, of course, only one of several possible measures that may be used.[7] All other appropriate measures, however, must be similarly based on the measurement of variability in operating earnings. The major limitations of this particular measure are its dependence on historical data and the necessity of estimating the expected earnings trend in the period used.

INCORPORATING BUSINESS RISK INTO THE PDV FRAMEWORK

With the inclusion of business risk, there is the possibility that the operating stream of earnings that the analyst expects will not materialize, and this may adversely affect the PDV of the future stream of benefits that he expects to receive. In the case of common stock this would entail a capital loss when the investor went to sell his stock. In an extreme case this could mean bankruptcy and total loss to the shareholder. In

---

[6] Some analysts may want to use the semivariance in their analysis, maintaining that deviations above expectations do not really expose the investor to risk. The semivariance is a measure of dispersion for all observations less than the expected value:

$$\text{Semivariance} = \sqrt{\sum_{j=1}^{n} (X_i - \bar{X})^2 P_i}$$

where $X_i < \bar{X} \} X_i = X_i$
$X_i > \bar{X} \} X_i = \bar{X}$

[7] Other possible measures of variability in earnings include the mean absolute deviation and the standard error of the estimate. For example, see Bank Administration Institute, *Measuring the Performance of Pension Funds,* 1968; P. Cootner and D. Holland, *Risk and Rate of Return,* The M.I.T. Press, Cambridge, Mass., 1964; A. Conrad and I. Plotkin, "Risk-Return United States Industry Pattern," *Harvard Business Review,* March-April, 1968.

the case of fixed income securities, the presence of business risk as measured by the deviation from expected earnings may impair the firm's ability to meet its interest or amortization payments. The more variability in operating income, the greater the chance of bond default. In the evaluation of either security, the presence of business risk increases the risk to the investor. In more conventional terms, the quality of the earnings stream is less. In order to compensate for this additional risk, the investor must demand a higher return.

Because business risk is independent of the other risks in the PDV framework, it may be added to the other risks to get the total risk involved with the particular stream of future benefits. Therefore, it is necessary to add a measure of business risk to the real interest rate and the purchasing power risk in the discount factor. This discount factor r now comprises all three risks covered so far and is

$$r = i + p + b$$

where i equals the real interest rate (including interest rate risk considerations), p equals the purchasing power risk premium found in the pure interest rate, and b equals a measure of business risk. We can include the business risk factor in the discount factor for the same reasons that we include the other factors. Just as the real interest rate and the purchasing power risk decrease the value of the analyst's projected earnings stream, so also does business risk.

To illustrate the point, let us take the following example. There is a 5-year bond that promises to pay $50 per year in interest at the end of each of the next 5 years and be redeemed at the end of 5 years for $1,000. In the market place a 5-year United States government bond is yielding 5 percent. If the rate of inflation is expected to be 3 percent per year in the next 5 years, the purchasing power risk premium is 3 percent, and the real interest rate 2 percent. If the bond were a United States government bond, there would be no business risk, and the discount factor would be

$$\begin{aligned} r &= i + p \\ &= 0.02 + 0.03 \\ &= 0.05 \end{aligned}$$

The PDV of the government bond would be

$$\begin{aligned} \text{PDV} &= \frac{50}{(1 + 0.05)} + \frac{50}{(1 + 0.05)^2} + \frac{50}{(1 + 0.05)^3} + \frac{50}{(1 + 0.05)^4} \\ &\quad + \frac{50}{(1 + 0.05)^5} + \frac{1{,}000}{(1 + 0.05)^5} \\ &= \$1{,}000 \end{aligned}$$

If the same bond were being offered by a steel manufacturer, business risk would be present. If the measure of business risk were the 0.06 computed in the example in Table 12.2, the discount factor would be

$$r = i + p + b$$
$$= 0.02 + 0.03 + 0.06$$
$$= 0.11$$

The PDV of this bond would be

$$\text{PDV} = \frac{50}{(1+0.11)} + \frac{50}{(1+0.11)^2} + \frac{50}{(1+0.11)^3} + \frac{50}{(1+0.11)^4} + \frac{50}{(1+0.11)^5} + \frac{1{,}000}{(1+0.11)^5}$$
$$= \$778.45$$

If a firm with only 0.03 business risk offered the same bond, the PDV of the bond would be

$$\text{PDV} = \frac{50}{(1+0.08)} + \frac{50}{(1+0.08)^2} + \frac{50}{(1+0.08)^3} + \frac{50}{(1+0.08)^4} + \frac{50}{(1+0.08)^5} + \frac{1{,}000}{(1+0.08)^5}$$
$$= \$880.08$$

The inclusion of business risk in the discount factor adjusts the value of the expected stream of benefits so as to compensate the investor for undertaking the business risk. The larger the business risk associated with a particular stream, the larger the discount factor.

SUMMARY

In the consideration of business risk, we move from the risks associated with general financial market conditions, that is, real interest rate risk and purchasing power risk, to risks that are particular to individual firms. Business risk is independently determined from the other risks in the PDV framework. Business risk is a function of the operating conditions and the variability that they impart to the firm's stream of operating income and expected dividends. Business risk itself is divided into two categories: internal and external. Internal business risk is associated with operating conditions that can be managed within the firm and is reflected in the operating efficiency of the firm. External business risk is associated with the operating conditions imposed on the firm by circumstances beyond its control, such as the political and economic environment in which it operates. The variability imparted to the operating income by the operating conditions also exposes the investor to the risk of loss. Deviations from the expected stream of future benefits caused by business risk may decrease the present discounted value of the stream and cause capital loss to the investor.

The attempts to measure business risk have generally followed the industry classifications system. In the extreme form, this system implies that business risk among firms in the same industry is equal but that business risk among industries is different. This approach has not only proved cumbersome in practice but has also had very little empirical support. Instead, it is suggested that the measure of residual variance of actual operating income from expected operating income, scaled by the average of the expected income for the period, be used as a surrogate measure for business risk.

If this measure of business risk or some similar quantifiable measure is used, the PDV framework may be adjusted to give explicit consideration to business risk. Because business risk is independent of the other risks, the analyst must add it to the other risks to derive the total risk attached to any particular income stream. This may be done by including the measure of business risk in the discount factor. When this is done, the higher the business risk, the higher the discount factor and the lower the PDV for any particular stream of benefits. Therefore, the investor will have been rewarded for the additional risk.

QUESTIONS

12.1 Define business risk. What influences business risk?

12.2 What is external business risk? Describe the major external business risk factors.

12.3 What is internal business risk? Describe the general categories of internal business risk.

12.4 Describe the usual procedure used among analysts to measure the degree of business risk associated with a firm. What are the shortcomings of such a system?

12.5 What are the advantages of using the standardized residual variance method of business risk measurement? What are the disadvantages?

PROBLEMS

12.1 Compute the deviation of expected operating earnings from actual operating earnings as a percentage of actual operating earnings for the farm equipment manufacturer cited in the chapter during each of the normal, recession, and boom periods. The farm equipment manufacturer wishes to reduce the variability in earnings by diversifying. What would be the percentage of deviation in operating earnings if the farm equipment manufacturer merged with the chewing gum manufacturer?

12.2 Five years ago, a firm's operating income was $4 per share. This was expected to increase at $0.10 per year during the following 5 years. Compute the residual variance and the business risk for the firm from the following actual per share operating income.

Year	1	2	3	4	5
Operating earnings per share	$4.10	$4.00	$4.20	$4.50	$4.90

REFERENCES

Gonedes, Nicholas J. "A Test of the Equivalent-Risk Class Hypothesis," *Journal of Financial and Quantitative Analysis,* 4:159–177, June, 1969.

Hubbard, Charles L., and Clark A. Hawkins. *Theory of Valuation,* Scranton, Pa.: International Textbook Company, 1969.

Lindsay, John R., and Arnold W. Sametz. *Financial Management: An Analytical Approach,* Homewood, Ill.: Richard D. Irwin, Inc., 1967.

Mayer, Robert W. "Analysis of Internal Risk in the Individual Firm," *Financial Analysts Journal,* 15:91–95, November, 1959.

Modigliani, Franco, and Merton H. Miller. "The Cost of Capital, Corporation Finance and the Theory of Investment," *The American Economic Review,* 48:261–297, June, 1958.

Robichek, Alexander A., and Steward C. Myers. *Optimal Financing Decisions,* Englewood Cliffs, N.J.: Prentice-Hall, Inc., 1965.

Sauvain, Harry C. *Investment Management,* 3d ed., Englewood Cliffs, N.J.: Prentice-Hall, Inc., 1967.

Solomon, Ezra. *The Theory of Financial Management,* New York: Columbia University Press, 1963.

Van Horne, James C. *Financial Management and Policy,* Englewood Cliffs, N.J.: Prentice-Hall, Inc., 1968.

Weston, J. Fred, and Eugene F. Brigham. *Managerial Finance,* 2d ed., New York: Holt, Rinehart and Winston, Inc., 1966.

13
Financial Risk

Financial risk is associated with the method used by the firm to finance its investments and is reflected in its capital structure. The addition of debt to a pure equity capital structure introduces variability into the pattern of net earnings and expected dividends per share beyond that already imparted by business risk. As debt becomes a larger percentage of the capital structure, more fixed claims on the income stream are sustained by the firm, and the firm is said to be *leveraged*. The presence of these fixed claims causes the amount of the dividend stream that eventually reaches the stockholder to be more variable for any given situation than would have otherwise been the case. Whatever would have been the variability in the earnings without debt is magnified when debt is present.

Financial risk, as we are concerned with it in this chapter, arises only when there is debt in the capital structure. This is opposed to the concept of the business risk that is present as long as the firm is in business, regardless of how the firm is financed. Both risks account for variability in earning and expected dividends, and both are associated with some deviation from expected benefits. The business risk deviation is reflected in the operating earnings, that is, earnings before interest and taxes. By using operating income, the analyst can examine the stream of earnings before the fixed claims have exerted any influence on the income stream. Financial risk is concerned with the deviations introduced by the addition of debt to the capital structure. To measure financial risk, it is necessary to separate the effect of each form of risk from the total deviation in expected earnings.[1] One commonly used measure of financial risk is the debt-equity ratio. It is usually assumed that an increase in the debt-equity ratio reflects increased financial risk. Although the

[1] For simplicity of explanation, we assume that there are no income taxes.

debt-equity ratio is a measure that is independent of any business risk, it does not necessarily reflect the variability in the earnings per share because of debt in the capital structure. One of the aims of this chapter is to explore a method of measuring financial risk based on the variability in earnings after interest but before taxes.

Financial risk is independent of the other risks in the PDV framework. Business risk may be present when financial risk is not if the firm has no debt financing. As in the case of business risk, however, it is unique to the individual firm and does not evolve from the risks present in the general financial markets. Financial risk may be incurred only when debt is added to the capital structure and is unaffected by pure interest rate risk and purchasing power risk, although the latter two risks may appear in the cost of the debt. For example, it is possible that the cost of a firm's debt may increase, even if the percentage of debt in its capital structure remains unchanged because of upward movements in all interest rates. Such increased debt costs should never be confused with an increase in financial risk. Only when the potential for variability in the earnings is increased because of the addition of debt to the capital structure is financial risk increased.

This chapter demonstrates that a leveraged firm is exposed to potentially more volatility in its earnings per share and has a greater potential for deviating from its expected trend in earnings per share than an unleveraged firm. The theoretical implications of this volatility on the value of the common stock, bonds, and the firm itself is explored. Finally, financial risk is incorporated into the PDV framework by a measure that attempts to separate the business and the financial risk effects on the variability of earnings.

FINANCIAL LEVERAGE

Financial leverage is the introduction of debt or other fixed income liabilities into the capital structure in an attempt to increase the return to the shareholders. By selling debt to finance a specified dollar amount of investment, the firm needs less equity or fewer shares outstanding to command the same amount of assets. This implies that the profit base is larger for each outstanding share. If the return on the assets purchased by debt is larger than the cost of the debt, the shareholders receive the difference. Without putting up more equity funds, the shareholders have received a larger return. But financial leverage is a double-edged sword in that if the return on the assets purchased by debt is less than the cost of the debt, the shareholders are required to make up the difference and so receive less than if the asset had been purchased without debt or not purchased at all.

We can, perhaps, best grasp this concept of financial leverage if we examine the example in Tables 13.1a and 13.1b. Continuing with the farm equipment manufacturer in the previous chapter, we assume that he needs $2.5 million in assets to generate the sales in Tables 13.1a and 13.1b. Without debt, this firm can finance this $2.5 million by selling 100,000 shares of stock at $25 per share. During normal years, the firm earns 10 percent on its investment. During recession years, the firm earns only 6.4 percent, and during boom years the firm earns 15.8 percent. Let us assume in this hypothetical firm a 10 percent growth in earnings per share for the next 3 years. According to Table 13.1a, the farm equipment manufacturer earns $2.50 per share in the normal year, $1.60 per share in the recession year, and $3.95 per share in the boom year with 100,000 shares outstanding.

TABLE 13.1a Financial Leverage
Farm Equipment Manufacturer, Inc. (Without Debt)

		Year			
		1	2		3
		Normal	Recession		Boom
Sales		$1,000,000	900,000		1,161,111
Fixed costs	650,000		650,000	650,000	
Variable costs	100,000		90,000	116,111	
Total costs		750,000	740,000		766,111
Operating earnings		250,000	160,000		395,000
Interest		0	0		0
Net earnings		250,000	160,000		395,000
Expected net earnings		250,000	275,000		302,500
Deviation		0	115,000		92,500
Net earnings per share (100,000 shares)		$2.50	$1.60		$3.95
Expected net earnings per share		2.50	2.75		3.02
Deviation per share		0	1.15		0.93

In contrast, Table 13.1b depicts the identical firm under the identical circumstances except that the $2.5 million in assets is financed with $1.25 million in 8 percent debt and 50,000 shares of stock sold at $25 per share. This means that the firm has committed itself to pay $100,000 per year in interest to the bondholders but, at the same time, has reduced the number of shares needed to finance the firm to 50,000.

What has this done to earnings per share? Table 13.1b reveals that earnings per share in the normal year have now jumped to $3. How could this have occurred when nothing has changed except the addition of debt? The answer is twofold. First, the firm has earned 10 percent on the assets that it bought with money borrowed at 8 percent. This means that stockholders have received a 2 percent profit differential on the $1.25 million that the firm borrowed to finance the asset purchase or an additional $25,000 per year. Second, the firm has command over the same $2.5 million of assets it had before with only half the number of shares outstanding. This means the additional $25,000 per year that accrues to the shareholders because of financial leverage is divided among fewer shares. With only 50,000 shares outstanding the additional $25,000 is equal to $0.50 per share, which represents the difference between the normal year per share profit without financial leverage and with financial leverage.

TABLE 13.1b Financial Leverage
Farm Equipment Manufacturer, Inc. (With Debt)

		Year 1		Year 2		Year 3
		Normal		Recession		Boom
Sales		$1,000,000		900,000		1,161,111
Fixed costs	650,000		650,000		650,000	
Variable costs	100,000		90,000		116,111	
Total costs		750,000		740,000		766,111
Operating earnings		250,000		160,000		395,000
Interest		100,000		100,000		100,000
Net earnings		150,000		60,000		295,000
Expected net earnings		150,000		175,000		202,500
Deviation		0		115,000		92,500
Earnings per share (50,000 shares)		$3.00		$1.20		$5.90
Expected earnings per share		3.00		3.50		4.05
Deviation per share		0		2.30		1.85

Financial leverage does not always add to the per share earnings. It may have a negative effect if the return to the assets purchased with the borrowed funds is less than the cost of the debt. According to Table 13.1b, the firm earned only $1.20 per share in the recession year when financial leverage was present. This is $0.40 per share less than the

$1.60 per share earned when the financial leverage was not present. The explanation for the lower earnings per share is similar to the explanation for the higher earnings experienced in the normal year. During the recession year the return on the assets purchased with the $1.25 million borrowed at 8 percent was only 6.4 percent. This means that 1.6 percent of the cost of the debt, or $20,000, must be paid to the bondholders from funds that would otherwise have gone to the stockholders. Because there are only 50,000 shares outstanding, each share is penalized $0.40, the difference between the $1.60 earned without financial leverage and the $1.20 earned with financial leverage.

Financial leverage magnifies not only the decline in earnings per share but also the increases. For example, Tables 13.1a and 13.1b reveal that the jump in sales for the boom year leads to a much larger earnings per share when debt is used. With financial leverage, earnings per share jump to $5.90 in the boom year, compared with $3.95 when financial leverage is not present.

Although the use of financial leverage may promise higher earnings per share, it also brings with it greater risk. Note from Tables 13.1a and 13.1b that the variability in earnings per share is substantially higher for the leveraged situation than for the unleveraged situation. The maximum expected earnings are also higher in the leveraged situation. Without leverage, earnings per share vary from a low of $1.60 to a high of $3.95, with average earnings per share at $2.68. With financial leverage, earnings per share vary from a low of $1.20 to a high of $5.90, with an average earnings per share of $3.39. This variability in earnings per share imparts greater potential deviation from what the investor expects earnings per share to be and exposes the investor to greater risk. This is illustrated in Tables 13.1a and 13.1b. Without leverage, the deviations in earnings per share are $1.15 for year 2 and $0.93 for year 3. With financial leverage, the deviations in earnings per share are $2.30 in year 2 and $1.85 in year 3. The higher the debt-equity ratio, the greater the potential for deviation from the expected earnings per share, and the greater the financial risk associated with this particular firm's securities.

FINANCIAL LEVERAGE AND SECURITIES PRICES

Financial Leverage and Stock Prices

Financial leverage has an effect on the price of both the common stock and the bonds of the firm that issues debt. We first turn our attention to the effect on common stock prices. As seen from the example in Tables 13.1a and 13.1b, financial leverage may increase expected earnings and, therefore, expected dividends per share and the potential deviation of actual earnings and dividends per share from expected earnings and dividends per share. The increase in expected earnings per share should increase the present discounted value of the stock, for now each share may anticipate a larger future stream of benefits. On the other hand, the same financial leverage that causes an increase in expected earnings per share also exposes the investor to the greater risk of not realizing the expected stream of benefits. This greater risk exposure should increase the discount factor in the PDV framework and lead to a lower present discounted value or share price for any given stream of earnings. Thus, we see that financial leverage elicits opposing forces within the PDV framework of share price evaluation. If the effect of financial leverage is to increase the expected earnings and dividends per share more than to increase the discount factor, the PDV of the share rises. If the increase in the expected earnings and dividends per share is less than the increase in the discount factor, the PDV of the share must fall. This may be demonstrated with the farm equipment manufacturer. Without financial leverage, this company could be expected to earn the stream in column 2 (from Chapter 12); with financial leverage, the expected earnings stream would be the higher one of column 3:

(1) Year	(2) Expected earnings per share (no leverage)	(3) Expected earnings per share (leverage)
1	$2.50	$3.00
2	2.75	3.50
3	3.02	4.05
4	3.32	4.45
5	3.65	4.89
6	4.02	5.38
7–25	4.00	5.00

Assuming that all earnings are paid as dividends,[2] the PDV of the unleveraged earnings dividend is

$$PDV = \frac{2.50}{(1+0.15)} + \frac{2.75}{(1+0.15)^2} + \frac{3.02}{(1+0.15)^3} + \frac{3.32}{(1+0.15)^4}$$
$$+ \frac{3.65}{(1+0.15)^5} + \frac{4.02}{(1+0.15)^6} + \sum_{j=7}^{25} + \frac{4.00}{(1+0.15)^j}$$

PDV = $22.38

[2] Although we could assume any payout ratio and use the resulting implied dividends in the PDV evaluation without altering the concept.

Financial leverage and securities prices

In the leveraged situations expected earnings and dividends would rise and the discount factor would increase, for example, to 16 percent. The PDV of the leveraged stream would be

$$\text{PDV} = \frac{3.00}{(1+0.16)} + \frac{3.50}{(1+0.16)^2} + \frac{4.05}{(1+0.16)^3} + \frac{4.45}{(1+0.16)^4}$$
$$+ \frac{4.89}{(1+0.16)^5} + \frac{5.38}{(1+0.16)^6} + \sum_{j=7}^{25} \frac{5.00}{(1+0.16)^j}$$

$$\text{PDV} = \$28.95$$

The PDV has increased, because the increase in expected dividends exceeded the increase in the discount factor. In this instance, leverage has worked to the advantage of the stockholder.

Unfavorable Leverage

Leverage may also work to the disadvantage of the stockholders, despite an increase in earnings and expected dividends. For example, if the discount factor had risen to 20 percent when debt was introduced into the capital structure, the PDV would have been

$$\text{PDV} = \frac{3.00}{(1+0.20)} + \frac{3.50}{(1+0.20)^2} + \frac{4.05}{(1+0.20)^3} + \frac{4.45}{(1+0.20)^4}$$
$$+ \frac{4.89}{(1+0.20)^5} + \frac{5.38}{(1+0.20)^6} + \sum_{j=7}^{25} \frac{5.00}{(1+0.20)^j}$$

$$\text{PDV} = \$19.89$$

The value of the shares would now be less than in the unleveraged situation.

Leverage and Risk

We also see that the leveraged situation exposes the investor to increased risk for which he must be compensated. The downside stock price potential for the PDV of the farm equipment manufacturer's leveraged stream of future earnings and implied dividends is greater than the potential downside risk for the unleveraged stream. In Chapter 12 we saw that the PDV of the farm equipment manufacturer's expected dividends (ex ante) was $22.38 and that the PDV of the actual dividends (ex post) was $17.34. The unleveraged stream had a price decline of $5.04.

The PDV of the leveraged stream has a greater price decline, because leverage magnifies variability in the expected earnings and dividend streams. For example, the expected leverage stream is higher than the expected unleveraged stream, and the actual leveraged stream deviates more from the expected than the actual unleveraged stream, as illustrated below:

Year	Expected unleveraged earnings	Expected leveraged earnings	Actual unleveraged earnings	Actual leveraged earnings
1	$2.50	$3.00	$2.50	$3.00
2	2.75	3.50	1.60	1.20
3	3.02	4.05	3.95	5.90
4	3.32	4.45	1.60	1.20
5	3.65	4.89	2.50	3.00
6	4.02	5.38	2.75	3.30
7–25	4.00	5.00	3.00	3.50

The PDV of the expected leveraged stream, assuming a discount factor of 0.16 and dividends equal to earnings is

$$\text{PDV} = \frac{3.00}{(1+0.16)} + \frac{3.50}{(1+0.16)^2} + \frac{4.05}{(1+0.16)^3} + \frac{4.45}{(1+0.16)^4}$$
$$+ \frac{4.89}{(1+0.16)^5} + \frac{5.38}{(1+0.16)^6} + \sum_{j=7}^{25} \frac{5.00}{(1+0.16)^j}$$

PDV = $28.95

The PDV of the actual leveraged stream is

$$\text{PDV} = \frac{3.00}{(1+0.16)} + \frac{1.20}{(1+0.16)^2} + \frac{5.90}{(1+0.16)^3} + \frac{1.20}{(1+0.16)^4}$$
$$+ \frac{3.00}{(1+0.16)^5} + \frac{3.30}{(1+0.16)^6} + \sum_{j=7}^{25} \frac{3.50}{(1+0.16)^j}$$

PDV = $19.16

If the investor had purchased the stock based on his earnings and dividend expectations for the leveraged situation, he would have paid $28.95 for a stream of benefits that was actually worth only $19.16. In the leveraged case, the investor has been exposed to a downside risk of $9.79; in the unleveraged case he has been exposed to a downside risk of $5.04. As in the case of business risk, the difference between the PDV of the expected stream (ex ante) and the PDV of the actual stream (ex post) represents the potential risk to the investor. The greater the difference, the larger the financial risk, and the larger must be the financial risk factor f.

Finanical Leverage and Bond Prices

Financial leverage has an analogous effect on bond prices. Because interest payments on the bond are fixed, financial leverage cannot alter the stream of expected future benefits, as it does in the case of common stock. The presence of fixed income claims on the earnings stream, however, increases the possibility that any given earnings are insufficient to cover the larger total interest payments. As the ratio of debt to equity increases, the potential variability in earnings per share also increases. This increased variability means that there is greater likelihood that in any one year, current income is insufficient to meet these fixed claims on income. It is reasonable to assume that as the debt-equity ratio rises, the discount factor in the PDV for the firm's bonds rises and puts downward pressure on the firm's bond prices.

OPTIMAL FINANCIAL LEVERAGE[3]

If the use of financial leverage raises the discount factor of both equity and debt, why does the firm use financial leverage at all? The answer is that the firm is trying to maximize its equity value. In this effort, the firm attempts to finance the assets, which generate the earnings, with the lease average cost (smallest discount factor) of capital; that is, the firm attempts to combine debt and equity financing, so that the average cost of all financing is the lowest attainable.

We may measure the average overall cost of capital by using the weighted average of the cost of each type of capital. For example, using the book value of debt and equity, the overall cost of capital k_0 would be

$$k_0 = 0.50(0.10) + 0.50(0.05)$$
$$= 7.5\%$$

In general symbols the overall cost of capital k_0 equals the weighted average of the cost of equity k_e and the cost of debt k_d:

$$k_0 = \frac{D}{D+E}(k_d) + \frac{E}{D+E}(k_e)$$

where D = book value of debt in capital structure
E = book value of equity in capital structure

The firm's objective is to minimize k_0.

---

[3] There remains disagreement as to the exact influence of debt on the firm's cost of capital, which is beyond the subject matter of this text. For more detailed discussions of the cost of capital see E. Solomon, *The Theory of Financial Management*, Columbia University Press, New York, 1963; F. Modigliani and M. Miller, "The Cost-of-Capital, Corporation Finance and the Theory of Investment," *American Economic Review*, June, 1958, pp. 261–297; J. F. Weston and E. Brigham, *Managerial Finance*, Holt, Rinehart and Winston, Inc., New York, 1969, chap. 11.

With a given amount of assets that generate a given stream of expected earnings, the firm endeavors to finance these assets at the least cost. Assume that the firm may choose any of the combinations of debt and equity scheduled below, where D is the percentage of debt in the capital structure and E the percentage of equity in the capital structure:

E	k_e, percent	D	k_d, percent	D/E	k_o, percent
100	10	0	5	0	10
90	10.5	10	5	1/9	9.95
80	11.0	20	5	2/8	9.80
70	11.5	30	5	3/7	9.55
60	12	40	5	4/6	9.20
50	15	50	6	5/5	10.50
40	18	60	8	6/4	12
30	20	70	10	7/3	13
20	25	80	13	8/2	15.40
10	30	90	20	9/1	21

In this example, the value of the equity is maximized at the debt-equity ratio of 40/60, where the overall cost of capital is minimized.[4] Note that as more debt is introduced into the capital structure, the cost of

---

[4] To demonstrate that the market value of the equity is maximized where the average cost of capital is minimized, assume a 10 percent return on investment and the interest rates found above:

(1) D/E	(2) Equity	(3) Debt	(4) Earnings	(5) Interest	(6) (4) − (5) Earnings for common	(7) k_e	(8) (6) ÷ (7) Equity value
0	$1,000	$ 0	$ 100	$ 0	$100.00	10.0%	$1,000.00
1/9	1,000	111	111	5.55	104.45	10.5	1,004.30
2/8	1,000	250	125	12.50	112.51	11.0	1,022.70
3/7	1,000	428	142.80	21.40	121.40	11.5	1,055.60
4/6	1,000	666	166	33.30	132.70	12.0	1,105.80
5/5	1,000	1,000	200	60.00	140.00	15.0	933.30
6/4	1,000	1,500	250	90.00	160.00	18.0	888.90
7/3	1,000	2,333	333	233.00	100.00	20.0	500.00
8/2	1,000	4,000	500	520.00	...	25.0	...
9/1	1,000	9,000	1,000	1,800.00	...	30.0	...

Note that the highest equity value occurs at the least overall cost of capital, not merely at the lowest cost of equity.

equity rises in response to the additional financial risk. The cost of debt does not rise until substantial amounts of debt have been introduced into the capital structure, because lenders envision no additional financial risk as the firm increases debt to 40 percent of its capital structure. At the first introduction of debt into the capital structure, the lower cost of the debt brings down the overall cost of capital, despite the rise in the cost of equity. This downward trend in the cost of capital continues until the optimum debt-equity ratio is reached. From that point on, the overall cost of capital increases. Graphically this is illustrated in Figure 13.1. K_e starts to rise as financial leverage is introduced into the capital structure; at first k_d remains constant. This implies that the weighted average cost of capital k_o starts to decline as debt is introduced into the capital structure. After the optimum point, k_e accelerates quite rapidly because of increased financial risk, and k_d also begins to rise rapidly because of increased financial risk. This reverses the downward trend in the overall cost of capital, and k_o begins to rise. With further introductions of debt into the capital structure, the rise in k_o accelerates.

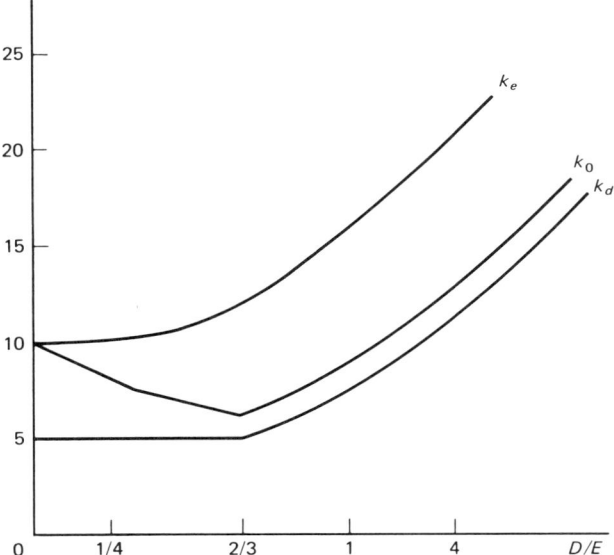

Figure 13.1. Effect of debt on the cost of capital.

FINANCIAL RISK IN THE PDV FRAMEWORK

Financial risk is another risk that the investor faces when he purchases a financial asset. As in the case of the other risks, it is independently determined by its own particular factors. In this case, financial risk is a function of the firm's financing methods. The degree of financial risk associated with any security is not influenced by what occurs in the other risks that we have considered.

As the degree of financial risk to which the investor is exposed increases, the expected stream of future benefits becomes less valuable and the discount factor in the PDV framework must be increased. The increase in the discount factor penalizes the worth of the stream of future benefits and, as in the case of the other risks, brings about an appropriate adjustment in the stock price to compensate for the added risk. Because financial risk is independent of the other risks, we may add the appropriate measure of risk to the other risks to derive total risk. In our terms this means that the discount factor r is equal to the sum of the real interest rate, the purchasing power risk, business risk, and financial risk. In symbols

$$r = i + p + b + f$$

Thus, the PDV evaluation framework would be

$$\text{PDV} = \sum_{j=1}^{n} \frac{D_j}{(1 + i + p + b + f)^j}$$

The precise measure of financial risk to be used, however, must still be decided. Up to now we have basically associated a higher debt-equity ratio with increased financial risk. Although it is true that higher debt-equity ratios are associated with increased financial risk, they do not describe the real essence of financial risk; that is, they do not measure the deviations in actual earnings and implied dividends from expected earnings and implied dividends caused by the variability in earnings associated with financial risk. What we need to measure are the deviations from expected earnings caused by financial leverage in a selected time period. A similar procedure was used to measure business risk in Chapter 12.

Following the same reasoning that we used to measure business risk, we can take a measure of financial risk as the earnings per share after interest but before taxes. This should include all fluctuations that are caused by the fixed income claims. We can then compare this actual earnings per share figure with what we had anticipated and determine the residual variance. Finally, we can relate this residual variance to the average expected earnings after interest to adjust for the scale factor. This procedure is illustrated in Table 13.2. The expected earnings per share for a 5-year period are in column 2, and the actual earnings per share for the same 5-year period are in column 3. The squared deviation of the actual from the expected is in column 4. The residual variance is approximately 0.50. When this is divided by the average of the expected earnings, we arrive at a potentially useful, although certainly not definitive, measure of the total financial and business risk associated

TABLE 13.2 Standardized Residual Variance in Earnings per Share

(1) Year	(2) Expected earnings	(3) Actual earnings	(4) Deviations	(5) Deviations squared
1	3.00	3.00	0.00	0.00
2	3.30	2.30	+1.00	1.00
3	3.60	2.50	+1.10	1.21
4	3.90	4.40	−0.50	0.25
5	4.25	4.50	−0.25	0.06
	18.05			2.52

Residual variance = $2.52/5 \cong 0.50$
Standardized residual variance = $0.50/3.61 \cong 0.139$
Scale factor = $18.05/5 = 3.61$

with any particular security. It must be noted and may be readily seen from the example in Tables 13.1a and 13.1b that the deviations of earnings per share that we have just constructed are caused in any form by the presence of both business and financial risk. From Table 13.1a, it is apparent that deviations in earnings per share already existed before the addition of debt to the capital structure, as reflected in Table 13.1b. The introduction of debt added further potential deviation. When we derive the deviations in earnings per share, we have captured the effect of both business and financial risk. The only way to separate the two effects is to subtract the business risk, as measured by the residual variance in operating income, from the residual variance in earnings per share. The difference is financial risk, as derived in Table 13.3.[5]

TABLE 13.3 Calculation of Financial Risk

Scaled average deviations in earnings per share	0.139
Scaled business risk (from Table 12.2)	0.060
Financial risk	0.079

SUMMARY

Financial risk is associated with the method used by the firm to finance its assets. The higher the percentage of debt in the capital structure,

---

[5] As in the case of the business risk measure, there are several possible measures of variability that may be used. See footnote 5, Chap. 12. Also, as in the case of the business risk measure, this financial risk measure is a historical indicator of expected financial risk and may be inaccurate if there is reason to suspect a fundamental change in future earnings variability.

the greater is the exposure to financial risk. It was demonstrated that the addition of debt to the firm's capital structure increases the potential for variability in earnings and expected dividends per share and potential deviation from expected earnings and dividends per share. It was also shown that financial leverage is a two-edged sword in the sense that it can increase as well as decrease the expected earnings. The effect of financial leverage on stock prices may also be favorable or unfavorable. If the use of debt sufficiently increases the expected earnings and dividends to offset the rise in the discount factor, the stock price should rise. If the use of debt does not sufficiently increase the expected earnings and dividends to offset the rise in the discount factor, the stock price should fall.

Within the PDV framework financial risk is treated, as are the other risks associated with the purchase of a financial asset. Because financial risk is determined independently of the other risks, it may be added as another element to the discount factor. We can measure financial risk by deriving the average deviation in earnings per share after interest payments but before taxes and subtracting the average deviation in operating earnings from this figure.

QUESTIONS

13.1 What is financial risk?
13.2 What is financial leverage? Explain the positive effects of financial leverage on earnings per share.
13.3 Explain the effect of financial leverage on stock prices.
13.4 What is downside risk?
13.5 Are bonds affected by financial leverage? If so, explain.
13.6 What is meant by the optimal level of financial leverage?
13.7 Why is financial risk measured on an after interest before tax basis?

PROBLEMS

13.1 Compute the financial risk of a firm from the following data:

Year	Actual earnings	Expected earnings
1	1.50	1.80
2	3.00	2.00
3	3.00	2.25
4	2.90	2.40
5	3.10	2.50

The firm's business risk is 9 percent. Based on the information provided, explain your opinion of the stock as an investment opportunity.

13.2 Illustrate the effects of financial leverage on earnings per share in each period when the firm changes its debt-equity ratio from 0 to 1. The firm's present capital structure is composed entirely of $2,000,000 (100,000 shares) in common stock and its cost of debt is 10 percent.

	Normal	Recession	Boom
Operating earnings	$300,000	$200,000	$500,000
Tax (50%)	150,000	100,000	250,000
Net income	$150,000	$100,000	$250,000

13.3 Compare the earnings per share deviation in Problem 13.2 for the financially leveraged case. Earnings per share, for the nonfinancially leveraged case are $1.50, $1.00, and $2.50 respectively. Earnings per share are expected to be 10 percent higher in the leveraged case.

REFERENCES

Findlay, M. Chapman, III, and Edward E. Williams. *An Integrated Analysis for Managerial Finance,* Englewood Cliffs, N.J.: Prentice-Hall, Inc., 1970.

Hubbard, Charles L., and Clark A. Hawkins. *Theory of Valuation,* Scranton, Pa.: International Textbook Company, 1969.

Lindsay, John R., and Arnold W. Sametz. *Financial Management: An Analytical Approach,* Homewood, Ill.: Richard D. Irwin, Inc., 1967.

Peterson, D. E. *A Quantitative Framework for Financial Management,* Homewood, Ill.: Richard D. Irwin, Inc., 1969.

Solomon, Ezra. *The Theory of Financial Management,* New York: Columbia University Press, 1963.

Van Horne, James C. *Financial Management and Policy,* Englewood Cliffs, N.J.: Prentice-Hall, Inc., 1968.

Weston, J. Fred, and Eugene F. Brigham. *Managerial Finance,* 3d ed., New York: Holt, Rinehart and Winston, Inc., 1969.

Appendix 13A
Summary of PDV Evaluation Framework

SUMMARY OF PDV EVALUATION FRAMEWORK

Let us summarize the PDV evaluation framework as we have constructed it. We started with the present discounted value of the security's future stream of benefits $F_i (i = 1, n)$ as the basic worth of any financial asset. The PDV of any financial asset was then

$$(13A.1) \quad \text{PDV} = \sum_{i=1}^{n} \frac{F_i}{(1+r)^i}$$

To explain the PDV at a point in time, we developed procedures for estimating the future stream of benefits F_i and for establishing the appropriate discount factor r. In the case of common stock, the stream of future benefits is the expected dividends D_i from now until infinity, where dividend expectations are derived from earnings estimates. Any expected growth in the future stream is incorporated into the dividend forecasts as increased dividend estimates. The PDV of a stock is then

$$(13A.2) \quad \text{PDV} = \sum_{i=1}^{\infty} \frac{D_i}{(1+r)^i}$$

The appropriate discount factor r comprises the real interest rate factor i, the purchasing power risk premium p, the business risk factor b, and the financial risk factor f. The real interest rate reflects the time value of money, including interest rate risk considerations. The purchasing power risk premium is the increment in the discount factor needed to compensate the stockholder for his anticipated loss of purchasing power because of inflation. The business risk factor is the increment in the discount factor needed to compensate the stockholder for the risk

Summary of PDV evaluation framework

(variability) imparted to the stream of future dividends by the operating nature and environment of the company. The financial risk factor is the increment in the discount factor needed to compensate the stockholder for the risk (variability) imparted to the stream of future dividends by the debt financing of the company. The PDV of a stock is then

$$(13A.3) \quad \text{PDV} = \sum_{i=1}^{\infty} \frac{D_i}{(1+i+p+b+f)^i}$$

Although Equation (13.3) may explain the PDV of a stock at any given point in time, the change in PDV from this point to some future date is explained by the change in either the expected future stream or the components of the discount factor r, where $r = i + p + b + f$. A shift in the expected stream, given everything else constant, moves the PDV in the same direction as the shift in the expected stream. A shift in any one of the components of the discount factor (i, p, b, or f), given everything else constant, moves the PDV in the opposite direction.

GROWTH MODEL REVIEWED

In Chapter 3, we explored a growth model shorthand for the PDV evaluation framework in which the expected stream of future dividends D grows at a constant rate g from now until infinity. The model is

$$(13A.4) \quad \text{PDV} = \frac{D_1}{r - g}$$

It is worth briefly noting the implications of retained earnings on this model as opposed to the PDV framework.

Retained earnings finance the expansion of earning assets that enable the future stream of dividends to grow. The practice of retained earnings, however, increases the risk attached to the future stream. When earnings are retained instead of being paid out in dividends, the hope is that future dividends will be larger. But whether future dividends are actually increased because of the retention of earnings in the present is not a certainty. If, for example, the projects in which the retained earnings are invested do not prove so profitable as had been anticipated, the expected increase in dividends will not materialize. In other words, the further into the future the actual payment of the dividend to the stockholder, the greater the possibility that today's sacrificed dividend will not be compensated for in larger future dividends.[1] Because the

---

[1] M. Gordon, "Optimal Investment and Financing Policy," *Journal of Finance*, May, 1963, pp. 264–272.

policy of retaining earnings postpones the receipt of the dividend, it increases the risk. The higher the present percentage of earnings retained, the greater the risk.

In the PDV framework, this increased risk because of retained earnings is accounted for in the estimate of each future year's dividends. Several of the procedures developed in Chapters 5 to 7 may be used to adjust the future earnings estimates for this risk. In contrast, the growth model—Equation (13.4)—does not incorporate this risk into the estimation of the future dividends, for the dividends are fixed in the model at D_1. Therefore, this risk must be accounted for in the discount factor r.

This risk attached to the retention of earnings may be incorporated into r in the following manner:

$$r = i + p + b + f + a'\,(1 - D_1/E_1)$$

where $a'\,(1 - D_1/E_1)$ is a function of the rate of retention or 1 minus the payout ratio. As the percentage of retained earnings increases, the discount factor increases by some proportional amount a'. Also, as the percentage of retained earnings increases, the expected rate of growth g increases, because the earning assets are able to expand more rapidly with the larger reinvestment. Both r and g are now functions of the retained earnings percentage and will increase, although probably not in the same proportion, as the percentage of retained earnings increases. The growth model shorthand is thus

$$(13\text{A}.5) \quad \text{PDV} = \frac{D_1}{i + p + b + f + a'(1 - D_1/E_1) - g}$$

Part Four

The first three parts of the text have been devoted to establishing the theme that runs throughout security analysis. Once we have firmly grasped the essentials of the PDV evaluation framework, it is possible to come to grips with the basic considerations in the evaluation of any financial asset.

Now we must turn our attention to variations on the theme. Within the spectrum of financial assets are hybrids and variations that may impose certain adjustments to the basic theme. If we are to remain attuned to the pertinent factors in the evaluation of these particular securities, we must familiarize ourselves with these variations.

First, we turn our attention to the variations and hybrids that occur in bonds. Chapter 14 considers bond ratings, the call privilege, the conversion option, and the municipal bond. Each topic is discussed in light of how its individual characteristics bear on the evaluation procedure and what methods of analysis are available to evaluate these securities.

Chapter 15 concerns itself with the variations and hybrids of equity securities. These include preferred stocks, warrants, options, new issues, secondary distributions, bankruptcy, dilution, and mergers. Each topic is examined as to how it differs in form from the normal equity security and how it may be evaluated.

Chapter 16 devotes itself to the analysis of investment companies, particularly mutual funds. These shares are a special case of an equity security that must be evaluated in light of its representation of ownership in a diversified portfolio of securities.

14
Special Situations—Bonds

Prior to this chapter, we have considered all bonds as long-term debt instruments that promise to pay a fixed annual sum as interest for a stated period of time and then be redeemed for the face value of the bond at maturity. Although it is true that the description above captures the essence of what a bond is, there are numerous variations on the basic concept. For example, the bond may be secured by real property, or it may be unsecured, with the reputation of the issuer as the only security.

The exact terms of a bond are set forth in the corporate bond contract, that is, the bond indenture. The indenture usually specifies a trustee who is mutually satisfactory to both the lender and the borrower and who administers the terms of the indenture. The indenture usually specifies such items as the interest to be paid, the maturity of the debt, and any limitations that may be placed on the borrower's ability to pay dividends, make sinking fund payments, engage in merger activity, maintain adequate working capital, or sell further debt. The indenture also contains provisions that specify the nature and type of collateral, if any, the mechanics of interest and principal payments, and any special features, such as sinking funds, call provisions, and conversion options.

The most commonly found variations in bonds are in the collateral provisions and the special terms of call provisions and conversion options. When a bond is backed by real property collateral, it is said to be secured. Collateral provisions give the bondholder a lien on the property of the borrower. In the case of default, in which the borrower is unable to meet interest payments or otherwise fulfill the terms of the indenture, the bondholder has the right to receive any proceeds from the sale of the collateral. In today's economic environment, the worth of such a provision is unclear. The future stream of benefits promised to the bondholder is unlikely to be more secure because he has the privilege of receiving the proceeds from the sale of the borrower's assets. Only in the case of reorganization or liquidation is the security provision likely to be of any significance.

In reorganization, a trustee is appointed by the courts to determine the earning power of the firm and to establish a new capital structure under which the firm will be able to operate. In the process of establishing this new capital structure, the trustee distributes new securities to the old bondholders and stockholders according to their priority. Those with the most secured liens on the firm's valuable property have the highest priority and usually fare the best in the reorganization.

In liquidation, in which the assets of the firm are sold to pay off the creditors, among the firm's security holders, the secured bondholder has first claim on the proceeds from the sale of the collateral. This usually proves to be less of a loss than is involved with the unsecured bonds, although substantial loss may still be incurred.

There are several commonly used types of secured and unsecured bonds that offer varying degrees of security coverage. The mortgage bond offers as collateral some real property of the borrower. This may be a building, machinery, and so on. Mortgage bonds may be senior or junior, depending on the priority that they have in the claim on the asset. The first priority is the senior bond, which generally offers more security than the junior bond. The collateral bond offers as security the bonds or stocks of another company. The chattel bond is commonly used to finance transportation equipment, and the piece of equipment itself is the collateral. The debentures are the unsecured bonds of the firm and have the lowest priority among the bonds. The debenture may be subordinated to other debt securities outstanding, including previously issued debentures, or it may just be junior to the secured bonds.

The special features of the bonds with which we concern ourselves in this chapter are the call provision and the conversion option. The call provision gives the borrower the option of paying off the bond before maturity. Usually this option may be exercised only at a call premium that gives the investor a bonus above the face value of the bond if it is redeemed before maturity. We examine the implications of the call privilege and its effect on the bond's price.

The conversion option gives the bondholder the right to exchange the bond for the common stock of the corporation. A bond that has this feature is a convertible bond. This exchange option means that the convertible bond takes on some of the characteristics of the common stock as well as of the bond. We examine how the hybrid nature of the convertible bond affects the evaluation of the security and what techniques may be used for investing in convertible bonds.

We also investigate the characteristics of the municipal bond. These bonds, issued by state and local governments, have individual peculiarities which distinguish them from the corporate bond and which must be considered in evaluating their investment worth. The risks associated with municipal bonds are derived from operating conditions that do not readily avail themselves to the same analysis as corporate bonds. The return to municipal bonds is also different, because they are not subject to federal taxation. We explore how these factors may influence the investor's evaluation procedure and what evaluation techniques are available to the municipal bond investor.

CORPORATE BONDS

Investor experience with bonds has varied substantially since 1900. Combing the studies of Hickman[1] and Atkinson,[2] we get a picture that shows both the secular and cyclical default record of corporate bonds.

According to Hickman, there seem to be long-term waves of improvement and deterioration in bond quality. Hickman found that the percentage of par amounts of bonds offered going into default at any time in their life span was highest among the bonds offered in the first decade of the twentieth century, declined among bonds offered in the early 1920s, rose again for bonds offered between 1928 and 1933, and declined thereafter. In total, 17.3 percent of the outstanding par value of bonds defaulted between 1900 and 1943.[3] This compares with less than 10 percent default on the average par amount of outstanding bonds from 1945 to 1965 and less than 0.1 percent on the average outstanding par amount of bonds in 1965.[4] Of course, the earlier record is distorted by the presence of the Depression, and the post-Second World War period has not experienced an economic setback of such magnitude.

Cyclically, the default record of corporate bonds has not been what we normally expect. Particularly since 1945, defaults have not been concentrated in any part of the business cycle; that is, bond defaults have occurred almost randomly in the cycle. It seems as if the relatively mild recessions of the post-Second World War period have not forced corporations to default on their debt obligations. What has happened is that in both the pre-Second World War and postwar periods, the default rate is associated with the activity in the sale of bonds, not in the date of default. The default rate has been highest among those bonds

---

[1] W. B. Hickman, *Corporate Bond Quality and Investor Experience,* National Bureau of Economic Research, Princeton University Press, Princeton, N.J., 1958.

[2] T. R. Atkinson, *Trends in Corporate Bond Quality,* National Bureau of Economic Research, Columbia University Press, New York, 1967.

[3] Hickman, *op. cit.,* p. 10.

[4] Atkinson, *op. cit.,* p. 48.

which were sold at the peak volume in bond sales. Apparently, investor confidence during the year before and the year of the peak in business activity leads to overconfidence in the ability of marginal firms to meet new debt obligations. In this overconfidence, investors purchase the marginal offerings, only to experience default when the euphoria of the boom subsides. Atkinson concluded that "the process whereby bonds are offered [at the peak in the business cycle] and . . . subsequently default continues to be associated with the business cycle."

Bond Ratings

The Standard & Poor's Corporation and the Moody's Investor Service, Inc., publish ratings on bonds. They attempt to rank bonds in a descending order of quality that, in their opinion, reflects the probable risk of default and the potential magnitude of loss. The ratings are shown in Table 14.1 and descent in alphabetical order with AAA and Aaa the highest ratings. The ratings of A and higher indicate investment grade issues. The ratings of BBB signify a medium grade bond that borders on the investment grade quality. BB ratings are assigned to lower medium grade issues, and B rated bonds are considered speculative. CCC and CC grade bonds are considered outright speculations, and C rated bonds are income bonds (usually issued in reorganization and on which interest is paid only when earned) that are not paying interest. DDD and below are bonds that are in default. The ratings in one agency compare with those in the other, so that a S&P AAA is equivalent to a Moody's Aaa, although the two agencies do not necessarily agree on the quality of a particular bond and may assign different ratings to the same bond.

TABLE 14.1

Standard and poor's				Moody's		
AAA	BBB	CCC	DDD	Aaa	Baa	Caa
AA	BB	CC	DD	Aa	Ba	Ca
A	B	C	D	A	B	C

In their attempt to rate bonds, the rating agencies look at such factors as the adequacy of earnings to cover interest and amortization, lien protections, which include such considerations as priority, the adequacy of the property, and the indenture provisions as to limitations on new debt, dividend payments, and merger activity. In addition, the agencies look at the nature of the industry and its expected performance, the strength of the company, and the marketability of the bonds. Depending on what the agency sees in these factors, it then subjectively assigns a rating to the bond.

The record of the agencies has been reasonably good. From 1900 to 1943, the occurrence of default increased as the rating quality decreased (see Table 14.2). The default rate as a percentage of par value rose from 6 percent in the AAA and AA ratings to 13 percent in the A rating and to 42 percent in the BB and below ratings. The record since 1945 is difficult to judge because of the limited number of defaults and their concentration in the railroad industry. The agencies also exhibited a good record of downgrading the rating quality of a bond before it defaulted.

TABLE 14.2

Agency rating	Default rate	Promised yield	Realized yield
AAA	5.9	4.5	5.1
AA	6.0	4.6	5.0
A	13.4	4.9	5.0
BBB	19.1	5.4	5.7
BB and below	42.4	9.5	8.6

SOURCE: W. B. Hickman, *Corporate Bond Quality and Investor Experience*, National Bureau of Economic Research, Princeton University Press, Princeton, N.J., 1958, p. 10.

The ratings themselves have exhibited cyclical tendencies. Hickman found that the rating agencies tended to upgrade their ratings during the upward phases of the business cycle and to downgrade their ratings during the contractionary phase. The net volume of bonds upgraded by the agencies tended to expand in the business expansion and decline in the business contractions. A partial explanation for this cyclical pattern lies in the sensitivity of the various financial ratios used by the agencies to the business cycle. As the financial ratios change with the business cycle, the agencies respond by changing their ratings. Since 1945, this cyclical pattern among the ratings has not been so evident.

Another rating system explored by Hickman was the market rating system. In this approach, the bonds were rated in terms of the premium that the promised yield represented over the pure interest rate yield that prevailed at the time of offering. The default rate rose as the premium on the offered bond rose. Hickman concluded that the premium on the bond at the offering was a good indicator of the probable quality that the bond would have at redemption. Atkinson claims, however, that the search for higher returns in the post-Second World War period has "driven down yields on the poorer quality bonds, so that it is likely spurious indications of the recent trend in quality are obtained from the use of the market rating."

Investment Implications

When broad aggregates and samples of bonds were used, Hickman found that the realized yield on all bonds equaled the yield promised at the offering. The realized yield includes the capital gains and losses that the bonds experienced when they were either redeemed at a premium or extinguished at a loss. These capital gains and losses played a substantial role in the investors' experience with bonds. The capital gains were sufficient to offset any losses experienced by investors, so that, on average, the realized yield equaled the promised yield when the bonds were held to maturity.

The capital losses experienced rose as the quality of the bond offered declined. The higher promised yield on the lower quality bonds, however, was not completely offset by the higher capital losses. In terms of realized yields, the lower quality bonds actually returned more to the investor than the higher quality bonds. Hickman found the result as illustrated in Table 14.2.[5] From Table 14.2, it is apparent that promised yields and the default rate rose with a decrease in the quality of the bond. Accompanying the increased default rate were increased capital losses that tended to drag down the realized yield from the promised yield. Among the higher quality bonds, the promised yield was actually increased because of capital gains.

The investment implications from these observations are that a high grade bond portfolio, in the aggregate, experiences low default risk and loss rate, and comparatively stable prices. In addition, the high grade portfolio experiences low promised and realized returns. In contrast, the low grade bond portfolio experiences high promised yields and, if the risk is sufficiently diversified, high realized yields. At the same time, the low grade portfolio also experiences high default and loss rates, as well as price instability.

For the small investor, who is unable to diversify sufficiently, the advantages of the high grade portfolio outweigh the disadvantages. With capital gains and losses playing such a large role in the realized yield, the small investor may penalize his realized return if he encounters a default or loss situation. On the other hand, the large investor, who would not be hurt so much by default in a few of his holdings, because he has sufficiently diversified, could actually improve his expected real-

[5] Hickman, *op. cit.,* p. 10.

ized yield by purchasing lower grade bonds for their higher yields. This strategy seems to be at work in the portfolios of the large life insurance companies, who specialize in acquiring the lower grade bonds and holding them to maturity.

Earnings Coverage

One of the most commonly used indicators of bond quality is the times fixed charges earned ratio. This ratio reflects the ability of the firm to meet its fixed charges, such as interest, on its debt. The concept is to determine how much of its earnings are available to pay fixed charges and to relate this figure to the fixed charges. The amount of earnings available is usually calculated as the firm's net income before taxes and debt interest. We use income before taxes, because loan interest is paid before taxes and comes out of the earnings stream before taxes. We use earnings before interest payments, because these payments, before they are paid, are available to meet interest charges.

The fixed charges are usually the interest on the debt. In most cases, the sinking fund and amortization requirements are not included in the fixed charges, because the sinking fund payments are covered by depreciation charges and bondholders usually do not force the firm into bankruptcy if it is temporarily unable to retire the debt. If the sinking fund is mandatory, however, the payments should be included in the fixed charges. Because the default on any of the firm's outstanding debt, regardless of whether it is junior or senior to the particular bond of the bondholder, can threaten the safety of all bonds, the fixed charges on all outstanding debt should be used.

Once the net earnings before interest and taxes and the fixed charges are computed, the former figure is divided by the latter to arrive at the times charges earned ratio. For example, if the net earnings before interest and taxes was $1 million and the fixed charges were $100,000, the times fixed charges earned ratio would be 10. But this is a relative measure. Is 10 times sufficient earnings coverage? The answer depends on the individual circumstances of the bond. One check for the analyst is to determine how stable this earnings coverage has been over the years, especially in the recession years. If the firm's earnings are prone to large fluctuations, the earnings coverage might disappear in the recession years. Another check is to compare the earnings coverage of this situation with similar situations. The historical record may indicate the sufficiency of coverage. Hickman's study showed that there was a sharp increase in the default rate when the income before taxes to fixed charges ratio dropped below approximately 4.0 times.

The increased use of leasing to finance the firm may also affect the interpretation of the times fixed charges earned ratio. Rents incurred under leases represent a fixed charge and should be included in the denominator of the ratio. The numerator (earnings before interest and taxes) should also be adjusted to incorporate the lease payments that are available for fixed charges before they are paid. The analyst may separately consider the earnings coverage of fixed charges before and after lease payments if he believes that the situation warrants it. As a general rule, however, because the failure to meet lease obligations may be just as damaging to the company's ability to generate future earnings as a failure to meet interest payments on its debt, the analyst should concern himself with the earnings coverage of all fixed charges, including lease payments.

The times fixed charges earned ratio is difficult to interpret in the sense that it provides only a relative measure of bond quality when we are interested in an absolute measure. We want to know the chances of the firm's being unable to generate sufficient cash to meet all its obligations in a given period. The times fixed charges earned ratio does not give us a bearing on the firm's cash-generating ability or the probability attached to a cash flow insufficient to meet cash outflow.

Cash Flow Analysis

To meet these objections to the times fixed charges earned ratio, the use of cash flow analysis with attached probabilities has been suggested.[6] Cash flow analysis in this framework examines all sources of funds, including net sales, borrowings, and any other source that brings cash into the hands of the firm. It also examines the cash uses that include the cost of goods sold, selling and administrative expenses, dividends, retirement of debt, and so on. We determine from and to where all cash that passes through the control of the firm goes and establish any interrelationships among the sources and uses.

The next step is to assign to each of the sources and uses the probability that in a recession each will decline by a certain percentage. For example, the analyst may decide that in a recession sales have a 0.2 probability of declining 20 percent, a 0.4 probability of declining 10 percent, and a 0.4 probability of declining 5 percent. Accompanying the sales decline is the possibility that expenses will decline in some proportion to sales. For example, the analyst may decide that expenses have a 0.8 probability of declining in a 1 to 1 relationship with the percentage change in sales and a 0.2 probability of declining in an 0.8 to 1 relationship with the percentage change in sales. The analyst then determines what the cash flow would be under each possible combination of changes in each source and use of funds. For example, assuming $5 million in sales and $4 million in expenses, the possible recession

---

[6] G. Donaldson, *Corporate Debt Policy,* Harvard Graduate School of Business, Boston, 1961.

combinations of sales and expenses (assuming no depreciation and taxes) would be as follows:

Combination	Sales (change)	Expense (change)	Cash flow
1	$4 mil (−20%)	$3.2 mil (−20%)	$0.8 mil
2	4 (−20%)	3.36 (−16%)	0.64
3	4.5 (−10%)	3.6 (−10%)	0.9
4	4.5 (−10%)	3.68 (− 8%)	0.82
5	4.75 (− 5%)	3.8 (− 5%)	0.95
6	4.75 (− 5%)	3.84 (− 4%)	0.91

When all the other sources and uses changes are incorporated into the combinations and applied to the actual figures, the analyst arrives at a cash flow of each combination.

By multiplying (assuming independent changes) the probabilities attached to each of the changes in each combination, the analyst can determine the probability that the particular combination will occur. For example, assume that the probabilities attached to the combination in changes in sales and expenses by the firm's management are as follows:

Combination	Cash flow	Probability sales change, percent	Probability expense change, percent	Probability of combination, percent
1	$0.8 mil	20	80	16
2	0.64	20	20	4
3	0.9	40	80	32
4	0.82	40	20	8
5	0.95	40	80	32
6	0.91	40	20	8
				100

This probability distribution implies that combination 1 has a 16 percent chance of occurring, combination 2 a 4 percent chance, and so on. When the probabilities of all the other sources and uses are incorporated into the computations, the analyst arrives at the probability of a particular cash flow's occurring.

Looking at the possible cash flows that may occur under the various combinations of changes, the analyst can determine how many of the possible cash flows fall below the level needed to maintain the firm's debt service and can sum the probabilities of these occurrences. This summed probability represents the probability that the cash flow will be inadequate in a recession year. For example, if the projected cash outflow were $.9 million, we could say that there was a 28 percent probability (the sum of the probabilities to combinations 1, 2, and 4) that the firm would not generate a sufficient cash flow to meet its cash requirements in a recession. If, however, the firm has $200,000 of cash, we could then say that there was only a 4 percent probability (combination 2) of the firm's being unable to meet its cash requirements during a recession. This information provides the analyst with quantitative estimates of the firm's debt capacity. The probability of inadequate coverage may also be used relatively in comparing it with other firms' probability of inadequate coverage.

Other Bond Considerations

Among other considerations that are peculiar to bonds and may have some bearing on their evaluation are the lien provisions (claims on specific assets), the size of the issuer and marketability of the issue, the capitalization, and the working capital position. Lien provisions have become less and less common in recent years, as it became apparent that they had little to do with the risk of default. In fact, it seems as if the risk of default is equally as great if not greater with a secured bond than with an unsecured bond, because the firms that are initially weaker are the ones that have to resort to lien provisions in order to sell their bonds. The only time that the provisions seem to be of value is in reorganization or liquidation.

It has been claimed that the size of the issue and the marketability of the bond may have a bearing on its value.[7] If, because of market imperfections, the individual seller depresses the price of the bonds, there is a market risk. The larger the size of the issue and the more actively traded, the less likely that the seller will have to depress the price to rid himself of the bonds. Marketability is of some significance only if the issue is small or if the bondholder has to liquidate a relatively large position in a short time.

The capitalization and working capital position of the firm may have some bearing on the evaluation of the bonds. The debt/equity ratio may give an indication of the excessive use of debt that may impair the position of the company. The debt/equity ratio is a relative measure, however, and may be misleading unless compared with an absolute standard. The working capital position would reveal the cash reserves available to meet debt service if the expected cash flow did not materialize. Even prosperous firms sometimes experience embarrassing cash shortages that impair their ability to maintain their debt service. A strong working capital position is an indication that the firm is able to tide itself over

[7] L. Fisher, "Determinants of Risk Premiums on Corporate Bonds," *Journal of Political Economy,* June, 1959, pp. 217–237.

the cash shortage without undue risk to the bondholders. Of course, an analysis of the working capital position is no substitute for a complete cash flow forecast.

Bond Evaluation

We are now in a position to integrate the various factors of bond quality discussed above into the PDV evaluation framework. The value of a bond, like that of any financial asset, is the sum of the expected stream of future benefits discounted back to the present at a rate that appropriately reflects the time value of money and the quality of the promise to pay the interest and redeem the bond. For example, if Basic Incorporated had outstanding a 5 percent bond that would mature 5 years from now at $1,000, the value of the bond would be

$$\text{PDV} = \frac{\$50}{(1+r)} + \frac{\$50}{(1+r)^2} + \frac{\$50}{(1+r)^3} + \frac{\$50}{(1+r)^4} + \frac{\$1,050}{(1+r)^5}$$

where $r = i + p + b + f$

Using the same measures of interest rate risk, purchasing power risk premium, business risk, and financial risk developed in Chapters 4 to 13, it is now possible to evaluate this bond. For example, if $r = 0.10$, the PDV of the bond would be

$$\text{PDV} = \frac{\$50}{(1+0.10)} + \frac{\$50}{(1+0.10)^2} + \frac{\$50}{(1+0.10)^3} + \frac{\$50}{(1+0.10)^4} + \frac{\$1,050}{(1+0.10)^5}$$
$$= \$45.45 + 41.30 + 37.55 + 34.15 + 652.05$$
$$= \$830.50$$

If our evaluation of the bond were greater than its market price, we should be potential buyers of the bond. On the other hand, if the market price were above our evaluation, we should be potential sellers of the bond if we owned it. If we were forecasting the future value of the bond under expected future market conditions or a new operating environment for the company, we should evaluate the stream of interest and redemption payments at the r expected to prevail then and compare this evaluation with the current market price to make a buy or sell decision.

It is obvious that a bond, as well as a stock, has interest rate risk and a purchasing power risk premium, because the promised reward to each is disbursed over time. It is equally obvious that the promise to repay and redeem the bond, like the payment of the expected dividends for the stock, reflects the business and financial risk of the borrower. The myriad of various protective provisions of the indenture, however, may force us subjectively to alter the general evaluation technique of the PDV model in some circumstances. For example, the company's first mortgage bonds with their more protective covenants and liens may be considered less risky than the same company's subordinated debentures. In this case, the r should be appropriately smaller for the mortgage bond than for the debenture by some subjectively determined amount. As the protection of the mortgage covenant increases, such as in the case of increased bankruptcy risk, the difference between the r for the mortgage bond and that for the debenture should increase. In the more typical cases, in which, for all intents, the mortgage provisions offer little if any additional protection, because the chance of their being used is so minimal, the difference between the discount factor for each bond should also be minimal.

Sinking Funds and Default Bonds

Some bonds require or give the issuer the option to redeem some of the bonds periodically. For example, a $10 million bond issued in 1970 and maturing in 1990 may require that $500,000 of the bonds be retired each year until 1990, when all the bonds are redeemed. This implies that the investor may not be investing his money for a 20-year period, as implied in the maturity date, but in the equivalent of a bond portfolio, part of which matures each year. The price of the bond may then be viewed as the "sum of the present values of the streams of interest and principal of the portfolio of serial bonds of different maturities discounted by yields imputed by investors on bonds of these maturities."[8] Referring to the PDV framework, we can expect that a sinking fund bond will, each year, return some of our principal along with some annual interest payment. By computing what we expect that the return of principal and interest will be each year of the bond after giving effect to the expected retirement of some of the bonds, we can arrive at the expected stream of future benefits. We can then discount this stream by the prevailing rates in the term structure of interest rates that correspond to the years in which we expect to receive the streams of interest and principal. The PDV of this stream is equivalent to the price of the bond. If the investor expects interest rates to rise in the future, he favors a bond with mandatory sinking fund retirement provisions, because he is able to reinvest the principal that is returned to him before the maturity date at a higher interest rate. If he expects lower interest rates, he favors bonds without mandatory or optional sinking fund retirement provisions.

The default bond (one on which no interest is being paid) is dealt in what is generally known as a *flat basis*. This means that the purchaser

[8] F. Jen and J. Wert, "The Effect of Sinking Fund Provisions on Corporate Bond Yields," *Financial Analysts Journal,* March-April, 1967, pp. 125–131. As a rule of thumb, the proportion of one's bondholding retired through a sinking fund in any one year should, on average, be equal to the proportion of one's holdings in relation to the total issue. This approximation implies that, on average, an equal installment sinking fund designed to retire the bond at maturity gives the bond an average life of one-half its total maturity.

of the bond is not entitled to any accrued interest (see Glossary). The defaulted bond has stopped paying interest, and these missed interest payments are forever lost to the bond. Hickman's study showed that investors who had purchased bonds after they defaulted and held them to maturity actually realized a higher rate of return, on average, than those investors who held bonds that did not go into default, for a sufficient number of defaulted bonds recovered in quality and price to afford large capital gains to a portfolio of defaulted bonds. A study of the performance of defaulted bonds from 1950 to 1966[9] showed that the return on flat bonds in the period was 6.8 percent and ranged from −1.9 to 32.4 percent for the intervening years. The same study also found a high degree of correlation between the return on common stock and the return on flat bonds, because the interest payments on flat bonds are, as in the case of common stock dividends, dependent on the firm's earnings.

DEFERRED CALL PRIVILEGE

The call privilege is an option provision in the bond that allows the issuer to buy back the bonds from the bondholders at a stated price before scheduled maturity. It differs from the sinking fund option in that the entire issue is usually called for redemption. In most cases, this option may be exercised only at a call premium that gives the bondholder a bonus above the face value of the bond. When this call option is deferred through specific restrictions prohibiting redemption of the issue for a specified period, the call privilege is said to be deferred. The advantage of the deferred call privilege to the investor is that it guarantees that a length of time will elapse before the call can occur and assures the investor of the bond's particular interest rate. When interest rates are high in relation to what they may be expected to be, it is advantageous to the investor to lock himself into a bond issue that cannot be retired in the event that interest rates decline.

The value of a deferment to the investor is dependent on the present interest rate and what the investor expects interest rates to be during the period of the deferred call privilege. The deferred call privilege is of little or no value to the investor who anticipates that future interest rates will be higher than the rate on the bond issue during the deferment period. Only if the expected interest rate during the deferment period is sufficiently low to justify the issuer's calling the bond and refunding it with a new issue at a lower rate is the deferment worth anything to the investor. When it becomes profitable for the issuer to refund the bond, the issuer calls the outstanding issue and thus deprives the bondholder of the higher interest rate that he thought that the bond would provide him until maturity. It becomes profitable for the bond issuer

[9] E. Baskin and G. Crooch, "Historical Rates of Return on Investment in Flat Bonds," *Financial Analysts Journal,* November-December, 1968, pp. 95–97.

to retire the issue when the present value of the savings in interest during the remainder of the issue's life more than offsets the expenses of refunding and any call premium that has to be paid.[10]

If the investor anticipates a sufficient decline in interest to warrant the issuer's calling the issue, the value of the deferment to the investor is the present discounted value of the additional interest that the bondholder received during the deferment period above what he would receive, including any call premium, at the expected lower interest rate. For example, if interest rates were now 7 percent and were expected to drop to 5 percent within 1 year, the value of a deferment of 5 years in the call option would be the present discounted value of the 2 percent interest differential for the 4 years remaining in the deferment period after the interest rates declined,[11] as illustrated below. If there were a call premium, the value of the deferred call privilege would be the present discounted value of the difference between (1) the sum of the 7 percent received for 1 year, the call premium received at the end of 1 year, and the 5 percent received for 4 years and (2) the 7 percent received in each of the next 5 years.

If the discount rate were 10 percent, the value of the deferred call privilege would be as follows:

Deferred privilege income stream	$70.	$70.	$70.	$70.	$70.
Callable bond income stream	$70.	$50.	$50.	$50.	$50.
Difference in income streams	0	$20.	$20.	$20.	$20.

$$\text{Value of deferred call privilege} = \frac{\$0}{} + \frac{\$20.}{(1+0.10)^2} + \frac{\$20.}{(1+0.10)^3} + \frac{\$20.}{(1+0.10)^4} + \frac{\$20.}{(1+0.10)^5}$$

$$= \$57.64$$

Empirical investigation has confirmed that in recent years deferred call privileges have affected the yield of bond issues.[12] Pye found that

---

[10] F. Jen and J. Wert, "The Value of the Deferred Call Privilege," *National Banking Review*, March, 1966, pp. 369–378; R. Johnson, "The Value of the Call Privilege," *Financial Analysts Journal*, March-April, 1967, pp. 134–138.

[11] As an alternative to a deferred call, investors may demand a higher call premium. A sufficiently high call premium may prevent the issuer from even calling the bond, or, if called, the bondholder may receive a sufficient gain to offset much of the loss in yield if forced to reinvest at a lower interest rate.

[12] G. Pye, "The Value of Call Deferment on a Bond: Some Empirical Evidence," *Journal of Finance*, December, 1967, pp. 623–636; and F. Jen and J. Wert, "The Effect of Call Risk on Corporate Bond Yields," *Journal of Finance*, December, 1967, pp. 637–651.

the effect of a 5-year deferment on the bond yield was significantly negative. In fact, the effect of the 5-year deferment was almost equal to an improvement in the quality rating of a bond from A to AAA. Specifically, he found that the yield difference between a freely callable bond issue and a bond issue with a deferred call privilege became larger as the general level of interest rates rose and as the length of the deferment grew. The yield to maturity on a freely callable 30-year bond was almost 1 percent higher than for a bond with a deferred call privilege during periods of high interest rates.

This raises the question whether it has been more profitable when high interest rates prevail for the investor to buy the freely callable bonds that carry higher coupon rates, the deferred call privilege bonds that carry a lower yield, or previously issued bonds that are selling at a discount (below par value). Jen and Wert found that the promised high yields of the freely callable bonds were not realized by the investor, because during the period studied so many of them were called and refinanced with lower-yielding bonds. In fact, the results showed that realized interest on these bonds with promised higher yields was only slightly more than that on bonds offered in periods of moderate interest rates, unless the freely callable bonds promised a yield of more than 1 percent higher. The implications for the investor are that he should consider either already outstanding bonds that are selling at a discount, for they are unlikely to be called, or bond issues with deferred call privileges during periods of high interest rates if he wishes to maximize his yield to maturity. Of course, the results of these empirical studies are influenced by the period involved. At other times, when investors may anticipate sustained periods of high interest rates, realized yields on the freely callable bond issues may increase, for the issuer will find no advantage in quickly retiring the issue. The number of called bonds will decrease and the length of time that high-yielding, freely callable issues are allowed to remain outstanding will grow. If investors anticipate high interest rates for the entire deferment period, there is no value to the deferred call privilege.

CONVERTIBLE BONDS

The convertible bond is a hybrid security combining the features of straight debt and common stock. It is straight debt in the form of a bond that offers the investor annual interest payments plus the return of his principal at maturity. It is common stock in that the bondholder has the option to convert the bond into a specific number of common shares of the company. If the price of the common stock rises, the option to convert the bond into common stock becomes valuable and dominates in the evaluation of the bond.

As a straight debt instrument, the convertible bond has a present discounted value and is exposed to the risks in the PDV evaluation framework. The straight bond value of a convertible bond is identical with the value of a straight bond of the same company. The straight debt value of the convertible bond is unaffected by a decline in the price of the common stock and provides a floor under which the market price of the bond will not fall. Of course, the straight bond value is not immune from interest rate, purchasing power, business, and financial risks. In other words, the floor may vary over time. If any of the risks to which the bond is exposed increased, the value of the bond as straight debt would decrease. It is possible that the floor may also rise, however, if the risks associated with the bond decrease. The floor is the value of the bond as straight debt in the marketplace, and this value can change.

The conversion value of the convertible bond is a function of the price of the common stock and the number of shares into which the bond is convertible. If P were the price of the common stock and S the number of shares into which the bond was convertible, the conversion value of the bond would be $C = P \times S$, and the conversion ratio would be $S = C/P$. For example, if S equaled 100 and P equaled $10, the conversion value of the bond would be $1,000. Usually, S is fixed at the time of the original bond offering, so that the conversion value varies with P. The higher P, the higher is the conversion value. The lower P, the lower is the conversion value. It is possible for the conversion value to be above, below, or equal to the straight debt value of the bond. For example, if the market value of the bond as straight debt were $1,000, the conversion value of the bond in this example would be equal to the straight bond value. If P rose to $20 per share, the conversion value of the bond would be $2,000, or double the straight bond value. If P fell to $5 a share, the conversion value would be $500, or half of the straight debt value.

It is not uncommon to find convertible bonds selling at a market value in excess of the straight bond and the conversion value. The excess of market value over the conversion value of the bond is known as the premium over conversion value, and the excess of the market value over the straight bond value is known as the premium over bond value. A convertible bond is likely to sell at a premium over conversion value, because it reduces the risk of directly owning the common stock while not reducing the reward potential, provided that the conversion value is higher than the straight bond value. For example, if P were $20 per share and S were 100 shares, the conversion value of the debt would be $2,000, where in the example the straight bond value is $1,000. If P fell to $5 per share, the market value of the bond would fall to the straight bond floor of $1,000, whereas a direct investment in 100 shares of the common stock would fall to $500. The downside risk in the convertible bond investment would be 50 percent, or a fall from $2,000 to $1,000; the downside risk of a direct investment in the common stock would be 75 percent, or a fall from $2,000, to $500. At the same time, the upside potential for the convertible bond is as great as that of the common stock. For example, if P rose to $25 from $20 per share, the convertible bond would sell for at least its conversion value of $2,500, and the common stock would also sell for $2,500. Because of this reduced risk exposure without any forfeiture of potential reward, the investor should be willing to pay a premium for the convertible bond investment.[13]

Evaluation of Convertibles

Figure 14.1 illustrates Brigham's hypothetical model of a convertible bond.[14] The straight debt value of the bond is represented by the line BXM. As discussed in the previous section, BXM is the maximum price at which the bond can sell, regardless of the associated stock price. Note that the BXM line slopes upward in time until it equals the face value M. This configuration occurs because the bond is usually first issued at an interest rate that is below the current rates on similar bonds with no conversion feature. Investors are willing to buy these bonds at the lower interest rate, because the conversion feature is of value. In time this discount from the value of a similar bond without a conversion feature is erased. This occurs because the closer the maturity, when the bond will be redeemed at face value, the less is the penalizing effect of the time value on the money to be received at maturity. Finally, at maturity there is no more time to wait for the money and no discounting for time, and the value of the bond as straight debt is equal to M.

The conversion value of the bond is represented by the CXC_t line. As discussed in the previous section, the conversion value is a function of the associated stock price and the number of shares into which the bond is convertible. It is assumed the associated stock price will increase in time at some constant rate of growth, so that the conversion value CXC_t will rise each year in continual increasing amounts until the bond is called in year N. Thus, we arrive at the upsweeping configuration of the CXC_t line.

The market price of the bond is represented by the line MM'. This is the price at which the bond is traded. In time it, too, will rise in

---

[13] In an analogous manner, investors may be willing to accept a lower yield on a convertible bond than on a straight bond of the same quality because of the potential value of the conversion feature. The potentially more valuable the conversion feature, the lower the yield that investors should be willing to accept.

[14] E. Brigham, "An Analysis of Convertible Debentures: Theory and Some Empirical Evidence," *Journal of Finance,* March, 1966, pp. 34–35.

an upsweeping configuration similar to that of the CXC_t line. Clearly, however, the market price cannot lie below the conversion value for if it did, investors would buy the bond and convert until the purchase of the bonds drove their price above the conversion value. Note, however, that the MM' line does not rise so rapidly as the CXC_t line, and, eventually, the two merge at M'. We discuss the reasons for this shortly. The shaded area between CXC_t and MM' represents the premium over conversion value for the bond. This shaded area represents the premium that investors are willing to pay for this bond. Note that to the left of X, the straight debt value of the bond is greater than the conversion value and the shaded area represents the premium over bond value.

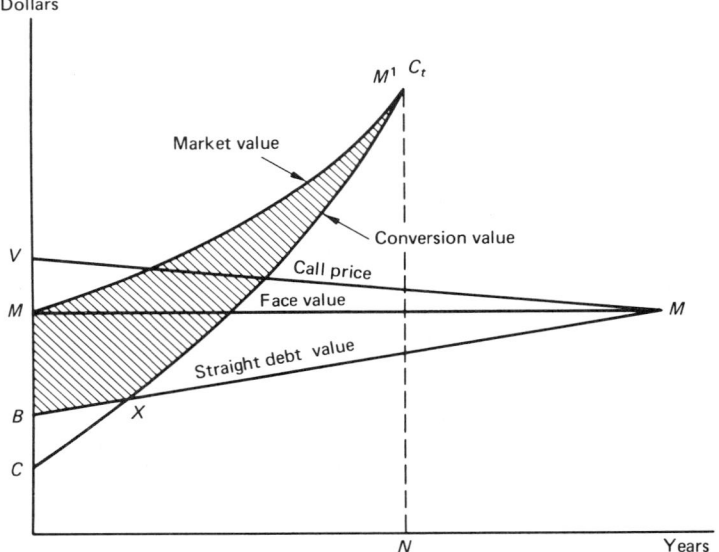

Figure 14.1. Hypothetical model of a convertible bond.

(From E. Brigham, "An Analysis of Convertible Debentures: Theory and Some Empirical Evidence," Journal of Finance, March, 1966, p. 37.)

The VM line is the call price, the price that the company is obligated to pay if it redeems the bonds before maturity and they are not converted. The call price usually is at a premium over the face value of the bond, but the call premium usually declines at periodic intervals in time until it disappears at maturity. This declining call premium causes the VM line to slope downward.

It is important to note that the premium over conversion decreases with the passage of time until at the call date N the market value and the conversion value are identical. One reason that the premium narrows and eventually disappears is that bondholders realize that the issue is callable. If the bond is called, the bondholder must either convert the bond into the stock, which is only worth the conversion value, or have the bond redeemed for its straight debt value, both of which are lower than the market value. As time passes and the conversion value of the bond rises, it becomes more likely that the issuer will call the bond. As the chances of the bond's being called and the accompanying loss increase, the potential bond buyer is less willing to pay so large a premium as previously paid. A second factor that increases the potential loss to the bondholder as the conversion value rises is that the straight debt value floor becomes farther and farther away. This exposes the investor to a larger potential loss if the price of the common stock declines. A third reason for the narrowing of the premium is the relationship between the yield on the bond and on the stock. As we have seen from the examples, once the conversion value exceeds the straight debt value floor, the price appreciation of the bond and that of the stock move in tandem. The dividend on the stock may change, however, whereas the interest payment on the bond is fixed. If the dividend on the common stock increased, the yield on the stock would also increase, but that on the bond would not. Therefore, the attractiveness of holding the bond instead of the stock would diminish, and the premium that investors are willing to pay would narrow.

The yield that the investor expects to receive on this bond is the discount rate that equates the sum of the annual interest payments to be received until the bond is called in year N and the terminal conversion value of the bond in year N. In equation form this is

$$(14.1) \quad M = \sum_{t=1}^{n} \frac{I}{(1+k)^t} + \frac{TV}{(1+k)^N}$$

where M = price of bond
TV = terminal value of bond: call price if surrendered on call, maturity value if redeemed, conversion value if converted, or market price if sold
I = dollars of interest received annually
N = number of years that bond was held
k = discount rate

In order to solve this equation, the investor must estimate what he believes that the terminal value will be and for how many years he expects to hold the bond. According to Brigham, the terminal value of the bond is defined by corporate policy, because a sufficient number of firms have a definite policy of forcing conversion when the conversion value rises a certain amount above the call price, usually 20 percent. The investor, according to this thinking, might be able to determine corporate policy if he examined the firm's performance on previous convertible bond redemptions or by questioning the firm's management. If the investor can satisfactorily determine at what terminal value the firm is likely to force conversion, he can estimate the number of years N that it will take the bond to reach this conversion value at a specified growth rate, that is, in the stock price, how many years it will take the present conversion value to reach the terminal conversion value. The computation of N may be illustrated graphically, as in Figure 14.1, where N may be read as the number of years that it takes the CXC_t line to reach C_t. Mathematically, Brigham suggests that the N may be computed in the following manner. If M is the issue price, P_c the conversion price, and P_0 the initial stock price, then

$$(14.2) \quad C_t = \frac{P_0}{P_c}(1+g)^t M$$

but because C_t equals the terminal conversion price when $t = N$,

$$(14.3) \quad TV = \frac{P_0}{P_c}(1+g)^N M$$

Because we know P_0, P_c, M and can estimate g and TV, we can solve for N by referring to the compound interest tables or to the following equation:

$$(14.4) \quad N = \frac{(\log P_c - \log P_0) + (\log TV - \log M)}{\log (1+g)}$$

Once we have solved for N, we can solve the original equation (14.1) for k. If k, the expected return, is equal to or greater than the return on other securities of equal risk, the investor purchases this convertible bond.

Others[15] have suggested that a convertible bond is worth the greater

---

[15] William Baumol, B. Malkiel, and R. Quandt, "The Valuation of Convertible Securities," *Quarterly Journal of Economics*, February, 1966, pp. 48–59. According to these authors the value of the convertible C is equal to either

$$C \geq P(t)S + \int^{\bar{B}/P(t_0)S} \int (i,t_0)[\bar{B} - i(t)P(t_0)S] \, di(t)$$

where the first term on the right side of the inequality is the conversion value and the second term is the expected value of the difference between the straight bond value $\bar{B}$ and lower expected future conversion values $[i(t)P(t_0)S]$

or $\quad C \geq \bar{B} + \int_{\bar{B}/P(t_0)S}^{\infty} \int (i,t_0)[i(t)P(t_0)S - \bar{B}] \, di(t)$

where the first term on the right side of the inequality is the straight bond value and the second term is the expected value of the difference between the conversion value and lower expected straight bond values.

of (1) the conversion value plus any expected value of the straight bond floor feature or (2) the straight bond value plus any expected value of the conversion privilege. In the first instance, any time that the straight bond feature is expected to prevent the market price from falling as low as it normally would if it were determined by the conversion value, the worth of the straight bond feature must be added to the conversion value. The estimated worth is the expected value of all future such occurrences. In the second instance, where the conversion value exceeds the straight debt value, the expected value of all such future occurrences must be added to the value of the bond as straight debt. The investor should, therefore, be willing to pay the present discounted value of the stream of interest payments plus the greater of the computed values he expects to prevail when he sells the bond.

Investment Implications

It has been suggested that an inverse relationship between the premium over conversion value and the premium over bond value exists among most convertibles.[16] As illustrated in Figure 14.2, high premiums over conversion value are associated with low premuims over bond value. This is apparently caused by the narrowing of the premium over conversion value as the market price rises. As the market price rises, the downside risk increases, narrowing the premium over conversion that investors are willing to pay. At the same time, because of the rising market value, the price of the bond is pulling farther away from the straight debt value floor, and the premium over bond value increases. The relationship between the two premiums may be plotted, as in Figure 14.2, with the relationship line computed as the regression line that best describes the plotted points, at a given point in time. If any convertible bond fails to conform to this relationship by not lying closely along the relationship line in Figure 14.2, the analyst has reason to investigate the cause. If the deviant observation lies above and to the right of the line, it implies that the market is willing to pay an unusually large premium for this issue, and the analyst is alerted to look for special, usually favorable characteristics in the firm's prospects. If the deviant observation lies below and to the left of the line, the analyst is alerted to look for reasons why the market is placing a lower than expected premium on the bonds. If the analyst can satisfy himself that the market is unduly penalizing these bonds, he may feel that they are attractive investments. The advantage of this type of analysis is that it gives the analyst a standard reference when comparing convertible bonds. The analyst must be aware, however, that the relationship line may shift up or down as the market changes its evaluation of convertibles in general.

[16] A. Bladen, *Techniques for Investing in Convertible Bonds,* Solomon Brothers and Hutzler, New York, 1966.

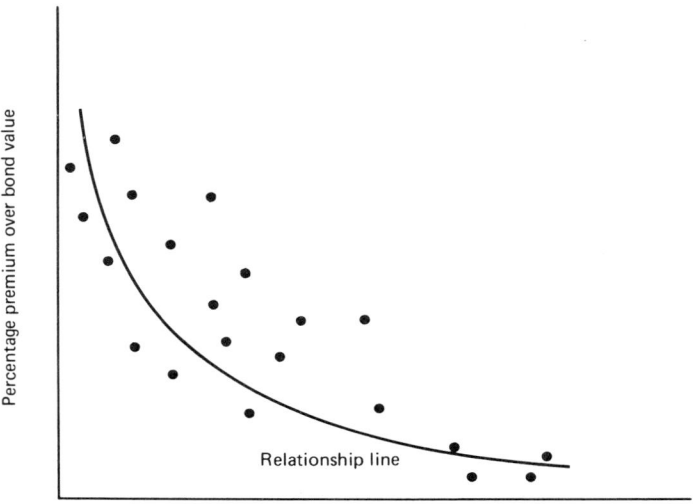

Figure 14.2.

We may illustrate this particular technique of convertible bond analysis with the data in Table 14.3, which contains the conversion and straight debt value of the convertible bond as of June 8, 1970. When these values are compared with the market price of the bond, we obtain its percentage premium over conversion and straight debt values from which we plot the trade-off curve in Figure 14.3. Note that the freehand curve in the figure roughly describes the relationship of the two premiums. As the premium over conversion increases, the premium over bond value tends to decrease, exhibiting the trade-off characteristics that we should expect to find among convertible securities. Two observations, however, the Greyhound $6\frac{1}{2}$'s of 1990 and the Air Reduction $3\frac{7}{8}$'s of 1987, lie far to the left of the trade-off curve. This should imply to the analyst that investors are demanding significant discounts in both the straight debt and conversion value to purchase these bonds, and he should be alerted to search for further clues as to why.

In the case of new convertible bond issues, a combination of a low premium over bond value and a low conversion price in relation to the prevailing market price may be indicative of investors' pessimistic attitudes toward the firm. The combination of the two implies that the investors are not expecting to benefit very much from the conversion value and must make up the difference by keeping the interest rate close to the straight debt rate. The low conversion price implies that investors are anticipating a slow growth pattern and are attempting

TABLE 14.3 Convertible Bonds, June 8, 1970

Issue	Coupon, percent	Maturity	Bond price	Yield to maturity	Straight bond value	Bond value premium, percent	Conversion price	Stock price	Conversion: Value	Conversion: Premium, percent
Air Reduction	3⅞	8/87	62	7.99	61	1.6	31¼	15⅞	50¾	22.2
Alcoa	5¼	9/91	83½	6.72	68⅜	22.1	85	53¼	62⅝	57.8
Armour	4½	9/83	82⅞	6.45	65	27.5	51.14	42½	83⅛	−0.3
Ashland Oil & Ref.	4¾	8/93	64	8.26	62⅜	2.6	50	20¾	41½	54.2
AVCO	5½	11/93	56	10.63	56	0	54	14⅞	27½	103.6
Baxter Labs.	4¾	3/90	84½	6.10	64⅛	31.0	38½	23⅝	61⅜	37.6
Burlington Inds.	5	9/91	96½	5.28	92⅝	3.9	39	36⅛	64⅛	50.4
Celanese	4	4/90	69	6.89	55¾	23.7	96	55	57¼	20.5
Cluett Peabody	4¼	9/84	85¼	5.81	63¼	34.4	20¾	17⅝	85¼	0
Del Monte	5¼	3/94	74¼	7.61	63½	16.9	39	21⅜	54¾	35.6
Eastern Airlines	5	11/92	49⅞	11.12	49⅞	0	50	13⅜	26¾	86.4
Fruehauf	5½	4/94	79½	7.33	62½	27.0	46¼	29⅜	63½	25.2
General Instrument	5	10/92	50	11.10	50	0	67	14	20¾	40.9
Greyhound Corp.	6½	1/90	78⅞	8.78	71⅞	9.7	18⅜	14	76¼	3.4
Int'l Min. & Chem.	4	1/91	45	10.65	45	0	53.20	10¼	19¼	133.7
Kerr-McGee	3¾	5/92	67⅛	6.61	52⅝	27.5	76½	67⅛	56⅝	18.5
McGraw-Hill	3⅞	5/92	54	8.57	54	0	62½	14⅛	22⅝	138.6
Owens-Illinois	4½	11/92	80⅛	6.14	60⅝	32.1	59	41⅛	69¾	14.7
Penn-Dixie Cement	5	10/82	64	10.21	64	0	29¼	11¼	38½	66.2
Purex	4⅞	1/94	57½	9.38	57½	0	34.83	11¾	33¾	70.3
Reynolds Metals	4½	3/91	64½	8.05	59	9.3	61.96	26½	42¾	50.8
Union Pacific	4¾	4/99	77⅝	6.47	61	27.3	57.14	33¼	58¼	33.3
Utah Construction & M	5	11/92	136	3.07	64½	21.1	32.17	43⅝	135⅝	0

SOURCE: Moody's Bond Survey, Convertible Bonds.

to decrease the waiting period until the conversion value brings them some reward. If investors had been anticipating a high growth rate for the firm, they would have been willing to accept a higher conversion price relative to the present market price for the same annual interest payment, because the conversion value would increase at a faster rate. Conversely, at the same interest rate, the investor is willing to accept a higher conversion price relative to the present market price if rapid growth is anticipated. The more rapid the growth, the more quickly any set conversion price becomes valuable, and the higher is the annual reward to the bondholder. The analyst may take combinations of unusually high interest rates and low conversion prices as a signal to intensify his investigation of the firm.

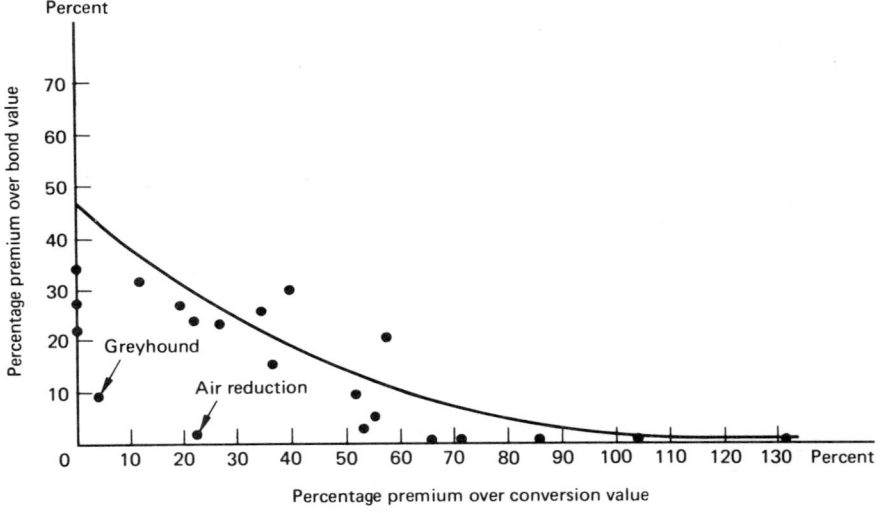

Figure 14.3. Convertible bond trade-off.

The convertible bondholder is also interested in knowing when to convert into common stock. Usually, the bondholder converts once the return to the common shares into which the bond is convertible is greater than the return to holding the bond. For example, a $1,000 5 percent convertible bond returns $50 per year in interest plus any increase in the market value of the bond. If the bond were convertible into 100 shares, the bondholder would convert once the dividend income plus the price increase in 100 shares of the common stock was greater than the return to the bond. As we have seen, once the price of the common stock moves above the conversion price, in this case $10 per share, the market value of the bond based on its conversion value increases in tandem with the common stock price. This means that the investor gets the same capital appreciation from either the bond or the stock. The only difference in the return to the bondholder is that between the annual interest payment on the bond and the dividend on the 100 shares of common stock. In the example, when the dividend exceeds the $50 annual interest payment, the bondholder is better off with the stock than with the bond and converts.

MUNICIPAL BONDS

There are several distinctive features of municipal bonds. The most obvious is the freedom of interest receipts from federal income taxes. Thus, the real value of the interest to the municipal bondholder is the annual payment that he receives plus any savings that he experiences by not paying federal income taxes on this interest, although any capital gains are taxed at regular capital gains tax rates. For example, a $25 per year tax-exempt interest payment to a person who must pay 50 percent of his additional income to the federal government is equivalent to $50 of annual income on which he must pay taxes. Therefore, when the investor is evaluating municipal bonds, he must consider the tax-exemption advantage before he is able to compare municipal bonds with other investments. The higher the individual's marginal tax bracket, the more valuable the tax-free interest. Other features, which are not generally found in corporate bonds, include the overlapping jurisdictions of various municipal districts that issue bonds. Thus, the same population and area may be responsible for a multiplicity of obligations. The general inability of municipal bonds to be sold quickly and in large amounts at prevailing prices is another distinguishing feature.[17]

There are two basic types of municipal bonds. The general obligation bond, which is secured by the full faith, credit, and taxing power of the issuer, and the revenue bond, which is backed by the revenues derived from the project that the issue was used to finance. An example of a revenue bond is the bond used to finance the construction of toll roads and bridges, in which the revenue from the tolls is used to maintain the debt.

Revenue bonds are exposed to interest rate risk, purchasing power risk, business risk, and financial risk in the sense that the project must prove its economic worth by generating sufficient income to maintain the debt service.

General obligation bonds are also exposed to interest rate risk, purchasing power risk, business risk, and financial risk. The concept of business risk when applied to the community, however, must be modi-

---

[17] See References at the end of the chapter for more detailed discussions of these special features.

fied. We are now dealing with a broader interpretation that involves the character of the people, economic environment of the area, the social and political problems of the people, and other concepts that are hard to incorporate into specific measurements. Although there is a resemblance between the business risk of a corporation and the municipality, the analysis of the municipality is of mushrooming complexity.

Because of this complexity, municipal bond ratings, which parallel those of corporate bonds, have come under criticism. Among the criticisms have been the following:

1. The ratings cover only a limited number of outstanding bonds and issuers.
2. The ratings are expressed in such broad trends as to be difficult to interpret.
3. The basis for a rating is vague.
4. There is no way of relating the ratings to the market.
5. The present bond rating system is confusing.[18]

In an attempt to overcome some of these criticisms and problems, analysts have been searching for quantitative measures that would provide a reasonable profile for municipal bond quality ratings. One attempt[19] to discriminate between lower quality bonds (Ba and lower) and higher quality bonds (Baa and higher) found that the following variables were reasonably good discriminators of municipal bond quality:

1. Debt/assessed value
2. Logarithm of the area's population (demographic considerations)
3. Tax collection rate
4. Bond quality of the state in which the municipality is located

For example, the following statistics were available in *Moody's Municipal and Government Manual* for Howard County, Texas:

Population	1950	26,722
	1960	40,139
Assessed property value	1968–1969	$78,557,440
Bonded debt	1968	1,310,000
Tax collection rate	1968	96.7%
State of Texas rating	1969	Aaa
Howard County rating	1969	Baa

[18] R. Goodman, "Municipal Bond Rating Testimony," *Financial Analysts Journal,* May-June, 1968, p. 63.

[19] J. Horton, Jr., "A Statistical Rating for Municipal Bonds," *Financial Analysts Journal,* March-April, 1969, pp. 72–75.

From these statistics it is apparent that the area's population is growing and, with this growth, more capable of generating the tax revenue necessary to pay the interest and amortization on the county's debt. The debt to assessed value ratio is relatively small and stands as a reasonably good sign of the area's conservative attitude toward debt and of substantial assets in back of the debt. The high tax collection rate of 96.7 percent indicates a well-functioning collection system capable of raising funds to repay the debt obligation. The high rating of the state of Texas, according to this list of indicators, enhances the quality of the bond, most likely because the state is in a position to aid Howard County through its good credit rating if the county is unable to sustain its debt burden.

This is by no means a definitive list, and much more testing must be done. Other measures that are commonly used are the municipality's net debt per capita, the relation of debt service to annual revenues, the trends in debt and debt retirement policy, the limitations on the debt and taxing powers, and the ratio of taxes to aggregate income. The trend in municipal bond rating seems to be toward statistical rating systems that untangle the maze of data and coordinate it into a systematic and objective profile based on a selected number of indicative variables.

SUMMARY

In this chapter, we have attempted to explore some of the variations which may exist in bond characteristics and which may have some influence on the usual bond evaluation procedures. The first section was devoted to an introduction to the historical performance of bonds and bond ratings. According to the empirical studies, the portfolio of higher quality bonds experienced, in the aggregate, a lower default and loss rate, comparatively stable prices, and relatively low promised and realized yields. On the other hand, the lower grade bond portfolio experienced, in a sufficiently diversified portfolio, higher promised and realized yields in addition to a greater occurrence of default risk and increased price instability. On average, over all bonds, the capital gains exactly offset the capital loss, and the promised yield equaled the realized yield.

The times fixed charges earned ratio provided a historical indication of bond quality; when, in the period studied, this ratio dropped below 4.0 times, there was a large increase in default risk. The times fixed charges earned ratio itself, however, was found to be difficult to interpret, and the cash flow analysis of corporate debt capacity was suggested as an alternative measure. In the cash flow analysis approach, the procedure is to determine the probability of the cash flow's being inadequate to meet debt service.

Other bond provisions, such as liens, were considered. It was concluded that the presence of a lien on specific assets did not, in general, reduce default but served only as an advantage in the case of reorganization or liquidation.

The value of the deferred call privilege was examined. It was concluded that its value depended on the investor's expectation of interest rates during the length of the deferment period. If the investor expected interest rates to fall enough to make it profitable for the issuer to call the issue, the value of the deferred call privilege was the present discounted value of the difference between the interest rate that the bondholder would have received if the bond had not been called and that which he would have received if he were forced to reinvest the proceeds of the redemption in a lower yield bond.

Convertible bonds take their value from their characteristic as a straight bond or as a claim on common shares, depending on which is higher. Their value as a straight bond acts as a floor under the price of the bond and reduces the risk of investing, without penalizing the potential return. This explains why convertible bonds generally sell at a premium over their bond value and their conversion value. By comparing the premium over conversion value with the premium over bond value, the analyst can construct a standard of reference with which to evaluate convertible bonds. The yield to convertible bonds is the present discounted value of the stream of annual interest payments and the terminal value of the bond at the call date. The call date is estimated as the number of years that it would take for the conversion value of the bond to grow to some specified redemption value.

The most important characteristic of municipal bonds is their tax-exempt status, which makes it necessary to adjust the income stream before evaluating the bond. Only if this adjustment were made could the municipal bond be compared with other bonds. Some of the criticisms of the present municipal bond rating systems are causing analysts to look toward systematic, objective rating systems based on selected measures of bond quality.

QUESTIONS

14.1 What is a bond indenture?

14.2 Distinguish between a secured and unsecured bond. What are some examples of secured bonds?

14.3 Explain the call provision and the conversion option.

14.4 What factors do bond rating agencies consider in rating a bond?

14.5 How should the times fixed charges earned ratio be used to indicate bond quality effectively?

14.6 What is the aim of cash flow analysis?

14.7 What is a sinking fund bond? Why would an investor choose to invest in a sinking fund bond?

14.8 What is meant by "dealt in flat"?

14.9 Explain the call privilege attached to a bond.

14.10 Of what advantage is the deferred call privilege to the investor?

14.11 Under what conditions would a bond issuer wish to call the outstanding bonds?

14.12 What is a convertible bond?

14.13 Explain how the price of a convertible bond is a reflection of either a firm's straight debt instruments or common stock.

14.14 Define conversion value premium and bond value premium.

14.15 Explain the real value of the interest paid to a municipal bondholder.

14.16 Describe the two basic types of municipal bonds. What are the respective risks of each?

PROBLEMS

14.1 An analyst has estimated that during a recessionary period the sales for a particular company have a 0.3 probability of declining 5 percent, a 0.4 probability of declining 10 percent, and a 0.3 probability of declining 15 percent. Expenses are estimated to have a 0.9 probability of declining in a 1 to 1 relationship with the percentage change in sales and a 0.1 probability of declining in a 0.8 to 1 relationship with the percentage change in sales. Sales have been $5 million; expenses have been $3 million. What is the probability that the firm will be able to pay its $175,000 annual interest payment to its bondholders by a multiple of 10 or greater.

14.2 A 7 percent corporate bond becomes callable in 4 years at 105. The present interest rate of 7 percent has dropped to 6 percent, and remains at this level until the bond is called. Compute the value of the deferment to the investor if the issue is expected to be called.

14.3 Convertible bonds of a particular company are selling at $1,000. The price is expected to increase regularly, so that in four years the bond will be selling at $1,200, at which time the issue is expected to be called. The bond pays $50 interest annually. The discount rate of other securities of equal risk is 6 percent. Should an investor purchase the bond?

REFERENCES

Atkinson, Thomas R. *Trends In Corporate Bond Quality,* New York: Columbia University Press, 1967.

Baskin, Elba F., and Gary M. Crooch. "Historical Rates of Return on Investments in Flat Bonds," *Financial Analysts Journal,* 24:95–97, November-December, 1968.

Baumol, William J., Burton G. Malkiel, and Richard E. Quandt. "The Valuation of Convertible Securities," *Quarterly Journal of Economics,* 80:48–59, February, 1966.

Balden, A. *Techniques for Investing in Convertible Bonds,* New York: Solomon Bros. and Hutzler, 1966.

Brigham, Eugene F. "An Analysis of Convertible Debentures," *The Journal of Finance,* 31:35–54, March, 1966.

Cretien, Paul D., Jr. "Convertible Bond Premiums as Predictors of Common Stock Price Changes," *Financial Analysts Journal,* 25:90–95, November-December, 1969.

Dougall, Herbert E. *Investments,* 8th ed., Englewood Cliffs, N.J.: Prentice Hall, Inc., 1968.

Fundamentals of Municipal Bonds, Washington, D.C.: Investment Bankers Association of America, 1963.

Fisher, L. "Determinants of Risk Premiums on Corporate Bonds," *Journal of Political Economy,* 67:217–237, June, 1959.

Goodman, Roy M. "Municipal Bond Rating Testimony," *Financial Analysts Journal,* 24:59–65, May-June, 1968.

Harries, Breton W. "Standard & Poor's New Policy," *Financial Analysts Journal,* 24:68–71, May-June, 1968.

Hickman, Walter Braddock. *Corporate Bond Quality and Investor Experience,* Princeton, N.J.: Princeton University Press, 1958.

Horton, Joseph J., Jr. "A Statistical Rating Index for Municipal Bonds," *Financial Analysts Journal,* 25:72–75, March-April, 1969.

Jen, Frank C., and James E. Wert. "The Value of the Deferred Call Privilege," *The National Banking Review,* 3:369–378, March, 1966.

―――. "Imputed Yields of a Sinking Fund Bond and the Term Structure of Interest Rates," *The Journal of Finance,* 21:697–714, December, 1966.

15
Special Situations—Equities

As in the case of bonds, there are special situations which arise in the evaluation of equity securities and which necessarily alter the conceptual evaluation framework. The major categories of special equity situations are (1) the securities that represent a purchase option on the common stock, such as warrants and options; (2) the unexpected alteration of the firm's operating circumstances by merger or bankruptcy; and (3) the disruption of the market equilibrium by such occurrences as a stock exchange listing.

This chapter explores the impact of merger and acquisition activity on the value of the acquiring firm. We look at the effect that a merger might have on the acquiring firm's expected earnings pattern and on its business and financial risk. We also discuss the methods that are used to determine the price that the acquiring firm pays for the acquired firm and attempt to establish some standard of evaluation with which to compare the purchase price. We look at the empirical evidence and decide what are the investment strategy implications.

Next, we discuss the characteristics of the warrants, explore briefly the important factors in their evaluation, and set forth the resulting implications for the investor. Options to buy or sell common stock and some of the factors determining their value are also discussed.

The last section of the chapter deals with the characteristics and investment performance of the stocks of bankrupt companies, the effects of potential earnings dilution, the effects of exchange listing on the New York Stock Exchange, and the price performance of new issues.

MERGERS AND ACQUISITIONS

Although the law distinguishes among several methods of consummating a merger, it is only necessary for our purposes to use the term "merger" as it is most commonly used to mean the acquisition of one company by another. For financial analysis, however, it is important to distinguish among the mergers by their various economic implications. Among economic definitions, there are three basic types of merger: horizontal, vertical, and conglomerate. The horizontal merger is the acquisition of one firm in a particular industry by another firm in the same industry. For example, the merger between two steel companies is a horizontal merger. A vertical merger is the acquisition by a firm of its supplier of raw materials or of its distributors. If we envision the chain of commerce running from the raw materials producer to the manufacturer to the retailer, the acquisition by any one of another is a vertical merger. For example, the acquisition by an automobile manufacturer of his steel supplier is a vertical merger. The conglomerate merger is a firm's acquisition of another firm in an unrelated industry. For example, the acquisition of an automobile parts distributor by a motion picture production company is a conglomerate merger.

There are two main concerns in evaluating the effect of a merger on the stock price of the acquiring company: (1) what will be the effect of the merger on the firm's expected pattern of future earnings, and (2) what will be the effect of the merger on the discount factor r at which the future stream of benefits is capitalized? The merger's effect on earnings can arise from any of several areas that can affect the firm's earnings capacity. Among the more common areas of operations in which beneficial effects of a merger might be realized are the enlarged base from which to do research, the acquisition of management skills, economies of scale, and the expansion of product line and distribution channels. Larger total profits might accrue to the company if the firm were able to undertake a greater research effort, and a greater research effort is more easily mounted by a relatively large company than by a smaller one. The larger company has the resources to see the research through and to diversify the research risk over several projects, thereby increasing the chances of success. Because the returns to a successful research project are rather high, one successful project may be more than sufficient to offset the costs of the unsuccessful projects and still return a profit to the firm. If sufficient command of the market is achieved through the merger, the merged firm may be in a position to garner monopoly profits.

With the acquisition of another firm, the acquiring firm inherits a management structure. The inherited management structure may strengthen the management of the existing firm. For example, one firm with strong upper management might find it advantageous to merge with a firm with strong middle management. This may be particularly true in the case of rapidly growing younger firms that are guided mainly by one innovating entrepreneur. The firm may have advanced beyond the size that he, as an individual, can successfully manage the firm.

The economies of scale that accompany a merger might be significant in raising earnings. For example, the merged firm would need one efficient plant instead of two less efficient plants. The merger might also produce an expansion of the firm's product line and distribution channels that would increase earnings. The acquisition of a complementary line of products could mean that one salesman could now sell the same products to each customer that two salesmen had previously been selling. For example, the acquisition of an aspirin manufacturer by a bandage manufacturer could mean that one salesman would sell both products to the drug store. The druggist may be willing to increase his purchases from the company, because he now has a complete line of merchandise, and he has the convenience of "one-stop shopping."

There are still other factors that might affect the earnings. The speed with which a merger enables a company to grow may be an important factor. For example, it may take up to several years before a new plant or facility can be built, but through merger, the company can acquire already existing facilities and be in production the next day. From a competitive viewpoint, it might be advantageous to establish customer relations quickly before a competing firm does, and the speed of the acquisition process could provide this edge. In some instances it may be less expensive to acquire the assets through an exchange of stock than it would be to sell the firm's securities, raise the money, and purchase the assets for cash or build them. The acquisition process usually avoids the expenses of a public underwriting. Because the exchange of stock is usually tax-deferred to the acquired firm, whereas the cash purchase is not, the acquired firm might be willing to sell at a lower price for stock than for cash.

The effect of the merger on the company's earnings may be more than just a combining of the earnings of the two before their merger. In any of the areas mentioned, the effects of the merger may be to make the combination of the two companies potentially more profitable than either of the two was on an individual basis. In this case, the whole is worth more than the sum of the parts. This concept has become known as *synergism*. It is the analyst's responsibility to determine the synergistic effects of the merger in addition to merely combining the records of the two companies into one. Of course, there may be a time lag before the effects of synergism begin to be reflected in the earnings of the merged firm. For example, the combination of the New York Central Railroad and the Pennsylvania Railroad into the Penn Central Company promised large benefits to earnings from the elimination of duplicate facilities and administrative services, which, at least in the early stages of the combination, failed to emerge because of problems in combining operations and has forced the merged railroad into bankruptcy. The delay in the expected savings forced investors to adjust their expectations of when they would receive the benefits and had an adverse effect on the price of the stock.

The accounting procedures used in the merger may also affect the company's future earnings. According to opinion 16 of the Accounting Principles Board, the merger may be treated either as a purchase or as a pooling of interests. The pooling of interests method is applicable if the merger is accomplished by an exchange of common stock between independent companies. The financial application of this method allows the merged company to combine the assets, liabilities, stockholders' equity, and operating results of the separate companies by adding the historical-cost–based amounts and prior earnings together. For example, assume that company A and company B had the following balance sheets and earnings and that company A exchanges 10,000 of its shares for company B's shares. The merged company A and B would have the following balance sheet and earnings:

	A	B	A and B
Current assets	$ 50,000	$ 50,000	$100,000
Fixed assets	100,000	100,000	200,000
Total assets	150,000	150,000	300,000
Current liabilities	25,000	25,000	50,000
Long-term debt	100,000	0	100,000
Total debt	125,000	25,000	150,000
Stockholders' equity	100,000	100,000	200,000
Total earnings	50,000	25,000	75,000
Number of shares	20,000	10,000	30,000
Earnings per share	$ 2.50	$ 2.50	$ 2.50

The purchase method is applicable in those instances in which the combination is accomplished by the exchange of cash, other assets, liabilities, or by the choice of the purchase method when exchanging common stock. The financial treatment of the method requires that the acquired asset be valued, for the purposes of the merger, at cost in the case of a cash or liabilities payment and at the fair value of the acquired asset when the payment is in shares. The fair value of the asset may be determined by either the fair value of the shares given in exchange or the fair value of the asset acquired, "whichever is more clearly evident." Any amount paid in excess of the fair value of the asset is allocated to goodwill, which is an attempt to measure the intangible assets acquired in the purchase, such as management talent, that are the reasons that the acquiring firm is willing to pay in excess of the acquired assets' net worth. For example, assume that company C and company D have the following balance sheets and earnings and that C issues 1,000 shares worth $50,000 in the purchase of D:

	C	D	C and D
Current assets	$ 50,000	$10,000	$ 60,000
Fixed assets	100,000	25,000	125,000
Goodwill	0	0	20,000
Total assets	150,000	35,000	205,000
Current liabilities	25,000	5,000	30,000
Long-term debt	0	0	0
Stockholders' equity	125,000	30,000	175,000
Total liabilities	150,000	35,000	205,000
Earnings	18,000	2,000	20,000
Number of shares	9,000	1,000	10,000
Earnings per share	$ 2.00	$ 2.00	$ 2.00

In this case, company C has exchanged $50,000 worth of stock for the $30,000 net worth of company D. If it is clearly evident to the accountant that the fair value of the acquired assets of company D is only $30,000, there is a discrepancy between the increase in the assets acquired and the increase in the stockholders' equity accounts. Because the assets and liabilities sides of the balance sheet must balance, the asset goodwill is created to effect the balance. This makes the dollar amount of the combined firm's depreciable assets of the separate firms.

This increase in depreciable assets means that future earnings may be smaller because of larger depreciation charges. If goodwill is created or the fair value of the assets increased because of the purchase, the preferred accounting procedure is periodically to charge against income an amount over the estimated life of the asset. If the charges against income are substantial enough, the potential earnings benefits of the merger could be eliminated. To avoid this, some firms charge off goodwill against capital or earned surplus, despite the general disapproval of the accounting profession.

Merger and Earnings Forecasts

In addition to considering the combination and synergistic effects of the merger, the analyst must estimate the merger effects on the earnings per share growth pattern of the merged company. The analyst must divide his estimate of the combined earnings by the number of shares to arrive at a per share estimate for the combined company. The number of shares to be outstanding after the merger is consummated depends on the exchange ratio, which is the rate at which the acquiring company issues its shares for each share of the acquired company. For example, the acquiring company might be issuing two of its shares in exchange for each of the acquired firm's shares. In this case the exchange ratio would be 2 to 1. We explore, later in this chapter, some of the considerations that are involved in determining the exchange ratio, but for the present we assume a certain exchange ratio and discuss its effects on the expected future earnings of the company.

The immediate effect of a merger by an exchange of stock may be an increase, decrease, or no change in the earnings per share. For example, consider the effect on the earnings per share of the surviving company in the following illustration:

	ABC	XYZ
Present earnings	$10,000,000	$1,000,000
Present shares (mil)	5	1
Present earnings per share	$ 2.00	$ 1.00
Stock price	$20.00	$20.00

If ABC had agreed to acquire XYZ in an exchange ratio of 1 to 1, that is, ABC will give the stockholders of XYZ one share of ABC stock for each share of stock, the total number of ABC shares outstanding after the merger would be 6 million. Earnings per share for the surviving company would be $1.83, as computed below:

Surviving company ABC	
Earnings	$11,000,000
Shares (mil)	6
Earnings per share	$1.83

The immediate effect of the illustrated merger on earnings per share has been a dilution of $0.17 per share for ABC.

The immediate effect could have been an increase in the earnings per share of the surviving company if the exchange ratio had been different. For example, if the exchange ratio had been $\frac{1}{10}$ of a share of ABC for each share of XYZ, the total number of shares outstanding for the surviving company after the merger would be 5,100,000, and the earnings per share of the surviving company would have been increased from $2 to $2.16. But the analyst is really more concerned with the future earnings per share than with the immediate effects of dilution. The effects of the merger on the future pattern of earnings depends on the exchange ratio and the initial dilution that it may cause, the relative size of the merging firms, the relative earnings growth rates of the two companies, and any synergistic effects. The larger the exchange ratio in excess of the ratio of market prices, the more shares the surviving firm has outstanding after the merger and the greater the immediate dilution. Thus, any growth that may occur in future earnings starts from a lower per share base, and it takes a period of time for the surviving firm's earnings per share to regain the dilution that immediately followed the merger. The length of time necessary to regain the dilution depends on the rate of growth in the earnings per share of the surviving company, which, in turn, is the result of the relative rates of growth in earnings for each of the merger partners and the relative size of the merger partners at the date of merger.

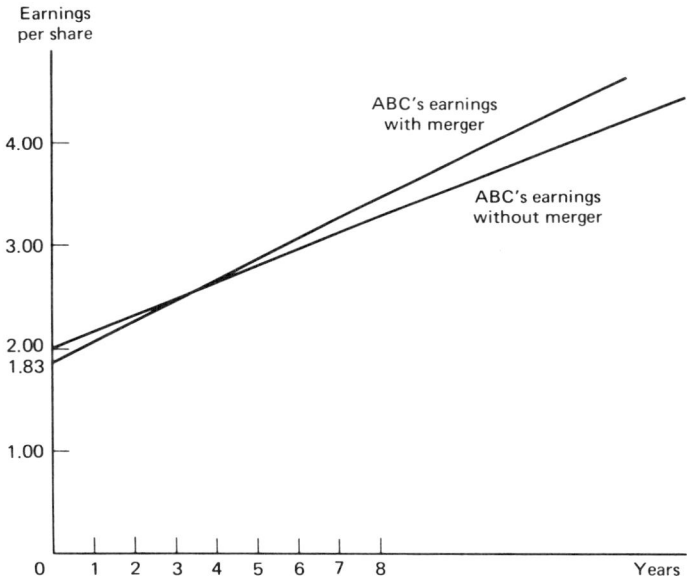

Figure 15.1. Effect of merger on future earnings per share.

This may be illustrated by referring to Figure 15.1. The effect of the initial dilution is to reduce present earnings per share from $2 to $1.83. Without the merger, ABC's earnings per share were expected to grow at 5 percent per year from the $2 level. With the merger, the earnings per share are expected to grow at 8 percent per year from the $1.83 level. The increase in the expected rate of growth is computed as the weighted average of the growth rates of each company before the merger based on the relative size of the earnings. In this example we assumed that the XYZ Company was expected to grow at 38 percent per year, so that the weighted average growth rate would be 8 percent ($1 million $\times$ 0.38 + $10 million $\times$ 0.05)/$11 million.

Applying the weighted average growth rate, which must be adjusted to include the effects of synergism, to the $1.83 earnings per share base, it may be seen that it will take approximately 3 years until the immediate dilution effect of the merger is overcome by the increased growth rate. The analyst who is trying to estimate the merger's effect on earnings must look beyond the immediate effects of the merger and concentrate on the pattern of earnings that will prevail after the merger. The analyst may expect and must look for the merger's effect on both the magnitude of the earnings per share and on the growth pattern.

Through mergers the firm can create a growth pattern in its earnings. The strategy is for a high price/earnings ratio company to acquire a company at a lower price/earnings ratio. After the exchange of shares, the acquiring high price/earnings ratio company's earnings per share will have risen. The acquiring company's earnings per share will rise every time that the process is repeated, as long as its price/earnings ratio is higher than the acquired company's price/earnings ratio at the date of the exchange. For example, if company D acquired company F, the surviving company D would have experienced an increase in reported earnings per share:

	Company D	Company F
Present earnings	$12 million	$6 million
Shares (mil)	4	3
Earnings per share	3.00	2.00
Exchange ratio	⅓	1
Price per share	$48.00	$16.00
	Surviving company D	
Earnings	$18.00	
Shares (mil)	5	
Earnings per share	3.60	

As can be seen from the example, the earnings per share of the surviving company D actually increased because of the merger. If the process is repeated enough times, the effect is to give the appearance of growth in the earnings per share. If, at the same time, the price/earnings ratio of the acquiring company remains the same or rises, the stock price should rise. As we discuss shortly, however, the merger effect on the price/earnings ratio may be quite substantial, and unless the effect of the merger on both the earnings and the discount factor is considered, no judgment may be made about the merger effect on the price of the stock.

Merger and the Discount Factor

Mergers affect not only the future earnings and expected dividend stream but also the business and financial risks associated with it. The variability in earnings caused by business risk may be lessened by merger. For example, a firm's earnings might be variable because the price of its raw materials varies substantially, as is the case of a copper wire fabricator who is dependent on an unaffiliated copper ore refiner for its basic raw materials. If the copper wire fabricator could vertically merge with the refiner, he would have a certain source of basic materials that would not fluctuate in price with supply and demand conditions in the world copper market. The variability in operating earnings could also be reduced by diversification across industry lines, such as in the case of conglomerate mergers. If, for example, a merger occurred between two firms, one of which had operating earnings that varied directly with the business cycle and the other of which had operating earnings that varied inversely with the cycle, the combined operating earnings of the two firms would be stable in the business cycle. This may be seen from the example in Table 15.1.

TABLE 15.1

	Normal	Boom	Recession
Company 1			
Sales (mil)	$10.00	$12.50	$ 7.50
Expenses	9.00	11.25	6.75
Operating income (mil)	1.00	1.25	0.75
Company 2			
Sales	10.00	8.00	12.00
Expenses	9.00	7.20	10.80
Operating income (mil)	1.00	0.80	1.20
Company 1 and 2			
Sales	20.00	20.50	19.50
Expenses	18.00	18.45	17.55
Operating income (mil)	2.00	2.05	1.95

The variation in operating earnings in the business cycle is much greater for each of the companies than for the combination of the two companies. Before merging, the operating income of company 1 ranged from $0.75 million in the recession year to $1.25 million in the boom year, and the operating income of company 2 ranged from $0.8 million to $1.20 million. After the merger of the two companies, the range in operating income shrunk to $1.95 to $2.05 million. When we think of business risk in terms of variability in operating income, it is obvious that the effect of a merger between company 1 and company 2 is to reduce business risk. Of course a merger between a firm with low business risk and a firm with high business risk increases the business risk for the low business risk firm and decreases that for the high risk firm, but the business risk associated with the combination of the two should be less than the sum of the independent risk associated with each company before the merger.

A merger also affects the financial risk associated with the stream of future benefits. The surviving firm may acquire the assets of the acquired firm in exchange for stock, debt, or a combination of both. The stock that is exchanged increases the equity position of the surviving company relative to the debt position. The debt that is exchanged increases the debt position of the surviving firm relative to the equity position. For example, assume that the following were the assets and liabilities of the two companies before a merger in which B exchanged $5 million in debt for A's stock:

Company A		Company B	
Assets	Liabilities	Assets	Liabilities
$5 (mil)	0 debt	$10 (mil)	0 debt
	$5 (mil) stock		$10 (mil) stock

After they merged, the combined balance sheet would as follows:

Company A and B	
Assets	Liabilities
$15 (mil)	$ 5 (mil) debt
	$10 (mil) stock

if company B had issued $5 million in debt to acquire company A. The debt/equity ratio of the combined company is 1/2, which is higher than the premerger debt/equity ratio, and the financial risk is increased. The earnings per share of the surviving company are subject to more fluctuation because of the introduction of debt into the capital structure. The reverse can occur. A firm with a substantial amount of debt could exchange shares for another company, and the surviving company would have a lower debt/equity ratio and less exposure to financial risk.

The analyst must be careful to determine the intent of the acquiring company before he can reach definite conclusions about the merger's effect on the firm's financial risk. In several instances, firms have exchanged shares for other firms specifically to increase the equity base of the surviving firm. This would seem at first as if the surviving firm's financial risk had decreased, but the actual intent of the acquiring firm had been to use the enlarged equity base as a basis for expanding its borrowing power. The intention is to expand its debt position back quickly to its original, if not greater, relation to equity.

Mergers and Stock Prices

The ultimate effect of the merger on the stock price is the result of the interaction of its effect on the expected future stream of benefits and on the discount factor in the PDV evaluation framework. If the merger increases (decreases) the expected stream of future benefits and everything else is held constant, the net effect should be an increase (decrease) in the stock price. If the merger increases (decreases) the business and financial risk of the firm without changing expectations about the future dividend stream, the stock price should fall (rise). If the merger increases the expected stream of future benefits and at the same time decreases financial and business risk, the stock price rises, because both effects tend to increase stock prices. If the merger effects are not obvious in that the stream of future earnings and dividend expectations moves in the opposite direction to the discount factor, the effect on the stock price depends on the magnitude of change in each. For example, if the relative increase in the discount factor is less than that in the expected stream of earnings and dividends, the price of the stock may be expected to rise. If, on the other hand, the relative increase in the expected earnings and dividends is less than that in the discount factor, the stock price may be expected to fall.

Exchange Ratio

In addition to judging the effect of the merger on the surviving company, the analyst is expected to make judgments on the exchange ratio. This requires that the analyst be familiar with the methods used to evaluate common stock in merger situations. The analyst may be called on for his judgment if he is assisting in the negotiations. As an outside investor, he may be required to forecast what the terms of the merger might be or to determine if the declared terms are reasonable, because the exchange ratio is the dominant factor in determining the stock price of the company to be acquired. Once the exchange ratio is declared, it is likely that the stock price of the company to be acquired will fluctuate in the proportions of the exchange ratio with the stock price of the acquiring company. For example, if the exchange ratio were one half-share of the acquiring company for each share of the company to be acquired, the stock price of the acquired company could be expected to rise $0.50 for every $1 rise in the stock price of the acquiring company.

The methods suggested for determining the exchange ratio involve evaluating the equity of the firm to be acquired and include asset evaluation techniques, capitalized income techniques, common stock market price techniques, and cash dividend methods.[1]

The asset evaluation method involves the determination of the book value of the common stock as a basis for computing the exchange ratio. We have already criticized the book value concept as not appropriately reflecting the economic worth of the assets. Asset value has little value in aiding the analyst in his judgment of the exchange ratio.

The capitalized income method seeks to determine what is the present discounted value of the future stream of earnings of the firm to be acquired. The reasoning behind this merger evaluation technique is the same as that behind the evaluation of a common stock share. The worth of any asset is the stream of future benefits expected to accrue to the asset, discounted to the present at an appropriate rate. The value of the acquired company to the acquiring company is the future stream of earnings discounted by the capital cost of the shares or debt to be exchanged. The acquiring company should be willing to pay up to the present discounted value of the stream. If the acquiring company pays less than this amount, it may be thought of as having acquired a bargain.

The common stock market price method evaluates the common equity of the acquired firm as the common stock price times the number of shares outstanding. The exchange ratio would be the ratio between the respective companies' stock prices. This method should reflect the relative economic worth of the merger partners as determined by the stock market. It has become common to merger activity, however, that the acquiring company pays a premium above the market value for the shares of the company to be acquired. This premium is the necessary enticement for the stockholders to exchange willingly their shares for those of the acquiring company and may reflect the increased benefits that the acquiring company expects to receive. It has been estimated,

---

[1] L. Dellenbarger, Jr., *Common Stock Valuation in Industrial Mergers,* University of Florida Press, Gainesville, 1966.

however, that the ratio of the market price of the two companies just before the initiation of merger discussions is the dominant factor in explaining the exchange ratio. The analyst should start his evaluation of the exchange ratio with a consideration of the market price relationship.[2]

The cash dividend relationship between the two prospective partners is another method of determining the exchange ratio but seems to have much less influence on the decision than the market price relationship. In the instance of a growth-oriented company, the analyst might expect the exchange to be made in convertible bonds or preferreds. By using these types of securities, the growth company can offer an equal dividend expectation to the dividend-oriented stockholders of the company to be acquired as well as participation in the growth prospects of the company. In this situation the dividend relationship between the two companies might be important in determining the dividend on the preferred; the market price relationship might be the dominant factor in determining the conversion price of the preferred.

If we choose to base our estimation of the exchange ratio on the common stock market price approach, it is possible to establish upper and lower limits within which the exchange ratio is likely to fall.[3] For example, assume that company A is negotiating the merger of company B and that the stock price of company A is

(15.1) $$P_a = \frac{(P/E_a)Y_a}{N_a}$$

where P_a = stock price of A
P/E_a = price/earnings ratio
Y_a = current earnings of A
N_a = total number of shares outstanding for A

Similarly, the stock price for company B is

(15.2) $$P_b = \frac{(P/E_b)Y_b}{N_b}$$

The expected market price per share of the combined firm should reflect the price/earnings ratio of the merged concern, which may be higher than the premerger P/E of either firm because of the synergistic effects, the combined earnings of the two firms, and the number of

---

[2] *Ibid.*, p. 140.
[3] Kermit D. Larson and Nicholas J. Gonedes, "Business Combinations: An Exchange Ratio Determination Model," *Accounting Review*, October, 1969, pp. 720–28.

shares outstanding after the merger. The postmerger share price may be expressed as

$$(15.3) \quad P_{ab} = \frac{(P/E_{ab})(Y_a + Y_b)}{N_a + (ER)N_b}$$

where ER is the exchange ratio of company A shares offered for one share of company B.

What is the maximum exchange ratio that the shareholders of company A are willing to offer the shareholders of company B? Clearly, the maximum offer is that which leaves the share price of company A unchanged from the price that prevailed before the merger; any offer that caused a lower market price would be rejected by company A's stockholders. In terms of Equations (15.1) and (15.2), the maximum exchange ratio offered occurs when P_a equals P_{ab}, which allows us to set the equations equal to each other and solve for ER_a as follows:

$$(15.4) \quad ER_a = \frac{(P/E_{ab})(Y_a + Y_b) - (P/E_a)(Y_a)}{(P/E_a)(Y_a)(1/N_a)(N_b)}$$

When Equation (15.4) is solved for ER_a, we obtain the maximum exchange ratio offer at which the share price of company A will be the same after the merger as before. Note, however, that ER_a depends on the price/earnings ratio that is expected to prevail after the merger (P/E_{ab}); as the P/E_{ab} increases, the maximum exchange offer from company A also increases. This may be illustrated as in Figure 15.2 as a rising ER_a.

We must now determine the minimum exchange ratio acceptable to the stockholders of company B. They, of course, will not be satisfied with any offer that will decrease the value of their holdings; that is, the postmerger price P_{ab} must at least equal the premerger price P_b of their stock adjusted for the exchange ratio, or $P_{ab} = P_b/ER$. Thus, we may set Equations (15.2) and (15.3) equal and solve as follows:

$$(15.5) \quad ER_b = \frac{(P/E_b)(Y_b/N_b)(N_a)}{(P/E_{ab})(Y_a + Y_b) - (P/E_b)(Y_b)}$$

The minimum acceptable ER_b also varies with P/E_{ab}, as did ER_a, but at a decreasing rate, as illustrated in Figure 15.2.

We are now in a position to compare the two acceptable levels of exchange ratios. On or below the ER_a line in Figure 15.2, the shareholders of company A are satisfied. On or above ER_b the shareholders of company B are satisfied. Therefore, negotiations should take place within the shaded area between the two lines. Of course, company A should bargain for an exchange ratio closer to line ER_b, and company B for an exchange ratio closer to ER_a; the final exchange ratio, of course, depends on the bargaining abilities of the two parties, but within this framework, the analyst should at least have an idea as to the limits of the exchange ratio.

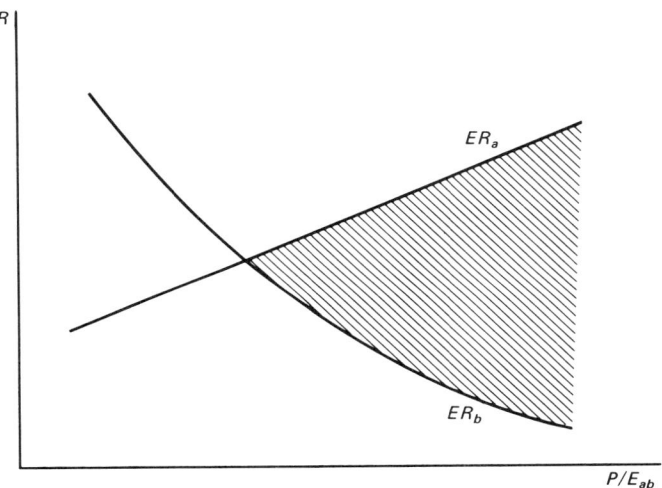

Figure 15.2. Exchange ratio limits.

(*From Kermit D. Larson and Nicholas J. Gonedes, "Business Combinations: An Exchange Ratio Determination Model," Accounting Review, October, 1969, p. 726.*)

Investor Experience and Mergers

The results of one study show that the price performance of the acquiring company before and after the announcement of the merger was not statistically different from that of companies in which there was no merger activity during the period. In this sample, however, the stock price performance of the companies to be acquired was appreciably higher than that of companies not engaged in merger activity.[4] This performance reflects the premium over the current market price offered the acquired company's stockholders by the acquiring company. Table 15.2 illustrates that from 3 months prior to the merger announcement (date 0 in Table 15.2) to the date of the consummation of the merger, the stock price performance of the acquired companies was superior to that of a control group of stocks that did not participate in merger activity during the period under study. The price appreciation in the 1-

[4] S. Block, "The Merger Impact on Stock Price Movements," *MSU Business Topics,* Spring, 1969, pp. 7–12.

month interval before the date of announcement was 17.01 percent. The returns in both periods to the acquired companies were far superior to those of the control group. Investors who were able to spot merger candidates more than 3 months before the announcement date generally did well.

TABLE 15.2 Stock Price Performance of Acquired Companies

Time before announcement, months	Acquired companies, percent	Control group, percent
9–6	+4.34	+3.66
6–3	+1.17	+5.06
3–1	+3.05	−1.87
1–0	+17.01	+3.08
0 to consummation	+9.69	+0.51

It is interesting to note that the price performance of the acquired companies offered a profit opportunity to the investor even after the announcement of the merger had been made. From the date of the announcement until the consummation of the merger, which averaged about 3 months, the price appreciation of the acquired company stocks averaged 9.69 percent. One possible investment technique that might be used to take advantage of this profit opportunity is the merger hedge. After the announcement, the investor could purchase the stock of the company to be acquired and, at the same time, sell the stock of the acquiring company short. When, at consummation, the stock of the acquiring company is exchanged for that of the acquired company, the investor returns the stock that he has borrowed to execute the short sale. The investor's profit is the difference between the price that he paid for the shares of the acquired company and the proceeds that he received from the short sell of the acquiring company's stock. By simultaneously selling the acquiring company's stock short and buying the acquired company's stock long, the investor has attempted to assure himself the profit represented by the difference between the two prices. There is the risk in any merger hedge that the merger may not be consummated and that the stock price of the company to be acquired would slide back to or below the level before the impact of the merger began to be felt. If this happened, the merger hedge would result in a loss, because the value of the stock that the investor had purchased in the company that was to have been acquired declines, and he would not receive the shares of the acquiring company needed to cover his short sale. The profit that he had expected to make by covering his short sale with these shares would disappear. It is also possible that a delay in consummating the merger may make the profit opportunity less appealing than alternative investments, for the time value of money would lessen the PDV of the profit.

WARRANTS

A warrant is a right to buy, at the warrant holder's option, a stated number of shares of stock at a specified price during a specified period of time. For example, the Tenneco, Inc., warrant allows the warrant holder the option of purchasing one share of Tenneco common stock at $32 until April 1979.

All warrants are characterized by provisions that specify the price at which they may be exercised, the number of shares that they entitle the holder to purchase, and the date at which they expire. The exercise price, such as the $32 per share in the Tenneco example, may be fixed for the life of the warrant or increase in predetermined steps during its life. In the latter case the exercise price would rise by a fixed amount after the passage of a stated period of time. The number of shares that may be purchased by the warrant holder for each warrant that he exercises may vary from fractions to many shares. For example, the Tri-Continental warrant entitles the warrant holder to purchase 2.83 shares at $22.61 each. The life of the warrant may vary from several days for those warrants which are about to expire to infinity for those warrants which have no expiration date. The Tri-Continental warrants, for example, have no expiration date. The warrants may be issued in conjunction with a bond issue, and when the investor must purchase the two together, the warrants are said to be attached. Some attached warrants are detachable in the sense that once the investor has the bond and the warrant, he may sell either one separately. Certain attached warrants are not detachable and may be sold only in conjunction with the bond. The warrant holder is not entitled to any of the dividends paid on the common stock, but if the common stock is split or a stock dividend is declared, the exercise terms of the warrant are usually adjusted to take account of this change. For example, if the Tenneco common stock were split two shares for one share held, the exercise price of the warrant would decline to $16 per share, and the number of shares one warrant could purchase would double.

To the investor many warrants offer investment leverage. For example, let us take the case of the investor who had $1,000 to invest in either the common stock of a company that was selling at $10 per share or the warrants of the same company that were selling at $2 per warrant and entitled the warrant holder to purchase one share of the common stock at $10 per share. With $1,000 the investor could buy either 100 shares of the common stock or 500 warrants. If the common stock price rose $5 to $15 per share and the warrants followed in tandem by also rising $5 to $7 per warrant, the value of the 100-share common stock investment would be $1,500; the value of the 500-warrant investment would be $3,500. The common stock investment would have had a profit of $500, or 50 percent; the warrant investment would have had a profit of $2,500, or 250 percent. Because of the lower price of the warrant and its tendency to move in tandem with the price of the stock, the warrants offered a greater potential reward than the common stock. At the same time, warrants also have a greater risk exposure. If in the example, the stock price fell $2 from $10, there is a 20 percent loss. In contrast, if the warrant price fell $2 from $2, there is a 100 percent loss.

Theoretical Warrant Value

The theoretical value of a warrant V_w can be determined by the following equation:

$$V_w = (P - O)N$$

where P = market price of one share of stock
O = exercise price of one share of stock
N = number of shares that may be purchased with one warrant

For example, if the price of the common stock of Tenneco were $35, the value of the warrant that is exercisable at $32 would be

$$(\$35 - \$32)1 = \$3$$

Theoretically, the warrant will not sell below this computed value, for at any price below this value an investor could buy the warrant, exercise it, and immediately sell the share that he had just purchased by exercising the warrant for a profit. He would continue to do this until his purchasing of the warrants sufficiently drove up their price and his selling of the common stock drove down its price to the point at which the warrant's theoretical value equaled its market price. Generally, the warrant's theoretical price is a floor under which the market price cannot fall. If, however, the stock price declines, the theoretical price floor falls.

Premium

It is common to find warrants selling at higher market prices than their theoretical value. The difference between the market price and the theoretical value is the premium. It has been observed[5] that the premium on warrants tends to increase as the common stock price declines and tends to decrease as the common stock price rises. Thus, even when the theoretical value of the warrant is zero, or negative, the market is still willing to pay some positive price for the warrant. The warrant's leverage is one reason that it may sell at a premium.

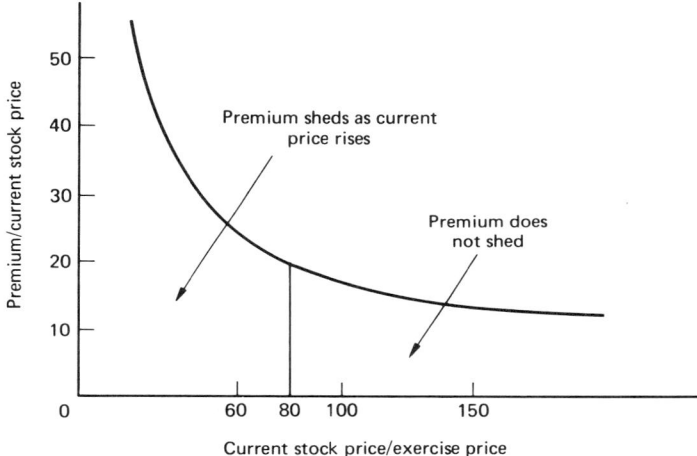

Figure 15.3. Warrant premiums and stock prices.

From this observed pattern of warrant premium behavior, Pease has suggested certain trading rules for the warrant investor.[6] From Figure 15.3, it may be seen that the ratio of the warrant premium to the current stock price rises as that of the current stock price to the exercise price falls. This implies that as stock prices decline, the decline in the warrants is dampened, because the premium on the warrant is growing. Conversely when the common stock price is rising, the upward price movement of the warrant is dampened by the *shedding* (decline) of the premium. Pease observed that after the common stock price reached 80 percent of the exercise price, the shedding of the premium lessened considerably, so that after the 80 percent figure had been reached, the dampening effect no longer greatly hindered the upward price movement of the warrant. At figures of 60 percent and below Pease observed that an upward price in the common stock would not be accompanied by

---

[5] F. Pease, "The Warrant: Its Power and Its Hazards," *Financial Analysts Journal*, January-February, 1963, pp. 25–32.

[6] *Ibid.*

so large a price movement in the warrant, because the warrant would be shedding its premium. Therefore, the warrant investor should concentrate his purchases in those warrants with a current stock price to exercise price ratio of at least 80 percent, because the upward price potential would not be penalized by the shedding effect and the downward price movement would be dampened by the buildup of the premium.

By concentrating strictly on such a trading rule, however, the investor may be overlooking certain other factors that may have an important bearing on the analysis of warrants. Among these may be the expected future price of the stock, the length of time before the warrant expires, and the potential dilution that may result from the exercise of the warrants. We must now turn our attention to some of the models of warrant evaluation that incorporate these considerations.

Warrant Evaluation Models

Warrant evaluation models have been developed that point out areas of investigation at which investors might look in determining warrant value. We look at two particular models in order to gather what are the pertinent variables and their importance in warrant price determination. Shelton[7] has suggested that warrant price is bounded as to how high or how low it may fluctuate when the associated stock is at a certain price. The lower boundary is determined by the theoretical value of the warrant. This means that, at a minimum, the warrant can sell for no less than zero when the computed theoretical value is negative and that as the stock price rises the theoretical value of the warrant also rises. This is illustrated in Figure 15.4. The upper boundary represents the warrant price that the investor feels would return a profit exactly equal to that which he can expect from the common stock and the price at which all the advantages of leverage to the warrant disappear. The investor is unlikely to pay this price, because the leverage of the warrant exposes it to more downside risk than the common stock and the investor demands a greater return for this greater risk exposure. As stock prices rise, the upper bound draws closer to the lower bound until, at about the point at which the stock price is four times the exercise price, the upper and lower bounds become one.

The forces that push the upper bound toward the lower bound are the diminishing leverage advantage and the higher dividends at the higher stock price. It generally occurs that by the time the stock price is four times the exercise price, there is little profit differential to be

---

[7] J. Shelton, "The Relation of the Price of a Warrant to the Price of Its Associated Stock," *Financial Analysts Journal,* May-June, 1967, pp. 143–151, and July-August, 1967, pp. 88–89.

gained by purchasing the warrant as opposed to the common stock. At the higher stock prices, both the warrant and the stock usually sell at prices that are relatively close to each other and usually move in tandem, so that the percentage gain in one is almost equal to the other. At these higher prices, it is also usually true that the dividend forfeited by the warrant holder is relatively large and that any leverage effect that may remain is offset by the dividend forfeiture. In Figure 15.4, we see the upper and lower bounds joining at the point at which the stock sells at four times the exercise price.

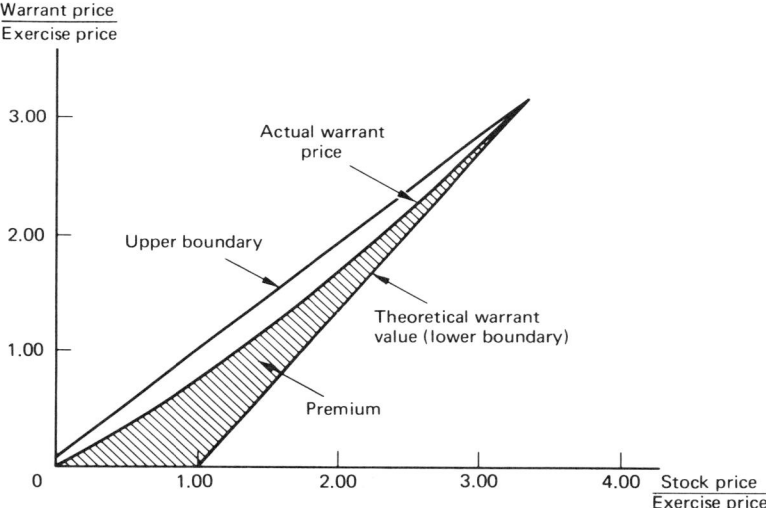

Figure 15.4. Warrant price relationships.

(From J. Shelton, "The Relation of the Price of a Warrant to the Price of Its Associated Stock," Financial Analysts Journal, May–June, 1967, p. 145.)

Between the upper and lower bounds, there is an entire spectrum of prices at which the warrant may sell. The actual warrant price is the price that includes the premium (shaded area in Figure 15.4) over the theoretical value. As we have seen, the premium tends to be greatest at the lower levels of stock prices and to shrink as the stock prices rise until the premium disappears and the actual and theoretical warrant prices coincide.

The factors that Shelton found to determine the premium at the various levels of stock price were the number of months before the warrant expired, the dividend yield on the common stock, and whether or not the warrant was traded on an organized exchange. Specifically, he found, by regression analysis, that the premium, which he expressed as a percentage of the distance between the upper boundary and the lower boundary, would be equal to

$$P = \sqrt[4]{\frac{M}{72}} (0.47 - 4.25Y + 0.17L)$$

where M = number of months remaining in warrant's life
Y = dividend yield on common stock
L = 1 if warrant were listed; 0 otherwise
P = premium (percentage of difference between boundaries represented by actual prices)

For example, if the distance between the upper boundary and the lower boundary were $4 and $P = 50$ percent, the premium would be $2 per share. The actual warrant selling price should then be the theoretical value plus the $2 premium.

We can illustrate Shelton's model with his application to Alleghany Corporation warrants. As a rough approximation, the upper limit, over an index price range in the associated stock, is three-quarters of the stock price. In this case, the Alleghany common was selling at $11 per share, and so the upper limit would be $8.25 (¾ × $11). The warrant entitled the holder to purchase one share at $3.75 without a time limit. The warrant theoretical value was $7.25 ($11.00 − $3.75). Thus, the warrant price had to be between $7.25 and $8.25. Shelton assumed that $M = 120$, the yield Y on the stock $= 0.018$, and because the warrant was listed, $L = 1$. Therefore

$$P = \sqrt[4]{120/72} \, (0.47 - 4.25)(0.018 + 0.176)$$
$$P = 0.64$$

that is, the warrant selling price SP should, according to Shelton's model, be the theoretical warrant value ($7.25) plus the premium, which is equal to 64 percent of the difference between the upper limit and the theoretical value:

$$SP = \$7.25 + 0.64(\$8.25 - 7.25)$$
$$SP = \$7.89$$

The implication for the analyst is that at a particular price for the stock, he can judge by this standard if the warrant selling price is out of line. If the value computed in this manner reveals that the warrant price should be more than what it presently is, the warrant could be considered undervalued. Conversely, if the computed value were below the selling price, the warrant could be considered overvalued. It is important to note that this analysis is predicated on the present price of the stock. If the stock price changed, so would the computed value for the warrant.

Another model for warrant evaluation was suggested by Kassouf.[8] He, too, bounds the area of possible warrant prices. The area bounded closely resembles that in Figure 15.3 and may be described by the following equation:

$$Y = (x^z + 1)^{1/z} - 1$$

where Y = warrant price divided by exercise price
x = stock price divided by exercise price
z = value of factors that determine premium

The upper boundary is determined where z equals 1, for there the value of the warrant is equal to the price of the common stock:

$$\begin{aligned} Y &= (x^1 + 1)^{1/1-1} \quad \text{where } z = 1 \\ &= (x+1)^0 \\ &= 1 \end{aligned}$$

Because, as we can see from the theoretical value of the warrant, the price of the warrant cannot exceed that of the common stock when both are related to the exercise price, this must be the upper boundary. The lower boundary is determined when z equals infinity:

$$\begin{aligned} Y &= (X^\infty + 1)^{1/\infty} - 1 \\ &= (x^\infty + 1)^{-1} \\ &= \frac{1}{(x^\infty + 1)} \\ &= \frac{1}{\infty} \\ &= 0 \end{aligned}$$

The actual values of the warrant, which include the premium, are determined when z takes on intermediary values between 1 and infinity. To determine z, it is necessary to determine what factors influence the premium. Once we can estimate z, we can compute a value for Y and the estimated selling price for the warrant.

Kassouf found, by regression analysis, that the factors that determined z were the number of months to expiration, the dividend yield on the common stock, and the potential dilution that would occur if

---

[8] S. Kassouf, "Warrant Price Behavior: 1945 to 1964," *Financial Analysts Journal*, January-February, 1968, pp. 123–126.

all the warrants that were outstanding were exercised. Specifically, Kassouf found that

$$z = 1.2221 + \frac{5.131}{T} + 14.8135R + 0.2765D + 0.4401\frac{X}{A} + 0.4131\log\frac{X}{X_j}$$

where T = number of months to expiration
 R = annual dividend yield on common stock
 D = number of warrants/number of shares
 X = price of common stock
 A = exercise price
 X_j = price of common stock 11 months before

Subscription Rights

On occasion, a firm offers its stockholders the right to subscribe (purchase) additional shares, within a short specified time period, at a stipulated price. Usually, the subscription (stipulated) price is below the current market price, so that the rights themselves have value and may be sold independently or together with the stock. Each shareholder is issued a right for each share of stock that he presently holds, although it usually takes several rights to subscribe to one additional share. For example, a rights holder may purchase one additional share at $30 per share for every 10 rights that he holds.

The value of one right V_r is part of the stock when it is sold together with the stock. To compute the V_r, itself, we must remove the value of the right from the stock price and compute how much per right the subscription price SP has saved us above the current market price MP minus the value of the one right included in the share $(MP - V_r)$. Therefore, the value of the right depends on the difference between the $(MP - V_r) - SP$ and the number of rights required R to purchase one additional share. For example, assume the following:

$MP = \$52$

$SP = \$30$

$R = 10$

The value of one right V_r would be

$$V_r = \frac{MP - V_r - SP}{R}$$

$$R(V_r) = MP - V_r - SP$$

$$R(V_r) + V_r = MP - SP$$

$$V_r = \frac{MP - SP}{R + 1}$$

$$V_r = \frac{\$52 - \$30}{11}$$

$$V_r = \$2$$

If the right is sold independently of the stock, that is, the value of the right has already been removed from the stock price, the stock price should be lower by the worth of the right—in this example $50. In this case, we do not have to remove the value of the one right from the stock price before computing the V_r, which would be computed as

$$V_r = \frac{MP - SP}{R}$$

$$= \frac{\$50 - \$30}{\$10}$$

$$= \$2$$

OPTIONS

An option is an indirect claim on a common stock that is similar to the warrant. The option assigns the right to the holder either to buy or sell a specified number of shares at a specified price within a stated time from the option issuer, who is usually an option dealer or an owner of the stock.

There are numerous types of options. Among the most common are the put, the call, the straddle, the spread, the strip, and the strap. The put option entitles the option holder to sell a stated number of shares at a stated price within a specified time period to the person from whom the option was purchased. For example, the option might specify that the holder had the right to sell to the option writer 100 shares of ABC Company at $50 per share before the next 6 months expired. The option purchaser hopes that the stock will decline in price and to profit by being able to buy the 100 shares of ABC Company at less than $50 per share sometime during the next 6 months and then sell these shares for $50 each to the option writer. For this right, the option holder pays the option writer a fee. Unless the market price at which the option buyer can purchase the shares of ABC Company is sufficiently low enough to cover the cost of the fee, he loses money.

The call is the reverse of the put. With the call the option holder has the right to buy the shares of ABC Company from the option writer. In this case, the option holder hopes that the price of the ABC Company shares will rise, so that he will be able to buy the shares from the option writer at a price below which they are currently selling and then sell them on the open market for a higher price. For example, the investor might purchase a call that entitles him to purchase 100 shares of XYZ Company at $15 per share any time within the next 3 months. For this call he might pay $150. If the price of the stock rose above $16.50 per share, the option holder could profit by requiring the option writer to sell him the shares at $15 per share and then resell them on the open market at a price above $16.50. The cost to the option holder would be the $1,500 for the shares plus the $150 for the call, or a total of $1,650; the sale of the shares would bring in more than $1,650. If the price of the stock did not rise above $16.50, the option holder would have lost money.

The straddle is two identical options, one a put and the other a call. The put and the call are on the same stock, for the same number of shares, the same price, and the same time period. With a straddle, the investor could profit by exercising both the put and the call if the stock price fluctuated sufficiently.

The spread is identical to the straddle except that the price at which the option holder may sell the shares to the option writer is below the prevailing market price and the price at which the option holder may purchase the shares from the option writer is above the prevailing market price. The strip is a combination of two puts and a call, and the strap is a combination of two calls and a put.

When one owns a put or a call, any dividends that are applicable to the associated common stock are also applicable to the option. For example, if during the life of a call a dividend of $1 is declared on the associated common stock, the call price is reduced by $1 per share. In the case of a put, the price at which the holder has the option to sell to the option writer is reduced by the same $1.

Option Value

The value of an option reflects the option purchaser's expectations of the future price of the associated common stock during the life of the option. This requires that he postulate a subjectively derived probability distribution of future market prices $\hat{P}_i$, such as illustrated in Figure 15.5.

Given this probability distribution, the potential purchaser is in a position to evaluate any option offered to him. Let us assume that he is offered an option with an exercise price of *EP* in the figure above. This means that any $\hat{P}_i$ to the left of *EP* are worthless to the option holder, because to the left of *EP* the market price of the stock does not exceed the price at which the option entitles the holder to purchase the stock. In other words, he could buy the stock at a lower price in the open market than he could by exercising his option. Conversely, all possible prices $\hat{P}_i$ to the right of the option price (the shaded area) make the option valuable, for now, by exercising the option to buy the stock at the *EP*, he is purchasing it at a lower price than the market price.

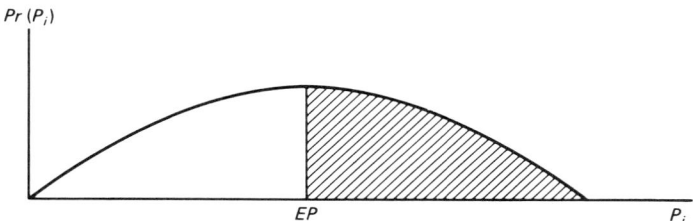

Figure 15.5. Estimated associated common stock price.

The expected value of the option price is then dependent on the profit that can be made at these favorable prices by exercising the option and selling the stock in the market for the higher price. For example, if the investor assumed the following probability distribution of future stock prices:

$\hat{P}_i$	$Pr(\hat{P}_i)$
$60	0.10
55	0.20
50	0.40
45	0.20
40	0.10

and $EP = \$45$, he would have a 0.10 chance of making a $15 profit, the difference between the market price of $60 and the *EP* of $45, a 0.20 chance of a $10 profit, a 0.40 chance of a $5 profit, and a 0.30 chance of no profit. Obviously, what we want to know is the expected profit from the option. In this example, the expected profit would be $5.50. This is not the final answer, however, because assuming that the profit will not be realized until the end of the option's life, we must discount the expected return for the time value of money. If, in this example, the option had a life of 1 year and the time value of money were 10 percent, the option value would be $5. The potential option holder should then compare this option value with the cost of the option. If the cost is less than $5, ignoring transactions costs, he would purchase the option; more than $5.00 and he would not purchase the option.

Option Investment Results

The simulated profit performance of option traders has been varied. Kruizenga's study[9] concluded that from 1946 to 1956 there was a high return to the option investment. Ninety-day call options on U.S. Steel returned about 9 percent, and 6-month calls returned about 35 percent. Most of the profit, however, was centered in the most bullish years. The results are rather unexpected, because the 6 months called had tax advantages not available to the 90-day option. The option buyers should have bid up the option price in their effort to gain the tax advantage.

Put options, on the other hand, did not prove to be profitable investments. A put purchaser would have lost money during the period. In comparison with a strategy of holding the stocks, the purchase of options had a lower return. This implies that the options were not the most attractive method of investing.

Boness' study[10] estimated that between 1957 and 1960 option purchasers lost some 60 to 80 percent per year and concluded that option purchasing was unprofitable. On the other hand, option writers succeeded in earning some 18 to 32 percent per year during the period studied if they were capable of committing a sufficiently large investment to the option market and frequently revised their offerings.

Both these studies may be misleading.[11] The obvious difference in specified time periods means that the results recorded then may not be indicative of present option performance. Both the studies did not consider transaction costs or taxes or the thinness of the option market, which may have prevented the option purchaser from actually completing all his transactions as simulated.

Option Price

What factors influence the price of the option? It has been suggested that the price of the call option relative to that of the associated common stock is affected by the expected rate of appreciation of the associated common stock, the variability of the price of the associated common stock, the trading volume, and the actual price of the associated common stock.[12]

The option price should naturally be higher, the larger the expected price appreciation in the associated common stock. A high expected

---

[9] R. J. Kruizenga, "Profit Returns from Puts and Calls," as reprinted in P. H. Cootner, *The Random Character of Stock Market Prices*, The M.I.T. Press, Cambridge, Mass., 1964.

[10] A. J. Boness, "Some Evidence of the Profitability of Trading in Put and Call Options," as reprinted in *ibid.*, pp. 475–496.

[11] B. G. Malkiel and R. Quandt, *Strategies and Rational Decisions in the Securities Option Market*, The M.I.T. Press, Cambridge, Mass., 1969, p. 20.

[12] *Ibid.*, pp. 26–31.

price appreciation would make the option seller more reluctant to sell a claim on his shares to another without some increase in the fee paid for this privilege. The option purchaser would be more willing to pay a higher fee for this privilege if he expected a large price appreciation in the associated common stock. These supply and demand pressures should force the option price higher.

The option price should increase as the variability of the associated common stock price increases. Increased variability means that it is more likely that sometimes during the option period the price of the associated common stock is sufficiently high to make the exercise of the call profitable. The more often the associated stock price rises to make the option valuable, the greater should be the worth of the option.

The option price should decrease as the number of shares outstanding increases, because a larger number of shares decreases the probability of large variation or swings in the associated share price. A smaller number of shares should allow a greater price movement in the stock. Also, the option price should increase as the trading volume in a stock increases, because large trading volume suggests that there is active market interest in the stock and any company news or general market movement is reflected in the price. The inactively traded stock may just languish for the entire option period, frustrating even the most carefully planned option investment.

The option price relative to the price of the associated common stock should decrease as the absolute market stock price rises. Apparently, the appeal of the option partly lies in its small cash outlay. Because the higher the price of the associated common stock, the higher the absolute option price, the appeal of the small cash outlay is lost when investing in options on higher-priced stocks.

We should expect the call option price relative to associated common stock price to be positively related to the volatility of the stock price, the trading activity, and the expected price appreciation and negatively related to the number of shares outstanding and the absolute stock price. The results of empirical work in this area[13] support the influence of these factors in determining the call option price in relation to the associated common stock price. The most significant of the factors seems to be the volatility of the associated common stock price.

BANKRUPTCY—ALTMAN'S MODEL

Certain income statement and balance sheet items have been found to be good indicators of corporate bankruptcy.[14] When taken as a profile

---

[13] *Ibid.*, pp. 29–31.

[14] E. Altman, "Financial Ratios, Discriminant Analysis and the Prediction of Corporate Bankruptcy," *Journal of Finance,* September, 1968, pp. 589–609.

of the corporation one annual financial statement before the declaration of bankruptcy, the following ratios have proved to be good indicators:

X_1 = working capital/total assets
X_2 = retained earnings/total assets
X_3 = earnings before interest and taxes/total assets
X_4 = market value of equity/book value of total debt
X_5 = sales/total assets

The combined profile of these ratios would be as follows, where z is an overall index of the profile:

$$z = 1.2X_1 + 1.4X_2 + 3.3X_3 + 0.6X_4 + 0.999X_5$$

When z is greater than 2.99, it seems that the firm is not in danger of going bankrupt; and when the value of z is below 1.81, the firm is very likely to go bankrupt. This is illustrated in Figure 15.6.

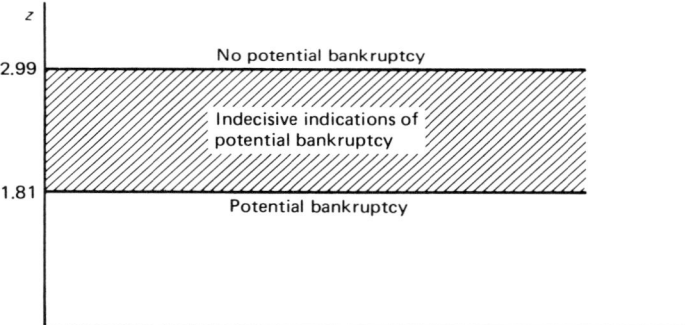

Figure 15.6. Altman's decision rules.

Each of the ratios in the profile reflects an aspect of the firm's financial position and earning power and has a bearing on the firm's ability to maintain its solvency. The working capital/total assets ratio X_1 reflects the firm's liquidity position. A firm that may be headed toward insolvency ordinarily has sustained losses in preceding years that have weakened its working capital position, particularly among the more liquid assets, such as cash and marketable securities. Eventually the working capital position may become so weak that the firm is forced into bankruptcy for failure to meet its everyday cash needs. By incorporating this variable into the overall index, the model catches the degree to which the weakening of the working capital position may indicate potential bankruptcy.

The retained earnings/total assets ratio X_2 reflects the cumulative profit during the life of the firm and usually the age of the firm, because the younger firms have had less time to build up substantial retained earnings. Because the incidence of bankruptcy is concentrated among the younger, less established firms, the use of this ratio in the profile contributes to the indication of potential bankruptcy.

The earnings before interest and taxes/total assets ratio X_3 is an indication of the firm's productivity. The essence of any successful venture is an ability to generate sustained earnings. Before impending bankruptcy the firm is likely to experience losses. These losses are an indication that the productivity of the firm's assets is low.

The market value of the equity/book value of total debt ratio X_4, which is defined as the market value of all the preferred and common stock to the current and long-term debt, reflects the degree to which the firm's assets can shrink in value until the debt exceeds the assets. Because the market value reflects more accurately the economic worth of the firm and the contractual debt of the firm remains constant, this ratio gives the analyst some indication of the economic worth of the equity in relation to the debt.

The sales/total assets ratio X_5 reflects the turnover or utilization of the firm's assets and their ability to generate sales. This measure is a good indication of management's ability to handle internal business risk. Poor management is one of the primary causes of business failure, and this is reflected in the importance of the measure in the computation of the overall measure z.

This particular profile of corporate variables proved a good indicator of bankruptcy as early as 2 years before the actual bankruptcy, although its accuracy improved as the date of bankruptcy was approached. During the 2 years before bankruptcy, each of the ratios reflected a deterioration in quality and began to show signs of corporate decay that accompany bankruptcy. Earlier than 2 years before the actual bankruptcy, however, the predictive quality of the profile greatly declined. This seems to imply that it may take 2 years before the situation deteriorates into bankruptcy, which, of course, allows sufficient time for detection and portfolio reconsiderations.

Although we are now equipped with insights into the indicators of corporate bankruptcy and shoud, theoretically, be able to detect impending bankruptcy, we must ask ourselves about the investment implications. Does the investor have a profit opportunity once the model has predicted bankruptcy, or has the market already anticipated the bankruptcy and negated any profit opportunities? What has been the price performance of the equity securities of bankrupt firms? According to Altman, the market value of the common stocks declined 45 percent from the time that the model first predicted bankruptcy until the actual failure date, which was an average of 15 months. The implications for the investor are significant. If he does not already own the stock, he should not commit himself to any purchase. If he does already own the stock, he would be advised to sell it on the first indication of bankruptcy and reinvest the funds elsewhere. If the investor is aggressive, he may attempt to profit from the situation by selling the stock short in anticipation of the price decline that should accompany the actual bankruptcy predicted in the model.

Another study by Altman[15] determined that the price performance of the equity securities of bankrupt firms was inferior to the general price performance of all stocks. The results showed that the investor who already owned the stock or purchased it 1 month prior to the failure date and held it for 10 years would have, on average, experienced a return that was only 76 percent of that experienced by stocks in general. During the 10-year sample period, only 19 percent of the bankrupt stock had a greater rate of return than the general market. The investor who purchased the stock 1 month after the actual failure, however, received a return approximately equal to that received by all stocks. In fact, among the more recent bankruptcies, the average return has outperformed the market, implying that the investor might profit by investing in selective bankrupt securities, perhaps those which have the highest overall index value 1 month after bankruptcy. The average return to an investor who bought bankrupt stocks 1 year after the actual failure, however, was about equal to the average return on all stocks.

This seems to imply that if the investor is to gain from the purchase of bankrupt stocks, the best time to purchase them would be shortly after bankruptcy. If the investor waits for 1 year to elapse, the profit opportunity is lost, because the market apparently very quickly bids up the stock prices of those bankrupt companies which are likely to recover.

OTHER CONSIDERATIONS

Other variations in the evelution of equity securities may occur in the instances of new issue, New York Stock Exchange listing, and potential dilution.

New Issues

It has been suggested that the pricing of new issues for which no market existed would be biased downward, offering the investor a profit oppor-

---

[15] E. Altman, "Equity Securities of Bankrupt Firms," *Financial Analysts Journal,* July-August, 1969, pp. 129–133; and "Corporate Bankruptcy Potential, Stockholder Returns and Share Valuation," *Journal of Finance,* December, 1969, pp. 887–900.

Other considerations   341

tunity when the stock was issued.[16] The undervaluation bias results because of the unseasoned nature of the security, the underwriter's bias to price the issue low so as to ensure the success of its sale, and to ensure that the exercise price of the stock options, which are given to the underwriter and the company's officials, is low. If the new issue is underpriced, it should quickly rise in price after the initial sale. The Reilly and Hatfield study showed that more than half of the new issues outperformed the general market. This in itself was not significant, but the price performance of the half that did outperform the market was more than sufficient to offset the price performance of those new issues which did not outperform the market, so that, on average, the return to the new issues was substantially higher than that to the general market. This above average performance for new issues occurred in the 1-week, 1-month, and 1-year periods after the initial offering, with the bulk of price appreciation coming almost immediately after the initial offering.

The return to new issues during the longer term was not so rewarding as the general market.[17] In a 10-year holding period there was no evidence to support a higher return to unseasoned new issues. The evidence seems to indicate that the return was lower than average. It had been expected that the return to the unseasoned new issues would be higher than that to stocks in general because of the greater risk attached to their purchase. In both the short- and long-run cases the results may have been influenced by the general market conditions. There seems to be some indication that the demand for new issues runs in cycles and that the price performance of the new issue immediately after the initial offering may be affected by the "receptiveness" of the market. At certain times a speculative fever erupts in new issues that sends their price to immediate premiums above the initial offering price. At other times the demand for new issues is slack, and the number of new issues is curtailed. The investment implications of these studies may be subject to wide variation depending on the "mood" of the market.

Dilution

When the firm has a senior security that is convertible into the common stock of the company at the option of the senior security holder, the earnings per share are subject to dilution. The analyst should know whether or not the market in general compensates for the potential dilution when it evaluates the common stock. If the market totally compensated for the potential dilution, the analyst could merely compute what

[16] F. Reilly and K. Hatfield, "Investor Experience with New Issues," *Financial Analysts Journal,* September-October, 1969, pp. 73–80.

[17] I. Friend, et al., *Investment Banking and the New Issues Market,* World Press, New York, 1967.

the earnings would be if all the outstanding convertible securities were converted and use these earnings figures in his evaluation. If the market does not totally compensate for the dilution factor, the analyst must be aware of this. It seems as if the market does take into consideration the potential dilution effect[18] by assigning a significantly lower price/earnings ratio to those stocks with potential dilution. In fact, the higher the potential dilution, the lower the price/earnings ratio. For every 1 percent increase in the potential dilution the price/earnings ratio seems to decline three-tenths of one point. When the potential dilution factor is taken into consideration, however, by using earnings per share after the conversion of all convertible securities, the influence of the dilution on the price/earnings ratio becomes insignificant, although what influence seems to remain seems to cause a lower than appropriate price/earnings ratio. The implication for the analyst is that in his evaluation he should use the earnings per share that would exist if all conversion had occurred.

Exchange Listing

The listing of a stock on the New York Stock Exchange may have some effect on the evaluation of the stock. It seems that a stock that trades on the New York Stock Exchange commands a premium above its identical counterpart that is traded over the counter.[19] This may arise because a listing assists in making the stock more marketable by assuring a wider distribution of the shares, more assurance against fraud and stock manipulation, and promulgation of information concerning the company. This does not affect the evaluation of a stock that is already listed or one that is not listed, unless the analyst is comparing the two. The only investment implication is in the one-time move of the stock from one to the other, usually from an unlisted to listed trading status. Such a move might give occasion to a spurt in the stock's price to bring the previously unlisted stock in line with other previously listed securities.

SUMMARY

In evaluating stocks there are several situations that sufficiently deviate from the standard PDV framework to warrant modifications in the evaluation analysis. Among the special situations are mergers and acquisitions, stock purchase warrants, options, and bankruptcy.

---

[18] E. Lerner and R. Auster, "Does the Market Discount Potential Dilution," *Financial Analysts Journal,* July-August, 1969, 118–121.

[19] J. L. O'Donnell, Jr., "Case Evidence of the Value of a New York Stock Exchange Listing," *MSU Business Topics,* Summer, 1969, pp. 15–21.

The merger may affect the value of the surviving company by altering either the expected earnings stream or the financial or business risk associated with it. The effect of the merger on earnings may be an immediate increase or decrease in the earnings per share. An immediate increase may give the appearance of growth and, if the discount factor is unchanged, an increase in the stock price. The image of a growing earnings stream garnered by merger activity, however, may prove illusionary if the firm is unable to continue an aggressive, successful merger campaign. Although the earnings may be initially diluted by the merger, the effect on the earnings stream must be judged over the longer horizon. The merger may actually cause a higher growth rate in the earnings per share that in the longer run may more than offset the immediate decrease in the earnings per share. In addition, there may be synergistic effects from the merger, so that the combined operations of the two firms may be more profitable than if each had continued separately.

The effect of the merger on the business and the financial risk of the firm may also be favorable or unfavorable. Business risk may be reduced if the merger leads to a lower variability in the operating income of the firm. This may be accomplished by merger by proper diversification, the securing of stable-priced raw material resources or product demand, and so on. Financial risk may be changed with the consummation of a merger if the capital structure is altered.

The determination of the exchange ratio in the merger seems to be primarily dependent on the market price of the stocks before the merger negotiations, although most of the time a premium above the market price that prevailed before the negotiations is paid by the acquiring company. This premium presents an investment opportunity for the investor who can spot merger candidates. From 3 months before the merger announcement there is, on average, substantial price appreciation in the stock price of the company to be acquired. Even after the merger announcement there remains a profit opportunity.

The evaluation of a warrant requires the investor to estimate the premium that will be paid above the theoretical value of the warrant. Investors are apparently willing to pay a premium for the warrant because of its leverage advantages. The premium seems to rise as the price of the associated common stock falls and to fall as the price of the associated common stock rises. The exact value of the premium at any particular stock price may depend on the number of months until the warrant expires, the dividend yield on the associated common stock, the listing status of the warrant, the potential dilution, and the recent price history of the common stock.

The stock option comes in many forms. Among the more common forms are the call, the put, the spread, the straddle, the strip and the strap. The value of the option seems to be mainly dependent on what the investor feels is the most likely future price of the associated common stock.

In the case of stocks of bankrupt firms, it seems as if a combination of certain financial ratios is an accurate predicator of corporate bankruptcy. These ratios are the working capital/total assets, sales/total assets, market value of the equity/book value of the debt, earnings before interest and taxes/total assets, and retained earnings/total assets. These ratios seem to predict bankruptcy as early as 2 years before the actual failure. This presents the investor with a profit opportunity by selling short as stock prices tend to decline quite sharply just before the actual bankruptcy. The historical evidence seems to support the sharp drop in stock prices just before actual failure but also reveals that the price of bankrupt stocks, if they are to recover at all, tends to bottom out shortly after the actual failure and, on average, appreciate more from this point than stock prices in general. After a year from the date of actual failure has elapsed, however, this greater than average profit opportunity seems to have disappeared.

QUESTIONS

15.1 Describe the three basic types of mergers.

15.2 What are the main concerns in evaluating the effect of a merger on the stock price of the acquiring company?

15.3 How might accounting procedures affect a merged company's future earnings?

15.4 What determines the effects of a merger on the future pattern of earnings?

15.5 Why would a high price/earnings ratio company seek a merger with a low price/earnings company?

15.6 Explain how a firm could reduce its financial risk by a merger.

15.7 Describe the possible effects of a merger on the stock prices of the surviving company.

15.8 Discuss the various methods for determining the exchange ratio.

15.9 Explain the merger hedge investment technique.

15.10 What is a stock warrant?

15.11 What factors are important in the analysis of warrants?

15.12 According to the literature cited, what determines the upper boundary of the warrant price?

15.13 Explain why a warrant's upper bound approaches its lower bound as the stock's price rises.

15.14 What factors did Kassouf use in determining the value of the warrant premium?

15.15 What are subscription rights?

15.16 Explain each of the following options: (a) put, (b) call, (c) straddle, (d) spread, (e) strip, and (f) strap.

15.17 With reference to Figure 15.5 on page 335, why are prices to the left of EP worthless to the option holder?

15.18 What determines the expected value of the option price?

15.19 List the factors that would cause the price of an option to increase.

15.20 Discuss the significance attached to each of the variables in Altman's bankruptcy model.

15.21 What investment implications stem from Altman's bankruptcy model?

15.22 Why do new issues have a tendency to be undervalued?

15.23 What measures should an analyst consider to compensate for the effects of dilutions?

PROBLEMS

15.1 What are the earnings per share for the surviving company if the exchange ratio is two shares of A for one share of B? Compare this with ES of B. Assume that A is the surviving company:

	A	B
Present earnings (mil)	2.5	5
Present number of shares (mil)	0.2	0.65
Assets (mil)	10	20

15.2 Compute the growth rate of the surviving company from the following information:

	A	B
Assets	4,000,000	1,000,000
Growth rate	5%	8%

What would be the growth rate if the merger were expected to have synergistic effects of 125 percent?

15.3 Company B is acquiring A on a dollar for dollar book value basis. Compute the surviving company's debit/equity ratio:

Company A		Company B	
Assets	Liabilities	Assets	Liabilities
$10 (mil)	$ 0 debt	$20 (mil)	$10 (mil) debt
	$10 (mil) stock		$10 (mil) stock

Compare the ratio with the debt/equity ratio of Company B.

15.4 Compute the theoretical value of a warrant if the stock is selling at $20 per share, the exercise price of the warrant is $25 per share, and the warrant will purchase five shares. What is the premium on the warrant if it is selling for $2.

15.5 Using Shelton's model, compute the percentage premium on a listed warrant from the following information. There are 18 months remaining in the life of the warrant, and the yield on the common stock, which is listed on a national exchange, is 5 percent.

15.6 What would be the premium for the warrant in Problem 15.5 if its lower boundary were $2 and its upper boundary $6? If the theoretical value were $3, what would be its selling price?

15.7 If Z in Kassouf's model were equal to 2, compute the warrant price when the exercise price is $10 and the stock price $12.

15.8 What is the value of a right if the current market price, ex rights, is $30, the subscription price is $25, and 10 rights are required to purchase one share?

15.9 Determine the financial soundness of a company using Altman's model and the following financial information:

Current liabilities	4
Current assets	5
Total assets	10
Retained earnings	4
Sales	20
Taxes	0.5
Debt at 10%	0.2
Income (after interest, before taxes)	1
Number of shares outstanding	1
Current market price of stock	$12 per share

There is no preferred stock, and no dividend is paid on the common stock.

REFERENCES

Alberts, William W., and **Joel E. Segall** (eds.). *The Corporate Merger,* Chicago: University of Chicago Press, 1966.
Altman, Edward I. "Corporate Bankruptcy Potential, Stockholder Returns and Share Valuation," *The Journal of Finance,* 24:887–900, December, 1969.
———. "Bankrupt Firms' Equity Securities as an Investment Alternative," *Financial Analysts Journal,* 25:129–133, July-August, 1969.
———. "Financial Ratios, Discriminant Analysis and the Prediction of Corporate Bankruptcy," *The Journal of Finance,* 23:589–610, September, 1968.
Block, S. "The Merger Impact on Stock Price Movements," *MSU Business Topics,* 17:7–12, Spring, 1969.
Boness, A. James. "Elements of a Theory of Stock-Option Value," *The Journal of Political Economy,* 72:163–175, April, 1964.
Bracken, Jerome. "Models for Call Option Decisions," *Financial Analysts Journal,* 24:149–151, September-October, 1968.
Cohen, Jerome B., and **Edward D. Zinbarg.** *Investment Analysis and Portfolio Management,* Homewood, Ill.: Dow Jones-Irwin, Inc., 1967.
Dellenbarger, Lynn E. *Common Stocks Valuation in Industrial Mergers,* Gainsville: University of Florida Press, 1966.
Donaldson, Gordon. "New Framework for Corporate Debt Policy," *Harvard Business Review,* 40:117–131, March-April, 1962.
Fredman, Albert J., and **James E. Wert.** "An Analysis of Secondary Distributions," *Financial Analysts Journal,* 24:165–168, November-December, 1968.
Furst, Richard W. "Does Listing Increase the Market Price of Common Stocks," *The Journal of Business,* 43:174–180, April, 1970.
Goudzwaard, M. B. "Conglomerate Mergers, Convertibles, and Cash Dividends," *Quarterly Review of Economics and Business,* 9:53–62, Spring, 1969.
Guthmann, Harry G., and **Archie J. Bakag.** "The Market Impact of the Sale of Large Blocks of Stock," *The Journal of Finance,* 20:617–632, December, 1965.
Hayes, Samuel L., and **Henry B. Reiling.** "Sophisticated Financing Tool: The Warrant," *Harvard Business Review,* 47:137–150, January-February, 1969.
Kassouf, Sheen T. "Warrant Price Behavior, 1945–1964," *Financial Analysts Journal,* 24:123–126, January-February, 1968.
Lerner, Eugene M., and **Rolf Auster.** "Does the Market Discount Potential Dilution," *Financial Analysts Journal,* 25:118–121, July-August, 1969.
Leveson, Sidney M. "Have We Solved the Dilution Problem?," *Financial Analysts Journal,* 24:69–70, September-October, 1968.
Malkiel, Burton Gordon, and **Richard E. Quandt.** *Strategies and Rational Decisions in the Securities Options Market,* The M.I.T. Press, Cambridge, Mass.: 1969.
McKenzie, Robert R. "Convertible Debentures, 1956–65," *The Quarterly Review of Economics and Business,* 6:41–51, Winter, 1966.
O'Donnell, J. "Case Evidence of the Value of a New York Stock Exchange Listing," *MSU Business Topics,* 17:15–21, Summer, 1969.
Pease, Fred. "The Warrant: Its Powers and Its Hazards," *Financial Analysts Journal,* 19:25–32, January-February, 1963.
Shelton, John P. "The Relation of the Price of a Warrant to the Price of Its

Associated Stock," *Financial Analysts Journal,* 23:88–99, July-August, 1967.
———. "Warrant, Stock-Price Relations: Part I," *Financial Analysts Journal,* 23:143–151, May-June, 1967.

Snyder, Gerard L. "A Look at Options," *Financial Analysts Journal,* 23:100–103, January-February, 1967.

Taylor, Howard M. "Evaluating a Call Option and Optimal Timing in the Stock Market," *Journal of the Institute of Management Sciences,* 14:111–120, September, 1967.

16
Investment Companies

In recent years investment companies, lead by mutual funds, have experienced extremely rapid growth. Their numbers have proliferated, and their shares have become common items in the holdings of thousands of smaller investors. Probably the greatest capital market participation on the part of the average investor has occurred in the ownership of mutual fund shares. Because of their importance as investment vehicles, the investor and the financial analyst must be prepared to evaluate the shares of these investment companies.

There are, however, certain peculiarities of mutual funds and other investment companies that require modification of the evaluation framework. Like the warrant, the shares of the investment company are an indirect claim on the actual securities of the operating companies. This implies that the risk attached to the ownership of investment company shares arises from the securities portfolio and only indirectly and partially from the financial and operating characteristics of the operating company. The share price of the investment company is determined by the underlying net asset value of the portfolio. This means that the evaluation framework is not concerned with determining the share price as in the case of an individual stock or bond, for the mutual fund share price already reflects the value of its financial asset holdings. What we are interested in determining is how well the portfolio managers have done their task in providing shareholders with professional management, improved returns, and proper diversification.

The major positive arguments advanced by the mutual funds, which are of interest to us in this text, are that mutual funds give the investor (1) professional management and (2) proper diversification. Professional management is supposed to increase the return to the investor above that which he could expect to earn without it. Because the investor must purchase a portfolio over which he has little control when he purchases the fund's shares, any profit expectation must be based on the investor's opinion that the professional managers will increase the value of the portfolio. What the investor is doing in evaluating the fund is really evaluating the ability of the professional managers. Because it is obvious that professional managers vary in quality, the investor requires a tool that will aid him in evaluating the management.

This chapter concerns itself with methods of evaluating the management of investment companies, particularly mutual funds. The question of proper diversification is deferred to the part on portfolio analysis and investment techniques. The first part of this chapter is devoted to the types of investment companies. Then we explore some procedures for evaluating management and the implications for the potential fund purchaser. Finally, we briefly touch on some of the empirical evidence on the performance of the funds.

TYPES OF INVESTMENT COMPANIES

Most investment companies are engaged in the business of managing a portfolio of financial assets, ranging from mortgages to stocks. It is not the scope of this chapter, however, to examine any investment companies other than those which invest in stocks and bonds. These companies sell their own securities to investors and in turn invest the proceeds in the stocks of other companies. There are several types of investment companies that are generally divided into the two categories of closed-end and open-end.

Closed-End

The closed-end investment companies derive their name from their closed capitalization. Once these companies have sold their shares to the investor, they do not normally make frequent further share offerings. In this respect they are similar to the industrial corporation. Any further share offerings are usually by occasional underwritings, and the shares are not redeemed by the company. The owner of these shares must sell them in the open market, where the price is determined by the prevailing supply and demand for the stock.

The net asset value of the share is the proportional claim of the share on the net market value of the company's security portfolio, less any debt or current liabilities. It is not unusual for the shares to sell at a discount from the net asset value per share. This varies, however, among the closed-end investment companies with shares selling at a market price both above and below their net asset value. The net asset value of the fund seems to be the focal point in determining closed-end share prices and is used as a standard of comparison when evaluating share prices. The investor either adds or subtracts from this net asset figure according to his perception of the quality of the management. If the professional management seems to have an expertise that promises greater than average returns, the market assigns a premium to the shares, that is, sells above net asset value. If the management does not seem to have the expertise, the market assigns a discount to the shares, that is, sells below net asset value.

Dual Funds

The dual fund is a variation on the closed-end investment company, and like the closed-end investment company, its shares are traded in the open market. The dual fund has a specific duration like a bond (usually 15 years at inception), at the end of which its shares are redeemed. At the fund's inception two classes of stock are sold, each class having the same number of shares and the same dollar value. One class is the preferred or income shares. These shares are entitled to receive all the dividend income earned by the fund after expenses are deducted. The preferred shares are usually assured a minimum dividend, which if it is not paid, becomes a claim against the other class of shares. At the termination of the fund, the preferred shares are redeemed for an amount approximately equal to the original purchase price plus any unpaid, promised dividends. The other class is the capital shares. These shares are entitled to receive all the assets remaining at termination after the preferred has been redeemed.

The advantage to the holder of either class of shares is the ability to tailor the risk to one's own preferences while, at the same time, experiencing leverage. The capital shareholder, who is usually more willing to sustain risk exposure for the potential of larger returns, receives the capital gains not only from the capital gains–oriented stocks in the portfolio but also any capital gains that may accrue to the dividend-oriented stocks in the portfolio. This means that the capital share has a greater chance for a larger return, because the potential for capital gains is not restricted to a narrow, limited group of more speculative securities. This also means that the risk exposure to the capital shareholder is reduced, because the portfolio from which his potential capital gains arise is more diversified and combines the risk-offsetting qualities of the more dividend-oriented stocks. The same risk-reducing and return-enlarging effects occur in the preferred shares. Any dividends that may arise in the capital gains part of the portfolio will increase the dividend income of the preferred. At the same time, the speculative risks of the capital gains part of the portfolio will mesh with the risks of the dividend-oriented stocks to form a total portfolio of greater diversification and more balanced risk.

The potential disadvantage of the dual funds lies in the danger that the managers will concentrate their investments in one type of stock to the disadvantage of the other. An undue preponderance of investment in dividend stocks may so detract from the fund's ability to generate capital gains that the capital shares would suffer. The preferred shares, however, would benefit and would expect increasing dividends. Conversely, an undue preponderance of investment in capital gains stocks, which usually pay little or no dividends, will penalize the preferred shares. The capital shares, however, would benefit because of expected larger capital gains income.

The evaluation of the preferred shares would be very similar to that of a bond. The preferred shares would be valued at the present discounted value of the expected stream of dividends and the return of the principal on the termination of the fund. The preferred shareholder could expect increasing, decreasing, or constant dividends during the remaining life of the fund, depending on management's investment policies and acumen. It has been suggested that the price behavior of the preferred resembles that of a bond,[1] for as the preferred shares approach termination, they have to approach their redemption value. This may give the preferred share a price pattern that follows the yield curve and may give the preferred shareholder an opportunity similar to "riding the yield curve" (see Chapter 10) in bonds. The value of the capital shares is the present discounted value of the expected termination value of the fund's assets after the preferred shares have been redeemed.

Open-End

The open-end investment company is more commonly called the mutual fund. It is characterized, in contrast with the closed-end investment company, by its continuous selling and redeeming of its shares. These shares may be offered at net asset value, in which case the fund is known as a no load fund (no sales charge). If the fund has a sales charge, the cost of the shares is the net asset value plus the sales charge. A fund with a sales charge is known as a load fund. It is usual with load funds to add the entire sales charge for the purchase of the shares and the shares contracted for future purchase to the price of the first shares purchased. This is known as front loading and has the effect of immediately penalizing the purchaser and prevents him from realizing a profit as quickly as he would if the sales charge were spread over the life of the contractual period.

During the period of ownership, the shareholder is also charged a management fee and for all the expenses incurred in the operation of the fund. At redemption, the shareholder may also be charged a redemption fee that lowers the amount that he receives for his shares.

[1] J. Shelton et al., "An Evaluation and Appraisal of Dual Funds," *Financial Analysts Journal,* May-June, 1967, pp. 131–139.

Several of the mutual funds have specific investment objectives that distinguish them. The major types of funds are the diversified common stock (growth) fund, the balanced fund, the income fund, the industry-specialized fund, the international fund, and the hedge fund. The diversified common stock fund is generally capital gains–oriented and has a portfolio that consists mainly of common stocks. The balanced fund portfolio consists of a diversified selection of common stocks, preferred stocks, and corporate and government bonds. The income fund's primary objective is a high return on its portfolio. These funds concentrate on the higher-yielding securities and have not invested to any great extent in the growth-oriented stocks. The industry-specialized funds concentrate their portfolios in one or a few industries. The international funds are primarily restricted to the purchse of foreign securities. The hedge fund is not restricted, as are most of the other types of funds, to only the cash purchase of securities. The hedge funds are chartered to engage in generally more speculative practices, such as short selling, buying on margin, options, and letter stock (securities which are not registered with the SEC and cannot be marketed until registered). The objective of the fund affects management philosophy, as well as the return and the risk that the investor can expect.

MANAGEMENT EVALUATION

Because management is the major determinant of the performance of a mutual fund, the analyst must have some criterion for evaluating management. The analyst must use a criterion of either relative or absolute performance. With the relative performance measure, the analyst is asking how the performance of this particular fund compares with that of other funds during the same time period. With the absolute criterion of performance, the analyst is asking what management's ability to predict stock price movements is. In other words, does the manager have the ability to generate a return for the fund above what we should expect from a portfolio of a given level of risk.[2]

The return to the shareholder is the dividends, capital gains distributions, and the increase in the fund's share price (which directly reflects the value of the stocks in the portfolio) that he experiences during a particular time period. Much of this return is related to the performance of the market in general. Any diversified portfolio of securities that is representative of the market as a whole could be expected to fluctuate to the same degree as the market. The value of the professional manager

---

[2] Much of the discussion in this section is based on J. Treynor, "How to Rate Management of Investment Funds," *Harvard Business Review,* January-February 1965, pp. 63–79.

should be his ability to outperform the general market. To perform merely as well as the general market is of little value to the shareholder, for he would receive the same return from the purchase of a diversified list of securities without paying the manager's fee. So in judging the performance of a manager, the analyst must consider the manager's record in relation to the performance of the general market.

It is also possible for the performance of any fund to be affected, especially in the shorter term, by the degree of risk inherent in the portfolio. It may be reasonably expected that the more risk in a portfolio, the greater should be the return. The manager's performance, as measured solely by the return on the portfolio, may be improved with riskier investments and investment practices. For example, we should expect a larger return from a portfolio of all common stocks than one balanced between common stocks and high quality bonds. For a greater exposure to risk, the shareholder naturally demands more reward. In judging the manager's performance, it is necessary to consider the portfolio's risk and its effect on the fund's performance. The performance measure that we are seeking must tell us how we, as shareholders, have fared at a given level of risk. In relative terms, we may only compare the performance of the portfolio once the effect of risk exposure has been equalized among the portfolios.

How can we compare the fund's performance with that of the market? What we are looking for is a measure that relates the fund's performance to various levels in the general market performance, such as the Dow Jones Industrial Average, the Standard and Poor's 500 Stock Average, or the New York Stock Exchange Index. Such a measure would reveal the fund's performance in relation to the market's performance. The ideal fund would have a rate of return that rises rapidly and at a faster rate than the general market in the upswings and a rate of return that declines slowly and less rapidly than the market in the decline. In fact, the ideal fund would put its assets into cash or short-term Treasury bills (or in the case of a hedge fund, sell short) during declining market conditions and, therefore, should always experience a positive return. Figure 16.1 illustrates the relationship between the market rate of return and the ideal fund's rate of return.[3] The market's rate of return is on the horizontal axis, and the fund's rate of return on the vertical axis. When the market's rate of return increases in Figure 16.1, the fund's rate of return increases by a more than proportional amount. When the market's rate of return decreases, the fund's rate of return decreases by a less than proportional amount. In Figure 16.1 the fund's rate of return is 20 percent when the market's rate of return

---

[3] K. Cohen and F. Hammer, *Analytical Methods in Banking,* Richard D. Irwin, Inc., Homewood, Ill., 1966, pp. 375–376.

is 10 percent, and 10 percent when the market's rate of return is −10 percent. As the lower market returns, the ideal fund has a tendency to maintain a high rate of return, and as the high market returns, the fund has a tendency to achieve a still higher return. No fund is ideal, however, and the relationship between the market and the fund's performances has been linear, as illustrated in Figure 16.2. When the market returns 10 percent in general, fund A returns 10 percent, fund B returns 0 percent, and fund C returns 30 percent. This relationship between a given market return and a fund's return is the *characteristic line*.

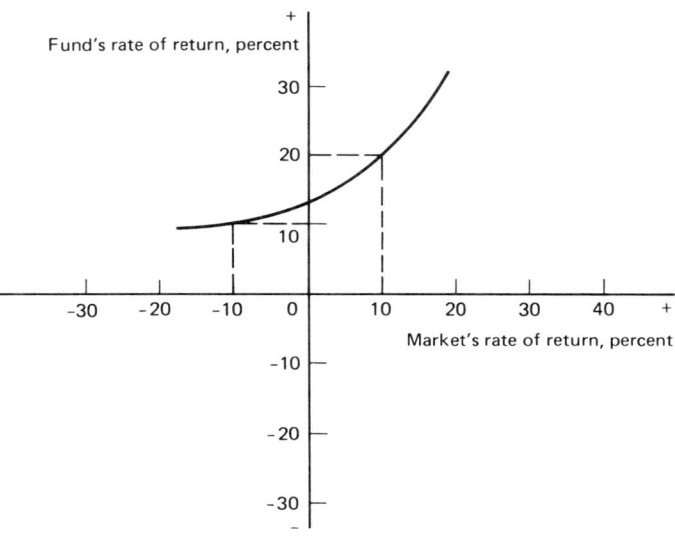

Figure 16.1. Ideal fund's performance in relation to the market's performance.

In time each fund establishes for itself this performance relationship with the market. The analyst can chart this characteristic line by plotting the fund's rate of return in any one year against the market's rate of return for the same year during a period of time and estimating the line.

This relationship also tells us about the portfolio's risk in relation to general market price movements. The slope of the line reflects the volatility in the fund's return. A steep slope would indicate that the fund is very sensitive to the general market. A slope of less inclination would imply that the fund's performance was not so sensitive to the general market. The more volatile the fund, the more risk inherent in the portfolio. In Figure 16.2, the slopes of the lines are the same for all three funds, implying that the risk is the same for all three funds. In comparing the three funds, the investor would prefer fund C, because it offered the best performance record in relationship to the market with the same risk exposure as the other two funds.

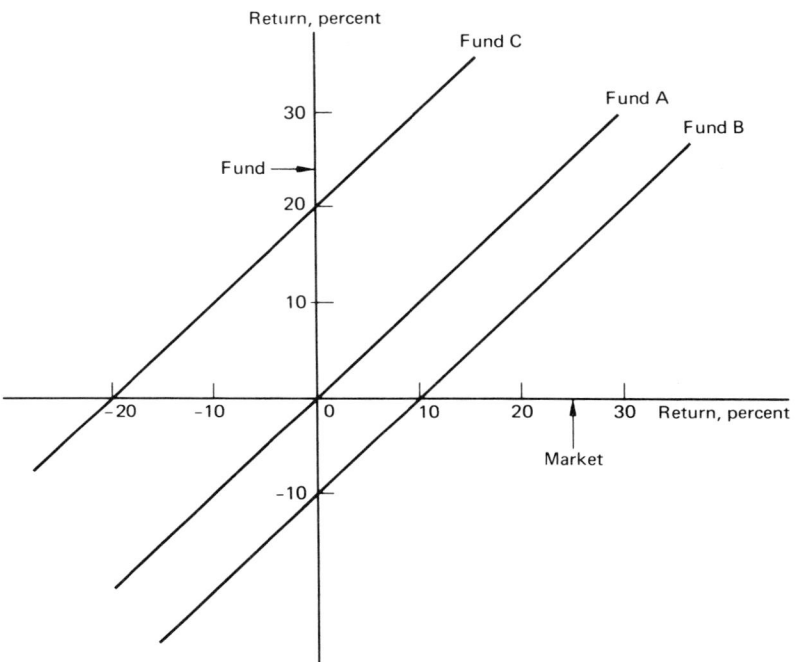

Figure 16.2. Fund and market performance.

Individual deviations in any one year from this market characteristic line reflect risks not related to the general market movements but to the particular securities held in the portfolios. When the deviations occur, it is an indication that the portfolio is not sufficiently diversified to minimize the risk that is unrelated to the general market price movements. We should, for example, expect an industry-specialized fund to deviate more from the characteristic line than a more broadly diversified fund. A fund that tends to deviate often from its line makes it difficult for the investor to estimate the risk attached to the purchase of these shares. Deviations above its line imply a greater than expected return for the prevailing market conditions; deviations below the line imply a less than expected return. A shift in the line up or down without a change in the slope would imply a change in management performance.

We can use the characteristic line to rank the funds in order of performance while still taking into consideration the effect of the general market and risk differentials. This is illustrated in Figure 16.3. The characteristic lines for funds 1, 2, and 3 are plotted. By relating the individual fund performance to the market performance, we have taken into

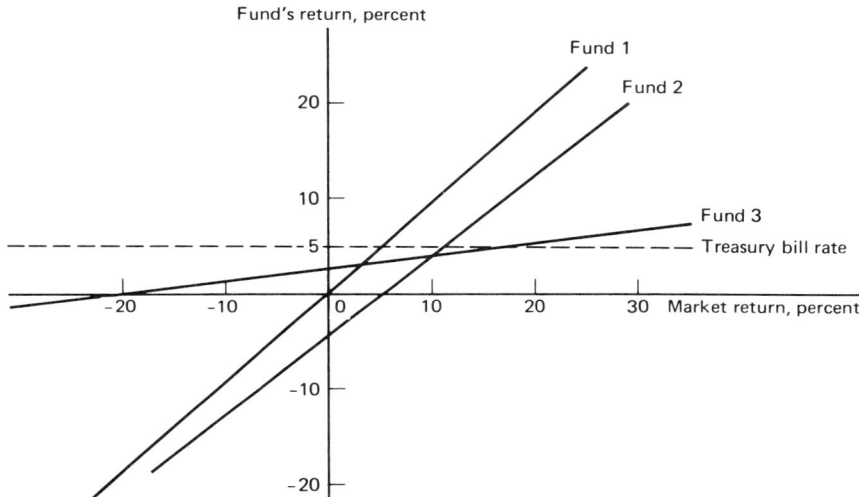

Figure 16.3. Ranking funds.

consideration the general market effect. To equalize the risk among the funds so that we may compare the performance records, we establish the pure interest rate available on an asset, such as a Treasury bill. In Figure 16.3 this is represented by the broken line drawn at the 5 percent rate of return level. The fund that is first to return the pure interest rate as the market rises (a movement to the right on the horizontal axis) is the highest ranked. In this case, fund 1 would be the first in rank, because it takes the smallest increase in the market to return the same as the pure interest rate. The other two funds must wait for a larger rise in the market before they return the pure interest rate. Note that although the characteristic line of fund 3 is less steep than the others, implying a lower risk exposure, it is not the first ranked, because the very fact that it is less risky precludes it from returning a performance as good as the pure interest rate until well after the other two funds have done so. In fact, the relative standing of fund 3 is third, behind funds 1 and 2, which return the pure interest rate long before fund 3. This ranking may change if the characteristic line shifts or the pure interest rate return changes.[4] This relative ranking brings into clear

[4] *Ibid.*, p. 378.

focus the necessity of considering the general market and individual fund risk when comparing funds.

PERFORMANCE RECORD

In terms of absolute performance, we wish to know if the professional manager is capable of producing returns above those which we should expect to receive from a portfolio equal in risk to that which he is managing. We should expect that the return on any portfolio would be equal to the pure interest rate plus a return to compensate for any additional risk.[5] The return on the fund's portfolio R_j should reflect the increased return that accompanies the increased risk $B_j(\bar{R}_M - R_F)$—see Figure 16.4. The fund incurs the additional risk when it purchases securities that are riskier than those which yield the pure interest rate.

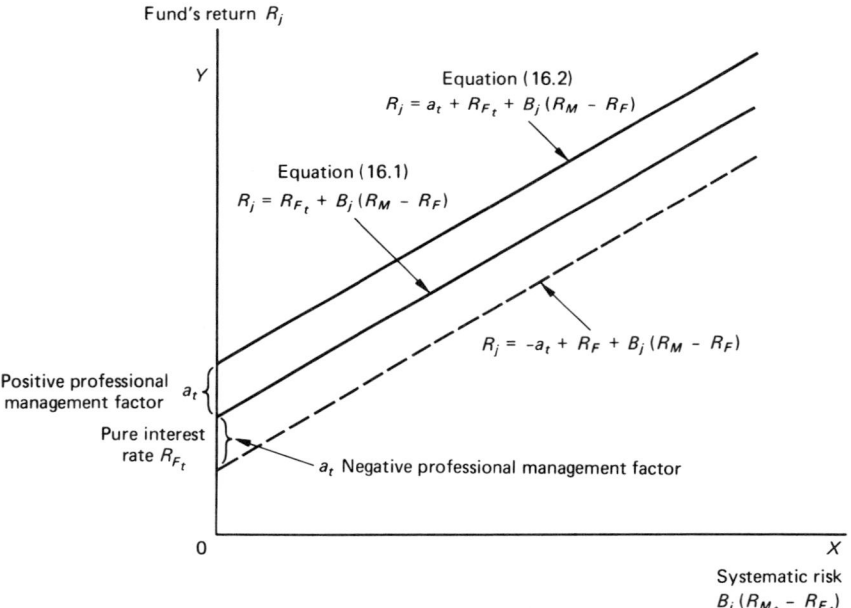

Figure 16.4. Mutual fund performance measures.

The particular portfolio of risk assets that the fund holds experiences a return that varies in some proportion B_j to the difference between the

[5] Much of the discussion in this section is based on M. Jensen, "The Performance of Mutual Funds in the Period 1945–1964," *Journal of Finance,* May, 1968, pp. 389–416.

return in the general market and the pure interest rate ($\bar{R}_M - R_F$). This difference may be envisioned as reflecting the systematic risk in the sense that it systematically reflects the greater risks attached to the larger return of the general market. Because the fund buys securities of more risk, its portfolio incorporates more of the systematic risk of the general market. The fund's portfolio can capture the entire return differential ($B_j = 1$) if it takes on a portfolio that is equal to a portfolio of all securities in the general market or more than the return differential ($B_j > 1$) if it takes on a portfolio of selected securities that are riskier than a portfolio of all market securities.

In more symbolic terms the return to the portfolio is

(16.1) $$R_{j_t} = R_{F_t} + B_j(\bar{R}_{M_t} - R_{F_t})$$

where R_{j_t} = return on portfolio
R_{F_t} = pure interest rate
B_{j_t} = systematic risk in portfolio j
$\bar{R}_{M_t}$ = expected return on market for all securities
t = time period

Equation (16.1) implies that the return on any portfolio is the pure interest rate plus a risk premium that is the amount of the return differential on the risk securities captured by the portfolio by the undertaking of systematic risk. This is illustrated in Figure 16.4. The mutual fund portfolio can take on more risk by advancing out the risk axis (X axis). It is expected that for every unit of more risk undertaken, the return to the portfolio R_j rises by a factor B_j. If no risk is undertaken, the portfolio is expected to return at least the pure interest rate R_{F_t}. It is hypothesized that it takes no particular professional management ability to increase the return R_j by increasing risk ($R_{M_t} - R_{F_t}$).

Any professional manager could be expected to have his portfolio return at least R_j. For the professional manager to exhibit any predictive ability, he must return more than R_j at each level of risk. If in time the fund manager had consistently performed better than R_j, there would be some constant factor that would make the actual return higher than R_j. We can represent this by a_j, where a_j is positive if professional management has improved on the expected return and negative or zero if professional management has not improved on the expected return. In equation form this would be

(16.2) $$R_{jt} = a_{jt} + R_{F_t} + B_j(\bar{R}_{Mt} - R_{Ft})$$

where a_j = effect of professional management

By estimating Equation (16.2) by regression analysis, Jensen found that a_j, the constant factor that he claimed reflected professional management's ability to forecast price movements, was negative ($-a_t$ in Figure 16.4). This implied that during the period that he sampled, the average fund performed worse than could have been expected with professional management. On average, Jensen concluded that the funds earned 1.1 percent less per year than they should have earned, given their degree of systematic risk. Only 39 out of 115 funds sampled showed a_j positive, implying that professional management improved on the expected return. The central conclusion seems to be that the average fund performed worse than could be expected without professional management, and if the investor is to purchase fund shares, he must be very selective in his evaluation of management.

Other studies[6] have reached similar conclusions. These studies have concluded that, on average, the mutual funds do not perform so well as expected, and in many instances a randomly selected portfolio actually outperforms the average mutual fund. Several studies have found that the expenses attached to the purchase of the mutual shares, particularly the sales load, have caused the funds to have a lower return on the shareholder's investment than he could have gotten from the general market averages. The investment implication here is that the no load funds, on average, offer a better opportunity for investment profit than the load funds do. Almost all the studies seem to agree that there are pronounced differences among the performances of individual funds. The *Wharton Study*, for example, concluded that "there was considerable variability in performance among funds of the same general type" as well as "pronounced differences in the performance of funds of different types." However, "during the period under study, performance records . . . on average conformed rather closely to the behavior of the securities markets as a whole."

OTHER PERFORMANCE MEASURES

Wiesenberger and Company has suggested in its publication, *Investment Companies*, that the performance of a mutual fund should be judged by its growth in assets per share and the dividends disbursed. Assuming that all capital gains distributions (the distribution to the shareholders from capital gains earned by the fund) are reinvested in the shares of the fund and all income distributions (the distribution to the share-

---

[6] I. Friend et al., *A Study of Mutual Funds*, prepared for the Securities and Exchange Commission by the Wharton School of Finance and Commerce, Report of the Committee on Interstate and Foreign Commerce, 87th Congress, 2nd Session, August 28, 1962; William Sharpe, "Mutual Fund Performance," *Journal of Business, Security Prices Supplement*, January, 1966, pp. 119–138; and I. Friend and D. Vickers, "Portfolio Selection and Investment Performance," *Journal of Finance*, September, 1965, pp. 391–415.

Other performance measures 361

holders from dividend income earned by the fund) are accepted in cash, Wiesenberger compares the sum of the assets per share at the end of the period, the capital gains distribution per share received during the period, and the income distribution received during the period with the assets per share at the beginning of the period to derive an index of the per share performance. In formula terms the index would be

$$(16.3) \quad \text{Index} = \frac{EA + DD + CD}{BA}$$

where EA = ending assets per share
DD = dividend distribution per share
CD = capital gains distribution per share
BA = beginning assets per share

If the index at the end of the period is greater than 1.0, the fund has provided a positive return to the shareholder during the period. If the index is less than 1.0, the fund has provided a negative return to the shareholder during the period. When compared with a similar index constructed from some general market measure, such as the Standard and Poor's 500 Stock Index, the shareholder receives an idea of the relative performance of his fund to that of the general market.

Although the Wiesenberger index is a reasonable measure of the return on a fund's assets during a given period, it does not consider the risk attached to any particular fund or such factors as management fees and broker's commissions. In an effort to judge the performance of mutual funds with some consideration to risk, *Forbes,* an investors magazine, has established a system of relative grades from A⁺ to D⁻ to reflect a fund's risk. Using periods of rising and declining markets, Forbes asks the question: in each of the periods did the fund do better than the market average, did it do worse than the market average, or did it merely keep abreast of them? Funds that managed to keep abreast of the market in all four "up" periods received a B⁺, funds that kept up in three periods got a B, two periods, a C⁺, one period, a C, no periods, a D. Funds that outperformed the averages in each of the four periods by more than 20 percent received an A⁺; those which were beaten by the averages by more than 10 percent received a D⁻. Similar ratings were applied to the four downside periods. This grading system, used in conjunction with a return on assets measure, provides a similar, although not so accurately derived, indication of Treynor's characteristic line. Those funds which received high grades in rising markets and low grades in falling markets could be classified as more volatile and riskier than their counterparts that received grades more indicative of consistently good performances in both types of market climate.

SUMMARY

Investment companies are corporations engaged in the managing of security portfolios. Among the types of investment companies are closed-end investment companies, which are characterized by closed capitalizations. The share price of the closed-end investment company is determined by the prevailing supply and demand conditions for the shares. The shares represent ownership of a portfolio of securities and have a net asset value. In many cases the shares sell at discounts from their net asset value. Where the prospects for the portfolio are very promising or the management exhibits a valuable expertise in a certain area, however, the shares may sell at a premium above their net asset value.

One type of closed-end investment company is the dual fund. This fund has two classes of securities outstanding. The preferred class is entitled to receive all the fund's income; the capital shares are entitled to receive all the fund's appreciation when the shares are redeemed at the fund's termination. The value of the preferred shares is the present discounted value of the expected stream of dividends and the return of the original investment at termination. The value of the capital shares is the present discounted value of the expected termination value of the fund's assets after the preferred shares have been redeemed.

The other major type of investment company is the open-end investment company. These are usually called mutual funds and are characterized by their continuous selling and redeeming of their shares. Among the more common types of mutual funds are the common stock fund, the balanced fund, the industry-specialized fund, the income fund, the international fund, and the hedge fund.

Because mutual funds are not engaged in any operating activities, such as a manufacturing company, they derive their risk solely from the management's handling of the portfolio. This means that we are forced to derive special methods of analysis to evaluate the fund. The two areas of concern are the management's ability to improve the return to the shareholder and the proper diversification of the portfolio. In order to evaluate management and compare the performances of different funds properly, the fund must be judged in relation to the performance of the general market, and the distorting influence of the various risk exposures among the different funds must be filtered out. One method of accomplishing this is to relate the fund's rate of return to the market's rate of return by establishing a characteristic line. This line tells us the fund's performance under various market conditions and the risk of each fund as measured by the volatility of the fund's share prices. By comparing these characteristic lines with the pure interest rate, the analyst can eliminate the distorting effects of different risk exposures and rank the funds according to their performance.

The performance records of the funds may be judged by determining whether they consistently outperformed what could be expected of a portfolio of risk equal to the ones they manage. Several studies on mutual fund performance attempted to evaluate the fund's record on this basis and concluded that the average fund performed more poorly than was expected of it. The variation in the performance of the funds was substantial, however, and a selected number of funds performed better than was expected of them.

QUESTIONS

16.1 What advantages do mutual funds offer the small investor?

16.2 Explain the organization of the closed-end, dual, and open-end investment companies.

16.3 Discuss the advantages and disadvantages of the three major types of investment companies.

16.4 Explain what is meant by front loading, and discuss its drawbacks.

16.5 Describe the objectives of each of the following funds: (a) income fund, (b) balance fund, (c) growth fund, and (d) hedge fund.

16.6 On what basis should a professional portfolio manager's success in managing a fund be evaluated?

16.7 Briefly describe the performance of an ideal fund.

16.8 What information is revealed by the slope of the characteristic line? What is indicated by individual deviations in the characteristic line?

16.9 According to the literature cited, what conclusions can be drawn about the performance of professionally managed funds?

PROBLEMS

16.1 Compute the percentage difference between the bid and ask prices of some of the mutual funds listed in the financial section of your newspaper. What is this difference called?

16.2 The characteristic lines of several funds are given by the following equations:

Fund 1	$FR_1 = MR_1$
Fund 2	$FR_2 = 3MR_2$
Fund 3	$FR_3 = 2MR_3 + 6$
Fund 4	$FR_4 = MR_4/2 - 5$
Fund 5	$FR_5 = MR_5 - 10$

where FR_n is the fund's return and MR_n is the market return. The yield on Treasury bills is 6 percent. Make the following comparisons by graphically ranking the funds:
  a. Which fund(s) is ranked first?
  b. Which fund(s) has the most risk?
  c. Which fund(s) experiences the most losses when the market return is zero?
  d. Which fund(s) is performing the best when the market return is zero?
  e. Which fund(s) is performing at least as well as the market as a whole?
  f. Which fund(s) has the least risk?
  g. Which fund is ranked last?
  h. Which funds have equal risk?

16.3 A fund is presently earning a 15 percent net return for its stockholders. The average return for all securities is 12 percent, and the pure rate of interest is 5 percent. The fund's portfolio consists of stocks that on the average give returns 150 percent higher than the average market return. Compute the effect of the fund's professional management.

16.4 The management of the fund in Problem 16.3 has suggested changing the fund to no load status. The fund is presently charging a 10 percent load charge. Compute the effect of the fund's professional management if the load charge is dropped.

REFERENCES

Cohen, Kalman J., and Frederick S. Hammer (eds.). *Analytical Methods in Banking,* Homewood, Ill.: Richard D. Irwin, Inc., 1966.
────── **and Jerry A. Pogue.** "Some Comments Concerning Mutual Fund versus Random Portfolio Performance," *The Journal of Business,* 41:180–190, April, 1968.
Friend, Irwin, et al. *A Study of Mutual Funds,* prepared for the SEC by the Wharton School of Finance and Commerce, published Aug. 28, 1962, by the U.S. Government Printing Office.
────── **and Douglas Vickers.** "Portfolio Selection and Investment Performance," *The Journal of Finance,* 20:391–415, September, 1965.
──────. "Re-evaluation of Alternative Portfolio-Selection Models," *The Journal of Business,* 41:174–179, April, 1968.
Gentry, James A., and John R. Pike. "Dual Funds Revisited," *Financial Analysts Journal,* 24:149–157, March-April, 1968.
Investment Companies, New York: A. Wiesenberger.
Jensen, Michael C. "The Performance of Mutual Funds in the Period 1945–1964," *The Journal of Finance,* 23:389–420, May, 1968.
McCandish, R. W., Jr. "Portfolio Evaluation: An Approach," *Financial Analysts Journal,* 23:147–150, November, 1967.
Mead, Stuart B. "Mutual Funds from the Investor's Viewpoint," *MSU Business Topics,* 15:45–53, Winter, 1967.

Netter, J., II. "Dual-Purpose Funds: One Month Later," *Financial Analysts Journal,* 23:85–87, July, 1967.
Schneider, Theodore H. "A Worksheet Technique for Measuring Performance," *Financial Analysts Journal,* 25:105–111, May-June, 1969.
Sharpe, William F. "A Linear Programming Algorithm for Mutual Fund Portfolio Selection," *Management Science,* 13:499–510, March, 1967.
———. "Mutual Fund Performance," *The Journal of Business,* 39:119–138, January, 1966.
Shelton, John P., et al. "An Evaluation and Appraisal of Dual Funds," *Financial Analysts Journal,* 23:131–139, May-June, 1967.
Sherman, John C. "A Device to Measure Portfolio Performance," *Financial Analysts Journal,* 22:106–108, January-February, 1966.
Sieff, John A. "Measuring Investment Performance: The Unit Approach," *Financial Analysts Journal,* 22:93–99, July-August, 1966.
Simon, J. L. "Does Good Portfolio Management Exist?" *Journal of the Institute of Management Sciences,* 15:B308–B324, February, 1969.
Treynor, Jack L. "How to Rate Management of Investment Funds," *Harvard Business Review,* 43:63–75, January-February, 1965.

Part Five

In Part V we concern ourselves with technical analysis. There are two main schools of thought. The fundamental school emphasizes the relationship between the stock price and earnings power of the firm. According to the fundamentalists, the stock price randomly fluctuates around some equilibrium value that reflects the future prospects of the company until new information changes them. The technical school, on the other hand, believes that there are trends or patterns in the movements of stock prices. According to the technicians, these trends are observable in the day-to-day price movements of the stock and, if carefully followed, reveal profit opportunities. It is not necessary for the technician to be aware of the company's earnings prospects, for all the necessary information is contained in the price pattern of the stock. We devote Chapter 17 to a discussion of the theory and the evidence on whether or not stock prices behave in a random manner or in a trend or pattern.

The major tools of the technician are his charts. With them he keeps track of the patterns and trends that he expects to find in stock price movements. Among the most commonly used charts are the point and figure chart and the bar chart. Chapter 18 examines the construction and interpretation of both kinds.

Chapter 19 examines the technical indicators that are used to forecast general market and stock price levels. Many of the technicians believe that certain characteristics of the market may be used to forecast the level of general stock prices. Among the more commonly used indicators are the advance-decline index, short sales ratio, and odd lot trading figures. Some technical indicators are used to forecast individual stock prices. These include insider trading figures, quarterly growth rate indexes, and stock splits.

17
Technical Analysis

Do today's stock prices contain any indication of tomorrow's? The advocates of the random walk theory of stock prices maintain that they do not. The advocates of the technical school maintain that they do. Who is right? Unfortunately, there is presently no definitive answer, but let us examine what each side has based its arguments on and the evidence that each has produced and decide for ourselves. We first explore the conceptual framework of the random walk and then that of technical analysis. Some of the numerous empirical studies are then examined, and the reader can make his own decision.

RANDOM WALK

The random walk theory, in its pure form, envisions a perfectly competitive market that operates very efficiently to bring the actual stock price in line with its present discounted value. This implies that, at any point in time, the equilibrium value, determined by the supply and demand for the stock, is a true representation of what the suppliers and demanders envision to be the value of the stock (its PDV), based on the information that they have. Because the market is efficient, all or a sufficient number of participants have the same information, so that the prevailing market price truly reflects the stock's present value. Any deviation from the equilibrium value is quickly erased, and the stock price is returned to the equilibrium price. The professional stock trader who is alert to these deviations seizes on them when they occur and forces the stock price back toward its equilibrium.

According to the random walk theory, a price change occurs only when the pertinent, underlying factors affecting the corporation or the financial markets change. This alters the equilibrium value, and the stock price almost instantaneously jumps to a new equilibrium level. It is this rapid spurt to the new equilibrium level in response to a new piece of information that distinguishes the random walk philosophy. This immediate adjustment means that all the known information is reflected in the stock price and that any further spurt in stock prices must be the result of another piece of information that was previously unavailable. The changes in stock prices are independent of one another, for the price changes are dependent on pieces of information that are themselves independent of one another. The stock market digests each piece of information separately and independently of other pieces of information, and each piece of information causes, by itself, a price change. For example, a stock might be selling at $20 per share based on all the known information. The next day the news of a copper strike might spurt the stock price to $28 per share, and, the day after, further news that the copper strike involved high grade ore might spurt the stock to $35 per share. The first spurt in the stock from $20 to $28 per share was caused by the initial news of the strike. The second spurt in the price from $28 to $35 per share was caused by the additional information on the quality of the strike. Each price spurt is independent of the other, because each came from a different piece of news that was immediately digested by the stock market. It should be noted that the independent pieces of information may come in rapid succession, as is often the case, and give the appearance of a rising price trend when each price rise is really independent of the other.

The essence of the random walk is that the stock price immediately and fully reflects the information as it is disseminated and that this immediate and full response to the information makes the price movements independent of one another. Today's price movement holds no information as to future price movements.

Because the prices are independent of one another, the next price may be higher, lower, or unchanged from the previous price. The random walk proponents point to the institutional factors of the present market to stress the logic of their position. They state that the competitive structure of today's financial markets forces this immediate price adjustment. The extremely rapid and efficient communications systems of today practically ensure a wide and rapid distribution of the information to bring an almost immediate reaction to any piece of information. The government and stock exchange regulations concerning full disclosure and the simultaneous release of information to all reinforce the tendency to a quick reaction. The presence of very large and influential professional managers who devote vast resources of time and money to gathering the information practically ensures a sufficiently informed market.

TECHNICAL ANALYSIS

Technical analysis maintains that stock prices do move in trends. According to the technician, these trends continue for an appreciable time and with sufficient repetition so that an astute evaluation of the trend reveals information about future prices.

The technician assumes that all variables that affect the value of the firm are reflected in the stock price. In this, he resembles the random walk theorists, who also believe that the stock price reflects the value of the firm, although the technician usually includes the irrational variables, such as psychological factors. But the technician differs from the random walk theorist when he contends that the dissemination of the information about these variables is not equal to all market participants. Some of the participants, he believes, receive the information before others. The first to receive the information initiates the price movement. As the information gradually spreads among the participants, the price movement gains momentum until eventually the piece of information is completely reflected in the stock price. In addition, the technician believes that this price movement occurs in some recognizable pattern that resembles previous price movement patterns.[1]

The presence of this information lag and its effect on stock price are the essence of the technician's art. He hopes to profit by detecting the price movement pattern in its earlier stages and by making his investments according to what the early price movements indicate to him that the later price movements will be. He is playing the lag, hoping to get in during the initial stages of the price movement and gain from the later stages.

This lag between the initial price reaction to the piece of information and the time that it is fully reflected in the stock price arises, according to the technician, because the market is not perfectly competitive. There are some market participants who receive the information first, such as corporation officials who may have access to privileged information. The less astute market participants may lag in properly evaluating even readily available public information, leaving the more astute to initiate the price movement. The initial price movement may be caused by psychological factors that do not show up in the fundamental analysis until later. Only technical analysis detects the psychological changes that are incorporated in the stock price movements and their implication for future price movements.[2]

The success of technical analysis also depends on the assumption that

---

[1] R. Levy, "Random Walks: Reality or Myth," *Financial Analysts Journal,* November-December, 1967, pp. 69–77.

[2] *Ibid.*

price movements occur in recurring patterns. The price movement at one time resembles that at a future date. There may be several distinct types of patterns, but they are liable to repeat themselves, according to the technician. We reserve the discussion of the particular types of patterns and their interpretation until the next chapter, but it is important to note now that unless the pattern is repeated in almost identical form with previous patterns, the technician is unable to gather any insight into future prices from today's prices. This gives technical analysis a self-verifying nature, for when the technicians see a pattern, they all react in the same fashion, causing the predicted result to occur.

EMPIRICAL EVIDENCE—RANDOM WALK[3]

The evidence in support of the random walk has emphasized the lack of measurable trends in stock prices and the lack of any relationship between changes in stock prices. This lack of any relationship has been observed in correlation tests, simulation tests, distribution pattern tests, run tests, and filter tests.

Correlation Tests

Efforts have been made to determine if price changes in one period are correlated with those in future periods. Empirical tests are conducted to search for a relationship similar to those in Figure 17.1. If prices in some future period $t+1$ were influenced by prices in the present period t, so that a price rise in period t meant a price rise in period $t+1$, a scatter diagram of the prices should resemble Figure 17.1a. If the effect of a higher price in period t is a lower price in period $t+1$, a scatter diagram of the prices should resemble Figure 17.1b. If there were no relationship between the prices in the two periods, the scatter diagram of the prices would resemble Figure 17.1c.

It is not necessary to use a scatter diagram to test for any correlation among the prices. The correlation coefficient is a more precise statistic that measures the relationship. If the correlation is as illustrated in Figure 17.1a, the correlation coefficient is positive, implying that a higher price in period t will lead to a higher price in period $t+1$. The closer this relationship, the higher the value of the correlation coefficient, until it reaches a value of 1 or a perfect one-to-one relationship between prices in each period. A negative value to the correlation coefficient implies that a higher price in period t will lead to a lower price

---

[3] See the references at the end of the chapter for the sources of these studies. The most comprehensive work on random walk is P. Cootner, *The Random Character of Stock Market Prices,* The M.I.T. Press, Cambridge, Mass., 1964.

in period $t + 1$. A perfect one-to-one negative relationship would have a correlation coefficient of minus 1, as shown in Figure 17.1b. If the relationship were random, as illustrated in Figure 17.1c, the correlation coefficient would be 0.

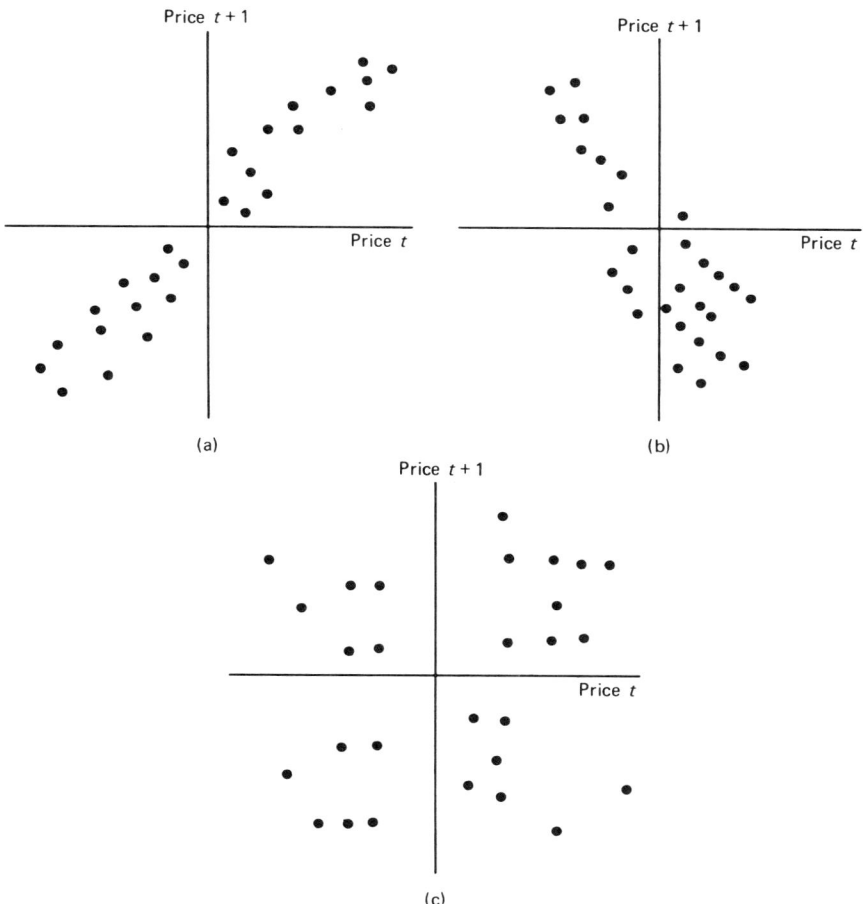

Figure 17.1. Scatter diagrams of possible price relationships.

The results of these correlation tests revealed no correlation coefficients that were statistically, measurably different from 0. All the results implied that scatter diagram 17.1c was the best representation of the relationship of price changes between periods. Table 17.1 illustrates the typical results. None of the correlation coefficients is significantly different from 0.

TABLE 17.1 Correlation Coefficients Between Daily Price Changes and Lagged Price Changes for Each of the Dow Jones Stocks

Stocks	\multicolumn{10}{c}{Lag, Days}									
	1	2	3	4	5	6	7	8	9	10
AlliedCh	.02	−.04	.01	−.00	.03	.00	−.02	−.03	−.02	−.01
Alcoa	.12	.04	−.01	.02	−.02	.01	.02	.01	−.00	−.03
Am Can	−.09	−.02	.03	−.07	−.02	−.01	.02	.03	−.05	−.04
Am T&T	−.04	−.10	.00	.03	.01	−.01	.00	.03	−.01	.01
Am Tob	.11	−.11	−.06	−.07	.01	−.01	.01	.05	.04	.04
Anacond	.07	−.06	−.05	−.00	.00	−.04	.01	.02	−.01	−.06
Beth Stl	.01	−.07	.01	.02	−.05	−.10	−.01	.00	−.00	−.02
Chrysler	.01	−.07	−.02	−.01	−.02	.01	.04	.06	−.04	.02
duPont	.01	−.03	.06	.03	−.00	−.05	.02	.01	−.03	.00
E Kodak	.03	.01	−.03	.01	−.02	.01	.01	.01	.01	.00
Gen Elec	.01	−.04	−.02	.03	−.00	.00	−.01	.01	−.00	.01
Gen Fds	.06	−.00	.05	.00	−.02	−.05	−.01	−.01	−.02	−.02
GenMot	−.00	−.06	−.04	−.01	−.04	.01	.02	.01	−.02	.01
Goodyr	−.12	.02	−.04	.04	−.00	−.00	.04	.01	−.02	.01
Int Harv	−.02	−.03	−.03	.04	−.05	−.02	−.00	.00	−.05	−.02
Int Nick	.10	−.03	−.02	.02	.03	.06	−.04	−.01	−.02	.03
Int Pap	.05	−.01	−.06	.05	.05	−.00	−.03	−.02	−.00	−.02
JohnMan	.01	−.04	−.03	−.02	−.03	−.08	.04	.02	−.04	.03
OwensIll	−.02	−.08	−.05	.07	.09	−.04	.01	−.04	.07	−.04
Proctr G	.10	−.01	−.01	.01	−.02	.02	.01	−.01	−.02	−.02
Sears Ro	.10	.03	.03	.03	.01	−.05	−.01	−.01	−.01	−.01
StOilCal	.03	−.03	−.05	−.03	−.05	−.03	−.01	.07	−.05	−.04
StOilNJ	.01	−.12	.02	.01	−.05	−.02	−.02	−.03	−.07	.08
Swift Co	−.00	−.02	−.01	.01	.06	.01	−.04	.01	.01	.00
Texaco	.09	−.05	−.02	−.02	−.02	−.01	.03	.03	−.01	.01
Un Carbide	.11	−.01	.04	.05	−.04	−.03	.00	−.01	−.05	−.04
UnitAirc	.01	−.03	−.02	−.05	−.07	−.05	.05	.04	.02	−.02
US Steel	.04	−.07	.01	.01	−.01	−.02	.04	.04	−.02	−.04
WestgEl	−.03	−.02	−.04	−.00	.00	−.05	−.02	.01	−.01	.01
Woolworth	.03	−.02	.02	.01	.01	−.04	−.01	.00	−.09	−.01
Averages	.03	−.04	−.01	.01	−.01	−.02	.00	.01	−.02	−.01

SOURCE: R. Brealey, *An Introduction to Risk and Return from Common Stock*, The M.I.T. Press, Cambridge, Mass., 1969, p. 13.

These correlation tests have been run in numerous variations, but none has produced a significant relationship. Several variations have been attempted on different prices, including commodity price, stock price indexes, and individual stock prices. Many different time periods have been tested to determine if there is any lagged relationship between prices. The results in Table 17.1 are lagged in days; others have lagged the relationship by weeks and longer periods and have found little indication of correlation. Still other studies have used price changes and price levels. These studies also did not find evidence of correlation between either price changes or price levels from one period to another.

Simulation Tests

Another attempt to test the randomness of stock prices was to compare the pattern of prices simulated from a random numbers table with that actually recorded for levels and changes in the Dow Jones industrial index.[4] If the randomly drawn pattern of prices resembles that of the actual prices, the implication is that stock prices are also random. The results of the experiment revealed an "unmistakable" resemblance between the actual and the randomly drawn patterns. Figure 17.2 reveals the similarity in patterns. Figure 17.2b, the random pattern of weekly price changes, closely resembles the actual weekly price changes in Figure 17.2a. The same jumbled pattern of price changes is evident in both figures, although the actual results have a slightly greater dispersion. Figure 17.2c, the actual pattern of weekly price levels, has the same type of pattern as Figure 17.2d, the randomly drawn pattern. Note the same type of formations in the random pattern as it rises to a peak, falls back before shortly rising to a still higher peak, only to fall back again, and make a futile effort to surpass the previous peak and then enter a long declining phase. In the jargon of the technician, this pattern is known as a head and shoulders. Because it was randomly generated as well as actually observed, the implication is that technical patterns may be the result of random stock price movements.

Distribution Patterns

If the price movements are random, a sufficiently large sample of price changes should produce a normal distribution pattern similar to that illustrated at the top of Figure 17.3. Several tests of this nature were performed on various stock and commodity prices, and the resulting distributions were very similar to the normal distribution. This implies that price changes are random and that the next price change is inde-

---

[4] H. Roberts, "Stock Market Patterns and Financial Analysis: Methodological Suggestions," *Journal of Finance,* March, 1959, pp. 1–10.

Technical analysis 376

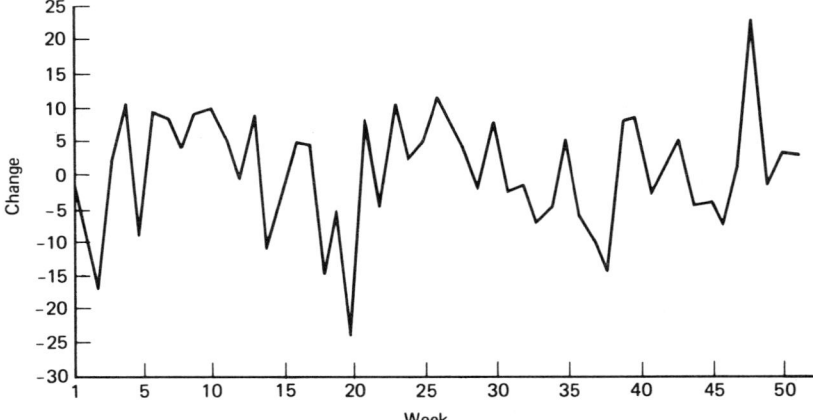

(a) Changes from Friday to Friday (closing) January 6, 1956 to December 28, 1956. Dow Jones industrial index.

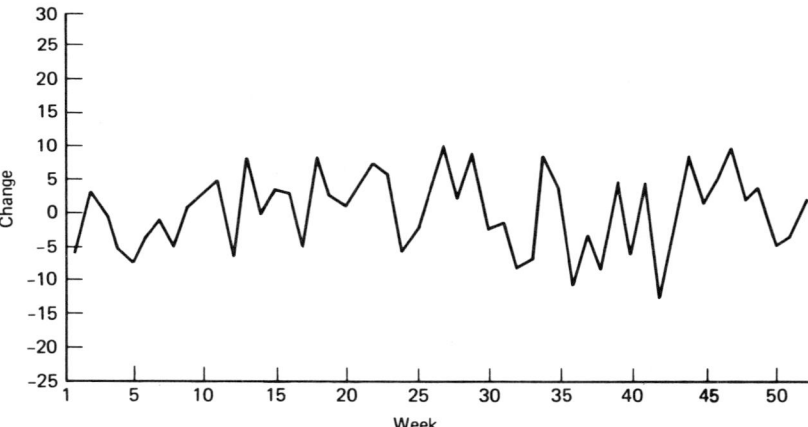

(b) Simulated market changes for 52 weeks.

Figure 17.2. Simulated versus actual stock price patterns.

(From H. Roberts. "Stock Market 'Patterns' and Financial Analysis: Methodological Suggestions," Journal of Finance, March, 1959.)

pendent of the last price change. Typical results found by Brealey[5] are illustrated in Figure 17.3. On occasion, however, studies have found outlying observations that do not conform to the shape of the normal distribution. These outlyers appear at the tails of the normal distribution

[5] R. Brealey, *An Introduction to the Risk and Return from Common Stock*, The M.I.T. Press, Cambridge, Mass., 1969.

Empirical evidence—random walk 377

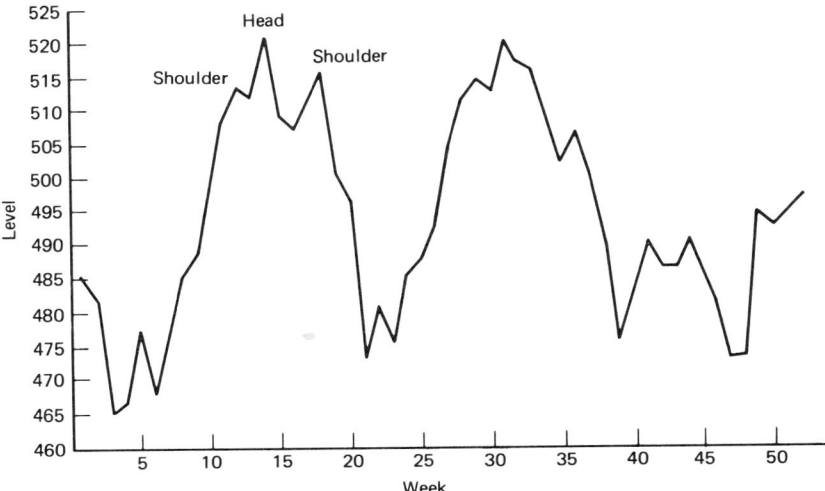

(c) Friday closing levels, December 30, 1955 to December 28, 1956. Dow Jones industrial index.

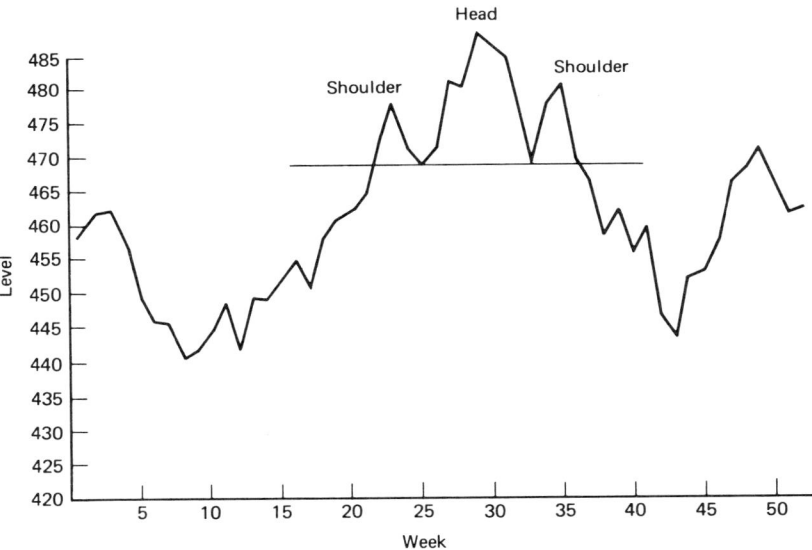

(d) Simulated market levels for 52 weeks.

Figure 17.2 (Continued)

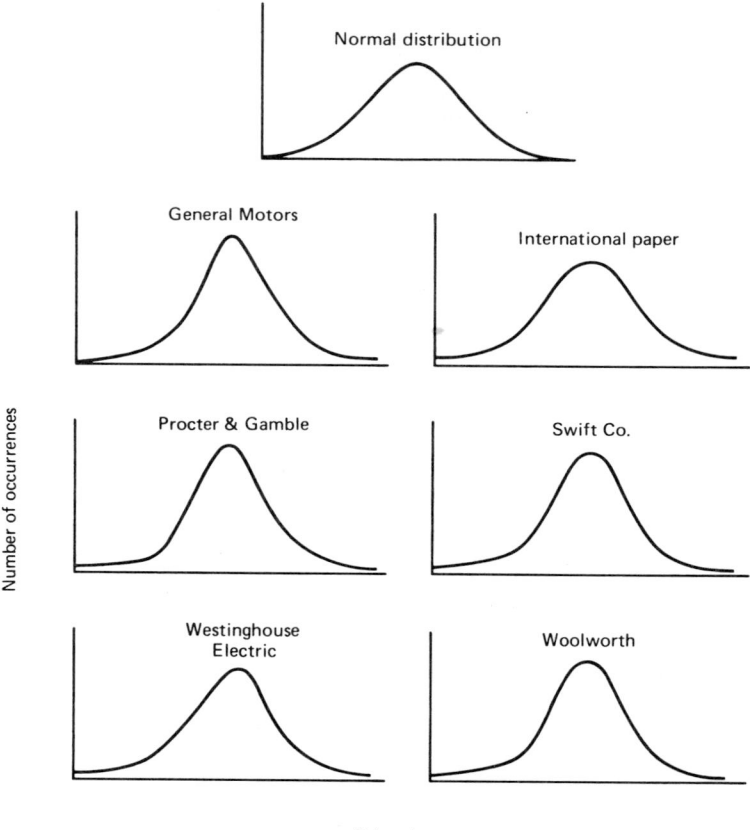

Figure 17.3. Normal distribution and distribution of daily price changes of six stocks.

(From R. Brealey, *An Introduction to Risk and Return from Common Stocks,* The M.I.T. Press, Cambridge, Mass., 1969, p. 10.)

with a frequency that should not exist in the normal distribution. The tendency has been to overlook these observations as of no importance to the general conclusion.[6]

Run Tests

Run tests were also applied to stock price changes to determine if there was a pattern. A series of price changes, which may be figuratively

[6] M. Kendall, "The Analysis of Economic Time Services, Part I," *Journal of the Royal Statistical Society,* 1963, pp. 11–25, as reprinted in P. Cootner, *The Random Character of Stock Market Prices,* The M.I.T. Press, Cambridge, Mass., 1964; and E. Fama, "Mandelbrot and the Stable Paretian Hypothesis," *Journal of Business,* 1963, pp. 420–429, as reprinted in Cootner, *op. cit.*

represented by pluses and minuses, where the + is a price advance and the — a price decline, might resemble the following:

++++----+-+--+---+---+---++++++

A run would be a consecutive sequence of the same symbol. When the actual runs that were observed in the market were compared with those which could be expected if price changes were randomly generated, there was no significant difference between the two. This enforces the conclusion that price changes occur in a random manner, independent of one another.

Filter Tests

A filter test attempts to determine if a price change of a certain percentage is indicative of further price change. A price change from a previous level may be random or may be the beginning of a price movement. If the price change is random, subsequent price changes should move back toward the original price, according to profit opportunities to the investor. If the price change is indicative of an incipient price shift to a new equilibrium level, the subsequent price changes should afford an opportunity for investment profit.

If the price change were indicative of a further price change, a trading rule could be developed that would produce superior profits. For example, if the investor believed that a price change of greater than 2 percent was indicative of a further price change, he would purchase the stock any time that the price rose more than 2 percent and sell it any time that the price declined more than 2 percent. If the investor were correct, he would, excluding transactions costs, experience profits superior to simply buying and holding the security during the same trading period.

To test whether a filter trading strategy would produce profits superior to the strategy of buying the stock and holding it for the entire period, the profit results of a portfolio using various filter levels was simulated from actual stock prices. In one test the trading strategy was:

If the daily closing price of a security moves up at least x%, buy and hold the security until its price moves down at least x% from a subsequent high, at which time simultaneously sell and go short. The short position is maintained until the price rises at least x% above a subsequent low, at which time one covers and buys. Moves less than x% in either direction are ignored.[7]

The profit performance of the portfolio at various filter levels (selected x% levels) was simulated and compared with the profit perfor-

---

[7] E. Fama and M. Blume, "Filter Rules and Stock Market Trading," *Journal of Business, Security Price Supplement,* January, 1966, pp. 226–241.

mance of the same portfolio using a buy-hold strategy. The results of one such simulation[8] are summarized in Table 17.2. The buy-hold

TABLE 17.2 Simulated Portfolio Performances Using Filter Test Rules

	Average annual rates of return per stock			
Value of x, percent	Return with trading strategy, percent	Return with buy-and-hold strategy, percent	Total transactions with trading strategy	Return with trading strategy, after commissions, percent
0.5	11.5	10.4	12,514	−103.6
1.0	5.5	10.3	8,660	− 74.9
2.0	0.2	10.3	4,784	− 45.2
3.0	−1.7	10.3	2,994	− 30.5
4.0	0.1	10.1	2,013	− 19.5
5.0	−1.9	10.0	1,484	− 16.6
6.0	1.8	9.7	1,071	− 9.4
7.0	0.8	9.6	828	− 7.4
8.0	1.7	9.6	653	− 5.0
9.0	1.9	9.6	539	− 3.6
10.0	3.0	9.3	435	− 1.4
12.0	5.3	9.4	289	2.3
14.0	3.9	10.3	224	1.4
16.0	4.2	10.3	172	2.3
18.0	3.6	10.0	139	2.0
20.0	4.3	9.8	110	3.0

SOURCE: R. Brealey, *An Introduction to Risk and Return from Common Stock*, The M.I.T. Press, Cambridge, Mass., 1969, p. 26.

strategy proved superior in all the filter values except the very lowest filter of 0.5 percent. The commissions on the transactions erased all profit advantage, however, for in the lower filter values the number of transactions increased substantially. The implication is that stock price movements are random and afford no opportunity for superior profit performance from the use of trading rules.

The decision rule may be modified in an attempt to capture price

[8] Brealey, *op. cit.*, p. 26.

movements from the equilibrium level rather than the previous close. In that case, the decision rule would be:

If the price of a stock exceeds a moving average of past prices by x%, go long and stay long, until it falls short of the moving average by the same margin, at which time sell.[9]

The results for this decision rule for thirty randomly selected stocks were similar to those of the previous decision rule. The profit performance of the thirty stocks under the buy-hold strategy was superior to the profit performance of the same stocks under the various filter values.[10] Again, the implication is that stock price changes are random and that there is little opportunity for superior profit performance by using technical analysis.

EMPIRICAL EVIDENCE—TECHNICAL ANALYSIS

The basis of the empirical evidence in support of technical analysis lies in the technicians' claim to have simulated a superior profit performance by trading strategies based solely on stock prices. One study by Levy[11] purports to show that using the techniques of relative strength ranks and portfolio upgrading, the return to a portfolio is larger than under the buy-hold strategy.

The technique of relative strength ranks is designed to spot stocks that seem to be in a price uptrend. The basic concept is to relate the stock's most recent price behavior to its previous price behavior. Those stocks with the strongest recent price behavior are ranked highest. Levy attempted to capture this price behavior concept by comparing the stock's most recent price with its average price for the last 26 weeks and the last 4 weeks. The stock with the highest price in relation to the average of its past prices was considered to be most the attractive for investment. The measure is intended to reflect strength in the stock. The assumption is that the strongest performers continue to show the strongest performance.

Taking the rankings of the stocks, Levy upgraded his portfolio by including only those stocks, from among 200 randomly selected, which ranked in the top 10 percent of his rankings (001 to 020) and eliminating any stock whose ranking fell below a certain specified rank (the cast-out level). In the first week of the portfolio's simulated existence,

[9] *Ibid.*, p. 27.
[10] J. Van Horne and G. Parker, "The Random Walk Theory: An Empirical Test," *Financial Analysts Journal*, November-December, 1967, pp. 87–92.
[11] Levy, *op. cit.*, pp. 69–77.

only the stocks in the top 10 percent (the first 20, that is, ranks 001 to 020) of the rankings were included. As time progressed, those stocks which fell below the cast-out level (lower than the 020 rank, in this case) were sold, and the proceeds were reinvested in those stocks then in the upper 10 percent of the rankings. Supposedly, this upgraded the portfolio by eliminating the weaker-ranked stocks and replacing them with the stronger, higher-ranked stocks.

The results are reported in Table 17.3. The portfolio had a higher return under the trading rules than a buy-hold strategy's return, as measured by the gross geometric average return of the 200 stocks for the same time period. The gross annual returns at all the cast-out levels exceeded the return to the buy-hold strategy. When the commissions were deducted, only the low cast-out strategy of 020 (the top 10 percent in the relative strength index) did not exceed the return to the buy-hold strategy. The 020 cast-out level was apparently too sensitive to minor fluctuations in the stock prices and triggered too many transactions.

TABLE 17.3 Results of Portfolio Upgrading with 10 Percent Relative Strength Selection and Trades Based on Relative Strength Cast-out Ranks

	Cast-out ranks						200 stock geometric average
	020	050	100	150	180	195	
Gross results, percent:							
Annual return	14.2	20.3	21.1	21.8	19.3	13.8	10.6
Average of 4-week returns	1.08	1.47	1.54	1.59	1.45	1.09	0.83
Standard deviation of 4-week returns	4.79	4.85	4.35	4.39	4.53	4.60	3.52
Net results, percent:							
Annual return	−3.2	11.1	16.3	19.1	17.8	13.2	10.6
Average of 4-week returns	−0.19	0.86	1.22	1.41	1.35	1.05	0.86
Standard deviation of 4-week returns	4.87	4.90	4.39	4.41	4.55	4.01	3.52

SOURCE: R. Levy, "Random Walks: Reality or Myth," *Financial Analysts Journal*, November-December, 1967, p. 72.

The risk, as measured by the standard deviation of the 4-week return, involved with the relative strength strategy, is greater for the trading strategy than for the buy-hold strategy. The increased return has been obtained with an increase in risk. To lessen the risk exposure, Levy has suggested that a proportion of the portfolio be invested in bonds. As the market rises, the proportion of bonds should be decreased, and as the market declines, the proportion of bonds should be increased. The results from this strategy, according to Levy, are that the risk is reduced below that of the randomly selected stock portfolio and the return remains higher than that of the random portfolio.

SUMMARY

There are two basic schools of thought concerning stock price movements. The random walk school maintains that stock price changes are independent of one another and that present stock price changes contain no indication of future stock prices. The random walk proponents base their belief on the competitive nature of the financial markets. All information is disseminated and quickly reflected in the stock price. The stock price does not move again until a new piece of information is released. The institutional factors of today's rapid and extensive communication system and full disclosure laws ensure the rapid and wide dissemination.

The technical school maintains that the dissemination is not wide and rapid but that information gradually spreads from the first, privileged few to receive the information to the rest of the market participants. As the news spreads, the stock price reacts until gradually the news is fully reflected in the stock price. The gradual adjustment in the stock price follows a historic pattern and allows the technician who detects the beginning of the pattern to forecast the future price.

The empirical evidence in support of the random walk thesis centers on the inability of various statistical techniques to discover any relationship between prices of different time periods. Correlation tests, chance models, runs tests, distribution patterns, and filter tests all find no relationship between the stock prices of different time periods.

The empirical evidence in support of technical analysis rests mainly on the results of a simulated portfolio that demonstrated a superior profit performance using only stock price–based trading rules. By using techniques that rank the recent price performance of individual stocks and by adding the strongest performers and eliminating the weaker ones, the technicians maintain that they observe a superior profit performance.

QUESTIONS

17.1 Explain the random walk theory.

17.2 How do price changes occur according to the random walk theory?

17.3 What assumptions are made under the technical analysis framework?

17.4 Compare and contrast the beliefs of the technician and the random walk theorists.

17.5 The technician is playing the lag. Explain.

17.6 What does the correlation coefficient measure?

17.7 If stock price changes are random, what distribution is represented? What do random stock prices imply?

17.8 What is the purpose of a filter test? Explain its construction.

17.9 Explain the technique of relative strength. On what assumption is the technique based?

REFERENCES

Alexander, Sidney S. "Price Movements in Speculative Markets: Trends or Random Walks," *Industrial Management Review*, 2:7–26, Spring, 1961.

Brealey, Richard A. *An Introduction to Risk and Return from Common Stocks*, Cambridge, Mass.: The M.I.T. Press, 1969.

Cootner, Paul H. "Stock Prices: Random vs. Systematic Changes," *Industrial Management Review*, 3:24–45, Spring, 1962.

Cootner, Paul H. (ed.). *The Random Character of Stock Market Prices*, Cambridge, Mass.: The M.I.T. Press, 1964.

Fama, Eugene F., and Marshall E. Blume. "Filter Rules and Stock-Market Trading," *The Journal of Business*, 39:226–241, January, 1966.

Houthakker, H. S. "Can Speculators Forecast Prices?" *The Review of Economics and Statistics*, 39:143–151, May, 1957.

Jensen, M. C. "Random Walks: Reality or Myth—Reply," *Financial Analysts Journal*, 23:69–85, November, 1967.

Levy, Robert A. "Random Walks: Reality or Myth," *Financial Analysts Journal*, 23:69–77, November-December, 1967.

——. "Random Walks: Reality or Myth—Reply," *Financial Analysts Journal*, 24:129–132, January-February, 1968.

Roberts, Harry V. "Stock-Market 'Patterns' and Financial Analysis: Methodological Suggestions," *The Journal of Finance*, 14:1–10, March, 1959.

Samuelson, Paul A. "Rational Theory of Warrant Pricing," *Industrial Management Review*, 6:13–31, Spring, 1965.

Van Horne, James, and G. Parker. "The Random Walk Theory: An Empirical Test," *Financial Analysts Journal*, 23:87–92, November-December, 1967.

Van Horne, James C., and George G. C. Parker. "Technical Trading Rules: A Comment," *Financial Analysts Journal*, 24:128–132, July-August, 1968.

18
Charting

The technical analyst uses charts to maintain an orderly record of stock prices and detect recurring patterns. The chart is the basic tool of the technician. If the investor believes that there is merit in technical analysis, he must be familiar with the construction of the various charts, the patterns that the technician sees in them, and the implication of these patterns for stock prices.

The most commonly used charts are the vertical bar chart and the point-and-figure chart. The vertical bar chart uses vertical lines to plot the range of a stock's price in a specific period, such as a day, week, or month. Using only a plot of the stock price and the volume, the chartist searches for recurring patterns that resemble the shape of saucers, pennants, flags, triangles, head and shoulders, diamonds, and so on. To the chartist, each of these configurations has implications for the near-future behavior of the stock price.

The point-and-figure chart attempts to depict the significant price changes rather than all stock prices. Every significant price change is systematically recorded in a prescribed manner until chart patterns and trends emerge, from which the chartist attempts to forecast future stock prices. The point-and-figure chartists look for triangles, resistance levels, triple tops, and so on.

This chapter explores the construction of both vertical bar and point-and-figure charts and the patterns that are commonly associated with technical analysis.

VERTICAL BAR CHARTS

Figure 18.1 illustrates a typical vertical bar chart. The time dimension is on the horizontal axis. The time period may be a day, a week, or a month. The vertical axis is usually divided into two scales. The lower scale measures the volume, and the upper scale the stock price range. The volume and the stock price are both recorded by vertical straight lines (bars). The volume line starts at zero on the vertical axis and rises straight up as the volume during the time period increases. The length of the stock price line reflects the stock price range for the period. The line is drawn from the point on the chart that corresponds to the low price of the range to the point on the chart that corresponds to the high price of the range. The wider the range, the longer the line. Some technicians place a tick across the range line to mark the closing price for the period.

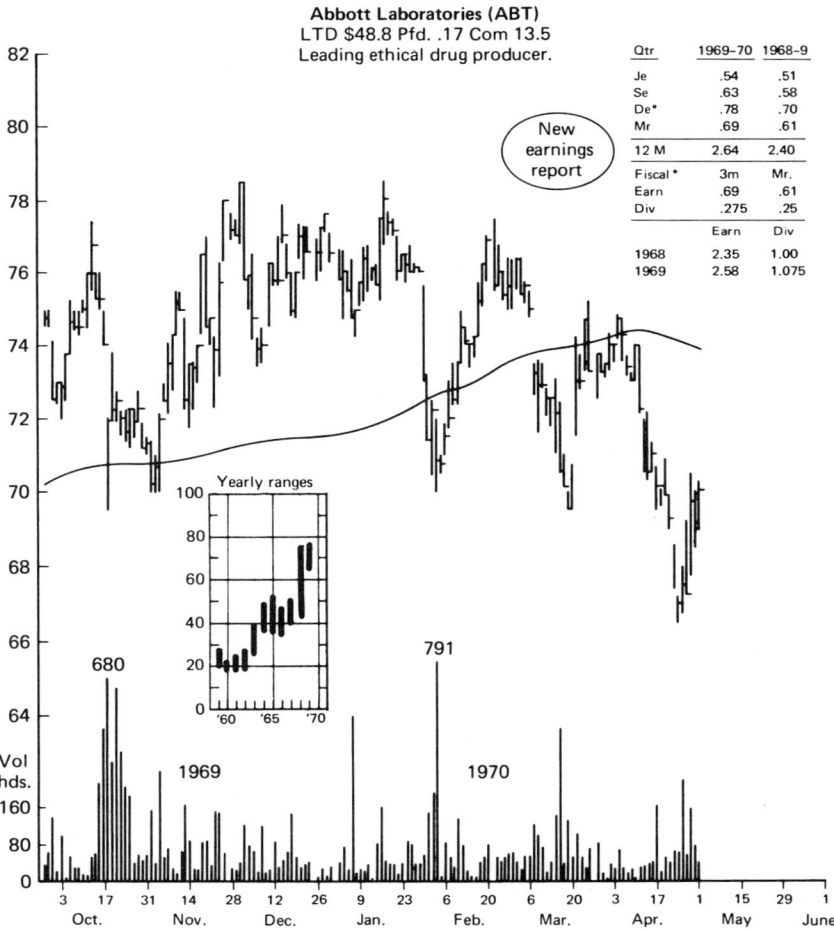

Figure 18.1. Vertical bar chart.

(*From Daily Basis Stock Charts, Trendline Corporation, New York, Oct.* 31, 1969.)

CHART PATTERNS[1]

The patterns used by the chartists are typically divided into three broad categories. The bullish patterns indicate a rising stock price, the uncertain patterns offer conflicting indications as to the direction of the next stock price change, and the bearish patterns indicate a declining stock price.

Bullish Patterns

Among the bullish patterns are the inverted head and shoulders, the saucer, the uptrend, the gap, and the flags. The inverted head and shoulders pattern, as illustrated in Figure 18.2, is recognizable by the two troughs in stock price that surround a deeper trough. The left shoulder rises from its trough to a peak and then falls into the head part, in which prices penetrate to still lower levels. From the lower levels of the head trough the stock price rises to a peak about in line with the previous peak, only to fall again to a trough that does not penetrate the previous lows. Technicians generally consider this pattern bullish when it is complete. The neckline is the straight line that joins the peaks that form the shoulders.

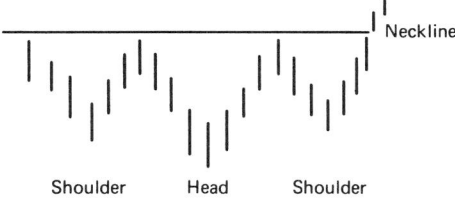

Figure 18.2. Inverted head and shoulders.

The volume that accompanies an inverted head and shoulders is considered to confirm the bullish indications if it is heavy during rising prices and low during declining prices, when the head and right shoulder are forming.

The stock price upswing that is expected to occur after the completion of an inverted head and shoulders is expected to be as great as the distance between the bottom of the head and the neckline.

---

[1] For a more detailed discussion of charting see D. Vaughn, *Survey of Investments,* Holt, Rinehart and Winston, Inc., New York, 1967, chaps. 18, 19, and William Jiler, *How Charts Can Help You in the Stock Market,* Commodity Research Publications Corporation, New York, 1962.

The saucer, as illustrated in Figure 18.3, is recognizable from the concave line that may be roughly traced out under the vertical stock price lines. Many times the similar saucer shape can be concurrently traced along the upper edge of the volume lines. According to chartists, it may take up to 3 weeks after the completion of a saucer formation for the stock to experience an upswing in price. During this interval, the stock price is expected to experience a slight decline on small volume. The expected stock price move, once the saucer has been formed, is equal to at least the radius of the saucer.

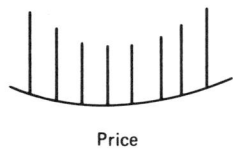
Price

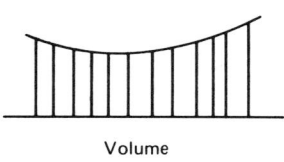
Volume

Figure 18.3. Saucer.

The trend line, as illustrated in Figure 18.4, is recognizable from the straight line that may be traced along the low points of the stock price bars and along the high points. Frequently, the stock price fluctuates between the two trend lines. A heavy volume on rising prices and a low volume on declining prices tend to confirm that the stock is still in its uptrend. A price reversal may be indicated if the volume rises on the declines and falls on the upswings.

The gaps, as illustrated in Figure 18.4, occur when the next day's trading range lies entirely below or above the previous day's. The bullish gaps that occur at the beginning of a price movement are called breakaway gaps. When the formation pattern is complete and the next price range gaps the previous price range on the upside, the indication is very bullish, for not only is the pattern complete, but the gap indicates that investors recognize the potential price increase and are bidding for the stock. The gaps that occur in the middle of an uptrend are known as measuring gaps. Because they are not connected with the completion of any pattern, they are not an indication of a change in the direction

Chart patterns   389

of prices. They indicate the price movement left in the current direction. The measuring gaps usually occur some two-fifths to one-half the distance of the entire upswing. The exhaustion gaps mark the termination of a stock price move. After a significant price increase from a bullish pattern, a downside gap accompanied by increased volume may be indicative of a reversal in the price trend.

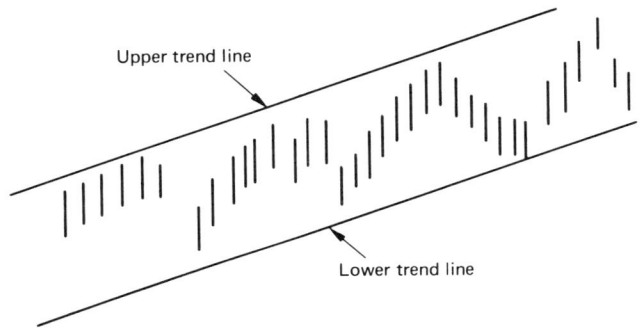

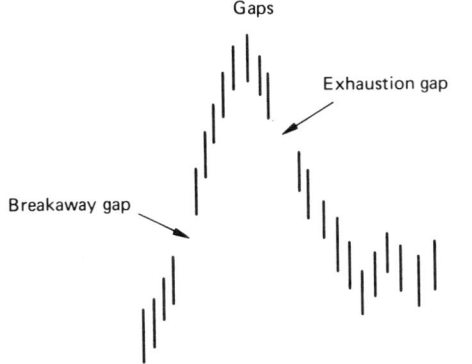

Figure 18.4. Trend line.

The pennant and the flag, as illustrated in Figure 18.5, are recognizable from the staff that is attached to a triangular or rectangular grouping of prices. A rising staff indicates a bullish pattern, and a falling staff a bearish pattern.

Uncertain Patterns

The triangle and the wedge, as illustrated in Figure 18.6, are recognizable from the lines that may be traced along the upper and lower edges of the stock price range bars. The triangle and the wedge occur when

Charting 390

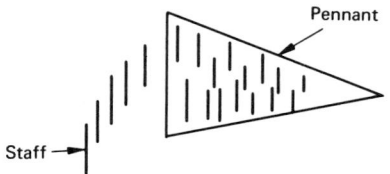

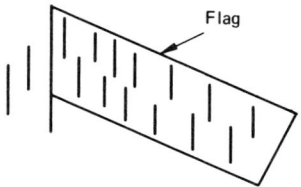

Figure 18.5. Pennant and flag.

the stock prices move progressively from a pattern of large fluctuations to small fluctuations. A rising wedge is formed by the two lines converging at a higher price than that at which the wedge started, and a descending wedge is formed by the two lines converging at a point lower than where they started. Triangles are formed when the two lines con-

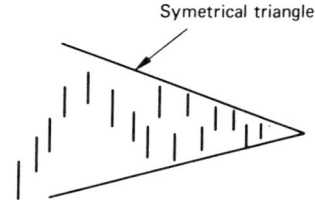

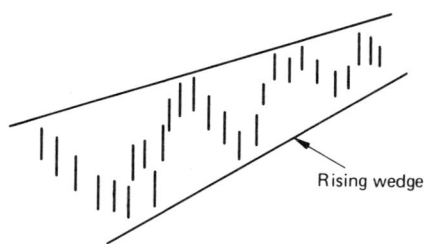

Figure 18.6. Triangle and wedge.

verge. The two lines may be converging from different angles. If the top line is descending and the bottom line is rising, the triangle is symmetrical. If the top line is horizontal and the bottom line rising, the triangle is rising. If the bottom line is horizontal and the top line declining, the triangle is declining. When the triangles or wedges are reversed, with the large end to the right and the small end to the left on the chart, the configuration is an inverted pattern.

The rectangle and box patterns are also uncertain indicators of future stock prices. The box and rectangle, as illustrated in Figure 18.7, are recognizable from the lines that may be traced around a stock price grouping to resemble the geometrical configurations.

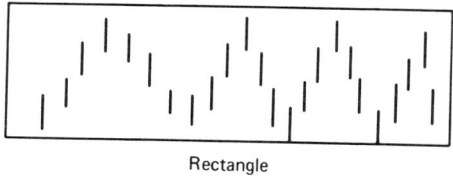
Rectangle

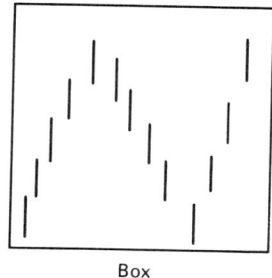
Box

Figure 18.7. Rectangle and box.

Bearish Patterns

Among the most commonly encountered bearish patterns are the head and shoulders, the double top, the triple and round top, the downtrend, and the inverted version of the bullish saucer.

The head and shoulders, as illustrated in Figure 18.8, is the inverse of the inverted head and shoulders. The left shoulder is formed by a rise and then a decline. The head is formed by a rise to a higher point than the preceding rise and a decline to about the same price level that existed at the beginning of the head formation. The right shoulder is formed by a rise that fails to penetrate the high price of the head and

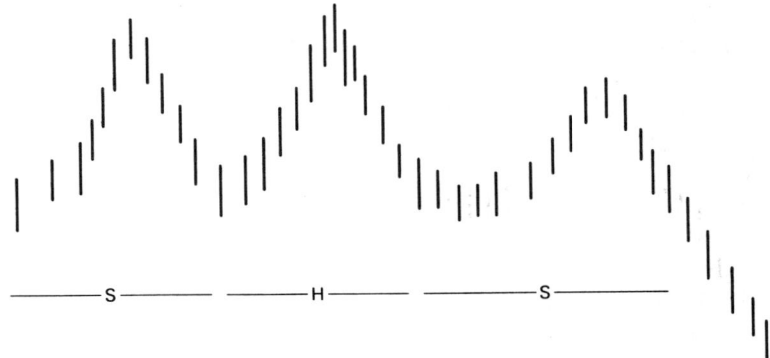

Figure 18.8. Head and shoulders.

then declines to a lower point than any of the other prices in the formation.

The double top, as illustrated in Figure 18.9, is characterized by a break in the upward trend line, followed by a series of stock prices slightly below the former high, a sudden spurt to another high close to the last one, and the inability to maintain an upward trend. In addition, the volume may confirm the approaching reversal by shrinking as the approach to the second high is made and expanding when the price retreats from the highs. The triple top, as illustrated in Figure 18.10, is a variant of the double top. Instead of two, there are three tops, each one characterized by a price decline through the trend line accompanied by an increase in volume and the failure to maintain any upward momentum or increased volume during price rises.

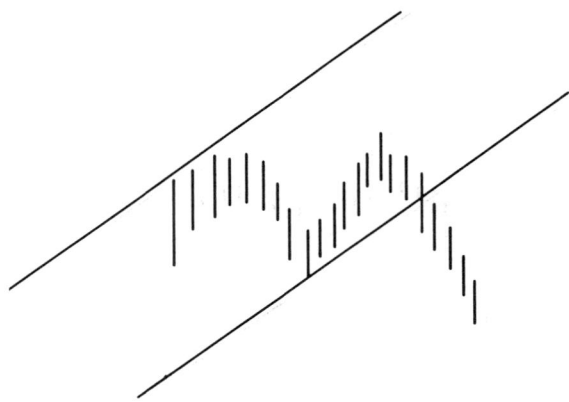

Figure 18.9. Double top.

Chart patterns 393

Figure 18.10. Triple top.

Other Chart Patterns

Besides the bullish and bearish patterns, the chartist looks for consolidation areas and support and resistance levels. The consolidation represents a period after a price movement in which the market is said to be digesting the movement. Usually, the prices in a consolidation period are closely grouped in the patterns of the triangles, boxes, wedges, or other uncertain patterns. Consolidation is the resting period between formations and is generally considered to be neither bullish nor bearish as long as the volume rises with price increases and decreases with price declines.

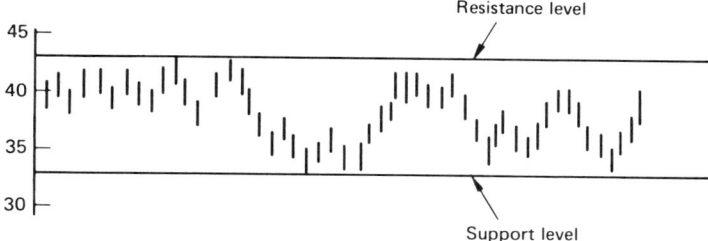

Figure 18.11. Resistance and support levels.

The resistance level is the price above which the stock has had trouble rising. The resistance level is characterized by a congestion of observations around the level but none above the level. In Figure 18.11, the resistance level is represented by the accumulation of stock prices at the $43 per share level. If the price breaks through this level, it is a bullish sign. According to the chartists, the stock is headed for a new, higher trading range. The chartists take this as a sign that the market is replacing the old equilibrium level, and the upper limit on the movement around the old equilibrium is no longer valid. When the resistance level is penetrated, it becomes the support level or the lower limit on the new trading range. Before a stock is considered to be in a downtrend, the support level must be penetrated. The support level in Figure 18.11 is $33.50.

POINT-AND-FIGURE CHART

The point-and-figure chart (p&f) is illustrated in Figure 18.12. The p&f chart differs from the vertical bar chart in that there is no time dimension, no volume figures, and only significant price changes, usually changes of ½ point or more, are recorded. The purpose of a p&f chart is to record significant price changes and their direction.

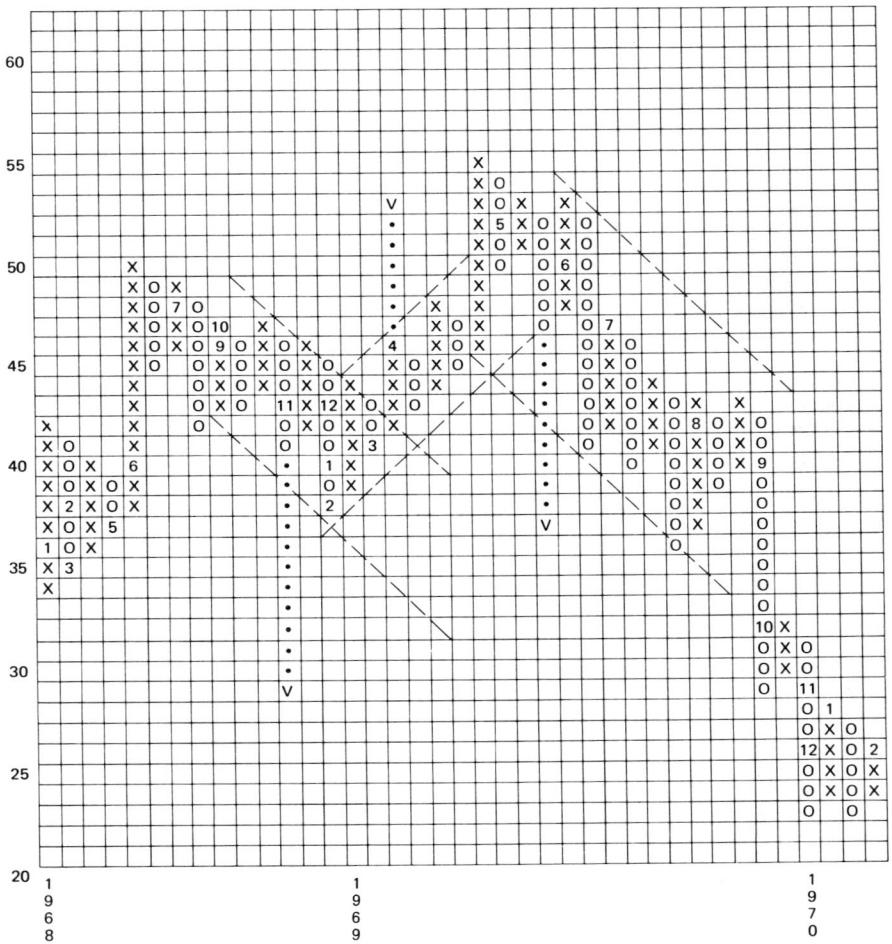

Figure 18.12. Point-and-figure chart: Ashland Oil (ASH).

Construction of the P&F Chart

The construction of the p&f chart is illustrated in Figure 18.13. The vertical axis represents the price change in gradations that are considered significant. In this case we are using gradations of one point, although other gradations may be used. Every time the price moves up through a whole point, such as the 85 or 86, an X is placed in the appropriate box. Every time the price declines through a whole point,

94							
93							
92							
91							
90							
89			X				
88	X		X				
87	X	0	X				
86	X	2					
85							
84							
83							

1970

Figure 18.13. Point-and-figure chart.

a 0 is placed in the appropriate box. Every time the direction of the price change reverses itself, we move to a new column. For example, if the following prices were charted, we should have the chart in Figure 18.13:

January 25	$85\frac{1}{8}$
January 26	$86\frac{1}{2}$
January 27	$86\frac{1}{2}$
January 28	$88\frac{1}{4}$
January 29	$87\frac{1}{4}$
February 1	$86\frac{1}{4}$
February 2	86
February 3	87
February 4	88
February 5	$89\frac{1}{4}$

The first entry on the chart is for the price increase between January 25 and January 26, because the change is greater than the one-point minimum needed to qualify as significant. The first entry is made in the first column of the chart at the 86 level, because this is the whole point through which the price has moved. There is no entry for January 27, because the price did not change by one point or more. The entry for January 28 requires two X's, one at the 87 level on the chart to represent the move up through the 87 level and one at the 88 level to represent the move, on the same day, through this level. Notice that the X's are made in the same column, because no change in direction has occurred in the price. On January 29, the price direction reverses by a point or more, and the entry is a 0 in the second column at the 87 level. The February 1 drop is recorded by a 2 (to indicate the second month of the year) at the 86 level. On February 3, the price direction changes again, and we move to the next column to begin recording the next series. To keep tract of the time reference, the year is usually marked on the horizontal axis, and the first entry of a new month is marked by the appropriate number, 1 to 12, as represented by the 2 in the second column. Soon, these entries take on patterns that are significant to the chartist.

P&F Patterns

Figure 18.14 illustrates some of the patterns that p&f chartists look for. Essentially the p&f chartist looks at areas of congestion or a narrow range in which significant price changes have occurred in search of breakthroughs to new high or low prices. If the breakthrough occurs on the upside, it is an indication of further price advances. If the breakthrough occurs on the downside, it is an indication of further price declines. If no breakthrough occurs, it is an indication of a continuing sideward price movement. Note the bullish signals in Figure 18.14. When the X's in any column rise above the previously highest X and the general congestion of the X's and O's, it is a signal to buy *b*. When the O's fall below the previously lowest O and the general congestion of the X's and O's, it is a signal to sell *s*. Note that the general congestion does not have to be lateral, that is, moving horizontally in a narrow straight band across the chart. The congestion may be in a downward or upward trend, such as the last two patterns at the bottom of Figure 18.14. If the X rises above the trend of the congestion, it is a signal to buy. If the O falls below the uptrend of the congestion, it is a signal to sell. The investor must be very careful, however, of what the chartists have called false signals. What may seem to be a breakthrough in either direction may prove only temporary, and the next significant move in the stock price may reverse the direction and lead to the very opposite signal. As in the case of the vertical bar charts, the area of congestion above the present price is the resistance level through which the upward price movements must break through, and it becomes the support level once the price breaks through.

Point-and-figure chart 397

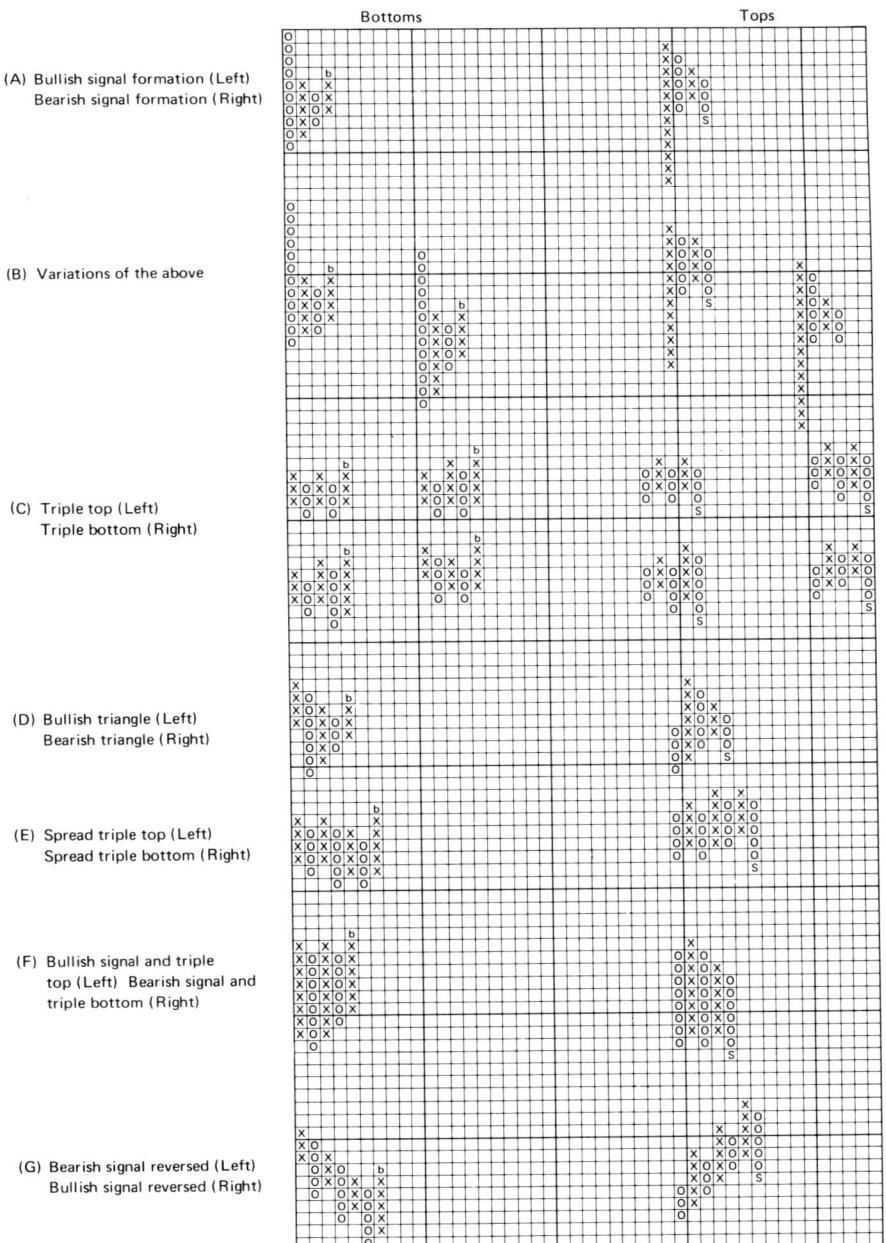

Figure 18.14. Point-and-figure chart patterns.

(*From D. Vaughn, Survey of Investments, Holt, Rinehart and Winston, New York*, 1967, p. 355.)

Some point-and-figure chartists claim that it is possible to estimate the extent of a price move once the breakout has been observed. Some do this by counting the number of columns in the area of congestion before the breakout and adding, if the breakout is on the upside, the number of columns, expressed in dollars, to the price at the area of congestion. This sum is the price to which the present movement, signaled by the breakthrough, is expected to go. If the breakout is on the downside, the number of columns is subtracted from the price in the area of congestion to derive the price level toward which the stock is heading. Others add or subtract the width of the area of congestion, that is, the number of rows instead of columns, to estimate the magnitude of the price movement.

SUMMARY

Charting is the technical analyst's method of maintaining a record of stock prices. From the charts he hopes to discern certain price and volume patterns that may indicate future stock prices.

The vertical bar chart periodically plots stock price ranges and volume, using vertical straight lines (bars). The higher the volume and the greater the range, the longer are the vertical price and volume lines. Using the bar chart, the chartist seeks patterns that may fall into three major categories: the bullish, the bearish, and the uncertain. The bullish patterns portend stock price increases and take on such configurations as inverted head and shoulders, a saucer, or a flag. The uncertain patterns give no clear indication of future stock prices and take on such shapes as boxes, rectangles, triangles, and wedges. The bearish configurations indicate declining stock prices and take on such shapes as the head and shoulders and the double and triple tops.

The point-and-figure chart attempts to record only significant price changes and their direction. Only if the price change is large enough is it recorded, and only if it reverses the direction of the price movement is there horizontal movement on the chart. The point-and-figure chartist seeks areas of congestion and indications that the price movement has broken out of these areas of congestion and is on its way to a new level.

QUESTIONS

18.1 What are the common charts used by the technician to analyze stock prices?

18.2 What are the typical bullish patterns? Briefly describe them.

18.3 What are measuring gaps and exhaustion gaps?

18.4 Describe some of the uncertain stock price patterns.

18.5 Describe the typically bearish stock price patterns.

18.6 Explain consolidation areas and resistance levels.
18.7 How does the point-and-figure chart differ from the vertical bar chart?
18.8 Explain the construction of the point-and-figure chart.
18.9 What patterns are important signals to the point-and-figure charts.

PROBLEMS

18.1 What would each of the following charts indicate to a chartist:

(a)

(b)

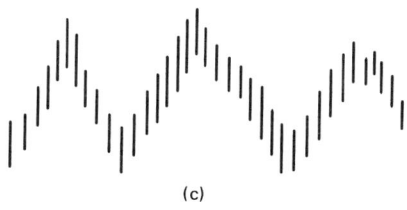

(c)

18.2 Construct a point-and-figure chart from the following prices:
14½
16⅜
15
14
16¾
17¼
18¾
19⅞
20 1
18⅝
17
Consider price changes of ±1 or more significant.

Charting   400

18.3 Analyze the following point-and-figure chart patterns:

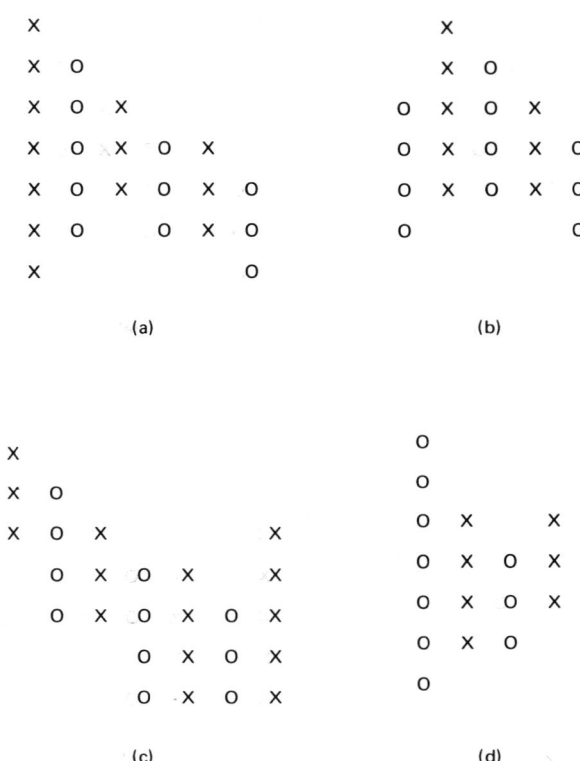

REFERENCES

Bishop, George W. *Charles H. Dow and the Dow Theory,* New York: Appleton Century Crofts, 1960.

Cohen, A. W. *The Chartcraft Method of Point and Figure Trading,* New York: Chartcraft, Inc., 1961.

Edwards, Robert D., and John McGee. *Technical Analysis of Stock Trends,* Springfield, Mass.: John McGee, 1964.

Jiler, William. *How Charts Can Help You in the Stock Market,* New York: Commodity Research Publications Corporation, 1962.

Lerro, Anthony J., and Charles B. Swayne, Jr. *Selection of Securities,* Braintree, Mass.: D. H. Mark Publishing Co., 1970.

Schulz, John W. *The Intelligent Chartist,* New York: WRSM Financial Service Corp., 1962.

Seligman, Daniel. "Playing the Market with Charts," *Fortune,* 65:118, 168 et seq., February, 1962.

―――. "The Mystique of Point-and-Figure," *Fortune,* 65:113–115, 178 et seq., March, 1962.

Trendline's Current Market Perspectives, New York: Trendline Corporation.

Vaughn, Donald E. *Survey of Investments,* New York: Holt, Rinehart and Winston, Inc., 1967.

Whellan, A. H. *Study Helps in Point and Figure Technique,* 2d ed., New York: Morgan, Rogers, and Roberts, Inc., 1966.

19
Technical Indicators

In addition to charting, technicians rely on numerous technical indicators for information on future stock prices. These technical indicators are measures that technicians feel indicate potential price movements of the market or a stock. The specific indicator may be derived from stock prices, the activities of market participants who are considered either highly informed or highly uninformed, or from the analyst's interpretation of market data that have been converted into an indicator.

Among the more commonly used technical indicators that we explore in this chapter are the breadth of the market or the advance-decline line, the odd lot index, the confidence index, insider transactions, and the premium on convertible bonds.

BREADTH OF THE MARKET (ADVANCE-DECLINE LINE)

Many technicians believe that the breadth of the entire market is a better measure of general market performance than the commonly used stock averages. These people maintain that the stock averages comprise only a part of the total number of stocks, and to get a true reading of the market, one must examine the price movements of all the stocks.

The measure that they suggest using is the breadth of the market. This is a cumulative index of the net differences between the number of advances and the number of declines in the daily trading of the New York Stock Exchange. The net advances or declines of one day are added to the previous, cumulated total, as illustrated below:

	Day 1	Day 2	Day 3	Day 4
Net advances (+)	200	100		
Net declines (−)			100	250
Index	+200	+300	+200	− 50

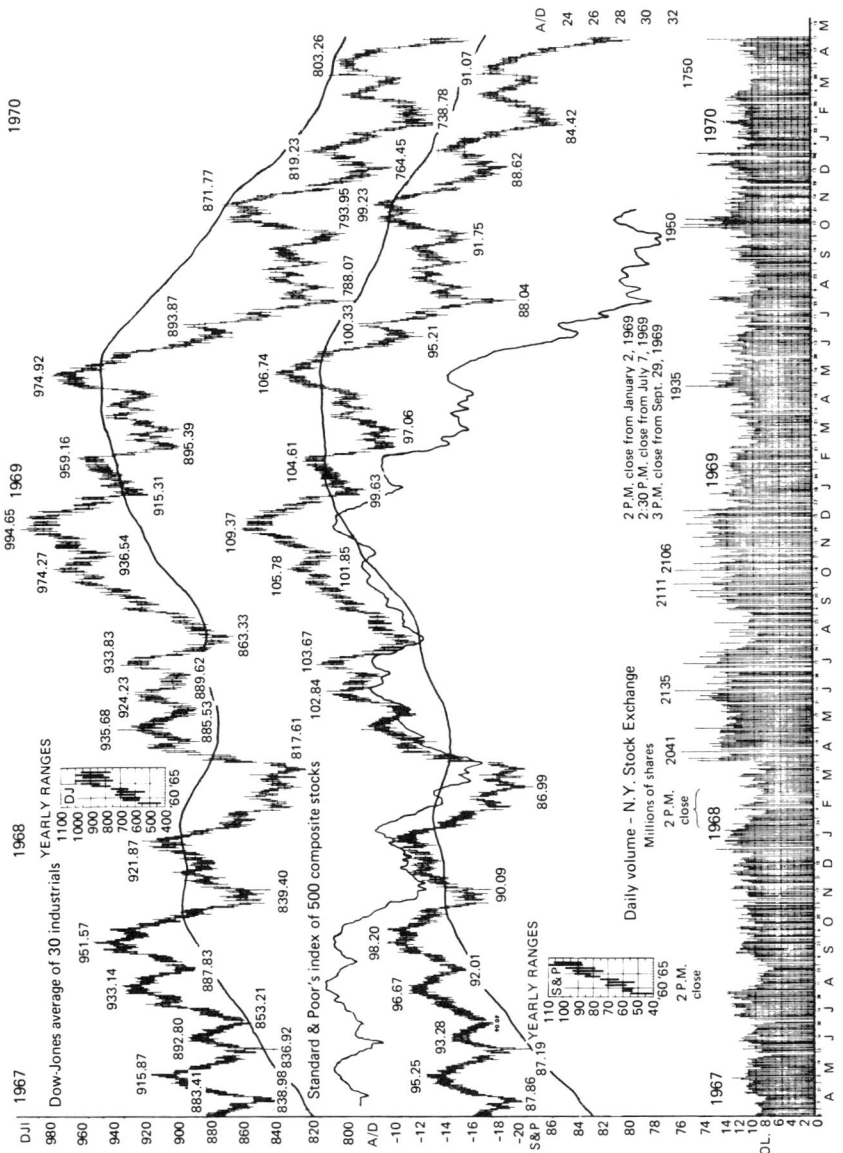

Figure 19.1. Advance-decline line compared with the Dow-Jones Industrial Average.

(From *Daily Basis Stock Charts, Trendline Corporation, New York.*)

The cumulative total may be positive or negative and may be continued for several years.

When this cumulative total is compared with the Dow Jones industrial average (DJIA), as illustrated in Figure 19.1, the technicians believe that it contains predictive insights into the future of the Dow Jones industrial average. The technician's reasoning seems to be that the Dow Jones industrial average, which comprises the more established industrial corporations, does not move simultaneously with the rest of the market. The rising market is envisioned as series of stocks rising to new price peaks. As the market gains in upward momentum, the number of new price peaks rises. Only as the market starts to lose its upward momentum does the number of new price peaks begin to taper off, for the weaker, more cyclically prone stocks are the first to feel the impending downturn. The cumulative breadth index, which includes these weaker stocks, begins to decline, but the Dow Jones industrial average continues to reflect the strength of the more established companies. This divergence between the Dow Jones industrial average and the breadth index is a signal of an approaching market decline.

The breadth index is also used to detect the beginnings of a market upswing. The technicians look for what is called a *selling climax*. Toward the end of a market decline, the technicians believe that there is a substantial increase in the volume and a rather large drop in price as panic spreads among investors and they rush to sell. During the selling climax, the cumulative breadth index experiences its sharpest decline, and the Dow Jones industrial average also experiences its sharpest decline. This last selling spurt is considered to be the last gasp of the market slide, and perhaps after a few weeks of rest, the next advance begins.

TRADING VOLUME

As we saw in Chapter 18, the technician looks to the trading volume of the market or the individual stock to confirm his opinions about the price pattern. Rising volume accompanying rising stock prices is a confirmation of a continuing uptrend in the stock. A rising volume with a declining stock price is considered to be a sign of stock price weakness.

The logic behind the volume indicator apparently lies in the relationship of supply and demand schedules. At the higher price, the technician feels that a larger supply is forthcoming. To maintain this higher price or advance further, there has to be a demand for the increased number of shares being offered. This means that volume has to increase. If the volume does not increase at the higher price, it is an indication to the technician that the demand will be insufficient to absorb the greater supply that he expects to be forthcoming at the higher price. The stock price will have to slip back to its former level to clear the market. Conversely, a declining price accompanied by declining volume will not be maintained, because the supply at the lower price has shrunk. Therefore, the increased demand at the lower price will not be met, and the stock price will return to its prior level.

The logic is reversed for a price rise on declining volume. There is not enough demand to purchase the increased supply expected at the higher price, and the higher price cannot be sustained. A declining price on expanding volume implies to the technician that the increased demand that he expects to find at the lower prices is being supplied. The increased supply at the lower prices is indicative of further price declines.

The problem in interpretation is that the technician is assuming that either the demand or the supply schedule shifts while the other remains steady. In reality, it is possible that both schedules are shifting at the same time in response to the same new information. In this case, the technician would really be unable to distinguish between the supply and the demand factors clearly, and the implications for future prices are vague.

SHORT POSITIONS

Traditionally, market participants have considered high or rising short positions as bullish indicators of future stock prices. The reasoning is that the short sale represented a potential demand for the stock, because eventually the short seller had to go into the market and purchase the stock to cover his short sale, that is, return the stock from whom it was borrowed. The potential demand for the stock from the short seller was considered high if the short interest (number of shares sold short), which is reported in the financial press as of the fifteenth of each month, was high in relation to the volume of shares traded.

The traditional view has been challenged by recent studies that indicate that stocks with high or rising short interest ratios[1] do not outperform the market and that the typical relationship between the short interest ratio and the general market averages may be negative.[2] A simulation of the performance of stocks with high or rising short interests did not outperform the general market averages during the same time period. The performance of a sample of stocks with high or rising short

---

[1] R. Smith, "Short Interest and Stock Market Prices," *Financial Analysts Journal*, November-December, 1968, pp. 151–154.

[2] J. Seneca, "Short Interest: Bullish or Bearish?" *Journal of Finance,* March, 1967, pp. 67–70.

interests was almost identical with that of randomly selected stocks. The performance of the ten stocks with the highest short interest and those with the most rapidly growing short interest also did not outperform the general market. The only distinguishing feature of the high short interest stocks was their higher price volatility, which implies that the investor is exposed to more risk in these stocks while not receiving any higher return.

The typical relationship discovered between the general market averages and the short interest ratio has been negative. This seems to imply that the short seller is an accurate forecaster of stock prices and that instead of a short sale's implying a bullish future, it is actually a good indication of a bearish future. Typically, the short seller, whom some consider to be more sophisticated than the average market participant, is correct in forecasting future price declines. It may be, however, that in the typical situation, characterized by unusually large short positions, the implications for future stock prices are bullish.[3] It is possible that the potential demand generated by unusually large short interest may outweigh the bearish implications of the short interest and cause a rally in the stock, as envisioned in the traditional view.

ODD LOT THEORY

The odd lot is a purchase or sale of a stock in an amount of less than 100 shares. The odd lot theory suggests that the relationship of odd lot sales to odd lot purchases is indicative of future price movements. When odd lot selling exceeds odd lot buying, it is an indication that the price will rise. When odd lot buying exceeds odd lot selling, it is an indication that the price will decline.

The logic behind the theory rests on the belief that the odd lotter, typically the uninformed, small investor, is usually wrong or late in his evaluation of the situation. The odd lotter usually purchases the stock after the effect of the news has been fully digested into the stock price and sells the stock when the worst is over and the stock is poised for a recovery. By doing the opposite of what the odd lotter is doing, the more sophisticated investor will be able to profit by taking advantage of the odd lotter's consistently wrong investment activity.

The evidence does not completely bear out the theory. In terms of the general averages, it has been observed that the odd lotter is actually correct in the timing of most of his transactions. It is just at the major turning points in the market that he is usually wrong. Throughout most of the rising market, the odd lot sales to purchase ratio is increasing,

---

[3] M. Hanna, "Short Interest: Bullish or Bearish?—Comment," *Journal of Finance,* June, 1968, pp. 520–523.

implying a correct policy of selling when prices rise, and throughout most of the declining market, the odd lotter is buying, implying a correct policy of buying when prices fall. Just before the peaks in the market, however, the odd lotter, probably carried away in his naïve enthusiasm and the apparent euphoria of the market, suddenly reverses himself and becomes an aggressive buyer. Just before the bottom of the decline, the odd lotter becomes discouraged and aggressively sells all the stocks that he has accumulated in the price decline. The major difficulty with using the odd lot sales to purchase ratio is in the interpretation of the ratio at the time that it actually occurs. The ratio has been known to give false signals that have lead to incorrect investment strategies.

The evidence on the use of the odd lot theory to predict the future price movements of individual stocks is contradictory.[4] The earlier tests reveal that the weekly odd lot sales/purchase ratios for individual stocks gave frequent buy and sell signals that were of little use in predicting price performance. The buy signal was defined as a switch by odd lotters from buying on balance (purchases exceed sales) to selling on balance (sales exceed purchases), and the sell signal was a switch by odd lotters from selling the stock on balance to buying the stock on balance. This switching occurred, on average, once every 5 weeks for each of the seventy-five companies in the study. Obviously, it occurred too frequently to indicate major turning points in the stock. When the signal was changed to a reversal in the 4-week moving average of the odd lot sales/purchase ratio, the frequency of the signals dropped, but there was no improvement in their ability to prevent future stock prices.

Another test[5] to determine the predictive quality of the odd lot sales/purchase ratio revealed some predictive qualities. Instead of using a reversal of the ratio for signals, the ratio had to move decisively upward or downward before the signal was given. By definition, this required a change in the 4-week moving ratio of 50 percent for a buy signal and 40 percent for a sell signal. The results, some of which are illustrated in Figure 19.2, showed that for the period studied, the buy signals were correctly indicative of future price increases. If the purchases had been made on the buy signals, the investor would have outperformed the market averages. The sell signals, however, were of little use in predicting future stock prices. From Figure 19.2, it can be seen that the odd lot buy signals actually precede the stock price increase

---

[4] T. Kewley and R. Stevenson, "The Odd-Lot Theory as Revealed by Purchase and Sale Statistics for Individual Stocks," *Financial Analysts Journal,* September-October, 1967, pp. 103–108, and by the same authors, "The Odd-Lot Theory for Individual Stocks: A Reply," *Financial Analysts Journal,* January-February, 1969. See also S. Kaish, "Odd Lot Profit and Loss Performance," *Financial Analysts Journal,* September-October, 1969, pp. 83–89.

[5] *Ibid.*

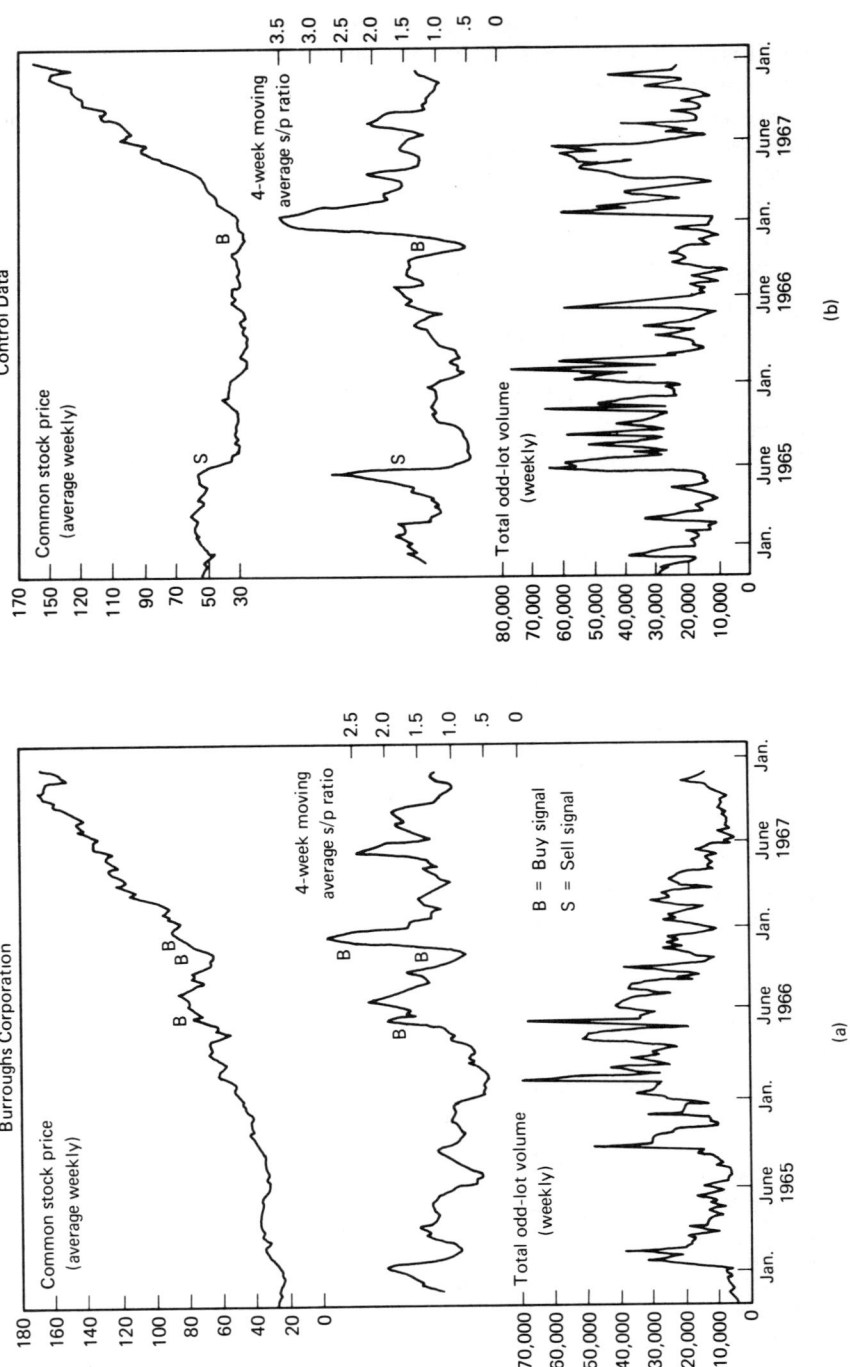

Figure 19.2. Stock prices and odd lot transactions.

(From T. Kewlwy and R. Stevenson, "The Odd-Lot Theory for Individual Stocks: A Reply," *Financial Analysts Journal*, January–February, 1969, pp. 102–103.)

in the case of both Burroughs Corporation and Control Data Corporation. It is interesting to note that, although there is no apparent relationship between the odd lot volume in the stock and the 4-week moving average of the sales/purchase ratio, there is a relationship between the stock price and the total odd lot volume. From Figure 19.2, the total odd lot volume for Control Data Corporation seems to have declined to a relatively low level for approximately 20 weeks before the stock price increase. It seems as if a low odd lot volume in a stock that previously had high odd lot volume may be a buy signal. Apparently, the odd lotters became discouraged with Control Data Corporation after many weeks of high trading activity and no significant price change. In the traditional view of the odd lotter, he became disenchanted and turned his attention elsewhere at the exact time that he should have been renewing his interest in Control Data, for 6 months later the stock price had a major advance.

INSIDER TRANSACTIONS

The insider transaction theory maintains that a careful study of the purchases and sales of the company's stock by its officers and major stockholders, as reported by the Securities and Exchange Commission's *Official Summary of Security Transactions and Holdings,* will reveal what these people believe to be the outlook for the company. In turn, this outlook should be indicative of future stock prices. The implication is that the insider has information about the company that, when made public, will affect the stock price. If the insiders are buying, the outlook for the stock is bullish. If the insiders are selling, the outlook is bearish.

The results of investigations of the predictive quality of insider transactions have been mixed. One study[6] concluded that "there is very little evidence that a definite relationship exists between insider transactions and subsequent price movements in relation to the general market level." The results showed that half of the insiders' transactions performed more poorly than the market and that half performed better than the market.

Another study, by Lorie and Niederhoffer,[7] concluded that intensive accumulation of stocks by insiders does pinpoint stocks that can be expected to outperform the market. In cases in which the number of insider purchases exceeded the number of insider sales by more than two, there was more than a 60 percent occurrence of superior market per-

---

[6] H. Wu, "Corporate Insider Trading Profits and the Ability to Forecast Stock Prices," as published in H. Wu and A. Zakon, *Elements of Investments,* Holt, Rinehart and Winston, Inc., New York, 1965, pp. 442–448.

[7] J. Lorie and V. Niederhoffer, "The Predictive Statistical Properties of Insider Trading," *The Journal of Law and Economics,* April, 1968, pp. 35–53.

formance. It was observed that insider transactions tended to follow patterns of consecutive purchases or consecutive sales. Any change in the direction of the pattern from consecutive purchases to sales or vice versa was viewed as an important clue to insider thinking and had a reasonable record of preceding large price changes.

CREDIT AND DEBIT BALANCES

The credit balance is the cash in investors' accounts at stock brokerage houses. When the investor sells a stock, he can either leave the cash there at no interest in anticipation of purchasing another stock or withdraw the cash to put it some place which pays interest. It is usually considered to be the unsophisticated investor who allows his credit balance to build up. The more sophisticated investor is expected to be more skillful in keeping his funds continually employed. Like his unsophisticated cousin, the odd lotter, the owner of the credit balance is expected to allow his balance to grow until just before the decline when he aggressively buys. The implication is that by doing the opposite to what the owner of the credit balance is doing, the sophisticated investor can profit.

In the opposite manner, the debit balance, the amount borrowed from brokerage houses to buy stocks on margin, is intended to reflect the attitudes of the more sophisticated investor who uses margins. Before a peak in the market, the sophisticated investor is expected to retrench and repay his debit balance. Before a trough in the market, the sophisticated investor is expected to buy aggressively, using his margin and expanding his debit balance.

MOVING AVERAGES

Many technicians prefer to use a moving average, usually of about 200 days, instead of the standard price indexes. They believe that this smooths out the random fluctuations, allowing them to detect the major trends and turning points. The problem is that the moving average is sluggish and rather slow to adjust. By the time that the moving average reveals a major reversal in trend, a good part of the reversal may have already occurred.

CONFIDENCE INDEX

The confidence index is the ratio of the yield on high grade bonds to the yield on lower grade bonds, that is, confidence index = high grade bond yield/low grade bond yield. The technicians believe that a rise in the ratio is indicative of a rise in stock prices and that a fall in the ratio is indicative of a decline in stock prices.

The reasoning behind the theory is that as the economy enters an expansionary phase, the bond investor should be willing to shift from the safer, lower-yielding bonds to the lower quality, higher-yielding bonds to get the higher interest. This bids up the price on the low grade bonds, thereby lowering their yield, narrowing the yield spread, and increasing the confidence index. If the economy is entering a declining phase, the yield spread widens and the confidence index declines. Because, the reasoning goes, the bond investor is the most astute of all investors, he is the first to react to a shift in the prospects for the economy. By watching the actions of the bond investor, the stock investor can get an early clue to the prospects for the economy and the stock market.

There is a danger of unwarranted reliance on the confidence index. There are other considerations in the determination of the yield and the yield spread than the demand of the professional bond investor. The effect of the Federal Reserve's monetary policy on the higher quality bond interest rates, the supply of various quality bonds, and the effects of inflation may offset the professional bond investor's effect on the yield spread.

DOW THEORY

The Dow theory contends that stock price movements are of two major types. The primary movement is the long-term trend. The secondary movement is a market price reaction within the primary movement. The secondary movement retraces substantial parts of the primary movement but is not larger than the part of the primary movement that it is retracing. Once the secondary movement stops, the market returns and exceeds its old level, and the primary trend continues. If the market does not exceed its previous high and then penetrates the most recent secondary movement's low, the market has reversed direction. The chart pattern of the movements is illustrated in Figure 19.3, which shows an upward primary trend. The first retreat from the primary trend is the secondary, declining trend, which stops short of the old low. After halting the secondary trend, the market rises to new highs, continuing the primary uptrend. On the next secondary trend, the market fails to recover to new highs and penetrates the previous lows, signaling a reversal in the primary trend.

To confirm the pattern of the Dow theory, the technician usually looks for both the Dow Jones industrial average and the Dow Jones transportation average to give similar signals. Only when the two give the same signal is the Dow theorist satisfied.

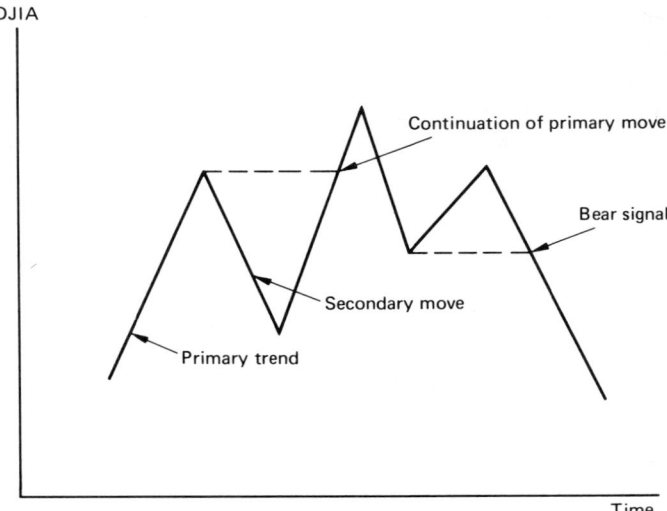

Figure 19.3. Dow theory chart.

The Dow theory does not claim to forecast how long the primary trend will last. It indicates only a reversal of the primary trend. It is also slow in confirming the reversal, for it may be months before the transportation average gives the same signal as the industrial average. If the primary trend is of short duration and not very steep, the Dow theorist may be too late to participate in the market uptrend and may be whipsawed between reversals in the primary trend.

NEW HIGHS TO NEW LOWS

The ratio of the number of new highs to new lows is used by some technicians to gain insight into future stock prices. If the ratio increases, the indication is bullish. If the ratio declines, the indication is bearish. The reasoning behind the ratio seems to be much the same as behind the advance-decline line. More and more stocks are expected to reach new peaks as the market gains in upward momentum. The upward momentum will gradually start to fade, with fewer and fewer stocks reaching new peaks while more and more stocks reach new lows. Many technicians believe that if the number of new lows exceeds the number of new highs, it is a signal of a reversal in a bull market, and vice versa.

CONTRARY OPINION

Many investors believe that if one moves in opposite direction to the prevailing opinion, he meets with success. The apparent rationale behind this factor is the observed factor that heights of giddy optimism have usually been followed by sobering reversals and that the depths of pessimism have been followed by better conditions. The difficulty lies in determining when the height of the pessimism or optimism has been reached. Many of these investors believe in buying out-of-favor stocks, those which seem to be in temporarily difficult times. One wonders, however, if they still own any trolley car company stocks.

TAX SELLING AND PAYMENT DATES

At certain times of the year it may be advantageous for investors to sell securities in order to establish a loss or a gain for income tax purposes. There may be large selling in stocks in which investors have a loss toward the end of the year, for recorded losses entitle the stockholder to tax benefits. At other times of the year, there may be selling pressure on the markets when investors sell stocks to raise money to pay their taxes.

STOCK SPLITS

When a stock is split, the holder of shares is given additional shares in some proportion to his present holdings. It has been observed that higher than usual returns accrue to these stocks in the months immediately prior to the split.[8] As can be seen from Figure 19.4a, the stock price starts to rise faster than the market as early as 29 months before the split and continues to rise at an increased rate as the date of the split approaches. After the split, the price performance of the stock is no different from that of the general market.

The apparent reason for the superior performance of the split stocks was the information contained in the split announcement, which occurred, on average, 44.5 days before the split took effect. The announcement confirmed investors' beliefs that the firm's prospects were improving. The superior price performance long before the split announcement may be taken as an indication that investors are anticipating improvement in the firm's prospects. The announcement leads investors to believe more firmly that they would be receiving increased dividends, which accompany most splits. The anticipation of increased dividends apparently caused the price of those stocks to rise. Those stocks which did raise their dividend did retain the stock price rise that they had experienced before the split and even rose a little further, as illustrated in Figure 19.4b. Those stocks which split and did not raise their divi-

---

[8] E. Fama et al., "The Adjustment of Stock Prices to New Information," *International Economic Review,* February, 1969, pp. 1–21.

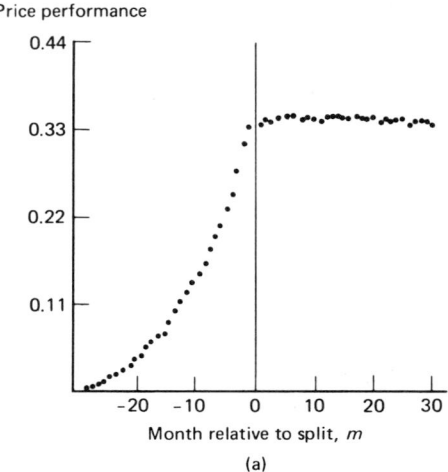
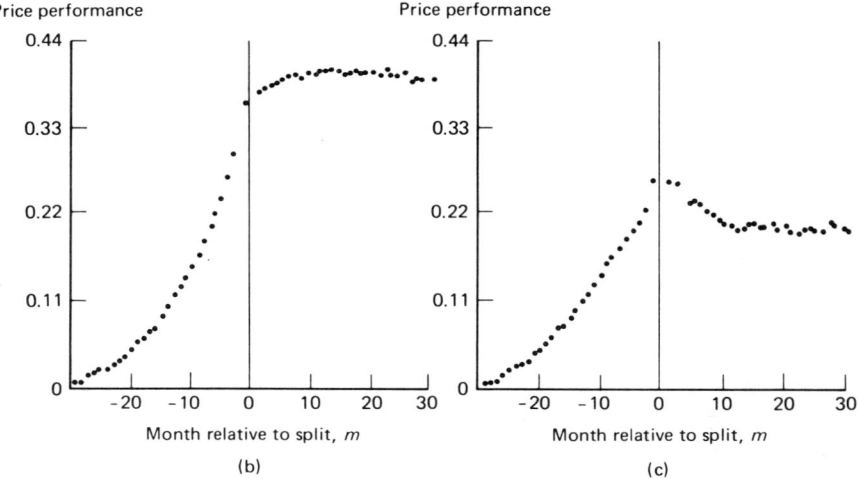

Figure 19.4. Price performance and stock splits, (a) cumulative superior price performance, (b) cumulative superior price performance for dividend increases, (c) cumulative superior price performances for dividend decreases.

(From E. Fama, "Efficient Capital Markets," *Journal of Finance*, May, 1970, p. 406.)

dend, however, lost almost all the price gains associated with the stock split, as illustrated in Figure 19.4c, and sank back to the price performance they had 5 months before the split.

The investment implications are that the investor who can spot the split candidate may experience a superior return. The stock must be purchased before the split announcement, however, because, as can be seen from Figure 19.4a, the price effect of the split is completed almost immediately on announcement.[9] The investor may obtain a superior performance after the split announcement only if the stock increases its dividend, as illustrated in Figure 19.4b, for those are the only stocks which continue to have a superior performance after the split. If the investor bought the stock after the split and the company did not raise its dividend, he would have had an inferior investment performance. The after split performance of all the stocks, whether or not they raised their dividend, was not, on average, greater than the general market. Because the investor is unaware beforehand of which firms will raise their dividends after a split and which firms will not, the purchase of a stock after the split announcement promises no better than average performance. Only if the investor can spot a stock split before the announcement does he outperform the market.

CONVERTIBLE BOND PREMIUMS DEVIATIONS

It has been suggested that the deviations in premiums on convertible bonds may be indicative of the future price of the associated stock.[10]

[9] D. Bellemore and L. Blucher, "A Study of Stock Splits in the Postwar Years," *Financial Analysts Journal,* November, 1956, pp. 19–26.

[10] P. Cretien, Jr., "Convertible Bond Premiums as Predictors of Common Stock Price Changes," *Financial Analysts Journal,* November-December, 1969, pp. 90–95.

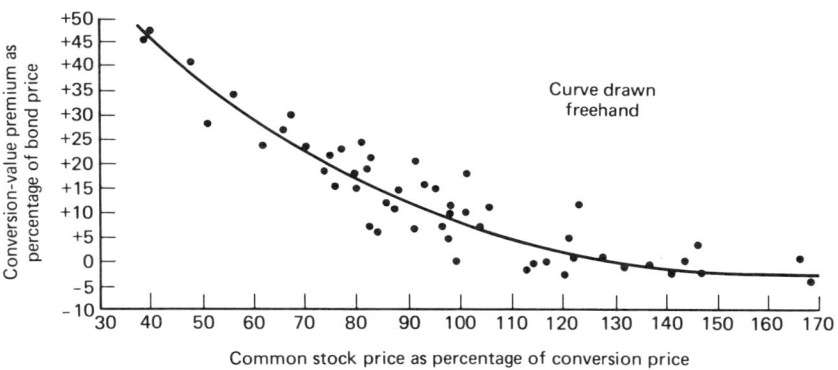

Observations based on data in *Moudy's Convertible Bonds* (Feb. 17, 1969).

Figure 19.5. Standard curve.

(*From P. Cretien, Jr., "Convertible Bond Premiums as Predictors of Common Stock Price Changes," Financial Analysts Journal, November–December,* 1969, *p.* 91.)

As we saw in Chapter 14, convertible bonds sell at a premium above conversion value that may be expressed as a percentage of the bond price. This may be compared with the common stock as a percentage of the conversion price, as illustrated in Figure 19.5. At any point in time, there should be a *standard curve* that expresses the relationship between the two values. Deviations in the conversion value premium as a percentage of the bond price above or below the standard curve indicate what the convertible bondholder believes is the outlook for the associated common stock. When the deviations are above the standard curve, it is a sign that the convertible bondholders are optimistic about the future price of the associated stock. When the deviations are below the standard curve, it is a sign that the convertible bondholders are pessimistic. When the deviations reverse direction, as illustrated in Figure 19.6, the implication is that the convertible bondholders have changed

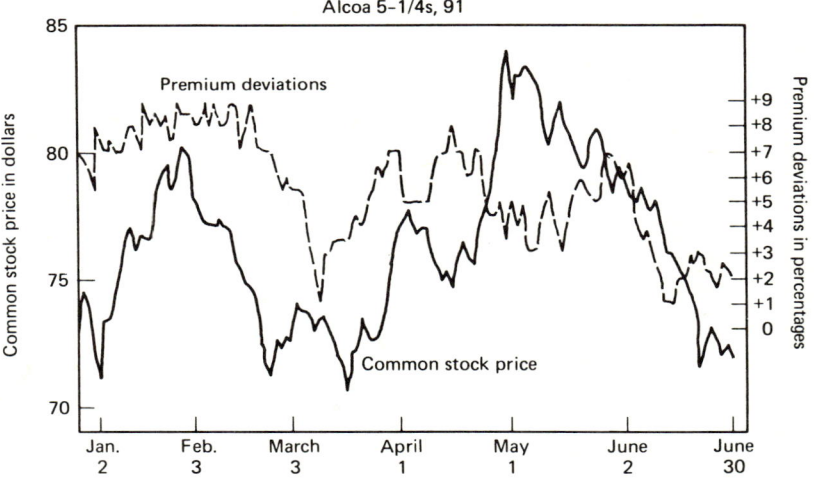

Figure 19.6. Stock price and premium deviations.

(From P. Cretien, Jr., "Convertible Bond Premiums as Predictors of Common Stock Price Changes," Financial Analysts Journal, November–December, 1969, p. 92.)

their outlook on the common stock. In Figure 19.6, the deviations made a sharp reversal upward on about March 10, which preceded the reversal in the common stock by almost a week. It may be possible to use the movements in the premium deviations to gather an indication of the future stock price. Caution must be exercised in interpreting the results, because the standard curve may shift, changing all the premium deviations and the implications for the common stock price.

EARNINGS PATTERNS

Studies have suggested that an examination of quarterly earnings will indicate which stocks may provide superior investment performance.[11] The attempt was made in these studies to "produce private information from the public record." The studies maintained that the information contained in the quarterly earnings statements was not fully digested by the market at the time of the report. The astute investor who could properly analyze the quarterly report could obtain a superior investment performance if he invested before the market belatedly digested the full effect of the quarterly report. This idea runs counter to the random walk theory, which maintains that all public information is fully and almost immediately reflected in the stock price.

One of the unique transformations on the quarterly earning data was the "increased momentum in relative earnings." This is a measure of the "acceleration in the rate of the company's earnings relative to the rate of change in the earnings for stocks in general." The results of a simulation that filtered out stocks according to this rule found that those stocks which reported accelerated growth in quarterly earnings outperformed the general market in the succeeding 6 months.

The other suggested unique transformation of the public data to gather an indication of future price performance was the use of quarterly earnings in relation to the stock price. Those stocks which had the highest quarterly earnings, both actually reported and deseasonalized, in relation to price were superior performers during the next 6 months. Those stocks with the lowest quarterly earnings in relation to price had an inferior performance.

Caution must be exercised in using this technical trading rule, as with all technical trading rules. The results of the simulations may be very dependent on the period under study and not indicative of a successful strategy in the present market environment.

SUMMARY

This chapter has briefly highlighted a number of the numerous technical indicators that may be used by technicians to judge future market prices.[12] Like all technical devices, each one requires a recurring pattern

---

[11] M. Kisor and V. Messner, "The Filter Approach and Earnings Forecasts," *Financial Analysts Journal,* January-February, 1969, pp. 109–115, and H. Lantane et al., "E/P Ratios v. Changes in Earnings in Forecasting Future Price Changes," *Financial Analysts Journal,* January-February, 1969, pp. 117–120, 123.

[12] A summary of technical indicators is included in G. Pinches, "The Random Walk and Technical Analysis," *Financial Analysts Journal,* March-April, 1970, pp. 104–110.

and an assumed lag between the time that the pattern emerges and the time that its effect is fully digested into the stock price. Obviously, if either the patterns change or the lag disappears, the technical indicator loses its usefulness. Because of this, extreme caution must be exercised in applying technical indicators.

The technical indicators that we explored included the breadth of the market, which attempts to judge the market by movements in the cumulative difference between the number of advances and the number of declines. Trading volume is expected to increase on stock price rises and decrease on stock price declines if the pattern is to remain bullish. The contradictory implications of the short position found that it typically reflected a bearish indication for the stock price, unless the short position was unusually large. The contradictory evidence on the odd lot theory found that the odd lot sales to purchases ratio was not a good indicator for superior investment performance, except in the case of buy signals from decisive, large changes in the ratio. The evidence on the predicative quality of insider transactions is also contradictory.

Other technical indicators are the credit and debit balances in brokerage house accounts. The confidence index, the Dow theory, which looks for secondary moves to confirm the continuation of the primary movement, the new highs to new lows index, the theory of contrary opinion, and the use of seasonal data are technical indicators.

Stock splits, as a technical indicator of stock prices, are associated with superior price performance. The investment implications of stock splits, however, do not seem to offer a profit opportunity, unless the stock split is anticipated before the split announcement is made. The premium deviations on convertible bonds above what could be expected revealed some tendency to foreshadow the movements in the price of the associated common stock. The information contained in the quarterly earnings may also be a technical indicator of stock prices. An accelerated rate of growth in the quarterly earnings above that experienced by stocks in general may indicate a future superior price performance, although again, the results of two studies differed on this point.

QUESTIONS

19.1 Describe the breadth of the market index.

19.2 How is the breadth of the market index used as a technical indicator?

19.3 How is the trading volume used as a technical indicator?

19.4 Why do market participants consider high or rising short positions bullish indicators?

19.5 Explain the logic behind the odd lot theory as a technical indicator.

19.6 How are credit and debit balances used as technical indicators?

19.7 What is the confidence index? How is it used as an indicator?

19.8 Explain the Dow theory.

19.9 What is a standard curve? Explain how deviations in convertible bond premiums are used as an indicator.

19.10 What assumption is made when using quarterly earnings patterns as an indicator of investment performance?

REFERENCES

Barker, C. Austin. "Stock Splits in a Bull Market," *Harvard Business Review,* 35:72–79, May-June, 1957.

Bellamore, D., and L. Blucher. "A Study of Stock Splits in the Postwar Years," *Financial Analysts Journal,* 12:19–26, November-December, 1956.

Biggs, Barton M. "The Short Interest: A False Proverb," *Financial Analysts Journal,* 22:111–116, July-August, 1966.

Drew, G. A. "Clarification of the Odd Lot Theory," *Financial Analysts Journal,* 23:107–108, September, 1967.

Fama, E., et al. "The Adjustment of Stock Prices to New Information," *International Economic Review,* 10:1–21, February, 1969.

Granville, Joseph E. *A Strategy of Daily Stock Timing for Maximum Profit,* Englewood Cliffs, N.J.: Prentice-Hall, Inc., 1960.

Hanna, Mark. "Short Interest: Bullish or Bearish? Comment," *The Journal of Finance,* 23:520–523, June, 1968.

"Is Short Selling Bullish or Bearish?" *Business Week,* Dec. 3, 1966, pp. 129–134.

Jones, Charles P., and Robert H. Litzenberger. "Quarterly Earnings and Intermediate Stock Price Trends," *The Journal of Finance,* 25:143–148, March, 1970.

Kaish, S. "Odd Lot Profit and Loss Performance," *Financial Analysts Journal,* 25:83–89, September-October, 1969.

Kewley, Thomas J., and Richard A. Stevenson. "The Odd-Lot Theory as Revealed by Purchase and Sale Statistics for Individual Stocks," *Financial Analysts Journal,* 23:103–108, September-October, 1967.

———. "The Odd-Lot Theory for Individual Stocks: A Reply," *Financial Analysts Journal,* 25:99–104, January-February, 1969.

Kisor, Manown, Jr., and Van A. Messner. "The Filter Approach and Earnings Forecasts," *Financial Analysts Journal,* 25:109–115, January-February, 1969.

Latané, Henry A., Donald L. Tuttle, and Charles P. Jones. "E/P Ratios v. Changes in Earnings in Forecasting Future Price Changes," *Financial Analysts Journal,* 25:117–120, January-February 1969.

Lorie, James H., and Victor Niedorhoffer. "Predictive and Statistical Properties of Insider Trading," *The Journal of Law and Economics,* 11:35–53, April, 1968.

Pinches, George E. "The Random Walk and Technical Analysis," *Financial Analysts Journal,* 26:104–110, March-April, 1970.

Seneca, Joseph J. "Short Interest: Bearish or Bullish?" *The Journal of Finance,* 22:67–70, March, 1967.

Smith, Randall D. "Short Interest and Stock Market Prices," *Financial Analysts Journal,* 24:151–154, November-December, 1968.

Wu, Hsiu-Kwang. "Corporate Insider Trading Profits and the Ability to Forecast Stock Prices," *Elements of Investments: Selected Readings,* New York: Holt, Rinehart and Winston, Inc., 1965.

Part Six

The preceding parts of this text have concentrated on security analysis, the evaluation of individual securities. We must now turn our attention to portfolio analysis.

Portfolio analysis examines the investment merits of an entire group of individual securities. To arrive at an evaluation of the entire group, we must determine the effect of the interactions among the individual securities on the entire portfolio. We must also establish the criteria that are used to evaluate the portfolio. Chapter 20 establishes the criteria to be used in the evaluation or construction of a portfolio and demonstrates the method for incorporating the interaction among the securities into the criteria.

Once the critera have been established, we must explore the portfolio management problems. These problems accompany the portfolio manager's efforts to construct a portfolio that meets the established criteria. Chapter 21 examines the areas in which portfolio management practices play an important role in matching the actual portfolio to the established criteria. Among the areas examined are the optimal size of the portfolio, the matching of the portfolio with the individual's investment objectives, the timing of investment decisions, the selection basis for the inclusion of individual stocks, the use of leverage in the portfolio, and the use of options in the portfolio.

Chapter 22 discusses various formula plans and aspects of institutional portfolio management. The formula plans establish specific rules for the timing of investments. These plans generally replace the portfolio manager's judgment in the areas of timing and allocation with mechanical rules. The objective, of course, is to improve on the performance of the portfolio by preventing rash or emotional actions on the part of the portfolio manager.

20
Portfolio Theory

The objective of portfolio theory is to establish the criteria for the evaluation of the entire portfolio. There are two basic criteria in determining the investment merits of a portfolio: (1) the return that one expects to receive from the portfolio and (2) the risk to which one is exposed in order to receive this return.

The question is, how do we quantitatively measure the expected return and the risk associated with each portfolio? Security analysis (Chapters 1 to 13) tells us the expected return and the risk to each security (as described in Chapter 21) but tells us little of the expected return and the risk associated with a group of individual securities. It is not sufficient to consider individual securities in isolation from one another when constructing a portfolio, for the various interactions among the individual securities may alter the investment attractiveness of the entire portfolio. We must examine the investment merits of the entire portfolio as a single entity, regardless of the attractiveness of its individual securities. The sum of the individual securities' merits does not have to equal the attractiveness of the portfolio as a single entity. The measures of expected return and risk that we seek tell us not only what each security is contributing to the entire portfolio's return and risk but also the effect of the interaction among the securities on both the return and the risk.

The specific measures that have been suggested[1] are the weighted average of the expected return on the individual securities in the portfolio and the variance or standard deviation of the return around the expected return. The standard deviation around the expected return measures the risk of the expected return's not being realized. The stan-

---

[1] H. Markowitz, "Portfolio Selection," *Journal of Finance,* March, 1952, pp. 77–91.

dard deviation measure includes the covariance among the individual securities that reflects the degree to which the returns among the securities are correlated. Generally, the more highly correlated the expected return of one security with another, the less the possible reduction in the total standard deviation. This chapter explores the specific computation of the expected return and the expected standard deviation.

Once we have the computed measures for each portfolios' expected return and the expected standard deviation, we are in a position to judge the relative merits of various portfolios. At each level of risk, there is one portfolio that has the highest return. This means that there is a series of portfolios, each of which offers the highest expected return for a given level of risk exposure. The portfolio manager must choose from among the various combinations of expected return and risk exposure the one portfolio that gives him the highest utility. It is, therefore, necessary to examine the portfolio manager's utility function and to compare it with the available portfolios to determine which portfolio maximizes his utility.

There are obviously limits as to how much risk one can avoid through portfolio diversification. The degree to which it may be possible to limit risk exposure is explored in this chapter.

In the last section of this chapter, the relationship between the expected return and the risk exposure level is explored. We call this relationship the risk function. We are interested in examining the form or shape of the risk function. There is some evidence that the shape may be linear, implying that there is a proportional trade-off between expected returns and risk exposure. There is also evidence to suggest that the function may be curvilinear, implying that there is either greater than or less than a proportional increase in the expected returns for an increased unit of risk.

PORTFOLIO CRITERIA

The two criteria for judging the investment attractiveness of a portfolio are the expected return and the level of risk exposure associated with the portfolio. The expected return is the weighted average of the return to each security in the portfolio, that is, where

R = expected return to portfolio
R_i = expected return to security i
X_i = proportion of total portfolio invested in security i

$$R = \sum_{i=1}^{n} R_i X_i, \text{ where } n = \text{total number of securities in portfolio}$$

For example, if there were two securities in the portfolio, as illustrated below:

Security number	Expected return R_i, percent	Proportion X_i, percent
1	10	25
2	20	75

the expected return to the portfolio would be

$R = R_1X_1 + R_2X_2$
$R = 0.10(0.25) + 0.20(0.75)$
$R = 17.5\%$

The expected return to the portfolio is 17.5 percent. The expected return to each security is the sum of its expected dividend and expected capital gain in a specified time period, usually expressed in annual terms. The expected returns to each security R_i are provided to the portfolio manager by the security analyst.

If the maximization of expected return were the criterion for the selection of the individual securities to be included in the portfolio, the portfolio in the illustration above would not be the most attractive. The highest return can be achieved by investing 100 percent of the portfolio in security 2. With the entire portfolio invested in security 2, the expected return would be 20 percent, an increase of 2.5 percent from the portfolio in the illustration. Using only the expected return criterion, the investor would always have a portfolio of one security, for there is always one security that has a higher expected return than any other.

The investor, of course, must also consider the risk involved with the portfolio. In the case of the one-security portfolio based on the highest expected return, the risk would be high. The possibility of the expected return's not being realized is probably very large. For example, one random occurrence could undermine the security analyst's projected return. The level of risk exposure is the probability of the expected return's not being realized. The investor requires that the security analyst not only provide him with the expected return but also with the probable range in which the return may actually occur. For example, the security analyst might project an expected return of 10 percent, with a 10 percent probability of actually being as low as 0 and a 10 percent chance of being as high as 20 percent. The distribution of the possible returns in this case might appear as follows:

Probability of occurrence	Possible returns, percent
0.10	0
0.20	5
0.40	10
0.20	15
0.10	20

The expected return is 10 percent, but there is a chance that the actual return may fall between 0 and 20 percent. Graphically, this distribution of possible returns is illustrated in Figure 20.1. The wider the range of possible returns for a particular expected return, the greater the level of risk exposure, for there is a greater chance of the expected return's not being realized.

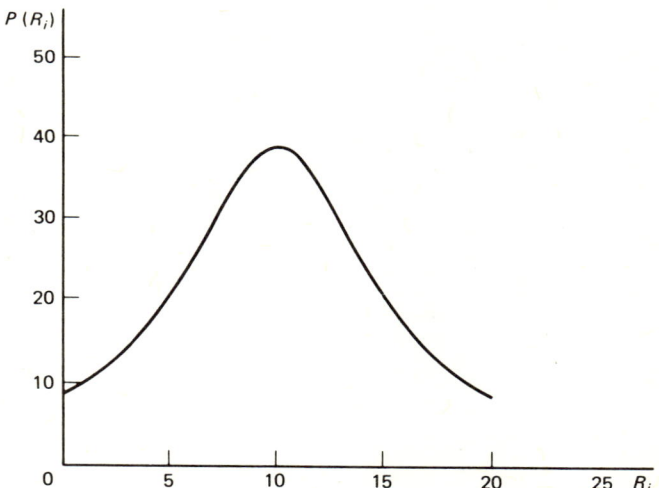

Figure 20.1. Probability distribution of possible expected returns.*

* The distribution is constructed as if the observation were continuous.

The standard deviation of the distribution illustrated in Figure 20.1 is a measure of the range in which the actual return might fall. The larger the standard deviation, the greater the chance of the expected return's not being realized and the greater the risk exposure. The standard deviation for the return in this illustration is slightly greater than 7. If we compare this security with another that also has an expected return of 10 percent but a standard deviation of 5, we can conclude that the latter is more attractive, because it offers the same expected return with less risk.[2]

When we attempt to derive the standard deviation for a portfolio of more than one security, we must also consider the effect of the interaction among the securities on the total risk. Obviously, there is a chance that the total risk may be reduced as another security is added to the portfolio. For example, the influence of the random occurrence that could make the security analyst's projected expected return incorrect for one of the securities may not affect the other security's expected return. The effect of the random occurrence on the expected return of the entire portfolio would thus be reduced.

The interaction among the securities in the portfolio depends on the degree to which the expected returns from the individual securities are correlated. The higher the degree of correlation, the less the possible reduction in the standard deviation and the lower the benefits of diversification. For example, if the two securities in this portfolio were both automobile manufacturers, we should anticipate that the actual return from one security would be highly correlated with that from the other. If the return from one dropped below the expected return, the return from the other would also, for the same random occurrence to the automobile industry would affect both securities in the same manner. On the other hand, if the expected returns from the two securities were negatively correlated, so that a decline in the actual return from one was accompanied by an increase in the return from the other, the effect of a random occurrence would be offset between the response of the two securities, and the expected return to the portfolio would be realized. With a larger chance of the expected return's being realized, the level of risk exposure is reduced.

The degree of correlation between the two securities is measured by the correlation coefficient. If the correlation were perfectly positive, so that a change in the actual return from one security was matched by a proportional change in the same direction by the other security, the correlation coefficient would be $+1$. If the correlation were perfectly negative, so that a change in one security was matched by an equal change in the opposite direction, the correlation coefficient would be -1. Less than perfect positive or negative correlation would be reflected

---

[2] The use of the standard deviation may be misleading, because it includes the returns above the expected returns as well as below. This implies that the investor is equally averse to returns that give him more than he expected and to returns that give him less. It is unreasonable to assume this, and it has been suggested that the semivariance of the deviation below the expected return be the risk measure. See K. Cohen and F. Hammer, *Analytical Methods in Banking,* Richard D. Irwin, Inc., Homewood, Ill., 1966, pp. 276–277.

in the correlation coefficient's being between $+1$ and -1. The greatest reduction in the standard deviation arises when the returns on the two securities are perfectly negatively correlated, although some reduction in the standard deviation is possible if the returns are less than perfectly positively correlated.

The possible reduction in the standard deviation, or risk measure, comes from the interaction between the two securities in reducing the range in which the possible returns may occur. This interaction among the securities is measured by the covariance between the two. The covariance is:

$$\sigma_{ij} = \rho_{ij}\sigma_i\sigma_j$$

where σ_{ij} = covariance between security i and security j
ρ_{ij} = correlation coefficient between security i and security j
σ_i = standard deviation of security i
σ_j = standard deviation of security j

The higher the degree of correlation between security j and security i and the higher the standard deviation of each security, the greater the covariance between the two securities. The larger the covariance, the smaller the possible reduction in the portfolio's standard deviation, as can be seen from the formula for the standard deviation of a portfolio of two securities:

$$\sigma_P = \sqrt{X_1^2\sigma_1^2 + X_2^2\sigma_2^2 + 2X_1X_2\rho_{12}\sigma_1\sigma_2}$$

where σ_P = standard deviation of portfolio
X_1 = proportion of portfolio in security 1
σ_1 = standard deviation of security 1
X_2 = proportion of portfolio in security 2
σ_2 = standard deviation of security 2
ρ_{12} = correlation of security 1 with security 2

The higher the covariance between the two securities, the larger the standard deviation of the portfolio. If the correlation coefficient is negative, the sum under the square root sign is reduced and so is the portfolio risk. If the correlation coefficient is zero, the returns on the two securities are independent, and the third term under the square root sign disappears. If the correlation coefficient is positive, the portfolio standard deviation is the same as if no diversification had occurred.

To illustrate the effect of the degree of correlation on the portfolio risk assume the following:

$\sigma_1 = 4$
$\sigma_2 = 7$
$X_1 = 0.5$
$X_2 = 0.5$

if $\rho_{12} = -1$,

$$\sigma_P = \sqrt{(0.5)^2(4)^2 + (0.5)^2(7)^2 + (2)(0.5)(0.5)(-1)(4)(7)}$$
$$\sigma_P = 1.5$$

if $\rho_{12} = -0.5$

$$\sigma_P = \sqrt{(0.5)^2(4)^2 + (0.5)^2(7)^2 + (2)(0.5)(0.5)(-0.5)(-0.5)(4)(7)}$$
$$\sigma_P = 3.041381$$

if $\rho_{12} = 0.0$,

$$\sigma_P = \sqrt{(0.5)^2(4)^2 + (0.5)^2(7)^2 + (2)(0.5)(0.5)(0)(4)(7)}$$
$$\sigma_P = 4.03$$

if $\rho_{12} = +1.0$,

$$\sigma_P = \sqrt{(0.5)^2(4)^2 + (0.5)^2(7)^2 + 2(0.5)(0.5)(1)(4)(7)}$$
$$\sigma_P = 5.5$$

Note that the lowest standard deviation for the portfolio occurs when the correlation between the two securities is -1. As the degree of positive correlation increases, the standard deviation of the portfolio rises. When the correlation coefficient is $+1$, the advantages of diversification disappear, for the standard deviation of the portfolio is then equal to the weighted sum of the standard deviations of each security. For example, the weighted sum of the standard deviations in this example is

$$\sigma_1 + \sigma_2 = X_1 \sqrt{(\sigma_1)^2} + X_2 \sqrt{(\sigma_2)^2}$$
$$= 0.5(4) + 0.5(7)$$
$$= 5.5$$

Note that the standard deviation of the portfolio when the two securities are perfectly positively correlated is identical with the standard deviation of the two securities taken independently. Diversification can reduce risk below the weighted sum of the standard deviation of each security for a given return only if the correlation among the securities is less than $+1$.

EFFICIENT SET

Each portfolio is now described by its expected return and its risk (standard deviation). Each possible combination of risk and expected return represents a portfolio that may be constructed from the available securities. All these possible combinations of expected return and risk compose the attainable set.[3] For example, the following may be the possible portfolio expected returns and risks:

Portfolio	Expected return, percent	Risk σ
A	15	13
B	13	8
C	10	4
D	8	3
E	5	4
F	5	9
G	10	12
H	10	9
I	7	8
J	9	7

Graphically, the attainable set of portfolios is illustrated in Figure 20.2. Each of the portfolios along or within line *ABCDEFG* is possible. It is not possible to have a portfolio outside of this perimeter, because no combination of expected return and risk exists there.

Among the various attainable portfolios, some are more attractive

[3] Markowitz, *op. cit.*, pp. 77–91.

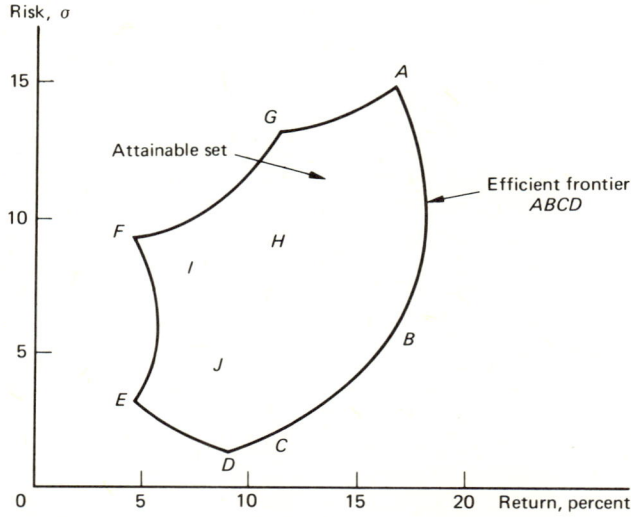

Figure 20.2. Attainable set of portfolios.

than others. For example, portfolio C is more attractive than either portfolio H or G, because C offers the same return as the other two at a lower risk exposure (standard deviation). Portfolio H, on the other hand, is more attractive than portfolio F, because H offers a higher return for the same amount of risk exposure. In general, any portfolio that offers a higher return for the same amount of risk or a lower risk exposure for the same return than another portfolio is more attractive than the other portfolio. Those portfolios which, from among all the attainable portfolios, offer the highest return at a particular level of risk are called *efficient portfolios*. Examples of efficient portfolios are portfolios A, B, C, and D, for at each level of risk no other portfolio offers a higher return. Line ABCD is the *efficient frontier* along which all attainable, efficient portfolios lie.

The portfolio manager selects his portfolio from the portfolios on the efficient frontier, for the selection of any other portfolio would not have the highest return for the level of risk exposure. The question still must be answered, which portfolio from among those which lie on the efficient frontier should the portfolio manager choose? The answer is, the portfolio manager should choose that portfolio which maximizes his utility. We must now attempt to measure his utility to determine which portfolio maximizes it.

Under the assumption of certainty, portfolio managers derive utility or satisfaction from the return that they receive. The typical manager is assumed to receive a greater satisfaction from a higher than a lower return. His total utility should increase with each additional dollar of return whether he falls on schedule I, II, or III, as illustrated in Figure 20.3. In each of these schedules, the portfolio manager's total utility, as measured on the vertical axis, increases as the return increases.

The differences in the slope of the schedules reflect the varying degree of marginal utility derived from a given increment in the return. The diminishing marginal utility of schedule I implies that this particular manager gains less than a proportional increase in utility from an increase in return. For example, the utility received from a return of $200,000 is not twice that received from $100,000. On the other hand, the particular manager whose utility function is represented by schedule III receives an increasingly larger satisfaction from the same increase in return. As illustrated in Figure 20.3, schedule III exhibits an increasing marginal utility of return, so that a manager with this schedule would receive more than a doubling in utility if the return doubled. Schedule II implies a constant marginal utility.

We can now compare the utility of a certain return with that of an expected (risky) return to demonstrate that the shape of the utility schedule reflects a preference for risk or certainty. Assume a hypothetical certain return of r_1 ($90) that lies on schedule I at point C in Figure

Portfolio theory 432

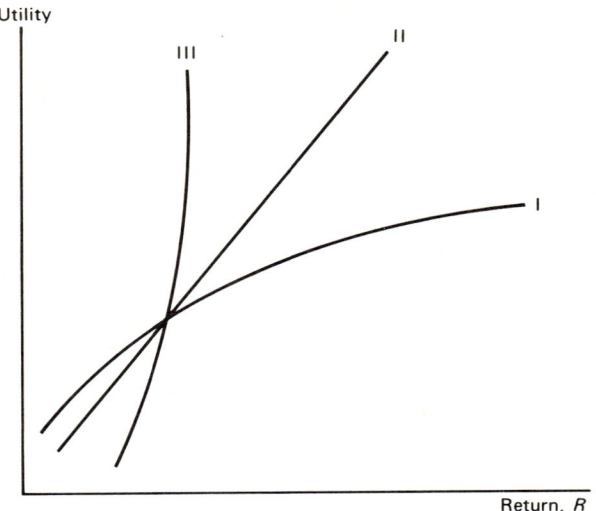

Figure 20.3. Utility function.

20.4 and gives utility U_1. For comparison purposes, assume that we have a portfolio consisting of two equally likely outcomes (50:50 chance), as represented by A ($60) and B ($120) in Figure 20.4. The expected return to this portfolio is also r_1 ($90). Although the certain return is equal to the expected return, however, the latter offers a lower utility U_2. The expected utility to the risky expected return is the aver-

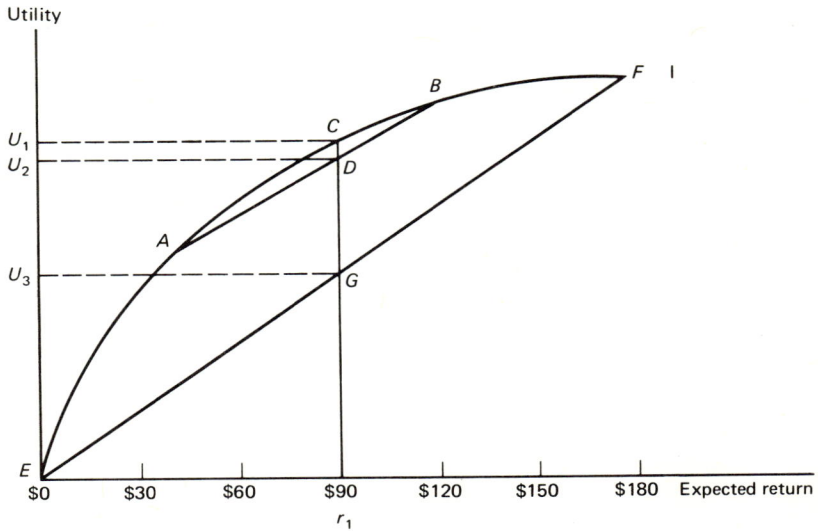

Figure 20.4. Preference for certainty.

age of the utility levels of the possible outcomes A and B. Because in schedule I, the higher possible outcomes have less than proportional increases in utility, the average utility must be less than that for the certain return. This is illustrated as point D in Figure 20.4. Point D represents the average of the utility levels associated with the possible outcome A and the possible outcome B. The utility corresponding to point D is less than the utility corresponding to point C, although both points have the same return.

As the risk increases, measured by the increase in the dispersion of the possible outcomes, the utility associated with a given expected return decreases. For example, assume that the two possible outcomes of the risky portfolio were E and F in Figure 20.4. The expected return would remain r_1 ($90), but the average of the utilities associated with these possible outcomes would be U_3, or less than the utility associated with either the less risky portfolio or the certain return. Because the portfolio manager has a diminishing marginal utility of return (schedule I), any risky combination has less utility than (lies below) the certain return, and the riskier the combination (the farther apart the two points connected), the less the utility received. Obviously, because the portfolio manager receives less utility from the same return as the risk increases, he may be said to be risk-averse.

In contrast to the risk-aversion preference of the manager with a diminishing marginal utility of return, the manager with an increasing marginal utility of return (schedule III) finds that he receives a higher utility from the riskier portfolios, as illustrated in Figure 20.5. Any risky combination has more utility than (lies above) the certain return, and the riskier the combination (the farther apart the two points connected) the greater the utility received from a given expected return.[4] Obviously,

---

[4] See M. Friedman and L. Savage, "The Utility of Choices Involving Risk," *The Journal of Political Economy*, August, 1948, pp. 279–304, for a discussion of the construction and shape of the utility function under risk. In this article it is suggested that the utility function may be S-shaped, as below:

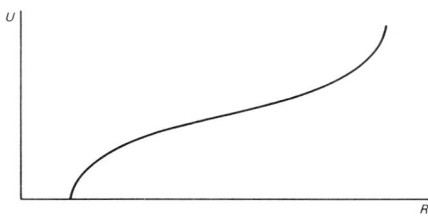

This could imply that the portfolio manager has a preference for certainty among the lower and intermediate levels of return and a preference for risk in the higher levels of return. The utility of the risky return may, in this case, be higher or lower than the equivalent certain return, depending on where the possible outcomes (the points to be connected) lay on the utility schedule and the average of the associated utilities.

since the portfolio manager receives more utility from the same return as the risk increases, he may be said to be a risk seeker.

It is difficult to imagine that the majority of investors could be risk seekers. It is even difficult to imagine that one rational individual would be a risk seeker. Rather, it may be safely assumed that the general market exhibits the characteristics of the risk averter and that portfolio preferences are based on the rational decisions of the risk averter. What risk-seeker effects are incorporated into the market should be quickly offset by the counteractions of the risk averters. Therefore, we consider the actions of the risk seeker irrational[5] and consider only the risk averter for the remainder of the chapter.

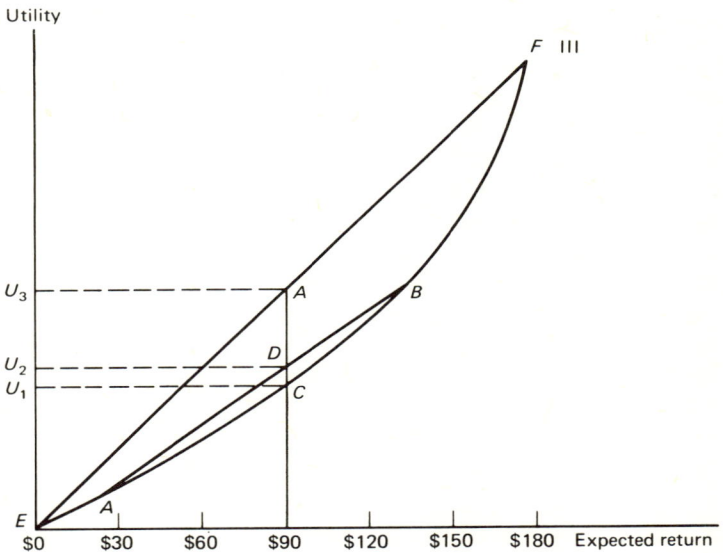

Figure 20.5. Preference for risk.

It is now possible to construct a relationship between the manager's utility function and his aversion to risk. Assuming that the manager is a risk averter, we can plot the various combinations of expected return and risk that give him a constant utility (the indifference curve). This is illustrated in Figure 20.6. The manager's total utility increases with an increase in the expected return and decreases with an increase in risk. In terms of Figure 20.6 an increase in the expected return moves

---

[5] William Sharpe, *Portfolio Theory and Capital Markets,* McGraw-Hill Book Company, New York, 1970, p. 193.

the curve to the right, and an increase in risk moves the curve to the left. These two opposing forces generate a constant utility at various combinations of expected return and risk. For example, assume that the combination of risk A and return A gives the same utility as the combination of risk B and return B, in Figure 20.6. This implies that the manager is satisfied with the increase in the expected return from A to B that compensates him for the increased risk from A to B. The schedule I is the indifference curve of this manager. On any point on this curve, the risk and expected return combination provides equal satisfaction. The indifference curve may be viewed as a trade-off between risk and the expected return necessary to maintain a constant utility. Most investors are risk averters, in that they demand higher expected returns for larger risks, and we assume risk aversion for the remainder of this chapter.

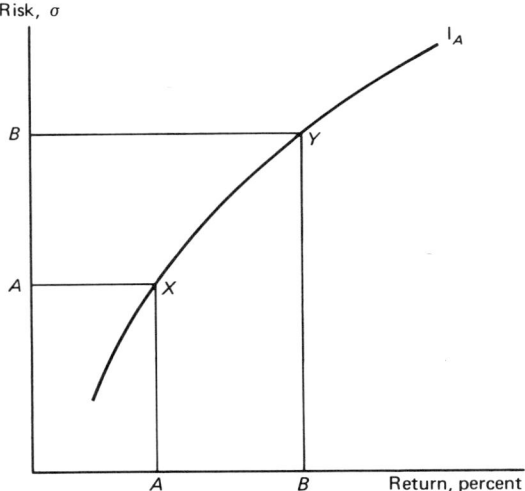

Figure 20.6. Indifference curve.

PORTFOLIO SELECTION

How can we determine a portfolio manager's aversion to risk? We know that he should insist on a higher return for more risk exposure, but to what degree should he be risk-averse? Each portfolio manager has his own degree of risk aversion, depending on his dislike for risk. We can query the manager about his dislike for risk and discover at which combinations of risk and expected return he is indifferent. The more conservative manager, one who is more averse to risk and demands a

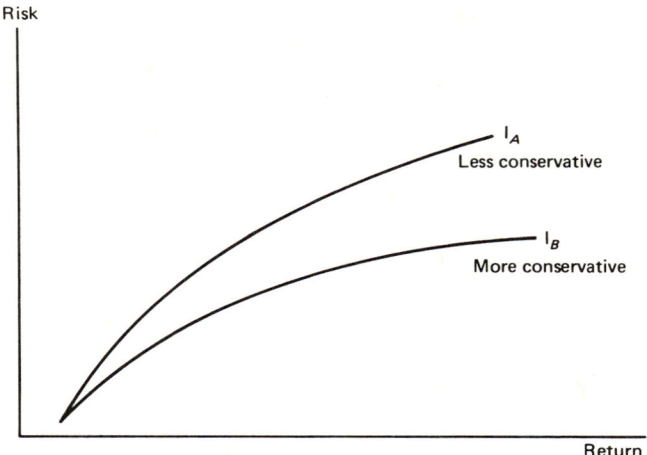

Figure 20.7. Comparison of indifference curves.

larger compensation for an increased risk exposure than another manager, demands a higher expected return with increased risk than the less conservative manager. In Figure 20.7, the more conservative manager has the less rapidly rising indifference curve.

Each portfolio manager has a series of indifference curves, as illustrated in Figure 20.8. The utility increases as the portfolio manager

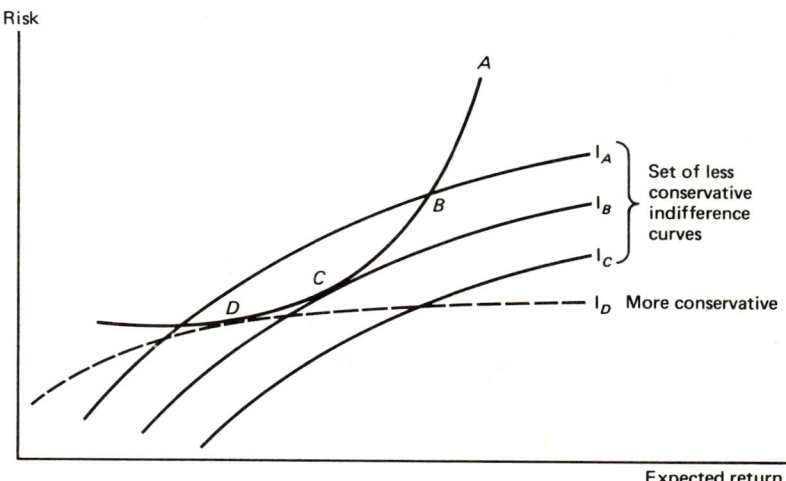

Figure 20.8. Selection of optimum portfolio.

moves down to the right, for as he moves to the right, the manager can achieve a higher expected return without an increase in risk.

The most attractive portfolio would be on the highest indifference curve. By comparing the indifference curve with the efficient frontier *ABCD*, we observe the portfolio that maximizes the manager's utility. In Figure 20.8, the point *C*, where a portfolio (in this case portfolio *C*) tangentially touches the indifference curve of highest utility, the manager's position is maximized.

A more conservative portfolio manager (I_D in Figure 20.8) might have selected portfolio *D* as the one that maximizes his utility. The point at which the efficient frontier tangentially touches the highest indifference curve determines the most attractive portfolio for the individual manager.

LIMITS OF DIVERSIFICATION

The degree to which portfolio diversification can reduce risk exposure (the standard deviation of the expected return) is limited to the extent that price movements among the securities in the portfolio are uncorrelated. If all stock prices were perfectly correlated and simultaneously moved in the same direction and magnitude, there could be no reduction in the risk of any portfolio. This is illustrated by the fact that when the correlation coefficient among stocks is $+1$, the standard deviation of the expected returns is identical with the weighted sum of the standard deviations of the individual securities. In the specific terms of the stock market, the broad, general price movements of the market, which are characterized by the large number of stock price movements in the same direction, lessen the risk-reducing potential of diversification.[6]

Those risks associated with the broad market price movements may be viewed as systematic risk that cannot be "diversified away." Those risks associated with the price movements which are not connected with the broad, general market price movements but are related only with the individual industry or stock, may be "diversified away." These latter, unsystematic risks may be reduced if less than perfectly correlated stocks are combined into one portfolio. By "diversifying away" the unsystematic risk, we can construct a portfolio equal in expected return to previous portfolios but with less risk exposure. The higher the degree of correlation among the price movements of stocks caused by some common general market factor, the less effective is diversification in lowering any portfolio's standard deviation of expected returns.

---

[6] J. Lintner, "Security Prices, Risk and Maximum Gain from Diversification," *Journal of Finance,* December, 1965, pp. 587–615, and William Sharpe, "Capital Asset Prices: A Theory of Equilibrium under Conditions of Risk," *Journal of Finance,* September, 1964, pp. 425–442.

SHAPE OF THE RISK FUNCTION

The shape of the risk function describes the relationship between an increase in risk and an increase in expected return along the efficient frontier. The efficient frontier in Figure 20.8 runs along line $ABCD$ (E is not included because it has a lower return and higher risk). Note that if the portfolio manager decided to move from portfolio D to portfolio C, he would gain proportionately more in expected return than he would add to his risk exposure. In other words, in the change from D to C the distance moved along the horizontal expected return axis is greater than that moved on the vertical risk axis. Moving from portfolio B to portfolio A on the same efficient frontier gives the exact opposite result. In this case, the increase in expected return is quite small compared with the larger increase in the risk exposure that accompanies the move.

The three basic forms that the risk function may take are illustrated in Figure 20.9. The linear form in Figure 20.9a implies that each time the expected return is increased, there is a proportionate increase in the level of risk exposure. Therefore, moving from one portfolio to another along the efficient frontier does not improve the risk-expected return relationship. The risk-rewarding form in Figure 20.9b implies that higher levels of risk exposure are more than proportionately rewarded. A portfolio of high risk could, under these circumstances, be expected to be more attractive to any portfolio manager whose utility function did not preclude the exposure to the higher levels of risk. The risk-penalizing form implies that the higher levels of risk exposure are less than proportionately rewarding. Any portfolio manager who, under these circumstances, chooses to remain in the high risk levels would not be expected to return a profit commensurate with the risk that he had exposed himself to.

The linear form receives its greatest support from Sharpe.[7] Sharpe suggests that in addition to the risk assets in the portfolio, there is also a riskless asset P that is expected to return the pure interest rate at which the portfolio manager can lend excess funds or borrow additional funds. This would mean, as illustrated in Figure 20.10, that the efficient frontier would no longer be line $ABCD$. Instead, it would be the straight line PCQ. It can be seen from Figure 20.10 that the portfolios that lie on the former efficient frontier between portfolios C and D are no longer efficient. The portfolios between P and C now have the same risk exposure but higher expected returns. The expected return to the portfolios between P and C is the weighted average of the expected return of the riskless asset and of portfolio C. Note that the portfolios between P and C offer a higher return than any portfolio of equal risk on line PDC. The addition of the riskless asset to the possible portfolios

[7] Sharpe, *op. cit.*, pp. 425–442.

has shifted the efficient frontier to the right. Among the portfolios from P to C, the investor is lending funds that are not invested in portfolio C by buying riskless debt. Among the portfolios from C to Q, the investor is borrowing in order to leverage his investment in portfolio C and, thereby, increase his expected return and risk.

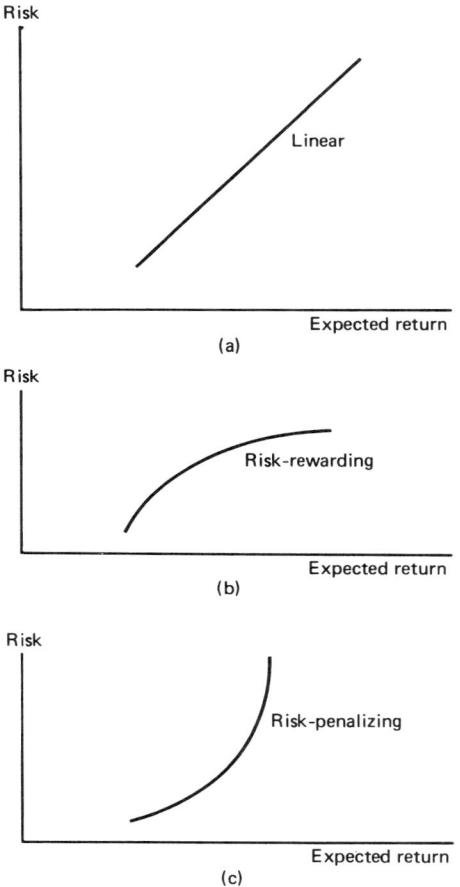

Figure 20.9. Possible risk functions.

In Figure 20.10, the securities markets cannot be in equilibrium, for now every investor attempts to maximize his risk-expected return relationship by purchasing various combinations of riskless asset P and portfolio C. In their attempt to move all their funds into portfolio C and asset P, the portfolio managers sell off portfolios A, B, and D. The price of these portfolios is driven down in the attempt, and their expected return is driven up. Thus, without changing the risk attached to these portfolios, their expected return is increased. This has the effect of moving these portfolios to the right in Figure 20.11 until line *ABCD* is flush with line *PCQ* and the efficient frontier is the straight line *PDCBA*. Now, the efficient frontier consists of those portfolios which lie on line *PDCBA* in Figure 20.11. The most attractive portfolio on the *PDCBA* frontier maximizes the manager's utility. For example, in Figure 20.11, the portfolio manager with a utility function of U_A will find a portfolio between points *D* and *C* as the most attractive; the manager with the utility function U_B will find a portfolio between points *C* and *B* to be the most attractive.

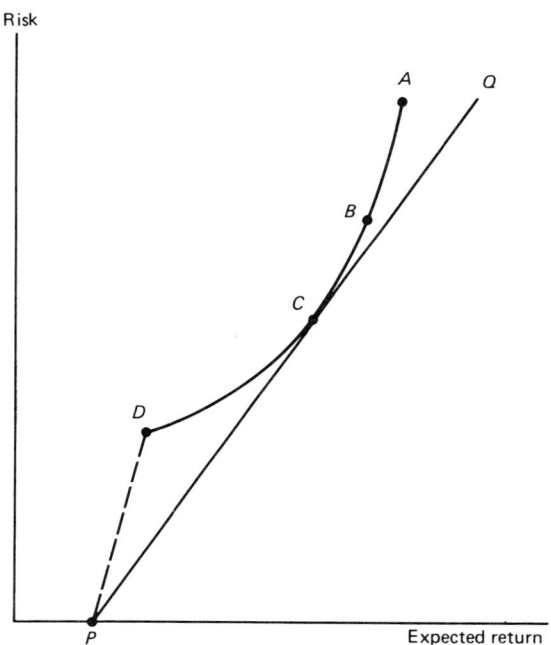

Figure 20.10 Efficient frontier with riskless asset.

The evidence on the shape of the risk function generally seems to support the linear shape.[8] The steepness of the slope of the line has varied in time and with different securities. The Soldofsky and Miller

---

[8] W. Sharpe, "Risk Aversion in the Stock Market: Some Empirical Evidence;" *Journal of Finance,* September, 1965, pp. 416–442, and R. Soldofsky and R. Miller, "Risk Premium Curves for Different Classes of Long-Term Securities," *Journal of Finance,* June, 1969, pp. 429–445.

study found for the 1950 to 1966 period that the portfolio manager who increased his risk exposure by 1 percent could have increased his expected return by almost 1.15 percent. In intervening periods, however, the relationship between increased risk and return varied. For example, between 1959 and 1966, an increase of 1 percent in the risk exposure resulted in a 0.93 percent additional return. Brealey[9] found

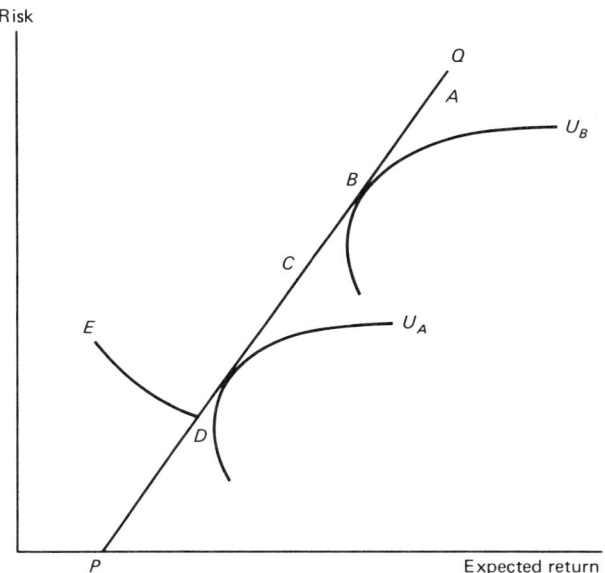

Figure 20.11. Efficient frontier with market equilibrium.

that the higher risk mutual funds did not provide commensurately higher returns, implying that the risk function may be risk penalizing. The evidence to date on the risk function seems to indicate that it may move from one shape to another, depending on the money and capital market environment.[10]

SUMMARY

Portfolio theory establishes a relationship between a portfolio's expected return and its level of risk exposure as the criterion for selecting the

---

[9] Brealey, op. cit., p. 52.

[10] A dissenting view on the risk-return relationship is offered in L. Richardson, "Do High Risks Lead to High Returns?" *Financial Analysts Journal*, March-April, 1970, pp. 88–99.

most attractive portfolio. The expected return is the weighted sum of the expected returns of the securities in the portfolio. The level of risk exposure is measured by the standard deviation of the expected returns. The standard deviation of the expected returns can be reduced by proper diversification, so that for every expected return there is one portfolio that has the lowest risk exposure. The reduction of the risk by diversification can be accomplished by combining into one portfolio securities whose price movements are less than perfectly, positively correlated. With less than perfect, positive correlation, the covariances among the price movements of the securities serve to lessen the standard deviation. The largest reduction in the standard deviation can occur when the securities in the portfolio are perfectly, negatively correlated. No reduction can occur when the securities are perfectly, positively correlated. The limit on diversification in the securities markets depends on the degree to which the price movements are correlated with a common market factor. The correlation that results from a response to a general market factor cannot be diversified away, because the prices of all securities move in tandem to this factor. The portfolio manager can only diversify away the price movements that are solely associated with the individual security.

This reduction in risk will continue to be sought by the portfolio manager until at each expected return there is one portfolio with the lowest risk exposure. And, vice versa, at each level of risk exposure there is one portfolio with the highest return. Portfolios that are attainable and conform to these standards form what is known as the efficient frontier. Along this frontier lie all the portfolios that will provide the highest expected return for this particular level of risk. From among these portfolios, the manager must select that one which renders him the highest utility.

The shape of the risk function, which describes the trade-off between increased risk and increased expected return, may be linear, risk-rewarding, or risk-penalizing. The evidence on the shape of the risk function tends to favor the linear form, but these findings also show that the shape and the position of the function may vary with the market environment and the security.

QUESTIONS

20.1 What are the two criteria for determining the investment merits of a portfolio?

20.2 Distinguish between security analysis and portfolio analysis.

20.3 How is the expected return of a portfolio computed? How might the expected return of a security be computed?

20.4 Within the context of portfolio management, what is associated with a large standard deviation of return?

20.5 How is the correlation among securities measured? What is the implication of security correlation? What degree of correlation is most desirable for a portfolio designed to minimize risk?

20.6 What is the covariance measure? Explain its effect on the portfolio.

20.7 What is the attainable set?

20.8 Describe the characteristics of portfolios that lie along the efficient frontier.

20.9 Explain each of the utility functions illustrated in Figure 20.3.

20.10 Explain why, in Figure 20.4, the expected utility is given at point U_2.

20.11 What is an indifference curve?

20.12 Explain the selection of a portfolio that maximizes the manager's utility.

20.13 Discuss the limits of diversification in terms of general price movements in the stock market.

20.14 Explain the implications of the three basic risk functions.

20.15 Explain why the introduction of a riskless asset to the portfolio would cause the efficient frontier to take the form of a straight line.

PROBLEMS

20.1 What is the expected return to a portfolio composed of the following securities?

Security	Expected return, percent	Proportion, percent
1	10	20
2	15	20
3	20	60

What would be the expected return if the proportion of each security in the portfolio were 25, 50, and 25 percent respectively?

20.2 Compute the risk on each portfolio in Problem 20.1 from the following information:

$\sigma_1 = 0.2 \quad c_{12} = 0.5$
$\sigma_2 = 0.3 \quad c_{13} = 0.1$
$\sigma_3 = 0.5 \quad c_{23} = -0.3$

$$\sigma_P = \sqrt{\sum_{i=1}^{N}\sum_{j=1}^{N} X_i X_j \sigma_{ij}}$$

20.3 Plot the attainable set of the following portfolios and the efficient frontier if the proportion of the securities in the portfolio cannot be changed:

Security	Expected return, percent	Risk, percent
1	5	3
2	7	2
3	10	1
4	12	2
5	14	3
6	15	3
7	13	7
8	18	5
9	8	8
10	22	7

20.4 The following equations are for the efficient frontier and a portfolio manager's indifference curve. Find the expected return and risk of his optimum portfolio:

Efficient frontier: $R_k = (R_t - 2)^2 + 2$
Indifference curve: $R_k = -(R_t - 6)^2 + 10$
where R_k = risk and R_t = return (both in percent)

REFERENCES

Baumol, William J. "Mathematical Analysis of Portfolio Selection," *Financial Analysts Journal,* 22:95–99, September-October, 1966.

Brealey, Richard A. *An Introduction to Risk and Return from Common Stocks,* Cambridge, Mass.: The M.I.T. Press, 1969.

Hanoch, Giora, and Haim Levy. "Efficient Portfolio Selection with Quadratic and Cubic Utility," *The Journal of Business,* 43:181–189, April, 1970.

Lintner, John. "Security Prices, Risk and Maximal Gains from Diversification," *The Journal of Finance,* 20:587–616, December, 1965.

———. "The Valuation of Risk Assets and the Selection of Risky Investments in Stock Portfolios and Capital Budgets," *The Review of Economics and Statistics,* 47:13–37, February, 1965.

Markowitz, Harry. "Portfolio Selection," *The Journal of Finance,* 7:77–91, March, 1952.

———. *Portfolio Selection: Efficient Diversification of Investments,* New York: John Wiley & Sons, Inc., 1959.

Merton, Robert C. "Lifetime Portfolio Selection under Uncertainty: The Continuous-Time Case," *The Review of Economics and Statistics,* 51:247–257, August, 1969.

Mossin, Jan. "Optimal Multiperiod Portfolio Policies," *The Journal of Business,* 41:215–229, April, 1968.

Samuelson, Paul A. "Lifetime Portfolio Selection by Dynamic Stochastic Programming," *The Review of Economics and Statistics,* 51:239–246, August, 1969.

Sharpe, William F. "Capital Asset Prices: A Theory of Market Equilibrium under Conditions of Risk," *The Journal of Finance,* 19:425–442, September, 1964.

———. "Risk-Aversion in the Stock Market: Some Empirical Evidence," *The Journal of Finance,* 20:416–422, September, 1965.

———. "Reply," *The Journal of Business,* 41:235–236, April, 1968.

Soldofsky, R., and R. Miller. "Risk Premium Curves for Different Classes of Long-Term Securities," *The Journal of Finance,* 24:429–445, June, 1969.

Treynor, Jack L., William W. Priest, Jr., Lawrence Fisher, and Catherine A. Higgins. "Using Portfolio Composition to Estimate Risk," *Financial Analysts Journal,* 24:93–100, September-October, 1968.

West, Richard R. "Mutual Fund Performance and the Theory of Capital Asset Pricing: Some Comments," *The Journal of Business,* 41:230–234, April, 1968.

21
Portfolio Management

In attempting to construct an efficient, optimal portfolio, the manager encounters administrative problems. These are construction considerations that must be handled if the portfolio is to conform to the optimization criteria. Portfolio management concerns the tactical decisions that must be made to construct a portfolio that is optimized and will continue to be optimal.

The major tactical considerations occur in the areas of (1) portfolio objectives, (2) portfolio size, (3) portfolio readjustment, (4) selection of individual securities, and (5) leverage. This chapter discusses these considerations and some of the ideas that have been suggested for coping with them.

The last section of this chapter explores the use of options in the portfolio as a method of increasing expected return.

PORTFOLIO OBJECTIVES

One of the first tasks of the portfolio manager, as an individual or as a manager for others, is to determine his or his client's investment objectives. Does he desire a portfolio that is capital gains-oriented or income-oriented? His preference probably depends on factors such as his age, his current income, his expenditure needs, and his tax bracket. Those who desire income-oriented portfolios generally require a supplement to their current income. Among these investors are the retired individual and others on relatively low or fixed income. Usually, these income-oriented investors are more averse to risk exposure, because they cannot afford to sustain a period of curtailed income. Thus, they are willing to sacrifice the higher expected returns for the lower risk exposure. To maximize their utility, these investors generally prefer the lower expected return-lower risk exposure portfolios on the efficient frontier, such as portfolio D in Figure 21.1. These particular portfolios on the efficient frontier frequently consist of the more dividend-oriented stocks and fixed income securities. There tends to be less risk attached to the expected return of these securities, and they cluster in the portfolios on the lower end of the efficient frontier.

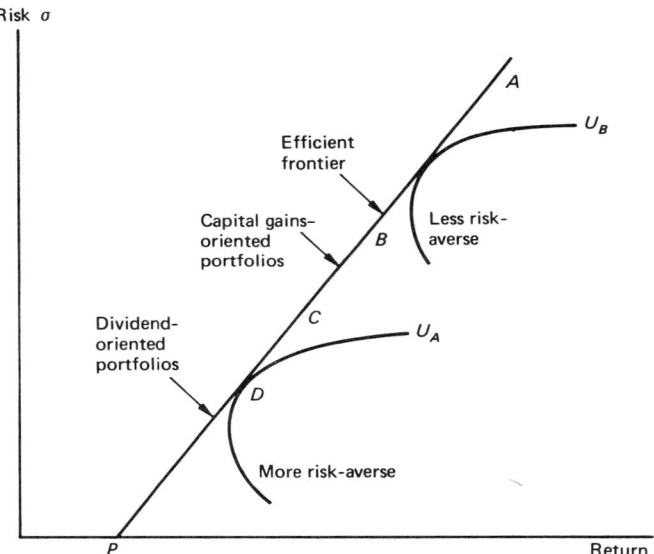

Figure 21.1. Portfolio objectives and the efficient frontier.

The capital gains-oriented portfolios tend to cluster at the other extreme of the efficient frontier, such as portfolio B in Figure 21.1. Here, the risk as well as the expected return is higher. Investors who seek the expected return through growth of their capital, rather than dividends, generally hold these portfolios. These investors are typically younger and less dependent on their portfolio to supplement their current income. They are also typically less averse to risk, for the loss of their invested capital usually has only a marginal effect on their present wealth status.

Between the extremes of the portfolios on the efficient frontier lie the portfolios that tend to combine the characteristics of both the income-oriented and the capital gains-oriented portfolio. Generally, the more income-oriented the portfolio, the less the associated risk exposure, for the expected return is derived from the more certain dividends and interest payments.

PORTFOLIO SIZE

What is the optimum number of securities in a portfolio? If too few securities are in a portfolio, the optimum reduction in risk by diversification may not be realized. If there are too many securities, the associated transaction costs may offset any expected diversification gains.

It has been suggested[1] that there is a relationship between the reduction in the standard deviation (risk) of the expected return on a portfolio and the number of securities in the portfolio. In general, the first few additional securities greatly contribute to the reduction in the standard deviation. Further additions to the portfolio contribute less and less to the reduction in the risk measure, until at the extreme, only the systematic risk of the general market remains. This is illustrated in Figure 21.2, which shows the reduction in risk decreasing as the number of securities in the portfolio increases, until, with a large number of securities, almost all the unsystematic risk, not derived from general market price movements, is eliminated, and only the systematic market risk remains.

[1] J. Evans and S. Archer, "Diversification and the Reduction of Dispersion: An Empirical Analysis," *Journal of Finance*, December, 1968, pp. 761–768.

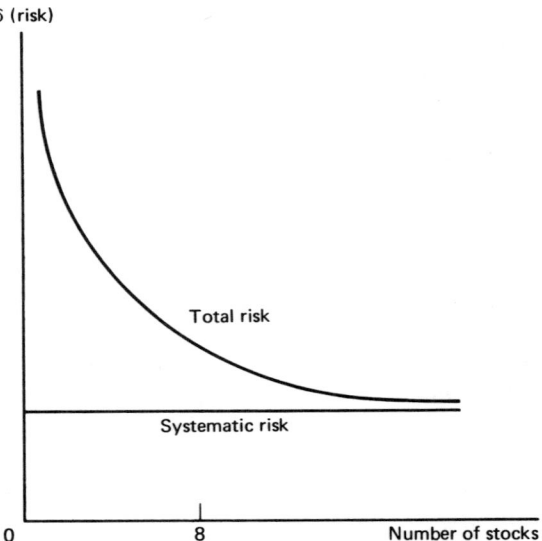

Figure 21.2. Relationship of risk to number of stocks.

(From J. Evans and S. Archer, "Diversification and the Reduction of Dispersion: An Empirical Analysis," Journal of Finance, December, 1968.)

There is also a relationship between the costs of the portfolio and the number of securities in it. There are certain costs, such as transaction expenses, attached to the addition of another security. If these costs offset the expected gains from the addition of this security, the addition of this security and further diversification are no longer justified.

The problem may be illustrated in the following example:

Portfolio	Expected return, percent	Standard deviation	Number of securities
1	16	5.69	20
2	16	5.75	15

Portfolio 1 is more efficient than portfolio 2 because it has a lower risk for the same expected return. But is it worth the extra cost of the five additional securities to reduce the standard deviation 0.06? The answer depends on the investor's cost in adding the five securities. If it is less than the expected gain, the further diversification pays. The results of Evans and Archer's work show that after approximately eight securities, the addition of another security only slightly reduces the risk. After eight securities are in his portfolio, the investor must have relatively low transaction costs to gain from further diversification.

The other portfolio size consideration is the absolute dollar amount. A large dollar portfolio seems to limit the flexibility of the portfolio manager. Obviously, a large dollar amount placed in the optimum number of securities of about eight leads to relatively large positions in each of the eight securities. The necessity of large positions limits the manager's ability to acquire or liquidate a security from his portfolio without upsetting the prevailing market price. The larger dollar portfolios seem to be at a disadvantage. They have little to gain from diversifying beyond eight securities but expose themselves to the risk of being unable to market their securities at the going price if they undertake to limit the number of securities in their portfolios.

READJUSTMENT

Once the portfolio size has been decided and the funds have been allocated among the securities in the portfolio, the manager should be on the efficient frontier. But what happens to his position on the efficient frontier if his expectations about future returns or risks change? A change shifts the efficient frontier and may then make the present portfolio less than optimal. For example, in Figure 21.3, the efficient frontier has shifted from $ABCDE$ to $A'B'C'D'E'$. Now the optimal portfolio is

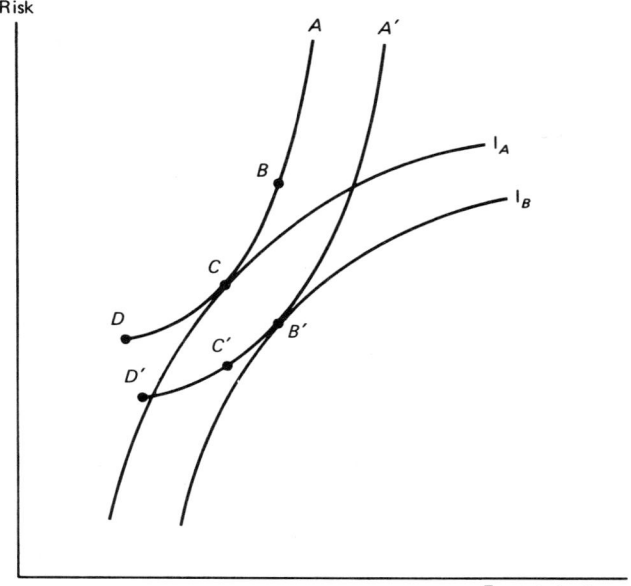

Figure 21.3. Shift in the efficient frontier.

B' instead of C. This change in the frontier could have arisen as security prices change or as new information is digested into the analyst's estimation of future risks and returns.

To move his portfolio to the new optimal portfolio in the new efficient frontier, the manager must weigh the advantages of moving against the cost of moving.[2] The major advantage of moving is to return the portfolio to an optimal position. The costs of moving depend on the extent of the necessary readjustment and the frequency with which readjustment occurs. If the necessary readjustment requires substantial changes in the portfolio, with a large number of shares to be sold and purchased, the associated transaction costs could offset any gain of returning to an optimum position. If frequent readjustment is undertaken, the cost of numerous transactions would again be high. It is, for example, conceivable that the portfolio needs daily readjustment as security prices change and new information becomes available. Perhaps, more realistically, the portfolio could require readjustment every 3 months, or every 6 months, or every year. The problems of readjustment are also present in the growing portfolio. An infusion of new funds may remove the portfolio from the efficient frontier, because the proportion of cash in the portfolio may become too great.

[2] Keith Smith, "Alternative Procedures for Revising Investment Portfolios," *Journal of Financial and Quantitative Analysis,* December, 1968, pp. 371–403.

There are several strategies that could be used when readjustment is necessary. One, the portfolio manager could do nothing; that is, he could buy and hold the securities without any readjustment. Two, he could restore the original proportions of the portfolio at the beginning of each review period. In this case, securities that now represent a larger proportion of the portfolio than they originally did would be sold in part, and the proceeds invested in those securities in the portfolio which now represent less than their original proportion. After this readjustment, all securities should be represented in their original proportions. No new securities would be added to the portfolio, and no securities that were originally included in the portfolio would be deleted. Three, he could make the complete transition from the present portfolio to the new optimal portfolio. This case could include adding new securities and deleting old securities from the portfolio. Four, the portfolio manager could perform a controlled transition; that is, he could gradually readjust from the present portfolio toward the optimal portfolio. Each time he added or dropped a security he would compare the benefits—in graphic terms, the distance moved from the present portfolio to one on a higher indifference curve—with the cost of the partial transition. Each change in the portfolio would bring new expected return and risk characteristics. These would be compared with those of the previous portfolio to determine if the transition will move the portfolio to a higher indifference curve. If the cost of the partial transition, including the costs of gathering the information about the new securities, exceeded the benefits, the portfolio manager would stop readjusting his portfolio. The objective for the manager is to make as much progress toward the optimal portfolio as possible before the expense outweighs the benefits.

The empirical evidence[3] on this point suggests that no one strategy is best at all times and in all market environments. There seems to be some advantage to the controlled transition readjustment strategy when revision is done on an annual basis. The complete revision strategy, however, does not materially differ from the buy-hold strategy. With shorter periods of portfolio revision—less than 1 year—the buy-hold and the controlled transitions readjustment strategies outperformed the other strategies, because they were the ones that limited the associated transaction costs. There is also evidence to suggest that the buy-hold strategy may allow risk reduction[4] that is unavailable to the other strategies that require shorter holding periods for any securities in the portfolio. The longer holding periods allow the random occurrences to be more completely dissolved into the results of the portfolio and increase the probability of a profitable performance.

[3] *Ibid.*
[4] R. Machol and E. Lerner, "Risk, Ruin and Investment Analysis," *Journal of Financial and Quantitative Analysis,* December, 1969, pp. 473–492.

SELECTION BASIS

How does the portfolio manager select the stocks for his original portfolio or his readjustments? In other words, how does he generate the expected return and risk measures used as inputs in the portfolio's construction. The original suggestion in portfolio theory was to require the security analyst to provide estimates of the expected return and risk for each security by using the PDV evaluation framework of the previous chapters. Thus, the security analyst is called on to give an estimated range of possible prices for the security at the end of the period along with the probability attached to each outcome. The analyst would construct such a probability distribution of possible future prices by using various combinations of estimated expected earnings and dividends, expected interest rates, purchasing power risk premiums, business risk, and financial risk in computing the expected PDV. For example, assume that the analyst forecasts the following possible values with their associated probabilities for dividends, the interest rate plus purchasing power risk premium factor, business risk, and financial risk:

Probability	$\hat{D}$	$(\hat{i}+\hat{p})$	$\hat{b}$	$\hat{f}$
0.10	0.80	0.07	0.02	0.01
0.20	0.90	0.06	0.02	0.01
0.40	1.00	0.06	0.02	0.01
0.20	1.10	0.06	0.02	0.01
0.10	1.20	0.05	0.02	0.01

Then the PDV of the various combinations would be as follows:

Probability	PDV
0.10	$ 8.00
0.20	10.00
0.40	11.11
0.20	12.22
0.10	15.00

which has an expected value of $11.18 and a standard deviation of 1.723 as inputs into the portfolio model.

If we assume that changes in stock prices are a function of some common market factor, such as interest rates, a simplified model[5] for

---

[5] W. Sharpe, "A Simplified Model for Portfolio Analysis," *Management Science*, January, 1963, pp. 277–293.

computing the expected return and the risk measure has been developed. The simplified model assumes that the expected return and the variation around it (the risk measure) are, for the most part, commonly determined by their relationship with some underlying market or economic factor. We have already seen in the earlier parts of this text that a large part of all security price movements is affected by changes in the real interest rate and purchasing power risk components of the discount factor. Changes in the pure rate of interest may cause changes in the discount factor and general changes in all security prices. We have, therefore, estimated a large part of price changes in all stocks by estimating changes in the one general factor that causes most of the general price movement. The assumption is that past changes in the general index caused a specific change in the return to each security. We can estimate this relationship and use it to forecast future returns. The more accurate the measurement, the less risk is attached to the forecast.

Assuming that the expected returns and the risks are commonly determined by some general market or economic factor I, we can relate the return R_i to any security in the following manner:

(21.1) $R_i = A_i + B_i I$

where R_i = expected return
A_i = constant parameter
B_i = relationship between general factor I and expected return
I = general factor, that is, the Standard and Poor's Stock Index or pure interest rate

Estimating Equation (21.1) by regression analysis, we can establish values for A_i, and B_i. If we then estimate I, we can generate an expected return for any security i by solving Equation (21.1) for R_i. For example, if the calculated regression were $R_i = 0.03 + 1(I)$, the expected return for security i would be 0.03 plus the increase in the general factor. If we estimate I, a market index, to rise 25 percent in the future period, we can anticipate that security i will rise by 28 percent. Other securities could rise by less than 25 percent, and still others more than 25 percent. The risk attached to achieving this anticipated return R_i is the historical variation Q_i in the relationship between R_i and I. Q_i equals the risk that the estimated R_i, in this case 28 percent, will not be realized. The larger Q_i, the greater the risk attached to the expected return R_i, for the greater the dispersion of possible returns around R_i. Graphically, Figure 21.4 illustrates the relationship between the general factor I and the expected return R_i. B_i is the slope of the line, and Q_i is the standard error of the estimate, a measure of the dispersion around R_i.

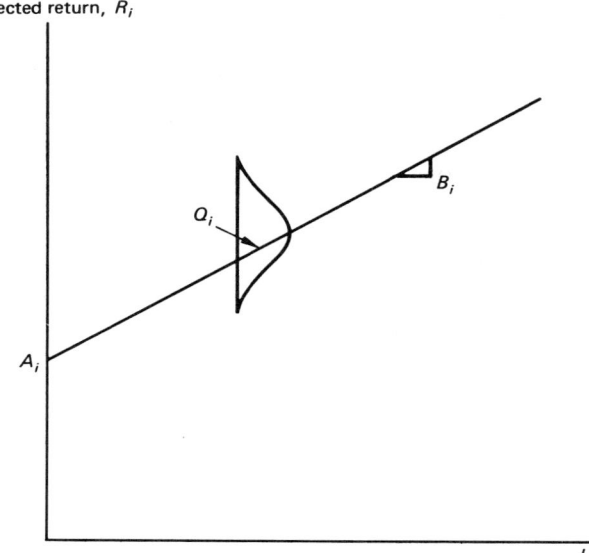

Figure 21.4. Relationship between R_i and I.

LEVERAGE

In addition to the other areas of portfolio management, the manager may have the option of borrowing funds to finance the purchase of additional securities. If the manager expects a higher return from his investments than the cost of borrowed funds, he also expects to increase his return on his investment with leverage. Leverage also increases the risk to the portfolio, however, because the variation in the expected return increases with the use of leverage. The exact degree to which the portfolio manager leverages is dependent on the utility that he receives from the additional expected return and risk associated with leveraging and on the legal and institutional restraints against borrowing. If the portfolio manager can receive a higher utility by leveraging, he presumably does so. Many legal barriers, however, may prevent the manager from borrowing either at all or as much as he desires. Many portfolios handled by institutional advisors, such as most mutual funds and trust funds, are prohibited from leveraging. The amount that an individual investor may borrow is regulated by the Federal Reserve System and constrained by the amount that lenders are willing to lend him.

The use of leverage enables the manager to expand the size of his optimal portfolio. The borrowed funds must be invested in the same securities and in the same proportions as the optimal portfolio if the manager is to remain on the efficient frontier. The borrowings allow a straight-line extension of the frontier from the optimal portfolio to the higher expected return and risk of the leveraged portfolio. The portfolios along this extension are larger versions of the optimal and are preferable to those lying on the old frontier to the left of the extension. Once the manager has decided on the characteristics of his optimal portfolio and his utility curve and has made the tactical decisions necessary in the problem areas of portfolio construction, he is prepared to explore possible methods of deriving still higher expected returns or lower risk from the portfolio. One suggested method has been the use of stock options.

STOCK OPTIONS AND THE PORTFOLIO

One suggested method[6] for returning a portfolio to its optimal position from a position to the left of the efficient frontier, as illustrated in Figure 21.5, is the use of stock options. In Figure 21.5, the present portfolio P_0 is not on the efficient frontier. The portfolio manager may sell a call option on a stock in his portfolio; that is, he sells the right for someone else to purchase, at a future date, the stock from his portfolio at a specific price. The amount that the manager receives for the call option increases the expected return to the portfolio. If the manager sells the option at a call price that does not alter the expected return from the security, the amount paid by the option purchaser is additional return to the portfolio. At the same time, if the sale of the option has not increased the risk of the portfolio, the effect of the increased expected return moves the portfolio to P_1 in Figure 21.5, closer to the efficient frontier.

If the call option is exercised and the portfolio manager must surrender the security, the composition of the portfolio is changed and the risk exposure altered. The effect of deleting the security from the portfolio may lower the risk exposure and move the portfolio to P_2 in Figure 21.5. Note that the expected return has not been changed by the deletion of the security. The effect might also be undesirable in that the remaining securities might have a greater risk exposure, and the portfolio may move to P_3. This seems unlikely, however, because the security deleted from the portfolio is immediately replaced by the cash that is paid to the portfolio manager when he surrenders the stock. Because cash has no risk of capital loss by itself and no correlation with the remaining securities, the level of risk exposure is unlikely to rise. If the cash is not reinvested, however, but instead allowed to remain idle, the sacrificed return may be anticipated to lower the expected return. The longer the cash is allowed to remain idle, the lower the expected return,

---

[6] K. Smith, "Option Writing and Portfolio Management," *Financial Analysts Journal,* May-June, 1968, pp. 135–138.

unless, of course, the manager anticipates declining securities prices and the cash position seems attractive.

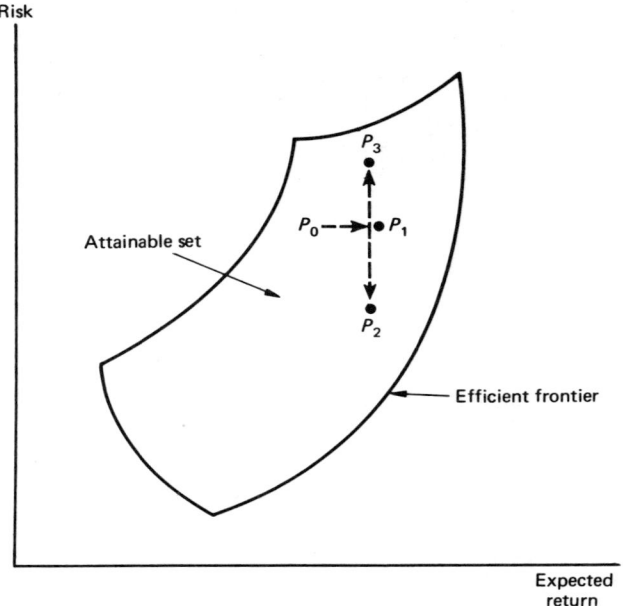

Figure 21.5. Stock option effect on portfolios.

If the sale of the call option alters the risk exposure as well as the expected return, the effect on the attractiveness of selling options must be more carefully examined. There is reason to suspect that the distribution around the expected return is altered.[7] When the manager sells call options on the stocks in his portfolio, he truncates his distribution of possible returns. All the possible returns above the exercise price of the option are no longer available to the portfolio. These returns belong to the option holder, because at any price above the exercise price, the option holder demands delivery of the stock. Assuming that an option is sold for *OP* with an exercise price of *EP*, the truncated distribution is illustrated in Figure 21.6. All the possible returns that before the sale of the option lay to the right of the exercise price have been sold to the option holder. The probability of these occurrences is incorporated into the return associated with the exercise price, because at any return to the right of *EP* the most that the portfolio will recieve is the exercise price.

[7] M. Chapman Findlay and S. Bolten, "The Use of Options in Portfolios," unpublished manuscript.

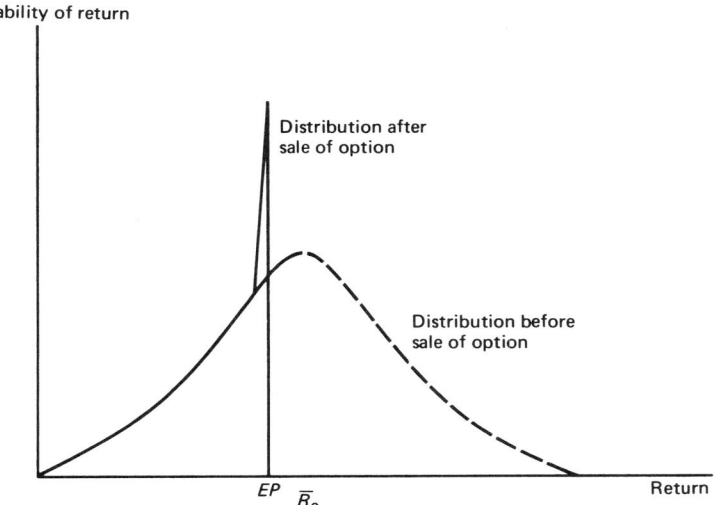

Figure 21.6. Truncated distribution.

The new distribution has a different expected return and different standard deviation from the previous one. The expected return and the standard deviation to the portfolio before the option sale are computed as we have previously done. For example, consider the following distribution of possible returns:

Return, percent	Probability
9	0.10
10	0.20
11	0.40
12	0.20
13	0.10

The expected return is 11 percent, and the standard deviation is 1.1 percent.

The expected return to the portfolio after the sale of the option is equal to the expected return of the truncated distribution plus the option premium,[8] which may be expressed as a percentage of original invest-

---

[8] For simplicity's sake, we contain the example to a stock that pays no dividend. If the stock paid dividends, the option seller would receive the dividends, but the exercise price would be reduced by the amount of the dividend, truncating the distribution even more.

ment in the stock, for example 2 percent. In the example, the truncated distribution might be as follows:

(1) Return, percent	(2) Option premium, percent	(3) Total return, percent (1) + (2)	(4) Probability
9	2	11	0.10
10	2	12	0.90

Note that each possible return has been increased by the option premium and that the probability of receiving a 10 percent return has risen to include the probability of all returns at or above 10 percent. The expected return is 11.9 percent, and the standard deviation is 0.30 percent. In this example, we have increased the expected return and decreased the risk by the use of options.

If we are to compare the portfolio before the sale of the option with the portfolio after the sale, we must consider the time factor involved in the receipt of the return. The expected return is not to be received until the end of the period. The option premium, on the other hand, is received at the beginning of the period. Because of the time value of money, the option premium is more valuable than the expected return to be received at the end of the period. In order to compare the portfolios, that portion of the expected return which is received at the end of the period must be discounted back to the present. In the example, the entire expected return of the prior portfolio must be discounted; in the after sale portfolio, only that portion of the return not connected with the sale of the option must be discounted.

We are now in a position to judge the relative merits of options in the portfolio. Assume that the portfolio before the option sale lies on the efficient frontier in an optimal position P_0, as in Figure 21.7, where the highest indifference curve is tangent to the frontier. If the option sale increases the expected return while, at the same time, reducing the standard deviation, the efficient frontier moves right to a higher indifference curve P_2. If the option sale reduces the standard deviation more than the expected return, however, the portfolio moves from P_0 to P_1 (a lower expected return and lower risk). Depending on the steepness and the magnitude of the movement from P_0 and the position of the efficient frontier, the portfolio after the option sale can be to the left P_1, to the right P_2, or to P_3 on the original efficient frontier. If the movement is to P_2, the sale of the option puts the portfolio on a higher indifference curve and is the appropriate course of action.

Stock options and the portfolio 459

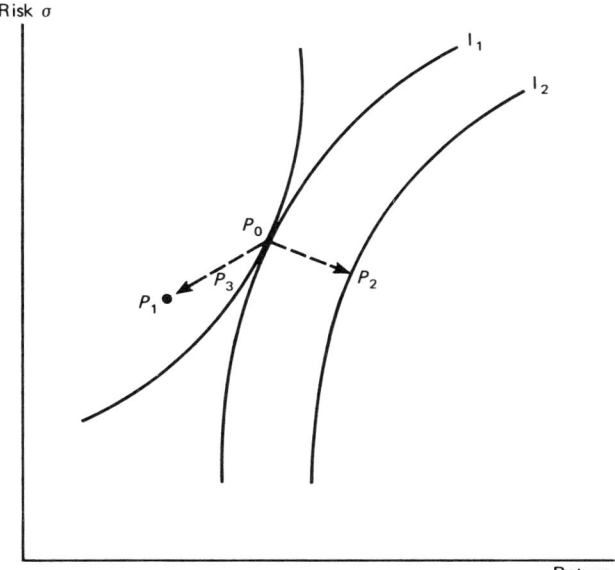

Figure 21.7. Option sale effect on portfolio.

Simulated experience with stock options[9] supports the use of stock options as an effective method of increasing portfolio returns. It is concluded that if the portfolio manager anticipates rising securities prices and has a diminishing marginal utility for money, his optimal strategy involves the selling of options on his portfolio.[10] If the portfolio manager anticipates no change in securities prices, his optimal strategy involves selling straddles.

If the portfolio manager anticipates rising securities prices and has an increasing marginal utility for money gains, the optimal strategy involves the purchasing of call options for the taxed investor. The implications for the tax-exempt investor are slightly different. Because the premium on an option sold by a tax-exempt investor is considered related business income (taxed) and that from the unexpired part of a straddle is short-term capital gain (not taxed), the optimal strategy is the purchasing of call options and the selling of straddles. But regardless of the individual portfolio circumstances, the use of stock options is a potential source of improving portfolio performance.

[9] B. Malkiel and R. Quandt, *Strategies and Rational Decision in the Securities Options Market,* The M.I.T. Press, Cambridge, Mass., 1969.
[10] *Ibid.,* p. 159.

SUMMARY

Portfolio management concerns the tactical decisions that must be made to construct a portfolio that is optimal and will continue to be so. This implies that the portfolio manager must consider the following: (1) the portfolio objectives, (2) the portfolio size, (3) portfolio readjustment, (4) the selection of individual securities, and (5) leverage.

The portfolio objectives should match those of the portfolio owner. Usually this involves concentrating funds in income-oriented or capital gains-oriented portfolios, depending on the manager's degree of risk aversion.

The portfolio size criterion determines the optimal number of securities in a portfolio. It is generally concluded that after a relatively few carefully selected securities are in the portfolio, most of the gains from diversification are accomplished. Any further gains may be offset by the associated transaction costs involved in acquiring the gains.

Readjustment decisions may be made whenever the portfolio ceases to be efficient. The gain from moving the portfolio back to an efficient position must be weighed against the offsetting transaction costs associated with the readjustment. The evidence seems to suggest that partial readjustment is the most effective.

The selection of individual securities may be simplified by deriving the expected returns and the associated risk measure from the correlation of a security's return to a general market or economic factor. The optimal degree of leverage that the portfolio manager desires depends on his expectation of future securities prices, his aversion to the additional risk associated with leveraging, and the legal and institutional limits on his borrowing capacity.

The use of stock options may improve a portfolio's performance. The sale of a stock option generally truncates the distribution of possible returns and alters the portfolio's expected return and risk. By comparing the expected return and risk of the portfolio without options with the expected return and risk with options, we can determine whether the use of options is desirable. Simulated portfolio results demonstrate that the use of stock options may improve portfolio results.

QUESTIONS

21.1 In what areas do the major tactical considerations occur?

21.2 Describe the income-oriented investor. Describe the nature of his portfolio.

21.3 What considerations must be made in determining the number of securities in a portfolio?

21.4 What problems do large portfolios (in terms of absolute dollar amounts) present?

21.5 What factors must the portfolio manager consider when readjusting his portfolio in response to a shift in the efficient frontier?

21.6 Explain the controlled transition method of portfolio readjustment.

21.7 Explain the logic behind the simplified model for computing the expected return and risk.

21.8 How does leverage affect the efficient frontier?

21.9 What is a call option?

21.10 What effect does a call option have on the distribution of possible earnings?

21.11 What is the expected return to the portfolio when a call option has been sold against a security position in it?

21.12 Under what conditions would the efficient frontier shift right when a call option has been sold?

PROBLEMS

21.1 Using a certain economic index as the independent variable in a regression equation, an analyst has been able to estimate the return and risk associated with a particular stock. What would be the expected return and range of expected returns within one standard deviation if the index is expected to increase 12 percent during the year and has a standard deviation of 0.02 percent and the regression equation is $R = 0.03 + 0.9\,(I)$?

21.2 Build a simplified selection model for one of the stocks listed on the NYSE, using the weekly changes in the stocks price and the NYSE index for the latest quarter.

REFERENCES

Baumol, William J. "An Expected Gain-Confidence Limit Criterion for Portfolio Selection," *Journal of the Institute of Management Sciences,* 10:174–182, October, 1963.

Block, Frank E. "Elements of Portfolio Construction," *Financial Analysts Journal,* 25:123–129, May-June, 1969.

Blume, Marshall E. "Portfolio Theory: A Step toward Its Practical Application," *The Journal of Business,* 43:152–173, April, 1970.

Clarkson, Geoffrey P. *Portfolio Selection: A Simulation of Trust Investment,* Englewood Cliffs, N.J.: Prentice-Hall, Inc., 1962.

Cohen, Kalman J., and Jerry A. Pogue. "An Empirical Evaluation of Alternative Portfolio-Selection Models," *The Journal of Business,* 40:166–193, April, 1967.

Dietz, Peter O. *Pension Funds: Measuring Investment Performance,* New York: Columbia University and The Free Press, 1966.

Dince, Robert R. "Portfolio Income: A Test of a Formula Plan," *Journal of Financial and Quantitative Analysis,* 1:90–107, September, 1966.

Evans, John L., and Stephen H. Archer. "Diversification and the Reduction of Dispersion: An Empirical Analysis," *The Journal of Finance,* 23:761–768, December, 1968.

Findlay, M. Chapman, III, and Steven E. Bolten. "The Use of Options in a Portfolio," unpublished manuscript, 1970.

Fisher, Lawrence, and James Lorie. "Some Studies of Variability of Returns on Investments in Common Stocks," *The Journal of Business,* 43:99–134, April, 1970.

Latané, Henry A., and Donal L. Tuttle. "Criteria for Portfolio Building," *The Journal of Finance,* 22:359–374, September, 1967.

Latané, Henry A., and William E. Young. "Test of Portfolio Building Rules," *The Journal of Finance,* 29:595–612, September, 1969.

Lintner, John. "Security Prices, Risk, and Maximal Gains from Diversification," *The Journal of Finance,* 20:587–616, December, 1965.

Machol, Robert E., and Eugene M. Lerner. "Risk, Ruin and Investment Analysis," *Journal of Financial and Quantitative Analysis,* 4:473–492, December, 1969.

Malkiel, Burton Gordon, and Richard E. Quandt. *Strategies and Rational Decisions in the Securities Options Market,* Cambridge, Mass.: The M.I.T. Press, 1969.

Sharpe, William F. "A Simplified Model for Portfolio Analysis," *Journal of the Institute of Management Sciences,* 9:277–293, January, 1963.

———. "Capital Asset Prices: A Theory of Market Equilibrium under Conditions of Risk," *The Journal of Finance,* 19:425–442, September, 1964.

———. "Risk-Aversion in the Stock Market: Some Empirical Evidence," *The Journal of Finance,* 20:416–422, September, 1965.

———. "Security Prices, Risk, and Maximal Gains from Diversification: Reply," *The Journal of Finance,* 21:743–744, December, 1966.

Smith, Keith V. "A Transition Model for Portfolio Revision," *The Journal of Finance,* 22:425–440, September, 1967.

———. "Alternative Procedures for Revising Investment Portfolios," *Journal of Financial and Quantitative Analysis,* 3:371–403, December, 1968.

———. "Needed: A Dynamic Approach," *Financial Analysts Journal,* 23:115–117, May-June, 1967.

———. "Option Writing and Portfolio Management," *Financial Analysts Journal,* 24:135–138, May-June, 1968.

22
Formula Plans

Formula plans are mechanical sets of rules designed to overcome the problem of timing the allocation of funds to specific securities. The plans attempt to force the manager into committing funds at relatively low securities prices and selling securities at relatively high prices. In their rigorous application of the timing decision, the plans do not maximize the utility or achieve an optimal portfolio for the investor. Generally, the criteria for portfolio optimization are relegated to secondary importance, and the other criteria for portfolio construction are usually assumed away. Consequently, the problems of portfolio objectives, size, readjustment to an optimal position, the selection of securities, and the use of leverage receive little attention. The management of a portfolio by a formula plan seems to be suboptimal and for this reason has fallen into disuse among the more sophisticated portfolio managers. These plans may still be useful, however, to the investor who lacks confidence in his ability to time his investment decisions.

This chapter examines four basic plans: (1) dollar cost averaging, (2) constant dollar, (3) constant ratio, and (4) variable ratio. The mechanics, advantages, and limitations of each are discussed.

DOLLAR COST AVERAGING

With the dollar cost averaging plan, the manager invests a fixed dollar amount at prespecified intervals during a long period of time. This plan forces the investor to commit funds in selected securities at different levels during the cyclical movements in the price. As the price declines, the manager acquires more shares for the fixed dollar amount than at a higher price. This means that the weighted average cost of the shares will be lower than the average price that prevails in the market. For example, assume that a manager invests $1,000 in a stock at three different prices during the year as follows:

Purchase	Price per share	Number of shares
1	$25	40
2	50	20
3	40	25
		85

The total invested is $3,000 for 85 shares. The average price paid per share is

$$\frac{\$3,000}{85} \text{ or } \$35.30$$

If an equal number of shares had been purchased at the three different prices, the average price paid per share would have been $38.33. Because of the dollar cost averaging method used to acquire the shares, the average price paid is less than that which prevailed in the market.

Advantages

The advantages of the dollar cost averaging plan are (1) low average price, (2) easy use, (3) fixed timing considerations, and (4) applicability to both rising and falling markets. We have already seen that the average price paid will be lower than the average market price during the price cycle. The simplicity of the plan is obvious. The manager must decide in advance the sum and the periodic intervals at which he will invest. Once this is decided, the implementation is mechanical. At no other time is a decision about when to invest required. During the price cycle, the dollar cost averaging approach should produce a lower average price paid per share than the average market price.

Limitations

There are several limitations of the plan. The extra transaction costs associated with frequent, small purchases raise the price of the shares. The higher per share commissions and additional odd lot fees encountered under this plan account for most of this expense. The plan contains no formal indication of when to sell; it is strictly a strategy for buying. It does not eliminate the necessity for selecting the individual stocks that are to be purchased. There is no indication of the appropriate interval between purchases. If the interval is too long, the manager may miss the cyclical fluctuations in market prices and fail to gain the averaging advantage inherent in the plan. The averaging advantage does not yield a profit if the stock price is in a downward trend. If the price is in a downward trend, so that it is continually declining—in the extreme, becoming worthless—the opportunity to sell the acquired shares for a profit will not materialize. The present market price may be lower than the previous prices at which any of the shares were acquired, so that if the shares were sold, the investor would have a loss. Further, it is often difficult to obtain the funds during declining markets.

The dollar cost averaging approach seems to work better with the more volatile stock prices.[1] In fact, the approach depends on a cyclical pattern in stock prices, without which dollar cost averaging would not produce a lower average price. For example, constant or rising stock prices produce only a constant average price or a rising average price with each additional purchase. A constantly declining price may produce a lower average purchase price but provide no profit opportunity. The approach is somewhat limited to a secularly rising stock price with intermediary cyclical patterns. Because this has historically been the pattern of most stock prices, the dollar cost averaging method has produced reasonable results. The more volatile stock prices decline and rebound farther, forcing the purchase of more shares at a lower price.

The best way to use the dollar cost averaging method and still avoid many of its limitations is to apply it to the purchase of a no-load mutual fund. The problems of high transaction costs, stock selection, and downward trend in stock prices are eliminated. The broadly based no-load mutual fund should experience a price movement similar to that of the general market, allowing the averaging effect to work. The investor has only to decide on the particular fund and the length of the interval between purchases.

CONSTANT DOLLAR PLAN

The constant dollar plan starts with a fixed amount of money invested in selected stocks or bonds or cash. When the prices of the securities rise, the manager sells a sufficient dollar amount of securities to return the total value of the investment in securities to the original dollar amount. For example, if the manager had a portfolio of $100,000 in stocks and their market value rose to $125,000, he would sell $25,000 of the securities. If the market value of the portfolio declined to $75,000, he would commit new funds to the purchase of $25,000 of securities. The major limitation of this approach is its constraints on profit potential during periods of continually rising or falling prices. The major advantage is the automatism with which this plan forces the man-

---

[1] J. Cohen and E. Zinbarg, *Investment Analysis and Portfolio Management*, Richard D. Irwin, Inc., Homewood, Ill., 1967, pp. 536–542.

ager to switch from stocks to defensive securities in a rising market, and vice versa.

CONSTANT RATIO PLAN

The constant ratio plan maintains a specific ratio of stocks and bonds or cash in the portfolio as prices change. For example, the investor might decide to maintain a portfolio balance of 50 percent stocks and 50 percent bonds. If the market value of the stocks in the portfolio rose above 50 percent of the portfolio's total value, the manager would sell a sufficient dollar amount of stock to restore the 50:50 balance. The plan's objective is to force the manager to lighten his investment in those securities which are heading toward a cyclical peak and to increase his investment in those financial assets which are heading for a cyclical trough. The restoration of the original balance might be done every time that the ratio deviates a certain percentage from the original ratio. For example, in this case, the manager might restore the original rates when the balance became 60:40.

The advantage of the constant ratio plan is the automatism with which it forces the manager to adjust countercyclically his portfolio. This approach does not eliminate the necessity of selecting individual securities, nor does it perform well if the prices of the selected securities do not move with the market. The major limitation to the constant ratio plan, however, is the use of bonds as a haven for money generated from the sale of the rising stocks. Because both stocks and bonds are money and capital market instruments, they tend to respond to the same interest rate considerations in the present discounted evaluation framework. This means, at times, they may both rise and decline in value at approximately the same time. There is limited advantage to be gained from shifting out of the rising stocks into the bonds if, in the downturn, both securities' prices decline. If the decline in bond prices is of the same magnitude as that in stock prices, most, if not all, of the gains from the constant ratio plan are eliminated. If the constant ratio plan is used, it must be coordinated between securities that do not tend to move simultaneously in the same direction and in the same magnitude.

VARIABLE RATIO PLAN

The variable ratio plan is similar to the constant ratio plan except that at varying levels of the market price, the proportions of the ratio change. When the price of stocks in the portfolio rises, a new ratio is adopted that decreases the representation of stocks in the portfolio and increases the proportion of defensive securities.

To implement the plan, the user is required to estimate a long-term trend in the price of stocks. Around this trend line, the manager constructs zones that represent a specified percentage of deviation from the estimated trend line. Associated with each one of these zones is a ratio of stocks to bonds that is held if the actual market level deviates sufficiently from the estimated market trend line to enter one of these zones. The zones above the trend line are connected with ratios that shift the portfolio's emphasis to the defensive securities (short-term bonds or cash). The zones below the trend line are connected with ratios that shift the emphasis to stocks. The plan takes its name from the variation in the ratios as stock prices move from zone to zone.

For example, consider the following ratios in relation to the deviations from the estimated trend line:

Deviation from trend line, percent	Ratio	
	Bonds	Stocks
+50	100	0
+40	90	10
+30	80	20
+20	70	30
+10	60	40
0	50	50
−10	40	60
−20	30	70
−30	20	80
−40	10	90
−50	0	100

As the deviations from the trend line rise (fall), the proportion of stocks in the portfolio is diminished (increased). This forces the portfolio manager to sell more aggressively stocks on the way up and to acquire more aggressively stocks on the way down than would be the case under the constant ratio plan.

We can graphically illustrate a variable ratio plan as in Figure 22.1. The solid trend line represents the investor's expectation of future stock prices. Zones 1 and 3 represent, respectively, 10 and 20 percent deviations above the expected trend, and zones 2 and 4 represent, respectively, 10 and 20% deviations below the expected trend. Starting at 40, the portfolio is 50 percent in stocks and 50 percent in bonds. Once the actual stock price index passes through a zone, such as point *a*, the portfolio is adjusted to the next proportion, in this case 60 percent bonds and 40 percent stocks. When the actual stock price index passes through point b, the proportion is again 50:50. Below point c the portfolio is 40 percent bonds and 60 percent stocks, and above point d it is again 50:50.

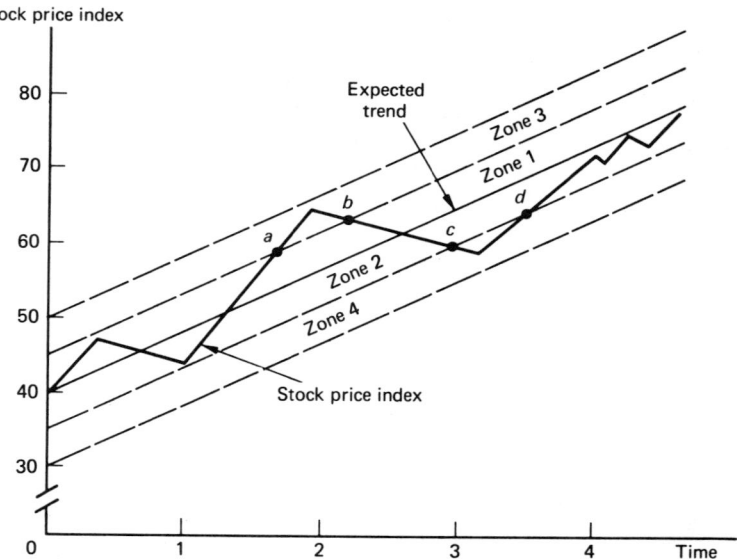

Figure 22.1. Formula planning zones.

The variable ratio plan does not have to use the trend in market prices; the same mechanical rules may be used if the deviations from the estimated dividend yield or the estimated price/earnings ratio are used. If the dividend yield deviates above (below) the estimated dividend yield by a certain percentage, a higher (lower) ratio of stocks to defensive securities is implemented. A similar system could be based on deviations in the price/earnings ratio.

Advantages

The major advantage of this plan is the automatism that it forces on the portfolio manager in emphasizing countercyclical portfolio changes. The manager cannot be emotionally swayed by the price swings in the market.

Limitations

The major limitations of the variable ratio plan are in the construction of the appropriate zones, trends, and ratios, the selection of specific securities, and the suboptimization of the portfolio. If the trend line that we use is not an accurate portrayal of what does happen, the counter-cyclical emphasis of the portfolio is destroyed. For example, if we foresee a falling trend when it actually rises, the deviations will be above the estimated trend line, and our portfolio will be concentrated in defensive issues during a rising market. If the zones are too small or the rates change the emphasis too rapidly, the portfolio will be concentrated in the defensive securities at a very early stage in the rising market and in the aggressive stocks at a very early stage in a falling market. This naturally limits the portfolio's performance. This approach, like all the other formula plans, does not optimize the manager's utility, because it deals only with the timing problem and disregards the other considerations in portfolio analysis.

SUMMARY

Formula plans are mechanical rules designed to solve the problem of timing the allocation of funds among the portfolio's possible investments. All the plans suffer from their emphasis on the timing problem to the exclusion of the other problems in portfolio analysis that have a bearing on optimizing the investor's position. Thus, these plans have limited application. Perhaps, the best remaining application is their use by the less sophisticated investor in acquiring shares of a selected no-load mutual fund.

QUESTIONS

22.1 Explain the mechanics and logic behind each of the formula plans. Be sure to include a discussion of the advantages and limitations of each plan.

22.2 Which kinds of stocks are best for the dollar cost averaging plan? Explain.

22.3 How might an analyst estimate the long-term trend in the price of a stock? How could he construct the zones that represent a specific percentage of deviation from the estimated trend line.

22.4 Why must the dollar cost averaging plan be used during a long period of time?

REFERENCES

Allen, Leon B. *A Method for Stock Profits without Price Forecasting,* Garden City, N.Y.: Doubleday & Company, Inc., 1962.

Amling, Frederick. *Investments: An Introduction to Analysis and Management,* Englewood Cliffs, N.J.: Prentice-Hall, Inc., 1965.

Ascher, L. W. "Dollar Averaging in Theory and Practice," *Financial Analysts Journal,* 16:51–53, September, 1960.

Cohen, Jerome B., and Edward D. Zinbarg. *Investment Analysis and Portfolio Management,* Homewood, Ill.: Dow Jones-Irwin, Inc., 1967.

Dince, Robert R. "Portfolio Income: A Test of a Formula Plan," *Journal of Financial and Quantitative Analysis,* 1:90–107, September, 1966.

Grodinsky, Julius. *Investments,* New York: The Ronald Press Company, 1953.

Leffler, George L. *The Stock Market,* 3d ed., revised by Loring C. Farwell, New York: The Ronald Press Company, 1963.

Appendix

From *Managerial Finance,* 2d ed., by J. Fred Weston and Eugene F. Brigham, Copyright © 1966 by Holt, Rinehart and Winston, Inc. Reprinted by permission. Table A also appears in the present text as Table 3.4, p. 31, and Table B also appears as Table 3.8, p. 35.

Appendix 472

TABLE A Present Value of $1 Due at End of *n* Years

Year	1%	2%	3%	4%	5%	6%	7%	8%	9%	10%	12%	14%	15%
1	.990	.980	.971	.962	.952	.943	.935	.926	.917	.909	.893	.877	.870
2	.980	.961	.943	.925	.907	.890	.873	.857	.842	.826	.797	.769	.756
3	.971	.942	.915	.889	.864	.840	.816	.794	.772	.751	.712	.675	.658
4	.961	.924	.889	.855	.823	.792	.763	.735	.708	.683	.636	.592	.572
5	.951	.906	.863	.822	.784	.747	.713	.681	.650	.621	.567	.519	.497
6	.942	.888	.838	.790	.746	.705	.666	.630	.596	.564	.507	.456	.432
7	.933	.871	.813	.760	.711	.665	.623	.583	.547	.513	.452	.400	.376
8	.923	.853	.789	.731	.677	.627	.582	.540	.502	.467	.404	.351	.327
9	.914	.837	.766	.703	.645	.592	.544	.500	.460	.424	.361	.308	.284
10	.905	.820	.744	.676	.614	.558	.508	.463	.422	.386	.322	.270	.247
11	.896	.804	.722	.650	.585	.527	.475	.429	.388	.350	.287	.237	.215
12	.887	.788	.701	.625	.557	.497	.444	.397	.356	.319	.257	.208	.187
13	.879	.773	.681	.601	.530	.469	.415	.368	.326	.290	.229	.182	.163
14	.870	.758	.661	.577	.505	.442	.388	.340	.299	.263	.205	.160	.141
15	.861	.743	.642	.555	.481	.417	.362	.315	.275	.239	.183	.140	.123
16	.853	.728	.623	.534	.458	.394	.339	.292	.252	.218	.163	.123	.107
17	.844	.714	.605	.513	.436	.371	.317	.270	.231	.198	.146	.108	.093
18	.836	.700	.587	.494	.416	.350	.296	.250	.212	.180	.130	.095	.081
19	.828	.686	.570	.475	.396	.331	.276	.232	.194	.164	.116	.083	.070
20	.820	.673	.554	.456	.377	.312	.258	.215	.178	.149	.104	.073	.061
25	.780	.610	.478	.375	.295	.233	.184	.146	.116	.092	.059	.038	.030
30	.742	.552	.412	.308	.231	.174	.131	.099	.075	.057	.033	.020	.015

Year	16%	18%	20%	24%	28%	32%	36%	40%	50%	60%	70%	80%	90%
1	.862	.847	.833	.806	.781	.758	.735	.714	.667	.625	.588	.556	.526
2	.743	.718	.694	.650	.610	.574	.541	.510	.444	.391	.346	.309	.277
3	.641	.609	.579	.524	.477	.435	.398	.364	.296	.244	.204	.171	.146
4	.552	.516	.482	.423	.373	.329	.292	.260	.198	.153	.120	.095	.077
5	.476	.437	.402	.341	.291	.250	.215	.186	.132	.095	.070	.053	.040
6	.410	.370	.335	.275	.227	.189	.158	.133	.088	.060	.041	.029	.021
7	.354	.314	.279	.222	.178	.143	.116	.095	.059	.037	.024	.016	.011
8	.305	.266	.233	.179	.139	.108	.085	.068	.039	.023	.014	.009	.006
9	.263	.226	.194	.144	.108	.082	.063	.048	.026	.015	.008	.005	.003
10	.227	.191	.162	.116	.085	.062	.046	.035	.017	.009	.005	.003	.002
11	.195	.162	.135	.094	.066	.047	.034	.025	.012	.006	.003	.002	.001
12	.168	.137	.112	.076	.052	.036	.025	.018	.008	.004	.002	.001	.001
13	.145	.116	.093	.061	.040	.027	.018	.013	.005	.002	.001	.001	.000
14	.125	.099	.078	.049	.032	.021	.014	.009	.003	.001	.001	.000	.000
15	.108	.084	.065	.040	.025	.016	.010	.006	.002	.001	.000	.000	.000
16	.093	.071	.054	.032	.019	.012	.007	.005	.002	.001	.000	.000	
17	.080	.060	.045	.026	.015	.009	.005	.003	.001	.000	.000		
18	.069	.051	.038	.021	.012	.007	.004	.002	.001	.000	.000		
19	.060	.043	.031	.017	.009	.005	.003	.002	.000	.000			
20	.051	.037	.026	.014	.007	.004	.002	.001	.000	.000			
25	.024	.016	.010	.005	.002	.001	.000	.000					
30	.012	.007	.004	.002	.001	.000	.000						

TABLE B Present Value of $1 per Year for *n* Years

Year	1%	2%	3%	4%	5%	6%	7%	8%	9%	10%
1	0.990	0.980	0.971	0.962	0.952	0.943	0.935	0.926	0.917	0.909
2	1.970	1.942	1.913	1.886	1.859	1.833	1.808	1.783	1.759	1.736
3	2.941	2.884	2.829	2.775	2.723	2.673	2.624	2.577	2.531	2.487
4	3.902	3.808	3.717	3.630	3.546	3.465	3.387	3.312	3.240	3.170
5	4.853	4.713	4.580	4.452	4.329	4.212	4.100	3.993	3.890	3.791
6	5.795	5.601	5.417	5.242	5.076	4.917	4.766	4.623	4.486	4.355
7	6.728	6.472	6.230	6.002	5.786	5.582	5.389	5.206	5.033	4.868
8	7.652	7.325	7.020	6.733	6.463	6.210	5.971	5.747	5.535	5.335
9	8.566	8.162	7.786	7.435	7.108	6.802	6.515	6.247	5.985	5.759
10	9.471	8.983	8.530	8.111	7.722	7.360	7.024	6.710	6.418	6.145
11	10.368	9.787	9.253	8.760	8.306	7.887	7.499	7.139	6.805	6.495
12	11.255	10.575	9.954	9.385	8.863	8.384	7.943	7.536	7.161	6.814
13	12.134	11.348	10.635	9.986	9.394	8.853	8.358	7.904	7.487	7.103
14	13.004	12.106	11.296	10.563	9.899	9.295	8.745	8.244	7.786	7.367
15	13.865	12.849	11.938	11.118	10.380	9.712	9.108	8.559	8.060	7.606
16	14.718	13.578	12.561	11.652	10.838	10.106	9.447	8.851	8.312	7.824
17	15.562	14.292	13.166	12.166	11.274	10.477	9.763	9.122	8.544	8.022
18	16.398	14.992	13.754	12.659	11.690	10.828	10.059	9.372	8.756	8.201
19	17.226	15.678	14.324	13.134	12.085	11.158	10.336	9.604	8.950	8.365
20	18.046	16.351	14.877	13.590	12.462	11.470	10.594	9.818	9.128	8.514
25	22.023	19.523	17.413	15.622	14.094	12.783	11.654	10.675	9.823	9.077
30	25.808	22.397	19.600	17.292	15.373	13.765	12.409	11.258	10.274	9.427

Year	12%	14%	16%	18%	20%	24%	28%	32%	36%
1	0.893	0.877	0.862	0.847	0.833	0.806	0.781	0.758	0.735
2	1.690	1.647	1.605	1.566	1.528	1.457	1.392	1.332	1.276
3	2.402	2.322	2.246	2.174	2.106	1.981	1.868	1.766	1.674
4	3.037	2.914	2.798	2.690	2.589	2.404	2.241	2.096	1.966
5	3.605	3.433	3.274	3.127	2.991	2.745	2.532	2.345	2.181
6	4.111	3.889	3.685	3.498	3.326	3.020	2.759	2.534	2.339
7	4.564	4.288	4.039	3.812	3.605	3.242	2.937	2.678	2.455
8	4.968	4.639	4.344	4.078	3.837	3.421	3.076	2.786	2.540
9	5.328	4.946	4.607	4.303	4.031	3.566	3.184	2.868	2.603
10	5.650	5.216	4.833	4.494	4.193	3.682	3.269	2.930	2.650
11	5.988	5.453	5.029	4.656	4.327	3.776	3.335	2.978	2.683
12	6.194	5.660	5.197	4.793	4.439	3.851	3.387	3.013	2.708
13	6.424	5.842	5.342	4.910	4.533	3.912	3.427	3.040	2.727
14	6.628	6.002	5.468	5.008	4.611	3.962	3.459	3.061	2.740
15	6.811	6.142	5.575	5.092	4.675	4.001	3.483	3.076	2.750
16	6.974	6.265	5.669	5.162	4.730	4.033	3.503	3.088	2.758
17	7.120	5.373	5.749	4.222	4.775	4.059	3.518	3.097	2.763
18	7.250	6.467	5.818	5.273	4.812	4.080	3.529	3.104	2.767
19	7.366	6.550	5.877	5.316	4.844	4.097	3.539	3.109	2.770
20	7.469	6.623	5.929	5.353	4.870	4.110	3.546	3.113	2.772
25	7.843	6.873	6.097	5.467	4.948	4.147	3.564	3.122	2.776
30	8.055	7.003	6.177	5.517	4.979	4.160	3.569	3.124	2.778

TABLE C Compound Sum of $1

Year	1%	2%	3%	4%	5%	6%	7%	8%	9%	10%
1	1.010	1.020	1.030	1.040	1.050	1.060	1.070	1.080	1.090	1.100
2	1.020	1.040	1.061	1.082	1.102	1.124	1.145	1.166	1.188	1.210
3	1.030	1.061	1.093	1.125	1.158	1.191	1.225	1.260	1.295	1.331
4	1.041	1.082	1.126	1.170	1.216	1.262	1.311	1.360	1.412	1.464
5	1.051	1.104	1.159	1.217	1.276	1.338	1.403	1.469	1.539	1.611
6	1.062	1.126	1.194	1.265	1.340	1.419	1.501	1.587	1.677	1.772
7	1.072	1.149	1.230	1.316	1.407	1.504	1.606	1.714	1.828	1.949
8	1.083	1.172	1.267	1.369	1.477	1.594	1.718	1.851	1.993	2.144
9	1.094	1.195	1.305	1.423	1.551	1.689	1.838	1.999	2.172	2.358
10	1.105	1.219	1.344	1.480	1.629	1.791	1.967	2.159	2.367	2.594
11	1.116	1.243	1.384	1.539	1.710	1.898	2.105	2.332	2.580	2.853
12	1.127	1.268	1.426	1.601	1.796	2.012	2.252	2.518	2.813	3.138
13	1.138	1.294	1.469	1.665	1.886	2.133	2.410	2.720	3.066	3.452
14	1.149	1.319	1.513	1.732	1.980	2.261	2.579	2.937	3.342	3.797
15	1.161	1.346	1.558	1.801	2.079	2.397	2.759	3.172	3.642	4.177

Year	12%	14%	15%	16%	18%	20%	24%	28%	32%
1	1.120	1.140	1.150	1.160	1.180	1.200	1.240	1.280	1.320
2	1.254	1.300	1.322	1.346	1.392	1.440	1.538	1.638	1.742
3	1.405	1.482	1.521	1.561	1.643	1.728	1.907	2.067	2.300
4	1.574	1.689	1.749	1.811	1.939	2.074	2.364	2.684	3.036
5	1.762	1.925	2.011	2.100	2.288	2.488	2.932	3.436	4.007
6	1.974	2.195	2.313	2.436	2.700	2.986	3.635	4.398	5.290
7	2.211	2.502	2.660	2.826	3.185	3.583	4.508	5.629	6.983
8	2.476	2.853	3.059	3.278	3.759	4.300	5.590	7.206	9.217
9	2.773	3.252	3.518	3.803	4.435	5.160	6.931	9.223	12.166
10	3.106	3.707	4.046	4.411	5.234	6.192	8.594	11.806	16.060
11	3.479	4.226	4.652	5.117	6.176	7.430	10.657	15.112	21.199
12	3.896	4.818	5.350	5.936	7.288	8.916	13.215	19.343	27.983
13	4.363	5.492	6.153	6.886	8.599	10.699	16.386	24.759	36.937
14	4.887	6.261	7.076	7.988	10.147	12.839	20.319	31.691	48.757
15	5.474	7.138	8.137	9.266	11.974	15.407	25.196	40.565	64.359

Year	36%	40%	50%	60%	70%	80%	90%
1	1.360	1.400	1.500	1.600	1.700	1.800	1.900
2	1.850	1.960	2.250	2.560	2.890	3.240	3.610
3	2.515	2.744	3.375	4.096	4.913	5.832	6.859
4	3.421	3.842	5.062	6.544	8.352	10.498	13.032
5	4.653	5.378	7.594	10.486	14.199	18.896	24.761
6	6.328	7.530	11.391	16.777	24.138	34.012	47.046
7	8.605	10.541	17.086	26.844	41.034	61.222	89.387
8	11.703	14.758	25.629	42.950	69.758	110.200	169.836
9	15.917	20.661	38.443	68.720	118.588	198.359	322.688
10	21.647	28.925	57.665	109.951	201.599	357.047	613.107
11	29.439	40.496	86.498	175.922	342.719	642.684	1164.902
12	40.037	56.694	129.746	281.475	582.622	1156.831	2213.314
13	54.451	79.372	194.619	450.360	990.457	2082.295	4205.297
14	74.053	111.120	291.929	720.576	1683.777	3748.131	7990.065
15	100.712	155.568	437.894	1152.921	2862.421	6746.636	15181.122

TABLE D Sum of an Annuity of $1

Year	1%	2%	3%	4%	5%	6%	7%	8%
1	1.000	1.000	1.000	1.000	1.000	1.000	1.000	1.000
2	2.010	2.020	2.030	2.040	2.050	2.060	2.070	2.080
3	3030	3.060	3.091	3.122	3.152	3.184	3.215	3.246
4	4.060	4.122	4.184	4.246	4.310	4.375	4.440	4.506
5	5.101	5.204	5.309	5.416	5.526	5.637	5.751	5.867
6	6.152	6.308	6.468	6.633	6.802	6.975	7.153	7.336
7	7.214	7.434	7.662	7.898	8.142	8.394	8.654	8.923
8	8.286	8.583	8.892	9.214	9.549	9.897	10.260	10.637
9	9.369	9.755	10.159	10.583	11.027	11.491	11.978	12.488
10	10.462	10.950	11.464	12.006	12.578	13.181	13.816	14.487
11	11.567	12.169	12.808	13.486	14.207	14.972	15.784	16.645
12	12.683	13.412	14.192	15.026	15.917	16.870	17.888	18.977
13	13.809	14.680	15.618	16.627	17.713	18.882	20.141	21.495
14	14.947	15.974	17.086	18.292	19.599	21.051	22.550	24.215
15	16.097	17.293	18.599	20.024	21.579	23.276	25.129	27.152
16	17.258	18.639	20.157	21.825	23.657	25.673	27.888	30.324
17	18.430	20.012	21.762	23.698	25.840	28.213	30.840	33.750
18	19.615	21.412	23.414	25.645	28.132	30.906	33.999	37.450
19	20.811	22.841	25.117	27.671	30.539	33.760	37.379	41.446
20	22.019	24.297	26.870	29.778	33.066	36.786	40.995	45.762
25	28.243	32.030	36.459	41.646	47.727	54.865	63.249	73.106
30	34.785	40.568	47.575	56.085	66.439	79.058	94.461	113.283

Year	9%	10%	12%	14%	16%	18%	20%	24%
1	1.000	1.000	1.000	1.000	1.000	1.000	1.000	1.000
2	2.090	2.100	2.120	2.140	2.160	2.180	2.200	2.240
3	3.278	3.310	3.374	3.440	3.506	3.572	3.640	3.778
4	4.573	4.641	4.779	4.921	5.066	5.215	5.368	5.684
5	5.985	6.105	6.353	6.610	6.877	7.154	7.442	8.048
6	7.523	7.716	8.115	8.536	8.977	9.442	9.930	10.980
7	9.200	9.487	10.089	10.730	11.414	12.142	12.916	14.615
8	11.028	11.436	12.300	13.233	14.240	15.327	16.499	19.123
9	13.021	13.579	14.776	16.085	17.518	19.086	20.799	24.712
10	15.193	15.937	17.549	19.337	21.321	23.521	25.959	31.643
11	17.560	18.531	20.655	23.044	25.733	28.755	32.150	40.238
12	20.141	21.384	24.133	27.271	30.850	34.931	39.580	50.985
13	22.953	24.523	28.029	32.089	36.786	42.219	48.497	64.110
14	26.019	27.975	32.393	37.581	43.672	50.818	59.196	80.496
15	29.361	31.772	37.280	43.842	51.659	60.965	72.035	100.815

TABLE D (Continued)

Year	28%	32%	36%	40%	50%	60%	70%	80%
1	1.000	1.000	1.000	1.000	1.000	1.000	1.000	1.000
2	2.280	2.320	2.360	2.400	2.500	2.600	2.700	2.800
3	3.918	4.062	4.210	4.360	4.750	5.160	5.590	6.040
4	6.016	6.362	6.725	7.104	8.125	9.256	10.503	11.872
5	8.700	9.398	10.146	10.846	13.188	15.810	18.855	22.370
6	12.136	13.406	14.799	16.324	20.781	26.295	33.054	41.265
7	16.534	18.696	21.126	23.853	32.172	43.073	57.191	75.278
8	22.163	25.678	29.732	34.395	49.258	69.916	98.225	136.500
9	29.369	34.895	41.435	49.153	74.887	112.866	167.983	246.699
10	38.592	47.062	57.352	69.814	113.330	181.585	286.570	445.058
11	50.399	63.122	78.998	98.739	170.995	291.536	488.170	802.105
12	65.510	84.320	108.437	139.235	257.493	467.458	830.888	1444.788
13	84.853	112.303	148.475	195.929	387.239	748.933	1413.510	2601.619
14	109.612	149.240	202.926	275.300	581.859	1199.293	2403.968	4683.914
15	141.303	197.997	276.979	386.420	873.788	1919.869	4087.745	8432.045

Glossary[1]

ACCELERATED DEPRECIATION: Depreciation methods that write off the cost of an asset at a faster rate than the write-off under the straight-line method.

ACCRUED INTEREST: Interest accrued on a bond since the last interest payment was made. The buyer of the bonds pays the market price plus accrued interest. Exceptions include bonds that are in default and income bonds.

ADVANCE-DECLINE LINE: see breath of market.

ALL OR NONE ORDER: A market or limited price order which is to be executed in its entirety or not at all. Bids or offers on behalf of all or none orders may not be made in stocks, but may be made in bonds when the number of bonds is fifty or more.

ALTERNATIVE ORDER-EITHER/OR ORDER: An order to do either of two alternatives—such as, either sell (buy) a particular stock at a limit price or sell (buy) on stop. If the order is for one unit of trading when one part of the order is executed on the happening of one alternative, the order on the other alternative is treated as cancelled. If the order is for an amount larger than one unit of trading, the number of units executed determines the amount of the alternative order to be treated as cancelled.

AMORTIZE: To liquidate on an installment basis; an amortized loan is one in which the principal amount of the loan is repaid in installments during the life of the loan.

ANNUAL REPORT: The formal financial statement issued yearly by a corporation to its shareowners. The annual report shows assets, liabilities, earnings—how the company stood at the close of the business year and how it fared profit-wise during the year.

---

[1] The terms defined here came from the following sources:
New York Stock Exchange, Glossary of Investment Language
Weston, F. and Brigham, E., *Managerial Finance,* 3d edition, N.Y., Holt, Rinehart & Winston, 1969.

Glossary 478

ANNUITY: A series of payments of a fixed amount for a specified number of years.

ARREARAGE: Overdue payment; frequently, omitted dividend on preferred stocks.

ARBITRAGE: Process of buying and simultaneously selling the same or equivalent securities in different markets.

ASSETS: Everything that a corporation owns or that is due to it: Cash, investments, money due it, materials and inventories, which are called current assets; buildings and machinery, which are known as fixed asets; and patents and goodwill, called intangible assets.

ATTAINABLE SET: All possible portfolios attainable within the constraint of the investor's funds.

AT THE CLOSE ORDER: A market order which is to be executed at or as near to the close as practicable.

AT THE OPENING OR AT THE OPENING ONLY ORDER: A market or limited price order which is to be executed at the opening of the stock or not at all, and any such order or portion thereof not so executed is treated as cancelled.

AVERAGES: Various ways of measuring the trend of securities prices, the most popular of which is the Dow-Jones average of 30 industrial stocks listed on the New York Stock Exchange.

BALANCE SHEET: A condensed statement showing the nature and amount of a company's assets, liabilities and capital on a given date. In dollar amounts the balance sheet shows what the company owned, what it owed, and the ownership interest in the company of its stockholders.

BALLOON PAYMENT: When a debt is not fully amortized, the final payment is larger than the preceeding payments and is called a "balloon" payment.

BANKRUPTCY: A legal procedure for formally liquidating a business carried out under the jurisdiction of courts of law.

BEARER BOND: A bond which does not have the owner's name registered on the books of the issuing company and which is payable to the holder.

BID AND ASKED: Often referred to as a quotation or quote. The bid is the highest price anyone has declared that he wants to pay for a security at a given time, the asked is the lowest price anyone will take at the same time.

BIG BOARD: A popular term for the New York Stock Exchange.

BLUE CHIP: Common stock in a company known nationally for the quality and wide acceptance of its products or services, and for its ability to make money and pay dividends.

BLUE SKY LAWS: A popular name for laws various states have enacted to protect the public against securities frauds. The term is believed to have originated when a judge ruled that a particular stock had about the same value as a patch of blue sky.

BOARD ROOM: A room for customers in a broker's office where opening, high, low and last prices of leading stocks are posted on a board throughout the market day.

BOND: Negotiable promissory note of corporation or public body.

BOND YIELD TABLE: Table of the average compound interest returns on bonds at various possible prices and coupon rates if held to maturity.

BOOK: A notebook the specialist in a stock uses to keep a record of the buy and sell orders at specified prices, in sequence of receipt, which are left with him by other brokers.

BOOK VALUE: An accounting term. Book value of a stock is determined from a company's records, by adding all assets (generally excluding such intangibles as goodwill), then deducting all debts and other liabilities, plus the liquidation price of any preferred issues. The sum arrived at is divided by the number of common shares outstanding and the result is book value per common share. Book value of the assets of a company or a security may have little or no significant relationship to market value.

BREAK-EVEN ANALYSIS: An analytical technique for studying the relation between fixed cost, variable cost, and profits. A break-even chart graphically depicts the nature of break-even analysis. The break-even point represents that volume of sales at which total costs equal total revenues (that is, profits equal zero).

BREATH OF MARKET: The cumulative index of the net differences between the number of price advances and declines.

BROKER: An agent, often a member of a stock exchange firm or an exchange member himself, who handles the public's orders to buy and sell securities or commodities. For this service a commission is charged.

BROKERS' LOANS: Money borrowed by brokers from banks for a variety of uses. Breath may be used by specialists and odd-lot dealers to help finance inventories of stocks they deal in; by brokerage firms to finance the underwriting of new issues of corporate and municipal securities; to help finance a firm's own investments; and to help finance the purchase of securities for customers who prefer to use the broker's credit when they buy securities.

BUSINESS RISK: The hazard of adverse economic developments in a corporation or a community which may cause unexpected variation in a firm's earnings.

CALL: (1) An option to buy (or "call") a share of stock at a specified price within a specific period. (2) The process of redeeming a bond or preferred stock issued before its normal maturity.

CALL LOAN: A loan which may be terminated or "called" at any time by the lender or borrower. Used to finance purchases of securities.

CALL PREMIUM: The amount in excess of par value that a company must pay when it calls a security.

CALL PRICE: The price that must be paid when a security is called. The call price is equal to the par value plus the call premium.

CALL PRIVILEGE: A provision incorporated into a bond or a share of preferred stock that gives the issuer the right to redeem (call) the security at a specified price.

CALLABLE: A bond issue, all or part of which may be redeemed by the issuing corporation under definite conditions before maturity. The term also applies to preferred shares which may be redeemed by the issuing corporation.

CALLING: The action of exercising the call privilege and redeeming securities prior to their maturity date.

CAPITAL ASSET: An asset with a life of more than one year that is not bought and sold in the ordinary course of business.

CAPITAL GAIN OR CAPITAL LOSS: Profit or loss from the sale of a capital asset. A capital gain, under current federal income tax laws, may be either short-term (6 months or less) or long-term (more than 6 months).

CAPITAL STOCK: All shares representing ownership of a business, including preferred and common.

CAPITAL STRUCTURE: The permanent long-term financing of the firm represented by long-term debt, preferred stock, and net worth (net worth consists of capital, capital surplus, and earned surplus). Capital structure is distinguished from financial structure, which includes short-term debt plus all reserve accounts.

CAPITALIZATION: Total amount of the various securities issued by a corporation. Capitalization may include bonds, debentures, preferred and common stock and surplus.

CASH FLOW: Reported net income of a corporation plus amounts charged off for depreciation, depletion, amortization, extraordinary charges to reserves, which are bookkeeping deductions and not paid out in actual dollars and cents.

CASH SALE: A transaction on the floor of the stock exchange which calls for delivery of the securities the same day. In "regular way" trades, the seller is to deliver on the fifth business day.

CERTIFICATE: The actual piece of paper which is evidence of ownership of stock in a corporation.

CENTRAL CERTIFICATE SERVICE (CCS): A department of Stock Clearing Corporation which conducts a central securities certificate operation through which clearing firms effect security deliveries between each other via computerized bookkeeping entries thereby reducing the physical movement of stock certificates.

CERTAINTY EQUIVALENTS: The amount of cash that someone would require with certainty to make him indifferent between this certain sum and a particular uncertain, risky sum.

CHARTIST: A technical analyst who uses graphic presentations of stock prices to predict future stock prices.

COLLATERAL: Securities or other property pledged by a borrower to secure repayment of a loan.

COLLATERAL TRUST BOND: A bond secured by collateral deposited with a trustee. The collateral is often the stocks or bonds of companies controlled by the issuing company but may be other securities.

COMMERCIAL PAPER: Short-term promissory notes of major corporations.

COMMISSION: The broker's fee for purchasing or selling securities of property for a client.

COMMISSION BROKER: An agent who executes the public's orders for the purchase or sale of securities or commodities.

COMMON STOCK: Securities which represent an ownership interest in a corporation. If the company has also issued preferred stock, both common and preferred have ownership rights, but the preferred normally has prior claim on dividends and, in the event of liquidation, assets. Claims of both common and preferred stockholders are junior to claims of bondholders or other creditors of the company. Common stockholders assume the greater risk, but generally exercise the greater control and may gain the greater reward in the form of dividends and capital appreciation.

COMPARATIVE BALANCE SHEET: A balance sheet in which each item is expressed as a percentage of the total assets or liabilities.

COMPARATIVE INCOME STATEMENT: An income statement in which each item is expressed as a percentage of total sales.

COMPOUND INTEREST: An interest rate that is applicable when interest in succeeding periods is earned not only on the initial principal but also on the accumulated interest of prior periods, Compound interest is contrasted to simple interest, in which returns are not earned on interest received.

COMPOUNDING: The arithmetic process of determining the final value of a payment or series of payments when compound interest is applied.

CONFIDENCE INDEX: The ratio of the yield on high grade bonds to the yield on low grade bonds.

CONGLOMERATE: A corporation seeking to diversify its operations by acquiring enterprises in widely varied industries.

CONSOLIDATED BALANCE SHEET: A balance sheet showing the financial condition of a corporation and its subsidiaries.

CONSTANT RATIO PLAN: A portfolio management plan which attempts to profit by adjusting stock-bond proportions to a fixed ratio.

CONVERSION PRICE: The effective price paid for common stock when the stock is obtained by converting either convertible preferred stocks or convertible bonds. For example, if a $1,000 bond is convertible into 20 shares of stock, the conversion price is $50 ($1,000/20).

CONVERSION RATIO: The number of shares of common stock that may be obtained by converting a convertible bond or share of convertible preferred stock.

CONVERTIBLE: A bond, debenture, or preferred share which may be exchanged by the owner for common stock or another security of the issuing firm.

CORNER: Buying of a stock or commodity on a scale large enough to give the buyer, or buying group, control over the price. A person who must buy that stock or commodity, for example one who is short, is forced to do business at an arbitrarily high price with those who obtained the corner.

CORRESPONDENT: A securities firm, bank or other financial organization which regularly performs services for another in a place or market to which the other does not have direct access. Securities firms may have correspondents in foreign countries or on exchanges of which they are not members.

COUPON BOND: Bond with interest coupons attached. The coupons are clipped as they come due and are presented by the holder for payment of interest.

COUPON RATE: The stated rate of interest on a bond.

COVERAGE OF FIXED CHARGES: The number of times available pretax earnings would cover bond interest and related charges.

COVERING: Buying a security previously sold short.

CREDIT BALANCE: The unborrowed cash in an investor's margin account.

CROSS-PRICE ELASTICITY OF DEMAND: The percentage change in demand for a product generated by the percentage in price of another product.

CUMULATIVE PREFERRED: A stock having a provision that if one or more dividends are omitted, the omitted dividends must be paid before dividends may be paid on the company's common stock.

CUMULATIVE VOTING: A method of voting for corporate directors which enables the shareholder to multiply the number of his shares by the number of directorships being voted on and cast the total for one director or a selected group of directors. Cumulative voting is required under the corporate laws of some states, is permitted in most others.

CURB EXCHANGE: Former name of the American Stock Exchange, second largest exchange in the country. The term comes from the market's origin on a street in downtown New York.

CURRENT ASSETS: Those assets of a company which are reasonably expected to be realized in cash, or sold, or consumed during the normal operating cycle of the business. These include cash, U.S. government bonds, receivables and money due usually within one year, and inventories.

CURRENT LIABILITIES: Money owed and payable by a company, usually within one year.

CURRENT RATIO: The ratio of a firm's current assets to its current liabilities.

CUSTOMERS' NET DEBIT BALANCES: Credit of New York Stock Exchange member firms made available to help finance customers' purchases of stocks, bonds and commodities.

DAY ORDER: An order to buy or sell which, if not executed, expires at the end of the trading day on which it was entered.

DEALER: An individual or firm in the securities business acting as a principal rather than as an agent. Typically, a dealer buys for his own account and sells to a customer from his own inventory. The dealer's profit or loss is the difference between the price he pays and the price he receives for the same security. The dealer's confirmation must disclose to his customer that he has acted as principal. The same individual or firm may function, at different times, either as broker or dealer.

DEBENTURE: A promissory note backed by the general credit of a company and usually not secured by a mortgage or lien on any specific property.

DEBIT BALANCE: The amount of borrowed funds in an investor's margin account.

DEFERRED CALL: The contractual inability of the bond issues to redeem the bond for a specific period.

DEPLETION: Natural resources, such as metals, oils and gas, timber, which conceivably can be reduced to zero over the years, present a special problem in capital management. Depletion is an accounting practice consisting of charges against earnings based upon the amount of the asset taken out of the total reserves in the period for which accounting is made.

DEPRECIATION: Normally, charges against earnings to write off the cost, less salvage value, of an asset over its estimated useful life.

DILUTION: Reduction in the actual or potential earnings per share by issuing more shares or giving options to obtain them.

DIRECTOR: Person elected by shareholders to establish company policies. The directors appoint the president, vice president, and all other operating officers. Directors decide, among other matters, if and when dividends shall be paid.

DISCOUNT RATE: The rate used in the discounting process; sometimes called capitalization rate.

DISCRETIONARY ACCOUNT: An account in which the customer gives the broker or someone else discretion, which may be complete or within specific limits, as to the purchase and sales of securities or commodities including selection, timing, amount, and price to be paid or received.

DISCRETIONARY ORDER: The customer empowers the broker to act on his behalf with respect to the choice of security to be bought or sold, a total amount of any securities to be bought or sold, and/or whether any such transaction shall be one of purchase or sale.

DIVERSIFICATION: Spreading investments among different companies in different fields. Another type of diversification is also offered by the securities of many individual companies because of the wide range of their activities.

DIVIDEND: The payment designated by the Board of Directors to be distributed pro rata among the shares outstanding. On preferred shares, it is generally a fixed amount. On common shares, the dividend varies with the fortunes of the firm.

DIVIDEND YIELD: The ratio of the current dividend to the current price of a share of stock.

DOLLAR COST AVERAGING: A system of buying securities at regular intervals with a fixed dollar amount. Under this system the investor buys by the dollars' worth rather than by the number of shares. If each investment is of the same number of dollars, payments buy more when the price is low and fewer when it rises. Thus temporary downswings in prices benefit the investor if he continues periodic purchases in both good and bad times and the price at which the shares are sold is more than their average cost.

DOW THEORY: A theory of market analysis based upon the performance of the Dow-Jones industrial and transportation stock price averages. The theory says that the market is in a basic upward trend if one of these averages advances above a previous important high, accompanied or followed by a similar advance in the other. When the averages both dip below previous important lows, this is regarded as confirmation of a basic downward trend. The theory does not attempt to predict how long either trend will continue, although it is widely misinterpreted as a method of forecasting future action.

DUAL FUND: A closed-end investment company with two classes of stock—an income oriented class and a capital gains oriented class.

EARNINGS PER SHARE: Total after tax earnings, after preferred dividends, divided by the average number of common shares outstanding during the period.

EARNINGS REPORT: A statement—also called an income statement—issued by a company showing its earnings or losses over a given period. The earnings report lists the income earned, expenses and the net result.

EARNINGS YIELD: Earnings per share expressed as a percentage of stock price.

EBIT: Abbreviation for "earnings before interest and taxes."

EFFICIENT FRONTIER: The set of possible portfolios, each of which has the highest expected return for a given level of risk.

EQUIPMENT TRUST CERTIFICATE: A type of security, generally issued by a railroad, to pay for new equipment. Title to the equipment, such as a locomotive, is held by a trustee until the notes are paid off. An equipment trust certificate is usually secured by a first claim on the equipment.

EQUITY: The net worth of a business, consisting of capital stock, capital (or paid-in) surplus, earned surplus (or retained earnings), and, occasionally, certain net worth reserves. Common equity is that part of the total net worth belonging to the common stockholders. Total equity would include preferred stockholders. The terms "common stock," "net worth," and "equity" are frequently used interchangeably.

EXCHANGE ACQUISITION: A method of filling an order to buy a large block of stock on the floor of the exchange. Under certain circumstances, a member-broker can facilitate the purchase of a block by soliciting orders to sell. All orders to sell the security are lumped together and crossed with the buy order in the regular auction market. The price to the buyer may be on a net basis or on a commission basis.

EXCHANGE DISTRIBUTION: A method of disposing of large blocks of stock on the floor of the exchange. Under certain circumstances, a member-broker can facilitate the sale of a block of stock by soliciting and getting other member-brokers to solicit orders to buy. Individual buy orders are lumped together and crossed with the sell order in the regular auction market. A special commission is usually paid by the seller; ordinarily the buyer pays no commission.

EXCHANGE RATIO: The ratio of the shares offered by the acquiring company for each share of the acquired company.

EX-DIVIDEND: A synonym for "without dividend." The buyer of a stock selling ex-dividend does not receive the recently declared dividend. Open buy and sell stop orders, and sell stop limit orders in a stock on the ex-dividend date are ordinarily reduced by the value of that dividend. In the case of open stop limit orders to sell, both the stop price and the limit price are reduced. Every dividend is payable on a fixed date to all shareholders recorded on the books of the company as of a previous date of record.

EX-RIGHTS: Without the rights. Corporations raising additional money may do so by offering their stockholders the right to subscribe to new or additional stock, usually at a discount from the prevailing market price. The buyer of a stock selling ex-rights is not entitled to the rights.

EXTRA: The short form of "extra dividend." A dividend in the form of stock or cash in addition to the regular or usual dividend the company has been paying.

FACE VALUE: The value of a bond that appears on the face of the bond, unless the value is otherwise specified by the issuing company. Face value is ordinarily the amount the issuing company promises to pay at maturity. Face value is not an indication of market value. Sometimes referred to as par value.

FEDERAL FUNDS: Interbank, overnight loans.

FINANCIAL ASSET: Any claim received in exchange for the transfer of funds.

FINANCIAL RISK: The variability imported to the earnings power of the operating entity because of the method of financing the asset acquisition.

FISCAL YEAR: A corporation's accounting year. Due to the nature of their particular business, some companies do not use the calendar year for their bookkeeping. A typical example is the department store which finds December 31 too early a date to close its books after the Christmas rush. For that reason many stores wind up their accounting year January 31.

FIXED CHARGES: A company's fixed expenses, such as bond interest, which it has agreed to pay whether or not earned, and which are deducted from income before earnings on equity capital are computed.

FLAT: This term means that the price at which a bond is traded includes consideration for all unpaid accruals of interest. Bonds which are in default of interest or principal are traded flat. Income bonds, which pay interest only to the extent earned are usually traded flat. All other bonds are usually dealt in "and interest," which means that the buyer pays to the seller the market price plus interest accrued since the last payment date. When applied to a stock loan, flat means without premium or interest.

FLOOR BROKER: A member of the stock exchange who executes orders on the floor of the exchange to buy or sell any listed securities.

FORECASTING RISK: The chance of an incorrect forecast of the future stream of benefits.

FORMULA INVESTING: An investment technique. One formula calls for the shifting of funds from common shares to preferred shares or bonds as the market, on average, rises above a certain predetermined point—and the return of funds to common share investments as the market average declines.

FREE AND OPEN MARKET: A market in which supply and demand are expressed in terms of price. Contrasts with a controlled market in which supply, demand and price may all be regulated.

FUNDED DEBT: Usually interest-bearing bonds or debentures of a company. Could include long-term bank loans. Does not include short-term loans, preferred or common stock.

GENERAL MORTGAGE BOND: A bond which is secured by a blanket mortgage on the company's property, but which is often outranked by one or more other mortgages.

GENERAL OBLIGATION: A municipal bond secured by the full faith, credit and taxing power of the municipality.

GILT-EDGED: High-grade bond issued by a company which has demonstrated its ability to earn a comfortable profit over a period of years and pay its bondholders their interest without interruption.

GIVE-UPS: Controversial practice under which brokers deliver portions of their commissions on large securities transactions to other brokers as compensation for favors done for the customer by the latter brokers.

GOOD DELIVERY: Certain basic qualifications must be met before a security sold on the exchange may be delivered. The security must be in proper form to comply with the contract of sale and to transfer title to the purchaser.

GOOD 'TIL CANCELLED ORDER (GTC) OR OPEN ORDER: An order to buy or sell, which remains in effect until it is either executed or cancelled.

GOODWILL: Intangible assets of a firm established by the excess of the price paid for the going concern over its book value.

GOVERNMENT BONDS: Obligations of the U.S. government, regarded as the highest grade issues in existence.

GROWTH STOCK: Stock of a company with prospects for future growth—a company whose earnings are expected to increase at a relatively rapid rate.

GUARANTEED BOND: A bond which has interest or principal, or both, guaranteed by a company other than the issuer. Usually found in the railroad industry when large roads, leasing sections of trackage owned by small railroads, may guarantee the bonds of the smaller road.

GUARANTEED STOCK: Usually preferred stock on which dividends are guaranteed by another company, under much the same circumstances as a bond is guaranteed.

HOLDING COMPANY: A corporation which owns the securities of another, in most cases with voting control.

HYPOTHECATION: The pledging of securities as collateral for a loan.

INACTIVE POST: A trading post on the floor of the New York Stock Exchange where inactive securities are traded in units of 10 shares instead of the usually 100-share lots. Better known in the business as Post 30.

INACTIVE STOCK: An issue traded on an exchange or in the over-the-counter market in which there is a relatively low volume of transactions. Volume may be no more than a few hundred shares a week or even less. On the New York Stock Exchange many inactive stocks are traded in 10-share units rather than the customary 100.

IN-AND-OUT: Purchase and sale of the same security within a short period—a day, week, even a month. An in-and-out trader is generally more interested in day-to-day price fluctuations than dividends or long-term growth.

INCOME BOND: Generally, a bond which promises to pay interest only when earned.

INCOME ELASTICITY OF DEMAND: The percentage change in demand for a product in response to a percentage change in income.

INDENTURE: A written agreement under which debentures are issued, setting forth maturity date, interest rate, and other terms.

INDEX: A statistical yardstick expressed in terms of percentages of a base year or years. An index is not an average.

INFLATION: An increasing price level.

INTEREST: Payments a borrower pays a lender for the use of his money. A corporation pays interest on its bonds to its bondholders.

INTEREST RATE RISK: The potential price change in a financial asset in response to a change in the interest rate.

INVESTMENT: The use of money for the purpose of making more money, to gain income or increase capital, or both. Safety of principal is an important consideration.

INVESTMENT BANKER: Also known as an underwriter. He is the middleman between the corporation issuing new securities and the public. The usual practice is for one or more investment bankers to buy outright from a corporation a new issue of stocks or bonds. The group forms a syndicate to sell the securities to individuals and institutions. Investment bankers also distribute very large blocks of stocks or bonds—perhaps held by an estate.

INVESTMENT COUNSEL: One whose principal business consists of acting as investment adviser and a substantial part of his business consists of rendering investment supervisory services.

INVESTMENT COMPANY: A company which uses its capital to invest in other companies. There are two principal types: the closed-end or mutual fund.

INVESTOR: An individual whose principal concerns in the purchase of a security are regular dividend income, safety of the original investment, and, if possible, capital appreciation.

ISSUE: Any of a company's securities, or the act of distributing such securities.

LEGAL LIST: A list of investments selected by various states in which certain institutions and fiduciaries, such as insurance companies and banks, may invest. Legal lists are often restricted to high quality securities meeting certain specifications.

LEVERAGE: The effect on the per-share earnings of the common stock of a company when large sums must be paid for bond interest or preferred stock dividends, or both, before the common stock is entitled to share in earnings. Leverage may be advantageous for the common when earnings are good but may work against the common stock when earnings decline. When a company has common stock only, no leverage exists because all earnings are available for the common, although relatively large fixed charges payable for lease of substantial plant assets may have an effect similar to that of a bond issue.

LIABILITIES: All the claims against a corporation. Liabilities include accounts and wages and salaries payable, dividends declared payable, accrued taxes payable, fixed or long-term liabilities such as mortgage bonds, debentures and bank loans.

LIEN: A claim against property which has been pledged or mortgaged to secure the performance of an obligation. A bond is usually secured by a lien against specified property of a company.

LIMIT, LIMITED ORDER OR LIMITED PRICE ORDER: An order to buy or sell a stated amount of a security at a specified price, or at a better price, if obtainable after the order is represented in the Trading Crowd.

LIQUIDATION: The process of converting securities or other property into cash. The dissolution of a company, with cash remaining after sale of its assets and payment of all indebtedness being distributed to the shareholders.

LIQUIDITY: The ability of the market in a particular security to absorb a reasonable amount of buying or selling at reasonably small price changes. Liquidity is one of the most important characteristics of a good market.

LISTED SECURITY: Security which is fully accepted for trading on a stock exchange.

LOAD: The portion of the offering price of shares of open-end investment companies which covers sales commissions and all other costs of distribution. The load is incurred only on purchase, there being, in most cases, no charge when the shares are sold.

LOCKED IN: An investor is said to be locked in when he has a profit on a security he owns but does not sell because his profit would immediately become subject to the capital gains tax.

LONG: Signifies ownership of securities: "I am long 100 U.S. Steel" means the speaker owns 100 shares.

MANAGEMENT: The Board of Directors, elected by the stockholders, and the officers of the corporation, appointed by the Board of Directors.

MANIPULATION: An illegal operation. Buying or selling a security for the purpose of creating false or misleading appearance of active trading or for the purpose of raising or depressing the price to induce purchase or sale by others.

MARGIN—PROFIT ON SALES: The profit margin is the percentage of profit after tax to sales.

MARGIN: The amount paid by the customer when he uses his broker's credit to buy a security. Under Federal Reserve regulations, the initial margin required in the past 20 years has ranged from 40 percent of the purchase price all the way to 100 percent.

MARGIN CALL: A demand upon a customer to put up money or securities with the broker. The call is made when a purchase is made; also if a customer's equity in a margin account declines below a minimum standard set by the exchange or by the firm.

MARKET ORDER: An order to buy or sell a stated amount of a security at the most advantageous price obtainable after the order is represented in the Trading Crowd.

MARKET PRICE: In the case of a security, market price is usually considered the last reported price at which the stock or bond sold.

MARKET RISK: The risk that a seller will not be able to find a buyer for the security.

MATCHED AND LOST: When two bids to buy the same stock are made on the trading floor simultaneously, and each bid is equal to or larger than the amount of stock offered, both bids are considered to be on an equal basis. So the two bidders flip a coin to decide who buys the stock. Also applies to offers to sell.

MATURITY: The date on which a loan or a bond or debenture comes due and is to be paid off.

MEMBER CORPORATION: A securities brokerage firm, organized as a corporation, with at least one member of the New York Stock Exchange who is a director and a holder of voting stock in the corporation.

MEMBER FIRM: A securities brokerage firm organized as a partnership and having at least one general partner who is a member of the New York Stock Exchange.

MEMBER ORGANIZATION: This term includes New York Stock Exchange Member Firm and Member Corporation. The term "participant" when used with reference to a Member Organization includes general and limited partners of a Member Firm and holders of voting and nonvoting stock in a Member corporation.

MERGER: Any combination that forms one company from two or more previously existing companies.

MIP: Monthly Investment Plan. A pay-as-you-go method of buying New York Stock Exchange listed shares on a regular payment plan for as little as $40 a month or $40 every three months. Under MIP the investor buys stock by the dollars' worth—if the price advances, he gets fewer shares and if it declines, he gets more shares. He may discontinue purchases at any time without penalty.

MONEY MARKET: Financial markets in which funds are borrowed, or loaned for short periods. (The money market is distinguished from the capital market, which is the market for long-term funds.)

MORTGAGE BOND: A bond secured by a mortgage on a property.

MUNICIPAL BOND: A bond issued by a state or a political subdivision, such as country, city, town or village. The term also designates bonds issued by state agencies and authorities. In general, interest paid on municipal bonds is exempt from federal income taxes.

MUTUAL FUND: See Investment Companies.

NASD: The National Association of Securities Dealer, Inc. An association of brokers and dealers in the over-the-counter securities business. The Association has the power to expel members who have been declared guilty of unethical practices.

NEGOTIABLE: Refers to a security, title to which is transferable by delivery.

NET ASSET VALUE: A term usually used in connection with investment trusts, meaning net asset value per share. It is common practice for an investment trust to compute its assets daily, or even twice daily, by totaling the market value of all securities owned. All liabilities are deducted, and the balance divided by the number of shares outstanding. The resulting figure is the net asset value per share.

NET CHANGE: The change in the price of a security from the closing price on one day and the closing price on the following day on which the stock is traded. In the case of a stock which is entitled to a dividend one day, but is traded "ex-dividend" the next, the dividend is considered in computing the change. The mark $+1\frac{1}{8}$ means up $1.125 a share from the last sale on the previous day the stock traded.

NET WORTH: The capital and surplus of a firm—capital stock; capital surplus (paid-in capital); earned surplus (retained earnings); and, occasionally, certain reserves. For some purposes, preferred stock is included; generally, net worth refers only to the common stockholder's position.

NEW ISSUE: A stock or bond sold by a corporation for the first time. Proceeds may be issued to retire outstanding securities of the company, for new plant or equipment or for additional working capital.

NONCUMULATIVE: A preferred stock on which unpaid dividends do not accrue. Omitted dividends are, as a rule, gone forever.

NYSE COMMON STOCK INDEX: A composite index covering price movements of all common stocks listed on the "Big Board." It is based on the close of the market December 31, 1965 as 50.00 and is weighted according to the number of shares listed for each issue.

ODD-LOT: An amount of stock less than the established 100-share unit or 10-share unit of trading: from 1 to 99 shares for the great majority of issues, 1 to 9 for so-called inactive stocks.

ODD-LOT DEALER: A member firm of the exchange which buys and sells odd lots of stocks. The odd-lot dealer's customers are commission brokers acting on behalf of their customers. There are one or more odd-lot dealers who, under current practices, are ready to buy or sell, for their own accounts, odd lots in any stock at any time. Odd-lot prices are geared to the auction market. On an odd-lot market order, the odd-lot dealer's price is based on the first round-lot transaction which occurs on the floor following receipt at the trading post of the odd-lot order.

ODD-LOT THEORY: A technical approach to stock trading which maintains the odd-lotter is consistently incorrect.

OFF-BOARD: This term may refer to transactions over-the-counter in unlisted securities, or to a transaction involving listed shares which was not executed on a national securities exchange.

OFFER: The price at which a person is ready to sell. Opposed to bid, the price at which one is ready to buy.

OPTION: A right to buy or sell specific securities or properties at a specified price within a specified time.

ORDERS GOOD UNTIL A SPECIFIED TIME: A market or limited price order which is to be represented in the Trading Crowd until a specified time, after which such order or the portion thereof not executed is to be treated as cancelled.

ORGANIZED SECURITY EXCHANGES: Formal organizations having tangible, physical locations. Organized exchanges conduct an auction market in designated ("listed") investment securities. For example, the New York Stock Exchange is an organized exchange.

OVER-THE-COUNTER: A market for securities made up of securities dealers who may or may not be members of a securities exchange. Over-the-counter is mainly a market made over the telephone. Thousands of companies have insufficient shares outstanding, stockholders, or earnings to warrant application for listing on the N.Y. Stock Exchange. Securities of these companies are traded in the over-the-counter market between dealers who act either as principals or as brokers for customers. The over-the-counter market is the principal market for U.S. government bonds and municipals and stocks of banks and insurance companies.

PAPER PROFIT: An unrealized profit on a security still held. Paper profits become realized profits only when the security is sold.

PAR: In the case of a common share, par means a dollar amount assigned to the share by the company's charter. Par value may also be used to compute the dollar amount of the common shares on the balance sheet. Par value has little significance so far as market value of common stock is concerned. Many companies today issue no-par stock but give a stated per share value on the balance sheet. Par at one time was supposed to represent the value of the original investment behind each share in cash, goods or services. In the case of preferred shares and bonds, however, par is important. It often signifies the dollar value upon which dividends on preferred stocks, and interest on bonds, are figured. The issuer of a 3 percent bond promises to pay that percentage of the bond's par value annually.

PARTICIPATING PREFERRED: A preferred stock which is entitled to its stated dividend and, also, to additional dividends on a specified basis upon payment of dividends on the common stock.

PASSED DIVIDEND: Omission of a regular or scheduled dividend.

PAYOUT RATIO: The percentage of earnings paid out in the form of dividends.

PENNY STOCKS: Low-priced issues often highly speculative, selling at less than $1 a share. Frequently used as a term of disparagement, although a few penny stocks have developed into investment-caliber issues.

PERCENTAGE ORDER: A market or limited price order to buy (or sell) a stated amount of a specified stock after a fixed number of shares of such stock have traded.

POINT: In the case of shares of stock, a point means $1. In the case of bonds a point means $10, since a bond is quoted as a percentage of $1,000. In the case of market averages, the word point means merely that and no more. A point in this average, however, is not equivalent to $1.

PORTFOLIO: Holdings of securities by an individual or institution. A portfolio may contain bonds, preferred stocks and common stocks of various types of enterprises.

PREFERRED STOCK: A class of stock with a claim on the company's earnings before payment may be made on the common stock and usually entitled to priority over common stock if company liquidates. Usually entitled to dividends at a specific rate—when declared by the Board of Directors and before payment of a dividend on the common stock—depending upon the terms of the issue.

PREMIUM: The amount by which a preferred stock or bond may sell above its par value. In the case of a new issue of bonds or stocks, premium is the amount the market price rises over the original selling price. Also refers to a charge sometimes made when a stock is borrowed to make delivery on a short sale. May refer, also, to redemption price of a bond or preferred stock if it is higher than face value.

PRESENT DISCOUNTED VALUE (PDV): The value today of a future payment or payments, discounted at the appropriate discount rate.

PRICE-EARNINGS RATIO: The current market price of a share of stock divided by earnings per share for a twelve-month period.

PRICE ELASTICITY OF DEMAND: The percentage change in the quantity of a product demand in relation to the percentage change in price for that product.

PRIMARY DISTRIBUTION: Also called primary offering. The original sale of a company's securities.

PRIME RATE: The rate of interest commercial banks charge very large, strong corporations.

PRINCIPAL: The person for whom a broker executes an order, or a dealer buying or selling for his own account. The term "principal" may also refer to a person's capital or to the face amount of a bond.

PROXY: Written authorization given by a shareholder to someone else to represent him and vote his shares at a shareholders' meeting.

PROXY STATEMENT: Information required by SEC to be given stockholders as a prerequisite to solicitation of proxies for a security subject to the requirements of Securities Exchange Act.

PURE INTEREST RATE: The interest rate on a financial asset with no associated business or financial risk—comprised of the real interest rate plus the purchasing power risk premium.

PUTS AND CALLS: Options which give the right to buy or sell a fixed amount of a certain stock at a specified price within a specified time. A put gives the holder the right to sell the stock: a call the right to buy the stock. Puts are purchased by those who think a stock may go down. A put obligates the seller of the contract to take delivery of the stock and pay the specified price to the owner of the option within the time limit of the contract. The price specified in a put or call is usually close to the market price of the stock at the time the contract is made. Calls are purchased by those who think a stock may rise. A call gives the holder the right to buy the stock from the seller of the contract at the specified price within a fixed period of time. Put and call contracts are written for 30, 60, or 90 days, or longer. If the purchaser of a put or call does not wish to exercise the option, the price he paid for the option becomes a loss.

Glossary 494

PURCHASING POWER RISK: The risk that the principal and income from investments will lose their purchasing power because price level inflation proceeds faster than capital values increase.

QUICK RATIO: The ratio of cash plus marketable securities and accounts receivable to current liabilities.

QUOTATION: Often shortened to "quote." The highest bid to buy and the lowest offer to sell a security in a given market at a given time. If you ask your broker for a "quote" on a stock, he may come back with something like "45¼ to 45½." This means that $45.25 is the highest price any buyer wanted to pay at the time the quote was given on the floor of the exchange and that $45.50 was the lowest price which any seller would take at the same time.

R^2: The coefficient of determination, a statistic which indicates the degree of accuracy with which the regression explains the actual observations.

RALLY: A brisk rise following a decline in the general price level of the market, or in an individual stock.

RANDOM WALK: A theory which claims stock prices are independent of one another.

RATIO ANALYSIS: Investment analysis by comparing a firm's balance sheet and income statement ratios to each other and to external data.

RATIO OF COLLATERAL TO DEBT: The number of times total stock margin debt is covered by total collateral value:

$$\frac{\text{Collateral Value}}{\text{Stock Margin Debt}} = \text{Ratio}$$

REAL INTEREST RATE: The interest rate on a loan with no business, financial or purchasing power risk. It is the rate charged for the use of money and equals the pure interest rate minus the purchasing power risk premium.

RECORD DATE: The date on which one must be registered as a shareholder on the stock book of a company in order to receive a declared dividend or, among other things, to vote on company affairs.

REDEMPTION PRICE: The price at which a bond may be redeemed before maturity, at the option of the issuing company. Redemption value also applies to the price the company must pay to call in certain types of preferred stock.

REFINANCING: Same as refunding. New securities are sold by a company and the money is used to retire existing securities. Object may be to save interest costs, extend the maturity of the loan, or both.

REGISTERED BOND: A bond which is registered on the books of the issuing company in the name of the owner. It can be transferred only when endorsed by the registered owner.

REGISTERED REPRESENTATIVE: Present name for the older term "customers' man." In a New York Stock Exchange Member Firm, a Registered Representative is a full time employee who has met the requirements of the Exchange as to background and knowledge of the securities business. Also known as an Account Executive or Customer's Broker.

REGISTERED TRADER: A member of the exchange who trades in stocks on the floor for an account in which he has an interest.

REGISTRAR: Usually a trust company or bank charged with the responsibility of preventing the issuance of more stock than authorized by a company.

REGISTRATION: Before a public offering may be made of new securities by a company, or of outstanding securities by controlling stockholders—through the mails or in interstate commerce—the securities must be registered under the Securities Act of 1933. Registration statement is filed with the SEC by the issuer. It must disclose pertinent information relating to the company's operations, securities, management and purpose of the public offering. Securities of railroads under jurisdiction of the Interstate Commerce Commission, and certain other types of securities, are exempted. On security offerings involving less than $300,000, less information is required.

Before a security may be admitted to dealings on a national securities exchange, it must be registered under the Securities Exchange Act of 1934. The application for registration must be filed with the exchange and the SEC by the company issuing the securities. It must disclose pertinent information relating to the company's operations, securities and management. Registration may become effective 30 days after receipt by the SEC of the certification by the exchange of approval of listing and registration, or sooner by special order of the Commission.

REGRESSION ANALYSIS: A statistical procedure for predicting the value of one variable (dependent variable) on the basis of knowledge about one or more other variables (independent variables).

REGULATION T: The federal regulation governing the amount of credit which may be advanced by brokers and dealers to customers for the purchase of securities.

REGULATION U: The federal regulation governing the amount of credit which may be advanced by a bank to its customers for the purchase of listed stocks.

RELATIVE STRENGTH: A technical trading strategy which maintains today's strongest performing stocks will also be tomorrow's strongest performing stocks.

REORGANIZATION: In bankruptcy the restructuring of a firm's capital structure and operating facilities under court protection.

RESISTANCE LEVEL: The upside price ceiling through which the price must penetrate.

REVENUE BOND: A municipal bond backed by the revenues of the project if financed.

RIGHT: A short-term option to buy a specified number of shares of a new issue of securities at a designated "subscription" price.

RISK FUNCTION: The relationship between the expected return and the associated risk.

ROUND LOT: A unit of trading or a multiple thereof. On the NYSE the unit of trading is generally 100 shares in stocks and $1,000 par value in the case of bonds. In some inactive stocks, the unit of trading is 10 shares.

SALVAGE VALUE: The value of a capital asset at the end of a specified period. It is the current market price of an asset being considered for replacement in a capital budgeting problem.

SCALE ORDER: An order to buy (or sell) a security which specifies the total amount to be bought (or sold) and the amount to be bought (or sold) at specified price variations.

SEAT: A traditional figure-of-speech for a membership on an exchange. Price and admission requirements vary.

SEC: The Securities and Exchange Commission, established by Congress to help protect investors. The SEC administers the Securities Act of 1933, the Securities Exchange Act of 1934, the Trust Indenture Act, the Investment Company Act, the Investment Advisers Act, and the Public Utility Holding Company Act.

SECONDARY DISTRIBUTION: Also known as a secondary offering. The redistribution of a block of stock some time after it has been sold by the issuing company.

SELLER'S OPTION: A special transaction on NYSE which gives the seller the right to deliver the stock or bond at any time within a specified period, ranging from not less than six business days to not more than 60 days.

SELLING AGAINST THE BOX: A method of protecting a paper profit. If one owns 100 shares of XYZ which has advanced in price, and he thinks the price may decline, he sells 100 shares short, borrowing 100 shares to make delivery. He retains in his security box the 100 shares which he owns. If XYZ declines, the profit on his short sale is exactly offset by the profit in the market value of the stock he has retained. He can close out his short sale by buying 100 shares to return to the person from whom he borrowed, or he can send them the 100 shares which he owns.

SERIAL BOND: An issue which matures in relatively small amounts at periodic stated intervals.

SHORT COVERING: Buying stock to return stock previously borrowed to make delivery on a short sale.

SHORT POSITION: Stocks sold short and not covered as of a particular date. On the NYSE, a tabulation is issued a few days after the middle of the month listing all issues on the Exchange in which there was a short position at the mid-month settlement date of 5,000 or more shares, and issues in which the short position had changed by 2,000 or more shares in the preceding month. This tabulation is based on reports of positions on member firms; books. Short position also means the total amount of stock an individual has sold short and has not covered, as of a particular date. Initial margin requirements for a short position are the same as for a long position. Proceeds from short sales are excluded entirely from this report. The initial margin required of the short seller, however, and profits and losses on short sales are reflected in stock margin debt.

SHORT SALE: A person who believes a stock will decline and sells it though he does not own any has made a short sale. For instance: One instructs his broker to sell short 100 shares of ABC. His broker borrows the stock so he can deliver the 100 shares to the buyer. Sooner or later one must cover his short sale by buying the same amount of stock he borrowed for return to the lender. If he is able to buy ABC at a lower price than he sold it for, his profit is the difference between the two prices—not counting commissions and taxes. But if he has to pay more for the stock than the price he received, that is the amount of his loss.

SINKING FUND: Money regularly set aside by a company to redeem its bonds, debentures or preferred stock from time to time as specified in the indenture or charter.

SPECIAL BID: A method of filling an order to buy a large block of stock on the floor of the New York Stock Exchange. In a special bid, the bidder for the block of stock—a pension fund, for instance, will pay a special commission to the broker who represents him in making the purchase. The seller does not pay a commission. The special bid is made on the floor of the Exchange at a fixed price which may not be below the last sale of the security or the current bid in the regular market, whichever is higher. Member firms may sell this stock for customers directly to the buyer's broker during trading hours.

SPECIAL OFFERING: Occasionally a large block of stock becomes available for sale which, due to its size and the market in that particular issue, calls for special handling. A notice is printed on the ticker tape announcing that the stock will be offered for sale on the NYSE floor at a fixed price. Member firms may buy this stock for customers directly from the seller's broker during trading hours. The price is usually based on the last transaction in the regular auction market. If there are more buyers than stock, allotments are made. Only the seller pays a commission on a special offering.

SPECIALIST: A member of the New York Stock Exchange who has two functions: First, to maintain an orderly market, insofar as reasonably practicable, in the stocks in which he is registered as a specialist. In order to maintain an orderly market, the Exchange expects the specialist to buy or sell for his own account, to a reasonable degree, when there is a temporary disparity between supply and demand. Second, the specialist acts as a broker's broker. When a commission broker on the Exchange floor receives a limit order, say, to buy at $50 a stock then selling at $60—he cannot wait at the post where the stock is traded until the price reaches the specified level. So he leaves the order with the specialist, who will try to execute it in the market if and when the stock declines to the specified price. At all times the specialist must put his customers' interests above his own. There are about 350 specialists on the NYSE.

SPECIALIST BLOCK PURCHASE: Purchase by a specialist for his own account of a large block of stock outside the regular Exchange market. Such purchases may be made in the regular market within a reasonable time and at reasonable prices, and when the purchase by the specialist would aid him in maintaining a fair and orderly market. The specialist need not fill the orders on his book down to the purchase price.

SPECIALIST BLOCK SALE: Opposite of the specialist block purchase. Under exceptional circumstances, the specialist may sell a block of stock outside the regular market on the Exchange for his own account at a price above the prevailing market. The price is negotiated between the specialist and the broker for the buyer. The specialist need not fill the orders on his book down to the purchase price.

SPECULATION: The employment of funds by a speculator. Safety of principal is a secondary factor.

SPECULATOR: One who is willing to assume a relatively large risk in the hope of gain. His principal concern is to increase his capital rather than his dividend income. The speculator may buy and sell the same day or speculate in an enterprise which he does not expect to be profitable for years.

SPLIT: The division of the outstanding shares of a corporation into a larger number of shares. A 3-for-1 split by a company with 1 million shares outstanding results in 3 million shares outstanding. Ordinarily splits must be voted by directors and approved by shareholders.

STANDARD DEVIATION: A measure of dispersion within a probability distribution.

STANDARD ERROR OF THE ESTIMATE: A measure of dispersion within the probability distribution of the regression estimates.

STOCK CLEARING CORPORATION: A subsidiary of the New York Stock Exchange which acts as a central agency for clearing firms in providing a "clearance operation" through which transactions made on the floor are confirmed and balanced and, also, a "settlement operation" which handles the physical delivery of securities and money payments.

STOCK DIVIDEND: A dividend paid in securities rather than cash. The dividend may be additional shares of the issuing company, or in shares of another company (usually a subsidiary) held by the company.

STOCKHOLDER OF RECORD: A stockholder whose name is registered on the books of the issuing corporation.

STOP LIMIT ORDER: A stop limit order to buy becomes a limit order executable at the limit price, or at a better price, if obtainable, when a transaction in the security occurs at or above the stop price. A stop limit order to sell becomes a limit order executable at the limit price or at a better price, if obtainable, when a transaction in the security occurs at or below the stop price.

STOP ORDER: A stop order to buy becomes a market order when a transaction in the security occurs at or above the stop price. A stop order to sell becomes a market order when a transaction in the security occurs at or below the stop price. Since it becomes a market order when the stop price is reached, there is no certainty that it will be executed at that price.

STOPPED STOCK: A service performed—in most cases by the specialist—for an order given him by a commission broker. Let's say XYZ just sold at $50 a share. Broker A comes along with an order to buy 100 shares at the market. The lowest offer is $50.50. Broker A believes he can do better for his client than $50.50, perhaps might get the stock at $50.25. But he doesn't want to take a chance that he'll miss the market—that is, the next sale might be $50.50 and the following one even higher. So he asks the specialist if he will stop 100 at ½ ($50.50). The specialist agrees. The specialist guarantees Broker A he will get 100 shares at 50½ if the stock sells at that price. In the meantime, if the specialist or Broker A succeeds in executing the order at $50.25, the stop is called off.

STREET: The New York financial community in the Wall Street area.

STREET NAME: Securities held in the name of a broker instead of his customer's name are said to be carried in a "street name." This occurs when the securities have been bought on margin or when the customer wishes the security to be held by the broker.

SUPPORT LEVEL: The downside price floor.

SWITCH ORDER-CONTINGENT ORDER: An order for the purchase (sale) of one stock and the sale (purchase) of another stock at a stipulated price difference.

SWITCHING: Selling one security and buying another.

SYNDICATE: A group of investment bankers who together underwrite and distribute a new issue of securities or a large block of an outstanding issue.

TAX-EXEMPT BONDS: The securities of states, cities and other public authorities specified under federal law, the interest on which is either wholly or partly exempt from federal income taxes.

TAX SELLING: Sales made to realize gains or losses for income tax purposes.

TECHNICAL ANALYSIS: A theory of stock prices which maintains there is a correlation between stock prices.

TECHNICAL INDICATOR: A term applied to the various internal market factor indicators; opposed to external forces such as earnings, dividends, political considerations and general economic conditions. Some internal factors considered in appraising the market's technical position include the size of the short interest, whether the market has had a sustained advance or decline without interruption, a sharp advance or decline without interruption, a sharp advance or decline on small volume and the amount of credit in use in the market.

TERM STRUCTURE: The relationship among the yields on bonds of equal quality but different maturity.

THIN MARKET: A market in which there are comparatively few bids to buy or offers to sell or both. The phrase may apply to a single security or to the entire stock market. In a thin market, price fluctuations between transactions are usually larger than when the market is liquid. A thin market in a particular stock may reflect lack of interest in that issue or a limited supply of or demand for stock in the market.

TICKER: The instrument which prints prices and volume of security transactions in cities and towns throughout the U.S. and Canada within minutes after each trade on the floor.

TIME ORDER: An order which becomes a market or limited price order at a specified time.

TRADER: One who buys and sells for his own account for short-term profit.

TRADING POST: One of 18 horseshoe-shaped trading locations on the floor of the New York Stock Exchange at which stocks assigned to that location are bought and sold.

TRANSFER: This term may refer to two different operations. For one, the delivery of a stock certificate from the seller's broker to the buyer's broker and legal change of ownership, normally accomplished within a few days. For another, to record the change of ownership on the books of the corporation by the transfer agent.

TRANSFER AGENT: A transfer agent keeps a record of the name of each registered shareowner, his or her address, the number of shares owned, and sees that certificates presented to his office for transfer are properly cancelled and new certificates issued in the name of the transferee.

TRANSFER TAX: A tax imposed by New York State when a security is sold or transferred from one person to another. The tax is paid by the seller. There is no tax on transfer of bonds.

TREASURY STOCK: Stock issued by a company but later reacquired. It may be held in the company's treasury indefinitely, reissued to the public, or retired.

TURNOVER: The volume of business in a security or the entire market. If turnover on the NYSE is reported at 10 million shares on a particular day, 10 million shares changed hands. Odd-lot turnover is tabulated separately and ordinarily is not included in reported volume.

TWO-DOLLAR BROKER: Members on the floor of the NYSE who execute orders for other brokers having more business at that time than they can handle themselves, or for firms who do not have their Exchange member-partner on the floor.

UNLISTED: A security not listed on a stock exchange.

UNLISTED TRADING PRIVILEGES: On some exchanges a stock may be traded at the request of a member without any prior application by the company itself. The company has no agreement to conform with standards of the exchange. Today admission of a stock to unlisted trading privileges require SEC approval of an application filed by the exchange. The information in the application must be made available by the exchange to the public. No unlisted stocks are traded on the New York Stock Exchange.

UP TICK: A term used to designate a transaction made at a price higher than the preceding transaction. Also called a "plus-tick." A stock may be sold short only on an up tick, or on a "zero-plus" tick. A "zero-plus" tick is a term used for a transaction at the same price as the preceding trade but higher than the preceding different price.

Conversely, a down tick, or "minus" tick, is a term used to designate a transaction made at a price lower than the preceding trade. A "zero-minus" tick is a transaction made at the same price as the preceding sale but lower than the preceding different price.

UTILITY FUNCTION: The relationship between the expected return and the satisfaction it generates.

VOTING RIGHT: The stockholder's right to vote his stock in the affairs of his company. Most common shares have one vote each. Preferred stock usually has the right to vote when preferred dividends are in default for a specified period. The right to vote may be delegated by the stockholder to another person.

WARRANT: A certificate giving the holder the right to purchase securities at a stipulated price within a specified time limit or perpetually.

WHEN ISSUED: A short form of "when, as and if issued." The term indicates a conditional transaction in a security authorized for issuance but not as yet actually issued. All "when issued" transactions are on an "if" basis, to be settled if and when the actual security is issued and the Exchange or National Association of Securities Dealers rules the transactions are to be settled.

WIRE HOUSE: A member firm of an exchange maintaining a communications network linking either its own branch offices, offices of correspondent firms, or a combination of such offices.

WORKING CAPITAL: Refers to a firm's investment in short-term assets—cash, short-term securities, accounts receivable, and inventories. Gross working capital is defined as a firm's total current assets. Net working capital is defined as current assets minus current liabilities. If the term "working capital" is used without further qualification, it generally refers to gross working capital. Net liquid assets with which a firm does business, roughly measured as current assets minus current liabilities.

WORKING CONTROL: Theoretically ownership of 51 percent of a company's voting stock is necessary to exercise control. In practice—effective control sometimes can be exerted through ownership, individually or by a group acting in concert, of less than 50 percent.

YIELD: Figuring the yield of a bond to maturity calls for a bond yield table.

YIELD CURVE: The relationship among the yields of bonds of equal quality but different maturity.

YIELD TO MATURITY: The annual return to a bond, including any annual accumulation or amortization.

YIELD SPREAD: The relationship among the yield on bonds of the same maturity but different quality.

Index

Accounts payable, 66
Accounts receivable, 64
    turnover, 67
Acquisitions (*see* Mergers and acquisitions)
Advance-Decline line, 402–403
Aggregate approach to earnings forecasting, 90
    economic indicator selection, 90
Altman's bankruptcy model (*see* Bankruptcy, Altman's model)
Altman, E., 337–340
American Stock Exchange, 16
Amortization, 57
Ando, A., 236
Annual Economic Report of the President, 91
Annuities, 33–34
Archer, S., 448
Arithmetic graph, 81
"Asked" price, 15
Assets, 64
    utilization ratio, 67
Atkinson, T. R., 281
Attainable set, 430–431
Auster, R., 342

Bach, G. L., 236
Balance of payments equilibrium, 175
Balance sheet, 64–69
Banker's Trust Investment Outlook, 190
Bankruptcy, 337–340
    Altman's model, 337–340
    and investment performance, 340
Bar charts, 385–393

Bar chart (*continued*)
    construction, 385–386
    patterns, 386–393
Base year, 85
Baskin, E., 291
Baumol, William, 156, 298
Bellemore, D., 415
"Bid" price, 15
Bing, R. A., 236
Bladen, A., 299
Block, S., 323
Blucher, L., 415
Blume, M., 379
Bond broker, 12
Bond evaluation, 289–290
Bond indenture (*see* Indenture)
Bond ratings, 283
    investment implications, 284
Boness, A. J., 336
Book value, 67–68
Box, 391
Breadth of the market, 402–403
Break-even analysis, 121–126
    high fixed cost versus low fixed cost, 125
Brealey, R., 374, 376, 380, 441
Brigham, E., 267, 295
Brown, Philip, 100
Business Conditions Digest, 22

Call option (*see* Options, call)
Call provision, 279, 291–293
Capital gain, 4
Capital gains model, 39–40
Capital loss, 4

Capital market, 3
  continuous, 7
  functions of, 10
  homogeneity, 4
  nonfunctioning, 8
Capital risk, 4
Capital structure, 68
Capitalization model, 40–44
Carelton, Willard T., 26, 45, 54
Carr, Hobart, 180
Cash, 64
Cash account, 12
Cash flow, 60
Cash flow analysis, 286–288
Certainty, 132
Certainty equivalent, 138
Certificates of deposit, 178, 182, 200–201
Chao, Lincoln, 86
Characteristic line, 355
Chart patterns, 387–393
  bearish, 391–393
    double top, 392
    head and shoulders, 391–392
    inverted saucer, 391
    triple top, 391
  bullish, 387–389
    inverted head and shoulders, 387
    saucer, 388
    trend line, 388–389
  uncertain, 389–391
    flag, 389
    pennant, 389
    rectangle, 391
    triangle, 389–390
    wedge, 389–390
Charting, 385–398
  point and figure, 394–398
  vertical bar charts, 385–393
Chattel bond, 280
Chou, Ya-lun, 86
Clearance, 15–16
Clendenin, J. C., 236
Coefficient of determination, 95–96
Cohen, J., 465
Cohen, K., 354, 427
Collateral, 279
Commercial paper, 183, 200–201
Commission broker, 12
Common size balance sheet, 70
Common size income statement, 63
Common stock evaluation, 39–47
  capital gains model, 39

Common stock evaluation (*continued*)
  capitalization model, 40
  dividend model, 39
  growth model, 47
Common-stock-market-price method (*see* Exchange ratio)
Compound growth rate, 83
Compound interest, 27–29
Comprehensive Bond Tables, 208
Confidence index, 410–411
Conrad, A., 254
Constant dollar plan, 465–466
Constant ratio plan, 466
Consumer Price Index, 175, 227
Contingency reserves, 61
Contrary opinion, 412–413
Conversion option, 280
Convertible bond, 280, 293–303
  premium deviations, 415–416
Convertible securities, 68–69, 293–303
  bond value, 294
  conversion value, 294
  effect on earnings, 68
  evaluation, 295
  premium, 294, 299–300
Cootner, P., 254, 372, 378
Correlation tests, 372–373
Cost of goods sold, 55
Cost push inflation, 228
Countercyclical response, 246
Covariance, 428
Credit and debit balances, 410
Creditor-debtor relationships, 119, 229–230
Credit proxy, 199
Critien, P., Jr., 415
Crooch, G., 291
Current ratio, 67

Dallenbarger, L., Jr., 320
DeAlessi, L., 236
Debentures, 280
Debt/equity ratio, 68, 260
Default bonds, 290–291
Deferred call privilege, 291–293
Deficit spending unit, 3
Delivery and clearance, 15
Demand analysis, 114
Demand for loanable funds (*see* Loanable funds framework)
Demand for money, 156
Demand-pull inflation, 226

Index 505

Depletion, 57
Depreciation, 57–60
  double declining balance, 57–58
  economic depreciation, 59–60
  straight-line, 57
  sum of the year digits, 58–59
Dilution of earnings, 69
  from conversion, 341
  in mergers, 314
  and stock evaluation, 342
Discount factor, 30, 151
Discount mechanism, 178
  borrowings, 204
Discretionary orders, 14
Dishoarding, 160
Distribution patterns, 375–376
Diversification, 245–246
  and business risk, 245–246
Dividend capitalization model, 40–41
Dividend model, 39
Dividend projections, 101–103
Dividend yield, 73
Dollar cost averaging, 463–465
  advantages, 464
  limitations, 464
Donaldson, G., 286
Double-declining balance, 57–58
Dow Jones Industrial Average, 404, 411–412
Dow theory, 411–412
Downward sloping yield curve (see Yield curve, types of)
Dual funds, 351–352
  advantages of, 351
  capital shares, 351
  preferred shares, 351
Durant, David, 45
Dynamic monetary policy, 180

Earnings coverage, 285
Earnings forecasting, 80–148
  aggregate approach, 90–98
  break-even analysis, 126
  compound growth rate, 83
  under dynamic conditions, 107–130
  graphic, 81–83
  moving average, 85–86
  ratios, 74
  return on investment approach, 98–99
  under risk, 131–148
  seasonality, 101
  simple growth rate, 83
  under stable conditions, 80–106

Earnings forecasting (continued)
  trend line, 86–90
Earnings patterns, 417
Earnings per share, 63
Ecletic framework (see Interest rate structures, term structure)
Economic depreciation, 59–60
Economic growth (see Federal Reserve System, goals)
Economies of scale, 311
Efficient frontier, 431
  with market equilibrium, 441
  with riskless asset, 440
Efficient set, 429–430
Eiteman, D. S., 236
Eiteman, W. J., 236
Elasticity of demand, 115–117
Equivalent risk class, 252
Eurodollars, 183
Evans, J., 448
Excess reserves, 204
Exchanges (see Securities exchanges)
Exchange listing, 342
Exchange ratio, 319–323
  methods of determination, 320
  negotiation limits, 321
Exhaustion gaps, 389
Expectation theory (see Interest rate structures, term structure)
Expected value, 136
  in earnings forecasting, 136
External business risk, 243–245

"Fair market value," 312
Fama, E., 378, 379, 413
Federal Funds, 183
Federal Reserve Bulletin, 22
Federal Reserve credit, 179, 194
Federal Reserve System, 155, 174–185
  goals, 174–177
  tools, 177–179
Federal taxes payable, 66
Fifo, 56
Fill or kill, 14
Filter tests, 379
Financial asset, 4
Financial leverage, 259–263
  example of, 261–263
  and security prices, 263–265
Financial statement analysis, 55–76
  balance sheet, 64–68
  income statement, 55–62
  retained earnings, 64

Findlay, M. Chapman III, 456
Fisher, L., 236, 288
Fixed charges earned ratio, 285–286
Fixed costs, 121
Flat basis, 290
Flat yield curve (see Yield curve, types of)
Float, 179
Floating supply, 73
Floor broker, 12
Floor trader, 12
Forbes, 361
Forecasting (see Earnings forecasting)
Forecasting under risk, 131–145
   analyst's record, 145–146
   certainty equivalent, 138–139
   expected value approach, 136–138
   sensitivity analysis, 138–142
   simulation, 142–144
Formula plans, 463–469
   constant dollar, 465–466
   constant ratio, 466
   dollar cost averaging, 463–465
   variable ratio, 466–469
Fourth market, 17
Free reserves, 182
Friedman, M., 433
Friend, I., 341, 360
Front loading, 352
Full employment (see Federal Reserve System, goals)
Full Employment Act, 174

General obligation bonds (see Municipal bonds)
Gibson, William, 230
GNP price deflator, 175, 227
Goodman, R., 304
Goodwill, 313
Gonedes, N., 252, 321
Gordon, Myron J., 43, 275
Government publications, 22
Grodinsky, Julius, 107
Gross national product, 90–91
Growth model, 47
Growth rate, 83
   compound, 83
   moving average, 85
   simple, 83
   trend line, 86

Hammer, F., 354, 427
Hanna, M., 406

Hatfield, K., 341
Hedge fund, 353
Hertz, David, 142
Hickman, W. B., 281, 284
Holland, D., 254
Homer, Sidney, 238
Horton, J., Jr., 304
Humped yield curve (see Yield curve, types of)
Hypothecation, 13

Income elasticity, 119–120
Income statement, 55–62
Income from subsidiaries and affiliates, 61
Indenture, 279
Indifference curves, 434–435
Industry life cycle, 107–112
   maturity stage, 111
   pioneering stage, 108
   stabilization stage, 112
Inflation, 226–229
   measures, 227–228
   patterns, 228–229
   types, 226–227
Inflation and stock prices, 235–238
   empirical evidence, 235
Insider transactions, 409–410
Interest coverage, 63
Interest rate determination, 158–159, 163–164
Interest rate forecasting, 189–193
Interest rate regulation, 178
Interest rate structures, 205–222
   term structure, 205–218
   yield spread, 218–220
Internal business risk, 245–250
Investment companies, 349–365
   closed-end, 350–351
      net asset value, 350
   dual, 351–352
   open-end, 352–365
      definition, 352
      management evaluation, 353–358
      performance measures, 360–363
      performance record, 358–360
      relative ranking, 356–358
   see also Mutual funds
Investment maturity state (see Industry life cycle)
Investment services, 21
Investory, 64
   turnover ratio, 66

Jen, F., 290, 292
Jiler, William, 387
Jensen, M., 358
Junior bonds, 280

Kaish, S., 407
Kassouf, S., 331
Kendall, M., 378
Kessel, R., 216
Kewley, T., 407
King, B., 155
Kissor, M., 417
Kruizenga, R. J., 336

Larson, Kermit, 321
Latané, H., 417
Lerner, Eugene, M., 26, 45, 54, 342, 451
Letter stock, 353
Leverage, 69, 259–262
  and financial risk, 260–263
  optimal leverage, 267–269
  in portfolio management, 454–455
  and risk, 265–267
  unfavorable leverage, 265
Levy, R., 371, 381
Liabilities, 66
Lien, 279, 288
Lifo, 56
Limited order, 14
Lintner, John, 101, 437
Liquidation, 280
Liquidity, 66–67
Liquidity preference, 155–159
Liquidity thesis of stock prices, 183–186
Loanable funds framework, 159–164
  demand, 162–163
  interest rate determination, 163–164
  supply, 160–162
Lorie, J., 236, 409
Listed, 12

Machol, R., 451
Malkiel, Burton G., 37, 205, 213, 217, 298, 336, 459
Management evaluation, 127
Margin, 13
  initial, 13
  maintenance, 13
Marginal utility of return, 431
Marketability, 288
Market order, 14
Market penetration, 14
Markowitz, H., 423, 430

Maturity stage (*see* Industry life cycle)
Mean, 134
Member bank reserves, 181, 195
Mergers, types of, 310
Mergers and acquisitions, 309–325
  effect on discount factor, 317–319
  effect on earnings, 313–317
  effect on stock prices, 319, 323–325
Messner, V., 417
Mieselman, D., 216
Miller, M., 267
Miller, R., 440
Modigliani, F., 267
Monetary base, 182, 194
Monetary indicators, 193–204
Money and capital markets, 3
Money supply, 181, 197
  and interest rates, 159
  and stock prices, 183–186
Moody's Investor Service, 21
Moore, Basil, 164
Mortgage bonds, 280
Moving average, 85, 410
  earnings growth, 85
  technical indicator, 410
Municipal bonds, 280–281, 303–305
  general obligation, 303
  revenue, 303
Murphy, J., 107
Mutual funds, 352–365; *see also* Open-end investment companies

Neter, J., 134
New high to new low ratio, 412
New issues, 340–341
New product demand, 126
New York Stock Exchange, 10
  history, 10
  membership, 12
  organization, 12
Nichols, Donald A., 235
Niederhoeffer, Victor, 100, 409
No load fund, 352
Nonconsolidated income, 61
Nonfunctioning market, 8
Nonprice competition, 115
Nonrecurring items, 61
Notes payable, 66

Odd lot, 13
Odd lot specialist, 12
Odd lot theory, 406–409
O'Donnell, J. L., Jr., 342

Official Summary of Security Transactions and Holdings, 409
Open market operations, 177
Operating income, 61
Operating margin, 62
"Opinion 16," 312
Options, 333–337
  call, 333
  investment results, 336
  in portfolio management, 455–460
  put, 333
  spread, 334
  straddle, 334
  strap, 334
  strip, 334
  value, 334–335
Option price, 336–337
Orders, types of, 13–15
Over-the-counter market, 16

Parker, G., 381
Payout ratio, 64, 102
Pease, F., 327
Perceived value, 9
Physical data, 70
Pinches, G., 417
Pioneering stage (*see* Industry life cycle)
Plotkin, I., 254
Point and figure charts, 394–398
  construction, 394–496
  patterns, 396–398
Polakoff, Murray, 164
Pooling of interests, 312
Portfolio balance effect, 164–168
Portfolio management, 446–460
  leverage, 454–455
  objectives, 446–447
  readjustment, 449–451
  security selection, 452–454
  size, 448–449
Portfolio selection, 435–437
Portfolio theory, 423–442
Premium on convertible bonds (*see* Convertible bond)
Present discounted value, 30–34
Price anticipation effect, 230–232
Price-dividend ratio, 41
Price-earnings ratio, 42, 47, 110
Price elasticity of demand, 115–117
  inelasticity, 117
  unit elasticity, 117
Price index, 175

Price stability (*see* Federal Reserve System, goals)
Primary market, 4
Prime rate, 183
Probability, 132–135
  distribution, 133
Product demand analysis, 114
Profit margin, 62
Projecting earnings (*see* Earnings forecasting)
Purchase, in mergers, 312
Pure interest rate, 154
Put (*see* Options, put)
Pye, G., 292

Quarterly reports, predictive quality of, 100
Quandt, R., 298, 336
Quick ratio, 67

R^2, 95–96
Random walk, 369–370, 372–381
  empirical evidence, 372–381
  theory, 369–370
Ratio analysis, 62–68
  commonly used ratios, 62–63, 66–68
  limitations of, 74–76
Real interest rate, 154, 229–232
Regional exchanges, 16
Registrar, 16
Regression analysis, 91–96
Reilly, F., 238, 341
Reorganization, 280
Reserves (*see* Member bank reserves)
Reserve requirements, 176
Resistance level, 393
Retained earnings, 64
Retention rate, 64
Return on investment, 67
Return on investment approach (*see* Earnings forecasting)
Revenue bonds (*see* Municipal bonds, revenue)
Richardson, L., 441
Riding the yield curve, 220, 221
Rights (*see* Subscription rights)
Risk, business, 4, 38, 241, 257
  definition, 242
  external, 243–245
  internal, 245–250
  measures of, 251–254
  definition, 132
  financial, 4, 39, 259–272

Index 509

Risk, financial (*continued*)
  measures of, 270–272
  and stock prices, 263–265
  forecasting, 4, 34, 138
  interest rate, 4, 36–37
  measurement, 132–134
  purchasing power, 225–239, 438
    premium, 154
    and stock prices, 233–235
Risk averter, 432–433
Risk-expected return relationship (*see* Risk function)
Risk function, 438
Risk seeker, 433–434
Roberts, H., 375
Round lot, 13
Run tests, 378–379

Sales, 55
Salvage value, 57–60
Savage, L., 433
Seasonality, 99–101
Secondary markets, 4
Secured bonds, 280
Securities exchange, 10–11
Securities and Exchange Commission, 17
Security analysis, 9
Segmented market theory (*see* Interest rates structures, term structure)
Sell-short, 14
Selling climax, 404
Semilogarithmetic graphs, 82
Semivariance, 254
Seneca, J., 405
Senior bonds, 280
Sensitivity analysis, 139–142
Shackle, G. L. S., 133
Sharpe, William, 360, 434, 437, 438, 440, 452
Shedding, 327
Shelton, J., 328, 352
Short interest, 405–406
Short sale (*see* Sell-short)
Short squeeze, 14
Simulation, 142–144
Simple annual growth, 83
Simple interest, 27
Simulation tests, 375
Sinking funds, 290
Smith, E. L., 236
Smith, K., 450, 455
Smith, R., 405
Soldofsky, R., 440

Solomon, Ezra, 54, 267
Sources and uses of funds statement, 70
Sources of information, 20–24
Specialist, 12, 15
Special situations, 279–344
  bonds, 279–306
  stocks, 309–344
Speculative demand, 157–158
Spread (*see* Options, spread)
Sprinkel, Beryl W., 183
Stabilization stage (*see* Industry life cycle)
Standard deviation, 134
  in portfolio theory, 424–429
Standard error, 95
Standard and Poor's, 21
Statistical Bulletin, SEC, 22
Stevenson, R., 407
Stock options and the portfolio, 455–460
Stockholder's equity, 68
Stock splits, 413–415
Stop order, 14
Straddle (*see* Options, straddle)
Straight-line depreciation, 57
Strap (*see* Options, strap)
Street name, 13
Strip (*see* Options, strip)
Subscription rights, 332–333
Supply and demand, effect on stock prices, 5–9
Support level, 393
Surplus spending unit, 3
Survey of Current Business, 22
Synergism, 311
Systematic risk, 359

Target payout ratio, 102
Tax loss carry forward, 61
Tax ratio, 667
Tax selling, 413
Technical analysis, 369–383
  and random walk, 369–370; *see also* Random walk
Technical indicators, 402–418
Term structure of interest rates, 205–218
  and stock prices, 206
  theories of (*see* Term structure theories)
Term structure theories, 212–218
  eclectic, 217–218
  expectation, 214–217
  liquidity premium, 216
  segmented markets, 212–214
Terminal year, 85

Third market, 17
Time horizon, 28
Time value of money, 26
Tobin, J., 156
Trade journals, 21
Trading volume, 404–405
Transfer agent, 16
Transactions demand, 156–157
Trend line, 86–89, 389
  intercept, 87
  problems with forecasting, 89
  slope, 87
  technical indicator, 389
  see also Chart patterns, bullish; Growth rate
Treynor, J., 353

Uncertainty, 132
U.S. Industrial Outlook, 91
Unsecured bonds (*see* Debentures)
Upward sloping yield curve (*see* Yield curve, types of)
Utility, 431–435

Value Line Investment Services, 22
Van Horne, J., 381
Variable costs, 121
Variable ratio plan, 466–469
Vaughn, D., 387
Vickers, D., 360
Volatility, 37

Wall Street Transcript, 20
Warrants, 325–332
  evaluation model, 328–332
  premium, 326–328
  theoretical value, 326
Wasserman, W., 134
Wert, J., 290–292
Weston, J. Fred, 267
Wharton Study, 360
Wholesale price index, 175, 227
Wiesenberger and Co., 360–361
Williams, J. Burr, 46
Wippern, R., 252
Working capital, 66
Wu, H., 409

Yamane, Taro, 86, 253
Yield, 4
  on selected securities, 202
Yield curve, 206–212
  applications of, 220–221
  derivation, 209–212
  informational content, 218
  types of, 209–210
Yield spread, 218–220
  cyclical behavior, 218–220

Zakon, A., 409
Zinbarg, E., 465